HOW IT WORKS
THE
WORLD OF
COMPUTERS AND
COMMUNICATIONS

Ian Graham

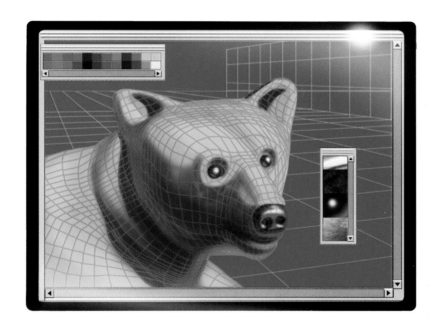

BARNES
&NOBLE
BOOKS
NEW YORK

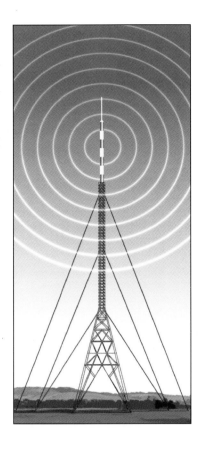

Series editor Elizabeth Miles
Designed by Paul Richards and Jenny Fry
Illustrations by Jeff Bowles,
Sebastian Quigley and Gerald Witcomb

This edition published by Barnes & Noble, Inc.,
by arrangement with Horus Editions Limited

1998 Barnes & Noble Books

ISBN 0-7607-0909-2

Printed in Singapore

98 99 00 01 02 M 9 8 7 6 5 4 3 2 1

HOW IT WORKS
CONTENTS

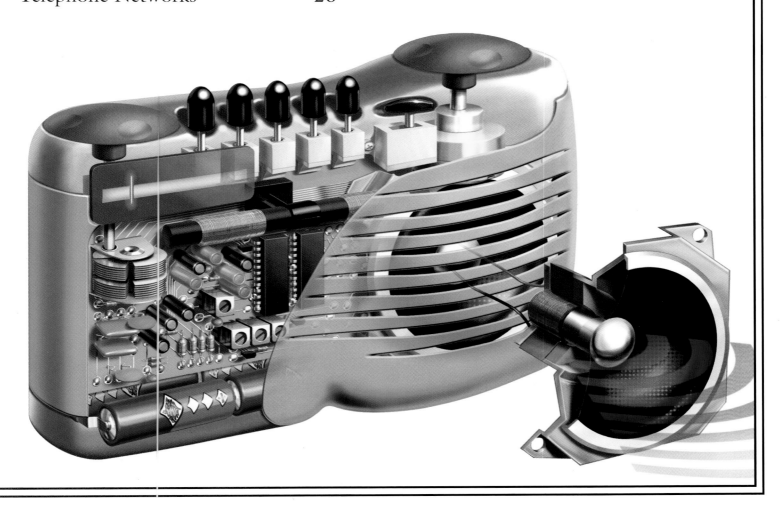

Printing

WE COMMUNICATE using words and pictures. Printing is the process of making lots of copies of the same words or pictures. Printing machines, called presses, work by coating a printing plate with ink and pressing it against paper so that the ink sticks to the paper. There are three main printing methods: letterpress, gravure, and lithography. In letterpress, raised parts of the printing plate are coated with ink and form the image or text on the paper. In gravure, the parts to be printed are formed by tiny pits in the metal plate. The plate is coated with ink and then cleaned to remove all the ink except for droplets that remain in the tiny pits. When the plate is pressed against paper, the paper soaks up the ink from the pits. Lithography (litho printing) relies on the fact that water and grease do not stick together. The part of the plate that will not be printed is moistened with water so that the greasy ink only sticks to the dry parts. Modern printing presses use the offset-litho printing method (*see right*).

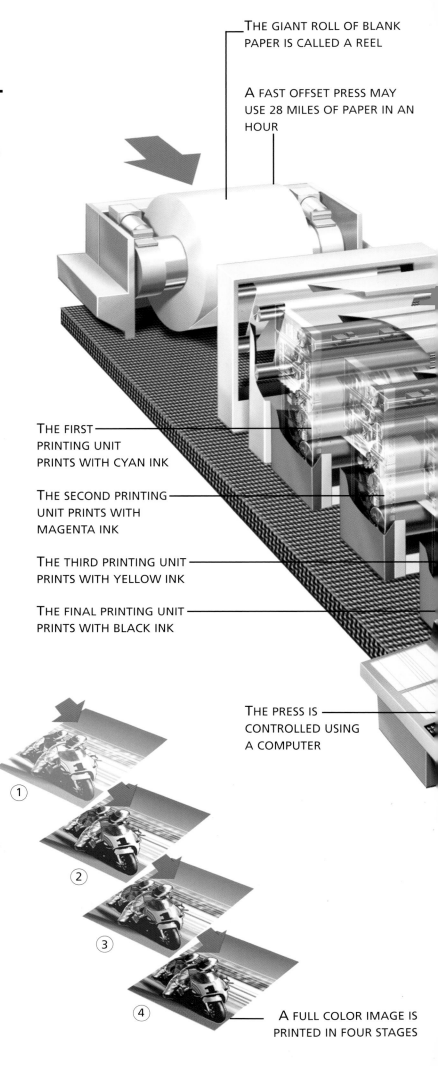

THE GIANT ROLL OF BLANK PAPER IS CALLED A REEL

A FAST OFFSET PRESS MAY USE 28 MILES OF PAPER IN AN HOUR

THE FIRST PRINTING UNIT PRINTS WITH CYAN INK

THE SECOND PRINTING UNIT PRINTS WITH MAGENTA INK

THE THIRD PRINTING UNIT PRINTS WITH YELLOW INK

THE FINAL PRINTING UNIT PRINTS WITH BLACK INK

THE PRESS IS CONTROLLED USING A COMPUTER

① ② ③ ④

A FULL COLOR IMAGE IS PRINTED IN FOUR STAGES

Printing in color

A printing press can print any color by using only four different colors of ink. The four colors are cyan (blue), magenta (purplish red), yellow, and black. Four separate printing plates are made so that each color can be printed on the paper separately as it makes its way through the press. The colored inks are never mixed. Instead, the four colors are printed as tiny dots which are so small they merge together on the paper to make different colors. The colors depend on the size and spacing of the dots.

In a printing press the cyan part of the image is printed first (1). Then the paper moves on to the next stage and the magenta part is printed on top of it (2). The paper moves on again and the yellow part is added (3). The process is completed by printing the black part (4).

A web offset press

This type of press, which uses the offset-litho method, is often used to print newspapers and magazines. Fast electric motors drive rollers which pull the paper through the press. The paper unwinds from a giant roll and then passes through a series of printing units. As in most printing presses, the printing plates are curved and fitted around rollers in each unit. There are four printing units in this press – one for each color.

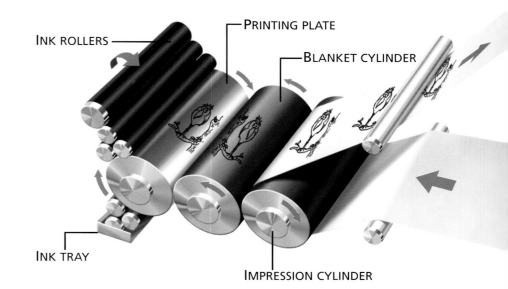

INK ROLLERS
PRINTING PLATE
BLANKET CYLINDER
INK TRAY
IMPRESSION CYLINDER

ELECTRIC MOTORS DRIVE THE PAPER THROUGH THE PRESS AT 2,460 FEET PER MINUTE

THE MOTORS, ROLLERS, AND CYLINDERS MUST NOT PULL THE PAPER TOO HARD OR IT WILL TEAR

THE PRINTED PAPER PASSES THROUGH A HEATED COMPARTMENT IN WHICH THE INK DRIES

Offset printing

In offset printing (*above*), the printing plate does not print directly on to the paper. Instead, the image on the printing plate is first transferred, or offset, on to a rubber-covered blanket cylinder. As the blanket cylinder turns, it prints the image on to the paper as it travels between the blanket cylinder and another cylinder called the impression cylinder.

A CUTTING AND FOLDING UNIT CUTS THE PAPER INTO FOLDED SHEETS

WHEELS SORT THE SEPARATE PRINTED SHEETS INTO COMPLETE NEWSPAPERS

CONVEYOR BELTS CARRY PRINTED NEWSPAPERS OUT OF THE PRESS

Taking Pictures

A CAMERA is a light-proof box with film inside and a lens at the front. The lens has an adjustable hole, or aperture, made from a ring of metal plates. When a photograph is taken the camera's shutter, which lets light on to the film, opens for a fraction of a second, and the lens focuses an image of the outside world on to the light-sensitive film. The amount of light falling on to the film can be adjusted in two ways: the shutter speed can be changed to alter the length of time that the shutter is open (for most photographs, the shutter is open for less than one hundredth of a second); or the aperture can be widened or narrowed. Electronic circuits in most cameras can measure the strength of light and set the aperture and shutter speed automatically.

The SLR
The SLR (Single Lens Reflex) is a popular type of camera. By the clever use of a mirror and a block of glass called a prism, it uses one lens to form both the image on the film and the image viewed through the camera's eyepiece. This means the same image that is seen in the eyepiece will appear on the photograph. Other types of cameras use two lenses, so if the camera is not held in just the right way the image on the photograph may not match the image seen in the eyepiece.

THE SHUTTER SPEED IS SELECTED BY TURNING A DIAL TO THE DESIRED SETTING

A SMALL LIQUID CRYSTAL DISPLAY SHOWS INFORMATION ABOUT THE CAMERA'S SETTINGS

THE EYEPIECE SHOWS A VIEW OF WHAT THE CAMERA IS POINTING AT

THE SHUTTER RELEASE BUTTON IS PRESSED TO TAKE A PHOTOGRAPH

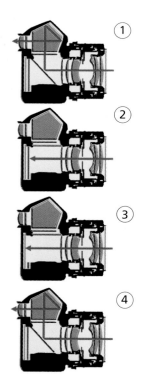

Pressing the button
Light coming in through the lens is reflected up to the eyepiece at the top of the camera by a mirror and a block of glass called a prism (1). To take a photograph, the shutter release button is pressed, causing the mirror to swing up and the diaphragm to close down to the correct size (2). Then the shutter itself opens to let light fall on the film (3). Finally, the shutter closes after a set time, the mirror drops down, and the diaphragm opens again to give a bright view through the eyepiece (4).

ELECTRONIC CIRCUITS MONITOR AND CONTROL THE CAMERA

BATTERIES POWER THE CAMERA'S ELECTRONIC CIRCUITS AND MOTORS

A MOTOR PULLS OUT A NEW PIECE OF FILM FOR EACH PHOTOGRAPH

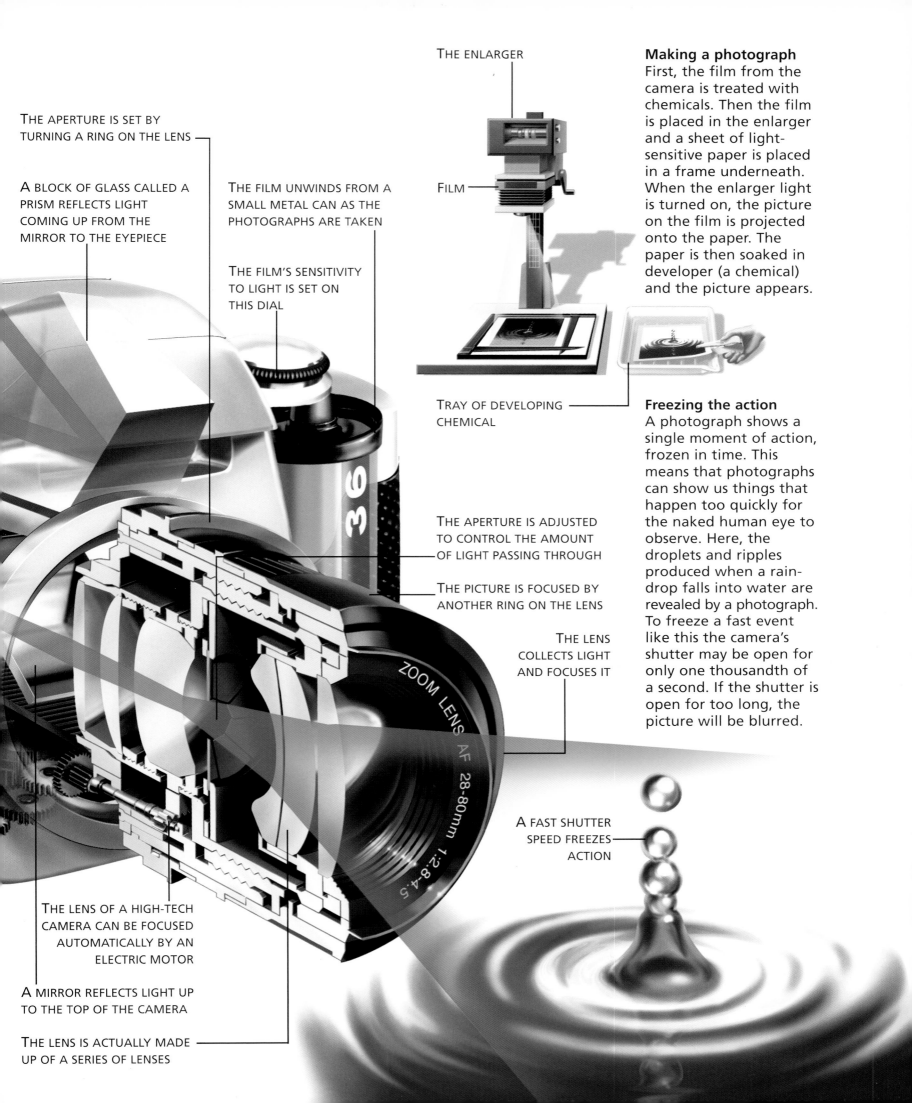

THE APERTURE IS SET BY TURNING A RING ON THE LENS

A BLOCK OF GLASS CALLED A PRISM REFLECTS LIGHT COMING UP FROM THE MIRROR TO THE EYEPIECE

THE FILM UNWINDS FROM A SMALL METAL CAN AS THE PHOTOGRAPHS ARE TAKEN

THE FILM'S SENSITIVITY TO LIGHT IS SET ON THIS DIAL

THE APERTURE IS ADJUSTED TO CONTROL THE AMOUNT OF LIGHT PASSING THROUGH

THE PICTURE IS FOCUSED BY ANOTHER RING ON THE LENS

THE LENS COLLECTS LIGHT AND FOCUSES IT

THE LENS OF A HIGH-TECH CAMERA CAN BE FOCUSED AUTOMATICALLY BY AN ELECTRIC MOTOR

A MIRROR REFLECTS LIGHT UP TO THE TOP OF THE CAMERA

THE LENS IS ACTUALLY MADE UP OF A SERIES OF LENSES

THE ENLARGER

FILM

TRAY OF DEVELOPING CHEMICAL

A FAST SHUTTER SPEED FREEZES ACTION

ZOOM LENS AF 28-80mm 1:2.8-4.5

Making a photograph
First, the film from the camera is treated with chemicals. Then the film is placed in the enlarger and a sheet of light-sensitive paper is placed in a frame underneath. When the enlarger light is turned on, the picture on the film is projected onto the paper. The paper is then soaked in developer (a chemical) and the picture appears.

Freezing the action
A photograph shows a single moment of action, frozen in time. This means that photographs can show us things that happen too quickly for the naked human eye to observe. Here, the droplets and ripples produced when a rain-drop falls into water are revealed by a photograph. To freeze a fast event like this the camera's shutter may be open for only one thousandth of a second. If the shutter is open for too long, the picture will be blurred.

Cameras in Space

A S LIGHT from distant stars and planets travels to the Earth's surface, our atmosphere bends it in different directions. It is this effect that makes the stars appear to twinkle. Unfortunately, it also prevents astronomers from taking clear photographs through their telescopes. Telescopes are often built on mountain tops so that there is less of the atmosphere above them, but the best place for them is above the atmosphere altogether, in space. The Hubble Space Telescope (*right*) is the biggest of these orbiting telescopes. It points its telescope deep into space. Cameras record the images produced. Cameras on board other orbiting satellites keep a constant watch on the Earth. Cameras carried by deep-space probes have photographed the planets and many of their moons. The probes send their photographs back to Earth by radio.

THE TELESCOPE RECEIVES COMMANDS AND SENDS DATA TO EARTH USING TWO DISH-SHAPED RADIO AERIALS

THE HUBBLE SPACE TELESCOPE ORBITS THE EARTH AT A HEIGHT OF ABOUT 373 MILES

THE PRIMARY MIRROR IS 8 FEET ACROSS AND MADE FROM ALUMINUM-COATED GLASS

TINY HEATERS WARM THE INSTRUMENTS WHILE THE TELESCOPE IS IN THE EARTH'S SHADOW

THE TELESCOPE'S TWO CAMERAS ARE HELD IN HERE

THE TELESCOPE'S IMAGE IS FORMED HERE

THE AFT SHROUD PROTECTS THE INSTRUMENTS AND MIRROR INSIDE IT

STAR TRACKERS CAN LOCK THE TELESCOPE ON TO ANY STAR AND HOLD THE TELESCOPE STEADY

BATTERIES SUPPLY ELECTRICITY WHEN THE TELESCOPE PASSES INTO THE EARTH'S SHADOW

TWO WING-LIKE SOLAR PANELS GENERATE ELECTRICITY FROM SUNLIGHT

The Hubble Space Telescope

The Hubble Space Telescope (HST) was launched by the Space Shuttle in 1990. Starlight entering the telescope is reflected by the primary mirror to the secondary mirror and then down the telescope to a package of cameras and other instruments.

Outside the atmosphere, it can take much clearer photographs than telescopes on Earth. The fuzzy image (*below left*) shows the star Melnick 34 as seen through a telescope on Earth. The sharp image (*below right*) shows the same star seen through the HST.

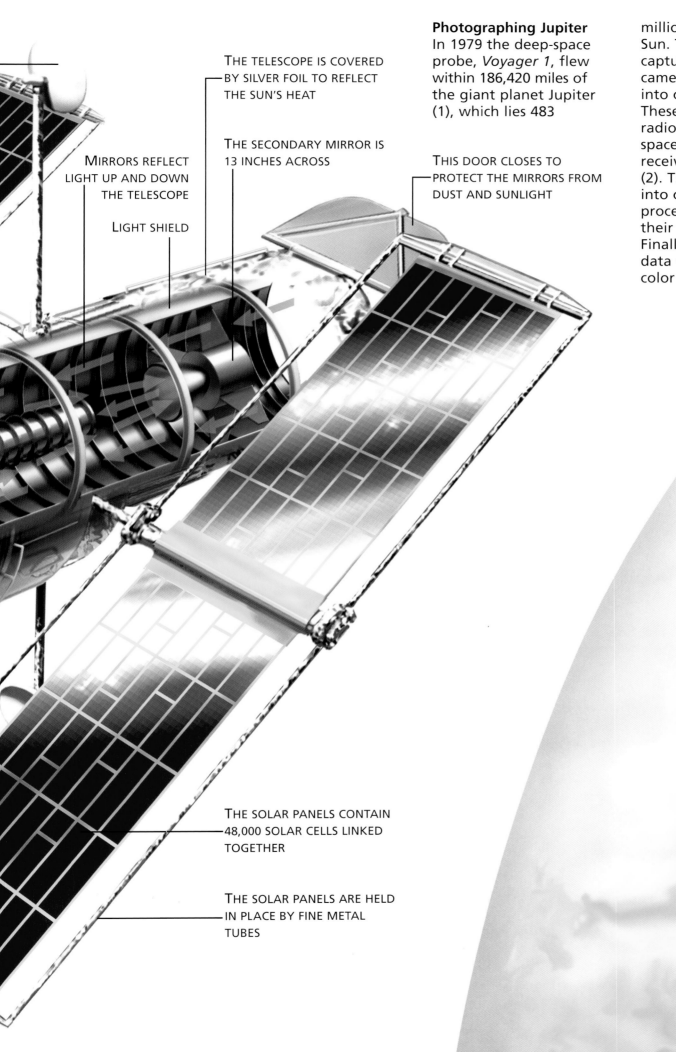

THE TELESCOPE IS COVERED BY SILVER FOIL TO REFLECT THE SUN'S HEAT

THE SECONDARY MIRROR IS 13 INCHES ACROSS

MIRRORS REFLECT LIGHT UP AND DOWN THE TELESCOPE

LIGHT SHIELD

THIS DOOR CLOSES TO PROTECT THE MIRRORS FROM DUST AND SUNLIGHT

THE SOLAR PANELS CONTAIN 48,000 SOLAR CELLS LINKED TOGETHER

THE SOLAR PANELS ARE HELD IN PLACE BY FINE METAL TUBES

Photographing Jupiter
In 1979 the deep-space probe, *Voyager 1*, flew within 186,420 miles of the giant planet Jupiter (1), which lies 483 million miles from the Sun. The images captured by its video cameras were converted into computer data. These were beamed by radio from the spacecraft to large receiving dishes on Earth (2). The data was fed into computers (3), and processed to improve their image quality. Finally, the processed data were used to make color photographs (4).

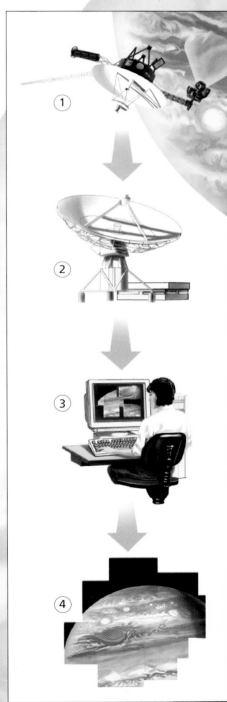

TV Cameras

TELEVISION CAMERAS turn images of the real world into electrical signals which can be broadcast and changed back into pictures by a television set.

Modern television cameras depend on a special type of chip called a CCD (Charge-Coupled Device). This is the part of a modern television camera that changes light into electricity. A CCD is covered by hundreds of thousands of light-sensitive points. When light falls on a CCD, it changes the voltage of these points according to how bright the light is. (Voltage is the force that makes an electric current flow.) Electronic circuits inside the camera read the voltage at every point on the CCD in a fraction of a second, making an electrical copy of the picture. Other circuits add extra information to mark the beginning and end of each line of the picture and each complete picture. The electrical signals from the camera, representing all the pictures it takes, can be broadcast live, or recorded on video tape ready to be edited and broadcast later.

Inside a TV camera
Light enters a television camera through a zoom lens. Pressing a switch turns on an electric motor that adjusts the lens to make the picture bigger or smaller. Light-sensitive devices inside the camera change the pictures from light into electrical signals. The camera operator aims the camera and makes sure that it is focused correctly by looking through the viewfinder. A tiny television screen shows the view through the camera's lens.

A MIRROR REFLECTS THE VIEWFINDER IMAGE OUT THROUGH THE EYEPIECE

THE CAMERA OPERATOR LOOKS THROUGH THE VIEWFINDER

A MICROPHONE CAN BE MOUNTED ON THE CAMERA TO PICK UP SOUND

PCM 16 bit 1.23.57.04

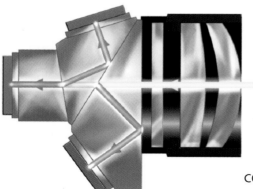

ELECTRONIC CIRCUITS CHANGE THE SIGNALS FROM THE CCDS INTO A TELEVISION PICTURE SIGNAL

A CUSHIONED SHOULDER PAD MAKES THE CAMERA COMFORTABLE TO HOLD

THE OPTICAL BLOCK SENDS THREE IMAGES TO THREE SEPARATE LIGHT SENSITIVE DEVICES

Splitting light
Light enters a television camera and passes through a specially shaped block of glass that splits it up into three beams. Coatings on the glass surfaces separate the incoming light into its red, green, and blue components. Three images – one red, one green, and one blue – fall on three CCDs. They produce the three signals that are combined by a television set to make a picture.

12

Satellite dish
Pictures from an outside broadcast are beamed to a control room by a microwave radio dish or satellite dish.

Editing computer
A computer can add captions to the pictures, or mix (combine) two or more television pictures together.

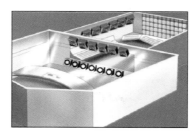

The control room
In a control room next to a studio, the director decides which pictures from the cameras to broadcast.

The transmitter
The pictures and sound from the studio are transmitted from a tower as radio signals. The radio signals spread out from the top of the transmitter tower at the speed of light.

THE VIEWFINDER MONITOR IS A TINY TELEVISION SCREEN

CAMERA-ON' INDICATOR LIGHT

LIGHT ENTERS THE CAMERA THROUGH THE LENS

A HOOD AROUND THE LENS STOPS STRAY LIGHT FROM ENTERING THE CAMERA

THE LENS IS MADE FROM SEVERAL LENSES WORKING TOGETHER

EXTRA CONTROLS ADJUST THE LENS

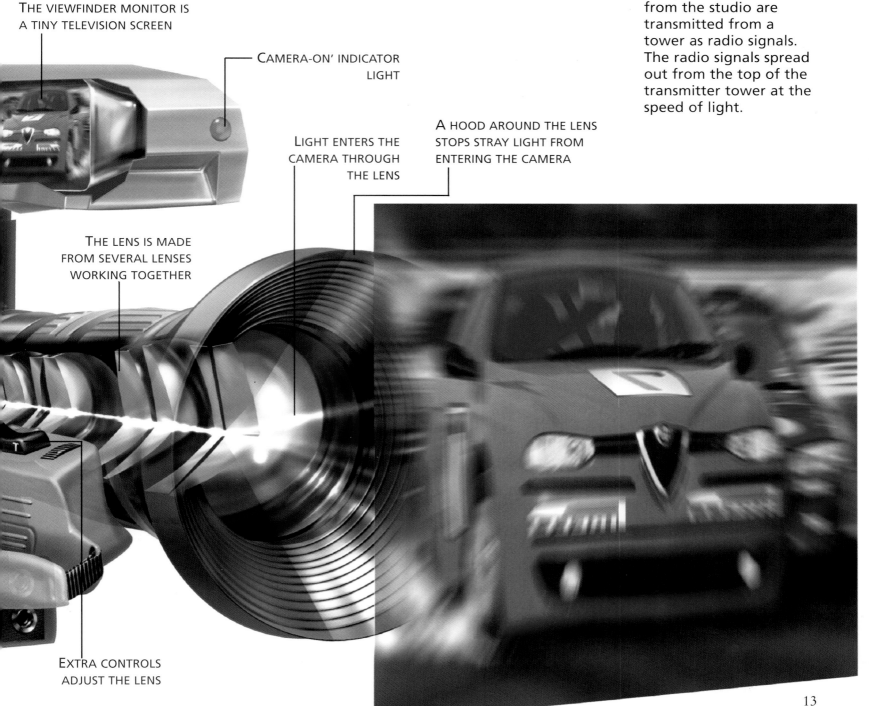

Televisions

A TELEVISION SET receives radio signals and changes them into sounds and pictures. The moving picture that appears on the screen is actually a series of still pictures that appear so quickly one after another (25 or 30 per second) that they seem to merge together and make a moving picture. In a fraction of a second, each picture is built up from hundreds of separate lines and each line contains hundreds of spots of light. The light comes from glowing chemicals, called phosphors, that are painted on the back of the screen. The phosphors glow when they are struck by three beams of electrons (electrically charged particles) that are fired from the back of the set. The electron beams sweep to and fro across the screen, tracing out the lines. The red, green, and blue phosphors are lit up by different electron beams. By varying the strengths of the beams, the three primary colors can be combined to make a whole range of colors.

Television on the move
The largest part of a television set is the glass picture tube. It makes a television set very heavy and fragile. The tube needs high voltages to work. This is because it has to send electrons at a high speed from the back of the tube to the front. It is now possible to build small television sets with thin, flat, lightweight screens that work on much lower voltages. This means they can be powered by batteries and carried in a car or a pocket, or even worn on a wrist.

AIR CIRCULATES FREELY INSIDE THE SPACIOUS CASE

HEAT ESCAPES THROUGH VENTILATION SLOTS IN THE CASE

THE TV CASE CUSHIONS THE TUBE FROM DAMAGING BUMPS AND KNOCKS

THE PICTURE IS MADE FROM TINY RED, GREEN, AND BLUE DOTS

MODERN TELEVISION SETS HAVE FLATTER SCREENS THAN OLDER SETS

PORTABLE TELEVISION SETS USE THIN FLAT SCREENS

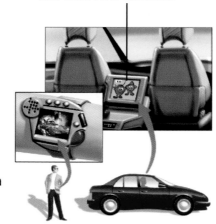

INDICATORS LIGHT UP TO SHOW THAT THE TELEVISION IS SWITCHED ON AND WORKING CORRECTLY

A DETECTOR HIDDEN BEHIND A RED FILTER RECEIVES COMMANDS FROM THE REMOTE-CONTROL HANDSET

A FEW ESSENTIAL CONTROLS ARE ON SHOW, WHILE OTHERS MAY BE HIDDEN BEHIND A FLAP

THE THREE ELECTRON BEAMS
PASS THROUGH A GRILL

ELECTRON BEAMS MAKE
PHOSPHORS GLOW

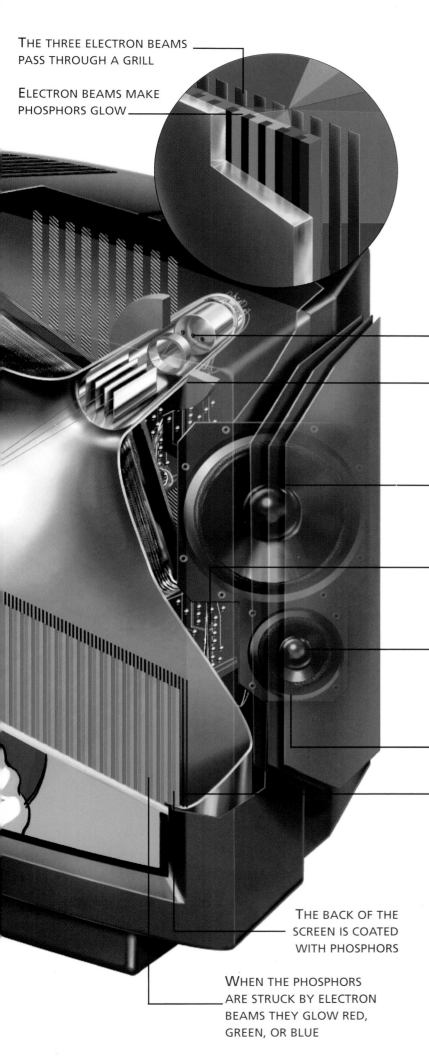

Red, green, and blue

The three electron beams pass through a metal sheet with holes or slots in it before they reach the screen. This ensures that one electron beam strikes only the phosphor that glows red, the second beam strikes only the green phosphor and the third beam strikes only the blue phosphor.

THE ELECTRON GUN FIRES
THREE BEAMS OF ELECTRONS
AT THE SCREEN

ELECTROMAGNETS AND
ELECTRICALLY CHARGED PLATES
MOVE THE BEAMS TO BUILD UP
THE PICTURE

A LARGE LOUDSPEAKER,
CALLED A WOOFER, MAKES
THE BASS (LOW FREQUENCY)
PART OF THE SOUND

CIRCUITS, OR ELECTRICAL
PATHWAYS ARE MADE ON
BOARDS THAT ARE EASY TO
REMOVE AND REPLACE

A SMALL LOUDSPEAKER,
CALLED A TWEETER, MAKES
THE HIGH FREQUENCY PART
OF THE SOUND

LOUDSPEAKERS ON BOTH
SIDES OF THE TELEVISION SET
PRODUCE STEREO SOUND

THE ELECTRON BEAMS PASS
THROUGH GUIDING HOLES OR
SLOTS BEFORE REACHING THE
SCREEN

THE BACK OF THE
SCREEN IS COATED
WITH PHOSPHORS

WHEN THE PHOSPHORS
ARE STRUCK BY ELECTRON
BEAMS THEY GLOW RED,
GREEN, OR BLUE

Receiving programs

Television signals reach our homes in three ways. The oldest and most common method is by a roof-top aerial (1). The aerial picks up signals broadcast from transmitters (2) dotted all over the country. Today there are two other ways of receiving television programs. Cable

television reaches the home along an underground fiber optic cable (3). Satellite television uses satellites (4) to beam programs directly into homes from space. The signals are received by a small dish aerial (5). One satellite can serve millions of homes. Cable and satellite television use signals that television sets were not designed to receive, so a decoder (6) is needed to change the signals into a form that television sets can use.

At the Cinema

A CINEMA FILM looks like a moving picture but is actually a series of still pictures. Each picture is slightly different from the one before. They are shown one after the other so quickly that our eyes and brain merge them together and we see them as one moving picture. The pictures that appear on the screen are produced by shining a light through film inside a projector. The picture is only one part of watching a movie. The sound is equally important. The latest movies have a digital soundtrack with six different sound channels.

FANS BLOW HOT AIR OUT OF THE PROJECTOR THROUGH METAL DUCTS (PIPES) TO KEEP IT COOL

DIGITAL SOUNDTRACK

The projector
An electric motor winds the film through the projector. Each frame (picture) is held in place for a moment and projected on to the screen by a bright light. A lens focuses the image. Then a spinning shutter cuts off the light and the film is moved on by one more frame. The intensely bright light inside the projector creates a lot of heat. To stop the projector from overheating fans constantly circulate cooler air.

Movie film
Movie film contains both pictures and sound. Two squiggly lines form one soundtrack. The same soundtrack in digital form is printed between the holes along one edge of the film. The soundtrack is picked up by shining a light through the edge of the film on to a photo-sensor.

A VERY BRIGHT LIGHT-BULB IS THE PROJECTOR'S LIGHT SOURCE

A SILVER REFLECTOR BOUNCES LIGHT FORWARD THROUGH THE FILM TO THE SCREEN

THE FILM UNWINDS FROM A
SPOOL

SHORT FILM SPOOLS ARE
ATTACHED TO THE PROJECTOR
(LONGER FILM SPOOLS ARE
MOUNTED ON A TABLE
BESIDE THE PROJECTOR)

SPRING-LOADED
ROLLERS TAKE UP ANY
SLACK IN THE FILM

THE LENS FOCUSES THE
PICTURE

A SPINNING SHUTTER CUTS
OFF THE LIGHT WHILE THE
FILM IS MOVING

FILM LEAVING THE
PROJECTOR IS WOUND
AROUND THE TAKE-UP SPOOL

The screen

The cinema screen is a reflective white surface on which the film is projected and focused. Black blinds on each side of the screen can be moved in or out to change the shape of the screen. Most movies are shot on film 35 mm wide, but other film sizes (16 mm and 70 mm) are also used.

Surround sound

Loudspeakers all around a cinema make sound reach the audience from every direction. Most of the speech comes from speakers behind the centre of the screen. Most of the music and background sounds come from speakers at each side of the screen. Sound effects come from the sides and rear.

SURROUND SPEAKERS LINE
THE REAR OF THE CINEMA

LOUDSPEAKERS BEHIND
CINEMA SCREEN

LARGE LOUDSPEAKERS
CALLED SUB-WOOFERS
PRODUCE THE BASS PARTS OF
A FILMS SOUNDTRACK

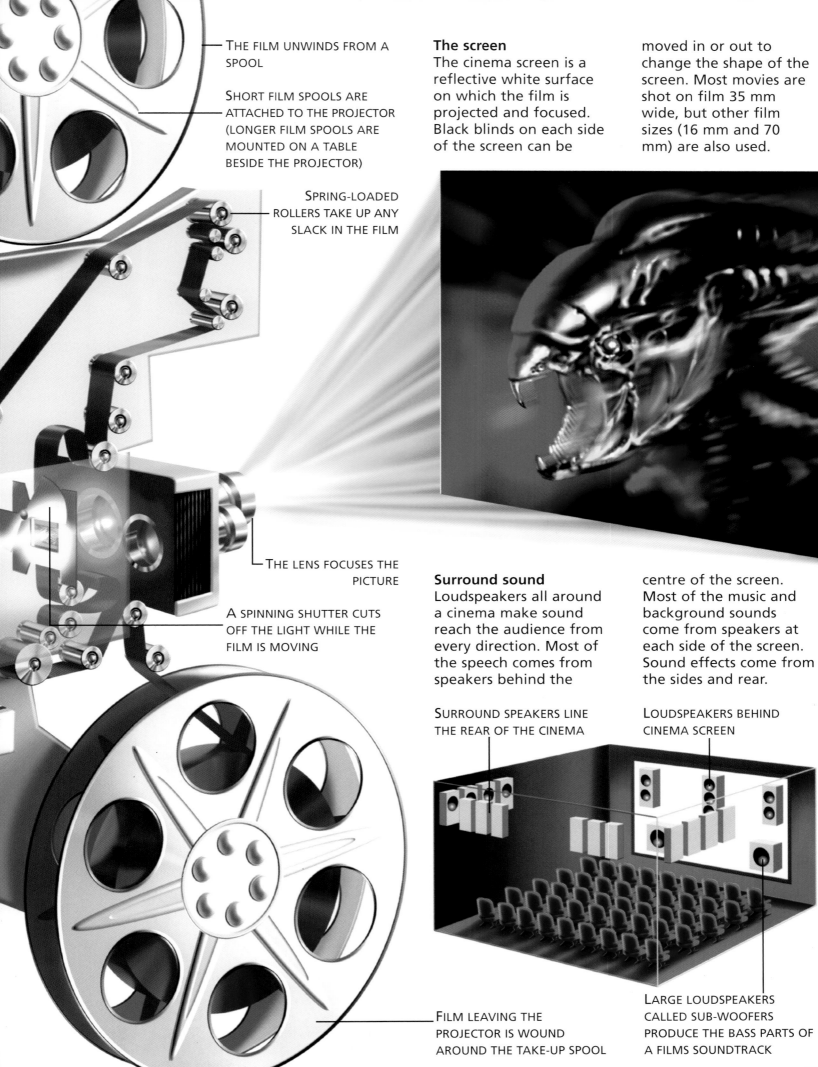

Tape Recording

TAPES STORE copies of sounds or pictures. Audio-tape records sound only. Video-tape records sound and pictures. The long, narrow ribbon of magnetic recording tape is wound around reels inside a plastic case called a cassette. Recording tape is a thin plastic film coated with powder made of microscopic, needle-shaped particles that can be magnetized.

A tape recorder's job is to change sounds or pictures into electric currents and then to change the electric currents into magnetic patterns on the tape. When a machine, such as the cassette player shown, plays the tape back, it works in the opposite way. It changes magnetic patterns recorded on the tape back into electric currents and converts them into sound. Most tape machines can both record and play.

Recording on tape

The magnetic particles on blank recording tape are magnetized in different directions, so they cancel out each other's magnetic force. When a tape recording is made, the recording head magnetizes the particles in to regular patterns, strengthening their magnetic force.

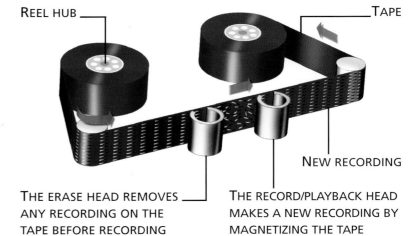

REEL HUB

TAPE

NEW RECORDING

THE ERASE HEAD REMOVES ANY RECORDING ON THE TAPE BEFORE RECORDING ON IT AGAIN

THE RECORD/PLAYBACK HEAD MAKES A NEW RECORDING BY MAGNETIZING THE TAPE

THE TOP OF THE PLAYER OPENS SO THAT A TAPE CASSETTE CAN BE LOADED

BATTERIES PROVIDE ELECTRICAL POWER FOR THE MOTOR THAT DRIVES THE TAPE AND THE ELECTRONIC CIRCUITRY

THE EARPIECES ARE PLUGGED INTO THE PLAYER

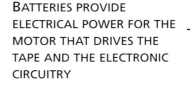

Video recording

A video recorder is a tape recorder that records sounds and pictures it receives from a television aerial. When a cassette is pushed inside the machine, a loop of tape is pulled out and wrapped round the video drum, which contains the recording and playback heads. The drum spins as the tape moves past. One spin of the drum records or plays one television picture.

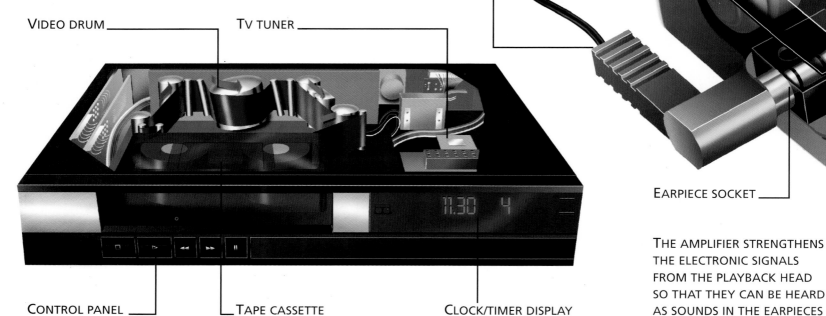

VIDEO DRUM

TV TUNER

CONTROL PANEL

TAPE CASSETTE

CLOCK/TIMER DISPLAY

EARPIECE SOCKET

THE AMPLIFIER STRENGTHENS THE ELECTRONIC SIGNALS FROM THE PLAYBACK HEAD SO THAT THEY CAN BE HEARD AS SOUNDS IN THE EARPIECES

11.30 4

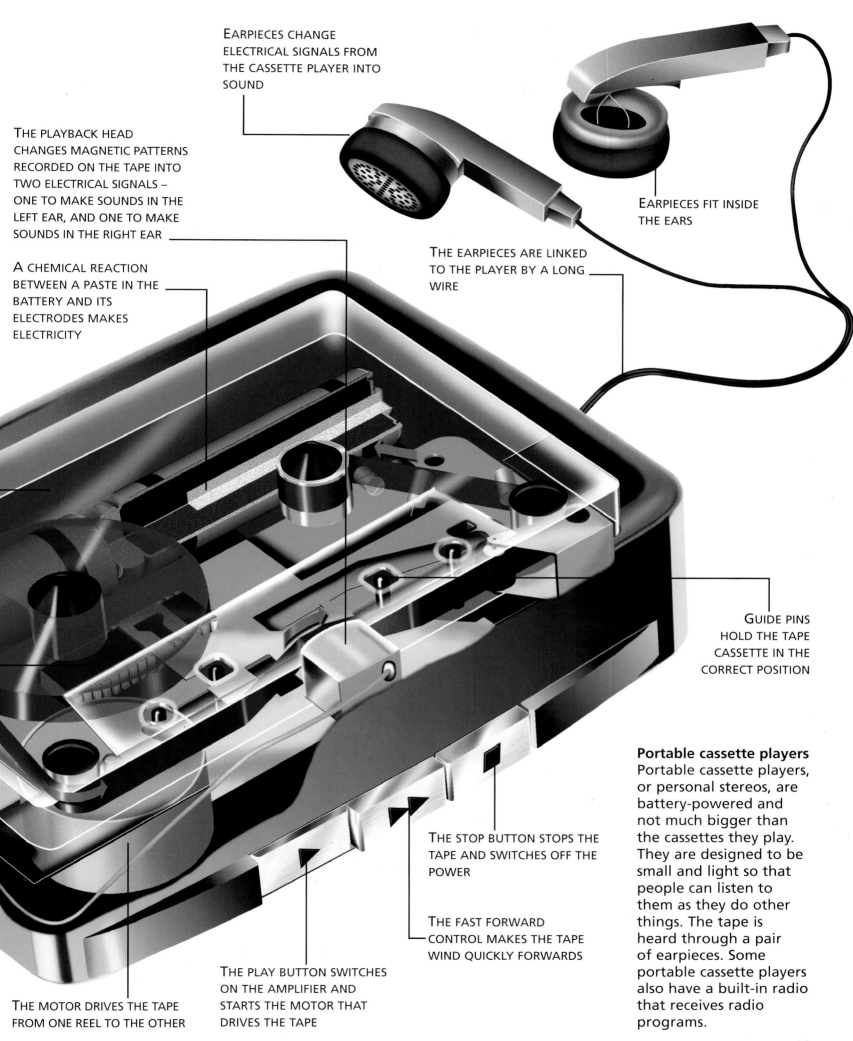

EARPIECES CHANGE ELECTRICAL SIGNALS FROM THE CASSETTE PLAYER INTO SOUND

THE PLAYBACK HEAD CHANGES MAGNETIC PATTERNS RECORDED ON THE TAPE INTO TWO ELECTRICAL SIGNALS – ONE TO MAKE SOUNDS IN THE LEFT EAR, AND ONE TO MAKE SOUNDS IN THE RIGHT EAR

A CHEMICAL REACTION BETWEEN A PASTE IN THE BATTERY AND ITS ELECTRODES MAKES ELECTRICITY

EARPIECES FIT INSIDE THE EARS

THE EARPIECES ARE LINKED TO THE PLAYER BY A LONG WIRE

GUIDE PINS HOLD THE TAPE CASSETTE IN THE CORRECT POSITION

THE STOP BUTTON STOPS THE TAPE AND SWITCHES OFF THE POWER

THE FAST FORWARD CONTROL MAKES THE TAPE WIND QUICKLY FORWARDS

THE PLAY BUTTON SWITCHES ON THE AMPLIFIER AND STARTS THE MOTOR THAT DRIVES THE TAPE

THE MOTOR DRIVES THE TAPE FROM ONE REEL TO THE OTHER

Portable cassette players
Portable cassette players, or personal stereos, are battery-powered and not much bigger than the cassettes they play. They are designed to be small and light so that people can listen to them as they do other things. The tape is heard through a pair of earpieces. Some portable cassette players also have a built-in radio that receives radio programs.

19

Compact Discs

COMPACT DISCS, or CDs, are small discs used to store high-quality recorded music or other sound. Sound is recorded on a CD as a pattern of microscopic pits. The pits are pressed into a silver-colored layer of metal under a protective, clear plastic coating. When a CD is loaded into a CD player, an electric motor spins the disc at high speed. A laser switches on and shines a narrow beam on the spinning disc. Reflections of the beam bounce back off the disc and are changed into electrical signals by a photo sensor and then into sound. The pattern of pits in a standard CD cannot be changed, so, unlike a tape cassette, the standard music CD is a 'read-only' disc, but there are also special recordable CDs.

Portable CD players
The electronic and mechanical parts of a CD player can now be made so small and light that portable CD players have become very popular. Portable CD players are available on their own or built into portable radio/cassette systems (*above*). Portable players are often fitted with anti-shock systems, so that the music continues playing even when the player is knocked and the laser is nudged out of position for a moment.

A CD SPINS AT 200 TO 500 TIMES A MINUTE

MUSIC IS RECORDED ON ONE SIDE ONLY

THE TRACKS OF PITS ARE LESS THAN TWO THOUSANDTHS OF A INCH APART

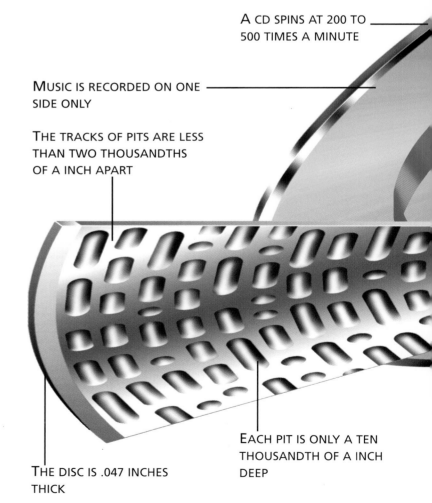

EACH PIT IS ONLY A TEN THOUSANDTH OF A INCH DEEP

THE DISC IS .047 INCHES THICK

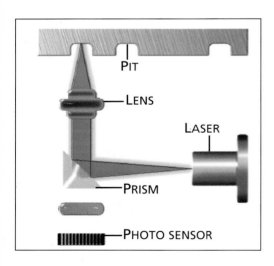

PIT
LENS
LASER
PRISM
PHOTO SENSOR

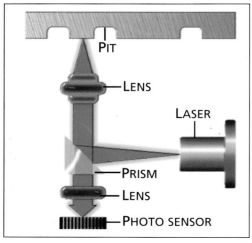

PIT
LENS
LASER
PRISM
LENS
PHOTO SENSOR

Playing a CD
A narrow beam is produced by a tiny laser underneath the compact disc. A lens focuses the beam on to a spot only one thousandth of a inch across. When the laser beam lands on a pit in the disc (*top left*), the rough surface of the pit scatters the laser beam in all directions. When the disc spins round a fraction more the laser beam falls on its smooth silver surface (*bottom left*). This makes a bright reflection bounce back from the disc through another lens and onto a photo-sensor. This changes the flashing reflections into a series of electrical pulses. The CD player then converts this stream of electrical code into sound.

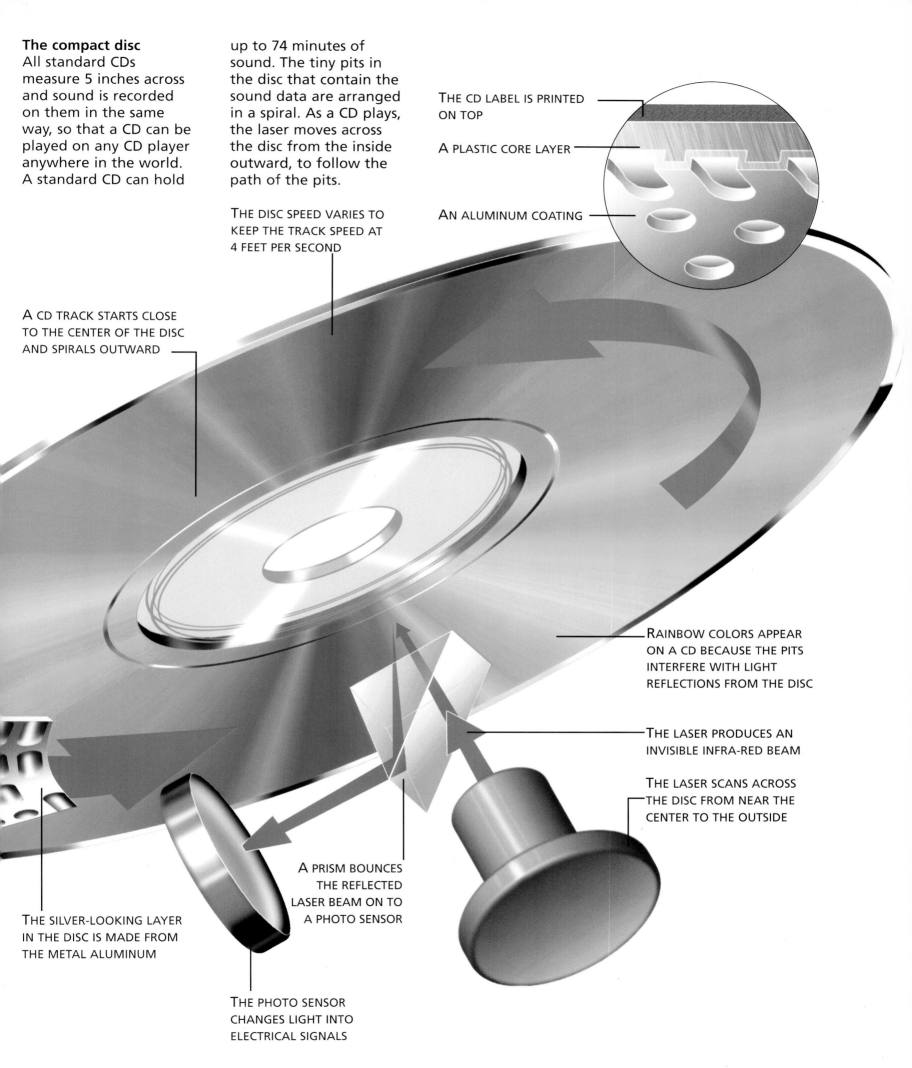

The compact disc
All standard CDs measure 5 inches across and sound is recorded on them in the same way, so that a CD can be played on any CD player anywhere in the world. A standard CD can hold up to 74 minutes of sound. The tiny pits in the disc that contain the sound data are arranged in a spiral. As a CD plays, the laser moves across the disc from the inside outward, to follow the path of the pits.

THE CD LABEL IS PRINTED ON TOP

A PLASTIC CORE LAYER

AN ALUMINUM COATING

THE DISC SPEED VARIES TO KEEP THE TRACK SPEED AT 4 FEET PER SECOND

A CD TRACK STARTS CLOSE TO THE CENTER OF THE DISC AND SPIRALS OUTWARD

RAINBOW COLORS APPEAR ON A CD BECAUSE THE PITS INTERFERE WITH LIGHT REFLECTIONS FROM THE DISC

THE LASER PRODUCES AN INVISIBLE INFRA-RED BEAM

THE LASER SCANS ACROSS THE DISC FROM NEAR THE CENTER TO THE OUTSIDE

THE SILVER-LOOKING LAYER IN THE DISC IS MADE FROM THE METAL ALUMINUM

A PRISM BOUNCES THE REFLECTED LASER BEAM ON TO A PHOTO SENSOR

THE PHOTO SENSOR CHANGES LIGHT INTO ELECTRICAL SIGNALS

Electronics

THE WORLD of modern communications relies on electronics to work. By electronics we mean the use of devices, called components, to control how electrons move in electric circuits. When electrons (invisible particles found in all atoms) move through a material, they produce an electric current. The electric currents used in communications carry information such as numbers, words, sounds, or pictures in a computer, or voices in a telephone. The electric currents flow around circuits and through the components. Components such as transistors and chips control the currents, switching them on or off, or making them larger or smaller.

All modern communications depend on electric currents and the electronic components that shape them. For example, in this electronic security system the sensors that detect a burglar breaking in communicate with the main control circuit by electric currents flowing along wires.

Resistor
A resistor is a component that resists the flow of electric current. It works by changing some of the electrical energy passing through it into heat.

Transistor
Transistors are used in two ways – as switches, turning electric currents on and off, or as amplifiers, making currents larger.

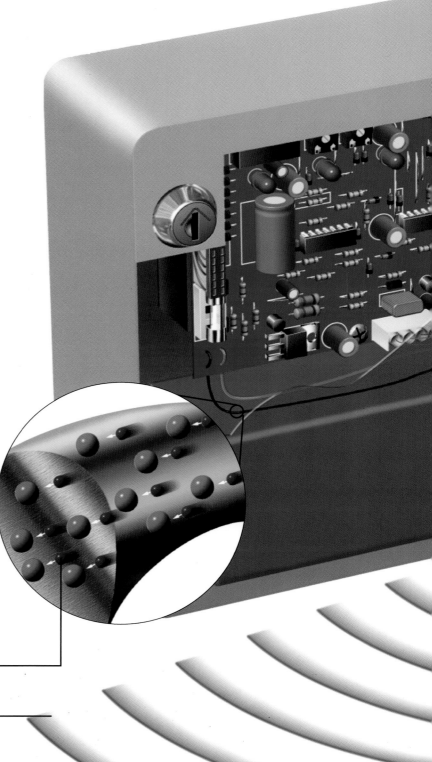

A WINDOW SENSOR IS ACTIVATED WHEN THE WINDOW OPENS

Electric current
An electric current is a flow of electrons from atom to atom through a material such as a copper wire. The more electrons that flow, the greater the current produced.

SENSORS ARE LINKED TO THE ALARM CIRCUIT BY WIRE

ELECTRONS JUMP FROM ATOM TO ATOM ALONG THE WIRE

SOUND WAVES

Fuse

A fuse is a thin piece of wire designed to melt if too much electric current flows through a circuit. It reduces the risk of electric shocks or fires.

Capacitor

A capacitor can store electricity for a time and then release it again. Capacitors can be used to smooth out variations in voltage.

Chip

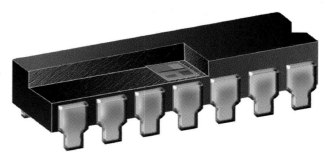

A chip, or integrated circuit, is a circuit constructed on a tiny sliver of silicon embedded in a block of plastic. Several chips can be linked together to form more complex circuits such as a computer. Different types of chips contain different electronic circuits. The type of circuit and what it is used for depends on what sort of electronic components it contains and how they are connected together.

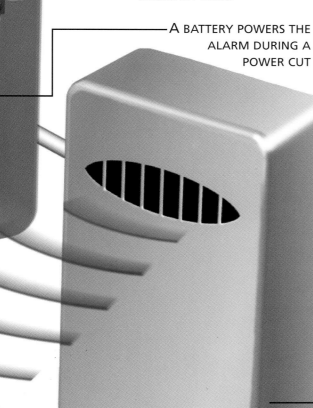

THE CONTROL BOX CONTAINS THE MAIN CIRCUIT BOARD

LEDS LIGHT UP TO SHOW WHICH PARTS OF THE SYSTEM ARE SWITCHED ON

CHIPS CONTAIN MOST OF THE SYSTEM'S ELECTRONIC COMPONENTS

ELECTRONIC COMPONENTS CHANGE THE ELECTRIC CURRENTS FLOWING THROUGH THEM

A BATTERY POWERS THE ALARM DURING A POWER CUT

A SIREN SOUNDS THE ALARM IF A BREAK-IN IS DETECTED

Electronic alarms

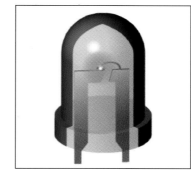

Homes and businesses are often protected by electronic security systems. All the windows and doors are fitted with sensors. These are switches that are operated when a window or door opens. Rooms may also be protected by motion sensors that detect movement. If someone enters a room after the alarm has been switched on, the circuit in the main control box detects which sensors have been activated and sounds the alarm.

Light emitting diode

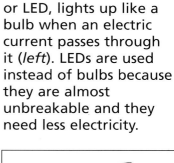

A light emitting diode, or LED, lights up like a bulb when an electric current passes through it (*left*). LEDs are used instead of bulbs because they are almost unbreakable and they need less electricity.

Transformer

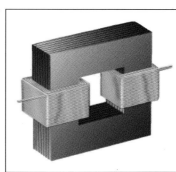

A transformer changes voltage. It is an iron frame with coils of wire wound round it. Electrical energy is supplied to the transformer by the primary coil. This coil creates a magnetic field, which makes a current flow through the secondary coil. Its voltage depends on the number of turns of wire in the two coils.

Telephones

TELEPHONES allow people to communicate with each other over long distances. A telephone does two jobs. When you speak into a telephone it changes the sound of your voice into a vibrating electric current. When a caller's voice arrives as an electric current, the telephone changes it back into sound waves. So, a telephone is really an energy converter. It converts (changes) sound energy into electrical energy and electrical energy into sound. A telephone also needs to be able to connect itself to one other telephone among all the millions of telephones in the world. For this it has a keypad or dial, so the caller can enter a unique number that identifies the other telephone. High-speed computers connect the many millions of telephone calls made every day around the world.

Inside the handset
When you speak into a telephone mouthpiece (*above right*), the sound waves from your voice make a thin sheet called a diaphragm, vibrate. This makes an iron armature vibrate too, which makes an electric current flow through a coil near a magnet. This current then travels down the telephone line to another telephone.

When an electric current is received by an earpiece (*right*), it flows through coils of wire. Magnetic forces produced by the coils make a nearby magnet vibrate. The magnet is linked to a diaphragm, which vibrates too, making the sound of the caller's voice.

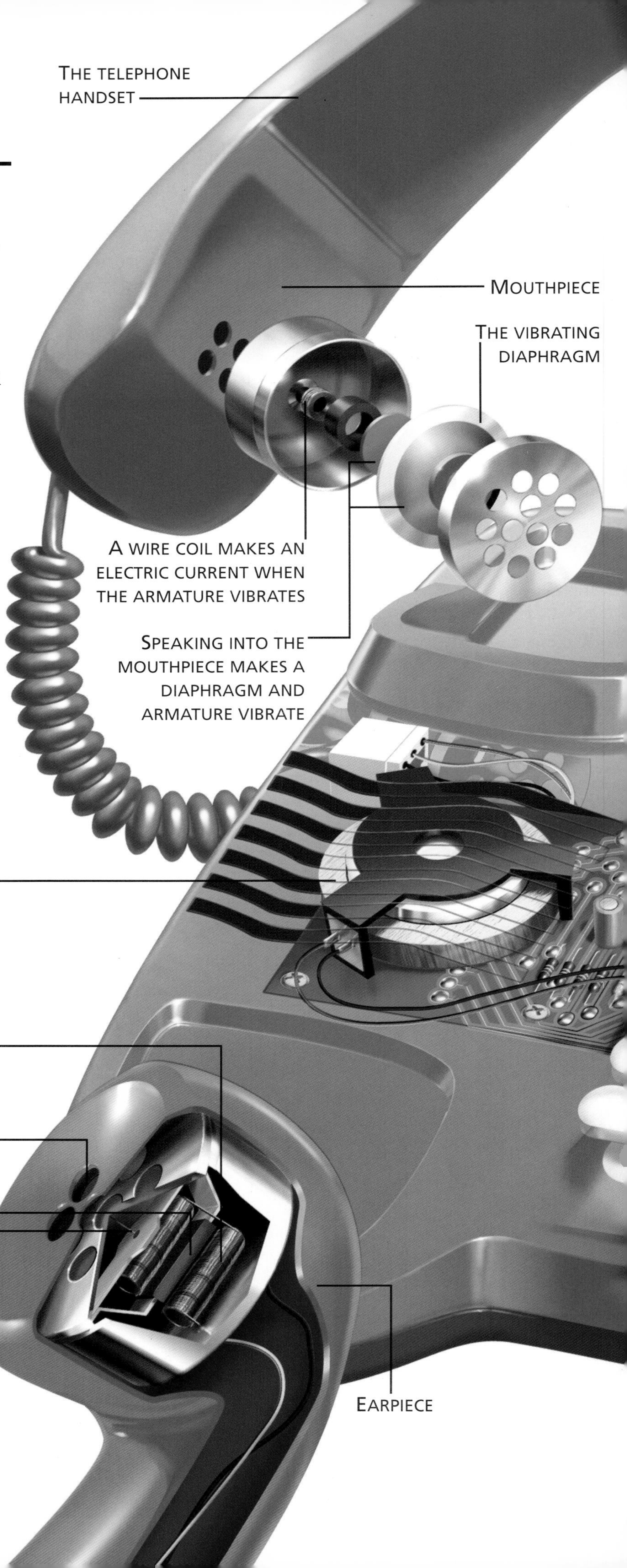

THE TELEPHONE HANDSET

MOUTHPIECE

THE VIBRATING DIAPHRAGM

A WIRE COIL MAKES AN ELECTRIC CURRENT WHEN THE ARMATURE VIBRATES

SPEAKING INTO THE MOUTHPIECE MAKES A DIAPHRAGM AND ARMATURE VIBRATE

THE TONE-CALLER 'RINGS' WHEN A CALL IS RECEIVED

ELECTRIC CURRENTS FROM THE CALLER MAKE WIRE COILS PRODUCE MAGNETIC FORCES

SOUND OUTLETS

MAGNETIC FORCES MAKE A MAGNET VIBRATE

A FINE WIRE TRANSFERS THE MAGNET'S VIBRATIONS TO THE DIAPHRAGM WHICH PRODUCES SOUND

EARPIECE

The telephone

Most telephones consist of a handset, containing a microphone and earpiece, and a base unit, containing a keypad and electronic circuits. Some types of telephone have a screen that shows the time and the number being dialled. Lifting the handset and pressing keys on the keypad tells the computer at the nearest telephone exchange which line to connect the telephone to. Extra control buttons allow the last number called to be dialed again by pressing one button, set the time on the display, or adjust the loudness of the ringing tone.

A CABLE CONNECTS THE TELEPHONE TO THE NEAREST EXCHANGE

A LIQUID CRYSTAL DISPLAY SHOWS THE TIME AND NUMBERS DIALED

Making a call

When you speak into a telephone, your voice is converted into an electric current which changes in time with your voice. It is an electrical copy of your voice. The electric current travels along the wire from your telephone to another telephone, which may be in the next street or on the other side of the world. There, the electric current is changed back into sound.

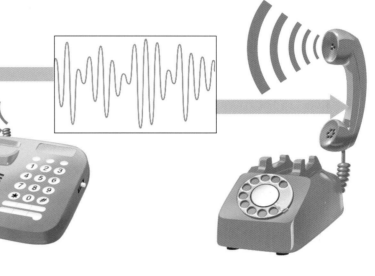

THE RINGING TONE CAN BE SWITCHED TO LOUD, SOFT, OR OFF

THE KEYPAD IS MOUNTED ON ITS OWN CIRCUIT BOARD

PRESSING A KEY CLOSES A SWITCH ON THE CIRCUIT BOARD BELOW

BUTTONS CONTROL EXTRA FUNCTIONS BUILT INTO THE TELEPHONE

ELECTRONIC COMPONENTS ARE LINKED BY METAL TRACKS

COMPONENTS AND TRACKS FORM PATHWAYS FOR ELECTRIC CURRENTS TO FLOW ALONG

THE '*' AND '#' KEYS CONTROL EXTRA FUNCTIONS

Fax machines

Facsimile transmission, or fax, machines send documents long distances by telephone. Motorized rollers pull each page into the machine. A light shines on it, line by line, and the reflections from the white parts of the paper are changed into coded electric signals. The signals are sent along a telephone line. At the other end, another fax machine uses the code to control a printer, which prints, line by line, a copy of the original page (*below*).

Telephone Networks

TELEPHONES ALL over the world are linked together in a very complicated global network. Cables, optical fibers, radio links, and satellites in space send millions of telephone calls back and forth every day.

In the past, telephone calls were connected by human operators using hand-controlled switchboards. Today, the telephone network is so big and complex that telephone calls are connected by computers.

All telephones used to be fixed in one place and connected to a telephone line by cable. Now we have mobile phones which are small enough to slip into a pocket and are linked to the telephone network by radio. People on ships at sea or flying in airplanes can make calls using satellite telephones. Even in the most remote parts of the world where there are no main power supplies, people can communicate using solar-powered telephones.

COMMUNICATIONS SATELLITES ORBIT HIGH ABOVE EVERY CONTINENT

RADIO SIGNALS SENT UP TO A SATELLITE ARE CALLED THE UPLINK

SIGNALS SENT DOWN FROM A SATELLITE ARE CALLED THE DOWNLINK

MOST COMMUNICATIONS SIGNALS TRAVEL UNDERGROUND OR BY RADIO, BUT SOME STILL TRAVEL ALONG WIRES ON POLES

MICROWAVES CARRY COMMUNICATIONS SIGNALS OVER LONG DISTANCES WITHOUT THE NEED FOR CABLES

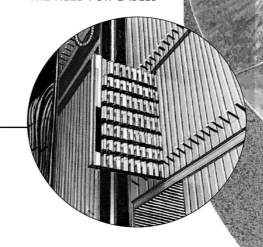

INSIDE A COMPUTERIZED TELEPHONE EXCHANGE

'DISH FARMS' LINK COMMUNICATIONS CENTERS WITH SATELLITES

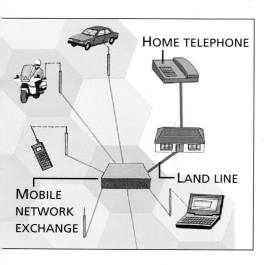

HOME TELEPHONE

LAND LINE

MOBILE NETWORK EXCHANGE

Mobile telephones
Areas where mobile telephones can be used are divided into a pattern of cells. Each cell has a radio antenna that can communicate with mobile telephones within the cell. When a mobile phone moves from one cell to another in the middle of a call, the call is automatically switched to the next cell. Mobile networks are linked to the rest of the international telephone system.

Telephone exchanges
Telephones are connected to telephone exchanges. Computers in automatic exchanges work out where each call is going to and connect it to the correct telephone line. If it is a long-distance call, the exchange connects it to another exchange. The computers work so fast, they can switch a call in a millionth of a second.

Satellites and cables

Communications satellites (1) allow airlines (2), military aircraft (3), and ships (4) to communicate with each other and with people on the ground. Telephone signals transmitted from an airliner by radio are picked up by a satellite orbiting far above it and passed on to a dish on the ground (5). Many thousands of telephone calls between continents are still carried by undersea cables (6).

MICROWAVES TRAVEL IN A STRAIGHT LINE FROM ONE DISH TO ANOTHER

MICROWAVE DISHES ARE MOUNTED ON TOP OF TALL TOWERS SO THAT THEY CAN 'SEE' FURTHER

OUR WORLD IS CRISS-CROSSED BY INVISIBLE RADIO SIGNALS CARRYING COUNTLESS TELEPHONE CALLS

SUBMARINE TELEPHONE CABLES USED TO BE METAL, BUT NOW THEY ARE OPTICAL FIBER CABLES

Optical cables

Metal telephone cables, which carry telephone calls as electric currents, are being replaced by optical fiber cables. Optical cables carry telephone calls as streams of light-flashes that travel along fine glass strands. The light reflects along the fibers core. Optical cables can carry many more telephone calls than metal cables. A pencil-thin optical cable containing 100 fibers can carry up to 200,000 conversations at the same time, and all travelling at the speed of light.

ONE SUBMARINE (UNDERSEA) TELEPHONE CABLE CAN CARRY 75,000 TELEPHONE CALLS

SUBMARINE TELEPHONE CABLES ARE LAID BY SHIPS WITH SPECIAL EQUIPMENT

CORE

OPTICAL FIBER

LIGHT BEAM

Satellites

COMMUNICATIONS satellites are spacecraft that beam radio signals around the world. These signals might be telephone calls, television programs, or computer data. All sorts of information can be changed into radio signals and sent anywhere on Earth at the speed of light in a fraction of a second. One communications satellite can handle tens of thousands of telephone calls. Radio signals sent from Earth into space are received by the satellite and then transmitted back down to Earth again. Radio equipment on a satellite needs electricity to work, so communications satellites have solar panels to make the electricity. They also have small thrusters to keep the satellite in the correct position, so that the antennas always point to Earth. If a satellite begins to drift out of position, the thrusters are fired to move it back again.

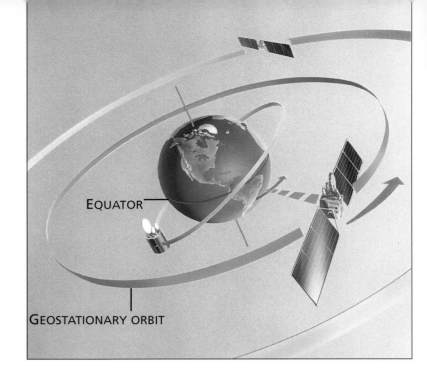

EQUATOR

GEOSTATIONARY ORBIT

Geostationary orbit
Satellites in space close to Earth have to keep flying very fast to stop gravity from pulling them down. Further away from Earth, where gravity is weaker, satellites can move more slowly. Most communications satellites circle the Earth 22,370 miles above the equator (an imaginary line around the Earth's middle). A satellite in this special orbit, called geostationary orbit, circles the Earth once every 24 hours. As the Earth also turns once every 24 hours, the satellite always appears to be at the same point in the sky.

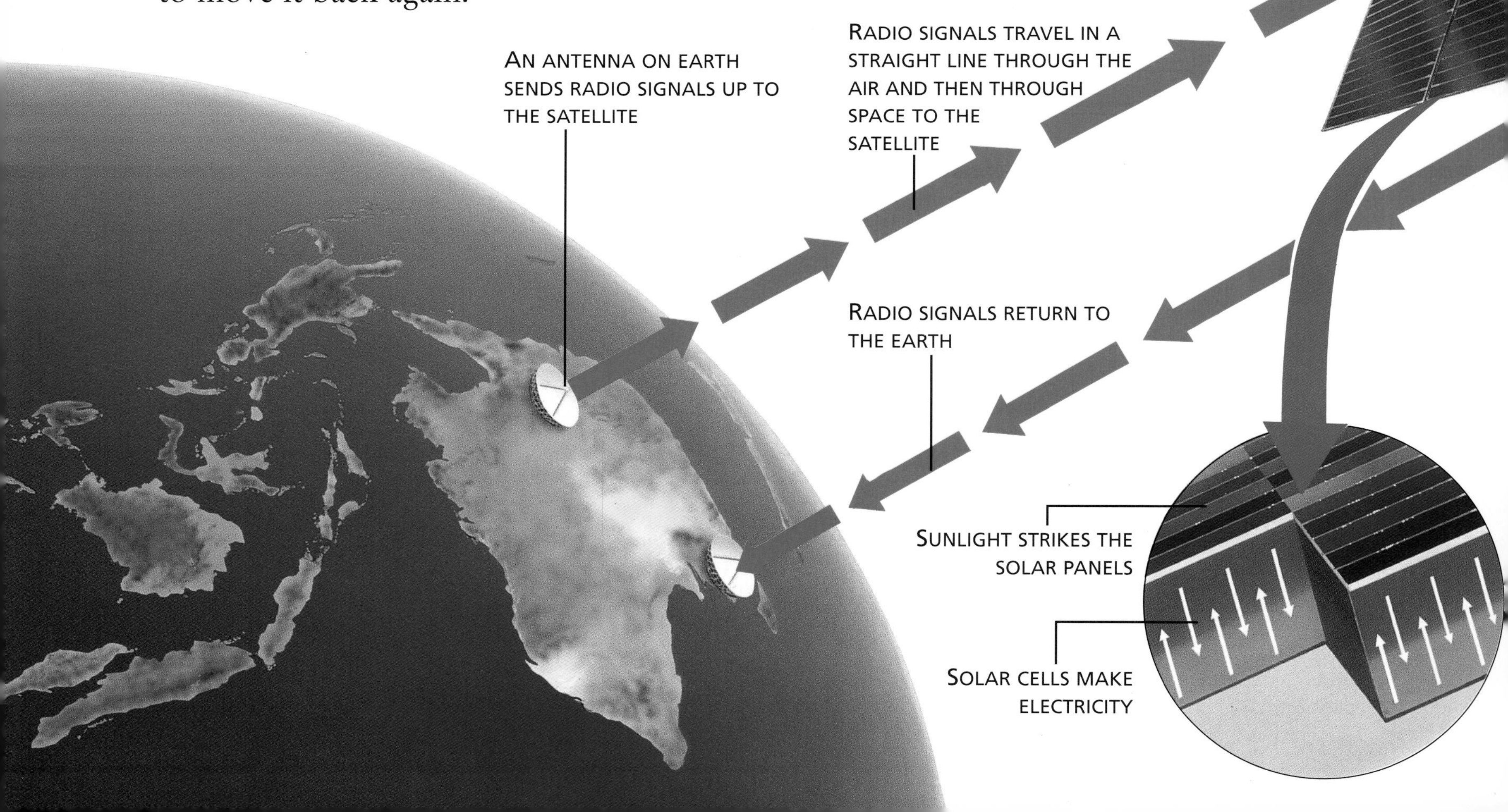

AN ANTENNA ON EARTH SENDS RADIO SIGNALS UP TO THE SATELLITE

RADIO SIGNALS TRAVEL IN A STRAIGHT LINE THROUGH THE AIR AND THEN THROUGH SPACE TO THE SATELLITE

RADIO SIGNALS RETURN TO THE EARTH

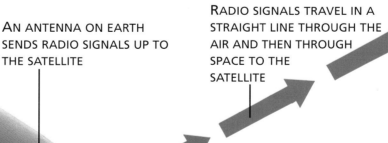

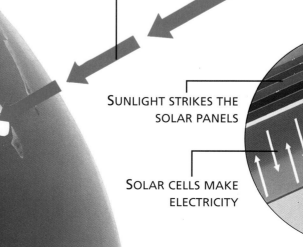

SUNLIGHT STRIKES THE SOLAR PANELS

SOLAR CELLS MAKE ELECTRICITY

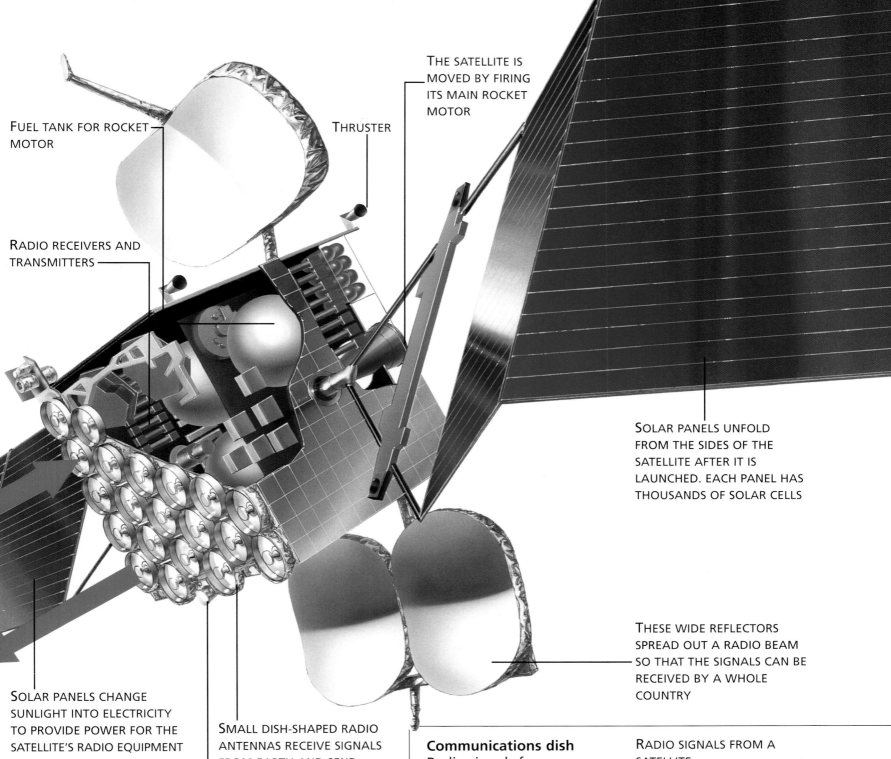

FUEL TANK FOR ROCKET MOTOR

THRUSTER

THE SATELLITE IS MOVED BY FIRING ITS MAIN ROCKET MOTOR

RADIO RECEIVERS AND TRANSMITTERS

SOLAR PANELS UNFOLD FROM THE SIDES OF THE SATELLITE AFTER IT IS LAUNCHED. EACH PANEL HAS THOUSANDS OF SOLAR CELLS

THESE WIDE REFLECTORS SPREAD OUT A RADIO BEAM SO THAT THE SIGNALS CAN BE RECEIVED BY A WHOLE COUNTRY

SOLAR PANELS CHANGE SUNLIGHT INTO ELECTRICITY TO PROVIDE POWER FOR THE SATELLITE'S RADIO EQUIPMENT

SMALL DISH-SHAPED RADIO ANTENNAS RECEIVE SIGNALS FROM EARTH AND SEND THEM BACK AGAIN

COMMUNICATIONS SATELLITES ARE FITTED WITH DIFFERENT TYPES OF RADIO ANTENNAS TO HANDLE DIFFERENT SIGNALS

Solar power

Communications satellites must work in space for many years. During that time, they have to make their own electricity. The electricity is made by solar cells. When light hits a solar cell, the cell behaves like a tiny battery and makes a small amount of electricity. Thousands of cells work together, making enough electricity to power the satellite's equipment.

Communications dish

Radio signals from satellites in space are received on Earth by dish-shaped antennas. The signals are very weak. A dish-shaped antenna strengthens them by collecting signals over a large area and then bringing them together in one small spot where the receiver is. The radio receiver may be held above the dish at the end of one or more legs, or it may be behind a hole in the middle of the dish.

RADIO SIGNALS FROM A SATELLITE

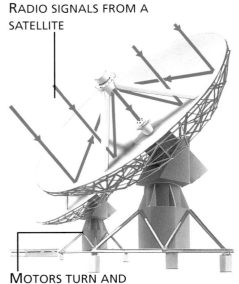

MOTORS TURN AND TILT THE DISH

Radios

A RADIO SET receives radio signals and changes them into sounds. First the signals are picked up by an antenna. The antenna might be a length of wire, a coil of wire, or a long metal rod. As the invisible radio waves stream past the antenna, they make tiny electric currents flow in the antenna. The radio set changes and amplifies (strengthens) these tiny currents so that they can make a loudspeaker work. Radio signals vibrate very quickly, about 100 million vibrations per second for a VHF (Very High Frequency) radio program. These signals 'carry' the sound signals. A radio set separates the sound signals from the radio signals and changes them into sound.

A radio antenna picks up dozens, perhaps hundreds, of radio stations. By turning a tuning dial or pressing a button, we can select just one of these stations to listen to.

Radio transmitters
Radio transmitting antennas broadcast radio signals in all directions. Antennas are often on the top of tall towers which stand on high ground. A large radio transmitter serving a wide area is very powerful. It may be equivalent to the power of 250 one-bar electric fires.

THE TUNING DIAL IS TURNED TO TUNE INTO DIFFERENT STATIONS

A NEEDLE ON A SCALE (OR SOMETIMES A DIGITAL DISPLAY) SHOWS WHAT STATION THE RADIO IS TUNED TO

THE RADIO CIRCUIT IS MADE FROM COMPONENTS FIXED TO A PRINTED CIRCUIT BOARD

Microphones
Microphones are used to broadcast sound, such as a person's voice, on the radio. A microphone changes sound waves into an electric current flowing along a wire. The sound waves make a thin sheet called a diaphragm vibrate. The diaphragm is fixed to a coil of wire inside a magnet. When the diaphragm moves, the coil moves too, and the magnet creates tiny electric currents in the coil. The electric currents change and vibrate in the same way as the sound waves.

A FOAM WINDSHIELD STOPS THE WIND FROM MAKING RUSHING NOISES

SOUNDS PASS THROUGH THE WINDSHIELD AND MAKE THE DIAPHRAGM VIBRATE

FIXED MAGNET

A MAGNET MAKES ELECTRIC CURRENTS FLOW IN A COIL OF THIN WIRE THAT VIBRATES WITH THE DIAPHRAGM

WIRES CARRY THE ELECTRIC CURRENTS AWAY

PORTABLE RADIOS ARE POWERED BY BATTERIES FITTED INSIDE A BATTERY COMPARTMENT

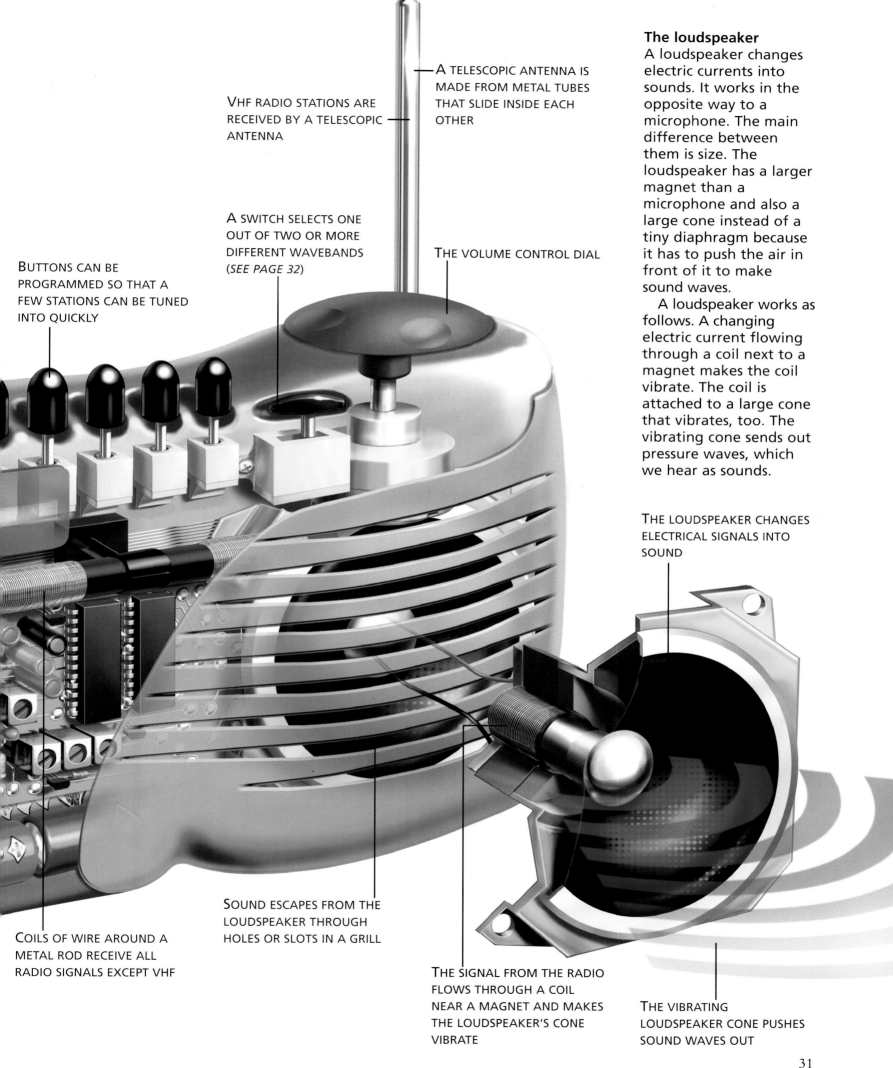

A TELESCOPIC ANTENNA IS MADE FROM METAL TUBES THAT SLIDE INSIDE EACH OTHER

VHF RADIO STATIONS ARE RECEIVED BY A TELESCOPIC ANTENNA

The loudspeaker
A loudspeaker changes electric currents into sounds. It works in the opposite way to a microphone. The main difference between them is size. The loudspeaker has a larger magnet than a microphone and also a large cone instead of a tiny diaphragm because it has to push the air in front of it to make sound waves.

A loudspeaker works as follows. A changing electric current flowing through a coil next to a magnet makes the coil vibrate. The coil is attached to a large cone that vibrates, too. The vibrating cone sends out pressure waves, which we hear as sounds.

A SWITCH SELECTS ONE OUT OF TWO OR MORE DIFFERENT WAVEBANDS (*SEE PAGE 32*)

THE VOLUME CONTROL DIAL

BUTTONS CAN BE PROGRAMMED SO THAT A FEW STATIONS CAN BE TUNED INTO QUICKLY

THE LOUDSPEAKER CHANGES ELECTRICAL SIGNALS INTO SOUND

COILS OF WIRE AROUND A METAL ROD RECEIVE ALL RADIO SIGNALS EXCEPT VHF

SOUND ESCAPES FROM THE LOUDSPEAKER THROUGH HOLES OR SLOTS IN A GRILL

THE SIGNAL FROM THE RADIO FLOWS THROUGH A COIL NEAR A MAGNET AND MAKES THE LOUDSPEAKER'S CONE VIBRATE

THE VIBRATING LOUDSPEAKER CONE PUSHES SOUND WAVES OUT

Radio Waves

RADIO WAVES are invisible waves of energy that travel through the air. We mainly use radio waves for communicating with each other. Both radio and television rely on radio waves to carry their sound and picture signals. In radio transmission a microphone changes sound into electrical signals. These signals are combined with a radio wave called a carrier wave and then transmitted. When received, the signals are separated from the carrier wave, amplified to make them stronger, and then fed into a loudspeaker. There are many different kinds of radio wave. Some radio waves hug the Earth's surface as they travel along. Others bounce off a layer of charged particles in the atmosphere called the ionosphere. Yet others pass into space and so can be used to communicate with satellites and astronauts.

COMMUNICATIONS SATELLITES RELAY RADIO SIGNALS FROM ONE PART OF THE EARTH TO ANOTHER

RADIO WAVES BETWEEN 3 INCHES AND 33 FEET LONG PASS THROUGH THE IONOSPHERE

THE IONOSPHERE REFLECTS SOME RADIO SIGNALS BACK TO EARTH

A RADIO SIGNAL SENT TO EARTH BY A SATELLITE IS CALLED THE DOWNLINK

THE LONGEST RADIO WAVES HUG THE EARTH'S SURFACE

A RADIO SIGNAL SENT UP TO A SATELLITE IS CALLED THE UPLINK

A DISH-SHAPED ANTENNA TRANSMITS A CONCENTRATED RADIO BEAM

SUBMARINES CAN COMMUNICATE BY RAISING A RADIO ANTENNA ABOVE THE WATER

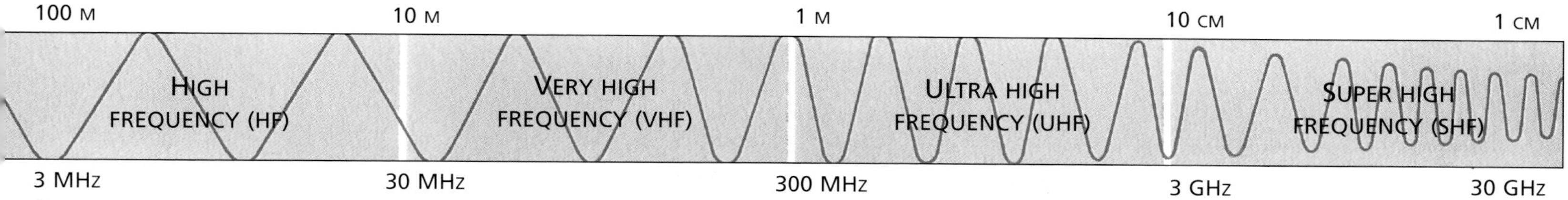

100 M		10 M		1 M		10 CM		1 CM
HIGH FREQUENCY (HF)		VERY HIGH FREQUENCY (VHF)		ULTRA HIGH FREQUENCY (UHF)		SUPER HIGH FREQUENCY (SHF)		
3 MHz		30 MHz		300 MHz		3 GHz		30 GHz

SOME RADIO WAVES CAN BE SENT BY BOUNCING THEM OFF THE IONOSPHERE

TALL TOWERS HOLD RADIO ANTENNAS HIGH ABOVE OBSTACLES

MICROWAVES ARE RADIO WAVES BETWEEN 0.39 INCHES AND 12 INCHES LONG

MICROWAVES TRAVEL IN STRAIGHT LINES FROM ONE ANTENNA TO ANOTHER

A MICROWAVE TOWER HAS MANY DISH ANTENNAS POINTING IN DIFFERENT DIRECTIONS

RADIO ANTENNAS ARE OFTEN PUT ON HIGH GROUND

UNWANTED REFLECTIONS FROM BUILDINGS AND HILLS CAN CAUSE INTERFERENCE

RADIO WAVES SPAN VAST DISTANCES WHERE IT WOULD BE DIFFICULT OR IMPOSSIBLE TO LAY CABLES

Wavebands

Radio waves of all lengths, called the radio spectrum, are divided up into a series of smaller bands according to their wavelength. The main wavebands that are used for radio communications are shown above. Radios can be tuned to pick up radio waves on different wavebands.

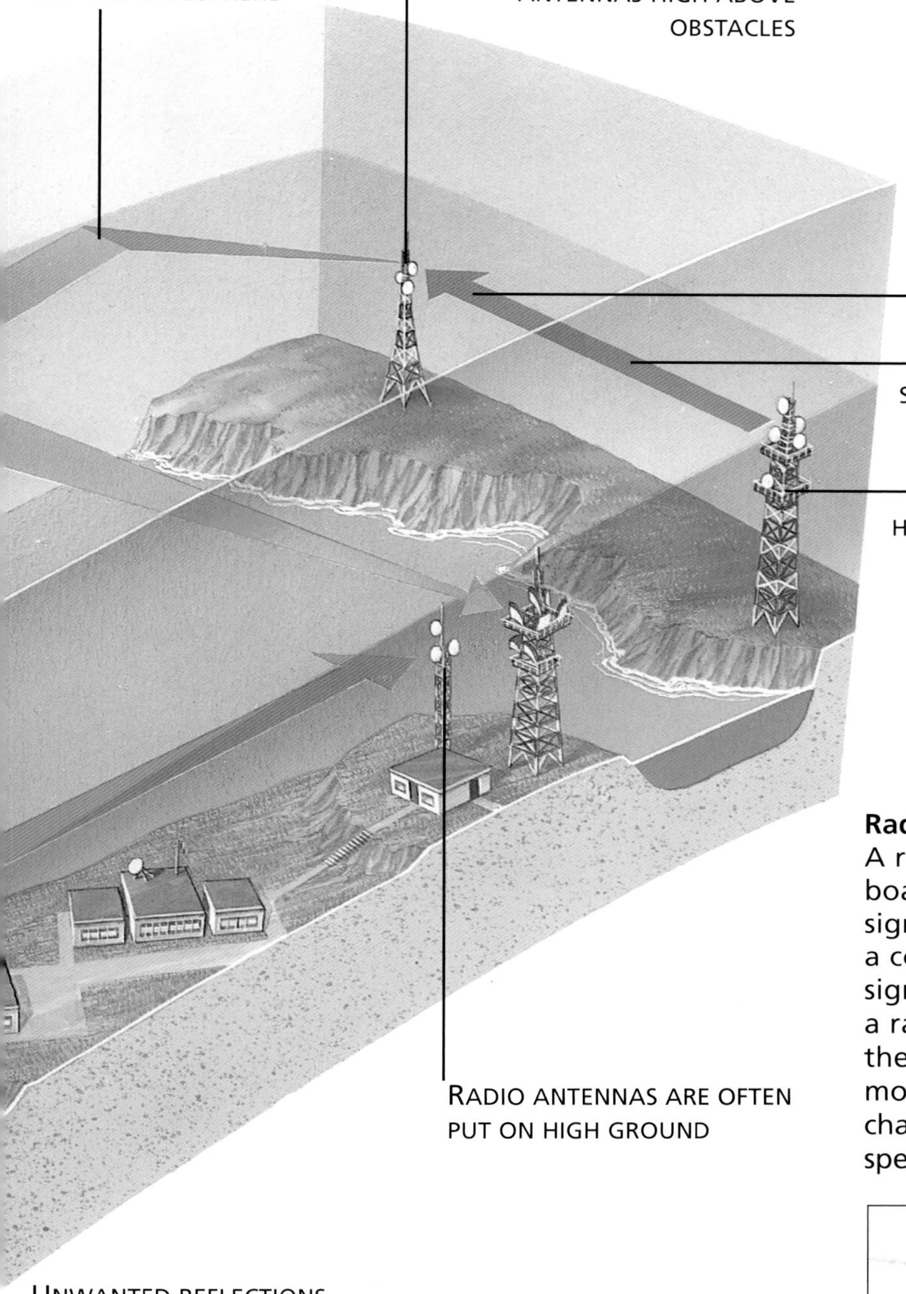

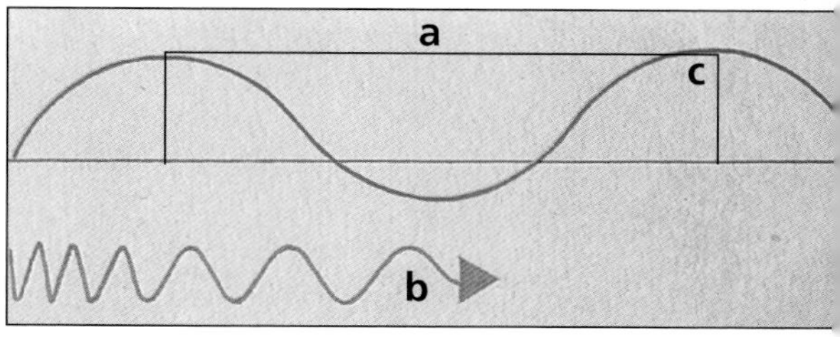

A radio wave

A radio wave has wavelength (a), frequency (b), and amplitude (c). When wavelength (the length of one complete wave) is multiplied by frequency (the number of waves passing a point in one second) the answer is equal to the speed of light. The amplitude is the size of the wave's peaks. Frequency is measured in hertz. One hertz (1 Hz) is one complete wave per second.

Radio control

A radio-controlled model boat is guided by radio signals transmitted from a control box. The signals are picked up by a radio receiver inside the model. They operate motorized controls that change the boat's engine speed or move its rudder.

CONTROL BOX

Radar

RADAR IS used to find distant objects, from storm clouds to aircraft, by bouncing radio waves off them. A radar transmitter sends out pulses of radio waves. If they hit an object, some radio waves are reflected back and are picked up by a receiver. Metal objects such as aircraft or ships produce the strongest radar reflections. The time it takes for a radar pulse to return to the receiver is used to calculate how far away an object is. This type of radar is called primary radar. Another type of radar, secondary radar, works in a different way. Secondary radar triggers a radio set to send out information. When a device called a transponder, carried by an airplane receives secondary radar pulses, it transmits a radio signal containing coded information about the plane. The latest military aircraft, called stealth planes, are designed so that they produce the smallest possible radar reflection, to make them difficult for an enemy to detect.

Secondary radar
Air-traffic controllers use radar to guide planes safely onward to their destinations. They need to know which plane is which on their radar screens, how high the planes are flying, and their destination. Every airliner carries a transponder in its belly which supplies air-traffic controllers with this information. When a plane's transponder receives the correct radar signal, it transmits the plane's flight number together with its height and destination.

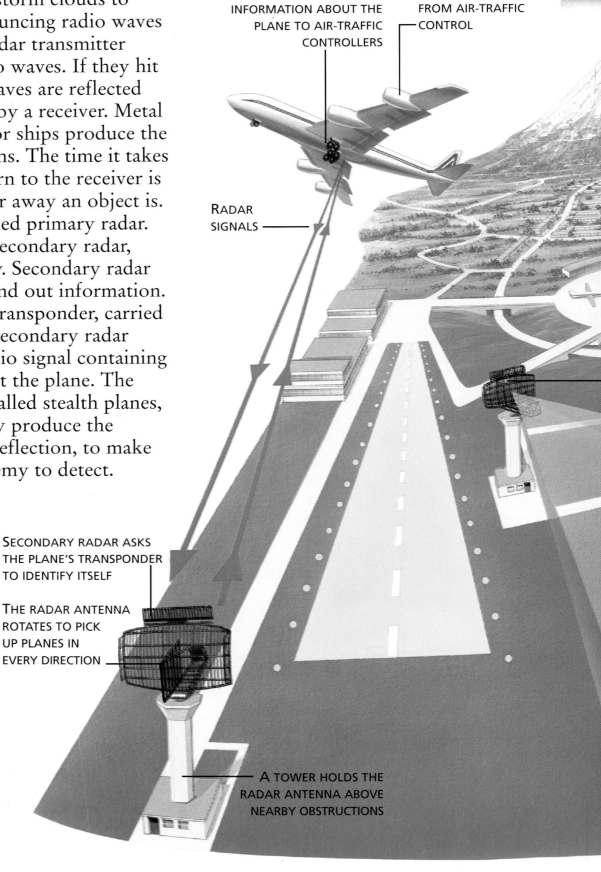

THE TRANSPONDER SENDS INFORMATION ABOUT THE PLANE TO AIR-TRAFFIC CONTROLLERS

AIRCRAFT CANNOT CHANGE HEIGHT OR DIRECTION WITHOUT PERMISSION FROM AIR-TRAFFIC CONTROL

RADAR SIGNALS

SECONDARY RADAR ASKS THE PLANE'S TRANSPONDER TO IDENTIFY ITSELF

THE RADAR ANTENNA ROTATES TO PICK UP PLANES IN EVERY DIRECTION

A TOWER HOLDS THE RADAR ANTENNA ABOVE NEARBY OBSTRUCTIONS

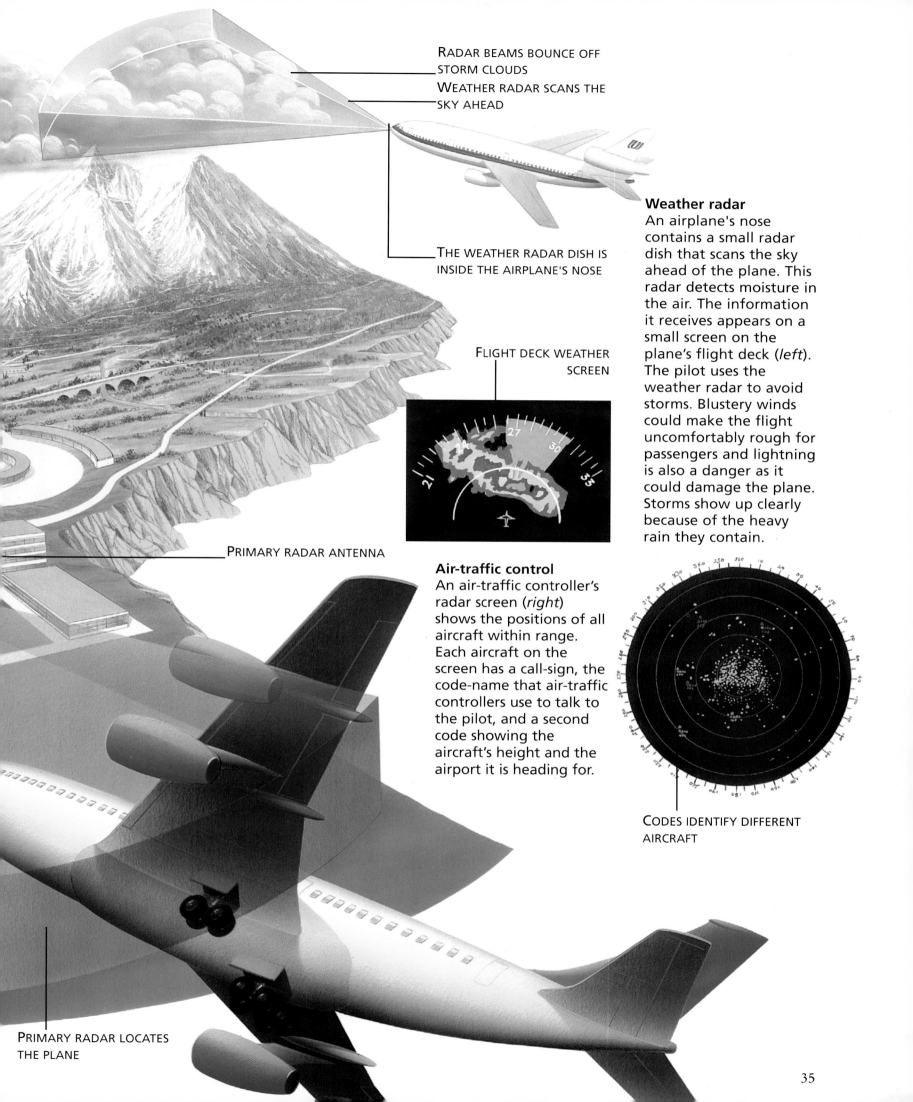

RADAR BEAMS BOUNCE OFF
STORM CLOUDS

WEATHER RADAR SCANS THE
SKY AHEAD

THE WEATHER RADAR DISH IS
INSIDE THE AIRPLANE'S NOSE

FLIGHT DECK WEATHER
SCREEN

PRIMARY RADAR ANTENNA

CODES IDENTIFY DIFFERENT
AIRCRAFT

PRIMARY RADAR LOCATES
THE PLANE

Weather radar

An airplane's nose contains a small radar dish that scans the sky ahead of the plane. This radar detects moisture in the air. The information it receives appears on a small screen on the plane's flight deck (*left*). The pilot uses the weather radar to avoid storms. Blustery winds could make the flight uncomfortably rough for passengers and lightning is also a danger as it could damage the plane. Storms show up clearly because of the heavy rain they contain.

Air-traffic control

An air-traffic controller's radar screen (*right*) shows the positions of all aircraft within range. Each aircraft on the screen has a call-sign, the code-name that air-traffic controllers use to talk to the pilot, and a second code showing the aircraft's height and the airport it is heading for.

Calculators

A CALCULATOR IS a machine designed to do arithmetic. In the past, calculating machines were big, hand-operated mechanisms with toothed wheels, levers, and dials. Today, calculators can be as small as a credit card and do complicated calculations in the blink of an eye because they work electronically. A battery or solar panel supplies the electric current. The machine calculates by processing pulses of electricity inside a microchip. The electric pulses represent numbers. All calculators are programmed to carry out the four basic tasks: addition, subtraction, multiplication, and division. Many calculators can do extra calculations such as finding the square root of a number. Some can do very complicated scientific calculations. Most have an extra electronic memory for storing numbers that are used again and again. A few calculators have a built-in printer that prints all the numbers entered and the results of calculations.

Making microchips

A pure crystal of silicon is cut into thin slices called wafers. Dozens of chips are made on each wafer by adding extra layers of chemicals in some places and eating away the surface in other places. Finally, each wafer is cut into separate tiny chips which are sealed inside plastic blocks for protection.

Inside a calculator

An electronic calculator contains a circuit board. Metal strips on the circuit board link all the chips and other components with the battery, keys, and display. Pressing a key closes a switch underneath it and completes an electric circuit, sending a series of electric pulses to the calculator's microchips. A memory chip stores the pulses and a processor chip does the calculations.

LIQUID CRYSTAL DISPLAY

A WIDE FLAT 'RIBBON' CABLE CONNECTS THE DISPLAY TO THE CIRCUIT BOARD

THE DISPLAY DRIVER CHIP CONTROLS THE DISPLAY

THE CENTRAL PROCESSOR CHIP DOES ALL THE CALCULATIONS

THE CHIPS ARE CONNECTED TO THE CIRCUIT BOARD BY METAL TERMINALS ALONG THE EDGES OF THE CHIPS

RESISTORS AND OTHER ELECTRONIC COMPONENTS CONTROL THE ELECTRIC CURRENTS FLOWING THROUGH THE CALCULATOR

TRANSISTORS SWITCH ELECTRIC CURRENTS FROM CHIP TO CHIP

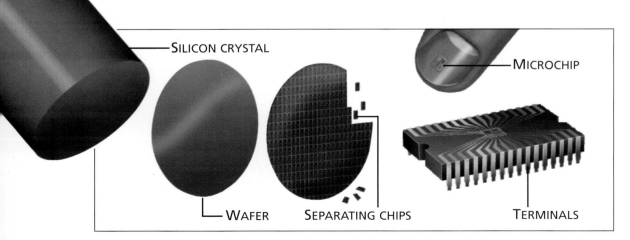

SILICON CRYSTAL

MICROCHIP

WAFER

SEPARATING CHIPS

TERMINALS

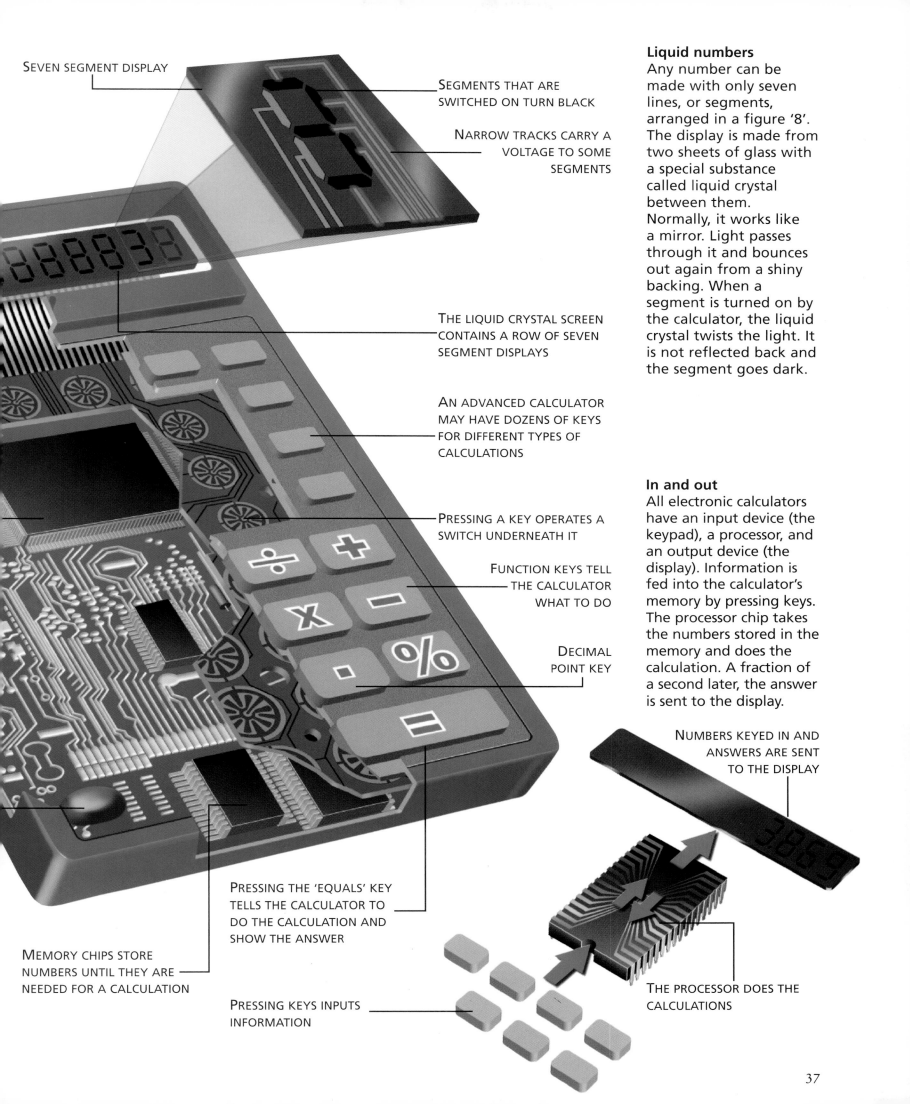

SEVEN SEGMENT DISPLAY

SEGMENTS THAT ARE SWITCHED ON TURN BLACK

NARROW TRACKS CARRY A VOLTAGE TO SOME SEGMENTS

Liquid numbers
Any number can be made with only seven lines, or segments, arranged in a figure '8'. The display is made from two sheets of glass with a special substance called liquid crystal between them. Normally, it works like a mirror. Light passes through it and bounces out again from a shiny backing. When a segment is turned on by the calculator, the liquid crystal twists the light. It is not reflected back and the segment goes dark.

THE LIQUID CRYSTAL SCREEN CONTAINS A ROW OF SEVEN SEGMENT DISPLAYS

AN ADVANCED CALCULATOR MAY HAVE DOZENS OF KEYS FOR DIFFERENT TYPES OF CALCULATIONS

PRESSING A KEY OPERATES A SWITCH UNDERNEATH IT

FUNCTION KEYS TELL THE CALCULATOR WHAT TO DO

DECIMAL POINT KEY

In and out
All electronic calculators have an input device (the keypad), a processor, and an output device (the display). Information is fed into the calculator's memory by pressing keys. The processor chip takes the numbers stored in the memory and does the calculation. A fraction of a second later, the answer is sent to the display.

NUMBERS KEYED IN AND ANSWERS ARE SENT TO THE DISPLAY

PRESSING THE 'EQUALS' KEY TELLS THE CALCULATOR TO DO THE CALCULATION AND SHOW THE ANSWER

MEMORY CHIPS STORE NUMBERS UNTIL THEY ARE NEEDED FOR A CALCULATION

PRESSING KEYS INPUTS INFORMATION

THE PROCESSOR DOES THE CALCULATIONS

Computers

A COMPUTER IS an electronic machine that takes in information, or data, and changes it by following a set of instructions called a program. Computer programs are also called software, while the computer itself is called hardware. Computers have four basic parts: input, memory, processor, and output. The input device, such as a keyboard, feeds instructions and data into the computer. The computer's memory then holds the information until it is needed. Software tells the processor what to do with the data and the results appear on an output device, such as a screen. The contents of the memory disappear when a computer is switched off, so important information is kept by recording it on a disc in the computer.

Computer screen

A computer screen works in the same way as a television screen. The picture is made of thousands of tiny points of light. Each point may be red, green, or blue. Any color can be made by mixing these three basic colors. The computer controls which colors appear at which points on the screen.

A COMPUTER CAN CREATE THREE-DIMENSIONAL PICTURES EVEN THOUGH THE SCREEN IS ALMOST FLAT

USING ONLY THREE BASIC COLORS A COMPUTER CAN PRODUCE ANY COLOR OR SHADE OF THE RAINBOW

Discs

Three main types of discs are used to store computer programs and data. Floppy discs and hard discs are magnetic. The third, the CD-ROM, is like a music CD. A personal computer may use all three types.

DATA CAN BE COPIED ONTO A FLOPPY DISC

THE KEYS ARE CONNECTED TO METAL STRIPS ON A BOARD CALLED A PRINTED CIRCUIT BOARD

A CD-ROM IS A COMPACT DISC THAT HOLDS COMPUTER INFORMATION

ONE WAY OF PUTTING INFORMATION INTO A COMPUTER IS TO TYPE IT ON THE KEYBOARD

A FLOPPY DISC IS USED BY PUSHING IT INTO THE COMPUTER HERE

PRESSING A KEY COMPLETES A CIRCUIT AND SENDS AN ELECTRICAL SIGNAL TO THE COMPUTER

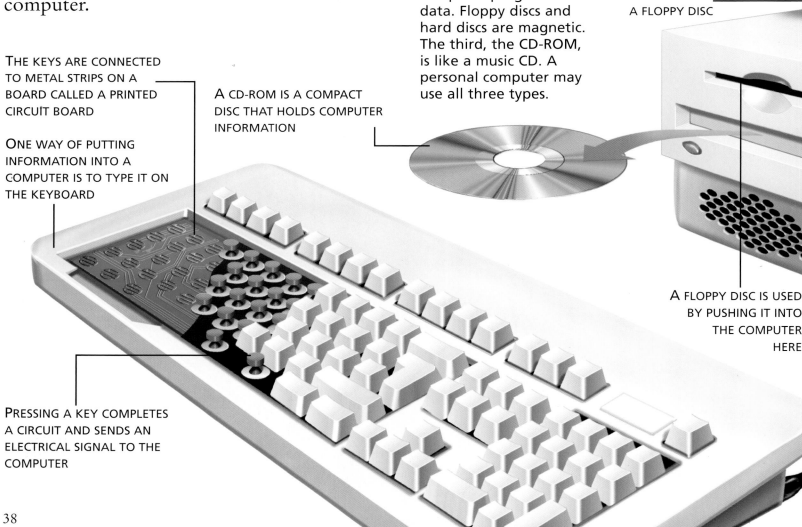

The microprocessor

A microprocessor is a computer's master control chip. It is also called the central processing unit, or CPU. All types of data or information are stored inside a computer as tiny pulses of electricity. The microprocessor controls where these pulses go and what they do. A clock controls how fast the microprocessor works. Computers work very quickly because their clocks tick millions of times every second.

CHIP

CHIPS ARE CONNECTED TO THE REST OF THE COMPUTER BY METAL LEGS (TERMINALS)

THE CHIP CONTAINS THOUSANDS OF TINY ELECTRONIC COMPONENTS

INFORMATION IS STORED IN THE RANDOM ACCESS MEMORY (RAM) CHIPS ONLY WHILE THE COMPUTER IS SWITCHED ON

The mouse

One way of controlling a computer is to use a device called a mouse. When a mouse is moved, a pointer on the computer screen moves too. The mouse is moved so that the pointer points at something on the screen. Then a button on the mouse is pressed to send information to the computer.

A FAN KEEPS THE COMPUTER'S CIRCUITS COOL

THE MICROPROCESSOR IS A COMPUTER'S MASTER CONTROL CHIP

A BALL UNDERNEATH A MOUSE ROLLS WHEN THE MOUSE IS MOVED

MOST COMPUTER MICE HAVE TWO CONTROL BUTTONS

A HARD DISC STORES INFORMATION LIKE A FLOPPY DISC, BUT A HARD DISC CANNOT BE TAKEN OUT OF THE COMPUTER

A SMALL LOUDSPEAKER CAN MAKE SOUNDS

THE BALL TURNS WHEELS WHICH TELL THE COMPUTER THAT THE MOUSE IS MOVING

THE MOUSE

Peripherals

COMPUTER equipment includes the computer itself and all the other machines and devices that may be connected to it. Pieces of equipment connected to computers are called peripherals. Peripherals include monitors, printers, modems, and scanners. A computer has a monitor, or screen, to show what the computer is doing. A printer enables information stored in the computer's memory to be turned into printed documents. A modem is used to connect a computer to a telephone line so that it can communicate with other computers. Modem is short for modulator-demodulator. A scanner changes a picture or printed text into computer data, a process called digitization. In the form of computer data the picture or text can be changed, stored, copied, and printed out.

Scanners

To feed a picture into a computer, it is placed, face down, on to a glass plate in a scanner. A cover is closed over it. A bright light shines through the glass on to the paper. The brightness of the reflection from the paper depends on what is printed on it. A motor moves the scan head, containing the light, down the length of the paper. It also relays the reflections, through a system of mirrors and lenses, on to light-sensors. Some scanners have the

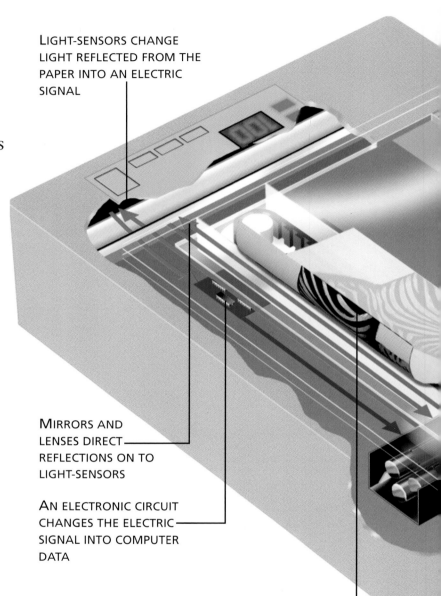

LIGHT-SENSORS CHANGE LIGHT REFLECTED FROM THE PAPER INTO AN ELECTRIC SIGNAL

MIRRORS AND LENSES DIRECT REFLECTIONS ON TO LIGHT-SENSORS

AN ELECTRONIC CIRCUIT CHANGES THE ELECTRIC SIGNAL INTO COMPUTER DATA

THE DOCUMENT TO BE SCANNED IS PLACED ON A GLASS PLATE

THE SCAN HEAD MOVES DOWN THE PAPER LIGHTING IT UP LINE BY LINE

Changing pictures

An image that has been scanned into a computer can be completely changed. Using a design or illustration program, all or part of any image can be changed in color, shape, and size. For example, these zebra's stripes in a scanned photograph have been altered to create a more colorful animal!

EVERY POINT IN THE SCANNED PICTURE CAN BE CHANGED BY A COMPUTER

light-sensors built into the scan head. The light-sensors convert the reflections into an electric signal. The brighter the reflection, the stronger the signal. This signal is then changed into electrical pulses that are sent to the computer.

A FLEXIBLE RIBBON CABLE LINKS THE SCAN HEAD TO THE SCANNER

CLEAN PAPER IS FED INTO THE LASER PRINTER

A RULER SCALE SHOWS WHERE TO POSITION THE DOCUMENT

THE DOCUMENT IS COVERED BY A LID TO KEEP OUT UNWANTED LIGHT

THE RUBBER BELT DRIVES THE SCAN HEAD DOWN THE PAPER

AN ELECTRIC MOTOR DRIVES A TOOTHED RUBBER BELT

THE SCANNER COMMUNICATES WITH A COMPUTER THROUGH A CABLE AND DATA CONNECTOR

Laser printers

Data sent by the computer to a laser printer turns a laser on and off. The laser produces a thin beam of light (1). A spinning mirror (2) reflects the beam onto an electrically-charged drum (3). Wherever light falls on the drum, the charge changes. Black toner powder sticks to parts of the drum, according to its charge pattern. Paper is pressed against the drum and takes up the toner (4). Finally, heated rollers bind the toner to the paper (5).

Modems

A modem changes computer data into electric signals that can be sent down a telephone line. At the other end of the line, another modem changes the signals back into computer data, which are fed into a second computer.

TELEPHONE LINE   A MODEM

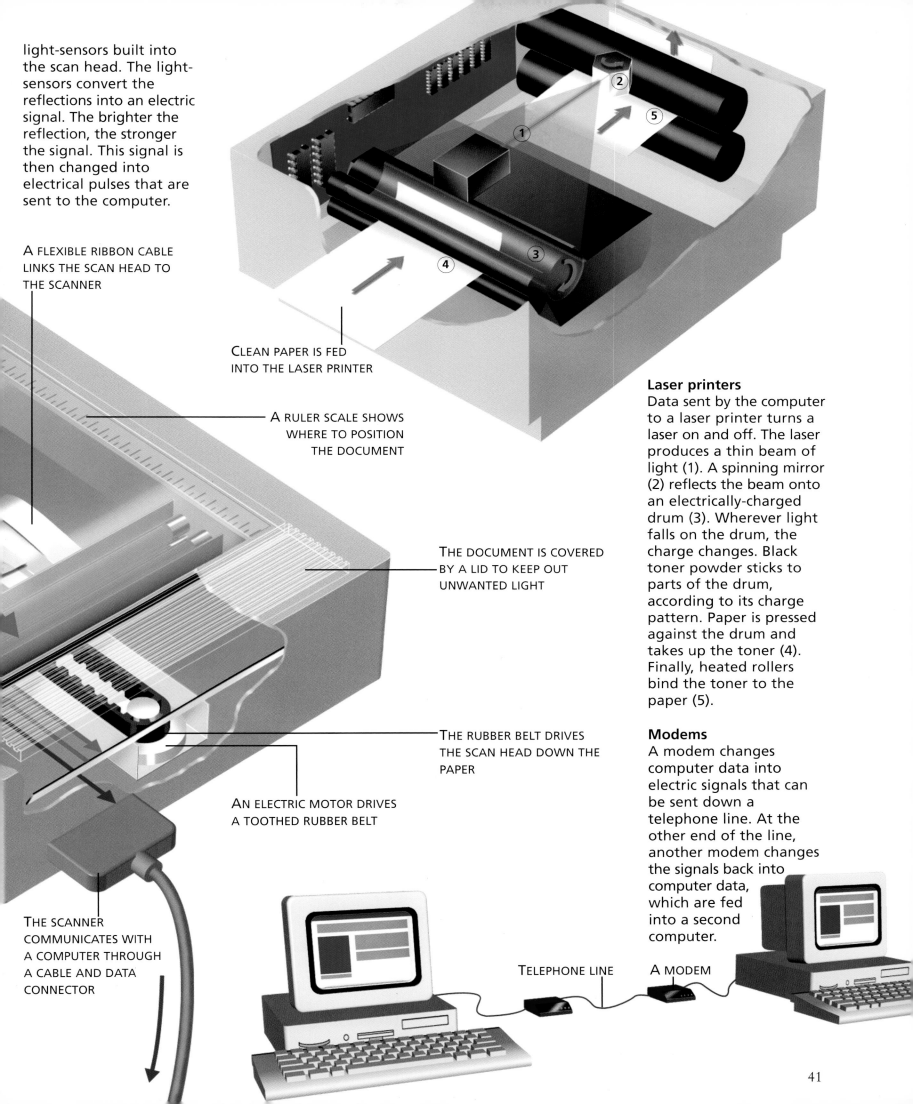

Using Computers

COMPUTERS can store and process, or manipulate, all sorts of information. The electric pulses that travel through their amazingly complicated circuits may represent numbers, letters, sounds, or pictures. They can process this information many millions of times faster than human beings. Because of this, they have become an essential part of almost every type of industry and business, as well as being very popular in the home. Their many uses include controlling machines, monitoring complicated power and transport systems, managing world-wide communications, providing access to vast amounts of information, and playing exciting computer games. They have also become very important in television and cinema because of their ability to create or change pictures that can look totally life-like.

A COMPUTER SYSTEM IN A MODERN RAILWAY CONTROL CENTER

Controlling trains

The control center for a modern railway system relies heavily on computers. Sensors along the tracks feed information to the control center, telling the computers where trains are and how the signals and points are set. The information appears as lights on a map of the railway network and on computer screens. Using the same computers, controllers can send out commands to change the points and signals.

THE COMPUTER GIVES THE SMOOTH SURFACES TEXTURE BY ADDING DETAIL, LIGHT, AND SHADE

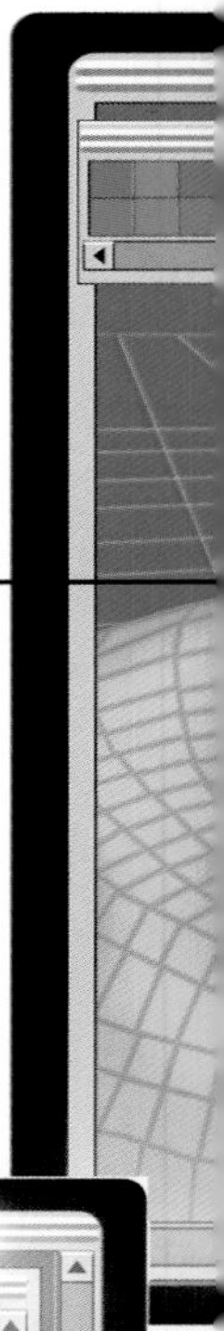

Creating characters

The first stage in creating a computerized, or virtual, character is building a clay model (1). The model is covered by a grid of lines. All the points where lines cross are entered into the computer. A copy of the grid, called a wire frame, appears on the computer screen (2). The computer changes the wire frame into a solid figure (3) by filling in the surfaces. Finally, the figure is animated, or made to move, and given different expressions (4).

A COMPUTER CHARACTER BEGINS AS A CLAY MODEL

①

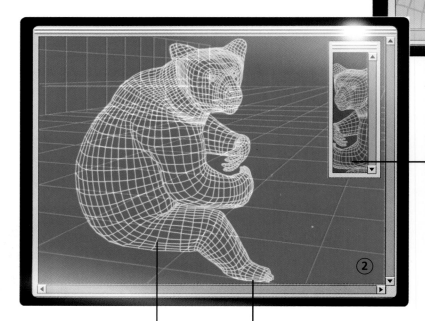

②

THE CHARACTER APPEARS ON THE COMPUTER SCREEN AS A SEE-THROUGH WIRE FRAME

THE CHARACTER'S SHAPE IS CHANGED UNTIL IT LOOKS EXACTLY RIGHT

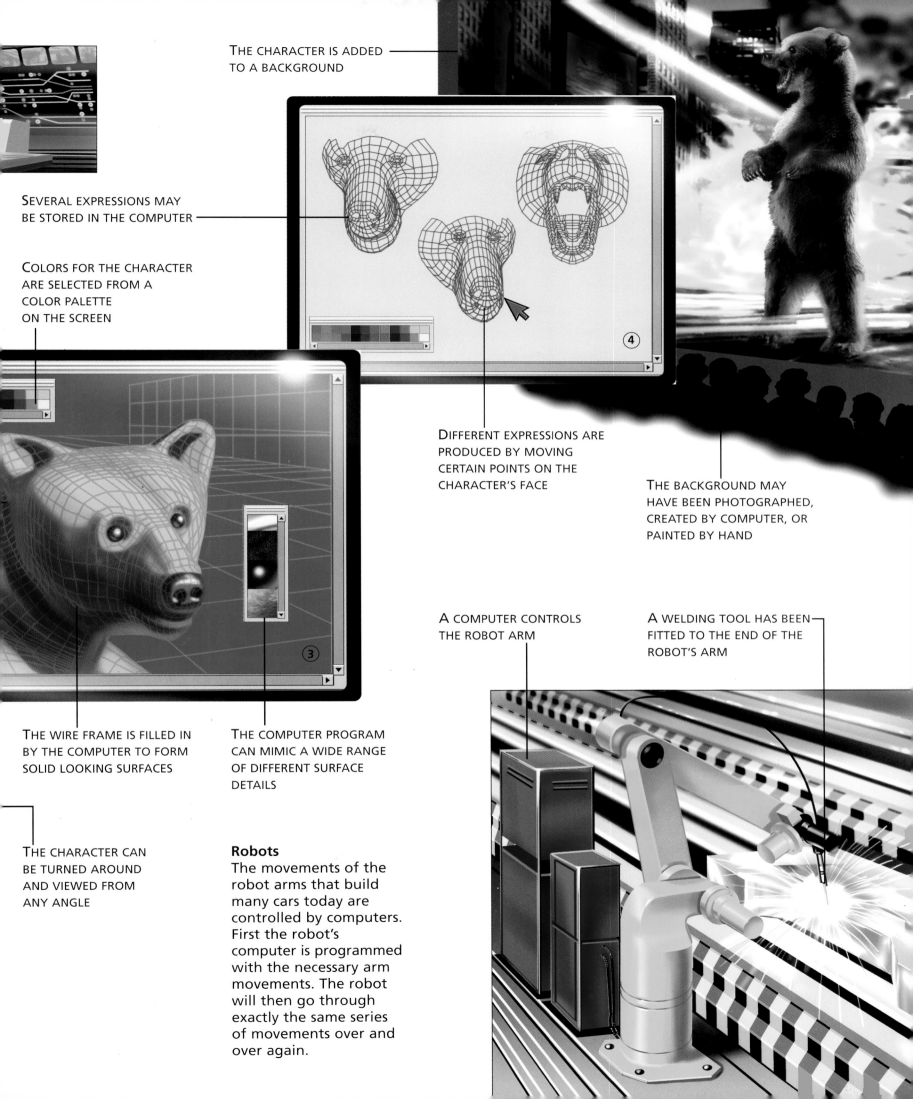

THE CHARACTER IS ADDED TO A BACKGROUND

SEVERAL EXPRESSIONS MAY BE STORED IN THE COMPUTER

COLORS FOR THE CHARACTER ARE SELECTED FROM A COLOR PALETTE ON THE SCREEN

④

DIFFERENT EXPRESSIONS ARE PRODUCED BY MOVING CERTAIN POINTS ON THE CHARACTER'S FACE

THE BACKGROUND MAY HAVE BEEN PHOTOGRAPHED, CREATED BY COMPUTER, OR PAINTED BY HAND

③

A COMPUTER CONTROLS THE ROBOT ARM

A WELDING TOOL HAS BEEN FITTED TO THE END OF THE ROBOT'S ARM

THE WIRE FRAME IS FILLED IN BY THE COMPUTER TO FORM SOLID LOOKING SURFACES

THE COMPUTER PROGRAM CAN MIMIC A WIDE RANGE OF DIFFERENT SURFACE DETAILS

THE CHARACTER CAN BE TURNED AROUND AND VIEWED FROM ANY ANGLE

Robots
The movements of the robot arms that build many cars today are controlled by computers. First the robot's computer is programmed with the necessary arm movements. The robot will then go through exactly the same series of movements over and over again.

Computer Networks

COMPUTER networks are groups of computers that can communicate with each other and exchange information.

One problem faced by scientists trying to use early computers was that the computers were not always in the right place. A computer in one place often contained programs or information needed by scientists working somewhere else. But there was no way of moving the programs or information to where they were needed. The answer was to connect computers together to form a network. To begin with, only scientists could use them, but once computers were connected to telephone lines, it became much easier to form bigger networks that covered longer distances. Businesses linked up computers within their offices and around the world. The most exciting development was when it became possible to connect small computers to the biggest computers in the world and use their super-fast computing power and vast memories.

SEVERAL COMPUTERS ARE LINKED TOGETHER TO FORM A LOCAL AREA NETWORK (LAN)

NETWORKS ARE LINKED TO EACH OTHER THROUGH DEVICES CALLED ROUTERS

TWO OR MORE LANS CONNECTED TOGETHER FORM A WIDE AREA NETWORK (WAN)

A CONNECTION TO A LAN IN ANOTHER BUILDING

ELECTRONIC MESSAGES TRAVEL FROM COMPUTER TO COMPUTER AS E-MAIL

A FILE SERVER HOLDS ALL THE MESSAGES IN ONE PLACE FOR COLLECTION

World Wide Web

The best known computer network is the Internet. This international network of computers allows anyone with an ordinary home computer to link up with other computers all over the world. The home computer must first be linked to a telephone line by a modem. The modem changes computer data into a form that can be sent down a telephone line. It also converts any information received by telephone back into computer data. One of the Internet's most exciting and useful features is the World Wide Web. It enables anyone to jump effortlessly between the millions of pages of information held in thousands of computers in different countries.

COMPUTERS AT A SERVICE PROVIDER COMMUNICATE WITH THE INTERNET

SERVICE PROVIDER'S COMPUTER SUPPLIES INTERNET SERVICES

SERVICE PROVIDER'S MODEM CHANGES ELECTRIC WAVES BACK INTO PULSES

ELECTRIC WAVES TRAVEL ALONG TELEPHONE LINES

THIS HOME COMPUTER IS LINKED TO A MODEM

A MODEM CHANGES COMPUTER DATA INTO ELECTRIC WAVES

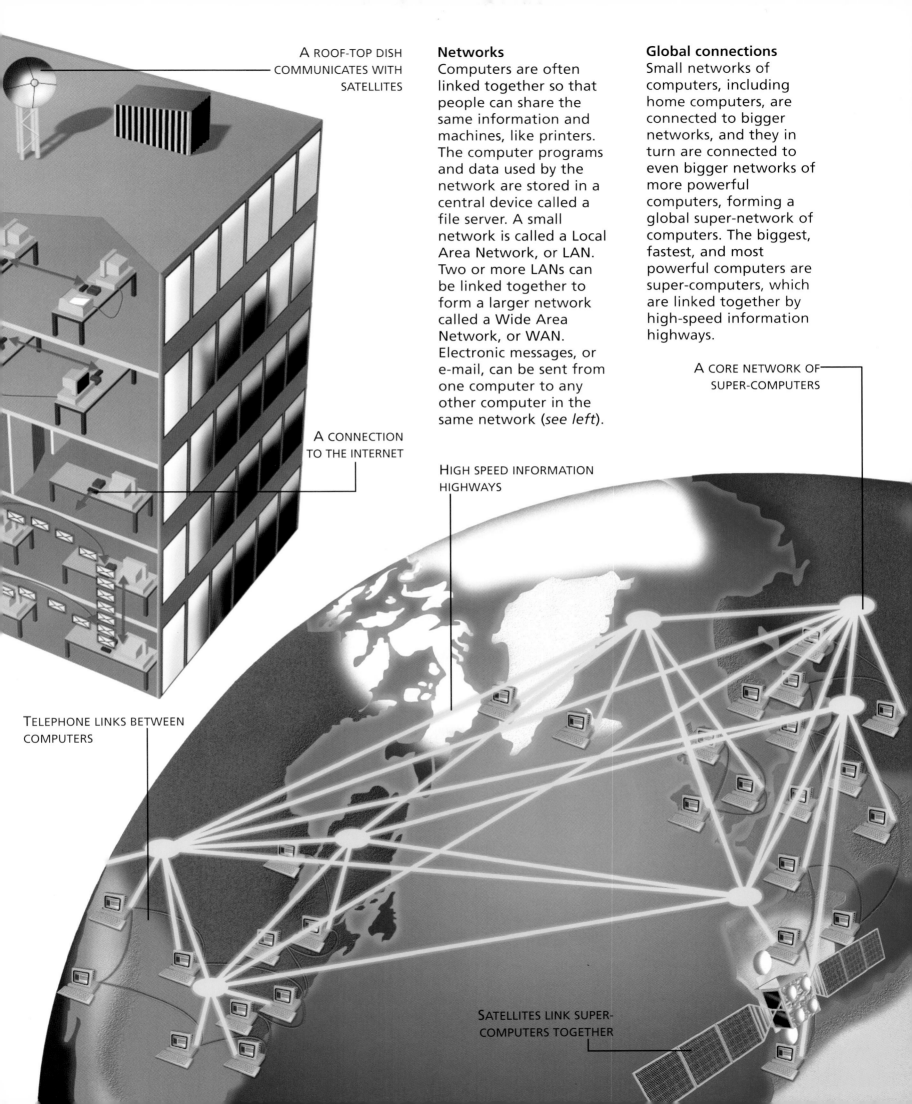

A ROOF-TOP DISH
COMMUNICATES WITH
SATELLITES

Networks
Computers are often
linked together so that
people can share the
same information and
machines, like printers.
The computer programs
and data used by the
network are stored in a
central device called a
file server. A small
network is called a Local
Area Network, or LAN.
Two or more LANs can
be linked together to
form a larger network
called a Wide Area
Network, or WAN.
Electronic messages, or
e-mail, can be sent from
one computer to any
other computer in the
same network (*see left*).

Global connections
Small networks of
computers, including
home computers, are
connected to bigger
networks, and they in
turn are connected to
even bigger networks of
more powerful
computers, forming a
global super-network of
computers. The biggest,
fastest, and most
powerful computers are
super-computers, which
are linked together by
high-speed information
highways.

A CORE NETWORK OF
SUPER-COMPUTERS

A CONNECTION
TO THE INTERNET

HIGH SPEED INFORMATION
HIGHWAYS

TELEPHONE LINKS BETWEEN
COMPUTERS

SATELLITES LINK SUPER-
COMPUTERS TOGETHER

Index

FOREWORD

We share the world with an extraordinary diversity of wildlife, the breadth and depth of which is, frankly, wonderful. As our ancestors traveled through the continents of planet Earth, they encountered amazing animals in each new area they explored. This "biogeography"—or how species are geographically distributed throughout different natural habitats—is something you can now experience for yourself in the following pages, by discovering which animals inhabit each continent's ecosystems. It is the aim of this book to present a visually compelling exploration of the world's ecoregions by summarizing the creatures that live there, as well as providing key facts about their life cycles and biology.

More than 40 ecoregions are described in depth, and all are complemented by a spectacular view of the animals—both the familiar and the less well-known—that inhabit them. By grouping species together within their natural habitats, it becomes easy to spot the top predators in each one, as well as the variety of creatures that live alongside them. Combining this global view with the very best the world of wildlife photography has to offer allows us to take you on a journey that can be completed in a variety of ways, but always at your own pace, and in the comfort of your home.

Most people are familiar with the animals, large and small, that share the regions in which we live. The current age of easy worldwide travel has allowed some of us to experience more exotic parts of the globe, where the animals are unfamiliar, different, and sometimes very strange indeed. Yet this diversity of habitats and organisms is, sadly, diminishing as the world becomes ever more populated with humans, and the impact of those increasing populations takes a heavy toll on natural areas worldwide.

The more we can learn about the diversity of wildlife on our planet, the easier and more effective it will be to design and implement conservation programs that ensure we retain species for future generations. As you make your way through this stunning compilation of our planet's amazing animals, enjoy the wonder and spectacle of life on Earth and take a moment to realize just how lucky we are to be a part of it—in our own time and place.

DON E. WILSON
SMITHSONIAN INSTITUTE, WASHINGTON, D.C.

ANIMAL HABITATS

Two-thirds of Earth's surface is covered by oceans. It is this abundance of water that enables the planet to support billions of living organisms, both in the seas and on the continents and islands that make up the land. The environment in which an organism lives is its habitat, and the huge range of habitats found on land are home to a vast number of plant species and a spectacular diversity of animals.

Geographers divide the world into ecoregions characterized by broad habitat types such as forest, grassland, wetland, desert, or polar zones. These can in turn be subdivided almost endlessly into more precise habitats, each supporting a unique community of plant and animals.

Climate exerts a powerful influence over each of the world's great ecoregions. Energy input from the Sun is greatest at the tropics, and the transfer of this energy via the atmosphere and oceans generates the currents of air and water that drive the world's weather systems. On land, weathering of rock leads to the formation of soil in which plants grow, forming the basis of ecological communities.

Variety of life

Biodiversity refers to the variety of life in a given habitat or ecoregion. As a rule, biodiversity increases toward the equator, with tropical forests and warm coastal seas registering the greatest numbers of species. Both poles are inhabited by comparatively few animal species, but in the Arctic, many animals live on land whereas in Antarctica, most animal life is found in the ocean.

Plants and animals become better adapted to their particular habitat through natural selection—those most suited to the environmental conditions survive in greater numbers and produce more offspring. This is a continuous process as habitats change slowly over time. Sudden events such as volcanic eruptions, floods, or human development can have catastrophic impacts, especially on species that are specialized to a certain way of life. So-called generalist species cope better with change, such as a fall or rise in temperature, but may be displaced by specialist species when conditions stabilize.

ECOREGION

The Alps comprise one of the world's best-known montane ecoregions. They extend into eight European countries, forming a snow-tipped arc that stretches from France and Italy in the southwest to Austria in the east.

CONTINENT

In southern Europe, the warm waters of the Mediterranean lap the coast and much of the land is covered by Mediterranean woodland and scrub. The soaring mountains of the Alps form a physical barrier, beyond which lies the colder, wetter north.

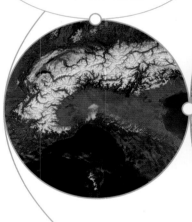

Scientists estimate that only
14 percent of species have been identified so far, and of those,
91 percent live on land

THE ALPS ECOREGION

If you pick any place on the planet, you will find a unique set of conditions, influenced by geography, latitude, and climate. This means the area, such as the Alps, will be home to a unique community of plants and animals.

HABITATS

The habitats of the Alps are found elsewhere in the world, but here their characteristics are contrasted by large differences in altitude. The grasses and herbs found in a high alpine meadow, for example, are very different from those in a lowland grassland.

FOOD CHAINS

One way all the plants and animals in a habitat interact is via a food chain. Plants convert the Sun's energy into food for growth and reproduction, and are eaten by herbivorous animals. These in turn become food for predatory or scavenging animals.

MOUNTAINS AND SCREE SLOPES

Mountains are effectively inland islands, where unique species can live and evolve in isolation. Slope habitats are heavily influenced by latitude, altitude, incline, aspect, and the underlying rock. Conditions above the tree line (beyond which no trees grow) are harsh.

EAGLE OWL

The Eurasian eagle owl is the top predatory bird in the Alps. It hunts mainly small mammals, but will also target other birds of prey.

MONTANE FOREST

Forests on mountains are banded according to altitude, with broadleaf trees dominating the warmer, lower slopes, and conifers thriving on higher ground up to the tree line. Because sloping, rocky ground is difficult to farm, mountainsides often retain more tree cover than flatter ground.

MARMOT

Alpine marmots spend the summer months feeding on lush grasses and herbs, building up fat to help them survive the long alpine winter.

ALPINE MEADOW

Where flooding or unstable ground prevent trees encroaching, grasses and herbs flourish in spectacular diversity. At high-altitude, there is a sudden burst of growth in spring and summer and the meadows are filled with blooms—an important food source for many animals.

DANDELION

As well as providing food for marmots, alpine dandelions are a welcome source of nectar for butterflies and bees.

FORESTS
The lungs of our planet

Roughly one-third of the world's land area is covered with trees. Some are the largest and longest-living organisms on Earth. Their roots, trunks, branches, and leaves form an uncountable variety of microhabitats, the character of which varies according to location. Dead and decaying leaves and wood also form a vital component of forest ecosystems, providing habitat and food, and releasing nutrients back into forest soils. Clearings left by fallen trees throng with light-loving ground plants and insects until new trees close the gap.

breaking them. By keeping their dark green leaves all year, they can make food whenever the Sun shines. The resin-filled leaves are distasteful to all but a few insects and so are not eaten even when food is scarce.

Farther south, winters are still cold, but summers are longer and warmer. Forests here are generally deciduous. The trees have broad leaves and spreading branches that maximize their ability to harvest light and get

Boreal and temperate forests

The wide range of climates in temperate areas supports coniferous, deciduous, broadleaf evergreen, and mixed forest. In the far northern boreal forests, winters are longer, temperatures lower, and snow fall more frequent—conditions to which coniferous trees are well adapted. Their triangular shape and narrow leaves prevent excess snow settling on their branches and

TEMPERATE CONIFEROUS

Nonflowering plants, such as conifers, produce their seeds in cones, which are released when dry conditions cause the cones to open. The tiny seeds of western hemlock are eaten by chickadees, pine siskins, and deer mice.

TEMPERATE BROADLEAF

The seasonal availability of some foods presents a challenge to woodland animals. Some, such as grey squirrels, solve the problem by hoarding nuts and seeds in tree holes and underground caches, to which they return in winter.

BOREAL

The hardy, evergreen conifers found in northern boreal forests provide less food than other trees due to the harsh climate and short growing season. In winter, when food is scarce, many animals migrate to warmer areas or hibernate.

SEYCHELLES ▷
Tropical rainforest on Silhouette Island, Seychelles, in the Indian Ocean.

energy from the Sun. However, such leaves also pose a risk in strong winds and heavy snow, so temperate broadleaf trees tend to produce thin leaves that are shed in the fall. The trees remain in an almost dormant state all winter and produce new leaves the following spring.

In the most southerly temperate areas, summers are long, hot, and dry, and winters are warm and wet. The broadleaf evergreen forest that grows in these climates ranges from the tall eucalypts of Australia to the shorter, more open woodland of parts of California and the Mediterranean.

Tropical forests

At the equator, the climate is warm and moist all year round, providing ideal conditions for plant growth and creating the most diverse of all terrestrial habitats. Trees and other forest plants grow in profusion forming vast rainforests, cloud forests, and montane forests that are green all year round. In the northern tropics, the forests of Southeast Asia are influenced by heavy monsoon rains, giving

FOREST DISTRIBUTION

Coniferous forests are generally found at higher latitudes and altitudes than temperate forests, and the boreal forest belt extends to the edge of the Arctic tundra. Tropical forests need warmth year-round and are centered on the equator.

■ Boreal forest   ■ Temperate forest   ■ Tropical forest

the region distinct wet and dry seasons. During the rains the forest is lush and green but in the dry season, many trees shed their leaves, allowing the sunlight to penetrate to the forest floor.

In areas where there is a long dry season, such as Madagascar and the Caribbean, tropical and subtropical dry forests are found. Composed mainly of broadleaved trees that shed their leaves to conserve water during dry spells, these forests are less diverse than other tropical forests. However, they are still home to a diverse community of animals adapted to cope with the demands of living in a hot, dry climate.

MEDITERRANEAN

Broadleaf evergreen forest is also known as Mediterranean forest, and typical trees include cork oaks, some species of pine, and eucalypts. Cork oaks are a particularly important habitat, providing food, shelter, and nesting sites for many species of animal.

TROPICAL DRY

Trees in tropical dry forests survive the long dry season by shedding their leaves, having thick bark, and deep roots that access groundwater. Many species have thorns or spines as a deterrent to animals that might try to feed on them.

TROPICAL MOIST

The dense canopy of the broadleaf trees growing in most tropical forests holds most of the forest's food. This means that many animals are adapted to life in the trees and are rarely seen at ground level. They include scarlet macaws and spider monkeys.

GRASSLANDS
Little shelter, but plenty of food

Where the climate is too dry to support trees, but wet enough for plants to grow, grasses and low-growing herbs dominate the landscape. These plants are highly diverse, and grassland habitats range from the high alpine meadows of Europe to tree-studded African savanna, tall grass prairies of North America, windswept Asian steppes, seas of head-height grass in India, China, and South America, and the dry desert scrublands of Australia. Today, they account for about 40 percent of the land area.

Temperate grasslands

The relatively flat terrain and scarcity of trees in temperate grassland gives rise to vast expanses of fairly uniform landscape across which strong winds can blow unimpeded. There are fewer habitats than in forests and, as a result, there are fewer animal species in temperate grassland, too. Grass is, however, able to support vast numbers of herbivores because, unusually in plants, its growth point is below ground level. As it is untouched by the animals that graze on it, grass regrows quickly after it has been cropped. This adaptation also allows grass to survive long periods without rain that kill many other plants.

In the past, grassland covered large tracts of the temperate world, but with the advent of agriculture, much of it has been used for growing crops—often with unforeseen consequences. Grass is unusual in that it channels most of its energy into growing roots rather than leaves. This allows grass to get the water and nutrients it needs and has

TEMPERATE GRASSLAND

Although grasses predominate, many herbaceous plants also grow in temperate grassland. Bright flowers attract insects, which in turn attract insect-eating birds. The grassland also provides food for mammals of all sizes, from bison to hares.

MONTANE GRASSLAND

These high-altitude grasslands occur at all latitudes. The plants and animals that live in these regions must be able to endure low temperatures, intense sunlight, and potentially harmful ultraviolet radiation. They include the guanaco of South America.

CUSTER STATE PARK ▷
The prairie habitat in South Dakota, provides a natural refuge for a herd of American bison.

the side-effect of stabilizing the soil it is growing in. When land such as this is plowed and the grass removed, the soil rapidly deteriorates and is blown away as dust, leaving only bare earth in its place.

Tropical grasslands

Scattered trees and scrub are a feature of tropical savannas, making them more diverse than their temperate counterparts. However, they cannot encroach far because, unlike grass, trees and scrub cannot survive the frequent fires that occur during the dry season. Although these fires appear destructive, the ash created provides soil nutrients that fuel the growth of fresh grass during the wet season that follows.

While some tropical grasses, such as bamboo and elephant grass, grow very tall, most savanna grassland provides little cover, making it difficult for both predators and prey to hide. Predators rely on stealth, speed, and sometimes cooperation to catch their food, whereas prey animals rely on spotting hunters before they get too close and running away. They do this by living in groups, which offers safety in numbers, and by relying on their senses. Prey animals have eyes on the sides of their heads for good all around vision, large swiveling ears, and an excellent sense of smell—hares are a good example.

GRASSLAND DISTRIBUTION

The largest temperate grasslands are the prairies of North America and the Asian steppes, which stretch from the far east of Europe to northern China. Tropical grasslands include those of sub-Saharan Africa and Brazil.

▦ Temperate grasslands   ▦ Tropical grasslands

SCRUB

In areas with long dry summers such as California and the Mediterranean, there is a transition zone between woods and grassland that is dominated by low, woody shrub vegetation. Also called heathland and chaparral, scrub offers more cover for animals.

TROPICAL GRASSLAND

These are usually warm year-round, with a long dry season followed by a short wet season that sees a spurt of plant growth. African savanna elephants help to maintain their habitat by eating woody shrubs and knocking down trees to feed on their leaves.

WETLANDS

Areas of land that are routinely inundated by fresh or salt water are often dominated by grasses, reeds, and sedges, while water hyacinths form free-floating mats of vegetation. Wetlands support many species, particularly birds.

EXTREME ENVIRONMENTS
Survival against the odds

Polar areas and deserts are some of the least hospitable habitats on Earth. The lack of rain and extreme temperatures create difficult conditions for life, and the few humans that live there lead a seminomadic existence. Today, several of these fragile, untouched ecoregions are under threat because of the discovery of oil, gas, and other minerals.

Polar regions

Much of the Arctic and Antarctica is effectively a desert gripped by ice. Winters are long and permanently dark and summers are short but, because the Sun never sets, there is a continual source of energy for plant growth. Where rock is exposed, the soil is virtually nonexistent, and usually at freezing point or below. Trees cannot survive here, and vegetation is limited to mosses, lichens, fungi, and a handful of flowering plants. This open, rather featureless landscape, called tundra, is found between 60–80 degrees north and

south of the equator. It is far more extensive in the northern hemisphere, covering large tracts of northern Canada and Russia. Similar areas on mountains above the tree line are called alpine tundra.

Polar regions may support a number of large land animals, but most are reliant on the sea for their food. This is because despite the icy conditions, sea life is plentiful. The cold waters of the Arctic and Southern oceans are rich in oxygen and the seabed provides

ALPINE TUNDRA

Found at altitudes of around 10,000 ft (3,000 m) with snow above and boreal forest below, alpine tundra is cold and windy and has sparse vegetation. Golden eagles hunt there during the summer as the open ground provides little cover for their prey.

ARCTIC TUNDRA

The Arctic poppy is one of the few flowering plants found on the Arctic tundra. The short growing season means the plant must grow, flower, and produce its seeds rapidly. It is usually pollinated by flies, but can self-pollinate if necessary.

POLAR

Polar regions may seem inhospitable, but their icy waters support several specialist mammal species, including walruses and seals. Small ice floes and broken pack ice are ideal habitat for bearded seals, for example, as they need easy access to the water to feed.

ANTARCTICA ▷
Snow covers the tundra on the northeast tip of the Antarctic Peninsula in winter.

plentiful nutrients. In summer, these oceans provide rich pickings for the many marine mammals and seabirds that migrate to these areas to feed and breed. The tundra also has summer visitors, such as reindeer that spend the winter sheltering from the cold in the taiga forest to the south, but return each summer.

Desert regions

Most of the world's great hot deserts, such as Africa's Sahara, are found in the subtropics, where dry conditions persist for months at a time. Others, such as the Mojave in the US southwest, are found on the dry leeward side of mountains. A few, such as the Atacama Desert in South America, are coastal and lack rain due to cold offshore water inhibiting cloud formation. Cold deserts are found in continental interiors and are very hot in summer and very cold in winter. All of these deserts are dry, receiving less than 6in (15cm) rain annually, and most are cloudless. The exception is coastal

DESERT AND POLAR ICE DISTRIBUTION

Deserts in the southern hemisphere tend to be less extensive than those in the north, which include the largest desert of all: the Sahara. Almost all of Antarctica and most of Greenland in the Arctic Circle is covered in ice-sheets.

Desert   Ice

desert, which can benefit from early morning fog drifting in from the ocean. Hot deserts, although hot all year, are cold at night as the lack of cloud cover allows heat to escape freely. Cold deserts also have large daily temperature fluctuations, but in winter, temperatures are below freezing and snow is not uncommon.

Plants growing in deserts must cope not only with lack of water and extreme temperatures, but also with soils that have little organic matter and few soil microorganisms. All desert plants and animals tend to restrict their reproductive efforts to periods of rainfall and show a range of adaptations to heat, such as being able to retain or store water, and many animals forage at night.

COLD DESERT

Despite the hostile treeless environment, limited rainfall, and enormous seasonal temperature differences, cold deserts are home to a variety of animals. Small mammals include the dwarf hamster, large ones the critically endangered Gobi bear.

COASTAL DESERT

In the early morning, coastal deserts benefit from moisture carried inland as fog. It is an important source of water for a number of arthropods and reptiles, some of which have adaptations to enhance water collection and storage.

HOT DESERT

Daytime temperatures in hot deserts are so high that even "cold blooded" arthropods, which are reliant on the Sun for warmth, seek shade to avoid the heat. Many animals, such as the deathstalker scorpion, avoid the Sun completely by being nocturnal.

AQUATIC ENVIRONMENTS
Planet Earth is really planet Ocean

More than 70 per cent of the Earth's surface is covered by water, which in its liquid form is essential for life. Water is continually circulating around the planet, evaporating from its surface and being carried as water vapour in the atmosphere until it falls again as rain. Around 95 per cent of the Earth's water is salt water, which is found in seas, oceans, and coastal lagoons as well a few isolated soda and salt lakes. The other 5 per cent is fresh water, which is seen in rivers and lakes, but also includes the ice held in polar regions and glaciers, and groundwater that is hidden from view. The challenges of life in fresh and salt water are very different and relatively few animal species are able to move from one to the other.

ranging from fast-flowing rivers and swampy wetlands to the relatively calmer but deeper water of many lakes. Organisms living in lakes and rivers must cope with strong currents, survive freezing conditions in winter, and endure summer droughts when some rivers and

Rivers and lakes

Fresh water is vital for life on land – without water plants cannot grow and animals would have nothing to drink. Rivers and lakes create diverse habitats

MANGROVES

These wetlands provide safe inshore nurseries for various marine animals as well as breeding sites and roosts for many bird species, including the scarlet ibis. These wading birds use their long, curved, sensitive bills to locate food in the soft mud.

LAKES

Lakes are often isolated, with little opportunity for new aquatic species to colonize them (unless introduced by humans). As a result they may have large numbers of endemic species or subspecies that have evolved to exploit the available habitats.

RIVERS

The steeper the gradient of a river, the faster the water flows and the stronger the current. More animal species tend to be found downstream, where slower-flowing water allows aquatic plants to grow. This increases the number of habitats.

CALIFORNIA COAST ▷
The sheer power of a breaking wave in Monterey Bay, US, is revealed.

shallow lakes disappear. Plants, including tree species, tend to grow where water flow is slow along stream and river banks or on islands in river channels. However, plants, such as water hyacinth, can cover large areas of fresh water. Animals may be confined to water – fish, for example – while others spend only part of their life there, including frogs, hippopotamuses, and dragonflies. Each species occupies a particular habitat, and together they create a distinct community unique to that particular river or lake.

Mangroves

Restricted to tropical and subtropical regions, mangrove swamps usually develop in intertidal areas on muddy shores, although some extend for some distance inland. Only mangrove trees can grow successfully in the waterlogged, salty mud and survive regular inundation by seawater. The different species have various adaptations that allow them to do this, including having prop roots for additional support in soft sediment, and the ability to filter out salt as it enters their roots, or to store it in their leaves and lose it when the leaves are shed. Mangrove swamp is the most endangered of the world's habitats due to large scale removal in recent years to make way for aquatic farming of fish, crustaceans, and molluscs.

Oceans and seas

Although the world's oceans are interconnected, numerous seas, each with their own distinct characteristics, exist within them. The sunlit upper waters of the ocean have the most organisms, and coral reefs are among the most biodiverse. However, ecoregions also exist much deeper, with food chains based on organic material drifting down from above or on bacteria able to manufacture food using chemical reactions that do not need sunlight. Coastal regions are extremely harsh environments for wildlife as rocks and sandy shores are periodically exposed to the air, and buffeting by waves can damage and dislodge organisms unless they are firmly anchored. Oceans support a huge variety of life, ranging from microscopic algae that underpin oceanic food chains to the planet's largest living animal, the blue whale.

COASTS

Exposure to the air twice a day and buffeting by the waves are just two features of coastlines that make them the most demanding of all habitats to live in. On rocky shores, many animal species have shells for protection and to retain moisture.

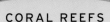

CORAL REEFS

Coral reefs provide plenty of food and hiding places. This means that reef fish are usually colourful and come in a multitude of shapes and sizes as, unlike oceanic fish, they do not need to be streamlined and fast to hunt or escape from predators.

OPEN OCEAN

Most life in the open ocean is found at or just below the surface as this is where most of the food is produced. Despite the vast expanse of this habitat, only around 5 per cent of the world's animal species live here.

British Columbia

A young grizzly bear searches for salmon during a
spawning run in a Canadian river. Its mother won't
be far as cubs don't become independent until
they are more than two years old.

North America

PEAKS AND PRAIRIES

North America

The world's third largest continent is bordered by the Pacific, Arctic, and Atlantic oceans, and the Caribbean Sea. Geographically, Greenland and the islands of the Caribbean are considered part of North America. Most of the continent occupies a single plate, with small parts of Mexico and California lying on the neighboring Pacific plate, which abuts the North American plate along the infamous San Andreas fault. The mountain ranges of the Western Cordillera have a profound influence on the climate of the west side of the continent. For example, rainshadow deserts form on the mountains' eastern flanks. Smaller, more ancient mountain ranges follow the eastern coast, while much of the interior of North America is low-lying. The vast north-south extent of the continent means it encompasses a wide range of climate types, from Arctic cold to tropical heat. Dominant ecosystems include tundra, boreal and temperate forest, prairie, desert, and extensive wetlands. These diverse habitats support an impressive range of animals, from the largest mammals—American bison and bears—to alligators living in the swamps and wetlands of the southeast.

KEY DATA

ECOSYSTEMS

Tropical broadleaf forest
Tropical dry broadleaf forest
Tropical coniferous forest
Temperate broadleaf forest
Temperate coniferous forest
Mediterranean woodland, scrub
Tropical, subtropical grassland
Temperate grassland
Wetland
Desert, scrub
Boreal forest/taiga
Tundra
Ice

AVERAGE TEMPERATURE

°F	°C
86	30
68	20
50	10
32	0
14	-10
-4	-20
-22	-30
-40	-40

AVERAGE RAINFALL

IN	MM
394	10,000
295	7,500
197	5,000
98	2,500
0	0

CANADIAN SHIELD

Extending north from the Great Lakes to the Arctic Ocean is one of the world's largest geologic continental shields (exposed Precambrian crystalline rocks). The rocks of the Canadian Shield have remained above sea level for almost 4 billion years. Soils form a thin layer or are absent as the rocks have been scoured by ice during repeated glaciations.

ALEUTIAN ISLANDS

An arc of 69 volcanic islands, largely treeless and fogbound, that support an array of plant life and seabird colonies.

Labels on map:

Greenland

Labrador Sea

Labrador

Davis Strait

Baffin Bay

Baffin Island

Hudson Strait

Péninsule d'Ungava

Ellesmere Island

Queen Elizabeth Islands

Parry Islands

Victoria Island

Hudson Bay

Banks Island

Great Bear Lake

Great Slave Lake

Lake Athabasca

Beaufort Sea

Mackenzie

Mackenzie Mountains

ARCTIC OCEAN

Rock...

Brooks Range

Mount McKinley (Denali) 6,194m

Yukon

Gulf of Alaska

Bering Strait

Bering Sea

Kodiak Island

Aleutian Islands

PACIFIC OCEAN

ATLANTIC OCEAN

Nova Scotia

Cape Cod

APPALACHIANS

The oldest mountains in North America include the Great Smoky and Blue Ridge ranges. The region is largely forested and has rivers rich in fish and invertebrates.

St. Lawrence

Lake Ontario

Niagara Falls

Lake Erie

Ohio

Appalachian Mountains

Blue Ridge

Tennessee

Alabama

Straits of Florida

The Everglades

Lake Okeechobee

Caribbean Sea

DEAN'S BLUE HOLE

Located in the Bahamas, the world's deepest salt water blue hole plunges to depths of 663 ft (202 m). A blue hole is a water-filled sinkhole formed by rainwater seeping into limestone bedrock. The entrance is now underwater.

BLUE DAMSELFISH

Lake Superior

Lake Huron

Great Lakes

Lake Michigan

Illinois

Mississippi

Arkansas

Mississippi Delta

Gulf of Mexico

Yucatan Peninsula

Lake Winnipeg

Manitoba

NORTH AMERICA

Great Plains

Missouri

Platte

Kansas

Red River

Rio Grande

Sierra Madre Oriental

Lago de Chapala

Sierra Madre del Sur

South Saskatchewan

Yellowstone

Sierra Madre Occidental

GULF OF CALIFORNIA

Also known as the Sea of Cortés, the Gulf of California lies between the west coast of mainland Mexico and the peninsula of Baja California. Around 800 species of fish are found in the gulf, but they are threatened by overfishing.

Mountains

Great Basin

Snake

Great Salt Lake

Colorado

Colorado Plateau

Grand Canyon

Sonoran Desert

Gulf of California

Baja California

Mount St Helens 2,549m

Mt Whitney 4,418m

Death Valley -86m

Mojave Desert

Sierra Nevada

Coast Ranges

Vancouver Island

WESTERN CORDILLERA

This chain of mountain ranges includes the Coastal Ranges, Rocky Mountains, and Sierra Nevada, and runs southeast from Alaska to western Mexico. Most of it formed millions of years ago as an ancient oceanic plate moved under the North American plate. This ancient plate has now almost completely disappeared.

continental (North American) plate

mountain range

subducting oceanic plate

GRAND CANYON

Carved by the passage of the Colorado River over 17 million years, the Grand Canyon is 277 miles (446 km) long and up to 1 mile (1.8 km) deep.

TORNADO ALLEY

Late spring on the lowlands of the Midwestern prairies, where there are no mountains to block air flow, creates the perfect conditions for tornadoes to form. These are columns of violently rotating air that develop within storm clouds and are in contact with the ground. The most powerful tornadoes occur almost exclusively in North America.

FEATURED ECOREGIONS

Canadian Arctic ≫p24–33
Tundra, ice

Yellowstone ≫p34–43
Temperate coniferous forest

Central Great Plains ≫p44–51
Temperate grassland

Sierra Nevada ≫p52–59
Temperate coniferous forest

Mojave Desert ≫p60–65
Desert, scrub

Florida Everglades ≫p66–73
Wetland: flooded grassland, mangrove

CANADIAN ARCTIC

A far northern place of ice and snow

The Canadian Arctic includes one of the world's largest archipelagos—36,563 islands, most of which are uninhabited by people. The easternmost islands are mountainous, becoming lower lying in the west. For much of the long, dark winter, land and sea are bound in a vast ice-scape, broken only by rocky island peaks and occasional polynyas —areas of sea that freeze late and thaw early. Polynyas are a vital resource for marine mammals including belugas and bowhead whales, which use them as breathing holes, and for seals and polar bears, which need to access the water from the sea ice. In summer, strong tides sweep the channels between the islands.

Frozen ground

On land, the top three feet of soil thaws briefly in summer, but the ground beneath is permanently frozen (permafrost). Plant life is limited to mosses, lichens, and around 200 species of grass, sedge, hardy forbs, and dwarf shrubs. Land mammals able to withstand the cold include reindeer, muskoxen, Arctic foxes, and lemmings. The number of invertebrate species is low, but mites and springtails become superabundant in summer, providing food for breeding migrant birds such as Arctic terns, ivory gulls, common eiders, and red phalaropes.

Melting of the permafrost releases methane and carbon, **increasing the rate of global warming**

ARCTIC TERN

Of 36 mammal species here, 17 are marine

This is a Land of the Midnight Sun—the Sun never sets in summer

LONG-DISTANCE TRAVELER
The Arctic tern travels further than any animal on the planet as it migrates between its Arctic breeding areas and the Antarctic. Many Arctic animals head south to avoid the winter– reindeer make a shorter but equally arduous trip to the tundra regions of Canada.

HOODED SEAL MOTHER AND PUP

TOUGH START IN LIFE
Newborn hooded seals feed on super-rich milk that enables them to increase their weight from 55–100 lb (25 to 45 kg) in just four days. After that, their mothers return to the sea to mate and feed. Each pup must learn to swim, dive, and hunt before it starves.

WOOD FROG

WINTER FREEZE
Wood frogs pass the winter dormant, their blood and skin frozen solid. To survive, they pump their cells full of a protective glucose syrup made by the liver. In contrast, Arctic cod have antifreeze proteins that prevent their blood freezing.

BANDED WOOLLY BEAR

Includes one of the world's largest archipelagos

SLOW AND STEADY
The Isabella tiger moth can breed in the High Arctic by having a long life cycle. Its woolly bear caterpillars hatch in summer and feed for a month. In winter, they freeze solid and lie dormant. They repeat the process for up to 14 years before pupating and emerging as adults that live for only a few days.

ARCTIC HARE

Birds come to the Canadian Arctic to breed, but leave before winter

WINTER WHITEOUT
Like other Arctic land mammals, the Arctic hare has exceptionally dense fur, which traps warm air close to the skin. In the south of its range in Newfoundland, hares molt into a gray-brown summer coat. Further north, where the thaw is negligible, they stay winter white all year.

FISH OF THE DAY
Arctic cod are not fished commercially, but feature in the diets of other predators. They are targeted from below by seals, belugas, and narwhals, and from above by birds such as guillemots, or murres, which dive to more than 330 ft (100 m), using their wings to "fly" underwater.

ARCTIC COD

LOCATION

The northernmost parts of the Canadian mainland and the islands, comprising part of the Northwest Territories and the mostly Inuit territory of Nunavut.

Greenland
ICELAND
Hudson Bay
C A N A D A
Edmonton
Vancouver

0 km 1000
0 miles 1000

CLIMATE

Temperatures are very low all year, only rising above 32°F (0°C) for 6-10 weeks in summer. Average annual temperatures are well below freezing, and virtually all precipitation falls as snow.

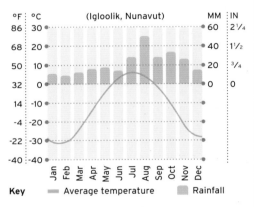

(Igloolik, Nunavut)

°F	°C		MM	IN
86	30		60	2¼
68	20		40	1½
50	10		20	¾
32	0		0	0
14	-10			
-4	-20			
-22	-30			
-40	-40			

Jan Feb Mar Apr May Jun Jul Aug Sep Oct Nov Dec

Key — Average temperature   Rainfall

GETTING WARMER

The Arctic is warmer now than at any time in the last 40,000 years, and the extent and duration of sea ice reduces every year. In 2007, the Northwest Passage linking the Atlantic and Pacific remained ice free for the first time in recorded history. This change in conditions can have profound effects on the growth of plankton, on which all marine life ultimately depends. The sea ice is vital to polar bears, which need it for hunting and breeding.

curved horns almost meet in middle of skull

Muskox
Ovibos moschatus

One of the few large mammals to roam the Arctic year round, the muskox is highly adapted to the cold. Its thick undercoat is covered by a coarse cloak of guard hairs over 24 in (60 cm) long, giving the animal its shaggy appearance. Its short, stocky legs and large hooves provide good traction on snow. The horns are used in defense and in dominance battles among bulls.

Musky males

Muskox herds are usually mixed-sex and can have 10 to more than 100 animals, although some bulls form bachelor herds or remain solitary. Herds are smaller from July to September, when dominant bulls control breeding harems of females. The bulls give off a musky odor during the mating season, giving the animal its name.

Muskox feed in lowland areas in summer, eating flowers in addition to their usual diet. In winter, they move to higher ground for easier foraging.

↔ 6–8 ft (1.9–2.3 m)
⚖ 440–900 lb (200–410 kg)
⊗ Locally common
🌾 Sedges, grasses, leaves
🏠 ⛰

N. North America, Greenland

▷ **FACING THE ENEMY**
When threated by predators such as wolves or a polar bear, muskoxen form a circle and face outward.

Fighting bulls' **collisions can be heard** up to **1 mile (1.6 km) away**

↔ 4–7 ft (1.2–2.2 m)
⚖ 265–660 lb (120–300 kg)
⊗ Endangered
🌾 Leaves, roots, bark, lichen
🏠 ⛰

N. North America, N. Europe, N. Asia

▽ **COLOR VARIATION**
High Arctic subspecies, such as the Peary caribou (*R. t. pearyi*), are smaller and lighter colored than caribou living at lower latitudes. Both male and female caribou have antlers that they shed and regrow each year.

branching antlers

outer coat of wool-like hair provides extra insulation

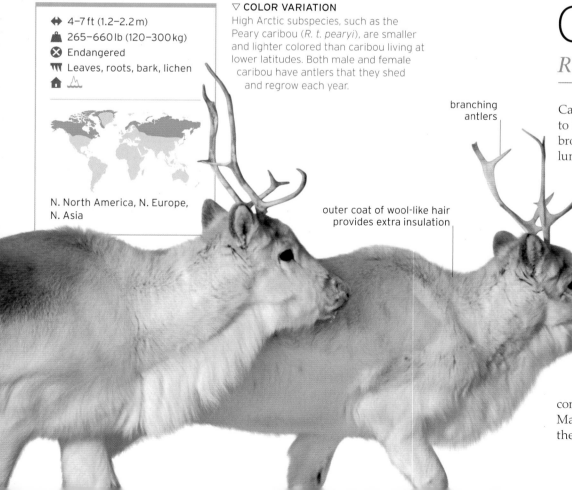

Caribou
Rangifer tarandus

Caribou (known as reindeer in Europe) are well adapted to life in the Arctic tundra. They have a dense coat and a broad muzzle that warms frigid air before it reaches the lungs. Caribou are strong swimmers, with broad, flat hooves. These provide stability on soft summer ground and act as snowshoes in winter, becoming harder and sharper-edged—ideal for cutting through snow and ice. Despite their broad hooves, they can run at up to 50 mph (80 km/h). They can see ultraviolet light, which helps them locate lichens and snow-covered vegetation on dark winter days.

On the move

Caribou are almost constantly on the move. Some migrate 3,000 miles (5,000 km) in a year—the longest distance any land mammal travels. Herds can be up to half a million strong, with smaller single-sex groups coming together to migrate during spring and fall. Males fight for control of harems of females in fall and the females give birth to a single calf in the next spring.

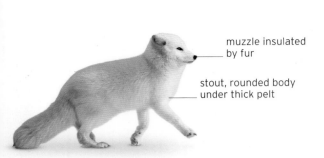

muzzle insulated
by fur

stout, rounded body
under thick pelt

Arctic fox
Alopex lagopus

Incredibly well-adapted to its harsh environment in the
Arctic Circle, the Arctic fox can survive temperatures as
low as -58°F (-50°C). Its dense fur is a few inches thick
during winter, insulating its short ears, muzzle, and
even the soles of its feet, which allows it to walk on
ice without slipping. In winter, most Arctic foxes grow
a white coat (some turn a steely blue) that lets them
blend into the snow.

Varied diet
Although it feeds on smaller mammals such as lemmings,
voles, and Arctic hares in summer, in winter the Arctic
fox may dig out seal pups from their under-ice birth
chambers. It will also follow polar bears and wolves to
feed on carcasses they leave behind. The Arctic fox is the
most common predator of Arctic birds such as snow
geese, but also eats fish, eggs, seaweed, and berries.

Mainly solitary, Arctic foxes may congregate around
carrion or fresh kills, and regularly raid garbage dumps
in northern Alaska. When not hunting, the Arctic fox
curls up in underground burrows during summer, while
in winter it tunnels into snow banks to escape blizzards.
Females give birth in spring to litters of as many as 14
kits, or pups. Both parents raise their young until around
August, when the family group disperses.

The Arctic fox has the **warmest pelt of any animal** found **in the Arctic**

△ **HUNTING IN
THE SNOW**
The Arctic fox listens for
movement below, then
leaps into the air before
plunging head-first to the
ground. This force breaks
through the snow to the
prey beneath.

↔ 21–22 in (53–55 cm)
🏋 9 lb (4 kg)
✖ Common
🍴 Small mammals, fish, birds
🏠 🏔

N. Canada, Alaska, Greenland,
N. Europe, N. Asia

◁ **SUMMER COAT**
Arctic foxes' white coats
thin and change color
to gray-brown in
summer to match
surrounding rocks and
low-growing vegetation
of the tundra.

▷ **AT HOME**
Snow dens protect young cubs from
the cold. The dens have one entrance
and often several chambers, and can
be up to 40 degrees warmer than
outside temperatures.

▷▷ **STRONG SWIMMER**
A polar bear's broad, partially webbed
forepaws make it a superb swimmer,
capable of covering up to 60 miles
(100 km) at a stretch, at speeds
of 6 mph (10 km/h).

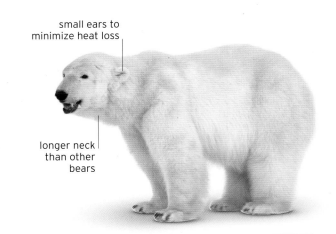

small ears to
minimize heat loss

longer neck
than other
bears

Polar bear

Ursus maritimus

The polar bear vies with the brown bear for the title of the world's largest living land carnivore. It is classified as a marine mammal, and its preferred hunting ground is Arctic pack ice. Superbly adapted to its environment, the polar bear has non-retractable claws and dimpled, partially furred foot pads that provide extra grip, allowing it to walk and run easily on ice.

The polar bear's body is covered in double-layered fur—the thickest of any bear species. The inner layer is a dense undercoat, while the outer fur consists of clear, hollow tubes that trap air for insulation. Since the tubes reflect all visible light, the outer coat makes polar bears seem white, allowing them to blend easily into snowy environments. Their skin is black and rests on a layer of blubber up to 4 in (10 cm) thick.

Feasting and fasting

Polar bears can live up to 25–30 years in the wild. Their lives alternate between feasting and fasting, and their intestines are adapted to process fat, which is easier to digest than meat and has more calories. They can also slow their metabolic rate when food is scarce. Their main diet is seals, but they occasionally hunt belugas or narwhals. When starving, they will also hunt walruses, but the risk of injury is high. They can smell prey up to ³/₄ mile (1 km) away, or up to 3¹/₄ ft (1 m) beneath ice.

Polar bears are generally solitary, except for breeding pairs or mothers with cubs. However, they will congregate around large food supplies such as whale carcasses. In fall, polar bears also gather together in "transition" areas such as southwestern Hudson Bay and Churchill, Canada to wait for the sea ice to form that allows them access to ringed seals swimming beneath the ice.

Polar bear territories are vast. Bears closest to the Canadian Arctic Islands have an average range of 19,000–23,000 sq miles (50,000–60,000 sq km), but those closer to the Bering Sea can cover up to 135,000 sq miles (350,000 sq km).

Winter births

Polar bears give birth to cubs every two to three years —one of the lowest reproductive rates of all mammals. Mating occurs from late March through May, but embryos may not start to develop until fall. Pregnant females must gain about 440 lb (200 kg) extra weight during summer to survive the winter, when they may have to go up to eight months without food. They dig maternity dens mainly in south-facing snowdrifts, where between one and four cubs are born in early winter. Most litters are of twins.

The adult female does not hibernate in the truest sense, but maintains a much warmer body temperature to care for her cubs. Even so, she neither eats, urinates, nor defecates during the months she is in the den. Mother and cubs do not emerge from their den until March or early April, when she leads them toward the sea ice in order to hunt.

Polar bears are capable of running as fast as an Olympic sprinter

◁ **MOCK BATTLE**
Young males often engage in playfighting–
sparring and trying to push each other over while
standing on their hind legs. Some of these males
may travel together for weeks or even years.

↔ 6–9 ft (1.8–2.8 m)
⚖ 880–1,500 lb (400–680 kg)
✕ Vulnerable
🍴 Seals, fish, birds, vegetation
🏠 ≋ ≋ ⛰

Arctic Ocean, N. Canada,
N. Russia

tusk grows
through
upper lip

Narwhal

Monodon monoceros

Narwhals are unique among whales in having a single long tusk, which is grown mostly by males. The tusk is, in fact, an elongated canine tooth that erupts mainly from the left side of the animal's upper jaw. It grows in a counterclockwise spiral, and is believed to be the reality behind the unicorn legends of medieval Europe.

While scientists once believed that the tusk's function was purely defensive, relating to dominance disputes over mating rights, recent research has revealed millions of nerve endings at the tusk's surface. These nerve endings allow the narwhal to detect changes in water pressure and temperature, as well as degrees of water salinity (saltiness). This discovery suggests that the characteristic rubbing of tusks by males may be a sensation- or information-seeking exercise—not simply "jousting." Tusks can grow to over 8 ft (2.5 m) long and are highly flexible, bending up to 1 ft (30 cm) in any direction without breaking. If a tusk is broken, new growth repairs the damage.

Super pods

Sociable animals, narwhals form small groups that often merge with others to form "super pods" of hundreds of whales. Individuals communicate by clicks, squeaks, and other vocalizations. Pods migrate each year, spending winters in and around the pack ice of the Arctic Ocean, and summers closer inland in bays or deep fjords. Their diet consists mainly of fish, such as halibut and cod, supplemented by squid.

Narwhals can **dive to remarkable depths,** some reaching 5,900 ft (**1,800 m**)

△ **TIGHT SQUEEZE**
Restricted space can cause pods of narwhals to merge as they swim along narrow channels that have opened in the sea ice.

▷ **UNICORNS OF THE SEA**
Male narwhals surface with their tusks pointing skyward. The dark staining is caused by algal growth.

Beluga
Delphinapterus leucas

small, rounded
flippers

The beluga is the only whale that is white in color when adult, a feature that helps it to hide from predators among the sea ice. If chased, the absence of a dorsal fin allows the beluga to escape by swimming away beneath the ice. It is also able to move its head up and down and from side to side because its neck vertebrae are unfused. Thick blubber makes up 40 percent of its body mass. Every summer it molts, shedding the outer layer of skin, partially by raking its body over pebbles in shallow waters. Highly social mammals, belugas are also extremely vocal—their wide repertoire of clicks, whistles, chirps, and squeals has earned them the nickname "canaries of the sea."

▷ **BLOWING BUBBLES**
Belugas amuse themselves by blowing bubble rings and then biting them. They may also produce bubbles if alarmed or surprised.

↔ 10–15 ft (3–4.6 m)
⚖ Up to 1.8 tons (1.6 metric tons)
✖ Near threatened
🍴 Fish, squid, shrimp
🏠 〰 〰 ⛰

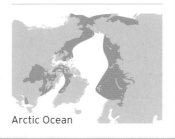
Arctic Ocean

Harp seal
Pagophilus groenlandicus

Named for their markings, harp seals are the most successful of all northern hemisphere seals, with numbers estimated at 8 million. Most inhabit icy northern waters, but some have migrated as far south as Virginia in the US and France. Mating occurs on pack ice in winter, and single pups are born from late February to mid March. Fast-moving on ice, harp seals are also good swimmers. Excellent eyesight and hearing make them formidable hunters, and also alert them to predators such as polar bears.

↔ 6 ft (1.8 m)
⚖ 286 lb (130 kg)
✖ Common
🍴 Fish, krill
🏠 〰 〰 ⛰

black head
markings of adult

▽ **HARP-SHAPED MARKINGS**
The dark markings on the sides of this adult seal curve upward to meet over the shoulders, forming a harp shape.

Arctic Ocean, North Atlantic

backward-directed
hind flippers

↔ 12–16 ft (3.7–5 m)
⚖ Up to 2 tons (1.8 metric tons)
✖ Near threatened
🍴 Fish, squid
🏠 〰 〰 ⛰

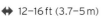

Arctic Ocean

oversized canine tooth

rough, heavily creased skin

Walrus

Odobenus rosmarus

This large marine mammal has a wide snout covered in hundreds of stiff, whiskerlike bristles called vibrissae, which help it to locate its food. Mollusks, such as mussels, are favorite foods, but walruses will eat the carcasses of young seals, usually when other food items are scarce.

The song of the walrus

Walruses travel in groups and "haul out" on land or ice. Females generally follow pack ice south in fall and north in spring, but most males stay all year in herds in the southern Arctic, only joining the females to mate. Bulls compete for mating locations by performing visual displays and intricate "songs," and also spar with their tusks. A successful bull will mate with several cows between December and March, and the females give birth to a single calf in spring the following year.

The average lifespan of walruses in the wild is 40 years. They can withstand icy conditions because of their thick skin and the presence of vast amounts of blubbery fat around their shoulders and neck.

A **walrus** can **slow** **its heartbeat** to survive in **icy water**

△ TOOTH PICKS
Walruses use their tusks in defense and also as handy "ice picks" that help them pull themselves onto ice floes or land. They punch breathing holes through ice with their tusks, which grow about 1/2 in (1 cm) a year throughout their lives.

▷ COLD COMFORT
Normally cinnamon-brown, walruses may turn pale after a long stay in icy water as blood vessels in their skin constrict to save body heat. In warmer weather, some walruses look pink as their vessels dilate to get rid of excess heat.

↔ 8–12 ft (2.4–3.7 m)
⚖ Up to 2.2 tons (2 metric tons)
✖ Not known
🦷 Mollusks, octopuses, fish
🏠 ≋ ≋ ⟍

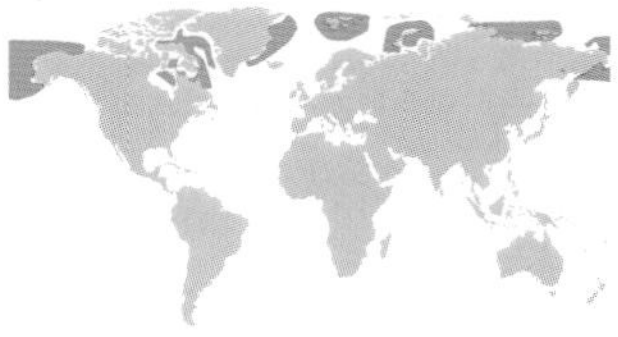

Arctic Ocean and coasts

Snowy owl

Nyctea scandiaca

mature male almost pure white

The snowy owl is a creature of the extremes, living in the High Arctic tundra. It is equipped with exceptionally thick plumage for insulation against the cold, the old males as white as a swan. Unusually among owls, females look different, with more dark spots and bars.

Winter wanderings

Snowy owls mostly feed on lemmings, surviving the long, dark Arctic winter and the extreme cold so long as they have food to eat. If food is scarce, they move south with regular winter migrations into central Canada and Siberia. Hundreds of snowy owls go farther south every few years as the populations of different lemming species boom and bust. Occasionally, they reach as far as Florida. Snowy owls breed every four or five years, with clutches of 3–13 eggs, and have barren years in between, so populations vary enormously.

long wings

↔ 21–28 in (53–71 cm)
⚖ 2–6 lb (1–2.7 kg)
✖ Common
🍴 Small mammals, birds
🏠 ⛰ ≋ ⬛ ⛰

N. North America, NE. Europe, and N. Asia

▷ **GRACEFUL FLIER**
"Snowies" are huge owls, flying low and silently between regular lookout perches on long, powerful, pointed wings.

heavily feathered legs and toes

Snow goose

Chen caerulescens

Snow geese breed in the extreme north of Arctic North America and migrate through western, central, and eastern states to winter in the far south. Hundreds of thousands of them stop to feed at regular "service stations," with large, noisy flocks making a spectacular sight. Despite the danger of being shot, they thrive on agricultural land, and they are highly sociable.

↔ 27–33 in (69–84 cm)
⚖ 5–8 lb (2.3–3.6 kg)
✖ Common
🍴 Grass, roots, seeds
🏠 ⛰ ≋ ⬛ ⛰
◉ North America; Wrangel Island, Russia

black-tipped wings

▷ **BRILLIANT WHITE**
Snow geese are found in two color forms: brilliant white (pictured) and blue-gray with a white head.

Arctic char

Salvelinus alpinus

Adapted to deep water and extreme cold, Arctic char are the most northerly of freshwater fish. A migratory, river-breeding form lives in the sea, and there is also a landlocked lake form. Spawning occurs at 39.2°F (4°C). Females scrape shallow nests, or redds, to lay their eggs in clean gravel.

↔ Up to 38 in (97 cm)
⚖ Up to 27 lb (12.3 kg)
✖ Common
🍴 Insects, crustaceans
🏠 ⛰ ≋ ⬛ ≋ ⛰
◉ N. North America, N. Europe, N. Asia, and Arctic Ocean

▷ **FIGHTING MALES**
During breeding season, males become aggressively territorial. They develop hooked jaws and sport brilliant red undersides.

YELLOWSTONE
America's forested geothermal wilderness

Lying within the South Central Rockies ecoregion and dominated by coniferous forest, Yellowstone was home to Native Americans for 11,000 years. Eighty percent of Yellowstone's forests consist of lodgepole pine, a tree so-named because its straight trunk is ideal for use as tipi poles.

Yellowstone was established as a national park in 1872—the first in the US and the world—and remains one of the largest, with more than 3,500 sq miles (9,000 sq km) of mostly pristine wilderness. The region is one of the last strongholds of American bison, and the reintroduction of the gray wolf in 1995 allows park managers to claim the area as the largest intact ecoregion in the northern temperate zone. The potentially damaging impacts of logging, hunting, and tourism are regulated, but not always successfully.

Hot springs and geysers

Around 1,700 species of plant live in the forests, meadows, and upland grasslands of the park, which also boasts mountains, lakes, rivers, and canyons. Yellowstone is also famous for being the world's largest center of geothermal activity—it has around half of the known geothermal features on the planet, including the Old Faithful geyser. People also visit the park in the hope of seeing animals such as grizzly and black bears and American beavers, whose tree-felling and stream-damming activities renew habitats such as pools, swamps, and meadows.

On average, **Old Faithful** produces columns of steam and water **every 67 minutes**

HOT SPRINGS

3 million visitors every year

THERMAL ACTIVITY
The localized effects of geothermal heat include extended plant-growing periods, thinner snow—allowing bison to graze in winter—and ice-free lakes, where waterfowl feed year round. The hot springs are also home to micro-organisms whose range of heat tolerances cause them to grow in distinctive bands.

MILLER MOTH

More than 350 major waterfalls and 500 geysers

MOTH FEAST
In summer, millions of miller moths (also known as army cutworm moths) migrate to Yellowstone to feed in alpine meadows. Their vast numbers attract grizzly bears, which consume up to 40,000 of the nutritious insects a day. The grizzlies often live on little else for up to three months.

67 species of mammal

WHITEBARK PINE

THE WHITEBARK ZONE
Open-canopied whitebark pine forests depend on a nutcracker prises open the cones to harvest the seeds and then caches them. The bird forgets about some of the seeds, which means they can germinate.

LANDSCAPE CHANGER

The loss of wolves from Yellowstone in the 1920s meant that within a few years its forests were being damaged by the increasing numbers of wapiti. In particular, quaking aspens failed to regenerate. Today, wolves are helping to control wapiti once more.

WAPITI

The world's first national park, established in 1872

FIERY BEGINNINGS

Lodgepole pines are adapted to cope with occasional wildfires. The trees burn rapidly, but their tightly closed cones require the heat of a wildfire to melt the resinous glue that seals them, releasing the seeds to germinate in the newly cleared area.

LODGEPOLE PINE

Yellowstone's supervolcano is the only one on land in the world

TOO MUCH COMPETITION

Named for the dramatic slash of scarlet on the lower jaw, cutthroat trout are threatened by habitat loss, disease, and competition from other fish species introduced for sport fishing. Those in Yellowstone are a separate subspecies. They are a key component of the diets of bald eagles and osprey, so the decline of this fish would also lead to a decline in these birds of prey.

YELLOWSTONE CUT-THROAT TROUT

LOCATION

The national park lies primarily within the western US state of Wyoming. It is part of the South Central Rockies ecoregion.

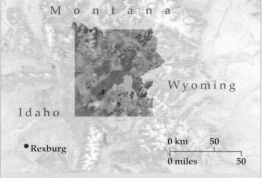

Montana

Wyoming

Idaho

• Rexburg

| 0 km | 50 |
| 0 miles | 50 |

CLIMATE

Yellowstone experiences a cool, temperate climate, with cool summers and long, cold winters. Precipitation is evenly spread throughout the year, falling as heavy snow between November and March.

(West Yellowstone, Montana)

°F	°C		MM	IN
104	40		80	3¼
86	30		60	2¼
68	20		40	1½
50	10		20	¾
32	0		0	0
14	-10			
-4	-20			

Jan Feb Mar Apr May Jun Jul Aug Sep Oct Nov Dec

Key — Average temperature ▮ Rainfall

SUPERVOLCANO

Around 640,000 years ago, a massive volcano erupted, which caused it to collapse and form the giant Yellowstone Caldera. The supervolcano beneath the caldera is still active, and the caldera is closely monitored for signs of increasing activity. Between 1,000 and 2,000 earthquakes and tremors are recorded in the area every year.

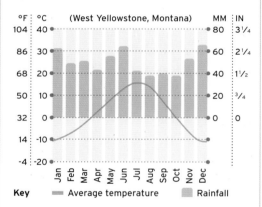

dish-shaped face

long front claws

Grizzly bear

Ursus arctos horribilis

All grizzlies are brown bears, but not all brown bears are grizzlies. This subspecies gets its name from its light-tipped fur, yet not all are "grizzled"—their coats range from whitish-blond to almost black. Their shoulder "hump" consists of muscles that make them efficient diggers and capable of inflicting strong blows with their forepaws.

Despite its often fearsome reputation, the bulk of a grizzly bear's diet comprises nuts, grasses, roots, seeds, and moths. Much of the meat they eat comes from carrion, but they hunt mammals ranging from ground squirrels to moose. Grizzlies prefer coniferous forests broken by fields and meadows with access to rivers. Good swimmers, they are skilled at catching trout, bass, and salmon.

Grizzly threat

Grizzlies mate in late spring to early summer. The female gives birth to up to four cubs, usually while hibernating, nursing them in her den until April or May. Cubs stay with their mothers for two to four years, and the main threat to youngsters is from adult male grizzlies. Once common throughout the western US, grizzlies now occur in small numbers only in Idaho, Montana, Washington state, and Wyoming, with larger populations in Alaska and Canada.

↔ 5–8 ft (1.5–2.4 m)
⬛ 132–727 lb (60–330 kg)
❌ Locally common
🍴 Berries, roots, carrion, fish
🏠 🌲🌲🌲 ⛰ 🌵 🌾

NW. North America

△ **FOOD FIGHT**
Grizzlies are powerful bears and competition for the best fishing spot can cause a fight to break out. However, most will stop before a serious injury occurs.

◁ **WHO'S THE DADDY?**
Female grizzlies will mate with several males in a breeding season and the cubs in the resulting litter may have different fathers.

large, sensitive ears help detect prey

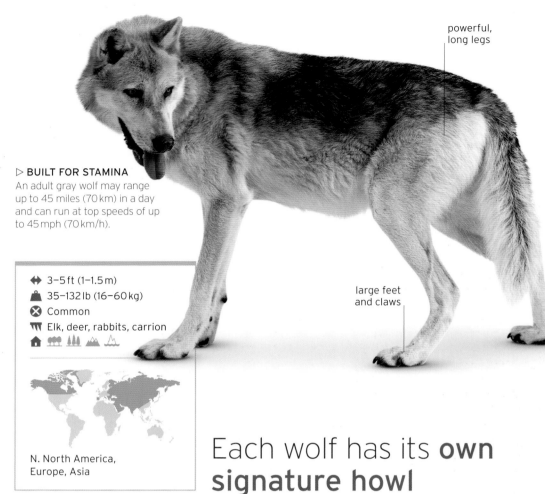
powerful, long legs

large feet and claws

Gray wolf
Canis lupus

Despite its name, the gray wolf can be black, brown, gray, or almost white. All gray wolves are pack predators, hunting large hooved mammals such as elk, deer, and caribou, and smaller prey such as rabbits and beavers. They also feed on carrion, particularly in winter.

An average wolf pack has seven to eight adults ruled by an alpha male and female. The alpha pair leads hunts, establishes territory, and chooses den sites, reinforcing the pack's bonds through vocalizations such as barks and howls. The alphas mate from January to March. After about three months, the female bears a litter of four to seven pups. The pack nurtures the pups until they are about 10 months old, when some will leave, traveling up to 500 miles (800 km), in search of other wolves.

Successful reintroduction
The light gray Rocky Mountain wolf subspecies (*C. l. irremotus*) was reintroduced to Yellowstone in 1995. Since the wolves' return, elk and deer are more mobile, letting trees and grassland regenerate.

▷ **BUILT FOR STAMINA**
An adult gray wolf may range up to 45 miles (70 km) in a day and can run at top speeds of up to 45 mph (70 km/h).

↔ 3–5 ft (1–1.5 m)
⚖ 35–132 lb (16–60 kg)
✖ Common
♜ Elk, deer, rabbits, carrion

N. North America, Europe, Asia

Each wolf has its **own signature howl**

↔ 26–43 in (66–109 cm)
⚖ 9–34 lb (4–15.4 kg)
✖ Common
♜ Rabbits, rodents, birds

S. Canada, US, Mexico

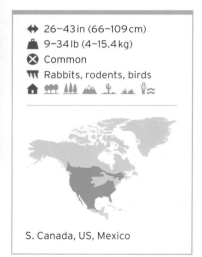

Bobcat
Lynx rufus

What the bobcat lacks in tail length it makes up in numbers. More bobcats live in North America than any other native cat species—estimates put the figure at more than a million. Also the most widely distributed cat, it is found as far north as British Columbia.

Adaptable cat
The secret to this tough little cat's success is adaptability. It prefers dense forests, but can easily survive in swamps, mountains, and deserts. Recently, it has added suburban and urban terrain to its habitats. This often brings it into conflict with humans, as it preys on domestic pets and small livestock. In the wild, rabbits form a large part of a bobcat's diet, but it also hunts rodents, birds, beavers, and small deer, mainly at dawn and dusk. At other times, it rests in dens hidden in thickets, hollow trees, or rocky crevices.

Like most cat species, the bobcat is solitary except during the mating season from December to April. After about a two-month gestation period, females give birth to litters of about three cubs, which remain with their mothers for eight months.

▷ **WINTER FREEZE**
Bobcats are more often seen in daylight hours during winter, when food is scarce. They are ambush predators, with markings that allow them to blend in with their surroundings.

Wolverine

Gulo gulo

Known as the glutton, albeit unfairly, the wolverine satisfies its voracious appetite by killing prey as big as deer. Its strong jaws rip open the toughest hides and crush the biggest bones in search of marrow. Although it is in fact a huge weasel, its heavy fur, sturdy legs, and large feet give the wolverine a bearlike appearance. It can walk on snow with its broad feet, and survive extreme conditions in remote forests, tundra, and mountains encircling the Arctic.

Wolverines store food after a big kill. Reindeer and caribou are dismembered and buried in snow or soil, or pushed into rock crevices and gullies. They mate in summer and two to four cubs are born the following spring.

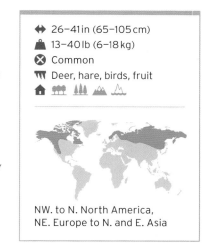

↔ 26–41in (65–105 cm)

⚖ 13–40lb (6–18 kg)

✖ Common

🦷 Deer, hare, birds, fruit

🏠 🌳🌳 🌲🌲 🏔 ⛰

NW. to N. North America,
NE. Europe to N. and E. Asia

▽ **ON THE GO**
Short, powerful legs and a supple, shuffling action help the wolverine cover long distances at a relentless pace in search of food, with minimum expenditure of energy.

◁ **PALMATE ANTLERS**
Male moose grow a new set of their massive antlers every summer. These have a covering of soft skin, or "velvet," which is shed by autumn, the mating season.

▽ **LOSING BATTLE**
This female moose managed to defend her week-old calf from a pack of wolves for 10 minutes, but, despite her superior size and power, they were able to drag the calf away from her.

Moose
Alces alces

pointed hooves for
digging in snow

The world's largest species of deer, the moose lives below the Arctic Circle, inhabiting coniferous and deciduous woodland, swamps, and lakes. In Europe, the moose is also known as the elk, whereas in North America—to add to the confusion—the elk is an entirely different species.

Solitary nomads

Unlike most other deer species, moose are mostly solitary, although females are accompanied by their calves. They do not defend territories, staying on the move all year round. Male moose select habitats that offer the greatest supply of food, while females choose habitats that provide the most cover for them and their young. Moose are diurnal browsers, and may be found cooling off in water during the hottest days of summer while feeding on lily roots and other aquatic plants.

They use their flexible upper lip to browse the freshest leaves and shoots. In winter, when leafy food is in short supply, they will kick away snow to get at moss and lichens underneath, chew on twigs of trees such as poplar and willow, and strip bark from trunks. Their wide hooves help them to walk on soft snow as well as wade through soft-bottomed lakes and swamps.

Male moose rut in the fall, and both sexes bellow to attract a mate. The females choose a mate by sizing up his antlers, which may span over 6 ft (2 m) and have up to 20 points each. Rival males frequently joust for mating rights. Female moose give birth to one or two calves the following summer, which are weaned after six months. A healthy adult moose has little to fear from predators other than humans as it can use its antlers or hooves to defend itself, but bears and wolves predate the much smaller calves.

↔ 8–10 ft (2.4–3 m)
⬛ 620–1,320 lb (280–600 kg)
✕ Common
🍴 Leaves, lichen, water plants, moss, bark

🏠 🌳 🌲 🌾≈

N. North America, N. Europe, N. and E. Asia

White-tailed deer
Odocoileus virginianus

Although widespread and found in large numbers, the white-tailed deer often stays out of sight. For most of the year, the deer live alone, occupying small home ranges of about a square mile. They set up home in swamps, woodlands, and scrubland—wherever there are plenty of shrubs to conceal them. They move slowly, constantly on the lookout for predators such as mountain lions. If danger appears, the deer whistle with alarm and bound away, waving their white tails to startle attackers.

The deer's territory provides all the food they need for the year, even in the northern fringe of their range where winters are long and severe. The deer do not leave when winter comes, but follow well-trodden paths through the snow looking for any greenery they can access. In winter, their coat is gray, but it thins in summer and turns red.

Spotted disguise
The females are ready to breed in fall, and males deploy their antlers to battle it out for the rights to each mate. Fawns are born in spring and lie hidden under shrubs while the mother is away feeding. They begin to follow their mothers in a month and are weaned when three months old. Their spotty coat, which helps them hide when young, is lost in the first winter.

↔ 4–6 ft (1.2–1.8 m)
⚖ 115–310 lb (52–140 kg)
✕ Common
🍴 Buds, leaves, twigs, cacti

S. Canada to N. South America

▷ **MATURE BUCK**
Only male white-tailed deer have antlers, growing a fresh set each year. A new point, or tine, is added with each growth.

short, thick fur protects from the cold

American pika
Ochotona princeps

The American pika looks like a cross between a guinea pig—with short legs and a large head—and a rabbit, with round ears and a whiskered face. Its long tail is hidden in fur. Lively in daylight, the animal bounds across scree slopes, pausing to make birdlike "cheeps" that warn of the presence of predators, such as coyotes, weasels, and stoats, or far-carrying "mews" to assert its territory. This consists of a foraging area and a den in a burrow or rock crevice. Pikas live next to a member of the opposite sex, giving a male–female patchwork of territories.

In summer, the pika gathers flowering stems, such as fireweed, and long grasses. These are stored in a pile near its burrow and left to dry. As winter approaches, the pika drags its hay pile deep into a rock cavity, keeping its food store safe from the snow. Pikas select plants that will decompose the most slowly to ensure their food store will last them through the winter. This animal is adapted to high, cold places, but climate change has squeezed it into an ever-shrinking range.

↔ 6–9 in (15–23 cm)
⚖ 4–6 oz (113–170 g)
✕ Locally common
🍴 Grasses, herbs

SW. Canada, W. US

▷ **MAKING HAY**
Pikas forage for grasses and herbs, eating some each day and caching the rest in their winter hay store.

Pikas use their **cheek glands** to **scent-mark their territory**

long whiskers enable beaver to feel its way in the dark

American beaver

Castor canadensis

△ **CLOSE LIPPED**
Beavers close their lips behind their incisor teeth when underwater so they can still nibble and gnaw on branches and stems.

North America's largest rodent, the American beaver, is a nocturnal "engineer" that alters landscapes throughout the continent, aside from desert areas and northernmost Canada. This stocky, big-skulled aquatic mammal fells trees by gnawing through the trunks, then arranges them into dams across streams or rivers, or uses them to build lodges for shelter. Its flat, scaly tail and webbed hindfeet make it a graceful swimmer, and a waterproof coat protects it from the winter cold.

Woody diet

The beavers' long, orange incisors, which never stop growing, are perfectly suited to their diet of woody bark, twigs, and stems. They also eat cambium, a soft tissue under the bark; favorite sources include birch, alder, and aspen, which they often store as winter food.

They live in small colonies, led by a male and female who mate for life. The female gives birth to three or four fully furred kits between April and June. The kits leave after two years to form their own colonies.

Beavers make their lodges along banks or lake shores, the most impressive being the island lodges in the middle of ponds. With an entrance only accessible underwater, these are the safest refuges from predators such as wolves and coyotes. They tailor their dams to rates of water flow, building straight ones for slow-moving water, and curved ones for faster currents.

▽ **MASTER BUILDER**
American beavers make their dams and lodges out of logs, branches, grass, and moss, plastered together with mud.

↔ 29–35 in (74–89 cm)
⚖ 24–57 lb (11–26 kg)
✗ Common
🌾 Woody bark, twigs, stems
🏠 🌾 ≈ ≈

North America

▷ **FISHING EXPEDITION**
The bald eagle, like other sea eagles, does not enter the water to catch prey; instead, it swoops down to snatch fish, live or dead, from the surface of a lake.

pure white hood

▷▷ **DOWNY CHICK**
Bald eagle chicks remain in the nest for 10–13 weeks, entirely dependent on their parents for food, protection, and shelter.

△ **BODY RIPPER**
The fiercely hooked bill is not used to kill prey, but to rip it into chunks that can be swallowed, and to tear the hide off the carcass of larger animals.

black-brown body

long talons

Bald eagle
Haliaeetus leucocephalus

The bald eagle is found only in North America, but its image is used as a symbol of power, grace, and durability worldwide. Like many birds of prey, its bold looks suggest a more swashbuckling lifestyle than is really the case, for it spends much of the time doing nothing, and much of its food is carrion. It is doing what big birds of prey do: conserving energy between bouts of hunting and gorging.

Life on the water's edge

There are eight species of giant sea eagles worldwide, including the Eurasian white-tailed eagle, the African fish or river eagle, and the spectacular Steller's sea eagle from far eastern Asia. All these species, including the bald eagle, have a powerful build and broad wings that are "fingered" at the tip when fully spread, a relatively short tail and a long head and neck, creating a crosslike shape in flight. Unlike golden eagles, bald eagles soar with their wings held flat. All sea eagles have bare lower legs and feet, with strong toes and sharp claws to grip and pierce their prey, as well as a strong bill to tear it to pieces.

Fish form a large part of the bald eagle's diet, but it also eats other prey. Bald eagles can catch and kill animals as large as sea otters and birds up to the size of a goose. In summer, many live on seabirds caught in coastal colonies. They are primarily birds of the water's edge, where such prey items—and all kinds of wave-tossed carcasses and scraps—can be easily foraged.

Living along the western seaboard of North America from Alaska to California, bald eagles penetrate far inland along rivers and around lakes. They breed across the far northern parts of Canada and in winter move south as far as Florida and the Gulf of Mexico—to wherever water can be found.

Bald eagles feed in small groups in winter if enough food is available, and nest in small defended territories, covering about $3/4$ sq mile (0.2 sq km). These sites can be grouped quite close together. Nests are built almost anywhere from near-flat ground to small slopes, cliffs, exposed crags, and trees.

Breeding pairs and trios

Each pair of bald eagles usually has several nests—one preferred nest, a huge heap of sticks, grass, and seaweed, can become as large as 13 ft (4 m) deep and 8 ft (2.5 m) across. Although two eggs are the norm, usually only one chick survives to fly. Up to three-quarters of the young die before they are a year old, and only one in ten reaches five years of age. Bald eagles can start breeding when four years old. However, unusually, half the adults are non-breeders and some form trios at one nest. Once grown, adults may go on to live long, productive lives, surviving for almost 50 years in the wild.

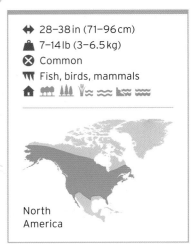

long, sharp
bill hook

↔ 28–38 in (71–96 cm)
⚖ 7–14 lb (3–6.5 kg)
✖ Common
🍴 Fish, birds, mammals
🏠 🌲 🌿 ≈ ≈ ≈

North America

The **bald eagle** was chosen as the **national bird of the US in 1782**

CENTRAL GREAT PLAINS
A rolling landscape, once covered in a sea of grass

Forming a broad band through North America almost to Mexico, between the Rocky Mountains and the Missouri River, the Central Great Plains was once an immense, gently rolling prairie landscape that was dominated by mixed grasses for millions of years. Succession by trees and scrub was kept down by wild fires and grazing by native herbivores such as American bison, pronghorn antelope, and prairie dogs. The prairies were also home to a variety of reptiles, birds, and invertebrates, and many of these animals were exploited sustainably by nomadic American Indian tribes.

Conversion to agriculture

As recently as the early 19th century, this vast area was still covered by grassland. Today, most of the fertile land is given over to agriculture. Overexploitation of arable land in the early 20th century led to the environmental and economic catastrophe in the 1930s known as the Dust Bowl, in which the topsoil was entirely lost from vast areas in a series of dust storms caused by drought and wind erosion. The land has mostly recovered sufficiently to support grazing, but the vast herds of bison that once roamed the prairies are largely gone, replaced mainly by domestic cattle.

A few pockets of relatively pristine prairie remain in the US and Canada, and in reserves such as the Wichita Mountains Wildlife Refuge in Oklahoma, surviving bison herds are protected. Even here, trees are few, and large vegetation is limited mainly to mesquite scrub and prickly pear cactus.

BECOMING A PEST
This beetle used to feed on a prairie weed Solanum rostratum, or spiny nightshade. But when settlers planted another Solanum species, the cultivated potato, the beetle changed its diet and became a notorious crop pest.

COLORADO POTATO BEETLE

BOOMING MARVELOUS
The spring mating rituals of the Greater prairie chicken are a new ecotourism attraction thanks to conservation efforts. Male birds compete at regular "booming grounds," making loud calls amplified by inflated air sacs on the neck.

PRAIRIE CHICKEN

ORNATE BOX TURTLE

Only 1% of the natural grassland survives

30 million bison once lived on the Great Plains

LIVING IN A BOX
The ornate box turtle is one of two terrestrial turtles on the Great Plains. They are named for their hinged lower shell, which can be clamped shut to protect the head and limbs from predators. However, many of them are killed trying to cross roads.

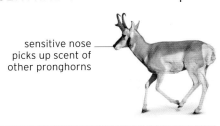
sensitive nose picks up scent of other pronghorns

Pronghorn
Antilocapra americana

The pronghorn is the fastest land animal in the Americas, with a top recorded speed of 54 mph (87 km/h). However, its defining feature is its horns. The forked, antlerlike headgear looks like that of a deer, and the pronghorn is also known colloquially as the American antelope. A deer sheds its antlers each year, while an antelope keeps one pair for life; the pronghorn keeps the bony core of the horn for life, shedding the keratin sheath over the bone each winter.

Home on the range
The pronghorn is the sole surviving member of the Antilocaprinae family, which had dozens of species five million years ago. Despite their unique horns, pronghorns share many features with other even-toed ungulates— a herd lifestyle, a diet of leaves and grasses, and long legs. The pronghorn population was devastated by hunting in the 19th century. Today, pronghorn herds survive in the remote parts of the American West, which is appropriate as it is the very beast mentioned in the anthemic western song "Home on the Range."

↔ 4–5 ft (1.2–1.5 m)
⬛ 66–176 lb (30–80 kg)
✖ Locally common
🌾 Forbs, leaves, grasses

W. and C. North America

A pronghorn can **leap 20 ft (6 m)** in a **single bound**

▽ **RACING AWAY FROM DANGER**
Pronghorns live in loose herds, with large males controlling mating territories in summer. They warn each other of danger with snorts and by raising their white rump hairs.

RESTORING DIVERSITY
The diminutive swift fox is a short-grass prairie specialist. Its disappearance from 60 percent of its range reflects wider ecological decline. Projects to restore habitat for this species will benefit others, including groundnesting birds.

SWIFT FOX

Encompasses Tornado Alley

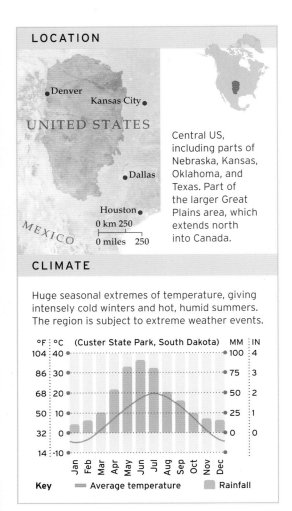

▷ **STAMPEDING HERD**
When alarmed, bison herds start to stampede and, at top speed, can reach 35 mph (60 km/h).

short, upturned
horn

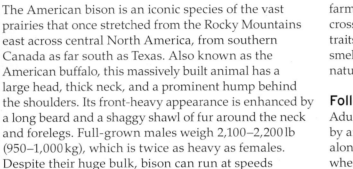

American bison

Bison bison

The American bison is an iconic species of the vast prairies that once stretched from the Rocky Mountains east across central North America, from southern Canada as far south as Texas. Also known as the American buffalo, this massively built animal has a large head, thick neck, and a prominent hump behind the shoulders. Its front-heavy appearance is enhanced by a long beard and a shaggy shawl of fur around the neck and forelegs. Full-grown males weigh 2,100–2,200 lb (950–1,000 kg), which is twice as heavy as females. Despite their huge bulk, bison can run at speeds of up to 35 mph (60 km/h). Both sexes have a pair of short, upturned horns.

Hunted almost to extinction

Bison used to live in huge, nomadic herds that roamed across long distances to graze. The population numbered many millions, with 30 million living on the Great Plains. They had long been hunted by Native American tribes, but during the 1800s, European settlers moved into the prairies and hunting for meat and hide accelerated. The bison's prairie habitat was converted to farmland, and by the 1880s, as few as 500–1,000 animals were left.

An end to hunting and the creation of national parks have raised the bison population to about 30,000 free-ranging animals, although the species only occupies less than one percent of its former range. There are about 500,000 domesticated bison on private ranches and farms. However, the domesticated stock have been cross-bred with cattle and have lost many of their wild traits. Wild bison have excellent hearing and sense of smell, which are essential for detecting their chief natural predator, the gray wolf.

Follow the grass

Adult females and young live in groups of 10–60, led by an older cow. The bulls form separate herds or live alone. The breeding season is from July to September, when the bulls rejoin the female-led herds. The bulls fight for mating rights and dominance, clashing heads in spectacular battles. The females give birth to a single calf after a 10-month gestation, usually in April or May when there is a fresh growth of spring grass.

Bison have complex stomachs with four chambers to help them digest large quantities of grass, and they spend long periods chewing the cud. They can paw aside snow to reveal grass below, but in harsh winters, they migrate to lower, snow-free areas.

Wood bison and wisent

Some of the bison found in Canada are a separate subspecies known as wood bison (*B. bison athabascae*). The largest free-ranging herd of this species is found in Wood Buffalo National Park. There is also a population of wild bison in the Bialoweza Forest on the Poland-Belarus border, and these may belong to a second species called the European bison, or wisent (*B. bonasus*).

△ **WINTER TRAVEL**
The bisons' thick coat and heavy mane protect them from the cold. They are so well insulated that even a dusting of snow on their back does not melt.

◁ **YOUNG BISON**
A calf can stand, walk, or run with its mother a couple of hours after it is born. The calves are weaned at about six months.

↔ 7–12 ft (2.1–3.5 m)
⚖ 770–2,200 lb (350–1,000 kg)
✕ Locally common
🌾 Grasses, sedges
🏠 ⛰

N., NW., and C. North America

An adult American bison could **leap over an adult human**

Black-tailed prairie dog
Cynomys ludovicianus

A large species of ground squirrel, black-tailed prairie dogs are highly social rodents. They live in "towns"—extensive networks of underground tunnels and chambers. A town houses hundreds of dogs, all organized into smaller groups called coteries. A coterie, made up of a dozen adults and their offspring, works together to maintain their patch of the tunnel and defend it from intruders. Coterie members share a scent, which marks them out from other groups.

Prairie dogs dig their tunnels deep enough to avoid winter frosts. Any loose earth pushed to the surface forms mounds around the tunnel entrances that are ideal for spotting predators.

▷ FAMILY UNIT
Pups emerge from under the ground at the age of six weeks and are looked after by every member of the coterie. Most males leave the group after their first winter.

- ↔ 14–17 in (36–43 cm)
- ⚖ 2–3 lb (0.9–1.4 kg)
- ⊗ Common
- ♨ Grass, sedge
- 🏠 ⬚ ⬚

SW. Canada to N. Mexico

Black-footed ferret
Mustela nigripes

This solitary, burrowing hunter is one of North America's rarest mammals. Numbers fell to 18 in the mid-1980s, but are now increasing again. About 90 percent of the black-footed ferret's diet is made up of prairie dogs. The ferrets dig their dens right in the middle of prairie dog communities, even setting up home in unused sections of their tunnel network. They can follow prairie dogs into their burrows, killing and eating them underground.

▽ DISTINCTIVE MASK
Male and female ferrets have a well-defined mask around the eyes from an early age.

- ↔ 16–20 in (41–51 cm)
- ⚖ 2–3 lb (0.9–1.4 kg)
- ⊗ Endangered
- ♨ Prairie dogs, mice, squirrels
- 🏠 ⬚ ⬚

Reintroduced to C. US

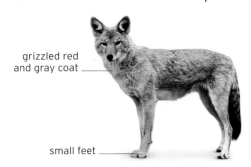

grizzled red
and gray coat

small feet

Coyote
Canis latrans

Most wild dog species face enormous pressure from
humans encroaching on their wide-ranging habitats.
However, the coyote is thriving, even encroaching on
human habitats as a proficient poacher of poultry and
scavenger of human garbage.

Somewhere between a fox and wolf in size, the coyote
has a highly adaptable lifestyle. Although it may form
packs to hunt large animals such as deer, mostly it is a
solitary hunter, targeting smaller prey—such as prairie
dogs—alone. Coyotes spend the day in an underground
den; they may dig their own den, but usually enlarge one
abandoned by badgers or ground squirrels.

Involved parenting
When raising offspring, coyotes set out their home ranges
by marking bushes and other landmarks with urine and
feces. They assert their claim on the territory with loud
yips and howls. Coyotes may form pair bonds that last
several years. Mating occurs in late winter, and about
six pups are born two months later. Both parents nourish
the youngsters with regurgitated food in the den.

Coyotes work with
American badgers
to hunt burrowing
rodents

◁ **HOWLING COYOTE**
Coyotes are noisy
animals, frequently
howling to lay claim
to a territory or greet
a family member.

↔ 29–37 in (74–94 cm)
⬛ 17–35 lb (7.7–15.9 kg)
✖ Common
🍴 Mammals, insects, fruit

North America
and N. Central America

Greater sage-grouse

Centrocercus urophasianus

America's largest grouse lacks a muscular gizzard and cannot digest hard seeds and shoots. It relies on various kinds of sagebrush for food and cover. During the breeding season, females watch males display at a lek, a communal display ground. They select the strongest males to mate with. A few dominant males mate with the females and hens lay six to nine eggs. The chicks are fully mobile after six to eight weeks, when families may move to winter ranges at lower altitudes in search of food.

↔ 19–30 in (48–76 cm)
⬛ 3–7 lb (1.4–3.2 kg)
✖ Near threatened
🎗 Sagebrush, insects
🏠 ⬛

W. to C. North America

▽ STRUT DISPLAY
When displaying at a lek, male sage-grouse rapidly inflate and deflate their breast air sacs to produce loud, far-carrying, bubbling, popping sounds. They also spread their pointed tail feathers.

Common garter snake

Thamnophis sirtalis

One of North America's most widespread reptiles, the common garter snake frequents all but very dry or very cold habitats. Across its cooler, northern range, individuals gather in burrows, caves, and similar sites to overwinter, conserving energy by slowing their metabolism. In late summer, females have litters of 10–70 babies.

↔ 20–49 in (51–125 cm)
⬛ 5–7 oz (141–198 g)
✖ Common
🎗 Worms, fish, amphibians
🏠 ⬛ ⬛ ⬛ ⬛ ⬛ ⬛
◉ North America

▽ STRIPES OR SPOTS
This species typically has three light stripes running lengthwise, but some garter snakes have rows of spots.

heavily keeled scales

Striped scorpion

Centruroides vittatus

By day, the striped scorpion lurks in damp nooks under rocks and logs, and in thick vegetation. It emerges at sunset to hunt, detecting prey by their smell and movement with the help of comblike sensory organs between its last set of legs. The scorpion then crushes victims with its pincers and kills them with its stinger.

Females produce young after an estimated gestation of about eight months. The 30–50 offspring are carried on their mother's back until they molt for the first time.

↔ 2–3 in (5–7.6 cm)
✖ Not known
🎗 Insects, spiders, centipedes
🏠 ⬛ ⬛ ⬛ ⬛
◉ C. North America to N. Central America

▷ PERFECT CAMOUFLAGE
The scorpion's coloring helps to hide it from predators as well as prey.

two broad stripes along back

black and white markings on wing tips

Monarch butterfly
Danaus plexippus

↔ 3–4 in (7.6–10.2 cm)
✕ Common
≣ Milkweed leaves, nectar
🏠 ▥

N. America to
N. South America

The beautiful monarch is a familiar sight in North America. In autumn, monarchs that live west of the Rocky Mountains migrate to coastal California, while those from the east of the Rockies fly south to a small highland area in Michoacán, Mexico. Survivors of the Mexican winter move north to Texas and Oklahoma in March, producing a new generation that spreads northward once more. Third and fourth generations continue the spread north through the US and Canada, and return south in autumn.

Predators beware
The monarch's bright, contrasted coloration advertises its unpalatability to predators. The caterpillar absorbs steroids from the sap of the milkweed plant that are toxic to predators. However, wasps and various birds can eat the caterpillar: orioles detect the poison and vomit after eating it, while grosbeaks have a degree of immunity and digest butterflies without suffering any harmful effect.

Monarchs are threatened by pesticide use in the US, which kills the milkweed plant, their food, and by logging in Mexico, which reduces their habitat and leaves them susceptible to cold and rain. The Monarch Butterfly Biosphere Reserve in Michoacán, where they overwinter, was declared a World Heritage Site in 2008.

▽ **MASS MIGRATION**
Millions of monarchs migrate south in fall. They use stored fat to fuel their flight, and may glide on air currents to save evergy.

▷ **FEEDING ON MILKWEED**
The milkweed plant sustains the monarch butterfly by supplying it with leaves, sap, and nectar.

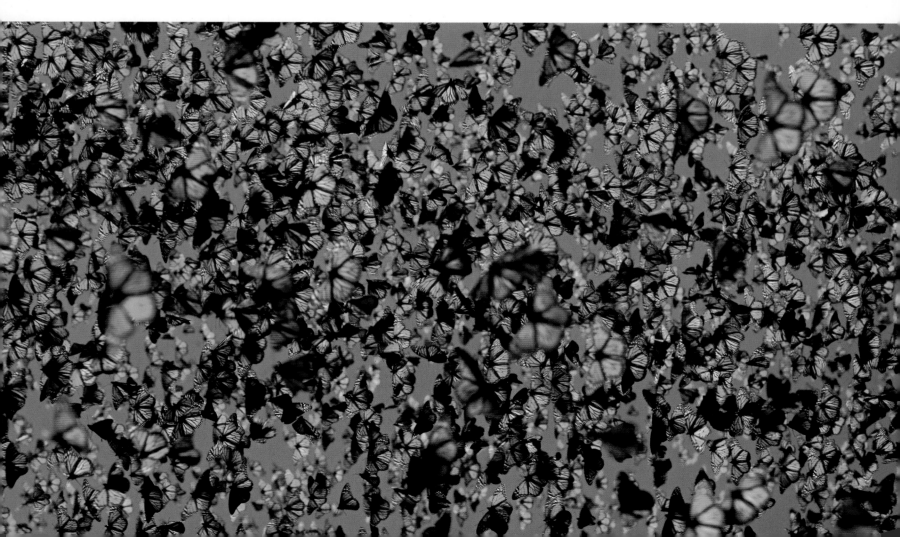

SIERRA NEVADA
California's snowy backbone

At around 4 million years old, the Sierra Nevada is a relatively young range of mountains, forming a dramatic crest 400 miles (650 km) long by 60 miles (100 km) wide along California's eastern edge. At the southern end lies Mount Whitney, the highest US peak outside Alaska at 14,505 ft (4,421 m). The region also boasts the largest alpine lake in North America—the famously clear Lake Tahoe—and three national parks: Yosemite, Sequoia, and Kings Canyon.

Forest and climate zones

The Sierra Nevada's western foothills are cloaked in savanna and deciduous oak woodland, but the rest of the range rising toward the east is dominated by coniferous forest, starting with juniper and Ponderosa and Jeffrey pines at lower altitudes. Giant sequoias start to appear at about 3,280 ft (1,000 m), and higher still, the forests are dominated by lodgepole pines, red and white fir, and eventually, whitebark pine. Finally, the trees give way to hardy alpine plants at about 10,500 ft (3,200 m). The forests are interspersed with rivers and lakes, wet and dry meadows, and extensive areas of brushland.

The wide range of altitudes and climates in the Sierra Nevada is reflected in the diverse wildlife. Animals living at higher altitudes, such as alpine chipmunks and pikas, must be able to tolerate low temperatures and snow for much of the year. The mountains are also home to both black and brown bears, bald eagles, and increasing numbers of American beavers.

PREDATOR IN DECLINE
Once widespread, this key forest predator has declined due to trapping. Fisher numbers in the Sierra Nevada remain worryingly low. Their loss from the ecosystem would affect the natural balance between predators and prey.

SUPERFOOD BONANZA
Sierra Nevada's rivers are important spawning grounds for Chinook salmon, and their spring breeding run provides a feeding bonanza for bears and other predators. However, overexploitation of the region's water resources threatens the species.

FISHER

CHINOOK SALMON

Home to the giant sequoia General Sherman, the second largest living thing

Has North

BLACK-BACKED WOODPECKER

BURNED FOREST
Black-backed woodpeckers exploit the aftermath of a fire, rapidly colonizing areas where dead wood teems with beetle grubs. As the area regenerates and beetle numbers decline, the birds gradually move on.

Bighorn sheep
Ovis canadensis

long hairs cover woolly coat

LOCATION

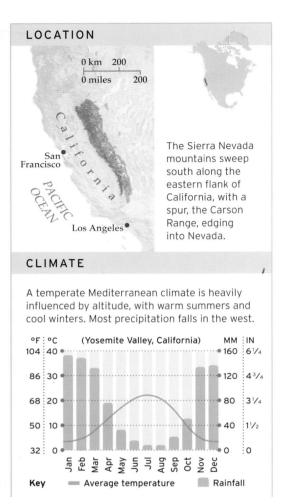

0 km 200
0 miles 200

The Sierra Nevada mountains sweep south along the eastern flank of California, with a spur, the Carson Range, edging into Nevada.

CLIMATE

A temperate Mediterranean climate is heavily influenced by altitude, with warm summers and cool winters. Most precipitation falls in the west.

°F	°C	(Yosemite Valley, California)	MM	IN
104	40		160	6¼
86	30		120	4¾
68	20		80	3¼
50	10		40	1½
32	0		0	0

Jan Feb Mar Apr May Jun Jul Aug Sep Oct Nov Dec

Key — Average temperature ▬ Rainfall

This North American wild sheep is named for the adult male's immense curling horns, which grow to more than 3 ft (1 m) in length. The rams establish a hierarchy based on horn size, with older sheep taking the lead. When it is too close to call, the rivalry is resolved with a head-butting battle. Females grow smaller horns that sweep back from the head. They are mainly defensive, used to deter predators such as eagles and pumas.

High living

In summer, bighorn sheep graze in high mountain meadows. They leap from ledge to ledge, never slipping on the steep, rough ground—their forked hooves split apart as they press down on the ground and grip the rock that fills the gap between them. As winter approaches, the chief ram leads his band of about 10 sheep to lower ground, where they join together to form herds of as many as 100 individuals. The hard outer rim of the bighorn sheep's hooves cut into snow and ice to provide a better grip. Breeding takes place in the valleys, and lambs are born in spring, a few weeks before the bands trek back up to the peaks.

↔ 3–6 ft (1–1.8 m)
⚖ 132–320 lb (60–145 kg)
⊗ Vulnerable
🌾 Forbs, grasses, shrubs
🏠 ⛰

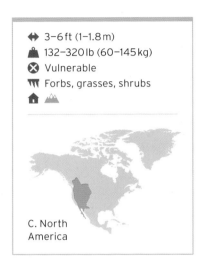

C. North America

▽ CURVED HORNS
The ram's horns keep growing, and can get so large that the tips impede its field of view. Older rams rub down the tips on a rock to keep them short.

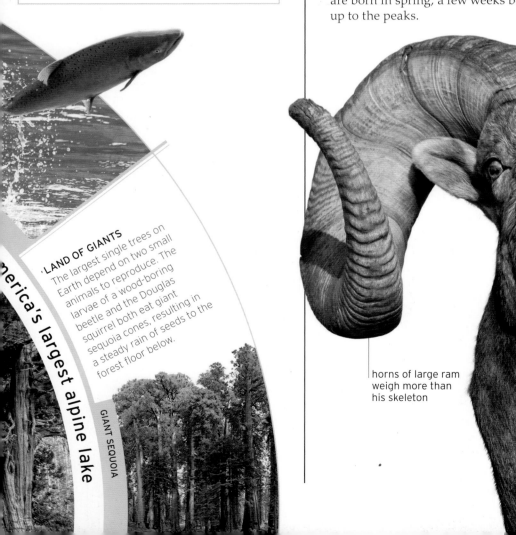

·LAND OF GIANTS
The largest single trees on Earth depend on two small animals to reproduce. The larvae of a wood-boring beetle and the Douglas squirrel both eat giant sequoia cones, resulting in a steady rain of seeds to the forest floor below.

America's largest alpine lake

GIANT SEQUOIA

horns of large ram weigh more than his skeleton

thick, sleek fur

powerful claws
for digging

Striped
skunk

Mephites mephites

About the size of a domestic cat, the striped skunk
is related to badgers, otters, and weasels. Skunks share
features such as a stocky, low-slung body with them,
but have the ability to spray a noxious chemical at
potential predators. This fluid is produced by the
anal scent glands under the tail. The skunk first lifts
its tail in the air like a flag and stamps the ground as
a warning. Should the aggressor stand its ground, the
skunk does a handstand, twists its body, and squirts
the liquid over its head at the attacker's face.

Opportunistic feeder

The striped skunk lives in a wide variety of habitats,
often near water. It will eat virtually anything,
including household garbage. Mostly solitary and
nocturnal, it can sometimes be spotted in the half-
light of dawn and dusk. Striped skunks breed from
February to March; females give birth in a burrow or
a den underneath a building or fallen tree. The young
become independent at about seven or eight weeks.

▷ **WARNING COLORATION**
The skunk's striking black-and-white coloration
with a bold white "V" running down its back
and tail, and its raised tail, serve as a warning
to potential predators.

△ **NEST RAIDER**
A striped skunk forages in a wild turkey's nest.
Skunks are adept at finding bird eggs, and often
eat an entire clutch at one go.

long,
bushy tail

↔ 22–30 in (56–76 cm)
⚖ 6–14 lb (2.7–6.4 kg)
❌ Common
🍴 Rodents, bird eggs, honey
🏠 🌳 🌲 🏔

C. Canada to N. Mexico

↔ 4–6 ft (1.2–1.8 m)
⚖ 120–660 lb (55–300 kg)
❌ Common
🍴 Fruit, nuts, vegetation
🏠 🌳 🌲 🏔

North America, N. Central
America

powerful limbs for tree climbing

American black bear

Ursus americanus

Smaller than grizzlies, black bears also have a straighter profile and are much better climbers. They prefer temperate forests, but can cope with humid Florida swamps as well as subarctic weather in Canada. True omnivores, they mainly feed on wild fruits, nuts, and vegetation, supplemented with insects, grubs, fish, and carrion—occasionally they hunt mammals too. Inquisitive and opportunistic, black bears also exploit garbage dumps and food left at campsites.

They are solitary except during the mating season, which takes place from mid-May to July. The cubs are born in a den from January to March, while their mothers are hibernating. Litters are usually made up of twins or triplets, but can contain as many as four or five cubs. Cubs remain with their mothers until they are around two years old.

Healthy numbers

American black bear numbers are about twice those of all the world's other bear species combined—despite the fact that it is native to just three countries: Canada, the US, and Mexico. Of 16 recognized subspecies, only the smallest, the Louisiana black bear (*U.a. luteolus*), is considered threatened under the US Endangered Species Act, due mainly to habitat loss and overhunting. The population of black bears seems stable in areas that are as diverse as their coat colors, which range from cinnamon, light gold, gray-blue, dark brown, and black to British Columbia's white-Kermode or "spirit bear" subspecies (*U.a. kermodei*).

△ **SCRATCH MY BACK**
Black bears often use trees as scratching posts, but bite and claw marks left on bark may mean certain trees also serve a territorial scent-marking purpose.

◁ **TREE CLIMBING**
Cubs are taught by their mothers to climb trees to escape danger—including attacks by adult male black bears.

△ **BATTLE WORN**
Black bears are shy and generally avoid humans, but both sexes will fight, kill, and sometimes even eat each other.

A black bear's **sense of smell** is **seven** times more **acute** than a **bloodhound's**

Alpine chipmunk
Tamias alpinus

Chipmunks are small, squirrel-like creatures of open spaces. Alpine chipmunks are found only in California's Sierra Nevada mountains, surviving above 8,000 ft (2,500 m) on broken cliffs and scree with abundant cavities and plentiful seeds of grasses, sedges, and stunted pines. They hibernate from mid-October to June to escape the worst of winter. They store little fat, but cache surplus food in summer and wake often to feed during winter, in between several days of torpor. Alpine chipmunks have no need to find and drink water as they get sufficient moisture from their food.

↔	6–7 in (15–18 cm)
⚖	1–2 oz (28–57 g)
✖	Locally common
⋔	Seeds, fruit
⌂ 🌲 ⛰	
◉	SW. US

◁ **ROCKY PERCH**
Deep, narrow crevices retain heat in high, exposed places, helping this small mammal to survive.

Mountain chickadee
Poecile gambeli

Tits, or titmice, are common worldwide. Several North American species are known as chickadees due to their "chick-a-dee" call. Active, acrobatic, social feeders, mountain chickadees join mixed flocks roaming high coniferous woods in search of food in fall and winter. A dispersed flock is more likely to find good feeding places than a lone bird, and many pairs of eyes are better at spotting danger.

↔	6 in (15 cm)
⚖	around 1/2 oz (10–18 g)
✖	Common
⋔	Seeds, small insects, spiders
⌂ 🌲 ⛰	
◉	N., W., and S. North America

distinctive white eyebrow

▷ **SOLE TARGET**
Should a predator such as a hawk appear, a lone chickadee would be its only target. It is much safer to be one of many in a flock.

heavy body

Turkey vulture
Cathartes aura

The turkey vulture is one of seven New World vultures, all of which scavenge dead animals and ride up-currents of warm air over vast areas. They soar on wings raised in a "V" shape for extra stability, their body weight slung low. Their slotted wingtips reduce turbulence—a feature copied by early aircraft designers.

Mutual dependence
While all vultures have excellent sight, few have a keen sense of smell. In forests, other vultures follow turkey vultures to locate carcasses hidden under trees because they can locate food by smell. When large carcasses are found, turkey vultures stand aside as bigger species with stronger beaks open up tough hides. All vultures prefer newly dead animals and avoid putrefying meat.

Turkey vultures that breed in the north migrate to the tropics in winter, but many stay in the southern US all year round. They breed in early spring in the south and in July or August farther north, laying their eggs on a cliff ledge, or sometimes in a hollow tree or dense thicket. Two eggs are incubated for up to 40 days, and the chicks are fed in the nest for about 10 weeks.

Turkey vultures can **smell newly dead** animals

25–32 in (64–81 cm)

2–5 lb (1–2.2 kg)

⊗ Common

Carrion

C. North America to S. South America

broad, fingered, two-tone wings

are head and hooked bill

strong bare legs and feet

◁ WIDE WINGS
Turkey vultures spread their wings when perched to allow the sun's heat to warm their body in the morning and to dry wet feathers. This keeps their plumage in good condition.

△ TOUCHING DOWN
Tail spread for control, wings beating as brakes, and eyes focused downward, the vulture thrusts its feet forward to absorb the shock as it brings its substantial weight in to land.

▷ **EGG TOOTH**
These day-old chicks still have the hard white egg tooth at the end of their beak, which they used to break out of their shell.

thick layer of feathers insulates body

Great gray owl

Strix nebulosa

▽ **WINGED WONDER**
A light body and broad wings allow slow, silent flight, and help the owl to maneuver with precision between trees. Special fringes on the wing feathers almost eliminate wing noise.

↔ 23–27 in (59–69 cm)
⚖ 2–4 lb (0.8–1.7 kg)
✖ Common
⋔ Voles, mice, birds, frogs
⌂ 🌲🌲 ⸺

N. and C. North America, E. Europe, Asia

This owl's thick insulation makes it look large, but its body is actually much smaller and lighter than the eagle owl or great horned owl. A less fearsome predator, the great gray owl focuses on small prey, often in difficult conditions. The disklike face, more than 20 in (50 cm) wide, suggests astonishingly acute hearing, although the owl's small eyes seem more suited to daylight than nighttime activity. Unusually for an owl, it hunts by day and at night. The facial feathers let sound through easily but protect what is hidden behind: an arc of stiff feathers that directs sound right into the assymetrically positioned ears. This helps the owl to locate the source of a sound with pinpoint accuracy.

Great gray owls watch and listen for voles from a perch, often a broken tree stump, and glide down silently to catch them, taking them by surprise. They can hear tunneling rodents under layers of snow, and penetrate 16–20 in (40–50 cm), plunging headfirst, with a final thrust of their deadly feet. Found mainly in the north, a small population of great gray owls remains in the Sierra Nevada of California.

wide facial disk

broad, fingered wings

short, broad tail

Mountain kingsnake

Lampropeltis zonata

The California Mountain kingsnake has an extensive distribution from Baja California, Mexico, north into Washington state. As its name suggests, the Sierra Mountain subspecies (*L.z. multicincta*) is restricted to that area. Living in uplands and mountains up to altitudes of 10,000 ft (3,000 m), this habitat generalist basks by day in remote gullies or on old logs; rests at night among boulders or tree roots; and shelters in burrows through winter.

False colors

Like most other kingsnakes, this nonvenomous constrictor has red or orange, black, and white or cream rings that mimic the coloration of the venomous coral snake to deter predators. A stealthy sight-and-smell predator, it hunts mainly lizards and small snakes. Other prey include birds, especially nestlings of towhees and thrushes, eggs, and less often, small rodents, frogs and other amphibians. It may squeeze a victim in its coils to subdue it before swallowing it whole.

↔ 20–47 in (50–120 cm)
🏋 Up to 3 lb (up to 1.5kg)
✖ Locally common
🍴 Small snakes, lizards, birds
🏠 🌲 ⛰
SW. North America

△ **TRICOLOR SNAKE**
Ready to strike if need be, the Sierra Mountain kingsnake displays its bright warning colors. Not all of the subspecies are alike; some have thinner or even no rings.

The kingsnake **eats other snakes**—even venomous young rattlesnakes

---

Ensatina

Ensatina eschscholtzii

A native of western US mountain forests, the ensatina salamander does not breathe air. This nocturnal amphibian has no lungs—all the oxygen it needs is absorbed directly through its moist skin. The nostrils on the snout are used purely for smelling. Ensatinas have poison glands in their tail, but predators such as raccoons have learned to eat the head, then body, and discard the tail.

Mating occurs during the cooler seasons, and in summer, pregnant females retreat into a damp nook to lay a dozen eggs. The young hatch out after about four months and have the same body form as an adult, rather than going through a larval tadpole stage. They leave the nest after the first autumn rains.

↔ 2–3 in (6–8 cm)
☁ Spring and summer
✖ Locally common
🍴 Worms, insects, spiders
🏠 🌳 🌲
🧭 W. US

△ **LIVING ON LAND**
Unusually for an amphibian, the ensatina salamander's entire life cycle is based on land.

Yellow-legged frog

Rana sierrae

back legs yellow underneath

Found in and around mountain pools and streams, the Sierra Nevada yellow-legged frog lives at altitudes of up to 11,800 ft (3,600 m). It spends winters hibernating at the bottom of frozen lakes. In summer, it hunts by day, rarely straying more than a metre or two from water.

Three species of yellow-legged frogs have now been identified, all with a pale yellow underside. The main difference between the three lies in their distinct mating calls. The breeding season begins after the spring thaw, and after mating, the females lay their eggs on aquatic vegetation. The tadpoles take three or four years to reach maturity.

△ **DEFENSIVE ODOR**
Yellow-legged frogs exude a pungent garliclike odor from their skin if they are picked up.

↔ 2–3 in (6–8 cm)
☁ Spring
✖ Endangered
🍴 Insects, spiders, worms
🏠 ⛰ 🌿 ≈
🧭 SW. North America

MOJAVE DESERT
The smallest and driest desert in the US

The Mojave Desert covers 25,000 sq miles (65,000 sq km) of alternating mountain ranges and flat, low-lying basins, mainly in southern California. The Mojave merges almost imperceptibly with the Sonoran Desert to the south and the Great Basin Desert to the north. Its extent is traditionally indicated by the range of an endemic yucca, the Joshua tree (see main photo). This distinctive plant is one of more than 200 found only in the Mojave, which make up a quarter of the desert's plant species.

Land of extremes
The Mojave Desert is dry because it lies in the rain shadow of the Rocky Mountains. It is a high desert, lying mostly at more than 1,970 ft (600 m) above sea level. Daytime temperatures are high, nowhere more so than

in Death Valley in the north, where at Furnace Creek on July 10, 1913, the atmospheric temperature reached 134°F (56.7°C), the highest ever recorded on Earth. Death Valley also holds the record for the lowest place in the US: Badwater Basin dips to 282 ft (86 m) below sea level. The name refers to a small spring, whose waters contain high levels of dissolved salts, making them undrinkable for humans. However, the spring does support other life, including pickleweed, a variety of aquatic insects, and the Badwater snail, another Mojave endemic. Other desert specialists living in the Mojave include the kangaroo rat, the desert tortoise, and the deadly Mojave rattlesnake.

BIDING THEIR TIME
Mojave ground squirrels survive droughts by not breeding and extending a form of dormancy known as estivation to eke out scarce food resources. Even so, populations frequently crash, but their numbers recover rapidly once the rains return.

MOJAVE GROUND SQUIRREL

DESERT BLOOM
Many desert plants are able to remain dormant for years, until sufficient rain falls for them to grow, flower, and set seed. Antelope Valley in the western tip of the desert is famous for the poppies and other flowers that bloom following the winter rains.

CALIFORNIA POP[...]

Average annua[...]

The hottest place in North America

More than 200 endemic plants

YUCCA MOTH

MUTUAL BENEFIT
The yucca moth is named for the plant that depends on it for survival. Females lay eggs in yucca flowers, then pollinate them by forcing pollen into the stigma. When the larvae hatch, they eat some of the developing seeds but the rest is left to grow.

Kit fox
Vulpes macrotis

black patch on either side of snout

Thanks to its huge ears, the kit fox has excellent hearing, which helps it locate prey ranging from insects to jackrabbits and lizards. Oversized ears also keep this desert dweller cool by thermoregulation: their huge surface area releases large amounts of heat during the hottest months, keeping the animal's body temperature within comfortable limits.

Survival skills
North America's smallest wild canid has other desert survival skills. The soles of its feet are fur-lined, lending traction but also keeping the pads from burning on hot terrain. Mainly nocturnal, the kit fox avoids the heat as well as predators, such as coyotes, by spending the day inside one of many burrows that it either digs or takes over from animals such as prairie dogs. It also makes dens in manmade structures such as storm drains.

Kit foxes are mainly monogamous, but pairs do not necessarily share the same den and they always hunt alone. A female bears an average of four young per litter, which stay with her for five to six months.

↔ 18–22 in (46–56 cm)
⚖ 4–6 lb (1.8–2.7 kg)
✖ Common
🍴 Rodents, hares, insects
🏠 🌵 🌿

SW. North America

Kit foxes rarely drink, obtaining **moisture** from their food

▽ **CHANGING COAT**
The kit fox sports a rusty-tan to buff gray coat in the summer. It takes on a silvery gray hue in the winter.

LOCATION

The Mojave Desert lies between the Sonoran and Great Basin deserts, mostly in southeastern California.

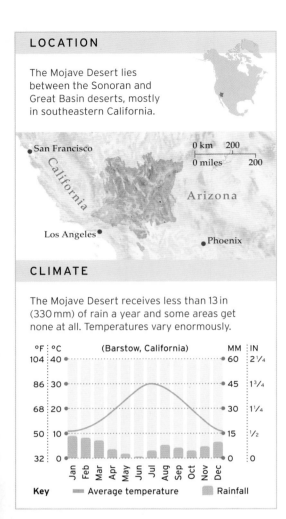

San Francisco

California

0 km 200
0 miles 200

Arizona

Los Angeles

Phoenix

CLIMATE

The Mojave Desert receives less than 13 in (330 mm) of rain a year and some areas get none at all. Temperatures vary enormously.

°F	°C	(Barstow, California)	MM	IN
104	40		60	2¼
86	30		45	1¾
68	20		30	1¼
50	10		15	½
32	0		0	0

Jan Feb Mar Apr May Jun Jul Aug Sep Oct Nov Dec

Key ▬ Average temperature ▪ Rainfall

AVOIDING THE HEAT
Red spotted toads lie dormant underground in dry periods, but after rain falls, they emerge by the thousands in the cool of the night. Females lay their eggs in small, temporary pools. They hatch in three days, and the tadpoles quickly develop into toads.

rainfall of 7 in (178mm)

RED SPOTTED TOAD

▷ **VOCALIZATIONS**
Small cats cannot roar as the big cats do. Instead, pumas snarl and hiss when annoyed and purr when content.

round head
with erect ears

large paws relative
to overall size

buff-colored,
thick fur

Puma
Puma concolor

North America's largest cat has more than 40 common names, including mountain lion and cougar. It is not classified as a big cat, but as the largest of the small cats. Once found across the US, it has now virtually disappeared from eastern and midwestern areas. Pumas farthest from the equator tend to be larger than those closer to it. Coat color also varies with geography; the most northern pumas are silver-gray, while those in southerly, humid climates tend to be reddish brown.

Previously elusive and solitary, pumas used to avoid contact with humans whenever possible, although they had been known to kill people when cornered. However, attacks recorded in North America have risen sharply since the 1990s, with hikers, mountain bikers, and skiers particularly at risk.

Flexible feline
Highly adaptable, pumas can live in habitats as diverse as deserts and tropical rainforests. This adaptability also extends to their diet. Although hoofed mammals are preferred—especially by mothers with cubs to feed —pumas hunt rabbits, feral pigs, insects, birds, mice, coyotes, and even other pumas. Although active during the day, they hunt mostly at dawn and dusk.

Female pumas can breed all year round. Males and females stay together for a few days when the female is in season. The male then leaves in search of other potential mates, playing no part in raising his offspring. In about three months, the female gives birth to two or three spotted cubs, which stay with her for up to 18 months. At 12–14 weeks, the cubs' spots begin to fade.

↔ 34–60 in (86–155 cm)
⚖ 75–160 lb (34–72 kg)
✖ Common
Ⅲ Mammals

W. and S.
North America,
Central
America,
South America

△ **AGILE AND ATHLETIC**
A puma's powerful hind legs allow it to bound up to 40 ft (12 m) when running, and leap up 18 ft (5.4 m) from the ground.

Black-tailed jackrabbit

Lepus californicus

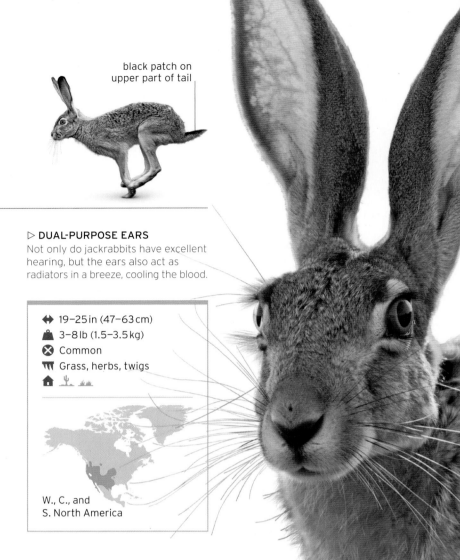

black patch on upper part of tail

large ears laced with fine blood vessels

Despite their name jackrabbits are in fact hares, not rabbits, with an above-ground lifestyle and a preference for outrunning predators, rather than diving into a burrow. A muscular, flexible body and long, powerful hind legs and feet act as a spring, giving the jackrabbit great speed and acceleration from a standing start.

Black-tailed jackrabbits are widespread in semiarid regions with sagebrush and creosote bush, and other open shrubland. They avoid searing heat by being active mostly at night. Unusually for hares, they occasionally burrow to escape excessive heat.

Precocious young

Females give birth to three to five fully furred, open-eyed young, called leverets, which are active soon after birth. Females can breed when under a year old, but the rate of predation is high—animals from pumas and coyotes to hawks and rattlesnakes eat jackrabbits. In favorable conditions, their numbers increase rapidly, but they fall again as food becomes scarce.

▷ **DUAL-PURPOSE EARS**
Not only do jackrabbits have excellent hearing, but the ears also act as radiators in a breeze, cooling the blood.

↔ 19–25 in (47–63 cm)
⚖ 3–8 lb (1.5–3.5 kg)
✕ Common
🌾 Grass, herbs, twigs
🏠 🌵 🌿

W., C., and S. North America

Greater roadrunner

Geococcyx californianus

lighter throat and chest with dark stripes

Roadrunners are predominantly ground-dwelling birds that belong to the cuckoo family. They have long, strong, bare legs, with two toes facing forward and two backward—a feature not seemingly ideal for fast running. Roadrunners favor semidesert regions with open spaces as well as dry, bushy cover, but have spread into moister, greener habitats with scattered trees. They are weak fliers but can get up onto treetops, wires, or roadside poles. Roadrunners eat lizards and mice, as well as small snakes and birds, snapping them up in their beak. This moisture-rich diet is an advantage when drinking water is scarce. They also conserve moisture by excreting excess salt from a gland near the eye, rather than wasting water in expelling it via the kidneys.

↔ 22 in (56 cm)
⚖ 12 oz (340 g)
✕ Common
🌾 Lizards, snakes, mice, birds
🏠 🌿 🌵 🌳

S. North America

◁ **DESERT RUN**
The roadrunner is well adapted to life in the fast lane. It walks and runs through the desert, trying to flush out prey.

Gila monster

Heloderma suspectum

fat tail stores food and water

A Gila **bite is painful** but **rarely fatal** to humans

shiny, beadlike scales

Solidly built, strong, slow, solitary, and secretive, the Gila (pronounced "hee-luh") is North America's largest native lizard—and one of very few that are venomous. Toxins from the Gila's modified salivary glands flow into a victim by capillary action along grooved teeth in the lower jaw, aided by its tenaciously chewing grip. As a result, the Gila has few natural predators.

Supersize meal

Gila monsters spend 90 percent of their time resting in a den in an appropriated old burrow, among roots, or under rocks. They feed on bird and reptile eggs, small mammals, birds (especially nestlings), reptiles such as lizards, and frogs and other amphibians, as well as bugs and worms. Given its energy-saving habits, and the ability to store fat in its tail, a sizeable meal lasts a Gila for weeks. A young Gila can eat one-half its own body weight in a sitting, an adult one-third. As a result, some Gilas eat as few as six times in a year.

Mojave rattlesnake

Crotalus scutulatus

rattle

A member of the pit viper family, this rattlesnake has bowl-like pits below the eyes that detect infrared (heat) in warm-blooded animals. Its potent venom is used both to subdue prey, such as rats and mice, and to defend itself. The warning rattle from which its common name is derived increases in size each time the snake sheds its skin.

The Mojave rattlesnake differs from its famous close cousin, the western diamondback rattlesnake, in that the back markings fade earlier toward the tail and its white tail rings are wider than the black ones.

△ **MOJAVE GREEN**
Some Mojave rattlesnakes have an olive-green tinge—locals call them Mojave greens.

↔	3–4ft (1–1.2m)
⬛	4–9lb (1.8–4.1kg)
✖	Locally common
▥	Small mammals, lizards
🏠	🌿 🌾
◐	SW. North America, Central America

Couch's spadefoot

Scaphiopus couchii

skin mottled with dark markings

The spadefoot is named after the hard pads on its hind feet, which it uses to dig burrows in the sand. The toad spends months deep underground to avoid dry conditions. While underground, it retains the toxins that are usually expelled in urine. This creates a high chemical concentration in the toad's body, allowing water to be absorbed from the soil through its permeable skin.

Breeding takes place in the wet season. The toads come to the surface after the first heavy rains, and females lay their eggs in temporary pools. They hatch within 36 hours, and tadpoles mature into toadlets in 40 days.

△ **FEED AND BREED**
As well as breeding, the toads spend the nights above ground hunting for as much prey as they can find.

↔	2–4in (5–10cm)
💧	Rainy season
✖	Common
▥	Insects, spiders
🏠	🌿 🌾
◐	S. US, Mexico

▷ **BURYING HER EGGS**
Females lay 5 to 10 eggs in summer and bury them in dry soil. The young, which are about 6 in (15 cm) long, hatch nine months later.

▽ **BEADED BODY**
Gila scales are rounded and slightly domed. The pattern of black with pink, red, or orange patches—unique on each individual—warns potential predators of its toxic bite.

↔ 16–24 in (41–61 cm)
⚖ 3–5 lb (1.4–2.3 kg)
⊗ Near threatened
🍴 Eggs, small birds, mammals
🏠 🌵

SW. US,
N. Mexico

Desert blond tarantula

Aphonopelma chalcodes

Lacking good vision, this desert hunter is at great risk of predation during the day. For this reason it remains in its burrow and waits for night to fall. In the dark, touch is the tarantula's main link to its surroundings. It uses its feet and mouthparts to detect vibrations caused by passing animals that touch a network of silk threads radiating from the entrance of its burrow. The spider lies in wait for prey, then rushes out and kills it with a venomous bite.

Mating quest

Tarantulas grow slowly, reaching sexual maturity at 10 years. Males then search for mates, delivering a silk sac of sperm to each female they find. The eggs are laid on a silk sheet at the sun-warmed mouth of the burrow. Spiderlings stay in the burrow for a few days only.

▽ **HAIRY HUNTER**
The tarantula's body hairs are sensory but also have a defensive function. When threatened, the spider uses its back legs to flick barbed, irritating hairs at its attacker.

dark abdomen

pale hairs on legs

↔ 2–3 in (5–7.6 cm)
⊗ Not known
🍴 Crickets, grasshoppers, small lizards
🏠 🌵

SW. North America

FLORIDA EVERGLADES
The largest wetland wilderness in the US

The Everglades is a complex of low-lying, densely vegetated wetlands incorporating a mosaic of habitats. The region lacks the scenic grandeur of some other US national parks, but an area in the south was granted protected status in 1934 on account of its unique ecology and biodiversity. The diverse array of interlinking habitats are defined by the depth, quality, and salinity of the water, and the frequency and duration of flooding.

River of grass

The park's coastal ecosystems include estuaries, tidal mangrove swamps, and coastal prairies dominated by salt- and drought-tolerant succulent plants. These give way inland to prairies and sparsely canopied forests of fast-growing slash pine, which are periodically razed by fire. The prairies are interspersed with lower-lying areas almost permanently inundated with

water flowing slowly south from Lake Okeechobee toward Florida Bay. These wet sawgrass prairies—known locally as the river of grass—include areas of sluggish open water, or sloughs, and cypress swamps. Small patches of slightly higher ground support hammocks of hardwood forest with trees including tropical mahogany and temperate oak, usually dripping with ferns and airplants (epiphytes).

More than 300 species of fish live in the Everglades, along with the largest breeding populations of tropical waders in North America. The region is also home to 50 species of reptile, including the American alligator and the threatened American crocodile.

SHARK NURSERY
Baby bull sharks are vulnerable to predation, so females enter low-saline rivers to give birth. In doing so, they endure physiological stress that would kill most marine fish. Young bull sharks eventually migrate to warmer offshore waters.

BULL SHARK

CYPRESS SWAMPS
Pond and bald cypresses thrive in swamps, forming dome-shaped clusters, with smaller, less stable trees at their edge. The largest trees in the middle are stabilized by buttress roots. Aerial roots with distinctive "knees" may play a role in respiration.

BALD AND POND

The only place in the world where alligato

North America's only subtropical wetland

FLORIDA PANTHER

PREDATOR IN PERIL
The Florida panther, a subspecies of puma, is the most endangered mammal in the Everglades—fewer than 100 remain. Its dwindling numbers have been boosted by other subspecies of puma introduced from Texas.

LOCATION

0 km 200
0 miles 200

ATLANTIC OCEAN

Florida

Orlando

Tampa

Gulf of Mexico

Miami

The southern tip of the Florida peninsula, mainly south of Lake Okeechobee. The greater Everglades ecosystem extends north to Lake Kissimmee.

CLIMATE

The Everglades are tropical, with two seasons: warm and dry from December to April, hot and wet from May to November.

°F	°C	(Florida City)	MM	IN
104	40		260	10¼
86	30		195	7½
68	20		130	5
50	10		65	2½
32	0		0	0

Jan Feb Mar Apr May Jun Jul Aug Sep Oct Nov Dec

Key ■ Average temperature ■ Rainfall

West Indian manatee

Trichechus manatus

With their bulgy bodies, broad heads, and wide, whiskery muzzles, West Indian manatees resemble walruses, but their closest living relatives are the elephant and the tiny, hooved, rodentlike hyrax. Gentle and slow-moving, manatees never haul out on land and cannot survive in cold conditions. They graze on salt- and freshwater plants, an activity that, along with their shape and docile nature, has earned them the nickname "sea cow".

↔ 8–13 ft (2.4–3.9 m)
⚖ 440–1,320 lb (200–600 kg)
✖ Vulnerable
🌾 Seagrasses, aquatic plants

SE. US to NE. South America, Caribbean

◁ **LANGUID PACE**
Manatees swim slowly, surfacing every three to five minutes to breathe. When resting, they can stay underwater for as long as 20 minutes.

Northern gray fox

Urocyon cinereoargenteus

Slight, quick, and agile, the gray fox is a capable climber, often resting as high as 59 ft (18 m) in trees out of reach of predators such as coyotes and dogs. Mainly nocturnal and a solitary hunter, it preys on rabbits and rodents in the winter, but its diet varies with the season and, like most foxes, it will eat almost anything it comes across. Both parents raise the pups, which are independent by fall.

↔ 22–26 in (56–66 cm)
⚖ 5–12 lb (2–5.4 kg)
✖ Common
🌾 Rodents, birds, insects

North America to N. South America

◁ **BARKING CALL**
The gray fox has a wide range of vocalizations, including yapping barks, screams, and growls.

↔ 24–37 in (60–95 cm)
⚖ 6–23 lb (2.7–10.4 kg)
✖ Common
🍴 Small animals, berries, eggs

S. Canada to
Central America

▷ **MASKED BANDIT**
The black "bandit" mask
around a raccoon's eyes
reflects its opportunistic
behaviour. It can climb,
dig, and manipulate
doors and latches
with its forepaws.

pale gray to almost black fur

Northern raccoon

Procyon lotor

Dexterous, intelligent, and adaptable, the northern raccoon is found in practically every North American environment, from swamp to mountains, urban streets to farmland. Once a tropical animal that foraged mainly along riverbanks, it has changed into a pan-continental species. Raccoons are now found in a variety of habitats, including deserts and mountains, where they were previously rare, but they prefer watercourses.

Adapt and thrive

"Flexible" describes this extremely successful omnivore best. Raccoons are optimal survivors, locating food in ponds and streams, in trees, and on the ground in the wild, as well as in gutters, garbage cans, and rooftops in cities. Insects, frogs, rodents, eggs, nuts, and berries make up their diet in the wild. In urban areas, they consume almost anything edible they come across—they even raid birdfeeders and outdoor feeding stations of domestic animals. Raccoons generally make their dens in hollow trees or burrows in the

wild, where they hole up during the day and emerge to hunt at dusk. They are just as willing to live in barns, crawl spaces, and attics. Raccoons thrive in towns and cities due to a plentiful supply of food and a lack of natural predators such as coyotes, bobcats, and pumas.

Master manipulator

Raccoons are exceedingly dexterous. The five toes on their forepaws function in the same way as human fingers, allowing them to grasp and manipulate food, as well as turn doorknobs and release latches. They are strong swimmers, relying heavily on their sense of touch—the sensitivity of which may increase underwater—when feeling around for prey such as frogs and shellfish. Even though its hindlegs are longer than its forelegs—giving it a hunched appearance— the raccoon can run at speeds up to 15 mph (24 km/h).

Females give birth to a litter of three or four young, from multiple fathers, called kits, in spring. The kits begin to follow their mother on her nocturnal forays when they are 8–10 weeks old, and remain with her until they are 13–14 months old.

An adult raccoon is **strong enough to hold a dog's head underwater**

△ **FEELING FOR FOOD**
With their agile, sensitive fingers, raccoons are adept at finding food underwater. Crayfish is a favorite food source.

◁ **TIGHT GRIP**
An adult raccoon can catch prey as large as trout. The raccoon keeps a tight grip on its slippery meal with its sharp claws.

kinked neck

broadly webbed feet

Anhinga
Anhinga anhinga

Found commonly in swamps and waterways, the anhinga is the Americas' equivalent of the similar African darter. It roosts on trees and mangroves, but leaves to feed soon after sunrise, flying to open water. It swims low in the water, head and neck raised, earning the alternative name "snakebird."

Spearfishing
With unusually dense bones and plumage that quickly absorbs water, the anhinga sinks easily and swims underwater for up to a minute. It does not have the powerful legs of the cormorants for active pursuit, but feeds more like an underwater heron, waiting for

a chance to spear a passing fish. Special vertebrae and neck musculature give its neck a permanent kink, and an instant, rapid forward stab. The anhinga then rises to the surface, shakes the fish free, and swallows it.

Anhingas nest in mixed colonies with other tree-nesting birds. The female builds the nest from twigs and reeds collected by the male. Up to six eggs are incubated for three to four weeks. The chicks are fed at first with pre-digested fish from the parents' throats and then whole fish. They leave the nest after six weeks, but remain dependent on their parents for a few more weeks.

slender head

silver-white markings on upperparts of wings

long, daggerlike bill

▽ **OUTSTRETCHED WINGS**
Anhingas display with one or both wings outstretched. They also regularly perch with open wings to help dry saturated feathers and to regulate their body temperature.

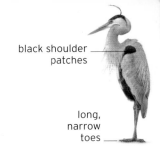

black shoulder patches

long, narrow toes

Great blue heron
Ardea herodias

The great blue heron is the largest wading bird in North America. Herons worldwide have a similar long neck, curled back between the shoulders in flight or when the bird is resting, but stretched out to grab a passing fish with a lightning strike of the long, sharp bill. Great blue herons are masters of "wait-and-watch" predation and patient stalking, standing like shadowy statues in the shallows for hours. They can be surprisingly aerobatic around their treetop colonies, where up to six eggs are incubated for 27 days. The chicks are fed by both parents for up to 80 days before they can fly. One subspecies, *A. h. occidentalis*, occurs in a pure white form in Florida.

◁ **PIERCED PREY**
Most fish-eating birds grasp prey in their bills, but anhingas are spear-fishers, piercing small fish with the upper mandible, and larger ones with both.

↔ 34–35 in (86–89 cm)
⚖ 3 lb (1.4 kg)
✖ Common
🏹 Fish
🏠 🌾 ≈ ≈≈

S. North America to C. South America

↔ 3–5 ft (0.9–1.5 m)
⚖ 5–6 lb (2.3–2.7 kg)
✖ Common
🏹 Fish, frogs, birds
🏠 🌾 ≈ 🍄 ≈≈

North America to N. South America

◁ **HIGH LIFE**
Great blue herons build their nests high on trees, safe from ground predators. They must be substantial enough for several chicks to grow to full size.

Purple gallinule
Porphyrio martinica

long, yellow legs and toes

Combining ease of movement on land and on floating leaves with the ability to swim like a duck, the gallinule is a waterside all-rounder that lives in tropical wetlands. It prefers dense vegetation with open channels and ditches. Its dishlike nest, made of grasses on a floating mat of weed or attached to reed stems, contains up to 10 eggs, which hatch after 20 days. The chicks feed themselves after a week, become independent three weeks later, and fly when five to seven weeks old.

▷ **QUICK STEPPER**
The gallinule spreads its weight through its elongated toes and steps quickly and rhythmically across floating vegetation. It also often climbs up more awkwardly through dense twigs.

↔ 11–14 in (28–36 cm)
⚖ 7–10 oz (200–284 g)
✖ Common
🏹 Seeds, fruit, invertebrates
🏠 🌾 🌿 ≈ ≈≈ 🍄

S. North America to South America

keeled scales on tail

alligators have a more rounded snout than crocodiles

American alligator

Alligator mississippiensis

This fearsome predator is restricted to wetlands and swamps of the southeastern US, and propels itself through water with its muscular, laterally flattened tail. On land, the American alligator can crawl on its underside or lift its body off the ground in a slow, waddling walk. If it draws its legs fully below its body, it can gallop for short distances, charging faster than many humans can run. Mostly a night hunter, it drifts or swims stealthily, then lunges at its prey.

Courtship and mating begin in April and May, with the males roaring and bellowing as low as they can to attract females. In August, 30–50 babies hatch in a nest mound of warm decomposing vegetation gathered by the mother. She listens for the hatching babies' chirps, helps them out of the nest, and carries them in her mouth down to the water. Size, power, and a thick skin mean an adult alligator has little to fear, but the young are vulnerable to predators and are protected by their mother for up to three years.

↔ 10–13 ft (3–4 m)
⚖ Up to 660 lb (300 kg)
✗ Locally common
🍴 Fish, waterbirds, mammals

SE. US

▷ **POWERFUL JAWS**
The alligator grabs its prey with about 80 conical teeth set in powerful jaws. A characteristic large tooth in the lower jaw fits into a socket in the upper jaw.

Common snapping turtle

Chelydra serpentina

Ranging as far north as Alberta, Canada, and as far south as the US Gulf Coast, some snapping turtles have even been seen in the Rocky Mountains—no mean feat for an animal that prefers to spend most of its time in muddy freshwater lakes and rivers.

As the name suggests, the snapping turtle bites. Highly aggressive on land, it is prone to snapping the heads off other turtles or taking a bite out of anything it comes across. The shells of older snapping turtles are usually covered in algae, enhancing their camouflage as they hide in wait for prey. Adults sometimes travel long distances overland and can end up as traffic fatalities, whereas hatchlings are vulnerable to attack by raccoons, herons, and skunks, as well as other turtles.

brown or olive to black upper shell

△ **FEROCIOUS SNAPPER**
Given their pugnacious temperament and tough carapace, adult "snappers" have few enemies and can live up to 40 years.

↔ 10–19 in (25–48 cm)
⚖ Up to 35 lb (16 kg)
✗ Common
🍴 Fish, mammals, plants

C. and E. USA

Golden silk orbweaver

Nephila clavipes

The golden silk orbweaver is one of the largest American web-spinning spiders. It builds a strong, semipermanent web between trees in swamps and woodlands. The web of a mature female may be 3 ft (1 m) wide, not including the anchoring strands. The species is named after the yellow-tinged silk of the web, which may transmit the green light reflecting off surrounding plants, making it harder to see when in the shade. When lit by the sun, the silk's gold color may attract flower-seeking insects, such as butterflies and bees, which become the spider's victims.

↔ ½–3 in (1.25–7.5 cm)
✖ Not known
🌾 Insects
🏠 🌳 🌿≈

S. North America to South America

◁ **LITTLE AND LARGE**
The male golden silk orbweaver, seen here next to a potential mate, is a fraction of the female's size.

Costa Rica
Flying high above the tropical rainforest a
scarlet macaw spies some brightly colored
flowers in the canopy. These large parrots
only breed in tree cavities.

Central and South America

LAND OF THE JAGUAR

Central and South America

Collectively, Central and South America constitute more than 7 million sq miles (18 million sq km) of incredibly varied terrain and climate. Forming South America's backbone is the world's longest mountain range, the Andes, which at its highest point reaches almost 23,000 ft (7,000 m) above sea level. The massive lowland drainage basin of the Amazon River and its tributaries is filled with lush rainforest, and at the continent's center is the world's largest tropical wetland, the Pantanal. The south and east of South America tend to be

drier and feature highland plateaus covered with wooded savanna and wide, grassy plains. This range of habitats has resulted in a huge diversity of plant and animal species, many of them found nowhere else.

Historically, the Central American isthmus has been an important bridge for the exchange of land animals between North and South America. It is also a vital flight path for birds migrating along the Pacific Flyway between Alaska, in North America, and Patagonia, in South America.

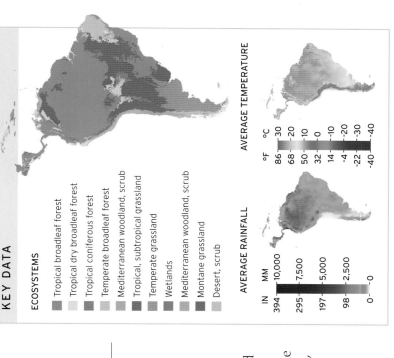

KEY DATA

ECOSYSTEMS

- Tropical broadleaf forest
- Tropical dry broadleaf forest
- Tropical coniferous forest
- Temperate broadleaf forest
- Mediterranean woodland, scrub
- Tropical, subtropical grassland
- Temperate grassland
- Wetlands
- Mediterranean woodland, scrub
- Montane grassland
- Desert, scrub

AVERAGE TEMPERATURE

°F	°C
86	30
68	20
50	10
32	0
14	-10
-4	-20
-22	-30
-40	-40

AVERAGE RAINFALL

IN	MM
394	10,000
295	7,500
197	5,000
98	2,500
0	0

AMAZON RAINFOREST

The largest rainforest on Earth dominates the northern half of South America. Estimated to be at least 55 million years old, the Amazon is home to a dazzling diversity of animal and plant life. It contains around 10 percent of the world's known species and is a refuge for jaguars, harpy eagles, and pink dolphins, as well as thousands of bird and butterfly species.

LAND LINK TO NORTH AMERICA

Formed around 3 million years ago, the isthmus allows movement of land animals between the continents.

COSTA RICAN RAINFOREST

Ecotourists flock to view the beautiful jungles and their wildlife.

GALAPAGOS ISLANDS

These volcanic islands are formed by a mantle plume—columns of molten rock rising

CARIBBEAN ISLANDS

The Caribbean has more than 7,000 islands and around 9% of the world's coral reefs.

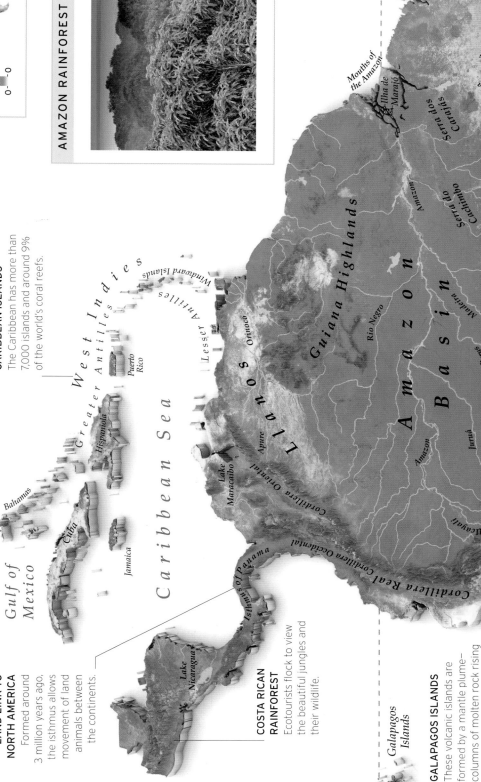

ATLANTIC OCEAN

EQUATOR

Mouths of the Amazon

Ilha de Marajó

Serra dos Carajás

Serra do Cuchimbo

Amazon

Guiana Highlands

Rio Negro

Madeira

A m a z o n   B a s i n

Jaruá

Amazon

Orinoco

Ucayali

West Indies

Windward Islands

Greater Antilles

Lesser Antilles

Puerto Rico

Hispaniola

Apure

L l a n o s

Cordillera Oriental

Lake Maracaibo

Caribbean Sea

Bahamas

Cuba

Jamaica

Isthmus of Panama

Cordillera Occidental

Cordillera Real

Gulf of Mexico

Lake Nicaragua

Galapagos Islands

PHYSICAL BARRIERS

Geographic barriers such as rivers separate animal populations, limiting their distribution and encouraging separate species to develop. Two capuchin species are separated by the Paraná and Araguaia rivers. Genetic evidence indicates that these populations separated 2 million years ago.

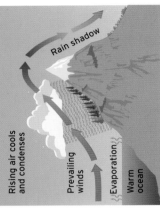

AZURA'S CAPUCHIN

ANDEAN RAIN SHADOW

Much of the south-eastern part of the continent is dry due to the rain shadow cast by the Andes. Winds from the Pacific Ocean rise and cool over the mountains, causing the water vapour they contain to fall as rain on the windward (west) side of the mountain range.

Rain shadow

Rising air cools and condenses

Prevailing winds

Evaporation

Warm ocean

FERTILE GRASSLANDS

The rich temperate grasslands of the Argentine pampas are home to many unique animals.

STRAIT OF MAGELLAN

Fish move through this sea passage between the Pacific and Atlantic oceans.

Brazilian Highlands

São Francisco

Serra do Espinhaço

Serra da Mantiqueira

Serra Dourada

Serra Dourada

Serra do Roncador

Serra do Mar

Serra de Maracaju

Serra do Caiapó

Serra Geral

Planalto de Mato Grosso

Pantanal

Paraguay

Paraná

Paraguay

Paraná

Uruguay

Lagoa dos Patos

Mirim Lagoon

ATLANTIC OCEAN

Gran Chaco

Mesopotamia

Río de la Plata

Pampas

Rio Grande

Lago Poopó

Lake Titicaca

Altiplano

Salar de Uyuni

Atacama Desert

Cerro Ojos del Salado 6,880m △

Sierras de Córdoba

△ *Cerro Aconcagua 6,959m*

Andes

Patagonia

Falkland Islands

Tierra del Fuego

Cape Horn

PACIFIC OCEAN

ATACAMA DESERT

The Atacama is the driest desert in the world—in some parts of the desert, no rainfall has ever been recorded. Nevertheless, around 500 species of plants and a few arthropods, amphibians, reptiles, birds, and mammals have adapted to survive here. These include scorpions, salt flat lizards, Humboldt penguins, and Andean flamingos.

VALLE DE LA LUNA

FEATURED ECOREGIONS

- Costa Rican Rainforest »p78-83
  Tropical, subtropical moist broadleaf forest
- Andean Yungas »p84-89
  Tropical, subtropical moist broadleaf forest
- Amazon Rainforest »p90-99
  Tropical, subtropical moist broadleaf forest
- The Pantanal »p100-07
  Wetland: flooded grassland
- Andean Altiplano »p108-13
  Montane grassland, shrub
- Argentine Pampas »p114-21
  Temperate grassland
- Galapagos Islands »p122-29
  Desert, scrub

COSTA RICAN RAINFOREST
A tropical eco-paradise

Costa Rica may be small, but it punches above its size in terms of biodiversity—it contains 5 percent of all species on just 0.3 percent of the world's land mass. The Costa Rican rainforest is a lush tropical jungle, with verdant foliage, rivers, and waterfalls, and teems with an exotic array of animal life. Many of this rainforest's inhabitants are dazzlingly beautiful—butterflies and hummingbirds flit among trees that are adorned with glorious blooms. A diverse array of orchid species are found here, considering the ecoregion's comparably small size.

This bountiful biodiversity is due to Costa Rica's location on the land bridge between North and South America, which gives it representatives from both continents. There is also a range of ecological niches in the country—as well as the rainforest, there are damp cloud forests at higher altitudes, dry forests, and mangrove swamps.

Conservation leader

Costa Rica leads the world in terms of protecting its wild heritage. Around a quarter of the country is designated as national parks or protected areas, and Costa Rica has been praised as a model of responsible ecotourism as people flock here to see the region's myriad of monkey species and unique mammals like sloths. The rate of deforestation has dramatically decreased since the 1960s and some areas have been successfully reforested. Costa Rica has also pioneered payments to landowners for environmental services to support conservation measures and to keep the rainforest intact.

HIGH RISER
Trees that emerge high above the main rainforest, such as kapok, benefit from sunlight that doesn't reach lower parts of the rainforest. Nectar-feeding bats pollinate its flowers, and fluffy seeds are blown on the wind to new areas.

KAPOK TREE

IF THE BILL FITS
The flowers of heliconia plants are almost exclusively pollinated by hummingbirds that visit to drink the flowers' rich nectar. The two have coevolved so that heliconias with deeper flower tubes are only pollinated by the species that has a long enough bill.

HUMMINGBIRDS

Home to more than 5% of the world's species > More than 50 species of hummingbird

HARPY EAGLE

HUGE HUNTER
The harpy eagle hunts monkeys and sloths among the rainforest canopy. Its short, broad wings make it easier for a bird of its size to maneuver, and its long talons and powerful feet allow it to catch and lift large prey.

LOCATION

Costa Rica is located on the Central American isthmus between North and South America.

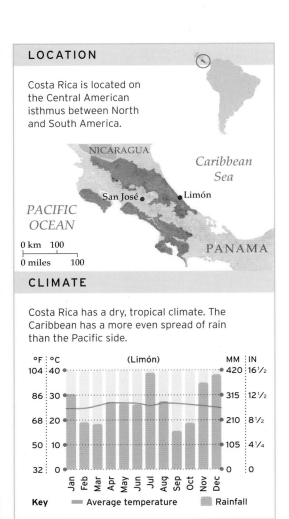

NICARAGUA

Caribbean Sea

San José • Limón

PACIFIC OCEAN

PANAMA

0 km 100
0 miles 100

CLIMATE

Costa Rica has a dry, tropical climate. The Caribbean has a more even spread of rain than the Pacific side.

°F	°C	(Limón)	MM	IN
104	40		420	16½
86	30		315	12½
68	20		210	8½
50	10		105	4¼
32	0		0	0

Jan Feb Mar Apr May Jun Jul Aug Sep Oct Nov Dec

Key ▬ Average temperature ▬ Rainfall

UMBRELLA SPECIES
The black-headed bushmaster viper preys on small mammals, such as spiny rats and marsupials, and lays its eggs in burrows made by other animals. Conservation of this species would benefit many others.

750,000 species of insect

BUSHMASTER VIPER

Honduran white bat
Ectophylla alba

This tiny white bat lives in rainforests where large-leafed heliconia plants are plentiful. Feeding on fruit at night, they roost during the day in tents that they construct by nibbling either side of a leaf's midrib so that the sides collapse, forming an inverted V that protects them from rain and sun. Their snow-white fur is tinted green as sunlight filters through the bright green leaves, thus camouflaging them from potential predators.

↔ 2 in (5 cm)
⚖ ¼ oz (7.5 g)
✕ Near threatened
🍽 Fruit pulp, fig seeds
🏠🌳

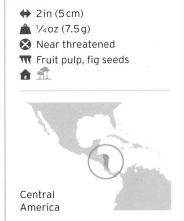

Central America

◁ **LEAF TENT**
Honduran white bats roost in groups of 4–10, usually a single male and his harem of females, underneath a leaf 6 ft (2 m) off the ground.

Hoffmann's two-toed sloth
Choloepus hoffmanni

Sloths live in slow motion to conserve energy. Their metabolism is about 50 percent slower than that of other similarly sized mammals. Their intestine is shorter than a carnivore's—a trait usually associated with a fast-acting digestion—yet the plant-based diet takes 6–21 days to be digested. This, however, allows sloths to extract the maximum nutrition from low-energy food and may also help neutralize toxins. Awkward and vulnerable on the ground, where the sloth descends once a week to defecate, the algae in its fur conceals it in the trees from predators such as harpy eagles and jaguars.

↔ 22–30 in (56–76 cm)
⚖ 9–19 lb (4–8.6 kg)
✕ Common
🍽 Leaves, buds, fruit, sap
🏠🌳🌳🌴

Central America, N. and W. South America

▷ **HANGING AROUND**
Sloths spend most of their lives in trees, where they eat, sleep, mate, and give birth—all while dangling upside down from their huge, hooked claws.

distinctive chainlike rosettes

Ocelots are **good swimmers** and will **catch fish, turtles, and frogs**

short, dense fur

Ocelot
Leopardus pardalis

The ocelot is the largest of three small, spotted cats native to Central and South American forests. Its patterned coat and stealthy, mainly nocturnal, habits ensure that the cat is rarely seen. Much of what we know about the species comes from analyzing its droppings, and radio-tracking. Ocelots have been tracked traveling long distances at night, with adult females ranging up to 3 miles (4 km) and males 5 miles (7.5 km).

Lone ranger

Ocelots become active in the late afternoon, and hunt by patrolling areas of thick cover. They prefer to feed on small ground-dwelling rodents, particularly rats, but can take young deer, wild pigs, and sloths. More unusual prey include lizards, land crabs, birds, fish, and frogs. Ocelots are agile climbers, often resting in trees during the day. Like most cats, they are solitary—adults socialize only during the breeding season. An adult male's home range overlaps with that of several females. The females breed once every two years and usually give birth to just one cub after 80 days.

◁ **AMBITIOUS HUNTER**
Ocelots will catch prey half their weight, such as green iguanas. To avoid the reptile's claws and lashing tail, a hunting ocelot will aim for the fleshy throat for a quick dispatch.

front paws larger than rear paws

▷ **DAPPLED FUR**
The ocelot's spotted coat provides excellent camouflage among foliage. In the past, this species was heavily hunted to supply the fur trade.

↔ 20–39 in (50–100 cm)
⚖ 25–35 lb (11.5–16 kg)
✖ Common
〽 Mammals

S. North
America
to S. South
America

Resplendent quetzal
Pharomachrus mocinno

Quetzals are a group of glossy birds found in tropical forests. The resplendent quetzal is the most extravagantly plumed, but when perched, upright, still, and silent, its long, green back makes it inconspicuous in the forest. It mostly eats fruit, especially wild avocados, but will occasionally feed on insects, small frogs, lizards, and snails.

Pairs are territorial, and they carve out a nest hole in a rotting tree. The female lays one or two eggs, which are incubated by both parents for 18 days. The male and female also take turns feeding the chicks; however, often only the male continues to do so for the last few days before the chicks can fly.

↔ 14–26 in (35–65½ cm)
⚖ 7–8 oz (200–225 g)
✖ Near threatened
〽 Fruit, insects

Central
America

▷ **SPLENDID PLUMES**
Resplendent quetzals are aptly named after the vibrant tail feathers of breeding males.

Common morpho
Morpho peleides

When viewed at rest with its wings folded up, the common morpho's wings are brown with several large eyespots. However, in flight, the upper wings produce a startling display of iridescent blues and turquoises. Visible even in the thick foliage, the shimmering wings allow the butterflies to spot one another—males keep their distance, while females seek out mates.

↔ 4–5 in (9.5–12 cm)
✖ Not known
〽 Juices of ripe fruits

Central
America
to N. South
America

white marks
on dark
fringe

◁ **VARIOUS FORMS**
Common morphos vary greatly in color and form, with different markings on the wing margins and fringes, and there are several subspecies.

black-and-yellow-
ringed eyespots

Red-eyed tree frog

Agalychnis callidryas

bright green upper body
provides camouflage

orange feet hidden
when at rest

The red-eyed tree frog is an iconic rainforest amphibian. As its name suggests, it has striking red eyes, although these are usually hidden from view. To camouflage itself against leaves, it makes itself look small by tucking its legs against the body so that only the green upper surfaces are in view. The eyes are shut to conceal the telltale red irises. When a predator gets too close, the frog flashes its eyes wide open, startling it momentarily. As it leaps to safety, extending its legs to a full stretch, it reveals yet more hidden color on its flanks and thighs.

Agile climber

The red-eyed tree frog is a nocturnal insect hunter. The vertical diamond shape of its iris shows that it is focused on tracking the vertical movements of insects marching up and down tree trunks. Like all frogs, the tree frog is a good jumper, but it also climbs up trees, gripping branches with the suction cups at the tips of its fingers and toes. Unlike most frogs, the red-eyed tree frog can swim, although the adult spends most of its life in trees. It visits water regularly—often just the puddles formed on leaves—to absorb water through the thin skin on its belly.

Show of strength

Mating takes place in the rainy season. Males, who adopt prominent perches, initiate courtship through a croaking call. They also quiver their body so much that the surrounding leaves begin to shake. This show of strength attracts females, and when one gets near, all the males in the area fight to mate with her. The winner fertilizes her egg clutches as she lays them on leaves in several batches.

distinctive blue
and yellow markings
on sides

▷ **FLASH COLOURING**
The bright blue and yellow flanks of the red-eyed tree frog are only visible when the frog is on the move. The flash of colour startles predators as the frog makes a hasty escape.

◁ MATING PAIR
The male clambers on to the female's back to mate. Mating takes several hours, with the smaller male clinging to the female as she searches for places to lay her eggs.

△ FROGSPAWN
The red-eyed tree frog's eggs are laid on a leaf hanging over a pond or a stream. When the tadpoles emerge, they fall into the water below.

vertical pupil

pads on toes help with grip

2–3 in (4–7 cm)
Summer
Locally common
Insects

Central America

Red-eyed tree frogs can **lighten and darken their skin color** for camouflage or to **signal a change in mood**

ANDEAN YUNGAS
A species-rich forest reaching into the clouds

The Andean yungas ecoregion covers the eastern slope of the Andes mountain range, from 3,300-11,500 ft (1,000-3,500 m). It is sandwiched between the lowlands of the Amazon basin and Gran Chaco grasslands to the east and the high plateau of the Andean altiplano to the west. The yungas features dramatically varied topography with high ridges and steep-sided valleys created by mountain rivers. The range in altitude produces different climatic zones, which in turn create various habitat types, including moist lowland forest, deciduous and evergreen upland forests, and subtropical cloud forests.

A hotspot for diversity

Among the more than 3,000 species of plants are tree ferns, bamboo, Peruvian pepper trees, and the coca bush. Coca leaves have been chewed or brewed as a tea for centuries by the people of the Andes to counter the effects of altitude sickness. In addition to the vast array of plants, around 200 species of vertebrate live here. The Andean yungas is known as a biological hotspot because it is home to many endemic species and because species from neighboring ecoregions—such as the Amazon rainforest—also live here.

Native species are often restricted to "altitudinal belts," which means they are only found at certain altitudes, either because they cannot physically cross certain geographic barriers such as rivers or mountains, or they only eat vegetation that grows at certain altitudes.

RECENT DISCOVERY
New species are still being discovered in the yungas. This dead-leaf toad is so-called because its body shape and coloration is perfectly camouflaged against dead leaves on the forest floor. It was described and named in 2014.

DEAD-LEAF TOAD

ORCHID HAVEN
The yungas contains 200 species of orchid, with a high level of endemism. They are particularly numerous in cloud forests as damp conditions allow epiphytes to thrive on tree trunks and branches. There are also lithophytes that grow on rocky cliffs.

MONKEY ORCHID

> 3,000 plant species > New species still being foun

Many species unique to the region

LONG-WHISKERED OWLET

SMALL STRANGER
With a population of around 350-1,000, the long-whiskered owlet was discovered in 1976 in Peru. It measures just 6 in (15 cm) in height. Its whiskery face inspired the Latin name of its genus, *Xenoglaux*, which means strange owl.

LOCATION

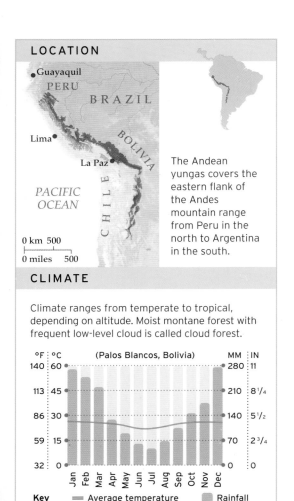

The Andean yungas covers the eastern flank of the Andes mountain range from Peru in the north to Argentina in the south.

CLIMATE

Climate ranges from temperate to tropical, depending on altitude. Moist montane forest with frequent low-level cloud is called cloud forest.

(Palos Blancos, Bolivia)

°F	°C	MM	IN
140	60	280	11
113	45	210	8¼
86	30	140	5½
59	15	70	2¾
32	0	0	0

Jan Feb Mar Apr May Jun Jul Aug Sep Oct Nov Dec

Key — Average temperature ▇ Rainfall

Mountain tapir

Tapirus pinchaque

short, extensible trunk

The mountain tapir is the smallest, most endangered of all four tapir species—fewer than 2,500 are thought to survive in the wild. It makes its home high in the Andes, where its fur, which grows to 2 in (5 cm) thick, has earned it the nickname "woolly tapir."

Snorkeling for safety

Short, stocky legs and splayed toes make the mountain tapir sure-footed and agile, capable of negotiating steep slopes and dense undergrowth. Like other tapirs, it hides in thickets by day, feeding mainly at dawn and dusk. It has a keen sense of hearing and smell, and flees when threatened, often hiding underwater and using its trunk like a snorkel to breathe until danger passes. Tapirs call to each other with shrill, high-pitched whistles that are often mistaken for birdsong.

↔ 6–7 ft (1.8–2.1 m)
⚖ 330–440 lb (150–200 kg)
⊗ Endangered
🌱 Leaves, herbs, grasses, fruit

NW. South America

◁ **LONG STRIPES**
Young tapirs are often called "watermelons on legs" due to their camouflage markings, which allow them to blend in with dappled sunlight.

SMALLEST DEER
The tiny pudu is the world's smallest deer, standing 15 in (38 cm) tall at the shoulder. It relies on a network of tunnels and well-trodden paths through the yungas vegetation to give it protection from predators.

NORTHERN PUDU

Most areas are protected

▷ **GRIPPING SNOUT**
The mountain tapir feeds using its flexible nose to grasp vegetation, dispersing up to 86 species of plant seeds in the process of eating and digestion.

distinctive white lips

soles of feet are soft and sensitive

Silky anteater
Cyclopes didactylus

fine, dense
fur

The world's smallest anteater is not much longer than a human hand. Seldom seen, silky anteaters live on trees, feed from sunset to sunrise on as many as 5,000 ants each night, and rest through the day. While the nocturnal habit protects them from humans, these anteaters are preyed upon by harpy eagles, hawks, and spectacled owls.

Silken disguise
Silky anteaters live in silk floss trees, which provide the perfect camouflage for the anteater with its long, fine, smoky-gray fur. Each front foot of the anteater has two enlarged claws, which are perfect for climbing and digging into tree-ant nests but must be turned inward for it to move on the ground. Although the silky anteater rarely comes to the ground, it walks well on flat surfaces and has been seen crossing roads. It also has a prehensile tail and specially adapted hindfeet that wrap firmly around branches, allowing it to move through the canopy.

After mating, a single baby anteater is born in a leaf-lined nest usually situated in a tree hollow. Both parents raise the baby, feeding it regurgitated ants. Males carry the babies on their backs.

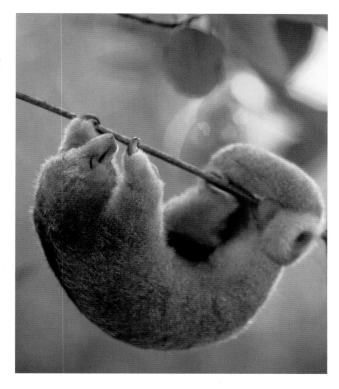

↔ 7–9 in (16–21 cm)
🏋 6–13 oz (175–357 g)
✖ Common
🐜 Ants, termites, ladybugs

Central America to N. South America

◁ **FAST ASLEEP**
The silky anteater spends its daylight hours sleeping high in the safety of trees, often simply hanging from its hooklike front claws, prehensile tail, and wraparound hindfeet.

Coati
Nasua nasua

Coatis move easily between different environments. Although terrestrial, coatis mate, give birth, and sleep in trees. Good climbers with powerful forelegs, they rotate their ankle joints to descend headfirst from trees, but easily jump from branch to branch, using their long tails for balance. They are also good swimmers. Strong claws and a flexible nose make them expert foragers.

Female coatis form bands of up to 65 animals. During the mating season, each band is joined by a male, which mates with all receptive females, then departs. Litters of one to seven young are born in spring and early summer. The females rejoin their band once the youngsters can walk and climb.

▽ **HEALTHY APPETITE**
Active and inquisitive members of the raccoon family, coatis feed on everything from small mammals, birds, and insects to fruit and leaves.

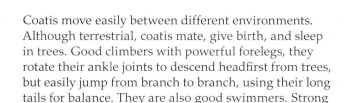
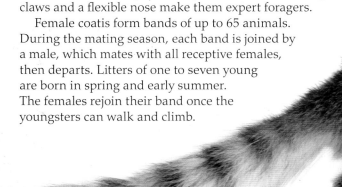

↔ 17–23 in (43–58 cm)
🏋 5–16 lb (2–7.2 kg)
✖ Common
🐜 Fungi, berries, insects, mice

W. South America

banded tail

4–6 ft (1.3–1.9 m)

132–390 lb (60–175 kg)

Vulnerable

Fruit, succulent plants, birds

W. South
America

creamy white
markings

Spectacled bear

Tremarctos ornatus

South America's only bear is also one of its largest
land mammals. Just 2–3 ft (60–90 cm) high at the
shoulder, they make their homes in a variety of
Andean habitats, ranging from cloud forests to
high-level grasslands bordering rainforests.
Spectacled bears spend much of their time in trees,
where they build a platform of sticks to sleep on
and forage from. They eat fruit, flowers, and
succulent plants. They also sometimes hunt
insects, birds, and small rodents.

The bears are solitary except during the
mating season, from April to June, when a
male and female stay together for up to two
weeks. Cubs are born from December to
February. Males do not play any part in
raising the young, and may even kill
cubs. While pumas and jaguars prey
upon the cubs, the greatest threat to
the species comes from habitat loss
and hunting by humans.

▷ **DISTINCTIVE MARKINGS**
The spectacled bear gets
its name from the cream
or yellow markings around
its eyes. These markings
often extend down
to its chest.

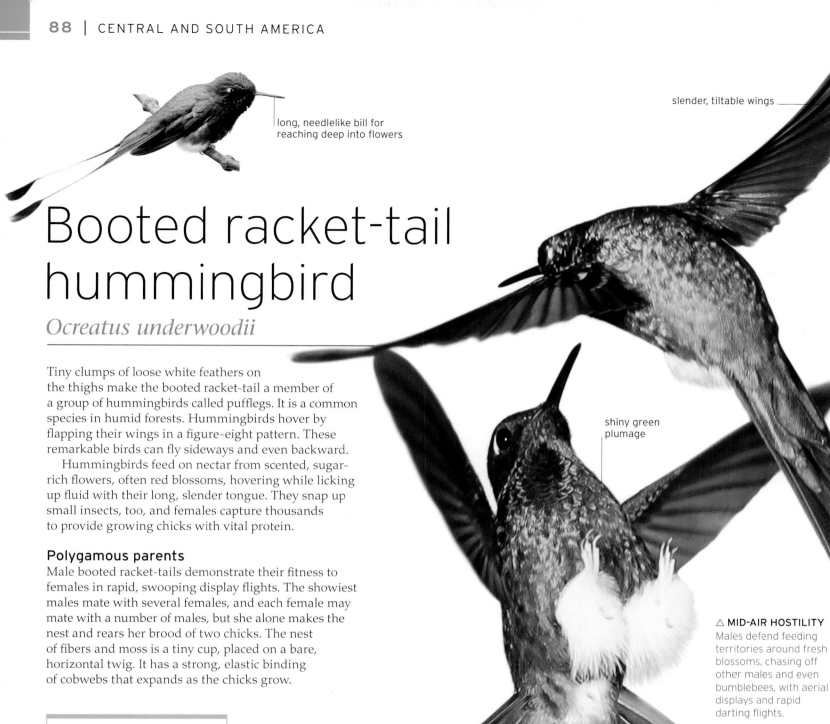

long, needlelike bill for
reaching deep into flowers

slender, tiltable wings

Booted racket-tail hummingbird

Ocreatus underwoodii

Tiny clumps of loose white feathers on
the thighs make the booted racket-tail a member of
a group of hummingbirds called pufflegs. It is a common
species in humid forests. Hummingbirds hover by
flapping their wings in a figure-eight pattern. These
remarkable birds can fly sideways and even backward.

Hummingbirds feed on nectar from scented, sugar-
rich flowers, often red blossoms, hovering while licking
up fluid with their long, slender tongue. They snap up
small insects, too, and females capture thousands
to provide growing chicks with vital protein.

Polygamous parents

Male booted racket-tails demonstrate their fitness to
females in rapid, swooping display flights. The showiest
males mate with several females, and each female may
mate with a number of males, but she alone makes the
nest and rears her brood of two chicks. The nest
of fibers and moss is a tiny cup, placed on a bare,
horizontal twig. It has a strong, elastic binding
of cobwebs that expands as the chicks grow.

shiny green
plumage

△ MID-AIR HOSTILITY
Males defend feeding
territories around fresh
blossoms, chasing off
other males and even
bumblebees, with aerial
displays and rapid
darting flights.

↔ 7–9 in (17–23 cm)

⚖ ⅛ oz (3 g)

✪ Common

🌿 Nectar, insects, spiders

🏠 🌳 ⛰

NW. to W.
South
America

long tail adornment
of male

Booted racket-tails **beat their
wings 60 times per second**
when hovering

Andean cock-of-the-rock
Rupicola peruvianus

In sheltered, moist ravines and river valleys high in the cloud forests of the Andes, male Andean cock-of-the-rocks gather to display for the benefit of the watching females. A chorus of squawks accompanies the rather awkward performance, drawing attention even to birds deep within the forest canopy. The males are at risk of predation during courtship, with various forest cats, birds of prey, and snakes likely to attack them. At other times, they are quiet and inconspicuous.

Mud nests

Females, which are not as colorful as the males and have less exaggerated crests, make a cup-shaped nest of mud and saliva, plastered against a rock or inside a small cave. They incubate two eggs for up to a month and feed the hatchlings on their own. The cock-of-the-rock's main diet consists of a range of fruits, supplemented with a supply of insects.

↔ 12–13 in (30–32 cm)
🏋 7–10 oz (200–275 g)
⊗ Locally common
🍴 Fruit, insects
🏠 🏞

N. to W. South America

◁ **DISPLAYING MALE**
Males compete in communal displays in a tree, bowing, flapping their wings, and calling discordantly. Their actions and sounds intensify if a female appears.

Trueb's cochran frog
Nymphargus truebae

Trueb's cochran frog is a species of glass frog, so-called because its skin is translucent on the underside, making it possible to see its bones and internal organs. This tiny native of the Andean cloud forest is nocturnal, sleeping through the day on leaves in the treetops. The green of the leaves shows through the frog's skin, helping it to blend in easily and stay hidden.

Females lay eggs on leaves above pools of water, and the males guard them until they hatch. The tadpoles plummet into the water below, where they feed among the detritus at the bottom.

yellow-spotted green skin

△ **LONG LIMBS**
Trueb's cochran frog is wide-skulled and long-limbed. Its eyes are placed at the top of the head.

↔ ⁷/₈–1 in (22.5–25 mm)
🏋 Not known
⊗ Not known
🍴 Insects
🏠 🏞 ⛰
🧭 S. Peru

Crimson longwing
Heliconius erato

Known for its wide, rounded black wings with flashes of red on the upper surface, the crimson-patched longwing is a highly variable butterfly with no fewer than 29 subspecies. Each subspecies has a unique wing pattern, some without any red markings. The species as a whole is found all over Central and South America.

To complicate things further, every subspecies mimics the coloring of the subspecies of another equally variable longwing called the common postman, or *Heliconius melpomene*, that lives in the same habitat.

↔ 2–3 in (5.5–8 cm)
⊗ Common
🍴 Pollen and nectar
🏠 🏞 🌳 ⛰ 🌿
🧭 Central and South America

crimson wing band

▷ **PERUVIAN NATIVE**
The crimson longwing subspecies pictured lives in the lowland forests of Peru.

AMAZON RAINFOREST

One of the most productive ecosystems on Earth

The Amazon is the world's largest tropical rainforest, covering 2.1 million sq miles (5.5 million sq km) of the drainage basin fed by the long and winding river that shares its name. The rainforest is among the most productive and biodiverse ecosystems on the planet, containing around 10 percent of all the world's known species and potentially many more that have yet to be discovered. The huge variety of plants provides a multitude of habitats and food for a myriad of different animal species. It is also important because it stores large amounts of carbon—110–154 billion tons (100–140 billion metric tons) —that would otherwise be in the atmosphere.

Life among the layers

Overwhelmingly green to look at, with bright flashes of color from flowers, fruit, monkeys, and birds, the rainforest consists of several different layers. The tallest trees project above the main rainforest canopy, which itself forms the middle layer. This layer is the most diverse, and beneath it lie the understory and then ground level, where much less light—and moisture—penetrates. The lush jungle foliage slows the speed of rain falling to the forest floor, where deep soil and decaying plant matter act like a sponge, holding water and slowly releasing it to streams and rivers.

Vegetation can be **so thick, rain** may take **10 minutes to reach the ground**

FIRE ANTS

LIVING RAFT
Many parts of the Amazon rainforest flood periodically, presenting a problem for creatures that nest underground such as fire ants. During floods, members of the ant colony form a raft out of their own bodies on which eggs, larvae, and queen are kept safe and dry.

Been in existence for 55 milion years

AGOUTI

The world's largest tropical rainforest

SEED DISPERSER
The agouti is one of the few animals able to gnaw through the tough fruit of the Brazil nut to release its seeds. When fruits are abundant, it hoards surplus seeds for later, often far from the parent tree, where they may be forgotten about and grow into new trees.

PARA RUBBER TREE

Covers 40% of South America

RUBBER BOOM
The bark of the Para rubber tree is cut to release milky latex sap. This sap is used to make products such as rubber boots and latex gloves, or is chemically treated to produce tougher items such as tires.

NATURAL HABITAT

In its native Amazon, the cane toad is regulated by many predators. As an introduced species in Hawaii and Australia, however, this poisonous amphibian breeds out of control.

CANE TOAD

Contains around 390 billion trees of 16,000 different species

CLIMBING AROUND

Colorful and pheasant-sized as adult birds, with an impressive headcrest of feathers, as chicks, hoatzins have two claws on each wing, which they use to climb through waterside vegetation until they are able to fly. They lose the claws before adulthood.

HOATZIN CHICK

An estimated 2.5 million species of insects live here

ENVIRONMENTAL MONITOR

Two species of Amazon river dolphin, the pink river dolphin and the tucuxi, are good indicators of the health of the freshwater ecosystems they inhabit. Fewer dolphins are found where there is existing river degradation, such as poor water quality and overfishing by large human populations.

PINK RIVER DOLPHIN

LOCATION

The Amazon rainforest stretches across nine South American countries: Brazil, French Guiana, Suriname, Guyana, Venezuela, Colombia, Ecuador, Peru, and Bolivia.

VENEZUELA

COLOMBIA
Bogotá

0 km 500
0 miles 500

ATLANTIC OCEAN

Manaus

PERU

PACIFIC OCEAN

BRAZIL

Brasília

CLIMATE

The Amazon rainforest's climate is tropical and humid. Although all months are wet, rainfall is greatest between December and April, when more than 8 in (200 mm) of rain falls on average each month in Manaus, the region's largest city.

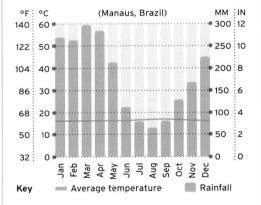

(Manaus, Brazil)

°F	°C		MM	IN
140	60		300	12
122	50		250	10
104	40		200	8
86	30		150	6
68	20		100	4
50	10		50	2
32	0		0	0

Jan Feb Mar Apr May Jun Jul Aug Sep Oct Nov Dec

Key ■ Average temperature ■ Rainfall

DEFORESTATION

The Amazon rainforest is being felled at such a rate that an estimated 135 plant and animal species become extinct daily. The sustainable harvest of rubber and other wild products, such as Brazil nuts, helps to protect the rainforest from the devastating effects of total land clearance for projects such as soy plantations.

Emperor tamarin
Saguinus imperator

tail twice as long as
head and body

Tamarins are small monkeys with silky fur, and many species also have elaborate facial patterns, crests, beards, or mustaches. Notable, too, for its long orange-red tail, the emperor tamarin lives in small families in the lower and middle levels of rainforests, and these families often forage together with saddleback tamarins. Emperor tamarins eat a variety of plant food, particularly berries and other fruit, and flowers, nectar, tree sap, and leaves. They also hunt insects, snails, frogs, and small lizards, snatching prey off foliage with their dextrous hands. The female usually bears twins, which the father carries except when they are being suckled.

↔ 9–10 in (23–26 cm)
🏋 16 oz (450 g)
✗ Common
🍽 Fruit, nectar, insects

W. South
America

◁ **DROOPING MOUSTACHE**
Both adult male and female emperor tamarins have a flowing white moustache. The long white curls reach down as far as their forearms.

Pygmy marmoset
Cebuella pygmaea

This minuscule, hyperactive primate is the world's smallest monkey—a curled-up adult pygmy marmoset would fit into a human palm. Pygmy marmosets keep to dense thickets and tangles of vegetation in the lower levels of forests, hiding from predators such as other monkeys, forest cats, hawks, and snakes. They are exceptionally agile and, despite their tiny size, can leap up to 16 ft (5 m).

Pygmy marmosets live in small family groups, usually consisting of a breeding pair and up to seven or eight young of varying ages, and most births are twins. Unlike other marmosets, they don't move around their home range in a group when feeding during the day, but they spend the night sleeping together in a huddle. They feed mainly on the sugary gum or sap of trees, by gouging the bark with their sharp lower incisors and then lapping up the liquid that flows out.

△ **MANED MONKEY**
Pygmy marmosets have long cheek hair that forms a mane, hiding their ears from view.

↔ 5–6 in (12–15 cm)
🏋 3–5 oz (85–140 g)
✗ Common
🍽 Tree sap, invertebrates

W. South
America

↔ 20–25 in (50–63 cm)
🏋 11–20 lb (5–9 kg)
✗ Common
🍽 Fruit, leaves

NW. South
America

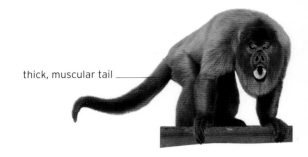

thick, muscular tail

Red howler monkey

Alouatta seniculus

The growling roars of red howler monkeys are among the most distinctive sounds of the Amazonian rainforest. Just before dawn, each troop starts to call from the treetops to announce ownership of their home range, and other groups in the area may reply. Adapted hyoid bones in the monkeys' throat amplify the sounds, which can be heard up to 3 miles (5 km) away. Both sexes roar. Male howlers react most to the calls of males in neighboring troops, while females respond most to the roars of other females, which are higher pitched.

Chunky monkeys

Red howlers are big, solid monkeys that move more slowly than many other monkeys. They typically spend most of their waking hours resting or digesting food in the forest canopy. Their prehensile tails have a bald patch near the underside of the tip to help grip branches. They feed on leaves and fruit—especially figs—and when they find a large fruiting tree, will guard it against rival groups. Red howlers periodically go to the ground to eat clay, which contains salts and minerals that help to neutralize toxins in the leaves they eat.

A red howler monkey troop usually has from three to a dozen members, led by an adult male that remains dominant for several years. Females mate for the first time when around five years old, giving birth to a single baby after a seven-month gestation. Babies cling to their mother's belly for the first month, then ride piggyback, and are independent at six months old. Despite their large size, red howler monkeys are preyed on by harpy eagles. On spotting danger, they quickly grunt warnings to alert the rest of the group.

△ **BEARDED MALE**
Adult male howler monkeys, which are much heavier than females, have a long, full beard.

▷ **URSINE HOWLERS**
Many howler monkeys are named after their predominant fur color. There are brown and black species as well as ones with red fur, such as the ursine howler (*A. arctoidea*).

Howler monkeys are the **loudest land animals**—their calls reach 90 decibels

↔ 4–6 ft (1.1–1.7 m)

🏋 70–270 lb (32–122 kg)

✗ Near threatened

🐾 Mammals, reptiles, birds

🏠 🌳 🌳 🌾 〰 🌲

Central America
to N. and C.
South America

▷ **ON THE PROWL**
A jaguar's broad, fur-soled paws make
no sound as it moves through dense
vegetation, and its dappled coat helps
it blend into the surroundings, making
this cat the ultimate stealth hunter.

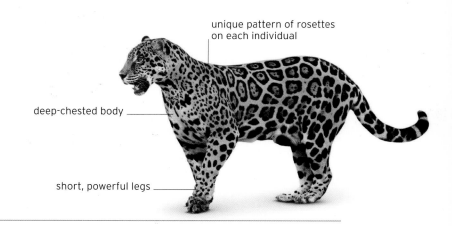

unique pattern of rosettes on each individual

deep-chested body

short, powerful legs

Jaguar

Panthera onca

The western hemisphere's largest feline is the least well-studied—scientists have no idea how many jaguars are left in the wild. This secretive cat once roamed forests from the southwestern US to Argentina, but it now occupies only about 45 percent of its original range, due to human intervention. Today, it is confined to 19 Latin American countries.

Formidable predator

The epitome of the opportunistic hunter, jaguars feed on a range of mammals, from deer and peccaries to coatis and monkeys. They also eat insects, fish, birds, caimans, anacondas, and eggs. There has been just one, recent, instance of a jaguar eating a human; however, when faced with habitat loss due to human encroachment, they will prey on livestock and domestic pets.

An efficient predator, the jaguar's immense jaw strength allows it to pierce the skull of its victims. It usually hunts at dusk or dawn, when its dappled coat provides maximum camouflage, but is more nocturnal where people are present. An adult male needs about 100 sq miles (260 sq km) of territory to hunt—this can range from humid rainforest, dry pine woods, swamp, scrubland, savanna, to desert.

Adult male jaguars can **break through bone and turtle shell** in a **single bite**

Like lions and tigers, jaguars can roar, but they communicate more frequently using coughs, growls, grunts, "huffs," and low moans.

Jaguars are solitary animals that only pair up to breed. Females give birth to one to four cubs, which are born with sky-blue eyes that turn green-gold in a few weeks. Their head and paws grow more quickly than the rest of their bodies. Cubs are independent at 15 months but may remain in their mother's territory until they are about two years old.

An estimated six percent of jaguars have a genetic mutation that gives them a "dark phase" coat color. Dark coated jaguars and leopards are called panthers, although the characteristic rosettes are still visible.

△ **SKILFUL SWIMMER**
Powerfully muscled legs make jaguars strong swimmers—one was seen crossing a river to attack a caiman basking on a sandbank.

▷ **AT THE WATER'S EDGE**
Generally considered a jungle creature, the jaguar can adapt to almost any habitat, provided there is water and prey nearby. In the wild, the jaguar's lifespan is 10–12 years.

oversized yet
lightweight bill

white bib on
black body

Toco toucan

Ramphastos toco

Few birds worldwide are as instantly recognizable as the toco toucan, with its huge, colorful bill. The long bill is useful for reaching fruit on the ends of branches that are too thin to support the toucan's weight. It can also be used to grab small reptiles, eggs and nestlings, and large insects, if fruit is scarce. The bill's bright color must act as a visual stimulus in social situations, although it is identical in both sexes. It also serves as a striking warning to predators.

Cool discovery

Scientists have recently discovered another use for the toco toucan's enormous bill: it has an important function as a radiator. When temperatures are high, the toucan can lose up to 60 percent of its body heat through the bill, which has a network of blood vessels

The toco toucan has the **largest bill of any bird**, relative to body size

that controls the flow of blood to its surface. In cool spells, the blood flow is restricted, allowing the toucan to conserve its body heat. During the night, it sleeps with the bill under a wing, to maintain heat.

Tocos are weak fliers. They flutter through the forest canopy, usually in pairs, to find fruiting trees. Tree cavities are often enlarged for the nest, in which two to four eggs are incubated by both parents. They defend the chicks from predators, such as snakes, as it takes several months for a chick's bill to be fully formed.

▽ PROMINENT BILL
Despite its size, the toco toucan's bill is comparatively light because it is mostly hollow, with a supporting framework of bony struts.

Scarlet macaw
Ara macao

Macaws are huge parrots with long tails and massive bills. The scarlet macaw—one of the largest members of this group—is a native of humid tropical forests. It lives in the dense tree canopy and communicates with far-carrying, ear-splitting screeches.

Scarlet macaws typically live in pairs—they pair for life—but often assemble in noisy groups, resting in tall trees. They eat nuts and seeds, cracking open tough shells with their powerful bills, as well as fruit, flowers, and leaves. Large flocks gather at vertical clay cliffs, where they scrape up the soil with their tongues. The minerals help to neutralize toxins in their food that would be fatal to most birds. In the wild, scarlet macaws can live for 50 years.

↔ 33–35 in (84–89 cm)
⚖ 2–3 lb (0.9–1.4 kg)
✖ Common
🐾 Nuts, seeds, fruit

Central America to N. South America

↔ 22–24 in (56–61 cm)
⚖ 18–30 oz (510–850 g)
✖ Common
🐾 Fruit, eggs, insects, frogs

NE. to C. South America

bare white skin on face

△ **STRONG FLIGHT**
Long, wide wings and powerful chest muscles help the scarlet macaw speed through the air, aided by its flexible tail.

Emerald tree boa
Corallus caninus

Well camouflaged among fresh green foliage, this nonvenomous tree boa has a wide head, powerful jaws, and very long, curved teeth. These are used to grab passing prey such as bats, arboreal rodents, lizards, and birds, while the snake remains securely anchored to a branch by its strong prehensile tail. Small victims are quickly swallowed whole, whereas more substantial prey is first suffocated by constriction.

Male emerald tree boas mature when three or four years old. They are slightly smaller and slimmer than females, which mature a year later. Mating occurs between May and July, and the female gives birth to 5–20 live young six months later. The baby boas are red or orange in colour, changing to green after about a year. There is no parental care.

↔ 5–6 ft (1.5–1.8 m)
⚖ Up to 7 lb (3.2 kg)
✖ Not known
🐾 Bats, rats, birds

N. South America

△ **READY TO STRIKE**
The emerald tree boa strikes out at airborne prey or hangs from a low branch to snatch its victim from the ground.

Dyeing poison frog
Dendrobates tinctorius

Dyeing poison frogs live on or near the forest floor and are mostly active by day. Males set up breeding territories and call for females, which may fight to win courtship rights. The winning female initiates mating by stroking the male's snout with her back feet. Six eggs are laid on a leaf and the male keeps them moist. The tadpoles hatch after about 14 days and both parents carry them on their backs to a bromeliad pool.

↔ 1–2 in (3–5 cm)
🌂 February, March
✖ Common
🎚 Ants, termites, spiders
🏠 🌳
◉ NE. South America

▷ **COLOR VARIETIES**
This pattern is typical of the species, with blue legs and belly, and broad yellow and black stripes on the back. Many other varieties exist using the same colors in different proportions.

Electric eel
Electrophorus electricus

long, cylindrical body

The electric eel is one of the largest freshwater fish in South America. It uses weak electrical pulses to find its way around and locate food in murky inland waters, such as rivers and ponds. It also produces larger electric shocks of around 600 volts that can kill other fish and even stun a human. The pulses are generated by organs of electrogenesis, which have about 5,000 to 6,000 modified muscle cells called electroplaques, running along almost the entire length of the fish's body.

↔ 7–8 ft (2–2.5 m)
⚖ 44 lb (20 kg)
✖ Common
🎚 Fish, shrimp, crabs
🏠 ≈
◉ N. South America

▷ **DECEPTIVE APPEARANCE**
Although it looks like an eel, the electric eel is a type of knifefish that shares a common ancestor with catfish.

Leaf-cutter ant
Atta cephalotes

↔ 1/16–3/4 in (2–22 mm)
✖ Common
🎚 Fungus
🏠 🌲 🏛

Central America to N. South America

Leaf-cutter ants live in extensive underground nests, with each colony consisting of millions of individuals. To feed the colony, small worker ants called "minimas" tend a fungus that grows on a mulch of cut leaves. This fungus can only survive inside the ants' nest, and needs their help to propagate. The pieces of leaf are cut and carried back to the nest by medium-sized "media" workers. The largest workers are called "maximas;"

they act as soldiers and guard the colony against intruders. The colony's single queen lays thousands of eggs every day.

▽ **HARD AT WORK**
A media worker can carry 50 times its own body weight. Leaf-cutters are also known as "parasol" ants because of the way they hold the leaves.

Goliath birdeater

Theraphosa blondi

Regarded as the largest spider in the world, this tarantula has a leg span that could cover a dinner plate, and a mass of about 6 oz (170 g), which far outweighs any of its rivals. Only Asia's giant huntsman spider has a larger leg span. Goliath birdeater females are much larger than the males. The name "birdeater" is based on a 1705 engraving by German naturalist Maria Sibylla Merian, which showed a Goliath birdeater devouring a hummingbird. The tarantula has 1-in- (2-cm-) long fangs, so it may be possible for it to prey on small birds, but its preferred diet is large insects and frogs and mice.

The Goliath birdeater lives in deep burrows on the forest floor and seldom climbs far off the ground. The males only live for three or four years, dying soon after mating for the first and only time, whereas the females can survive for 15 years or more. Each female lays 100–200 eggs and guards the brood constantly for about two months until the spiderlings hatch. If threatened, Goliath birdeaters can flick irritant hairs from their abdomen using their hind legs.

front legs and pedipalps raised in threat posture

↔ Up to 11 in (28 cm)
✖ Not known
🦷 Insects, frogs, mice
🏠 🌾 ⛰

NE. South America

◁ **DEFENCE STANCE**
When threatened, the spider raises up its front legs and shows off its hooked fangs. Defensive bites are "dry," saving venom.

fangs inject venom

The goliath birdeater detects its prey by **sensing vibrations** in the ground

THE PANTANAL
The world's largest wetland

The Pantanal is a vast area of tropical wetland, or swamp, making up 3 percent of the world's wetlands and spreading across 70,000 sq miles (approximately 180,000 sq km). It receives water from the Brazilian highlands and drains into the Paraguay River. Rich, silty soils support a broad complex of plants from the different ecoregions that surround the Pantanal, including the Amazon rainforest to the north and the Cerrado savanna to the east.

Wet and dry

Plant diversity in the Pantanal is particularly great because higher areas remain dry all year round and so maintain drought-tolerant trees, while lower-lying areas host plants that can cope with seasonal flooding, and some parts of the Pantanal are permanently underwater and so contain many aquatic plants. This diversity of

plant life presents great opportunities for animals in the region. However, there are few endemic species in the Pantanal, meaning that many of the animals are also found in neighboring ecoregions. This includes the Yacare caiman, although the Pantanal is its stronghold.

Wetlands act as natural water treatment systems, filtering and removing chemicals from the water, but they are susceptible to pollution from excessive run-off from agriculture and mining activities. Deforestation, infrastructure development, and cattle ranching also risk changing the Pantanal's water resources and so could alter its ecological balance.

MUTUALLY BENEFICIAL
Scented white flowers of the waterlily attract scarab beetles, which are trapped inside when the flower closes. They then pollinate the flower, which then loses its scent, turns pink, covers the beetles in pollen, then opens to release them.

GIANT WATERLILY

SUCCESS STORY
By the late 1980s, hyacinth macaws had declined to fewer than 1,500 individuals due to habitat loss and illegal capture of wild birds for the pet trade. Following stringent conservation measures, the population in the Pantanal has risen to more than 5,000.

HYACINTH MACA

LOWLAND TAPIR

KEYSTONE SPECIES
The lowland tapir is a keystone species in the Pantanal ecoregion. It plays a crucial role by dispersing seeds of many large fruiting plants, and by browsing, it clears areas in which the seeds can germinate.

80% of land is submerged during the rainy season > 159 species of mammal, 565 species

LOCATION

The Pantanal is located to the south of the Amazon river basin in central South America. Around 80% of it is in Brazil.

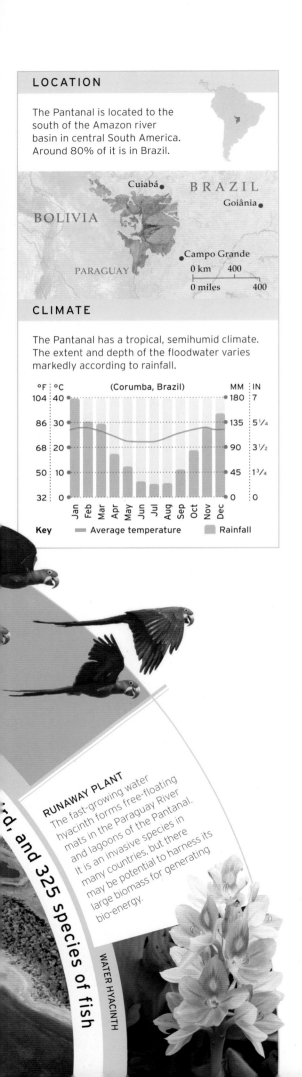

BRAZIL
Cuiabá
Goiânia
BOLIVIA
Campo Grande
PARAGUAY
0 km   400
0 miles   400

CLIMATE

The Pantanal has a tropical, semihumid climate. The extent and depth of the floodwater varies markedly according to rainfall.

°F	°C	(Corumba, Brazil)	MM	IN
104	40		180	7
86	30		135	5¼
68	20		90	3½
50	10		45	1¾
32	0	Jan Feb Mar Apr May Jun Jul Aug Sep Oct Nov Dec	0	0

Key   — Average temperature   ▬ Rainfall

RUNAWAY PLANT
The fast-growing water hyacinth forms free-floating mats in the Paraguay River and lagoons of the Pantanal. It is an invasive species in many countries, but there may be potential to harness its large biomass for generating bio-energy.

WATER HYACINTH

...rd, and 325 species of fish

White-lipped peccary
Tayassu pecari

large, sharp, interlocking canine teeth

One of the most social mammals, white-lipped peccaries move, feed, and rest together in herds ranging from five to hundreds of individuals. With jaws capable of cracking palm nuts, a group of peccaries can fend off natural predators such as jaguars. Human hunters, however, prey on herds, killing large numbers at a time, which has had a devastating impact on the species.

↔ 30–39 in (76–100 cm)
⚖ 55–88 lb (25–40 kg)
✖ Vulnerable
🍽 Fruit, nuts, small vertebrates

Central to South America

◁ GROUP IDENTITY
Peccaries spread rump scent-gland secretions among members to create a musky herd odor.

Capybara
Hydrochoerus hydrochaeris

↔ 4 ft (1.2 m)
⚖ 77–145 lb (35–66 kg)
✖ Common
🍽 Aquatic plants, bark, grasses

Related to guinea pigs, the capybara is the world's largest living rodent, closer in size to a large domestic dog. It is heavy bodied, with short but sturdy limbs, and almost no tail. This placid, sociable mammal spends much of its time in rivers and lakes, partly to avoid predators such as wild dogs, pumas, and jaguars. Partially webbed, hooflike toes make it an excellent swimmer, and its eyes, nose, and ears sit high on its head, allowing it to see and breathe while its body remains underwater.

N. and E. South America

coarse but sparse hair

◁ PRECOCIOUS YOUNG
Capybara pups can follow their mothers into water shortly after birth and are able to graze within a week.

Giant otter
Pteronura brasiliensis

stout whiskers detect prey movements in water

The world's largest otter is also one of the rarest—only a few thousand are thought to remain in the wild. Nicknamed the "river wolf," this sinuous, web-footed, muscular member of the weasel family is one of South America's largest predators. It is fiercely territorial—which it has to be—in order to protect itself and its family from caimans, jaguars, pumas, and other threats in and around the river systems it calls home.

Scent warning

Giant otters live in groups of up to 20 animals: a male and female—which mate for life—and their offspring. The parents dig a den in riverbanks or under fallen logs and trample a section of the bank around it. All of the group scent-mark the perimeter of their territory with their anal glands to deter intruders. They fish in and patrol a section of the river around their den.

Giant otters are sociable—grooming, hunting, playing, and sleeping together. They have up to nine different vocalizations, from intense territorial screeches to chirps and whistles. Most cubs are born during the dry season, in litters of one to six, and are cared for by both parents and older siblings. Young otters stay with their families until they are at least two and a half years old.

↔ 3–5 ft (1–1.5 m)
⬛ 48–70 lb (22–32 kg)
⊗ Endangered
🍴 Fish, frogs, small caimans

N. to C. South America

well-webbed toes

▷ **SINUOUS BODY**
The giant otter's long, sinuous body, webbed feet, and flattened, wide-based tail mean it is well-adapted for diving and swimming, but its short limbs make it ungainly on land.

Hooded capuchin
Sapajus cay

distinctive black cap

Hooded capuchins are medium-sized, highly sociable monkeys, common in the tropical forests of the Amazon basin in South America. They get their name from the distinctive cap of dark fur at the top of their head, which resembles the hairstyle of a Capuchin monk.

Forest acrobats

These energetic and acrobatic monkeys move quickly through the lower and middle layers of the forest in groups of about 10–20, staying in touch with each other using a variety of birdlike, high-pitched calls.

Capuchins are highly intelligent and use a variety of tools to obtain food. In the lush swamps of the Pantanal, there is no shortage of palm nuts, which make up part of their diet. In northern populations, capuchins have been observed to crack open tough palm nuts by knocking one rock against another, but this behavior has yet to be confirmed in the south.

↔ 16–18 in (40–45 cm)
⬛ 7–8 lb (3–3.5 kg)
⊗ Common
🍴 Fruit, leaves, small animals

N. South America

◁ **FEEDING ON FRUIT**
Clasping a prized piece of fruit, this hooded capuchin will eat it in the company of its troop.

▷ **HEAD FIRST**
The giant otter's diet consists mainly of fish, including characins, which are related to piranhas and catfish. They also eat frogs, snakes, and turtles.

Jabiru stork
Jabiru mycteria

massive, upswept bill

One of South America's largest birds, the male jabiru has a massive bill, measuring 12–14 in (30–35 cm). Social waterside birds, jabirus use their bill to detect underwater prey just like a spoonbill, sweeping it sideways, partly open. The male's naked black neck inflates in courtship and aggressive displays, giving the bird its name, which means "swollen neck" in the local Tupi-Guarani language. Nests are huge structures of sticks, constructed in busy, mixed colonies of waterbirds and used for several years. Two to five eggs are laid, and the young fly when 15 weeks old. They need parental care for three more months, so most pairs nest every other year. Jabirus may live for more than 35 years.

↔ 4–5 ft (1.2–1.5 m)
⚖ 11–15 lb (5–7 kg)
✕ Common
🍴 Fish, amphibians, reptiles

Central and South America

wide wingtips

▷ **SOARING AWAY**
Jabirus look ungainly, and flapping flight with such great weight and broad wings is hard work. However, they soar beautifully and efficiently in rising air.

broad, red collar of bare skin

short tail

long legs trail behind when flying

gray spatulate bill

color varies
with diet

Roseate spoonbill

Platalea ajaja

The only spoonbill in the Americas, of six species worldwide, the roseate is also the world's only pink spoonbill. It has the hallmark long, thick, flattened bill that broadens out into a round tip or "spoon." When feeding, the spoonbill sweeps its bill, partly open, from side to side through shallow water; the bill snaps shut when small fish, water beetles, shrimp, or snails touch the sensitive nerve endings inside the spoon. Nostrils located at the base of the bill help the bird breathe with its bill immersed. Roseate spoonbills feed in rivermouths, mangrove swamps, and freshwater marshes inland, often with other wading birds.

white neck stays
outstretched
in flight

Colonial nesters

Breeding pairs nest in mixed-species colonies in nearby mangroves, trees, or reeds. Both sexes incubate between one and five eggs, which hatch after 22–24 days. The chicks' bills are initially short, straight, and soft, only becoming spoon-shaped after nine days. Both parents feed and protect the chicks, which are never left alone. They beg noisily and reach inside the parent's open bill to take regurgitated food. The young take off on their first flight at six weeks old, and can fly well at seven or eight weeks.

↔ 28–33 in (70–85 cm)
⚖ 3 lb (1.4 kg)
✗ Common
🍴 Fish, crustaceans, mollusks
🏠 🏞 🌱 〰 🦐

S. North
America,
Caribbean,
South America

△ COURTSHIP RITUAL
Waving their wings and grasping bill tips, roseate spoonbills perform a courtship dance on the ground, in water, or even high in a tree.

long legs ideal
for wading

▷ STUNNING COLORS
Certain crustaceans in the roseate spoonbill's diet feed on algae that have carotenoid pigments, giving the bird its striking pink color.

Golden tegu
Tupinambis teguixin

A flexible diet of insects, spiders, and worms, and also vertebrates from fish to mice, eggs, fruits, and shoots allows this large lizard to colonize many habitats. The female lays 20–30 eggs in a foliage-lined burrow and may stay with them for the cold season until they hatch up to five months later.

- ↔ 40 in (100 cm)
- ⚖ 9 lb (4 kg)
- ✕ Not known
- ⋔ Insects, birds, mammals
- 🏠 🏔 🌾 🏘
- ◔ N. to C. South America

long toes, sharp claws

tail forms half the length of body

▷ **KILLER BITE**
Strong and often aggressive, the golden tegu has a bite that can even crush bone.

Green anaconda
Eunectes murinus

The world's bulkiest and most powerful snake, the green anaconda is a nonvenomous member of the boa constrictor family. It often lies in shallow water waiting to ambush animals that come to the water's edge to drink. The snake grabs its prey with sharp, back-curved teeth, and quickly wraps it into the muscular coils. Each time the victim breathes out, the coils tighten, and death is usually from suffocation or heart failure. Almost any vertebrate prey is taken. Mating occurs in the dry season. The female may eat her much smaller male partner to nourish her pregnancy.

- ↔ 20–33 ft (6–10 m)
- ⚖ Up to 550 lb (250 kg)
- ✕ Vulnerable
- ⋔ Reptiles, fish, mammals
- 🏠 🏔 🌾 ≈
- ◔ N. to C. South America

▷ **AMBUSH CAMOUFLAGE**
Patterned for swampy vegetation and forest undergrowth, the anaconda slides silently after quarry, or strikes from the water's edge.

Giant parrot snake
Leptophis ahaetulla

whiplike tail

Also called the lora or giant lora, this snake is only mildly venomous. It is active during the day and rests at night. Well-camouflaged among dense undergrowth, it ambushes prey, or pursues them with great speed. It also explores crevices, caves, and vegetation for food.

If confronted, it rears up, gapes its mouth, hisses, and makes mock strikes. The female lays and leaves three to five eggs in a safe place, usually in a tree hole or mossy branch fork.

- ↔ 1.5–2 m (5–7 ft)
- ⚖ 2–3 lb (1–1.5 kg)
- ✕ Common
- ⋔ Geckos, tree frogs, birds
- 🏠 🏔 🌿 ≈ 🌱

Central America to South America

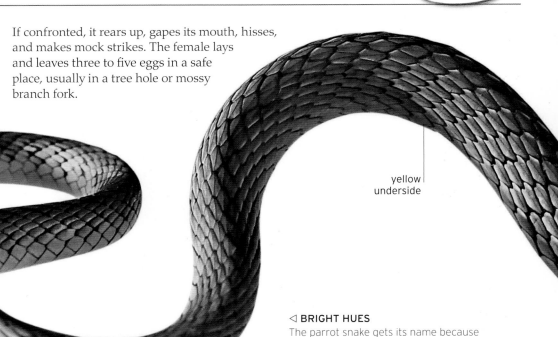

yellow underside

◁ **BRIGHT HUES**
The parrot snake gets its name because of its bright coloring: vivid green on the upper side and yellow underneath.

▷ **COMMUNAL FISHING**
Yacare caimans are often tolerant of others of their kind, crowding together at areas rich in sources of food, such as schools of fish, or at favored resting sites.

scales reinforced with bony plates

eyes and nostrils on top of head allow caiman to float low in water yet still see and breathe

broad snout

long, muscular tail

Yacare caiman

Caiman yacare

△ **TOOTHY GRIN**
The Yacare caiman has an average of 74 teeth. As the older ones fall out and leave gaps before replacement, the number may vary from 70 to 82.

▽ **BODY ARMOR**
Caiman have plates of bone, called osteoderms, that are embedded in the skin. These are smallest and most flexible on the head and underside of the body.

A close relative of the more northerly distributed common or spectacled caiman (*C. crocodilus*), the Yacare caiman is one of the major predators across much of its range. Its stronghold is the swampy wetlands of the Pantanal, where it is locally abundant, hauling out in large groups to bask on mats of floating plants or on banks. Its numbers here are counted in the millions—this may well be the largest crocodilian population on Earth.

Piranha prey

All five species of caiman are broad-snouted, Central and South American cousins of the North American alligator. The medium-sized Yacare caiman hunts mainly in water for snakes, amphibians, fish, and mollusks – in particular large water snails, called apple snails, that are crunched and swallowed in their shells. The local name "piranha caiman" may have arisen because the piranha makes up a considerable proportion of the Yacare caiman's diet. The name could also reflect its toothy appearance, similar to that of the piranha. It has sharp, conical teeth, and some of the larger teeth are still visible when its mouth is closed.

Finding new habitats

Before the global ban on the trade of wild crocodile skins in 1992, millions of Yacare caiman were killed during the 1970s and 1980s. This severe hunting pressure forced some Yacare caiman to move out of the wetlands and adapt to other habitats. These include drier grasslands, scrub, and even farmland, usually with an aquatic retreat such as a pool, ditch, or creek nearby. On land they lie in wait for passing lizards, birds, and mammals up to the size of capybara. In turn, younger Yacare caiman in particular fall prey to jaguars and anacondas.

Nesting on dry ground

The caimans' breeding peaks during the wet season when water levels are high. After mating, the female chooses a drier site, where she constructs a mound of heat-producing rotting vegetation in which to lay her eggs. The clutch size typically varies from 20–35. Incubation takes several weeks and the female usually guards the nest from raiders such as snakes, lizards, and hawks, but not so tenaciously as some crocodilians— the American alligator, for example. In some cases, the mother has left by the time the hatchlings emerge— which occurs mostly in March—so the young caiman must fend for themselves.

fourth tooth in lower jaw fits into socket in upper jaw when mouth closed

A caiman will get through up to **40 sets of teeth** in its **lifetime**

↔ 5–10 ft (1.5–3 m)
⬛ 55–120 lb (25–55 kg)
✖ Common
🍴 Fish, birds, mammals
🏠 🌿≈ ≈≈

C. to S. South America

ANDEAN ALTIPLANO
Silver salt flats hidden in the mountains

The Andean altiplano—literally, high plain—is the second largest mountainous plateau in the world after the Tibetan plateau in Asia. It is a landscape of extremes, surrounded by the mountains and volcanos of the central Andes. It has the world's highest navigable lake, Lake Titicaca, and the world's largest salt flat, the Salar de Uyuni. At an average altitude of 12,400 ft (3,750 m) above sea level, the air is thin, the sun is strong, winds can be fierce, and temperatures can fluctuate, making the altiplano a harsh place to live.

Harsh but fair

Despite the unforgiving conditions, the altiplano is also a land of strange beauty. The flat white expanse of the salt flats is, in places, adorned with three-foot-wide polygonal shapes created by the salt crystals, and incredible rock formations are sculpted by wind-blown sand. The mineral-rich lakes support flocks of flamingos numbering in the thousands, and the plains and slopes are home to herds of vicuñas, which are bred by Andean peoples for their wool, and llamas, bred for their wool, skin, and meat.

The Andean altiplano's vegetation, known as puna grassland, is dominated by grasses and shrubs, many of which form tussocks or cushions. Low-growing, mat-forming yareta plants and tall, branching cacti grow in the stony soils. The puna ecoregion is divided into wet, dry, and desert areas depending on the amount of rainfall they receive annually. One region in the center of the Andes receives a meager 16 in (400 mm) of rainfall a year and experiences an eight-month long dry season.

STARTLING SPECIALIST
This frog has evolved to survive in the most oxygen-impoverished lakes on Earth. Large folds of extra skin give it an extra-large body surface area. This allows it to maximize absorption of oxygen from the water and the atmosphere.

TITICACA WATER FROG

HARDY CROPS
Quinoa is well-adapted to the dry sandy soils of the altiplano and has been grown as a food crop by Andean peoples for thousands of years. The altiplano is one of few places where agriculture is practiced 11,500 ft (3,500 m) above sea level.

QUINOA

Lake Titicaca is the highest navigable lake

Uyuni is the largest salt flat on Earth

ANDEAN FLAMINGOS

THREE FLAMINGOS
Three of the world's six flamingo species live in the altiplano. James and Andean flamingos are found in the region year-round, staying warm near hot springs during winter. In the summer, they are joined by flocks of Chilean flamingos.

reddish brown legs

Culpeo
Pseudalopex culpaeus

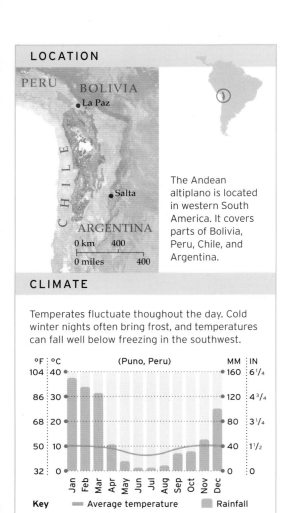

PERU
BOLIVIA
La Paz
CHILE
Salta
ARGENTINA
0 km   400
0 miles   400

The Andean altiplano is located in western South America. It covers parts of Bolivia, Peru, Chile, and Argentina.

CLIMATE

Temperates fluctuate thoughout the day. Cold winter nights often bring frost, and temperatures can fall well below freezing in the southwest.

°F	°C	(Puno, Peru)	MM	IN
104	40		160	6¹/₄
86	30		120	4³/₄
68	20		80	3¹/₄
50	10		40	1¹/₂
32	0		0	0

Jan Feb Mar Apr May Jun Jul Aug Sep Oct Nov Dec

Key — Average temperature   ▢ Rainfall

The second largest wild canid in South America, the culpeo is also known as the Andean fox, a name that reflects many of its characteristics. Like most fox species, it is an opportunistic hunter, feeding on wild berries as well as rodents and introduced European hares and rabbits. It also takes young domestic livestock such as lambs occasionally, which brings it into conflict with farmers.

↔ 2–4 ft (0.6–1.2 m)
⚖ 11–30 lb (5–13.5 kg)
✖ Locally common
🐾 Rodents, hares, fruit, insects
🏠 🌳 🏔 🌵

W. to S. South America

◁ **HOME IN THE ROCKS**
Culpeos are usually solitary, but mated pairs stay together for up to five months, making dens in caves, which both parents guard from predators.

Northern viscacha
Lagidium peruanum

The northern viscacha resembles a long-tailed rabbit, but this high-altitude rodent is more closely related to chinchillas. Its soft, ultra-dense coat protects it from frigid temperatures, while thin-walled arteries help it to survive in the oxygen-depleted conditions of the high Andes.

↔ 12–18 in (30–45 cm)
⚖ 2–4 lb (0.9–1.8 kg)
✖ Locally common
🐾 Grass, lichen, moss
🏠 🏔

W. South America

COVETED FUR
The long-tailed chinchilla's ultra-dense fur keeps it warm in the freezing temperatures of the high plateau. However, its fur became its downfall because chinchillas were trapped by hunters for the pet and fur trade. They are now critically endangered.

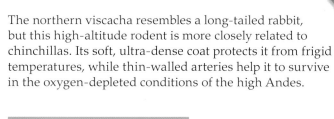

season lasts eight months

CHINCHILLA

whiskers around 6 in (15 cm) long

▷ **CLIFF DWELLER**
Viscacha colonies are often located on steep cliffs, which provide protection from predators—as well as being prime spots for basking.

Vicuña

Vicugna vicugna

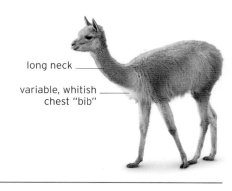

long neck

variable, whitish chest "bib"

A small, slender relative of the llama and the alpaca, the vicuña is well adapted to life in the high Andes. It lives in small family groups in arid meadows above 11,500 ft (3,500 m) and sometimes as high as 18,850 ft (5,750 m), but always below the snow line. In this environment, days are frequently sunny and warm, so tough thickets of grass can grow. At night, the thin air chills rapidly and temperatures plunge below freezing. The vicuña has a thick fleece of fine-layered hairs, which traps warm air around its body and keeps the cold out.

Unique teeth

The vicuña has unique teeth for a hoofed mammal. The front teeth (incisors) in its lower jaw grow constantly, like those of a rodent, and have enamel only on the front. The incisors are kept sharp by constant contact with the hard dental pad in the upper jaw as the vicuña relentlessly uses its molars to chew the tough grass. Vulnerable to attack on open grassland, vicuñas are always on the lookout for predators, such as foxes. They have excellent hearing and vision and when a predator is spotted, they give a warning whistle.

Families, led by a single male, consist of about five females and their young. The groups stay small, with only about 10 members, because the chief male drives away the young at the age of 10 months. Young vicuñas live alone or form single-sex herds until they start their own families at about the age of two. Unusually, vicuñas have separate feeding and sleeping territories, which are mostly marked out with dung. Vicuñas need to drink water every day so their feeding territory has to have a source of fresh water.

↔ 5 ft (1.5 m)
⚖ 88–120 lb (40–55 kg)
✖ Locally common
🌾 Grass
🏠 ⛰ 🌵 🌿 🌾

W. South America

△ PLAY FIGHTING
Young male vicuñas often play fight and bite each other. The fights become more serious as they reach sexual maturity, and the victor will join a female-only herd to start his own family.

▽ DAILY MIGRATION
Vicuña families spend the night in the relative safety of steeper slopes. They climb back down to graze in the high plains by day.

Titicaca grebe
Rollandia microptera

So adapted to life in water that it cannot fly and can barely stand, this flightless grebe is found only on lakes in the Lake Titicaca basin. Populations on separate freshwater lakes have lived in isolation for a very long time and are vulnerable to habitat change. A few thousand pairs live on reed-fringed lakes, with areas of open water, 9,850 ft (3,000 m) above sea level. The Titicaca grebe dives skilfully for fish—it mostly eats pupfish—and skitters across the water with raised wings. It can breed in any month of the year, making a platform of damp vegetation in which the female lays two eggs and can have several broods each year.

- ↔ 11–18 in (28–46 cm)
- 🏋 21 oz (595 g)
- ⊗ Endangered
- 🍴 Fish
- 🏠 ⛰ 🌾 〰

W. South America

◁ DAGGERLIKE BILL
Grebes have sharply pointed bills. The Titicaca grebe's bill has a red upper and yellow lower mandible.

Andean flicker
Colaptes rupicola

Flickers are New World woodpeckers, noted for their terrestrial feeding behavior, and the Andean flicker is the most terrestrial of them all. It is widespread in bushy habitats and open grassland at altitudes of 6,500–16,500 ft (2,000–5,000 m).

Barbed tongue
Andean flickers feed in groups on the ground, digging or scraping around grass tussocks with their large bills to reveal ants or beetle and moth larvae. They seize their prey with the barbed tip of their long, extendable tongue. Sociable even when nesting, they build a dozen or more burrows in road cuttings or sandy or earth cliffs. The 3–5 ft (1–1.5 m) long burrows lead to a 12 in (30 cm) nesting chamber that holds up to four chicks.

- ↔ 13 in (33 cm)
- 🏋 5–7 oz (142–200 g)
- ⊗ Locally common
- 🍴 Insect larvae
- 🏠 🌳 ⛰ 🌿

NW. to SW. South America

◁ FEMALE FLICKER
The striking black mustache combined with the red patch on the back of the neck identifies this flicker as female.

long, barred tail

bold, white ruff

Andean condor

Vultur gryphus

The Andean condor has the largest wing area of any bird, and its wingspan is more than 10 ft (3 m). Condors rely entirely on constant winds and rising thermal air currents to fly. They can glide great distances using gravity alone —energetic flapping is not an option for such a heavy bird. Fortunately, perpetual winds allow condors to search beaches, plateaus, and valleys, confident they can regain height easily.

Condors feed on carrion, using their strong bills to tear the hides and flesh. Unlike eagles and hawks, the condors' long legs are used simply for standing, not for killing prey. In the past, Andean condors mainly fed on vicuñas, guanacos, and seals, but nowadays they more often eat dead domestic livestock. Although no longer common, in their core range flocks of 30 or 40 condors still gather around large carcasses.

On the wane

Andean condors breed only once every two years and miss a year if food is short. The whole reproduction cycle is long and slow: females lay just one egg, which hatches after 56 to 58 days, and then it is six months before the chick can fly. Chicks rely on their parents for several months more. Young birds do not breed for six years, often more. Condors balance this low "output" with very low natural mortality—they can live for 70 years—but whole populations are extremely vulnerable to human persecution. They are simply unable to make up lost numbers quickly, if at all.

△ COMMUNAL ROOSTING
Groups of condors roost in remote caves and on sheltered ledges. In the morning, they leave their perch and rise effortlessly on thermal currents.

↔ 3–4 ft (1–1.3 m)
⚖ 24–33 lb (11–15 kg)
✖ Near threatened
🦅 Dead mammals
🏠 ⛰ 🌵 🌿

NW. to SW.
South
America

outspread flight
feathers

△ **PERFECT FLIGHT**
Gliding at speeds of up to 200 km/h
(125 mph), the Andean condor covers
extensive distances.

Fabian's lizard
Liolaemus fabiani

First identified as a distinct species in 1983, Fabian's lizard (also called Yañez's iguana) is endemic to the largest saltflat in Chile, Salar de Atacama. This lizard scampers around by day among the salty lumps and hypersaline shallows, even when surface temperatures exceed 113°F (45°C). It copes with drinking salty water by excreting excess salt from parts on its snout called lateral nasal glands—similar to its large cousin, the marine iguana. The lizard hunts flies, grabbing them in midair, but also takes beetles and other small prey.

Bars and stripes
Fabian's lizard has a big, strong head, a wide-gaping mouth, and robust limbs. Its "beaded" scales—small, smooth, shiny, and rounded—form 11 to 13 untidy, variable stripes or bars of black and sulfur-yellow to orange-red, on a speckly background along the flanks. This coloration fades on the underside.

Particularly aggressive about territory as well as mating partners, males display their striking side patterns to rivals. They also flick their limbs and tail, and clack their jaws at each other.

↔ 6 in (15 cm)
⚖ 1–2 oz (30–50 g)
✖ Not known
〰 Flies, beetles, other insects
🏠 ⛰

Chile (Salar
de Atacama)

▽ **AT HOME ON SALT**
Fabian's lizard is active by day among the salty accretions and saline pools. It snaps with lightning speed at passing flies.

△ **NOT FOR SHARING**
Males will deliver vicious bites when disputes over territory or females arise. Their jaws are even strong enough to draw blood through their tough scales.

ARGENTINE PAMPAS
One of the richest grazing areas in the world

The term pampas describes the wide, flat, grassy plains of southern South America, covering an area of more than 300,000 sq miles (750,000 sq km). It was named after a Quechua Indian word meaning flat surface. In North America, this sort of habitat is referred to as prairie and in Eurasia as steppe. The dominant vegetation comprises perennial grasses, such as stipas, and herbs.

Grasses are able to regenerate after the frequent wildfires, but few trees can survive them and so they are seldom found on the pampas. The scarcity of trees for shade and roosting has led to many animals burrowing underground for shelter.

Gauchos—cowboys—have herded cows, horses, and sheep on the grasslands for at least 200 years. The temperate climate and rich, fertile soils of the pampas also make it very good for cultivating crops such as soybeans, wheat, maize, and grape vines.

Overgrazing, habitat loss, and fertilizer use has diminished and degraded the natural pampas environment, making it less suitable for its native species. The Argentine pampas ecosystem is classified as an endangered ecoregion by the World Wide Fund for Nature (WWF) because none of the natural pampas is protected, despite plans by the Argentine government to create a national park.

Endangered ecosystem

Very little of the pampas remains pristine and undisturbed by human activity, and the original vegetation of coarse grasses has been greatly reduced.

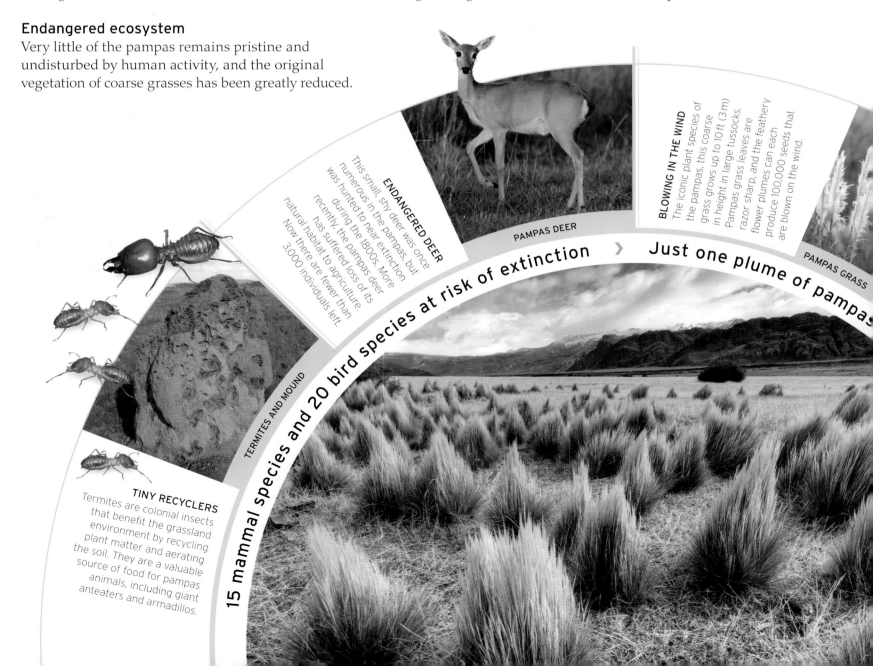

ENDANGERED DEER
This small, shy deer was once numerous in the pampas, but was hunted to near extinction during the 1800s. More recently, the pampas deer has suffered loss of its natural habitat to agriculture. Now there are fewer than 3,000 individuals left.

PAMPAS DEER

BLOWING IN THE WIND
The iconic plant species of the pampas, this coarse grass grows up to 10 ft (3 m) in height in large tussocks. Pampas grass leaves are razor sharp, and the feathery flower plumes can each produce 100,000 seeds that are blown on the wind.

PAMPAS GRASS

15 mammal species and 20 bird species at risk of extinction

Just one plume of pampas

TERMITES AND MOUND

TINY RECYCLERS
Termites are colonial insects that benefit the grassland environment by recycling plant matter and aerating the soil. They are a valuable source of food for pampas animals, including giant anteaters and armadillos.

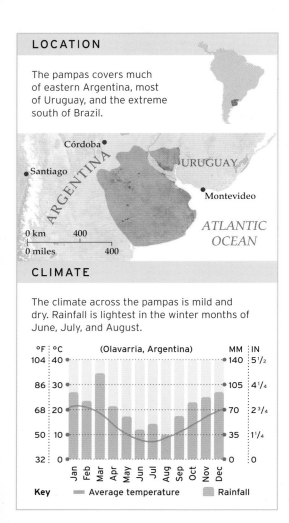

elongated finger bones support wing membrane

Vampire bat
Desmodus rotundus

As its name suggests, the common vampire bat feeds on blood, mainly of mammals such as tapirs, peccaries, agoutis, and sea lions along with domesticated species such as cattle and horses. Two other species of vampire bat, also living in Central and South America, feed predominantly on bird blood. The common vampire bat can crawl over the ground with amazing speed and agility, propped on its forearms and back legs. It usually lands close to a resting animal and uses its heat-sensitive nose pad to seek areas of warm blood vessels close to the skin. Once bitten, the anticoagulant properties of the bat's saliva help to keep the victim's blood flowing freely.

Reciprocal regurgitation

The common vampire bat has a communal roost in a hollow tree, cave, mine, or old building, which it shares with hundreds of others. Not only will adult females regurgitate blood to their offspring, they also share blood with hungry roost mates. Bats are more likely to help one another if they are related or have roosted together for a substantial amount of time. To judge whether a fellow bat is hungry, they engage in mutual grooming sessions that allow them to feel how distended each others' stomachs are before regurgitating.

↔ 3–4 in (7.6–10 cm)
⚖ ⁵⁄₈–2 oz (19–57 g)
✖ Common
🩸 Blood

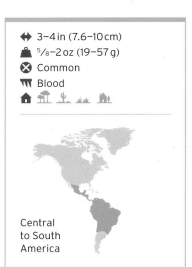

Central to South America

▽ BLOOD LICKER
The vampire bat's razor sharp teeth, long tongue, grooved chin, and short nose are all adaptations for getting access to and lapping up blood.

A vampire bat can **drink 50 percent of its body weight** in 30 minutes

black stripe with a white
or cream border

Giant anteater

Myrmecophaga tridactyla

The giant anteater has a large, tube-shaped skull but a small brain. It has poor eyesight, yet its sense of smell is 40 times greater than that of a human. The tiny mouth at the end of its snout contains no teeth, but its 2-ft- (60-cm-) long tongue is covered in microscopic spines and sticky saliva, which can lap up as many as 35,000 termites per day. The anteater shuffles when walking, yet runs quickly and swims well.

Ripping claws

Ants, termites, and their eggs make up most of the giant anteater's diet. It uses its powerful foreclaws to rip into anthills and termite mounds, and also against predators such as jaguars, pumas, or humans. A giant anteater is not aggressive but can defend itself well as it stands on its hindlegs—balancing its body on its massive tail—and lashes out with its clawed forelimbs. Solitary except when seeking mates, giant anteaters adapt their behavior according to their proximity to humans.

Those living near populated areas are generally nocturnal (the species is threatened by hunting), whereas animals in remote regions feed during the day. They sleep in the shelter of a bush or hollow, with their extremely bushy tail draped over their head and body for warmth.

Once they have mated, female giant anteaters give birth to one offspring after a gestation of about six months. The baby clings to its mother's back for much of its first year, and will stay with her until it is about two years old.

Giant anteaters **flick their tongues** in and out about **150 times per minute**

↔ 3–7 ft (1–2 m)
⬛ 49–86 lb (18–40 kg)
✖ Vulnerable
🐜 Ants, termites
🏠 🌳 🍄 🌾

S. Central
America to S.
South America

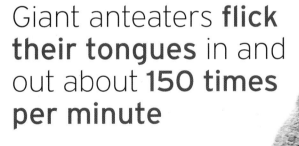

long, tubelike snout

△ ANT FEAST
A giant anteater feeds from one anthill only for a few moments before moving on to the next to ensure it does not exhaust its food supply.

◁ KNUCKLE-WALKER
Giant anteaters have a shuffling gait. They walk on the knuckles of their forelimbs whereas they keep the heels of their hindlimbs on the ground.

long, bushy, brown tail

Patagonian mara
Dolichotis patagonum

A mara looks like a small deer when on the move. When seated on its haunches, it could be mistaken for a giant rabbit. It is, however, a large, long-legged relative of the cavy, or guinea pig. Maras live in arid grasslands, where they spend the day grazing on sparse shoots and herbs. As temperatures drop at night, they retreat to burrows, which they dig using the sharp claws on their forefeet. While foraging, maras are preyed upon by foxes, pampas cats, and birds of prey. In defense, they operate in pairs— a male and female that stay together for life. While one feeds, the other keeps watch. If a threat is spotted, they gallop away, reaching a top speed of 28 mph (45 km/h).

↔ 27–30 in (69–75 cm)
⚖ 20–35 lb (9–16 kg)
✖ Near threatened
🌾 Grasses, herbs, seeds

S. South America

◁ LIFE IN A COMMUNE
Maras give birth in summer, which is also the rainy season. Pups are born in communal burrows occupied by several breeding pairs.

Six-banded armadillo
Euphractus sexcinctus

This native of the savannas digs out most of its food, such as roots, with its large forefeet. It also eats fallen fruit and licks up ants with its long, feathery tongue. The six-banded armadillo lives alone in burrows it digs about three feet into the ground. Marking territory with scent from a gland under the tail, it bites and scratches other armadillos that stray inside. The armadillo is a good swimmer, and swallows air before entering water to aid its bouyancy.

↔ 16–20 in (40–50 cm)
⚖ 7–14 lb (3.2–6.5 kg)
✖ Common
🌾 Roots, fruit, insects, carrion

C. to E. South America

▽ BODY ARMOR
The armadillo buries itself when it spots predators. The armored body plates protect any exposed upper body part, while the armadillo wedges itself into its burrow.

six-banded armadillos have six, seven, or eight bands

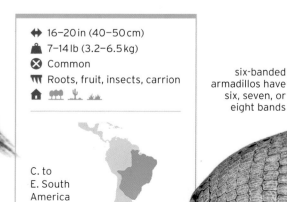

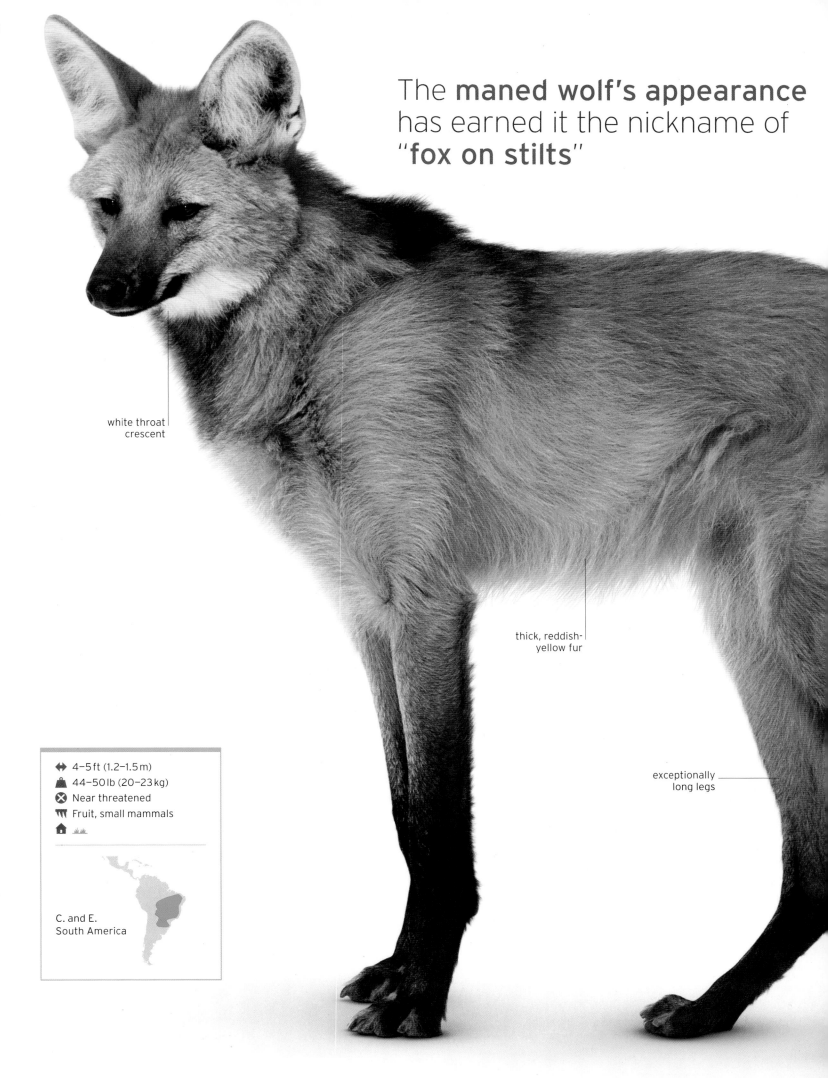

The **maned wolf's appearance** has earned it the nickname of **"fox on stilts"**

white throat crescent

thick, reddish-yellow fur

exceptionally long legs

↔ 4–5 ft (1.2–1.5 m)
⚖ 44–50 lb (20–23 kg)
✖ Near threatened
🍖 Fruit, small mammals
🏠 ⸛

C. and E. South America

Maned wolf

Chrysocyon brachyurus

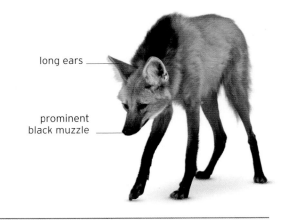

long ears

prominent
black muzzle

A slender fox- or wolf-like animal, the maned wolf has a different evolutionary lineage from both groups. This little-studied animal is probably an ancient relic that became an isolated species in South America thousands of years ago.

Superficially foxlike

Although not related, a resting maned wolf looks remarkably like a red fox. Large, whitish, triangular, and very mobile ears, and a white throat crescent beneath a prominent black muzzle, give it a distinctly foxlike look. Once it stands up and moves, however, it looks quite different with its high stance and long-striding walk.

The wolf has a long, black crest or rippling mane between the shoulders, and a striking white-tipped tail. Long legs allow it to move easily and see greater distances in the tall, dense grass in which it lives. It has a slightly awkward, undulating gait in open spaces, but in the long grass, it forces its way through with a slower, forward-reaching stride and short leaps.

Lone hunter

The maned wolf is a loner—more like a fox than a wolf —although several may gather where food is abundant. It uses its excellent hearing to locate, stalk, and pounce on prey, killing it by biting on or around the neck or spine. The wolf prefers mammals, mainly pacas—large rodents—and will eat armadillos, birds, and even fish. However, the maned wolf is remarkable for the large proportion of vegetable matter in its diet. It is fond of the tomatolike wolf apple, the fruit of the lobeira plant, and regularly eats various other fruits and roots. This fruit-rich diet is essential to the animals' health; when captive maned wolves have been given a pure meat diet, they have developed kidney and bladder stones.

Nightly patrols

Maned wolves create tracks through grassland by using regular routes in their nighttime patrols. They defend territories based on these paths, using strongly scented urine as a marker. Females give birth to between two and six pups, which are dependent on their parents for up to a year. The males may help feed the young.

Maned wolves are threatened by habitat loss, and are vulnerable to road traffic. They are sometimes killed by domestic dogs and are susceptible to their diseases, and myths about the medicinal value of their body parts sometimes lead to persecution by humans. Maned wolves require large areas of open ground, and are difficult to keep and even harder to breed in zoos. Their conservation relies on the protection of large areas of suitable habitat.

◁ **LONG-LEGGED ROAMER**
The maned wolf uses its long legs in an efficient, loping gait, covering long distances each night through its 12-20 sq mile (30-55 sq km) territory.

▷ **YOUNG PUP**
This pup, almost five weeks old and becoming increasingly inquisitive, will stay with the family group for up to a year.

△ **SOCIAL ENCOUNTER**
Prominent ears help maned wolves communicate: one lays them flat, in fear or submission, the other raises them, showing dominance.

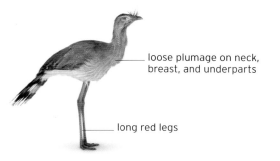

loose plumage on neck, breast, and underparts

long red legs

Red-legged seriema

Cariama cristata

Tall, long-legged, and gangly, seriemas share much of the same range and habitat as the larger rheas. They use the abundant termite mounds in grassy, savannalike scrub and bush as lookouts and song posts. The territorial males make the air ring with long series of loud yelps, with abrupt changes of pitch. These extraordinary sounds are audible over several miles. The head is flung back, bill wide open, almost touching the back at the loudest moments.

Short sprints

The red-legged seriema's short-toed feet are adapted for running—in short bursts of up to 25 mph (40 km/h)— to escape predators, and for pursuing and stamping on tough and lively prey. The seriema climbs around in the lower branches of trees or flies up higher to roost. The nest is built within reach of a short series of fluttering leaps. Otherwise, flight is infrequent and short-lived, with quick flaps of the wings followed by long glides.

Seriemas kill prey such as snakes by beating them on the ground with their bill. They are sometimes kept as "watchdogs" among chickens to keep them safe. Seriemas prefer open and bushy areas, so are not threatened by loss of habitat and, at times, may even benefit from deforestation.

↔ 30–36 in (76–91 cm)
🏋 3 lb (1.4 kg)
✖ Common
🍴 Lizards, birds, rodents
🏠 ᭞᭞

E. South America

permanently raised crest of feathers at base of bill

△ **THREAT DISPLAY**
Males sing loud duets to reinforce territorial claims. If they still chance to meet, they use ritual postures to settle differences without resorting to fighting.

◁ **DISTINCTIVE BILL**
A seriema's broad, hooked bill is its main tool, grabbing, manipulating, and breaking apart large prey such as lizards, snakes, and tough beetles.

finely barred body plumage

Burrowing owl

white speckles on brown body

Athene cunicularia

Short-grass prairies, sagebrush, and semidesert are the preferred habitats of the burrowing owl, but it will make do with cultivated ground, even golf courses and airfields. Roosting and nesting in holes, the owls may take over empty mammal burrows. They hunt by day and night, watching for prey such as small rodents from low mounds, bobbing and turning their heads to fix their victim's precise position. Viscachas and prairie dogs keep the grass short, giving the owls a better view.

- ↔ 8–10 in (20–25 cm)
- ⚖ 5–9 oz (141–255 g)
- ✖ Common
- 🍴 Insects, reptiles, birds

North America, Central America, and South America

Nests are **lined with dried dung**, perhaps to mask the owls' scent from predators

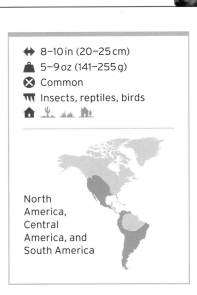

△ **IN THE BURROW**
Several pairs nest close together, each in a 3-ft- (1-m-) long burrow in soft ground containing between two and 12 eggs.

Greater rhea
Rhea americana

Open grassland is typical greater rhea habitat, where South America's largest bird hunts for large insects, reptiles, and seeds. Each male makes a nest and displays to attract six or seven females in succession. The females lay eggs in the nests, before moving on to mate with other males. Each male incubates 20–30 eggs and cares for the young by itself, or with a subordinate male "helper." Male rheas are very protective about their young, charging even at females during this period.

- ↔ 3–5 ft (0.9–1.5 m)
- ⚖ 33–66 lb (15–30 kg)
- ✖ Near threatened
- 🍴 Seeds, fruit, insects
- 🧭 E. and SE. South America

◁ **GROUNDED**
One of the world's large flightless birds, the rhea is more like Australia's emu than Africa's ostrich.

Argentine horned frog

hornlike projection

Ceratophrys ornata

This burly ground frog is also known as the Argentine wide-mouthed frog or the Pac-Man frog because of its tendency to gobble up anything that will fit in its immense mouth. The Argentine horned frog employs a sit-and-wait strategy to capture prey, lying hidden among fallen leaves with just its eyes and mouth showing. The frog's "horns" are small projections above the eyes, which disrupt the animal's body shape and help with camouflage. When suitable-sized prey comes within striking distance, the frog lunges forward and engulfs it within its cavernous mouth.

△ **FEARLESS DEFENDER**
The aggressively territorial Argentine horned frog will take on larger and more powerful encroachers fearlessly.

- ↔ 4–5 in (10–13 cm)
- 🌱 Spring
- ✖ Near threatened
- 🍴 Frogs, songbirds, snakes
- 🧭 SE. South America

GALAPAGOS ISLANDS
The island group that inspired the theory of evolution

The Galapagos is a remote archipelago of volcanic islands in the vast blue of the Pacific Ocean. These islands formed when the Earth's crust moved over a hot spot in the mantle (a warmer layer of semisolid rock below the crust), causing it to melt and form a sequence of volcanoes. Many erupting volcanoes reached the sea's surface before becoming extinct, and the cooled lava created the Galapagos Islands. Due to their remoteness from other land masses, these islands have unique endemic species found nowhere else on Earth.

The story of evolution
Charles Darwin, a British naturalist, traveled to the Galapagos Islands in 1835. What he saw there helped him develop his theory of evolution by natural selection, whereby species change as generations pass. Darwin saw fascinating examples of divergence—where animals on different islands had developed sufficient differences to become separate species. As a result, the Galapagos Islands have many unique animals, such as the various finches and giant tortoises.

Three major currents converge here, bringing nutrients and plankton that support fish, marine mammals, and seabirds. The islands are periodically affected by El Niño, which causes warmer and wetter conditions that can benefit plants and land animals, but is devastating to marine life.

DIFFICULT TO ESCAPE
Historically, there were no land-based predators on the Galapagos Islands and so this cormorant lost the ability to fly. Since the arrival of humans, its numbers have decreased because of introduced predators such as cats, dogs, and pigs.

FLIGHTLESS CORMORANT

PIONEER SPECIES
The lava cactus is quick to colonize the bare rock of lava fields. Its fleshy stems store water and are a valuable source of moisture for wildlife including land iguanas and tortoises. Cactus finches assist in populating new areas by distributing its seeds.

LAVA CACTUS

SALLY LIGHTFOOT CRAB

Approximately 127 islands and islets in total ›

A World Heritage Site since 1978 ›

CLEANER CRABS
Bright red Sally Lightfoot crabs have a mutually beneficial relationship with marine iguanas. They keep the resting iguanas clean by picking ticks and algae off their skin. The crabs eat what they find and so receive a reward for their work.

LOCATION

The Galapagos Islands lie in the Pacific Ocean, around 560 miles (900 km) due west of the coast of South America.

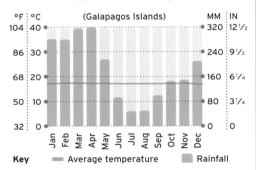

PACIFIC OCEAN

Galapagos Islands

Pinta
Marchena
Fernandina
San Salvador
Santa Cruz
Isabela
San Cristóbal
Puerto Isidro Ayora
Puerto Villamil
Puerto Baquerizo Moreno
Santa María
Española

0 km 100
0 miles 100

CLIMATE

The average temperature varies by a mere 1.26°F (0.7°C) throughout a year, whereas the rainfall varies drastically, especially during El Niño years.

(Galapagos Islands chart: °F/°C axis 104/40, 86/30, 68/20, 50/10, 32/0; MM/IN axis 320/12½, 240/9½, 160/6¼, 80/3¼, 0/0; months Jan–Dec)

Key — Average temperature — Rainfall

Galapagos sea lion
Zalophus wollebaeki

streamlined body

powerful fore flippers

Unlike its relatives, the true seals and walruses, the Galapagos sea lion is an otarid, or eared, seal. External ear flaps are one difference between otarids and true seals; another is the ability to work their hind flippers independently, which, along with stronger fore flippers, allows sea lions to move more easily on land. Like most sea lions, they can move rapidly due to their rotatable pelvis.

Colonies of curiosity
Highly social, sea lions are coastal mammals, feeding in ocean shallows before returning to the shore to sleep, rest, and nurse their young in colonies ruled by an adult male. Their inquisitive nature, particularly that of younger sea lions, brings them into contact with human activities such as fishing—often with fatal consequences. In addition, they are severely impacted by El Niño weather events: climatic changes that affect Pacific winds, ocean currents, and temperature patterns every few years, leading to a sudden depletion of fish in the area. During the El Niños of 1997–98, sea lion numbers in the Galapagos Islands fell by almost 50 percent.

↔ 4–5 ft (1.2–1.5 m)
⬤ 110–550 lb (50–250 kg)
✖ Endangered
🍴 Fish, squid, crustaceans

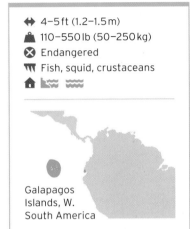

Galapagos Islands, W. South America

▽ **STRONG SWIMMERS**
Unlike true seals, which swim mainly by moving their rear flippers, sea lions use powerful, elongated front flippers to pull themselves along.

COMMON ANCESTOR
Seven species of colorful lava lizard live in the Galapagos; one species occurs on several islands, but the others are found on only one island each. Like the Galapagos finches, all lava lizard species evolved from a single ancestor.

endemic species identified

LAVA LIZARD

Sea lion **pups** start to develop **swimming skills** at **one to two weeks**

long tail used as rudder when flying

▽ **ATTENTION SEEKER**
The male's throat pouch expands into a red balloon as he sits on a treetop nest, displaying to female frigatebirds flying overhead.

Great frigatebird
Fregata minor

The great frigatebird looks almost prehistoric, with its long beak, forked tail, and huge, pointed, angular wings set in an inverted "W." It has the largest wing area to body mass, or the lowest wing-loading, of any bird. This, together with the large tail spread wide or closed to a single point, makes the frigatebird extremely stable as it soars effortlessly for hours, as well as supremely agile while dashing to grab flying fish or chase other birds. It also steals food from seabirds, especially boobies, harassing them until they regurgitate. The frigatebird flies over the sea, but avoids landing on water because it lacks fully waterproof plumage. It nests in trees on remote tropical islands in the Pacific, Indian, and South Atlantic oceans. Pairs take turns to incubate one egg for a period of 55 days.

↔ 34–41in (85–105cm)
⚖ 2–3lb (1–1.5kg)
✖ Common
🍴 Fish, squid, seabird chicks
🏠 〰〰

Tropical Pacific, South Atlantic, and Indian Oceans

inflated pouch

Frigatebirds **rarely land during the day,** except when breeding

Galapagos penguin
Spheniscus mendiculus

The only penguin that lives north of the Equator, the Galapagos penguin breeds mostly on the Fernandina and Isabela islands of the Galapagos archipelago. Swimming in the Cromwell Current by day, they exploit small schooling fish such as mullets and sardines—the cold ocean current provides a higher nutrient content than warm, tropical waters. The penguins visit land at night, when it is both cooler and safer for flightless birds. Like Antarctic penguins, they can flap their tiny wings to lose excess body heat.

Rare bird
The Galapagos penguin is one of the world's rarest penguins, with fewer than 1,000 breeding pairs. Their breeding season is regulated by the availability of food. Climatic events such as El Niño cycles warm the waters around the islands, reducing fish numbers as they depart for cooler waters. The resulting food shortage makes the penguins skip an entire breeding season.

Galapagos penguins are also threatened by pollution, intensive fishing, and predators such as cats and dogs that human settlers have brought to the islands.

↔ 21in (53cm)
⚖ 4–5lb (1.8–2.3kg)
✖ Endangered
🍴 Mullets, sardines
🏠 〰〰

Galapagos Islands

▷ **PARTNERS FOR LIFE**
Galapagos penguins mate for life. The female lays one or two eggs in deep rock crevices to keep them cool. Both parents take turns incubating them for a period of 38-40 days.

large feet fully webbed across four toes

Blue-footed booby
Sula nebouxii

The male blue-footed booby relies on his colorful feet to impress potential mates. The blue color is enhanced by pigments that come from a regular supply of fresh fish. The brighter the feet, the better nourished the male is, showing how good a provider he will be for offspring. Females tend to mate with younger males, as the brightness declines with age. Closely related to gannets, and more loosely to pelicans and cormorants, boobies have broad webbing across all four toes.

Survival of the fittest
About half of the world's blue-footed booby population is centered in the Galapagos Islands, although few young have been reared there recently. This is mainly due to a drop in the sardine population on which the booby feeds almost exclusively. The breeding season is short and the female lays two or three eggs, which hatch several days apart.

When there is enough food, the different sizes of chicks allow them all to be fed without much rivalry. Should food be scarce, the older, bigger chick kills its siblings and is more likely to survive. If more than one survives, the smaller chick will have as good a chance of becoming a productive adult.

↔ 30–35 in (75–90 cm)
⚖ 3–4 lb (1.3–1.8 kg)
✗ Common
🍴 Sardines, other fish
🏠

W. Mexico to NW. South America, Galapagos Islands

▷ **COURTSHIP DANCE**
Courting blue-footed boobies show off the brilliance of their webbed feet, lifting them alternately in a ritualized, waddling dance.

Waved albatross
Phoebastria irrorata

dull yellow bill

The only tropical albatross, the waved albatross, breeds on the Galapagos Islands and feeds off the coast of Ecuador and Peru. It forages up to 60 miles (100 km) from its nest, where fish are found close to the surface. Waved albatrosses use their long, slender wings to exploit air currents to travel far with little effort.

chestnut-brown plumage

↔ 34–37 in (86–93 cm)
⚖ 7–9 lb (3–4 kg)
✗ Critically endangered
🍴 Fish, squid, crustaceans
🏠
🧭 Galapagos Islands

△ **CALLING OUT FOR A MATE**
Albatrosses mate for life after an elaborate courtship ritual involving a precise sequence of moves, such as circling and bowing their bills.

Woodpecker finch
Camarhynchus pallidus

Finches in the Galapagos Islands have evolved into 15 distinct species, each with a different feeding strategy. In wet periods, the woodpecker finch feeds on abundant insects. However, in the hot, dry season it finds half its food by using a special tool—one of very few birds to do so. It wields a fine twig or cactus spine to remove grubs from crevices in bark or from tunnels bored into wood. The finch tests several tools and chooses the right one for the task, at times even snapping a twig to shorten it and make it more effective. It then goes on to use its favorite tool at several sites.

△ **BILL EXTENDER**
The woodpecker finch can use its bill to find grubs, but using a long spine means it can probe more deeply.

↔ 6 in (15 cm)
⚖ ¹¹⁄₁₆–¹¹⁄₁₆ oz (20–31 g)
✗ Locally common
🍴 Insects, larvae
🏠
🧭 Galapagos Islands

Galapagos tortoise

Chelonoidis nigra

five-toed forefoot

The Galápagos tortoise is famous both for its enormous size and for being one of the world's longest-lived animals. Six of the Galápagos Islands are home to 14 different kinds of this giant land reptile. Some experts regard them as subspecies or races; others class them as separate species in view of genetic studies. However, the Galápagos tortoise can be split into two types based on the shape of the shell. These are the large "domed" type, which have big, round shells, and the slightly smaller "saddleback", with an arched or saddlelike flare in the shell above the neck. This arch may be an adaptation to feeding in more arid habitats, where vegetation—such as the prickly pear cactus, a favorite food—is higher off the ground and can only be reached by craning the head and neck.

Partial migrators

On some islands, when the dry season begins, older males and some adult females leave the lowlands for the more humid highlands. It takes them two to three weeks to migrate about 4 miles (6 km), and they remain in the highlands until the rains return. The rest of the tortoises stay in the lowlands all year. The Galápagos tortoise's unhurried lifestyle, slow metabolism, and ability to store food energy and water mean it can survive for a whole year without eating or drinking if it has to.

Traditional nesting sites

Mating peaks from February to May—the rainy season —when the male becomes territorial and starts to sniff, pursue, nip, and ram the female. Female tortoises usually choose a traditional site near the coast and dig a hole in loose soil or sand to lay the eggs. She lays up to four clutches of between five and 18 eggs (the average is eight to 10 per clutch), then fills in the hole. The eggs take from four to eight months to hatch, depending on the temperature, and the babies may spend several days, even weeks, digging their way up to the surface. The eggs and hatchlings are threatened by introduced predators such as cats and black rats.

Galapagos tortoises are **exceptionally long-lived**, with **one female** living more than **170 years**

◁ **SADDLEBACK SHELL**
Galapagos tortoises have long, flexible necks. The above-neck flare of the shells of tortoises on the drier Española Island allows them to reach taller plants.

▷ **DOMED SHELL**
Domed-shelled tortoises are generally less territorial and more social. They often rest in groups or herds, in earthen scrapes called pallets.

↔ Up to 4 ft (1.2 m)
⚖ Up to 660 lb (300 kg)
⊗ Vulnerable
🌾 Cacti, grass, leaves, berries
🏠

Galapagos Islands

△ **SYMBIOTIC RELATIONSHIP**
Like other Galápagos reptiles, such as the giant tortoise, the marine iguana has a symbiotic relationship with the small ground finch, which cleans parasites from its skin.

high dorsal crest in older males

blunt snout

Marine iguana

Amblyrhynchus cristatus

The remote Galápagos Islands, straddling the Equator in the Pacific Ocean, are famed for their unique animals. The islands' marine iguanas are especially interesting, being the only marine lizard that feeds exclusively on seaweed.

Agile in water

Marine iguanas do not live in the sea but gather in colonies on rocky shorelines. They spend the early hours of daylight basking in the sun so that their bodies are warmed enough for a busy day of swimming and feeding. When ready, the lizards plunge into the deep water, diving to depths of 33 ft (10 m) to graze on the short seaweeds that grow on the sunlit rocks of the seabed. An iguana can stay under for an hour if it has to, but most feeding dives last a few minutes before the animal surfaces to breathe. With its plump body and short legs, the marine iguana is ungainly on land but very agile in the water. It has partially webbed feet, but swims mainly with the help of its flattened, oar-shaped tail, while the crest of spines along its back provides stability.

Warm on land

A marine iguana cannot remain in the sea for long. The chilly water begins to make it lethargic, and so it must get out of the water regularly to warm up in the sunshine. After eating it climbs back up the slippery rocks, gripping on with long, hooked claws. Its dark leathery skin helps it to absorb heat more quickly.

As it dries out, the body color becomes a paler gray, with blotches of orange, green, and other colors appearing. These are most pronounced in adult males, which develop vibrant coloring to attract mates. The colors are derived from the pigments in the seaweed they eat and, therefore, vary from island to island. The faces of male and female marine iguanas are also streaked with white. This is the excess salt consumed in their food, which is excreted through glands in the nose.

Along with boosting body temperature, the time spent on land is an opportunity for the iguanas to digest the tough seaweed. This is done with the aid of gut bacteria inside a bulbous fermentation chamber, hence the iguana's large and rotund figure.

Big not always best

Males can grow to twice the size of females, and they will guard a harem of mates from rivals during the breeding season. Conflicts are generally a show of bluff and bluster, with a dominant male bobbing his head at a rival, who normally withdraws. If he bobs back, however, the rivals will fight, each trying to shove the other away with his head. Large size helps with this, but is a hindrance in other ways. Bigger lizards take longer to warm up between foraging dives, and when seaweed cover in the water is low due to climatic events—such as El Niño—they cannot feed as often as their smaller counterparts.

△ **MARINE IGUANA COLONY**
Iguanas bask in the sunshine in colonies, their dark bodies helping them to both absorb the sun's warmth and blend in among the volcanic rocks and sand.

◁ **UNDERWATER MEAL**
The marine iguana gets all of its food from the seabed. It uses its hard, horny lips to scrape away the sea lettuce that grows on rocks.

↔ 20–40 in (50–100 cm)
🏋 2–24 lb (1–11 kg)
✖ Vulnerable
🌿 Seaweed
🏠 🌿〰

Galapagos Islands

When **food is scarce,** the marine iguana can **reduce its body size,** including **shrinking its skeleton** by 10 percent

Central Apennines
A gray wolf cautiously approaches a small herd of red deer, but they are alert to the predator's presence. Fewer than 1,000 wolves live in Italy and only in the Apennine mountains.

Europe

LAND OF ICE AND FIRE

Iceland lies on the volcanic seam of the mid-Atlantic ridge, where two tectonic plates are gradually growing and being forced apart. The land is dotted with active volcanoes, geysers, and glaciers.

AGRICULTURAL IMPACT

In Europe, ecological damage associated with human development is significant, with extensive urbanization, deforestation, and the conversion of land for agriculture.

FEATURED ECOREGIONS

ARCTIC OCEAN

Iceland

NORWEGIAN FJORDS
The landforms of the Norwegian coast, including flooded U-shaped valleys known as fjords, are among the most dramatic clues to northern Europe's glacial history.

Norwegian Sea

Faroe Islands

Shetland Islands

Orkney Islands

Scandinavia

Gulf of Bothnia

British Isles

Grampian Mountains

North Sea

Vänern

Gotland

Baltic Sea

Jutland

North Europ

Severn

Elbe

Thames

Vistula

Rhine

English Channel

E U R O P E

Ardennes

Bavarian Forest

WARMING CURRENT
A warm Atlantic current —an extension of the Gulf Stream—bathes the European coast, bringing a fairly stable climate, frequent rain, and mild temperatures to northern latitudes.

Brittany

Seine

Carpath

Loire

Black Forest

Danube

Tisza

Lake Geneva

Alps

Great Hungarian Plain

Bay of Biscay

Massif Central

Mt Blanc △ 4,807m

Rhône

Drava

Po

Apennines

Dinaric Alps

Cordillera Cantábrica

Pyrenees

Camargue

Adriatic Sea

Douro

Ebro

Tagus

Iberian Peninsula

Corsica

Balearic Islands

Sardinia

Sierra Nevada

M e d i t e r r a n e a n

Sicily

Ionian Sea

Etna △ 3,263m

MEDITERRANEAN SEA
Warm, salty, and almost landlocked, this sea has been adversely affected by fisheries and shipping, but still supports diverse underwater life.

Pelop

Malta

S e a

Barents Sea

Kola Peninsula

White Sea

Lake Onega

Lake Ladoga

Ural Mountains

Volga

Central Russian Upland

Don

Volga Uplands

Dnieper

Volga

Caspian Sea

Caucasus
El'brus
▲ 5,642m

Black Sea

Crete

URAL MOUNTAINS
Forming a natural boundary between Europe and Asia, the Urals run from the Arctic Circle to the dry temperate steppes of Kazakhstan.

PLAINS AND PENINSULAS
Europe

Europe is the western portion of the supercontinent of Eurasia, separated from Asia by the Black and Caspian seas, and the Ural and Caucasus mountains. It is a geologically and ecologically complex continent, with ancient glaciated uplands to the north and west, a vast plain sweeping east from southern England to Russia, and central uplands preceding the steep rocky terrain of the Alps—the longest mountain chain in Europe. Roughly half of the landmass comprises major peninsulas—Scandinavia, Jutland, Brittany, Iberia, Italy, and the Balkans—or large islands such as Great Britain, Ireland, and Iceland. The influence of the surrounding oceans and seas on climate is considerable.

Natural habitats and their plant and animal life occur in zones according to latitude. Tundra and coniferous forests dominate the north, giving way to deciduous forests, agricultural landscapes, mountains, and Mediterranean habitats in the south. Many species of bird and insect migrate annually between Asian breeding grounds and European wintering areas.

LIMESTONE CAVES

Karst landscapes, such as the Kras region of Slovenia and Italy, consist of thin, dry, alkaline soils above limestone bedrock with caves and underground rivers. Some are home to the cave salamander, or olm.

MANITA PEC CAVE

OLM

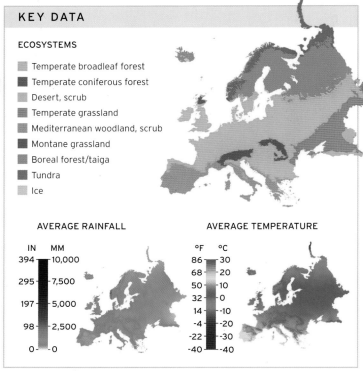

KEY DATA

ECOSYSTEMS

- Temperate broadleaf forest
- Temperate coniferous forest
- Desert, scrub
- Temperate grassland
- Mediterranean woodland, scrub
- Montane grassland
- Boreal forest/taiga
- Tundra
- Ice

AVERAGE RAINFALL

IN	MM
394	10,000
295	7,500
197	5,000
98	2,500
0	0

AVERAGE TEMPERATURE

°F	°C
86	30
68	20
50	10
32	0
14	-10
-4	-20
-22	-30
-40	-40

NORWEGIAN FJORDS
Sheltered havens of a convoluted coast

The coast of Norway is dominated by steep-sided valleys gouged out by glaciers over several ice ages. These were then flooded by the sea, forming long, narrow inlets with vertiginous rock walls known as fjords. The waters are fully marine, but sheltered, largely inaccessible from land, and often extremely deep. Despite their high latitude, the fjords usually remain ice-free all year thanks to the warming influence of the Gulf Stream. They support an abundance of resident and migratory fish, seals and porpoises, and sea birds, and the world's largest accumulation of deep-water coral reefs.

Cold-water corals

Deep-water corals were first discovered in 1869, but it took more than a century for their size and extent to be revealed. The main reef-forming coral in the Atlantic is *Lophelia pertusa*, and lophelia reefs more than 8 miles

(13 km) long and 100 ft (30 m) high have been found off the coast of Norway. Some of the reefs are thousands of years old. The reefs in the more shallow, but still cold waters of the fjords were discovered in 2000. They greatly enhance the ecological value of the fjords, giving shelter to a wide range of marine invertebrates and providing nursery and feeding areas for fish.

The mountainous land adjacent to and between the fjords is cloaked in coniferous and deciduous forests, dotted with glacial lakes and summer-grazing pastures in high valleys. Above 5,600 ft (1,700 m), the trees and meadows give way to alpine plants and snowy peaks.

SPAWNING GROUNDS
The Atlantic herring migrates to Norwegian fjords to spawn when it reaches five years. It is a key food item for several other fish, seals, cetaceans, and sea birds, and so all these animals suffer from overfishing of herring stocks by humans.

ATLANTIC HERRING

BOOM AND BUST
Norway lemmings can breed very quickly. When good conditions prevail, populations boom, leading to large-scale dispersal and the myth that lemmings hurl themselves into fjords to escape overcrowding. Populations crash due to limited food.

NORWAY LEMMIN

The largest lophelia reefs are mo

Sognefjord is the longest ice-free fjord in the world

WHITE-BACKED WOODPECKER

HAMMERED HOME
The relatively undisturbed coastal forests of Norway support dense populations of the white-backed woodpecker. Considered an indicator of healthy and mature ecosystems, its excavations provide nest holes for many other species.

LOCATION

Fjords occur along much of the western coast of Norway, with the largest and deepest between Stavanger and Trondheim.

CLIMATE

The climate is temperate and seasonal, but relatively mild owing to the influence of the Gulf Stream. Rain falls all year-round.

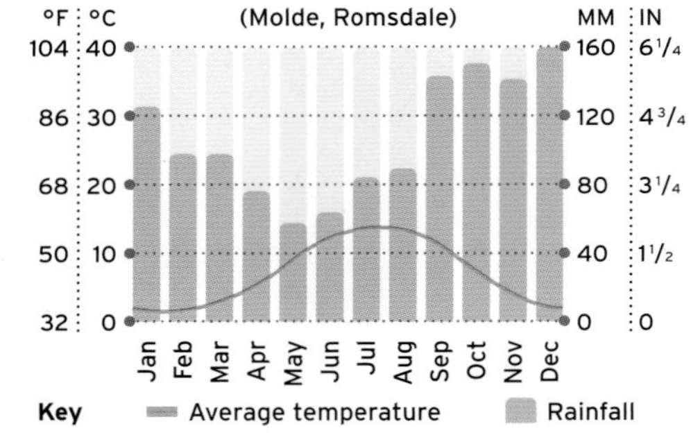

Gray seal

Halichoerus grypus

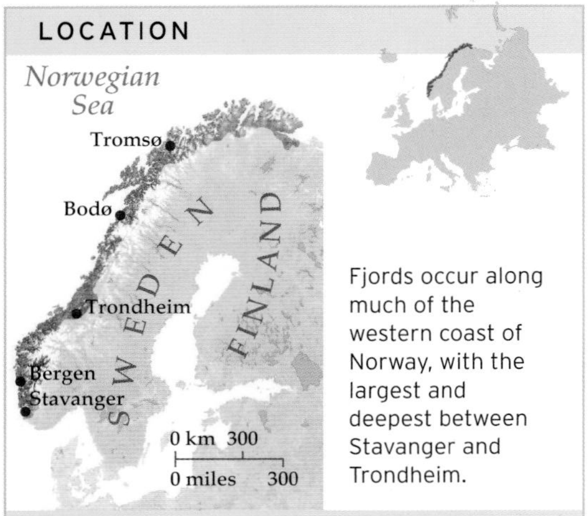

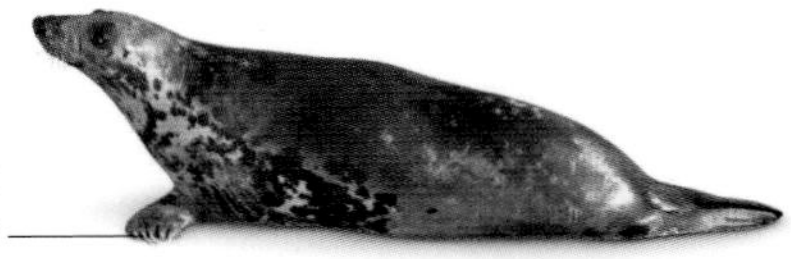

long, sharp claws on front flippers

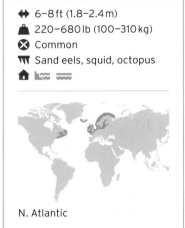

The gray seal is perfectly adapted to its cold-water environment. Up to 3 in (7.6 cm) of blubber gives this marine mammal excellent insulation, but it also diverts blood from the skin to vital organs. It hunts at depths of 200–985 ft (60–300 m), even in zero visibility, exhaling to collapse its lungs, then using its super-sensitive whiskers to track wakes left by sand eels and other prey.

- 6–8 ft (1.8–2.4 m)
- 220–680 lb (100–310 kg)
- Common
- Sand eels, squid, octopus

N. Atlantic

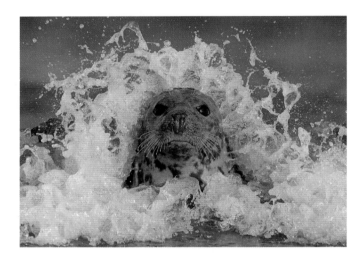

◁ **SURFING ASHORE**
Found in large colonies, gray seals haul out on beaches, ice, and rocky outcrops to rest, breed, molt, and give birth.

Harbor porpoise

Phocoena phocoena

Harbor porpoises frequent coastal areas, particularly cold-water shallow bays, where they search for food along the sea floor. Although often confused with dolphins, when viewed from a distance, porpoises have small dorsal fins, are more rotund, and lack a distinct beak. They also avoid boats, and seldom bow-ride.

- 4–7 ft (1.2–2.1 m)
- 99–165 lb (45–75 kg)
- Common
- Fish, squid, octopus

N. Pacific, N. Atlantic, Black Sea

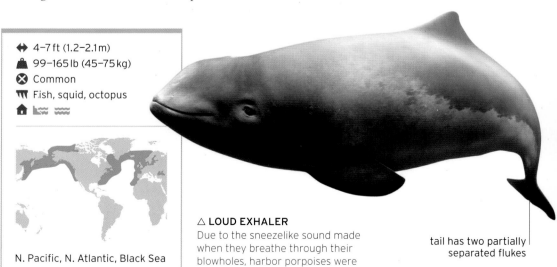

△ **LOUD EXHALER**
Due to the sneezelike sound made when they breathe through their blowholes, harbor porpoises were once known as "puffing pigs."

tail has two partially separated flukes

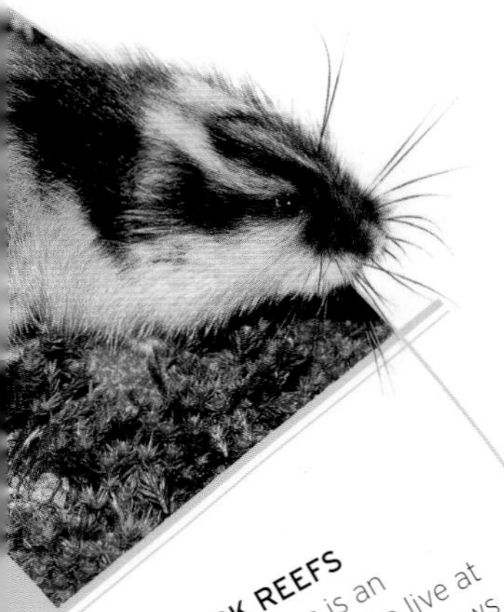

DEEP, DARK REEFS
Lophelia pertusa is an unusual coral, able to live at depth in cold water. It grows exceptionally slowly, feeding on dead plankton that drifts down from the sunlit waters above. Norway's coast hosts the greatest known density of lophelia reefs in the world.

than 8,000 years old

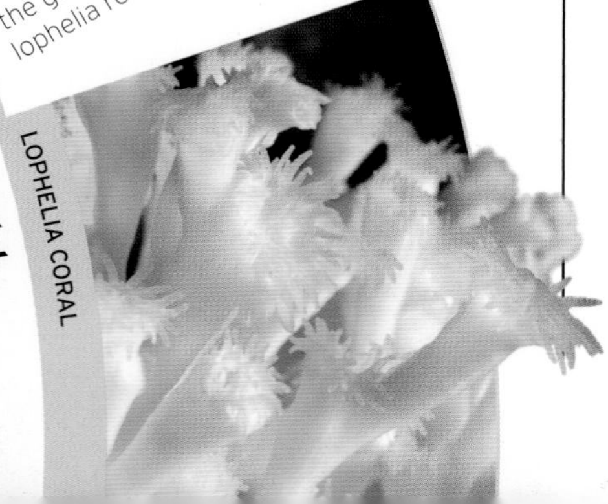

LOPHELIA CORAL

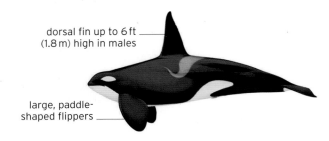

dorsal fin up to 6 ft
(1.8 m) high in males

large, paddle-
shaped flippers

Orca
Orcinus orca

The orca, or killer whatle, is not a true whale but the largest member of the dolphin family. Living up to 90 years, it is the only cetacean that regularly eats other marine mammals, including other dolphins.

Intelligent hunters

There are three types of killer whales: resident, transient, and offshore; each group has a different diet and lives in different areas. Resident orcas form the largest groups, or pods, and primarily hunt fish, squid, and octopuses. Transient orcas are the world's biggest predators of warm-blooded animals, feeding almost exclusively on marine mammals, including large whales, as well as seabirds such as penguins. The offshore orcas eat fish, especially sharks.

All types of orca are highly intelligent. Adults teach juveniles how to hunt: herding, stunning prey with tail strikes, and "wave-washing" seals off sea ice.

Orca pods range from just a few to 50 or more. An average pod generally includes smaller groups comprising a mature female and its female offspring. They communicate using a shared vocabulary of clicks, whistles, and pulsed calls (which sound like screams to human ears). Different populations have distinctive calls.

Orcas mate throughout the year, but most often in late spring and summer. After a 15- to 18-month gestation period—the longest of all cetaceans—females bear a single calf, usually born tail-first.

◁ **SURFACE BREACH**
Breaching, tail and flipper slaps, and "spy-hopping" –pushing only the head above water–are known forms of communication among orcas.

- ↔ 25–33 ft (7.5–10 m)
- ⚖ Up to 7.3 tons (6.6 metric tons)
- ✖ Not known
- 🍴 Fish, mammals, seabirds
- 🏠 ▬▬ ≈≈

Worldwide

King eider
Somateria spectabilis

This sea-going duck winters mostly north of the Arctic Circle and breeds on small lakes or rivers in coastal tundra and bogs. The king eider dives as deep as 115 ft (35 m) for food, but also tips forward to forage in the shallows. Courtship displays are ritualized, with the male's rump raised, tail depressed, and head and bill pushed forward.

- ↔ 19–25 in (48–63 cm)
- ⚖ 3–5 lb (1.4–2 kg)
- ✖ Common
- 🍴 Molluscs, crabs
- 🏠 ⛰ ≋ ≈≈ ▬▬
- ◉ Arctic Ocean, N. Pacific, N. North America, N. Europe, N. Asia

▽ **DIRECT FLIGHT**
King eiders have a swift, direct flight pattern with rapid wing beats. Large flocks tend to fly abreast, rather than one bird behind the other.

bright red bill and enormous yellow frontal shield of breeding male

Atlantic salmon
Salmo salar

Young Atlantic salmon spend a year, or more, in the upper reaches of clear-running rivers before swimming out to sea. Once at sea, the salmon follows coastal currents in search of food, and matures rapidly. After three or four years at sea, it locates its birth river by the unique smell of its water and journeys back to breed.

- ↔ 3–5 ft (0.9–1.5 m)
- ⚖ 5–20 lb (2.3–9.1 kg)
- ✖ Common
- 🍴 Fish, insect larvae,
- 🏠 ≋ ≈≈ ▬▬
- ◉ NE. North America, W. and N. Europe, N. Atlantic

◁ **HEADING UPSTREAM**
Many salmon die on the tough journey upstream, but survivors may make the trip three or four times.

↔ 11–12 in (28–30 cm)

🏋 14 oz (400 g)

⊗ Common

🦷 Sand eels, capelins, herring

🏠 ▨ 〰 ⋀

North Atlantic, Arctic Ocean

pale face darkens
in winter

▷ **FRESH CATCH**
Tiny sand eels hang in a row, held
in place by the puffin's muscular,
grooved tongue and inward-facing
serrations on the edges of its bill.

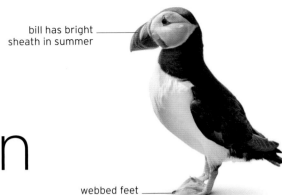

bill has bright
sheath in summer

webbed feet

Atlantic puffin

Fratercula arctica

Puffins are probably one of the most easily recognizable birds—particularly the Atlantic puffin, with its large, brightly colored, triangular bill. They are small, upright seabirds that come to land only to breed. They are less like penguins than their cousins the guillemots, which stand upright on their heels and tails, their legs set right at the back of the body. Puffins have more centrally placed legs and walk more easily.

Temporary finery

In spring, the puffin's bill sheath expands and gains its bright red summer colors. The number of yellow grooves in the red tip indicate the bird's age. By fall, the sheath is shed and the bill becomes smaller and duller for the winter. Without the need for the visual communication required at a breeding colony, the bill transforms into a practical tool for catching fish. Puffins dive deep for food, "flying" through the water with ease. They usually catch several small fish in a single dive, especially when collecting food for their chick.

Cliff-top colonies

Puffin colonies, some consisting of hundreds of thousands of pairs, spread over clifftop slopes and broken, rocky screes. Puffins from a colony often fly out over the sea in magnificent, swirling flocks to keep predators at bay and reduce the chances of individual puffins being killed. On land, they are noisy, at times aggressive, showing off their bright beaks and feet.

Puffins have a lifespan of 10–20 years, and they will often return to the same nest burrow year after year. If a new breeding pair cannot find an old burrow to occupy, they dig one with their feet, kicking out the soft soil until it is about 3ft (1m) deep. The female lays a single egg, which is held by either parent against a bare, hot "brood patch" under one drooped wing. The chick hatches after 36–45 days and both parents feed it for up to 60 days. The young puffin is then left alone and stands at the end of the burrow for several nights until it flies off to the sea. The synchronized timing of breeding leads to almost all adults leaving the colony together, so busy colonies become silent within a few days.

The **record number of sand eels** seen in an **Atlantic puffin's bill is 83**

◁ **UP IN THE AIR**
Atlantic puffins are capable of flapping their wings 400 times a minute, giving them a top speed of 55mph (90km/h).

△ **PUFFIN COLONY**
Adults fly up to 60 miles (100km) out to sea in search of fish for their chick, usually returning to the colony in groups.

SCOTTISH HIGHLANDS
Britain's last wilderness

The Highlands of Scotland are both culturally and ecologically distinct. The region encompasses ancient rocky mountains with highly complex geology, grassy plateaus, peat bogs, abundant small rivers and lochs, and remnants of native forest, as well as extensive plantations and vast swathes of heather moorland. Some authorities also classify the Hebridean islands as Highland areas, though most of these are relatively low-lying. The relative wildness of the region is due to the limited opportunities for intensive agriculture and a sparse human population.

Restoring native forest

The highest summits are well above the treeline, and include Britain's highest peak, Ben Nevis, at 4,409 ft (1,344 m), and the Cairngorm plateau resembles subarctic tundra in terms of plant and animal diversity. Meanwhile the lowlands bear the hallmarks of glaciation, with broad valleys, large meandering rivers, and extensive bogs. Most of the forest in the region is coniferous plantation containing non-native Norway and sitka spruce and Douglas fir, but forest managers are increasingly looking to restore more natural assemblages similar to the ancient Caledonian forest that once cloaked lower slopes in Scots pine, juniper, birch, willow, rowan, and aspen.

Other attempts to rebalance the region's ecology include the reintroduction of Eurasian beavers, extinct for 400 years, and a high-profile rewilding experiment on the private Alladale Wilderness Reserve, where the aim is to have gray wolves and brown bears living free within a substantial fenced area.

GROUSE MOORS
Vast areas of moorland are intensively managed to ensure an abundance of red grouse for shooting. Ruthless predator control and burning of heather to promote tender new growth for the grouse to eat are controversial practices.

RED GROUSE

BLANKET BOGS
Scotland holds a significant proportion of the world's blanket bogs, where peat is formed from dead moss, especially sphagnum. The amount of atmospheric carbon bound up in peat plays a key role in moderating climate change.

SPHAGNUM MOSS

WOOD ANT

Only 1.2% of ancient Caledonian forest remains, split across 84 sites

Ben Nevis is the

SMALL WONDERS
Wood ants perform vital ecological roles: aerating soil, dispersing seeds, controlling problem insects, and providing food for many other species. Their nests are also home to the tiny shining guest ant, woodlice, and chafer beetle grubs.

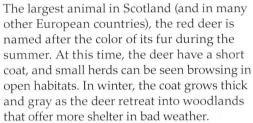

long, slender legs

Western red deer

Cervus elaphus

The largest animal in Scotland (and in many other European countries), the red deer is named after the color of its fur during the summer. At this time, the deer have a short coat, and small herds can be seen browsing in open habitats. In winter, the coat grows thick and gray as the deer retreat into woodlands that offer more shelter in bad weather.

Red deer live in single sex herds, but mixing is tolerated in winter. As spring arrives the males start to grow antlers, and the females give birth to spotted fawns. The rut begins in late summer. Dominant males control a harem of females, using a bellowing roar to keep them together. The weaker bucks, the young and the old, harass the females at the edge of the group, driving them toward the protection of the stronger males. The rut lasts until the arrival of winter, when the males shed their antlers, and the deer prepare for cold conditions once more.

mature buck has several points on each antler

antler bone grows 1 in (2.5 cm) per day

▷ **STANDING PROUD**
Females judge males by their antlers. Younger bucks have fewer points, or tines, while the antlers of aging males are less symmetrical.

△ **HEADS DOWN**
Rutting bucks try to avoid all-out combat. They walk side by side to size each other up and will only fight if neither backs down.

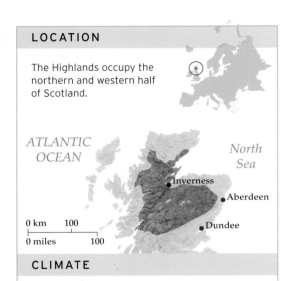

ATLANTIC OCEAN

North Sea

Inverness

Aberdeen

Dundee

0 km 100

0 miles 100

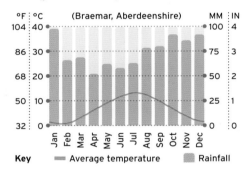

°F °C (Braemar, Aberdeenshire) MM IN

104 40 · · 100 4

86 30 · · 75 3

68 20 · · 50 2

50 10 · · 25 1

32 0 · · 0 0

Jan Feb Mar Apr May Jun Jul Aug Sep Oct Nov Dec

Key ▬ Average temperature ▮ Rainfall

ASSISTED RECOVERY
Water voles saw a huge decline in the UK in the late 20th century, partly due to heavy predation by introduced American mink. But because Highland river catchments are too exposed for mink, the voles have a refuge here.

highest mountain in Britain

WATER VOLE

↔ 8–10 in (20–25 cm)
🏋 7–17 oz (200–475 g)
✖ Common
🌾 Conifer seeds, nuts
🏠 🌳 🌲 ⛰

W. Europe to W. Asia

▷ **TUFTED EARS**
Unlike gray squirrels, red squirrels
have tufts on their ears, which
are particularly long in winter.

fluffy tail,
molts
annually

Eurasian red squirrel

Sciurus vulgaris

Eurasian red squirrels have remarkably varied coat
colors, with the upper coats ranging from very
light red to black. However, only the red form
occurs in the UK. Agile climbers, these rodents
can leap distances of up to 13 ft (4 m) and have
great vision, hearing, and sense of smell.

Focus on food

Red squirrels spend most of the day
feeding or caching food, such as seeds
and nuts. In the warmest hours of
summer, they retire to a drey, or
nest. They do not hibernate,
relying on their food stores to
survive winter, but they stay
in their drey in harsh weather.
Males compete for females, but
play no role in caring for young,
and, aside from mating, these
rodents live mainly independent lives.
Although found across most of Europe, they are
restricted to a few mixed woodlands in areas where they
have to compete with the larger, more successful gray
squirrel introduced from North America.

△ **EYES OPEN**
Squirrel kits spend their first weeks in a drey, lined
with soft moss and grass, opening their eyes at
around five weeks old.

Wildcat
Felis silvestris

thick coat with distinct dark stripes

At first glance, any of the 19 subspecies of wildcat could be mistaken for a domestic tabby—not surprisingly, as the African subspecies, *F. s. lybica*, is its ancestor. Look closely and differences emerge. European wildcats, for example, are generally larger than domestic cats, with longer, thicker coats, broader heads, and flatter faces. Their dark-ringed tails are also shorter, with blunt, black-tipped ends. In Europe, wildcats inhabit mainly mixed forests or broadleaved woods, but in other parts of the world, their habitats range from desert to alpine meadows.

Passing on hunting skills

Wildcats have excellent night vision and mainly hunt small mammals, although some subspecies occasionally hunt young deer. They are solitary and highly territorial, except when mating and rearing kittens—two to five is the usual litter size. As weaning begins, the mother brings live food to the den, often an old rabbit burrow or fox den, to teach the kittens to hunt. They become independent at five to six months. Hybridization is considered the main threat to this species as domestic cats readily breed with wildcats.

▷ STAY AWAY
Wildcats use urine and feces to mark their territories, but also communicate vocally, yowling and snarling to warn off intruders.

↔ 16–30 in (40–75 cm)
⚖ 5–16 lb (2–7.25 kg)
⊗ Common
🐾 Rodents, birds, reptiles
🏠 🌳 ⛰ 🌵 🌾 〰

Europe, W. and C. Asia, Africa

Scottish crossbill
Loxia scotica

crossed bill tips

green plumage of female

The Scottish crossbill is the only bird endemic to Scotland. A member of the finch family, it lives in the Scots pine forests of the Highlands, where it feeds almost exclusively on ripe cones, using its specialist bill to pry apart the scales so it can reach the seeds with its tongue.

Courtship begins in late winter or early spring, with flocks of males competing to see who can sing the loudest. Once a female selects a male, he touches his bill to hers, then feeds her. They build a nest of twigs high up in a pine tree and two to six eggs are laid, usually in March or April. Incubation lasts around two weeks, the male feeding the female all this time, and then both birds feed the chicks. They leave the nest after three weeks, but the parents have to feed them for 10 more days— until their bills are crossed.

Tough call

Two other species of crossbill also breed in the UK: the common crossbill, which feeds on spruce cones, and the slightly larger parrot crossbill, which specializes in tough pine seeds. Telling them apart is difficult, but they can be distinguished by their distinct calls.

↔ 6–7 in (16–17 cm)
⚖ 1–2 oz (36.5–49 g)
⊗ Locally common
🐾 Conifer seeds, buds
🏠 🌲 ⛰

NW. Europe (UK)

◁ SCOTTISH MALE
The male is red like the common and parrot crossbill males, but its muscular neck and large bill are intermediate between those two species.

broad, muscular body

Peregrine falcon
Falco peregrinus

Renowned for its skill in the air, the peregrine chases down prey, rising above and diving, or rolling over underneath to grasp the bird in its claws. Its spectacular "stoop" is a long, angled dive with wings folded in a teardrop shape, reaching speeds of 125–150 mph (200–240 km/h). In level flight, while sometimes outflown by a desperate pigeon, the peregrine puts on a burst of speed that few birds can match.

Formidable hunter
Hunting success is around 50–60 percent, but peregrines often chase birds without attacking them. They catch birds up to the size of a pigeon, and occasionally ducks and larger species. The decline of peregrines in the 1960s drew attention to the catastrophic effect of pesticides such as DDT, which is more concentrated further up the food chain. Birds of prey died or laid infertile or thin-shelled eggs. Peregrines have since recovered and often nest in towns, exploiting pigeon populations. They traditionally nested on cliffs, but high buildings are now used too.

tapered, pointed wing

↔ 14–20 in (34–50 cm)
⚖ 1–3 lb (0.6–1.5 kg)
⊗ Common
🐦 Birds
🏠 ⛰ ⛰ 🌵 🌾 〰 🏙

Worldwide

△ **BRACED TO LAND**
Landing peregrines swoop upward to lose speed, spread their wings and tail as air brakes, then thrust out their feet to take the shock of landing and to grasp the perch.

◁ **TINY PORTIONS**
Like most birds of prey, peregrines bring freshly killed animals back to the nest. They tear off a small piece of food and delicately offer it to a chick.

Western capercaillie

Tetrao urogallus

short, rounded wings

The capercaillie is the world's largest grouse. It survives mostly in old pine forests with an abundance of shoots and berries beneath the trees and in clearings close by. In summer, the birds look for food on the ground, but in winter, they often feed on shoots high up in trees. Male capercaillies gather and display in a lek to attract and impress the females, which then move away to nest.

Increasing deer, declining capercaillies

Capercaillie populations have declined almost everywhere, disappearing entirely from some forests. Climate change may play a role, but deterioration in capercaillie habitat is sometimes related to an increase in the deer population.

Capercaillies need a healthy growth of low shrubs, which provide essential cover and a rich diet. With too many deer browsing on these shrubs, capercaillies face a food shortage. High fences pose another problem. Because these birds can only fly low, many collide with fences intended to keep out deer and are killed.

↔ 24–34 in (60–85 cm)
⚖ 4–9 lb (1.8–4.1 kg)
✖ Common
🌾 Seeds, berries, shoots

N., W., and S. Europe, W. to C. Asia

▷ **VYING FOR ATTENTION**
A male capercaillie displays to impress females, while making croaking, gurgling, and cork-popping sounds.

Common adder

Vipera berus

The common adder is the most widely distributed member of the viper family and is the only venomous snake in northwest Europe. Its front upper fangs, folded back along the jaws, tilt down in an instant to strike immobilizing venom into prey. The adder's diet includes frogs, lizards, birds, voles, and other small mammals. It is not an aggressive snake, but it will bite a human if stepped on or handled. The bite is painful, and may cause swelling, but is rarely fatal.

Winter retreat

In their southern ranges, common adders stay above the ground and active all year. Further north, however, they spend the long cold winters together in large groups in a cave, burrow, or similar hideaway. They emerge from late spring to summer to mate. Females breed only once every two or three years and may mate with several males. The female gives birth to 10–15 live young who have to fend for themselves within hours of birth.

▷ **HOSTILE DANCE**
Male adders wrestle with each other to establish dominance. They raise up the front part of their body and attempt to push their opponent to the ground.

↔ 24–35 in (60–90 cm)
⚖ Up to 6 oz (180 g)
✖ Common
🌾 Small mammals, reptiles

Europe, C. to E. Asia

flat head

distinctive dark zigzag line running down back

THE CAMARGUE
Europe's most famous coastal wetland

The largest river delta in Western Europe forms where the Rhône River splits to enclose more than 360 sq miles (930 sq km) of salt marsh, low-lying islands and sand bars, saltwater lagoons, and reed beds. In 1986, the Camargue was officially designated as a wetland of international importance. It is also a UNESCO World Heritage Site.

Shifting landscape
The landforms of the Camargue shift continually, and the gradual accumulation of silt and sand means the delta is gradually growing. The coastal flats are stabilized by salt-tolerant sea lavender and glasswort. Further inland are juniper woodlands, and the north of the delta is stable enough to support agriculture including seasonal grazing for horses and cattle, rice paddies, and vineyards. Aside from the greater flamingos and semiwild horses for which the region is famous, the most conspicuous wildlife of the Camargue in summer is often the mosquitoes—reputed to be the most voracious in France. These deeply unpopular bloodsucking insects are nevertheless an important food resource for birds such as house martins, swallows, and alpine swifts. Other insect life includes more than 30 species of dragonfly, but it is birds for which the wetlands are best known. More than 400 species live in or visit the Camargue, and egrets, herons, and harriers that would turn heads elsewhere are almost ubiquitous.

CRAYFISH PROBLEM
Since it was imported in the 1980s, the American red swamp crayfish has reduced the abundance and diversity of aquatic invertebrates and amphibians through competition, predation, and transmission of the frog-killing chytrid fungus.

RED SWAMP CRAYFISH

ESSENTIAL GRAZERS
Repeated outbreaks of myxomatosis have greatly reduced the number of rabbits in the Camargue. While grazing by cattle and horses continues, they are less efficient than rabbits at halting the encroachment of more vigorous shrubs.

EUROPEAN RABB

30-plus species of dragonfly

CAMARGUE CATTLE

Parts protected as a Regional Natural Park since 1970

FREE-RANGE CATTLE
The handsome black cattle that live semiwild in the Camargue are bred for beef and for bullfighting. They are ecologically important as grazers, controlling the growth of emergent wetland vegetation and maintaining areas of open water.

LOCATION

The Camargue lies within the Rhône Delta, on the Mediterranean coast of southeastern France.

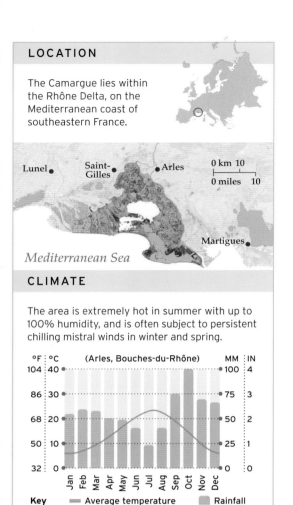

Lunel • Saint-Gilles • Arles

0 km 10
0 miles 10

Mediterranean Sea

Martigues •

CLIMATE

The area is extremely hot in summer with up to 100% humidity, and is often subject to persistent chilling mistral winds in winter and spring.

°F	°C	(Arles, Bouches-du-Rhône)	MM	IN
104	40		100	4
86	30		75	3
68	20		50	2
50	10		25	1
32	0		0	0

Jan Feb Mar Apr May Jun Jul Aug Sep Oct Nov Dec

Key — Average temperature ▬ Rainfall

THREATENED FISH
Eels were once the most common predatory fish in the Camargue, but they have declined here as elsewhere. This is due to a combination of pollution, the damming of their migration routes, and a parasitic nematode.

...than 400 species of bird

EUROPEAN EEL

Camargue horse

Equus caballus

compact stature

Although their exact origin is unknown, horses have lived in the salty marshlands of southern France, particularly around the Rhône Delta, for thousands of years. Today, Camargue horses live a semiwild existence as a protected breed. If described in horsebreeding terms, these small, compact horses are technically "gray" not white. When born, the foals are black or brown—the horses only turn gray at around four years old.

Water horses

Rugged and sturdy, Camargue horses are never stabled, nor are their hard hoofs ever shod. They survive extreme weather conditions partly by grazing on plants too tough for other herbivores. However, their even temperament and agility lead many to be tamed and ridden, and they are used to help manage the feral black Camargue cattle that also live in the wetlands.

↔ 7 ft (2.1 m)
⚖ 660–880 lb (300–400 kg)
✖ Endangered
🌿 Grass, leaves, herbs

S. Europe (Camargue)

Camargues are known in France as **"horses of the sea"**

▽ **RUNNING FREE**
Camargue horses naturally live in small herds, with the mares and foals usually led by a single dominant stallion.

adult has orange
bill with black
knob at base

large webbed feet
helps swan "run"
across water

Mute swan

Cygnus olor

While by no means silent—they make a snakelike hiss
when threatened, for example—mute swans are the least
vocal of all swans. Other swans make loud, bugling calls
when flying, but mute swans stay in touch in flight with
a different sound: their wings create a far-carrying,
deep, rhythmic, throbbing noise.

Mute swans are powerful enough to have few
predators as adults. Although an occasional fox or otter
may attack an unwary bird, swans have little need for
camouflage. Nor is there much demand for territorial
display because their huge size and white color stand
out. However, aggressive encounters are frequent. Mute
swans will allow younger swans into their territory but
chase away competitors. They arch their wing feathers,
curve back their necks, and thrust out their chests.
A charge toward another swan on water, powered by
thrusts of their big webbed feet, is fast and impressive.

Summer flocks

Large flocks of mute swans gather to molt and often to
feed in shallow, sheltered water or on open fields. Some
of these flocks persist through the summer with many
swans, even seemingly fully mature ones, not breeding.

Nesting pairs separate off and defend a territory in
spring, building a massive nest of reed stems and other
waterside vegetation. The young "ugly ducklings," or
cygnets, are drab gray-brown. It takes two to three years
for them to turn all-white and develop the bright orange
and black bill colors of the adults. Adult males have the
thickest necks and biggest bills, with a large basal knob.

The mute swan is one of the **heaviest flying birds** in the world

↔ 4–5 ft (1.2–1.5 m)
⚖ 21–27 lb (9.5–12 kg)
✗ Common
🌾 Vegetation, snails

Europe, W. and E. Asia

△ **TAKE OFF AND LANDING**
Getting airborne from water or land
requires a run to gather speed, before
the swan's wings can generate
sufficient lift. When coming in to land
on water, the large webbed feet and
wings act as brakes.

◁ **GOING FOR A RIDE**
Cygnets accompany their parents
for several weeks, sometimes taking
a ride on one of their backs while they
are still small.

Greater flamingo
Phoenicopterus roseus

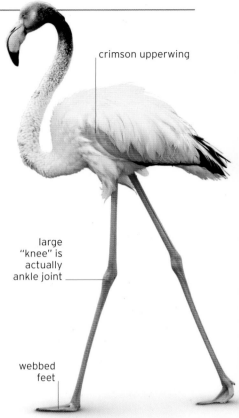

Flamingos feed unlike any other
bird. The angled bill, held upside
down and swept sideways,
works like a sieve, gathering tiny
invertebrates and algae from
the salty water. If disturbed,
flamingos run to take flight. The
slim body, long neck, and trailing
legs form a cross with the
crimson-and-black wings.

crimson upperwing

large
"knee" is
actually
ankle joint

webbed
feet

▷ **WALKING ON STILTS**
Long legs mean the greater flamingo
can wade in deep water with its long,
sinuous neck reaching down to its
toes to feed.

↔	4–5 ft (1.2–1.5 m)
🏋	Up to 9 lb (4 kg)
✕	Common
🌾	Krill, shrimp, algae
🏠	🌿 ≈ ≈
◉	SW. Europe, Asia, Africa

Pied avocet
Recurvirostra avosetta

The pied avocet has the most
upcurved bill of any European
bird. The delicate, sensitive,
slightly flat tip is swept
horizontally through soft, saline
mud, and tiny shrimp and other
creatures are located by touch.
  Few suitable natural nesting
sites of the pied avocet remain
in Europe, but many colonies
have formed on artificially
created lagoons and salt pans,
most of which are nature
reserves. In winter, the avocets
collect in flocks, hundreds
strong, on suitably mild,
wet, muddy estuaries.

↔	17–18 in (43–46 cm)
🏋	8–14 oz (226–400 g)
✕	Common
🌾	Crustaceans, insects
🏠	🌿 ≈ ≈ ▬
◉	Europe, Asia, Africa

▷ **OPEN NEST**
Avocets lay their eggs almost directly
on dried mud. Colonies are vulnerable
to predation despite the combined
defensive efforts of the adults.

turquoise patch on breast

long, triangular wing

European bee-eater
Merops apiaster

European bee-eaters live up to their name—their food largely comprises bees and wasps with minor variations according to location and season. The birds are partially immune to the insects' venom, but take care to remove the stings before swallowing the bees. They show a preference for the nonvenomous drones, particularly selecting such harmless food for their young.

Chorus singers

European bee-eaters can be seen roosting in rows on telephone wires, or in small groups on dead trees. Flying out to catch prey, they glide on flat, fully-stretched wings with bursts of quick beats. Even their calls draw attention—the chorus of rich, chirruping notes is a familiar sound in much of southern Europe. Migrating flocks sometimes number more than 100 birds, held together by almost constant calling.

Bee-eaters nest in colonies that range from a handful of nests up to hundreds, and large colonies are busy places bustling with noise and activity. Initially, the birds tend to fight while defending their nest hole and nearby perch. Breeding pairs may last for life, and their behavior is often interchangeable. It is only when the male feeds the female—helping to cement the pair bond and also to build up nutrients before egg-laying—that the sexes can be told apart. Four to seven eggs hatch after 20 days, and the chicks are fed in the nest for a month. The chicks continue to roost in the nest hole for a while after fledging, and families often migrate together in fall, spending the winter in Africa.

curved, dagger-shaped bill

▷ **CONTROLLED LANDING**
Bee-eaters have sleek and streamlined bodies. Their long, triangular wings and long tails allow them to maneuver with ease as they accelerate, twist, and turn to catch flying insects in mid-air.

wide tail with central spike

A bee-eater must **eat** about **225 bee-sized insects every day**

△ **MANIPULATING PREY**
A bee-eater turns bees and wasps in its bill, then rubs them against a branch to remove the sting or squeeze out their venom.

△ **NESTING HOLE**
Bee-eaters dig three-foot-long holes in earth banks or sandy ground, digging with their bills and kicking out spoil with their feet.

◆ 11in (28cm)
⚖ 2–3oz (56–85g)
✖ Common
🌾 Bees, wasps
🏠 🌳 🌲 🌾 〰

Europe, Africa,
W., C., and S. Asia

softly rounded head

TAGUS VALLEY
The great natural artery of Iberia

The principal river of Spain and Portugal passes through some of the most biodiverse landscapes in Europe, with a mixture of both European and North African plants and animals. The Tagus river begins its course in Spain's forested Alto Tajo Natural Park, cutting a series of dramatic limestone gorges. It winds past cereal fields, olive groves, and world-renowned vineyards and cork oak forests, and powers more than 60 hydroelectric dams. Then it cleaves its way through the spectacular canyons of the Monfragüe National Park, where birds of prey including the Iberian imperial eagle, black and griffon vultures, and European eagle owls are found.

Protected river

The river and its adjacent habitats remain protected as it passes into Portugal within the boundaries of the International Tagus Natural Park, which was created in 2000. Roughly 60 miles (100 km) from the sea, the valley opens out onto a broad floodplain, and emerges into one of the largest and most important wetlands in Europe. Here, extensive saltmarsh and creeks provide prime habitats for birds including the greater flamingo, little egret, purple heron, booted eagle, and Montagu's harrier. They also provide a major stopover point for birds migrating between Europe and Africa.

Commercial forestry is banned in most of the national parks that the river passes through, and work to eradicate introduced trees in Monfragüe National Park, especially eucalyptus, is ongoing.

DECLINING AMPHIBIAN
The European tree frog favors the open-canopied forests and meadows that flank sections of the Tagus. It uses pools and swamps to breed and so is affected by drainage and water pollution. Another factor in its decline is collection for the pet trade.

EUROPEAN TREE FROG

ENDEMIC EAGLE
The Iberian imperial eagle population fell to just 30 pairs in the 1970s as a result of habitat loss and collisions with powerlines. Thousands of pylons have since been modified and the population now numbers more than 600 adult birds.

IMPERIAL EAGLE

MEDITERRANEAN POND TURTLE

Longest river in Iberia at more than 620 miles (1,000 km)

45% of Tagus fish species

REPTILE REFUGE
The Mediterranean pond turtle is widely threatened by wetland drainage and pollution. It is protected under national and European law, and the Tagus Valley is considered an important stronghold for the species.

Western roe deer
Capreolus capreolus

narrow hooves

The smallest deer native to Europe, this species was the original Bambi—Walt Disney changed his character to the US white-tailed deer for the animated film. Roe deer spend most of their time in woodlands, but may occasionally move into open ground, especially around dawn or dusk when they are most active.

Mostly alone

Solitary for most of the year, roe deer gather for the rut in late summer. After establishing territories, males chase the females around the woodland, and their hooves flatten the underbrush, forming distinctive roe rings. Fawns are born 10 months later. The newborns lie hidden on leaf-littered ground, camouflaged in the dappled light by their white spots.

- ↔ 3 ft (0.9 m)
- 24–34 lb (11–15.5 kg)
- ✕ Common
- Grasses, sedges, forbs

Europe, W. Asia

▷ **ANTLER GROWTH**
Males shed their antlers in October and start to regrow them in November. By next year's rut, the last of the velvet skin is replaced by the hard bone beneath.

Iberian ibex
Capra pyrenaica

sturdy legs

This wild goat lives in the sparse oak woodlands that grow on rocky mountain slopes. With short legs giving a low center of gravity and wide, flexible hooves that navigate tiny footholds, the Iberian ibex can climb out of the reach of predators. In spring, the females and their young form a separate herd from the older males.

- ↔ 38–61 in (97–155 cm)
- 70–200 lb (31–90 kg)
- ✕ Locally common
- Grasses, forbs

SW. Europe

△ **PLACE OF SAFETY**
Iberian ibex climb a sheer cliff to escape predators. The herd is led to safety by an older individual that knows the best routes in the steep landscape.

LOCATION

The Tagus runs southwest across Spain's semiarid interior and central Portugal, to the Atlantic Ocean.

ATLANTIC OCEAN
PORTUGAL
Zaragoza
Madrid
S P A I N
Lisbon
0 km 100
0 miles 100

CLIMATE

Warm temperature, with most rain falling during the typically mild winters, while summers are hot and dry.

(Abrantes, Portugal)

°F	°C		MM	IN
104	40		120	4¾
86	30		90	3½
68	20		60	2¼
50	10		30	1¼
32	0		0	0

Jan Feb Mar Apr May Jun Jul Aug Sep Oct Nov Dec

Key ▬ Average temperature ▬ Rainfall

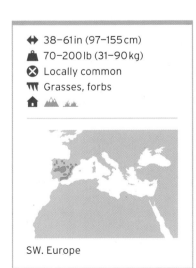

DEMAND FOR CORK
Cork oak forests have been carefully managed for centuries and comprise one of the most biodiverse habitats on earth. These unique ecosystems are vulnerable to a fall in global demand for cork.

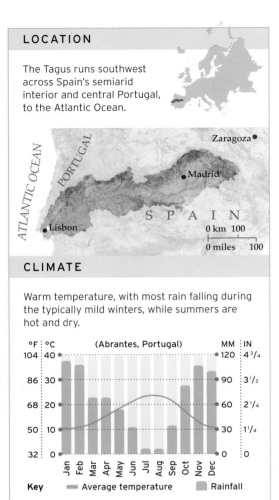

are found nowhere else

CORK OAK

Iberian lynx

Lynx pardinus

tufts of black hair on tip of ears

distinctive beard around face

The Iberian lynx is the most endangered cat on Earth. Once found throughout Spain and Portugal, as well as in southern France, fewer than 250 breeding adults are left in the wild, mostly confined to two tiny areas of southern Spain. This is largely due to human impact, but the lynx's highly specialized diet and habitat requirements have also contributed to its decline.

Reliant upon rabbits

This muscular, spotted wild cat has evolved to feed mainly on one animal—the European rabbit. In summer, rabbits make up as much as 93 percent of the lynx's diet, which means that if rabbit populations fall due to hunting or diseases, so do lynx numbers. If it has no other choice, the Iberian lynx will hunt rodents, hares, ducks, or even small deer, but it has become so specialized in its tastes that, without rabbits, its numbers inevitably decline.

Added to this is the increasing destruction of the lynx's habitat due to the rise in human population. The Iberian lynx prefers large areas of dense scrubland, such as heather interspersed with open pasture. Since lynxes are highly territorial and solitary as adults, maturing juveniles that leave their birth zones in search of their own territories face a high risk of being hit by traffic,

which in recent decades has increased dramatically in southern Spain. Even when they make it to adulthood, female lynxes will breed only after they establish their own territories.

Lynxes mate mainly during January and February, and before giving birth, a pregnant female will establish a den in a hollow tree, cave, or other sheltered spot, such as underneath dense bushes. Up to four cubs are born about two months later, although rarely more than two survive to weaning stage. Caring for her offspring puts an extra strain on the mother in many ways; a female lynx with cubs to feed needs to catch at least three rabbits a day, as opposed to the one she requires for herself. In addition, the female changes den sites frequently in order to keep the cubs safe. Like many species of wild cat, Iberian lynxes are primarily nocturnal, and spend the day resting away from the heat of the sun.

Future imperfect

Captive breeding programs and stricter hunting and development restrictions have led to a slight increase in Iberian lynx numbers, but conservationists are uncertain whether it will survive in the wild.

↔ 34–43 in (85–110 cm)

⬍ 22–29 lb (10–13 kg)

✖ Critically endangered

▥ Rabbits

🏠 🌲 ⛰ ≈

SW. Europe

▷ **BEARDED CAT**
Tufts of long, mainly black fur around the face give adult lynxes a bearded appearance, which makes their narrow jawline seem broader.

▷ **KILLING BITE**
Unlike larger cats, Iberian lynxes kill with a single bite, puncturing the rabbit's neck and severing its spinal cord.

▷ **MOTHER AND CUB**
Lynx cubs are weaned at 10 weeks and become independent at seven or eight months old, although they may remain with their mother for longer.

coat of stiff, sharp spines

European hedgehog

Erinaceus europaeus

With a coat of around 8,000 spines, the European hedgehog is one of the most recognizable—and most surprising—mammals. Earthworms, slugs, and snails feature in its diet, but its preferred food is insects, preferably ants and beetles. Stinging insects have little effect on it, and so it can even eat wasps and bees. A natural but variable resistance to venomous snakes allows it to eat adders as well. Hedgehogs spend daylight hours resting in shallow nests of leaves and twigs. At night they are highly active, covering up to 1 mile (2 km) as they forage for food.

Handle with care

Mating is tricky. A male circles a female, which hisses and snorts, initially. However, if the female flattens her spines by relaxing a special muscle, the male will mate with her several times before leaving in search of other females. Each year female hedgehogs have one or two litters of two to seven hoglets, born with white spines encased in fluid-filled skin. Once the fluid dissipates, the spines are revealed and are replaced by a darker set two to three days later. The banded adult spines appear when they are two to three weeks old. When threatened, hedgehogs roll up into a tight ball. They also cover their spines with foamy saliva in a practice known as "self-anointing"—but the reason for this is uncertain.

⬌ 8–11 in (20–28 cm)
⚖ 2 lb (1 kg)
✖ Common
🍴 Insects, slugs, bird eggs
🏠 🌳 🌿 🏘

Europe

△ **BUNDLED UP**
Piles of leaves, fallen logs or twigs, or garden compost heaps are favorite hibernation locations for hedgehogs in winter.

◁ **BLIND AT BIRTH**
Hoglets are born blind and remain blind, like these two youngsters, for between 11 and 14 days, at which time they begin to open their eyes.

Great crested grebe
Podiceps cristatus

Great crested grebes are renowned for their courtship rituals. One bird swims with the head and bill extended low on the water, then dives suddenly to reappear almost beneath its partner. The two perform "weed ceremonies" and dances. The nest is a mass of damp weed, which covers the eggs if a parent leaves the nest unattended. The stripy-headed chicks whistle to beg their parents for fish.

- ↔ 18–20 in (46–51 cm)
- ⚖ 1–3 lb (0.5–1.4 kg)
- ⊗ Common
- 🍽 Fish
- 🏠 🌾 ≈ ≈
- 🧭 Europe, Asia, Africa, Australia, New Zealand

▽ **MALE AGGRESSION**
Male great crested grebes may fight over territorial boundaries during the breeding season.

Hoopoe
Upupa epops

fan-shaped crest with black tips

Hoopoes spend most of their time foraging quietly on the ground, picking and probing with their bill in search of insects. Singing hoopoes spread their crests vertically, like a fan, giving low, far-carrying "hoop-hoop-hoop" calls from a tree or rooftop. They nest in tree cavities, which quickly become foul with the chicks' droppings and rotten food waste.

- ↔ 11 in (28 cm)
- ⚖ 3 oz (85 g)
- ⊗ Common
- 🍽 Insects, earthworms, snails
- 🏠 🌳 🌿 🏡
- 🧭 Europe, Asia, Africa

△ **SWIRL OF COLORS**
A hoopoe returning to its nest catches the eye in a flurry of black and white feathers.

Jeweled lizard
Timon lepidus

Europe's largest lizard—the jeweled, eyed, or ocillated lizard—gets its name from the blue "eyes" or rosettelike markings on its flanks. Its head and body are stocky, while the tapering tail makes up three-fifths of its length. The lizard hunts by day in mainly open, drier habitats. It hibernates in an old burrow or tree root for two to three midwinter months, and breeds in early summer. The female hides her clutch of 8–25 eggs in loose soil or undergrowth. If threatened by a predator, the jeweled lizard defends itself by opening its mouth and hissing. It also bites very hard and can be difficult to dislodge.

▽ **COLORFUL MALE**
The male jeweled lizard is larger and heavier, and more colorful, than the female.

- ↔ 20–32 in (51–81 cm)
- ⚖ Up to 1 lb (0.5 kg)
- ⊗ Near threatened
- 🍽 Insects, frogs, mammals
- 🏠 🌳 🏔 🌿 🏡

SW. Europe

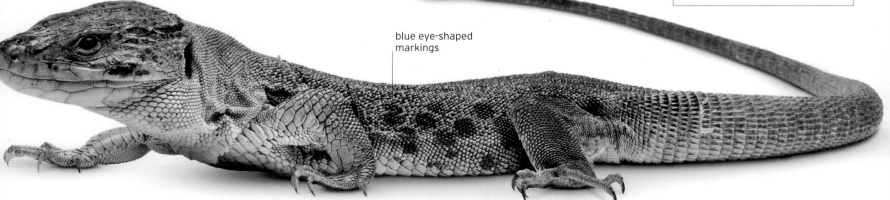

blue eye-shaped markings

THE ALPS
The mountainous heart of Europe

With an area of just under 77,000 sq miles (200,000 sq km), and 82 summits higher than 13,120 ft (4,000 m), the Alps form a natural climate barrier, dividing Europe into a cool, wet north and a warm, drier south. The mountains arc from France and Italy in the southwest to Austria in the east, and extend into eight countries. They rise from sea level to a peak of 15,771 ft (4,807 m)—the top of Mont Blanc, which straddles the French-Italian border.

Bountiful valleys

The Alps have several habitats, including glacial lakes, valleys, forests, high alpine meadows, and the slopes above the tree line. The meadows were created by specialist alpine plants colonizing rocky soil exposed by retreating glaciers. The region has been populated since prehistoric times, and a long history of mainly subsistence agriculture has changed the nature of the valleys and mountainsides to quite high levels. However, the steepness of the terrain and the need for trees to block avalanches means that large areas remain in a natural state. The Alps, therefore, support a rich diversity of plant and animal life, which, because of their location, are well studied. Of 13,000 plant species, 388 are endemic, and the Alps are also home to around 30,000 animal species.

Changing attitudes to wild carnivores and increasing forest cover are reflected in the gradual expansion of tiny remnant populations of gray wolf, European brown bear, and Eurasian lynx. However, these recoveries are not without problems—livestock, without protection, are easy prey for predators.

SMALL AND WHITE...
A symbol of the Alps, Edelweiss grows from 5,900 ft (1,800 m) to the snow line. The starlike pale leaves are covered in white hairs that insulate the plant from the cold and offer protection from drying winds and ultraviolet radiation.

EDELWEISS

MAKING A COMEBACK
Gray wolves were hunted to the brink of extinction across western Europe. However, changes in land use, habitat improvement, and legal protection in recent decades have allowed wolves to recolonize parts of their former range.

GRAY WOLF

ROSALIA LONGICORN BEETLE

Home to 75% of Europe's plant diversity > Covers 11% of Europe > More than 20%

WOODLAND BEAUTY
The spectacular Rosalia longicorn beetle has declined severely due to changes in forest management, which reduce the availability of dry dead wood in which the grubs develop. Unscrupulous collectors also take a toll.

LOCATION

The Alps cover 11 percent of Europe's land area, including most of Austria and Switzerland.

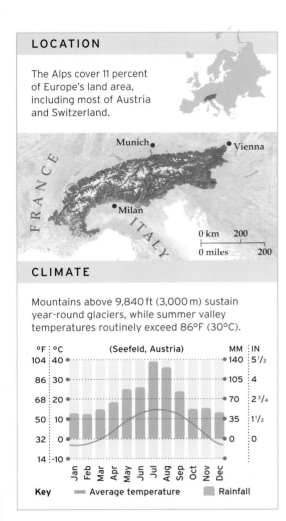

Munich • Vienna

FRANCE • Milan ITALY

0 km 200

0 miles 200

CLIMATE

Mountains above 9,840 ft (3,000 m) sustain year-round glaciers, while summer valley temperatures routinely exceed 86°F (30°C).

°F	°C	(Seefeld, Austria)	MM	IN
104	40		140	5½
86	30		105	4
68	20		70	2¾
50	10		35	1½
32	0		0	0
14	-10			

Jan Feb Mar Apr May Jun Jul Aug Sep Oct Nov Dec

Key — Average temperature ▮ Rainfall

Alpine chamois

Rupicapra rupicapra

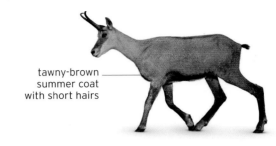

tawny-brown summer coat with short hairs

Agility is the trademark of the Alpine chamois—an adaptation to its rugged mountainous environment and a crucial survival skill when pursued by predators such as lynxes and wolves. A chamois' hooves provide maximum traction on slippery rocks, and even in snow-covered terrain, it can run, sure-footed, at speeds of up to 30 mph (50 km/h), leap upwards of 7 ft (2.1 m), and span 20 ft (6 m) in a single bound.

Lethal headgear

Both sexes have vertical horns ending in a sharp, hook-like curve, although the horns are slightly thicker in males. As well as wielding these against predators, males use their horns to fight each other for access to females. Unlike other hooved mammals that engage in head-to-head combat, male chamois attack each other's undersides and flanks, often with fatal consequences.

↔ 4 ft (1.2 m)

⚖ 55–132 lb (25–60 kg)

✕ Common

🌾 Grasses, forbs, leaves

🏠 🌲 ⛰ 🌱

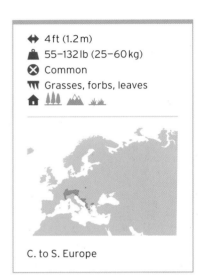

C. to S. Europe

A **newborn** chamois can **stand minutes after birth**, ready to follow its mother

◁ **MOUNTAINEERING EXPERT**
The chamois' thick winter coat provides excellent insulation. Their hooves have a thin, hard edge and softer, more pliable soles for grip, so they can negotiate the steepest, iciest terrain.

LOSS OF VARIETY
The alpine lakes are home to several subspecies of whitefish, which spawn in different levels of the lakes. Because fertilizer run-off has led to algal blooms, some of the subspecies have interbred and the whitefish diversity has declined.

of the Alps is protected

WHITEFISH

sharp claws used to scrape earth

Alpine marmot
Marmota marmota

▷ **SPARRING MALES**
Alpine marmots will defend their territory against intruders and to maintain their dominance in the group.

Alpine marmots are large ground-dwelling members of the squirrel family. They are of a sturdier build than their tree-dwelling cousins, with powerful legs for digging into hard, rocky ground. Most of their digits have sharp claws except the thumb, which has a nail.

Burrowing down

Alpine marmots live at altitudes of 2,000–10,500 ft (600–3,200 m), but more commonly over 4,000 ft (1,200 m). They create extensive deep burrow systems in alpine meadows and high-altitude pastures above the tree line. In the summer months, they feed during the day on lush grasses and herbs, accumulating fat that will see them through the long winter hibernation. Alpine marmots spend as many as nine months in a year hibernating, sealed in their hay-lined burrows for insulation as well as safety. Adults and older offspring cuddle up to younger animals to help maintain their body temperature, which drops as low as 41°F (5°C). While hibernating, alpine marmots breathe only one to two times each minute and their heartbeat drops to 28–38 beats per minute. They emerge in April when the mountains are still covered in snow. Dominant pairs mate soon after, and the young are born a month later.

Traditionally, alpine marmots were killed because their fat was thought to help with arthritis. They are still hunted for sport today.

▽ **MOTHER AND YOUNG**
Alpine marmots breed once a year, with litter sizes of one to seven. Mothers take on the main role of taking care of the young.

↔ 18–27 in (46–69 cm)
⬛ 5–14 lb (2.3–6.4 kg)
✖ Common
🌾 Grass, shrubs, herbs
🏠 ⛰ 🌱

C. Europe

Yellow-billed chough
Pyrrhocorax graculus

red legs

↔ 14–15 in (36–38 cm)
⚖ 6–9 oz (170–255 g)
✖ Common
🍽 Insects, fruit
🏠 ⛰ 🌾

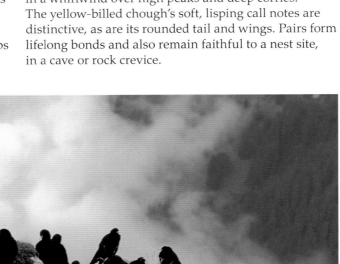

Europe, NW. Africa, W. to C. Asia

Skiers and climbers in the high Alps are familiar with this elegant member of the crow family, but flocks of yellow-billed choughs are sometimes seen at much lower elevations, especially in the Balkans. These choughs often visit tourist sites in search of extra scraps of food. They form flocks that are hundreds strong when feeding in green pastures or swirling effortlessly in a whirlwind over high peaks and deep corries. The yellow-billed chough's soft, lisping call notes are distinctive, as are its rounded tail and wings. Pairs form lifelong bonds and also remain faithful to a nest site, in a cave or rock crevice.

◁ **ON TOP OF THE WORLD**
Flocks of yellow-billed choughs settle on high ridges and forage on alpine pastures. In the Himalayas they can reach altitudes as high as 26,250 ft (8,000 m).

Ptarmigan
Lagopus muta

feathered feet

Unusually for a gamebird, the ptarmigan is monogamous. Pairs stay together to protect their growing chicks, although sexes often separate when they form winter flocks. A high-altitude bird in most of Europe, the ptarmigan lives much lower in the far north and northwest, commonly at sea level in Iceland. It is feared that climate change may wipe out southern populations on lower ranges, as their habitat and climate "envelope" rises above the available peaks.

Ptarmigans molt through a sequence of white, salt-and-pepper, gray-and-white, and beautiful mottled plumages, keeping pace with the change from white-out snow to the rich colors of rock, gravel, moss, and lichen in summer. Throughout the seasons they show white wings in flight, catching the light against blue skies—a vital clue for predators such as eagles.

↔ 13–15 in (33–38 cm)
⚖ 15–26 oz (425–737 g)
✖ Common
🍽 Berries, shoots, leaves, seeds
🏠 ⛰ 🌾

N. North America, C. and N. Europe, N. and C. Asia

▷ **SUMMER PLUMAGE**
The ptarmigan's mottled summer plumage offers camouflage, hiding it from golden eagles and Arctic foxes.

Golden eagle

Aquila chrysaetos

heavily feathered thighs

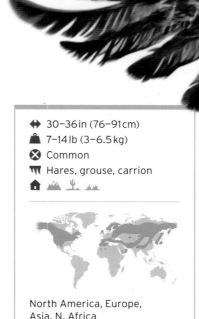

Golden eagles fly with incomparable skill and grace over mountain peaks and cliffs, and are often seen merely as dots over a distant high skyline. Their subtly curved wings are held in a shallow "V" as they soar high in the sky. They have excellent sight, several times more acute than a human's, and can see prey such as a mountain hare from 1–2 miles (2–3 km) away. They feed on whatever they can catch up to the size of a goose. In winter, they often eat dead sheep and deer, tearing the carcasses apart with their heavy, hooked bill. Golden eagles fare better on rich moors with plentiful prey than on colder, wetter peaks and forests.

Favorite eyrie

Pairing up for life, golden eagles have several nest sites, but one favored nest, or eyrie, in a tree or on a cliff ledge may become up to 13 ft (4 m) deep as sticks are added to the structure each breeding season. Courtship displays include high soaring, deep switchback undulations, and stunning stoops. In these long plunges with closed wings, the eagles reach extremely high speeds. The female usually lays two eggs, but the first-hatched chick often attacks its younger sibling, and frequently only the stronger, bigger chick survives.

Golden eagles can live for up to 38 years in the wild. However, in some parts of their range they are persecuted by humans and are under threat from activities such as illegal shooting, trapping, and the use of poisoned bait.

↔ 30–36 in (76–91cm)
⚖ 7–14 lb (3–6.5 kg)
⊗ Common
🐾 Hares, grouse, carrion
🏠 ⛰ 🌵 🌾

North America, Europe, Asia, N. Africa

broad wings for soaring and braking

△ **IN FOR THE KILL**
With its wings, tail, and talons stretched wide, this golden eagle swoops down onto its prey, attacking the animal from behind.

Midwife toad

Alytes obstetricans

Looking much like a common European toad at first glance, the midwife toad has a more pointed snout and vertical pupils. The toad's name refers to the way this small amphibian carries around fertilized eggs to keep them out of harm's way while they develop. However, the name is slightly misleading in that it is the male, not the female, that takes care of the next generation. During mating, the male glues the string of eggs to his rump and then delivers them to a pond a few weeks later in time for the tadpoles to hatch.

▷ **PATERNAL CARE**
The male midwife toad may carry the eggs of more than one mate. It secretes antibiotic mucus to protect the developing young.

↔ 1–2 in (2.5–5 cm)
☁ Spring and summer
⊗ Locally common
🐾 Insects
🏠 🌳 🌵 ≈ ≈ 🏠

W. to C. Europe

upcurved
wingtips

△ **SEEING OFF A FOX**
This immature golden eagle is
still big and strong enough to
chase away a red fox that has
tried to steal its meal.

powerful feet
for killing

Apollo
butterfly

Parnassius apollo

Although widespread across
Europe's mountainous regions,
this unusual member of the
swallowtail family is an
endangered species. Its color
pattern of pale wings dotted
with black and red spots is
so variable that dozens of
subspecies have been identified,
some of which are restricted to a
single alpine valley. Females lay
their eggs close to plants such as
stonecrop; the caterpillars eat
the leaves when they hatch.

red eyespot
on hind wing

△ **NECTAR OF THE GODS**
Adult Apollos can be seen drinking
nectar from flowers in mountain
meadows at the height of summer.

↔	2–4 in (5–10 cm)
✕	Vulnerable
♨	Leaves; nectar
⌂ ⛰	
◑	Europe, W. Asia

Large mountain
grasshopper

Stauroderus scalaris

This is the largest species of
grasshopper in Europe, and in
late summer, alpine meadows
resound with its whirring
stridulations, or "songs."
The bright green males sing
to attract the larger, drab
brown females.

↔	¾–1 in (1.8–2.7 cm)
✕	Common
♨	Grass, spurge, leaves
⌂ ⛰ ⛰ 🌾 ≈	
◑	Europe, E. to C. Asia

▷ **PREPARED TO JUMP**
Grasshoppers have long wings,
but instead of flying away from
danger, they usually jump, using
their large, powerful hind legs.

BAVARIAN FOREST
Europe's original deep dark wood

Germany's Bavarian Forest National Park and the Czech Republic's Bohemian forest combine to form the largest area of forest remaining in central Europe. The forest cloaks rolling mountains that, despite being relatively low, constitute a continental divide from which the headwaters of the Danube, Vlatva, and Elbe rivers drain in different directions. The mountains, gentle hills, curved valleys, and pockets of hard granite rock are evidence of a land carved by glaciers during the last ice age.

Ancient woodland
Much of the Bavarian forest is old-growth and undisturbed by humans, and conservation work in Germany's first national park aims to keep it untouched. Its plants and animals include several ice age relict species, such as the boreal owl, three-toed woodpecker, Norwegian wolf spider, and quillwort, a scarce semiaquatic fern.

The Bavarian forest has acidic soil and water. This is partly due to its cool, wet climate, but also to the overwhelming dominance of trees such as spruce, fir, and beech, which form closed canopies that block sunlight and warmth. These conditions limit opportunities for ground plants and some insect species to thrive, but fungi, mosses, and invertebrates associated with dead wood abound. Indeed, the forest boasts more than 1,300 species of mushroom, bracket fungus, and puffball. The ancient forest is also home to several large animals, including brown bears, gray wolves, lynxes, wild cats, roe deer, wild boar, capercaillies, and eagle owls.

CLEVER COMPETITOR
The porcelain fungus is a beechwood specialist. Its pale fruiting bodies appear in fall on dead wood, into which it secretes a chemical known as strobilurin. This inhibits the growth of other fungi, thus reducing competition.

PORCELAIN FUNGUS

Germany's first national park, created in 1970

DORMOUSE DUO
Two native dormice share the forest, using different zones to avoid competition. The tiny golden-furred hazel dormouse favors a complex matrix of low shrubs, while the much larger, silver-gray edible dormouse lives in the forest canopy.

HAZEL DORMOUSE

95% forest cover

LINKED FORTUNES
The cyclic boom and bust of roe deer populations has a dramatic effect on the reintroduced Eurasian lynx. Severe winters reduce deer numbers so the lynx lose out to the larger wolves, which work cooperatively to drive out competitors.

EURASIAN LYNX

3,693 invertebra

long, slender body

European pine marten

Martes martes

Pine martens can live in any tree-filled environment. Powerful forelimbs and strong claws allow them to leap from tree to tree in pursuit of small animals such as squirrels. Most of their hunting occurs on the ground, however, where they forage between dusk and dawn.

↔ 18–27 in (45–68 cm)
⚖ 2–4 lb (0.8–1.8 kg)
⊗ Common
🎋 Small mammals, berries

Europe to N. and W. Asia

◁ **SNOW PATROL**
In winter, pads on the marten's soles are covered with fur, which insulates its feet and provides traction in the snow.

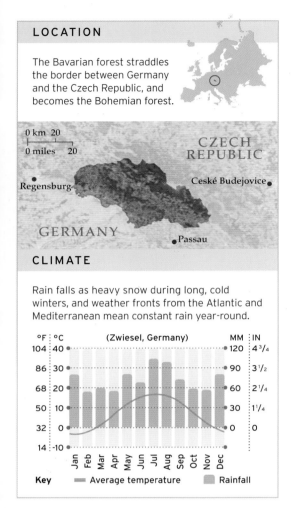
European badger

Meles meles

Badgers live in groups of six or more members, sharing the same sett—a system of underground tunnels, chambers, and toilet areas. Setts may evolve into huge networks over time. A sett is ruled by a dominant male, or boar, and one breeding female. The pair mate throughout the year, but a litter of one to five cubs is not born until February.

↔ 22–35 in (56–89 cm)
⚖ 22–36 lb (10–16 kg)
⊗ Common
🎋 Earthworms, fruit, birds

Europe to W. Asia

◁ **WHITE-STRIPED IDENTITY**
The badger's black-and-white striped face makes it instantly recognizable, but ginger-coated and albino (all-white) badgers have also been found.

short, powerful legs

MOSS SANCTUARY
Compared to flowering plants and ferns, the diversity of mosses in the national park is extraordinary. At around 490 species, this is 42 percent of mosses in Germany. They thrive because of the minimal human disturbance.

species recorded here

HAIRCAP MOSS

pale fur on throat and underside

muscular tail

Eurasian otter

Lutra lutra

Webbed feet and the ability to close their ears and noses underwater may mark them out as a semiaquatic member of the weasel family, but oddly enough, Eurasian or common otter cubs are not naturally drawn to water. In fact, female otters often have to drag their protesting cubs in for their first swim at around 16 weeks of age. However, once the initial shock has worn off, they quickly learn to love the water, spending hours play-fighting together in the shallows near the holt, or den, where they were born.

Staying dry

Once grown, their double-layered coats trap air bubbles for insulation in frigid waters, and the waterproof outer layer keeps them dry. Slender bodies and thick, tapered tails make them exteremely graceful swimmers, highly skilled at catching fish. They eat shellfish (particularly crabs), amphibians, and even water birds such as ducks. The year that the cubs spend with their mother is the longest time Eurasian otters live in a group. Otherwise, aside from mating, when a male and female may spend a week or so together, these highly vocal mammals lead solitary lives, staking out territories of 1–4 miles (1.6–6.4 km) along rivers, estuaries, lakes, streams, and ocean shores. Otters mark their territories with spraints, or droppings, usually on top of rocks, driftwood, or other debris near the water's edge.

On the lookout

Spraints and tracks are often the only signs of these highly vocal carnivores, because acute hearing, smell, and sight mean otters are more likely to be alert to a human being's presence and duck out of sight before the latter is aware they were ever nearby. The positioning of their eyes, ears, and noses toward the top of the head also means they can keep their bodies hidden from view underwater while they watch, until the coast is clear.

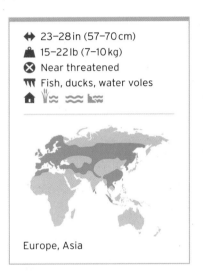

- ↔ 23–28 in (57–70 cm)
- 15–22 lb (7–10 kg)
- ⊗ Near threatened
- Fish, ducks, water voles

Europe, Asia

Otters that **hunt in coastal waters** need fresh water to **remove salt from their coat**

◁ **CLEAR VIEW**
Thick, double-layered fur keeps otters warm in icy conditions, and their long whiskers, called vibrissae, help them to locate prey in murky water.

△ **FRESH CATCH**
Fish make up about 80 percent of a Eurasian otter's diet. Adults eat up to 15 percent of their body weight in fish per day.

◁ **UNDERWATER DIVE**
Although the Eurasian otter is an exceptionally agile swimmer, it cannot hold its breath for long. Average dives last no more than 30 seconds.

Red fox
Vulpes vulpes

back of ear
often black

long, bushy
tail, or brush

Found throughout the northern hemisphere from sea level to 14,750 ft (4,500 m), in deserts, mountains, forests, farmland, and city centers, red foxes are the most widespread wild canines on the planet. They tailor their behavior and diets to suit highly diverse habitats. Small mammals make up a large part of the red fox's diet, but if rabbits, voles, and mice are scarce, it will eats birds, eggs, earthworms, beetles, and wild fruit such as blackberries.

Opportunistic hunters

Intelligent and territorial, these solitary hunters search for food from dusk until dawn. They are always ready to exploit landfill sites, compost heaps, garbage cans, bird feeders, and other easy sources of food. Excellent vision

and a keen sense of smell give all 44 subspecies of red foxes an edge when it comes to survival, as does a cooperative lifestyle when raising their young.

Once a dominant pair establishes a territory, mating occurs in early winter. The vixen digs out a den, or earth, in which she gives birth to four to six cubs around two months later. For the first three weeks, she stays with the cubs, relying on the male to bring her food.

▽ **MATED PAIR**
A vixen (left) and dog fox (right) race each other through deep snow in early winter, having spotted a potential meal.

↔ 18–36 in (46–91 cm)

⚖ 7–31 lb (3.2–14 kg)
❌ Common
🍖 Rabbits, voles, birds, fruit

Arctic, North America, Europe, Asia, and N. Africa

Wild boar

Sus scrofa

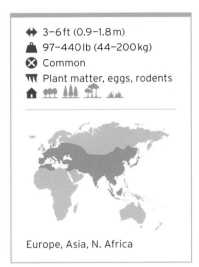

↔ 3–6 ft (0.9–1.8 m)
⚖ 97–440 lb (44–200 kg)
✖ Common
🍴 Plant matter, eggs, rodents
🏠 🌳🌲🌳🌿

Europe, Asia, N. Africa

The ancestor of most domestic pigs, the wild boar is an example of extreme species success. Now found on every continent except Antarctica, the highly adaptable wild boar is so prolific that it is often considered a pest, largely due to its impact on agricultural landscapes.

Sounders and solitary boars

Whether wild boar are solitary or social depends on their sex. Sows live in herds or "sounders" made up mainly of other females and their offspring. Sows only leave a sounder to give birth, returning as soon as their piglets—litter sizes vary from three to 12—are large enough to travel with the sounder. Sows may have two litters a year, and will protect all piglets in the sounder. Males only come into contact with other boar to mate, although they sometimes join sounders to feed.

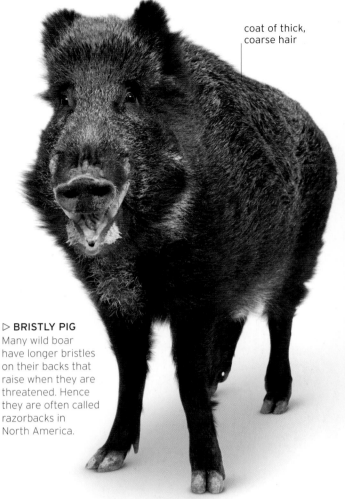

coat of thick, coarse hair

▷ **STRIPED PIGLETS**
Sows give birth to striped piglets that live in the sounder and are protected by the mother. Males leave their birth sounder at one or two years of age.

▷ **BRISTLY PIG**
Many wild boar have longer bristles on their backs that raise when they are threatened. Hence they are often called razorbacks in North America.

Black woodpecker

Dryocopus martius

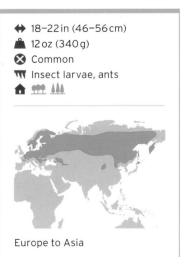

stiff tail used to maintain balance

Large woodpeckers have daggerlike beaks, crested heads, and stiff tails. A long outer toe turns outward or back, rather than the usual three-toes-forward, one-back shape of other perching birds, giving a better grip for climbing trees. Black woodpeckers need big trees—pine, oak, beech, or mixed forests are all occupied. In winter, they prefer wooded parks and yards. They chisel a new nesting cavity at the start of each breeding season. The eggs hatch in 12–14 days and the young can fledge after 24–28 days.

Noisy neighbors

Black woodpecker calls are loud and frequent, with strident, discordant laughing notes and high, long calls. They proclaim their ownership of a territory by "drumming"—a loud, deep, staccato sound produced by a rapid drumroll beat of the billtip against a branch.

△ **HARD AT WORK**
A female black woodpecker, with a smaller red cap than the male, chips away bark and living wood to get at the beetle larvae and carpenter ants inside.

↔ 18–22 in (46–56 cm)
⚖ 12 oz (340 g)
✖ Common
🍴 Insect larvae, ants
🏠 🌳🌲

Europe to Asia

Great crested newt

Triturus cristatus

This is the largest newt species in northern Europe. In summer, great crested newts hunt on land by night. In winter, they hibernate in sheltered spots or at the bottom of their breeding pools. Males court by arching their bodies and wafting their paddle-shaped tails. Females lay their eggs on submerged plants, each egg wrapped in a leaf for protection. The larvae hatch after three weeks and transform into the air-breathing form after about four months.

↔ 4–6 in (10–14 cm)
☁ Spring
✖ Common
〰 Larvae, worms
🏠 🌾≋
➤ Europe, C. Asia

▽ **BREEDING CREST**
Females are larger than males, but only males grow a crest during the spring breeding season.

distinctive black markings

Pale tussock

Calliteara pudibunda

heavily feathered antennae of male

crescent-shaped marking

This chunky moth is one of the most widespread moth species. It lives in the woodlands of Europe, where the adults (which do not feed) can be seen flying at night in late spring and early summer. Males use their antennae to sweep the air for the scent of mates. Eggs are laid on trees and hatch the following spring.

↔ 2–3 in (5–7 cm)
✖ Common
〰 Tree foliage
🏠 🌳 🏚
➤ Europe

▷ **TUFTED CATERPILLAR**
Some of the bristles are bunched into four distinct tufts.

↔ Average ¹/₂ in (12 mm)
✖ Common
〰 Pollen, nectar, honey
🏠 🌳 🌵 🏚

Europe, W., C., and SW. Asia, W., E., and S. Africa

△ **HARD AT WORK**
During construction of a new honeycomb, honeybee workers use their bodies to form a bridge across the gap.

▷ **PACKING POLLEN**
A forager bee packs pollen into her pollen baskets—a hollow section of each hind leg caged in by bristles.

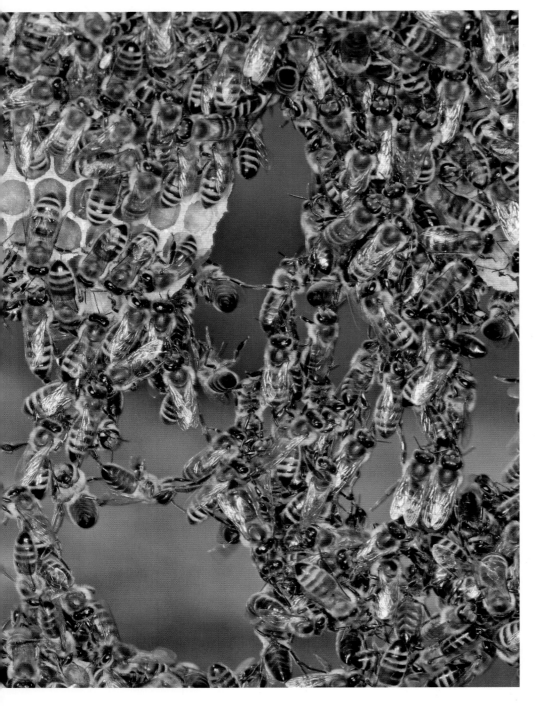

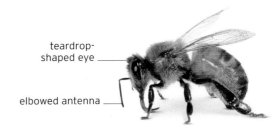

teardrop-shaped eye

elbowed antenna

European honey bee

Apis mellifera

Honeybees pollinate many flowering plants, including dozens of human food plants. They are social insects that live in wild colonies and in commercial hives, which are kept for honey production. Their natural range includes Africa, Europe, and the Middle East, but they have been introduced commercially into most parts of the world. Each colony is founded by a single queen, who rears her infertile daughters as workers. The workers extend and maintain the nest, raise more sisters, and make foraging trips to collect nectar and pollen from flowers.

Division of labor

A nest is typically built in a tree hollow. It consists of honeycomb—sheets of hexagonal cells made from wax. The cells are used as nurseries for larvae (and later, pupae) and for storing nectar and pollen. Honey is produced by workers regurgitating nectar and then fanning it until it dries out. Pollen is stored separately and provides food for the developing larvae. Honey is the main source of food for the rest of the colony.

Worker bees are infertile females that live for around four to five weeks. As they age, they graduate from duties in the nest to taking off on nectar-gathering flights to flowers. Foragers communicate the location of flowers to other workers back at the colony by a figure of eight "dance." In winter, numbers fall to 5,000, with the workers surviving on honey stores.

When a colony reaches a certain size, the queen flies off, taking half the workers with her. She leaves behind a new queen who flies off and mates with several males, collecting enough sperm to sustain her through a life that can be as long as five years, before flying back and taking over the colony.

△ **WORKER BEE PUPAE**
It takes 11 days for a worker bee egg to transform into a larva and then a pupa. The adult emerges at 21 days.

80,000 bees live in a colony in summer

enlarged, pronged
mandibles of male

Stag beetle

Lucanus cervus

This large forest insect is famed for the enormous mandibles of the male, which are used in jousting fights. They resemble the antlers used by male deer in battles of strength over potential mates, hence the name stag beetle. Females are smaller than males, and although their mandibles are more discreet, they can grip more strongly than the males. Like all beetles, both sexes have a hard, armored shell for protection.

Fueled by fat reserves

Adult stag beetles do not feed. Instead, they rely on their fat reserves built up while they were larvae living underground. They will, however, occasionally sip tree sap or juices from decomposing fruit using their smaller hairy mouthparts. Otherwise, the adults devote themselves to mating.

The males dig their way out of the ground in May or June, a week or so before the females. They establish a mating territory and use their "antlers" to fight off any late arrivals hoping to muscle in. The females walk from territory to territory, during which time they mate with several males. Adult life rarely lasts more than three months. The last thing a female does before she dies is find a suitable piece of rotting wood—usually decaying tree stumps or roots—where she lays about 20 eggs. Sometimes, females return to the site where they were larvae to lay their eggs.

Growing up underground

In total, a stag beetle lives for about six years. Most of this time is spent as a larva, eating wood rotting underground. The eggs hatch in August, and the tiny orange-headed grubs begin a five-year feeding session. It takes this long for a grub to reach full size and build up the crucial fat supply for the adult phase. When ready, the grub builds a cocoon chamber out of chewed wood fibers and turns into a pupa. In this form, it remains immobile for at least two months as its larval body is broken down and rebuilt as an adult. The pupa is protected by a hard case and the sex of the beetle can be identified—the large mandibles of a male are already visible. Pupation occurs in fall, but once emerged, the adult stays underground for the ensuing winter, readying itself to emerge the following summer.

The stag beetle population across the world is rapidly declining for many reasons, including changes in forest management that has led to the removal of dead timber. Increased urbanization is also a threat.

Stag beetles spend almost **their entire lives underground** as larvae

↔ 3 in (7.5 cm)
✗ Near threatened
🍴 Dead wood, sap, fruit juices
🏠 🌲 🌲

Europe, Asia

▷ **JOUSTING MALES**
The stag beetle fights to overturn the opposition. The mandibles have a series of prongs that give a good grip as the fighters try to flip their rival. However, injuries are rare.

◁ **FREQUENT FLIER**
Despite their large size and cumbersome appearance, stag beetles are frequent fliers. The males fly more often than the females, as they patrol their territories.

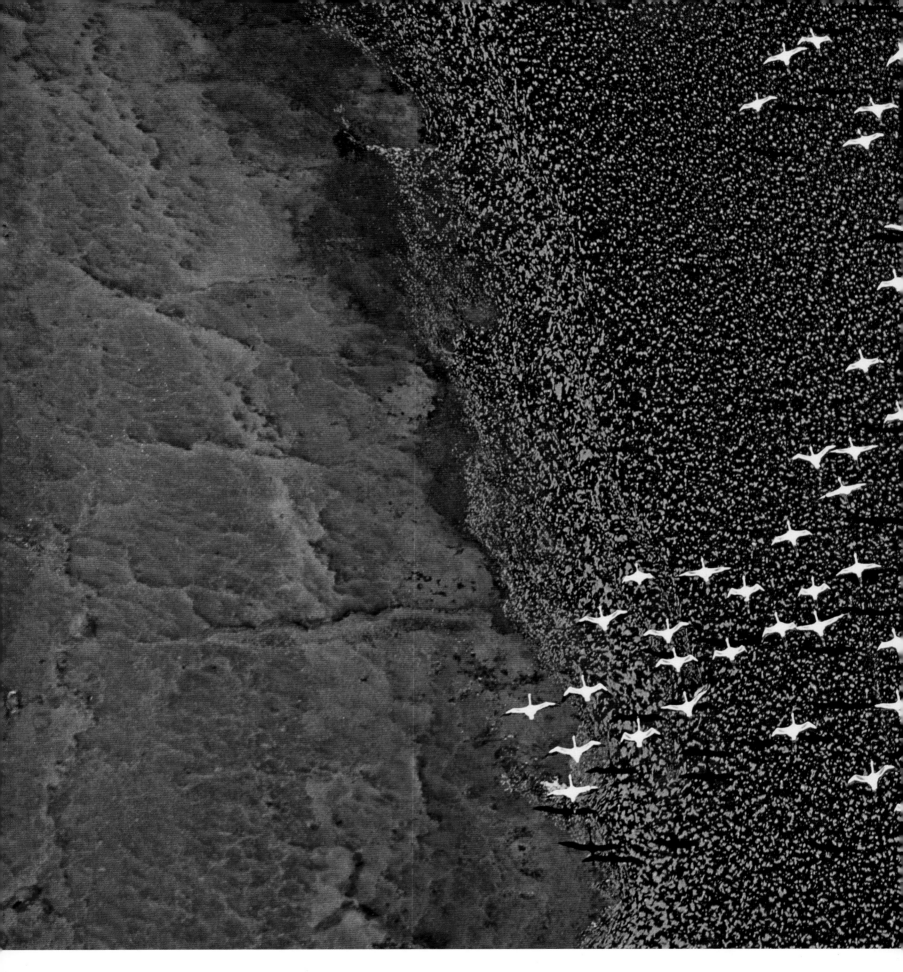

Great Rift Valley
Millions of lesser flamingos feed and breed around the edges of alkaline lakes in East Africa's Great Rift Valley. Flocks of adults fly in formation every day in search of fresh water to drink.

Africa

A SUNBAKED LAND
Africa

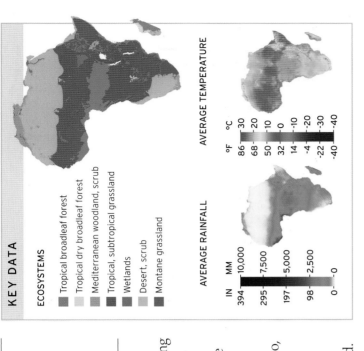

The second-largest continent, Africa covers 12 million sq miles (30 million sq km), and accounts for more than 20 percent of the world's land area. Dominated by sunbaked landscapes and tropical forest, Africa is famous for its wildlife. Even the rift valley lakes boast a spectacular diversity of cichlid fish that is every bit as impressive to zoologists as the large mammals of the Serengeti savannas are to tourists. Africa's habitats are some of the planet's most productive and biodiverse and include wetlands, uplands, and several major deserts as well as the forests and grasslands.

The eastern mountain ranges are part of the East African Rift, where the African plate is slowly splitting into two parts called the Somali and Nubian plates. The Great Rift Valley is one of its main arms. The Drakensberg range in South Africa marks the edge of a plateau that covers most of the south and east.

The continent is drained by several great rivers, including the Nile, Niger, Congo, Zambezi, Limpopo, and Orange. Some rivers never reach the sea. The Okavango feeds a vast inland wetland, while the Chari drains into Lake Chad in the Sahel from which the water evaporates or seeps into the ground.

ATLAS MOUNTAINS

The Atlas Mountains formed in a region where the African plate is colliding with the Eurasian plate to the north. The highest point is Mount Toubkal in Morocco.

SAHARA DESERT

The world's largest desert began to form 7 million years ago and is still growing. It covers about 30 percent of Africa's land area, limiting the north-south distribution of many species. Animals specially adapted to the dry conditions include the jerboa and fennec fox.

NILE DELTA

The vast Nile Delta fans out along 150 miles (240 km) of Egypt's Mediterranean coast. Its deep alluvial soils have been farmed for thousands of years.

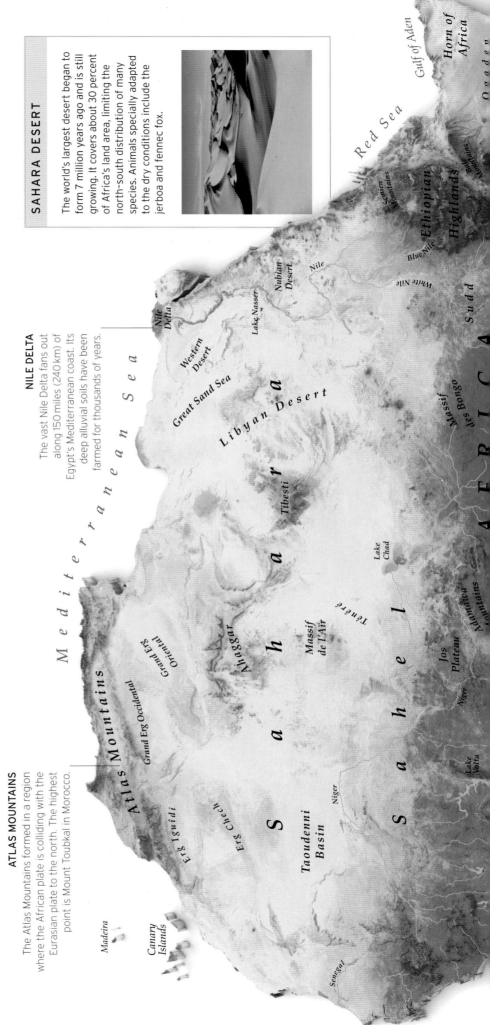

LAKE VICTORIA
The largest tropical lake in the world drains north into the Nile River. It supports Africa's largest inland fishery.

Comoro Islands

Madagascar

Zanzibar

Mozambique Channel

Lake Natron

▲ *Kilimanjaro 5,895m*

Great Rift Valley

Serengeti Plain

Lake Victoria

Lake Tanganyika

Great Rift Valley

Lake Nyasa

Zambezi

Victoria Falls

Lake Kariba

Limpopo

Congo Basin

Bié Plateau

Okavango Delta

Kalahari Desert

Drakensberg

Great Karoo

Namib Desert

Fynbos

Cape of Good Hope

Congo

INDIAN OCEAN

ATLANTIC OCEAN

São Tomé

COMMON REDSTART

SAHEL
The semiarid grasslands of the Sahel mark a transition between the desert and the savannas and forests further south. Enough rain falls during the wet season to allow this ecosystem to support great biodiversity and provide a stopping point for migrating birds.

NAMIB DESERT
Rainfall is so infrequent in the Namib that some specialist plants and animals rely solely on frequent sea fogs for moisture.

SARDINE RUN
During most winters, billions of sardines, or pilchards, travel up the east coast of South Africa. Single schools stretch for miles, and are the target of spectacular feeding frenzies attracting predators such as sharks, dolphins, and birds.

FYNBOS
This band of coastal and upland heath, flourishing in the Mediterranean climate of the Western Cape of South Africa, is a central component of the Cape Floristic Region. This tiny ecoregion is unmatched in biodiversity and endemic plants per square mile. Of 9,000 plant species known in the area, a staggering 6,200 occur nowhere else.

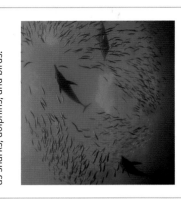

FEATURED ECOREGIONS

ETHIOPIAN HIGHLANDS
A hotspot of unique species in the roof of Africa

The largest area of land above 4,920 ft (1,500 m) in the whole of Africa, the Ethiopian Highlands rise to about nearly 15,000 ft (4,550 m) in the northeast of the continent. The region contains the Semien Mountains in the northwest and the Bale Mountains in the southeast, with part of the Great Rift Valley separating the two.

Loss of habitat

The area contains three distinct regions, differentiated by altitude. Up to about 5,900 ft (1,800 m) is dense montane forest, where the natural vegetation is dominated by evergreen trees, including myrrh, acacia, and juniper, and other conifers, with a shrub layer that includes wild coffee. Between 5,900 and 9,840 ft (1,800 and 3,000 m) is a region of montane grassland and woodland, which comprises a mosaic of forest, thicket, grassland, and brushlands and is home to ibex and gelada baboons.

Above the treeline, from 9,840 ft (3,000 m) upward, is montane moorland. The natural vegetation of this area is dominated by alpine shrubs and herbs. The densest collection of endemic wildlife, including mountain nyala and the world's rarest dog species, the Ethiopian wolf, is found here. All three regions have been severely impacted by human population increase and activities, mainly farming and unsustainable use of natural resources. As a result, an estimated 97 percent of the area's original habitat has been lost. Therefore, many of the plants and animals are being intensively studied and protected.

ARBOREAL BIRD
The colorful Prince Ruspoli's turaco feeds largely on figs and juniper berries. It is endemic to the Ethiopian Highlands, and its close association with the now fragmented montane forests of lower altitudes make it vulnerable to extinction.

PRINCE RUSPOLI'S TURACO

WINGED DRAGON
The Ethiopian highlander dragonfly is found only by clear mountain streams surrounded by forest, but its habitat is disappearing as a result of forest clearance and water pollution, and this endemic species is in danger of disappearing.

ETHIOPIAN HIGHL

Has 20 species of endemic mammals and 30 species of endemic birds

Only 3% of the

GIANT LOBELIA

ALL TOGETHER NOW
The giant *Lobelia* can grow to about 30 ft (9 m) high when flowering. Groups of *Lobelia* flower simultaneously after several years' growth, all producing a single flowering spike. They shed millions of seeds, then the plants die.

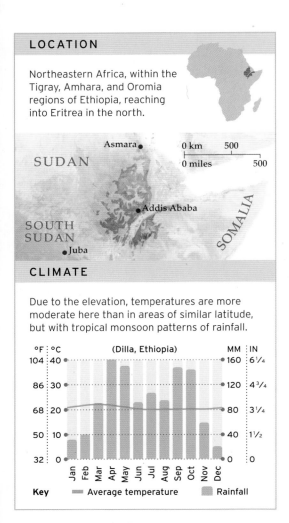

SUDAN · Asmara
Addis Ababa
SOUTH SUDAN · Juba
SOMALIA

0 km 500
0 miles 500

CLIMATE

Due to the elevation, temperatures are more moderate here than in areas of similar latitude, but with tropical monsoon patterns of rainfall.

(Dilla, Ethiopia)

°F	°C		MM	IN
104	40		160	6¼
86	30		120	4¾
68	20		80	3¼
50	10		40	1½
32	0		0	0

Jan Feb Mar Apr May Jun Jul Aug Sep Oct Nov Dec

Key — Average temperature ▇ Rainfall

UNDERGROUND GIANT
The giant mole rat lives alone, but in densities of up to 15,000 per sq mile (6,000 per sq km), so each burrow system overlaps many others. Insects and worms disturbed by the mole rats are eaten by alpine chats, which, in return, warn if Ethiopian wolves approach.

original vegetation remains

GIANT MOLE RAT

Ethiopian klipspringer
Oreotragus saltatrixoides

Unlike many other antelope species, where horns are either absent or smaller in females, Ethiopian klipspringer females grow the same spiked horns as the males. Klipspringers do not form herds, but move around their rock-strewn habitat in breeding pairs, marking territory with dung. The young are kept in hiding for two months and then follow the parents on feeding forays.

↔ 34 in (86 cm)
⚖ 11–35 lb (5–16 kg)
✗ Locally common
🌿 Leaves, flowers

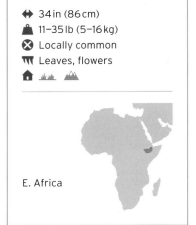

E. Africa

▷ **AGILE AND STURDY**
The klipspringer's "high-heeled" hooves allow it to perch all four feet in the smallest rocks as it moves around its rugged habitat.

speckled coat blends with rocks

short legs and narrow hooves

Mountain nyala
Tragelaphus buxtoni

spiraled horns

A relative of the kudu, not the lowland nyala, the mountain nyala migrates to higher altitudes in the dry season, but descends again when heavy rains arrive. Births peak after the end of the rains, with calves staying with their mother's herd until they are around two years old. Only males grow the tall "lyrate" horns.

↔ 7 ft (2.1 m)
⚖ 330–705 lb (150–320 kg)
✗ Endangered
🌿 Leaves, grasses, ferns, lichen

E. Africa

◁ **RELATED FEMALES**
Mountain nyalas live in small herds made up of females and their young. Mature males join them for the breeding season.

adult males have long, thick mane

Gelada

Theropithecus gelada

Geladas are cousins of the more common savanna baboons, which are found throughout much of sub-Saharan Africa. Geladas were widespread in Africa 50,000 years ago, but have gradually been squeezed out by competing subspecies of savanna baboon as well as human pressure. Today, geladas survive only in their remote highland refuge. They can forage on grasses—including roots—more efficiently than other baboons, surviving almost entirely on the grass of high-altitude meadows in the mountains of Ethiopia. A garnish of bulbs, seeds, fruit, and insects supplements this diet.

Signal patches

Most baboons have colorful patches of bare skin on their rears, which help to communicate mood, dominance, and breeding condition. Geladas spend most of their time sitting down, with their rumps hidden, while foraging on grasses within reach of their long arms. Perhaps this is why they have developed bare red patches on their chests. The male's patch mimics the female's, which mimics her own sexual skin and genitals with remarkable accuracy. This colorful area is used in both sexual and social interaction. "Social presenting"—a quick hind-end flash—among primates is a frequent peaceable signal, reducing aggression. Mimicry by males and non-estrous females helps enhance the message. Unless you are a gelada, however, it is hard to glean from a signal that a female is ready to mate.

Bachelor boys and bands

Geladas form herds several hundreds strong. Many males live in bachelor groups around the fringes of the herd until they are old enough to compete for dominance. The herd is comprised of several reproductive groups, or bands, each of which consists of an older male and his harem of females. They communicate using subtle facial signals and not-so-subtle "lip flicks" (see far right).

Geladas are also called **bleeding-heart baboons** after the **red patch on their chest**

△ **MOTHER AND INFANT**
Born helpless, baby geladas clamber over and ride on their mothers about a month after birth. Gelada families spend much time grooming.

▷ **ON TOP OF THE WORLD**
Geladas feed in meadows in Ethiopia, above 5,600 ft (1,700 m). They sleep in high rocky cliffs close by.

↔ 28–29 in (70–74 cm)

🏋 42 lb (19 kg)

✕ Locally common

🍽 Grass, roots, fruit

🏠 ⛰ 🌾

E. Africa

△ **STRIKING A POSE**

A male curls his lip in a "lip flick," exposing his gums and impressive teeth. This warns off rivals and reduces the need for physical aggression.

◁ **IMPRESSIVE MANE**

An adaptation to high-altitude cold, geladas are very heavily furred, especially around the head and upper body. The thick mane also increases the apparent size of a charging male.

Ethiopian wolf
Canis simensis

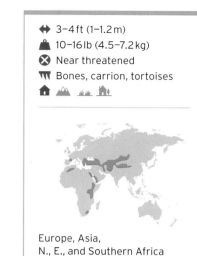

long, slender legs

A pack animal that mainly hunts alone, Africa's only wolf species is also the continent's rarest predator, and the world's most threatened canine: fewer than 500 adults are thought to remain in the wild. With its distinctive red coat and pointed muzzle, the Ethiopian wolf more closely resembles a fox. While on rare occasions a pack will work together to hunt a hare, this wolf is a specialist rat-catcher—up to 95 percent of its diet consists of small rats that live in the high African heathlands.

- ↔ 33–39 in (84–99 cm)
- 🏋 31–66 lb (14–30 kg)
- ✖ Endangered
- 〣 Rodents
- 🏠 ⋏

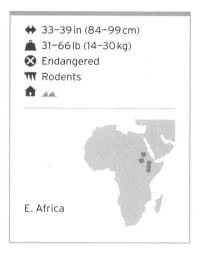

E. Africa

◁ **PACK LUNCH**
Pups mob adults until food is regurgitated for them to eat. All the adults in a pack care for the pups, although only the alpha female breeds.

- ↔ 3–4 ft (1–1.2 m)
- 🏋 10–16 lb (4.5–7.2 kg)
- ✖ Near threatened
- 〣 Bones, carrion, tortoises
- 🏠 ⛰ ⋏ 🏠

Europe, Asia, N., E., and Southern Africa

▽ **CLAIMING SUPERIORITY**
An adult lammergeier (right), although molting and unusually scruffy, reminds a juvenile who the boss is. The young bird shows the characteristic diamond-shaped tail.

Rufous sengi
Elephantulus rufescens

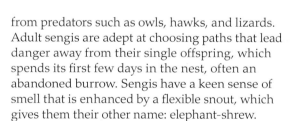

flexible snout to sniff out food

This sengi lives its life in literal "fast lanes"—it creates a network of trails that allow it to navigate its territory at high speed. Speed is essential; their metabolism is so rapid that sengis are constantly searching for food, and known pathways allow them to find prey in the most efficient manner possible. Trails also provide a handy escape route from predators such as owls, hawks, and lizards. Adult sengis are adept at choosing paths that lead danger away from their single offspring, which spends its first few days in the nest, often an abandoned burrow. Sengis have a keen sense of smell that is enhanced by a flexible snout, which gives them their other name: elephant-shrew.

- ↔ 5 in (12.7 cm)
- 🏋 2 oz (57 g)
- ✖ Common
- 〣 Insects
- 🏠 ⋏ ⋏

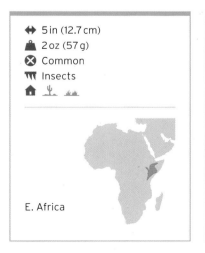

E. Africa

◁ **READY TO RUN**
Long hindlegs give sengis added power and maneuverability when attempting to outrun predators on their network of trails.

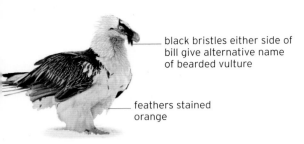

black bristles either side of bill give alternative name of bearded vulture

feathers stained orange

Lammergeier
Gypaetus barbatus

An ancient Greek playwright, Aeschylus, was allegedly killed when an eagle dropped a tortoise, mistaking his bald head for a stone. Myth turned the eagle into a lammergeier: the enormous vulture that carries bones (and sometimes tortoises) and drops them onto rocks to break open, exposing the marrow or flesh. Lammergeiers can swallow and digest shards of broken bone and eat gristly, bony scraps that other vultures leave behind, although flesh and skin of live prey such as tortoises and hares are preferred. With their huge wings and long tails, lammergeiers have a truly dramatic presence. This is often enhanced by a deep orange color brought about by iron oxide staining—they rub their feathers in red soil and rock dust and debris.

Highs and lows
Lammergeiers reach the summits of Africa's highest mountains and inhabit the most remote gorges, yet they frequently forage at town garbage dumps, where they are astonishingly agile at flying in congested spaces.

△ **EASY GLIDING**
A huge wingspan allows lammergeiers to glide almost endlessly with no effort. Occasionally they use a single, deep, emphatic wingbeat to adjust their course.

GREAT RIFT VALLEY LAKES
A global hotspot for freshwater diversity

The Great Rift Valley is part of a huge set of fissures in the Earth's crust that are expanding at a rate of about ¼ in (7 mm) a year and may eventually split Africa in two. The result is a sweep of low-lying land running from Jordan to Mozambique, which is flanked by some of the highest mountains in Africa. This land is dotted with lakes that include several of the oldest, largest, and deepest bodies of freshwater in the world. The rift valley splits into two branches in Kenya and Tanzania, between which lies Lake Victoria—the largest lake in Africa and the second largest freshwater lake in the world.

Fresh water, soda water

The Great Rift Valley lakes are generally stretched along the vertical axis of the rift. They differ widely in character, ranging from large, deep, and freshwater—like Malawi (also known as Nyasa), Tanganyika, and Turkana—to shallow and intensely mineralized and alkaline in the so-called soda lakes. Having been isolated from each other for millions of years, each lake has its own unique collection of aquatic animals. The deep waters of Lake Malawi, for example, which encompass a wide variety of habitats, are home to as many as 3,000 species of fish —more than any other lake in the world. The Great Rift Valley lakes also support large numbers of land-based animals and birds, such as pelicans and waders. The soda lakes—Natron, Bogoria, Nakuru, and Elementalia— are famous for their huge flocks of lesser flamingos.

UNDER THREAT
The lakes are home to the African spotted-necked otter and the smaller African clawless otter. Both are declining as a result of hunting for bushmeat, water pollution, and the introduced Nile perch, which eat the smaller fish on which the otters depend.

SPOTTED-NECKED OTTER

LONG-DISTANCE VISITORS
Huge numbers of migrant birds arrive at the lakes in fall, including familiar European species such as swifts, swallows, and wigeon. Some remain until March, feasting in and around the lakes; others pass through to wintering areas further south.

WIGEON

COMMON CARP

Home to 10% of the world's fish species – 3,000 in Lake Malawi alone ❯ Tanganyika is the

DOMINANT INTRODUCTION
The common carp was accidentally introduced to Lake Naivasha in 2001. It increased so rapidly that by 2010, it accounted for 90% of the lake's harvest, displacing a previously dominant introduction, the American red swamp crayfish.

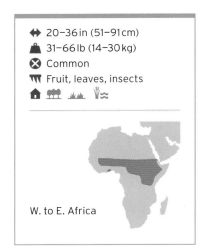

LOCATION

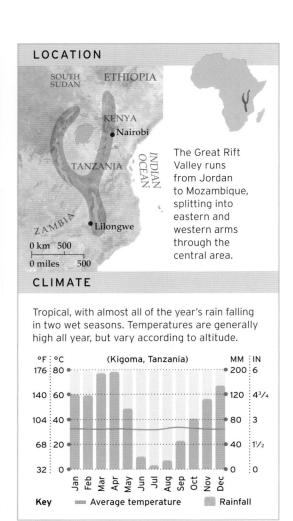

The Great Rift Valley runs from Jordan to Mozambique, splitting into eastern and western arms through the central area.

CLIMATE

Tropical, with almost all of the year's rain falling in two wet seasons. Temperatures are generally high all year, but vary according to altitude.

(Kigoma, Tanzania)

| Key | Average temperature | Rainfall |

Olive baboon
Papio anubis

Ever the opportunists, these intelligent, adaptable monkeys eat virtually anything they can get their hands on, from grasses to small animals and human refuse. They are also at home in many different habitats—even where there are few trees, such as rocky hills, semidesert, and open savanna.

Baboon society

Olive baboons live in large groups of up to 120 and spend most of their time foraging on the ground, often moving in columns. Adult males weigh twice as much as females, and have longer canine teeth and an impressive neck ruff, or mane. They fight for access to sexually receptive females, but usually only a few dominant males in each group manage to mate. Females can breed throughout the year, giving birth to a single baby after a gestation of around six months. It is carried by the mother, clinging to her belly, until it is around six weeks old and strong enough to ride on her back. Infants have black fur, which changes to grayish brown within a few months.

Because of their frequent crop-raiding, olive baboons are seen as pests and are widely persecuted by farmers. Their chief natural predators are leopards.

↔ 20–36 in (51–91 cm)

⚖ 31–66 lb (14–30 kg)

✖ Common

🍴 Fruit, leaves, insects

W. to E. Africa

▽ **MONKEYING AROUND**
Baboons are among the most playful of animals. They have an extended juvenile phase, during which they must learn the rules of their society.

CICHLIDS GALORE
Cichlids are famed for their diversity–Lake Malawi alone has some 800 species. Some have remarkable reproductive behaviors. Some males build elaborate nests to attract a mate, while some females are mouth brooders, carrying eggs and fry in their mouths.

orld's second-deepest lake

CICHLID

Adult male baboons are **efficient hunters**–they can catch hares, baby antelopes, **even other monkeys**

- ↔ 9 ft (2.7 m)
- ⚖ Up to 1.7 tons (1.5 metric tons)
- ⊗ Vulnerable
- 〽 Grass, aquatic plants
- ⌂

Africa

△ COMMUNAL POOL

Highly social, hippopotamuses live in groups or pods of 10–100 members, usually presided over by a dominant male. Other males are tolerated, if they are submissive.

▷ STAYING COOL

Along with regulating its body temperature in the hot African sun, water keeps a hippopotamus's skin from drying out and cracking.

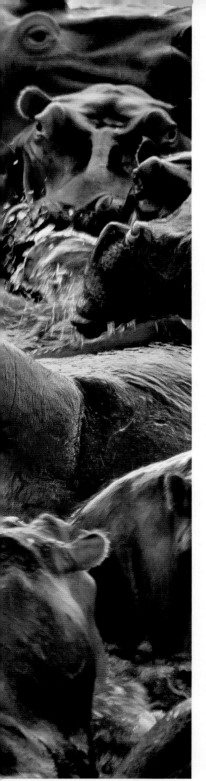

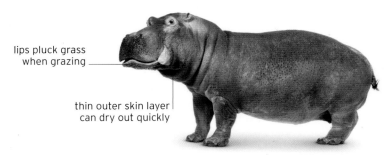

lips pluck grass
when grazing

thin outer skin layer
can dry out quickly

Hippopotamus

Hippopotamus amphibius

Although its name means "river horse," the hippopotamus, or hippo, more closely resembles the pig. In addition to similar teeth patterns, the two animals belong to the order artiodactyls—even-toed hoofed mammals. However, the hippopotamus's closest living relatives are not land mammals but whales and dolphins, with which it shared a common ancestor millions of years ago.

The hippopotamus is nearly hairless, and has an enormous mouth with teeth to match. Its bulky, barrel-shaped body makes it the Earth's third largest land animal, after elephants and rhinoceroses. Adult males weigh an average of 3,300 lb (1,500 kg) while females average 2,900 lb (1,300 kg). Despite its size and short, stocky legs, a hippo can sprint up to 18 mph (30 km/h). Speed, natural aggression, and 16–20-in- (40–50-cm-) long canine and incisor teeth that grow and sharpen themselves continuously make hippos one of Africa's most unpredictably dangerous species. They kill more people in Africa each year than any other mammal.

Walking underwater

As a semiaquatic animal, the hippopotamus spends its days in rivers, lakes, and swamps, where water and mud keep it cool and cover its skin in vital moisture. Water also supports its weight, and the animal can easily trundle or even leap along a lake bottom at speeds of up to 5 mph (8 km/h). However, even though a hippopotamus has webbed feet, it is not a strong swimmer; it cannot even float, so it stays in the shallows, closing its nostrils as it submerges, surfacing every 3–5 minutes to breathe.

Night grazer

Hippos feed at dusk, moving inland up to 6 miles (10 km) in search of the short grass that makes up the bulk of their diet. Adults consume as much as 150 lb (70 kg) of grass each night, pulling it up with their lips before crushing it with their large, grinding molars. The massive canines and incisors are only used in fighting and defense. Hippos "yawn" when threatened to show these teeth to their best advantage, opening their mouths nearly 180 degrees. Males defend territories by day, and it is thought that "dung-spinning"—performed mainly by males wagging their tails when defecating—is done partially as a territorial marking activity.

Mother and calf

Females can breed all year round, but most mating occurs in the dry season. Mating takes place in the water, with the female staying submerged for most of the process. A single calf, weighing up to 110 lb (50 kg), is born underwater and has to swim or be helped to the surface for its first breath. Baby hippopotamuses have sterile intestines, and must eat their mother's dung in order to obtain the bacteria they need for digesting grass. Juveniles are vulnerable to attacks by crocodiles, lions, and spotted hyenas.

△ BABY HIPPO
Calves are born and suckle underwater.
They often ride on their mother's back
if the water is too deep.

Hippo calls can reach up to **115 decibels**—as loud as **close-range thunder**

angled bill

extremely long legs

Lesser flamingo
Phoenicopterus minor

The lesser flamingo is an iconic bird of the African Rift Valley. Flocks hundreds of thousands strong turn whole landscapes pink at the steaming fringes of inhospitable alkaline lakes. In East Africa there are 3–4 million lesser flamingos; smaller populations live in southern Africa, including the Etosha Pan, and in India.

Incredible colonies

These monogamous birds breed in huge colonies on remote, caustic alkaline mudflats, exposed to searing heat, which are almost impossible for mammalian predators to reach. Their nests are small cones of mud and soda crystals, holding a single egg that hatches after 28 days. When two weeks old, chicks form herds of hundreds of thousands, attended by just one or two adults, leaving the parents free to find food. Chicks form lines up to 20 miles (30 km) long, and the nurseries are driven up to 30 miles (50 km) across burning mud to reach shallow freshwater lagoons.

Although a million or more flamingos may gather, only a small proportion breed each year. Of East Africa's 1.5 million pairs, an average of 319,000 breed, rearing 140,000 young. Half of them die before reaching breeding age, so to maintain the population, lesser flamingos require an adult lifespan of more than 20 years.

Natural mortality of full-grown birds, mainly from eagles and marabou storks, is low, but disturbance caused by tourism, including low-flying aircraft, may be more damaging, and there are increasing threats from pollution and industrial development.

↔ 32–35½ in (80–90 cm)

🏋 Up to 2 kg (4 lb)

✖ Common

🍴 Algae

🏠 Habitat

W., E., and S. Africa, S. Asia

△ **TAKING OFF**
Short daily flights take flamingos to fresh water for drinking, but longer nocturnal journeys between strings of alkaline lakes may lead them to fly hundreds of miles.

▽ **DIFFERENT DIETS**
Constant begging by flamingo chicks stimulates adults to produce a rich "crop milk," which is regurgitated to feed their young. The brilliant pink colors of the adult plumage are derived from the diet of algae.

Great white pelican
Pelecanus onocrotalus

Great white pelicans feed in flocks, herding fish into shallow water inside a tightening arc. Billfulls of water and fish are scooped up—the water spills out, but the fish rarely escape and are swallowed whole. Pelicans are massive birds but buoyant on water, and they are surprisingly elegant in the air, where they fly in synchronized lines, V-shapes, and huge flocks. In Africa, they will breed at any time of the year if the conditions are briefly favorable, nesting in colonies.

△ **FISH SCOOP**
A pelican's large, sensitive bill detects fish by touch. It then scoops up to 3 gallons (11 liters) of water, complete with prey, in its elastic pouch.

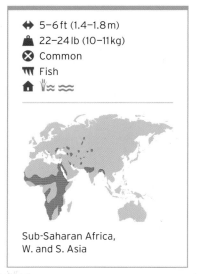

↔ 5–6 ft (1.4–1.8 m)
⚖ 22–24 lb (10–11 kg)
✕ Common
ⴲ Fish
⌂

Sub-Saharan Africa, W. and S. Asia

Gray crowned crane
Balearica regulorum

This spectacular crane used to be a common sight in East Africa's savannas and farmland. It strides majestically, picking seedheads and taking grasshoppers, locusts, worms, frogs, and lizards when it can. It has the typical crane dancing displays involving deep, rhythmic bowing movements with outspread wings, leading to dramatic leaps up to 8 ft (2.5 m) high.

Gray crowned crane pairs stay together for life and have large breeding territories. They nest in marshy places, clearing a large space by stamping on vegetation and gathering it into a huge central mound with a shallow cup to hold up to four eggs. These hatch after a month and the chicks quickly leave the nest. By the time they are three months old, the young are half the weight of an adult, but well grown and able to fly.

↔ 3–4 ft (1–1.1 m)
⚖ 7–9 lb (3–4 kg)
✕ Endangered
ⴲ Reptiles, insects, worms
⌂

E. to S. Africa

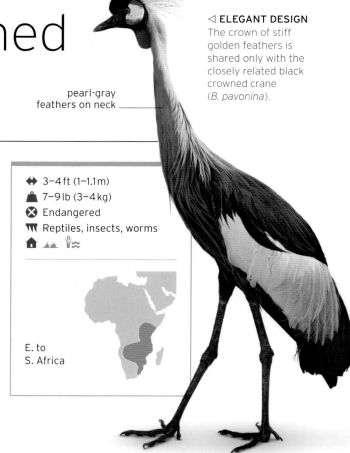

◁ **ELEGANT DESIGN**
The crown of stiff golden feathers is shared only with the closely related black crowned crane (*B. pavonina*).

pearl-gray feathers on neck

↔ 10–20 ft (3–6 m)
⚖ 880–1,760 lb (400–800 kg)
✖ Common
♈ Fish, mammals, birds

Africa, W. Madagascar

Nile crocodiles often **roll their eggs gently in their mouths** to help **hatching babies** emerge

dorsal scales reinforced by underlying bony plates (scutes)

◁ **RESTING CROCODILE**
When basking in the sun, crocodiles open their mouth to lose excess heat from its lining and their tongue.

long, keeled, powerful tail for propulsion

Shoebill
Balaeniceps rex

clog-shaped bill gives rise to name

Pointed, hooked, saw-edged, and spoon-shaped beaks, even pelicans' flexible pouches, are all used to catch fish. However, only one other bird has such a broad, deep, hook-tipped bill as the shoebill. The boat-billed heron's smaller bill helps it to fish by touch at night, whereas the shoebill fishes by sight during the day.

The shoebill moves remarkably delicately for a bird of its size, walking through waterside vegetation, bill tilted down so it can look for fish. The bill is also used to cool overheating eggs and chicks in the nest by pouring water over them. The nest is a huge, flat mound of wet vegetation in shallow water, among reeds or papyrus. The female usually lays two eggs. The chicks have to feed themselves on regurgitated fish dropped into the nest because of the adults' unusual bill structure.

▷ **HOOK-TIPPED BILL**
The broad, deep bill is adapted to grab fish, underwater vegetation, and mud in a swift open-mouthed lunge. Unwanted debris is then discarded.

↔ 4–5 ft (1–1.5 m)
⚖ 10–14 lb (4.5–6.5 kg)
✖ Vulnerable
♈ Lungfish, frogs

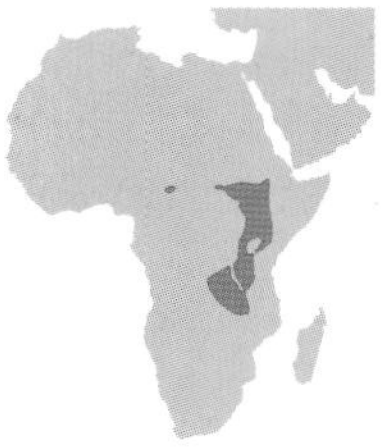

C. Africa

long, bare legs

Nile crocodile
Crocodylus niloticus

Among reptiles, only the saltwater crocodile (*C. porosus*) exceeds the Nile crocodile in bulk, but perhaps not in ferocity and size of prey taken. With a range extending to most wetland habitats south of the Sahara, the Nile crocodile is reputed to kill buffalo, giraffes, hippos, rhinos, and elephants. Typically, the Nile crocodile floats, loglike, close to animals at the water's edge, then it suddenly rears and lunges toward its victim, seizes the animal in its jaws, and pulls it under to drown.

It may spin in a "death roll" to dismember a struggling animal or large carcass. Land attacks also occur. The crocodile bursts from bushy cover in a "high walk" and may even "gallop" for short distances, reaching 9 mph (15 km/h) with its body held high off the ground.

Nile crocodiles form large groups at sunny basking sites or regular kill locations such as river crossings. Large males are dominant, while juveniles rank the lowest.

five toes (three-clawed) on front foot

fourth tooth in lower jaw can be seen even when mouth closed

△ **FORMIDABLE PREDATOR**
The Nile crocodile's eyes, ears, and nostrils are located high on the head, allowing it to float almost submerged in water, yet see, hear, and breathe.

Zebra mbuna
Maylandia zebra

This striped fish grazes on the thick algal mats that grow in the shallower areas in Lake Malawi. It feeds with its head held perpendicular to the rock, scraping away with its teeth to scoop up the algae and any tiny animals that live in it. Like many species of lake cichlid, the zebra mbuna is a mouth brooder, with the female carrying her eggs in her mouth for three weeks. She is unable to feed during this time, and once the fry have hatched, she will spit them out.

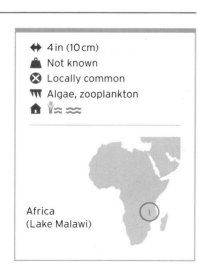

↔ 4 in (10 cm)
🏋 Not known
✖ Locally common
🍴 Algae, zooplankton
🏠 〰 〰

Africa (Lake Malawi)

△ **FISH OF MANY COLORS**
Light and dark male morphs are found in different parts of the lake. Females also vary in color, from pale orange to dark brown, but these variations are not restricted by location.

SERENGETI SAVANNAS
Home of the world's most famous migration

Grassland systems depend on natural or artificial factors that prevent natural succession to scrub and then forest. In the Serengeti, these factors are fire and grazing. This is a highly seasonal ecoregion, where the rain-induced growth of grasses such as red oat and couch grass supports vast herds of herbivores, which travel as the seasons progress, following the best grazing opportunities. When zebras, wildebeest, and Thompson's gazelles gather to migrate, their numbers seem uncountable and their movement unstoppable. Other significant species include elephant, giraffe, impala, and Cape buffalo. The herbivorous hordes support abundant predators and scavengers including big cats, hyenas, wild dogs, birds of prey, and vultures.

Changing but the same

The wildlife seen today is a fraction of that which existed 100 years ago. Human encroachment, mainly for agriculture, has greatly reduced the area of habitat available and this, along with hunting, has drastically reduced populations. Even so, the character of this ancient landscape and the cycles of life it shapes have changed little in millions of years. The land would be recognizable to the early humans whose remains have been discovered at sites such as Olduvai Gorge, which today lies within the Serengeti National Park.

The Serengeti is the **only ecoregion** in the world **still dominated by large mammals**

WILDEBEEST IN THE MASAI MARA

One of the seven natural wonders of the world

CIRCULAR MIGRATION More than 1 million wildebeest travel in search of fresh pasture each year. Late in the rainy season, they calve in the south of the Serengeti, where the grass is rich in phosphorus, a vital nutrient for lactating mothers. They then circle back toward the north and do not return for 10 months.

LIVINGSTONE'S TURACO

… animals and predators that hunt them

BIRDS, BEETLES, AND TREES Bruchid beetles eat fallen seeds of trees in riverside forests, but not seeds that have first been eaten by birds and passed in their droppings. Thus, fruit-eaters such as Livingstone's turaco help preserve the forests; if they decline, the trees decline.

CREMATOGASTER ANTS

Famed for its profusion of grazing …

RECIPROCAL BEHAVIOR A species of Crematogaster ant lives in the swollen thorn bases of whistling acacias. The ants feed on nectar produced near leaf bases and are safer from predation among the thorns. They defend the tree by biting any browser that tries to eat its leaves.

DUNG REMOVAL

Dung beetles are vital to the health of this ecosystem. They clear dung, recycle nutrients, and improve soil. As well as eating fresh dung, they roll it into balls and take it underground.

DUNG BEETLE AT WORK

Home to 7,500 elephants in 2014

Occupies 14% of Tanzania's land area

One of the oldest terrestrial ecosystems

STRATIFIED GRAZING

To avoid competing for food, grazing and browsing animals specialize in eating different plants or parts of plants. Zebras, for example, feed on older, tougher grasses than wildebeest, while giraffes browse from branches of acacia trees that no other animal can reach.

GIRAFFE FEEDING ON ACACIA BRANCHES

THE ROLE OF FIRE

Lightening striking dry vegetation can cause fire. This does not kill grasses because their growing points are safe in the soil, but it can kill trees, thereby preventing woodland from forming. White storks hunt insects fleeing the fire.

WHITE STORK HUNTING

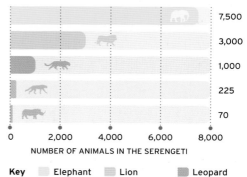

LOCATION

The Serengeti region covers 12,000 sq miles (31,000 sq km) of Kenya and Tanzania. The name is derived from a Masai term meaning endless plain.

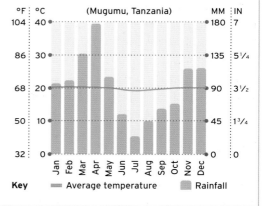

KENYA

• Musoma

• Mwanza

TANZANIA

0 km 50
0 miles 50

CLIMATE

The climate is warm and dry, with two wet seasons: the short rains in November and December, and the long rains from March to May. The highest rainfall is in the west, near Lake Victoria, and lowest in the rain shadow of the Ngorongoro uplands to the southeast.

(Mugumu, Tanzania)

°F	°C		MM	IN
104	40		180	7
86	30		135	5¼
68	20		90	3½
50	10		45	1¾
32	0		0	0

Jan Feb Mar Apr May Jun Jul Aug Sep Oct Nov Dec

Key — Average temperature ▬ Rainfall

THE FAMOUS FIVE

Big game hunters used to visit the Serengeti with the aim of shooting and killing the "Big Five"—a lion, leopard, elephant, rhinoceros, and Cape buffalo. Today, most tourists want to see and photograph the wildlife, and the cheetah has replaced the buffalo in the top five.

7,500
3,000
1,000
225
70

0   2,000   4,000   6,000   8,000

NUMBER OF ANIMALS IN THE SERENGETI

Key   Elephant   Lion   Leopard
       Cheetah   Black rhinoceros

mature male has thick, long mane

lioness has smaller head and a lighter build than male lion

Lion

Panthera leo

Lions are the most social species of cat. They form units called prides, consisting of a group of adult females that share a home range with their young and up to three adult males. Prides have just four or five members where food is scarce, such as the Namibian semi-desert, and at least a dozen in East Africa's prey-rich savannas—the record is 39. Prides often split into subgroups to search for food or explore their range.

Hunting as a team

Lions are the only big cats to hunt cooperatively. In larger prides, most kills are made by the faster, lighter females. Lions stalk grazing mammals in teams, leaping onto the back of prey or seizing its legs and rear, and delivering a suffocating bite to its throat when it is grounded. Kills are shared between pride members, and an adult consumes 33–44 lb (15–20 kg) of meat at a sitting. Because lions hunt mostly at night, they doze in the shade during the day. They also scavenge the carcasses of dead animals.

Synchronized litters

The lionesses in a pride become sexually receptive at the same time, resulting in synchronized births, after an average gestation of 110 days. Each female has up to

Lions can be **recognized** by their **whisker-spot patterns**, which are as **unique as human fingerprints**

six cubs in a litter, although two or three is usual. Male lions leave the pride that they were born into at 2–4 years old and form a coalition with several other males. These coalitions roam in search of prides to take over and lead, sometimes fighting a bloody battle to oust resident males. After a takeover, the new males kill any existing cubs in the pride so the lionesses come back into estrus and so are ready to mate again.

The population of lions in Africa has gone down from 100,000 just 50 years ago to fewer than 30,000 today. This is due to hunting, a decline in their prey, and persecution by local people in retaliation for attacks on their livestock. Lions have long since vanished from North Africa and the Middle East. In Asia, they now survive only in the Gir Forest area of northwest India.

▷ **KING OF THE SAVANNA**
Adult males develop a long, shaggy mane around their head and neck. Their territorial roar can be heard up to 3 miles (5 km) away.

△ **LIONESS WITH CUBS**
Cubs stay with their mother for 20-30 months, but they may suckle from several adult females in the pride until they are weaned.

▷ **HUNTING IMPALA**
When chasing prey, lionesses may accelerate to a speed of 28 mph (45 km/h). Such sprints are short; rarely more than 650 ft (200 m).

↔ 5–8 ft (1.6–2.5 m)
⚖ 330–550 lb (150–250 kg)
⊗ Vulnerable
🐾 Mammals, carrion
🏠 ⛰ 🌵 🌾

Sub-Saharan Africa (excluding Congo Rainforest), NW. India

black face line

ringed tail

hard foot pads and exposed claws

Cheetah
Acinonyx jubatus

The cheetah is built for speed. Its light, slender body and highly flexible spine help it to turn without losing its balance. Long muscular legs enable it to quickly reach strides of up to 23 ft (7 m). A small, short-muzzled head adds to its aerodynamics, and wide nostrils and large lungs enhance its breathing capacity. A large heart pumps blood to an optimal degree. Yet the cheetah is the least successful hunter among African cats—precisely because the adaptations that give it speed also restrict it in other ways. A short muzzle and small head lessen jaw strength. Its quick sprints can be sustained only for short distances, so it often fails to make a kill. High-speed bursts leave it overheated and in need of rest, so kills are easily stolen by other animals. For these reasons, cheetahs hunt mainly during the day to avoid stronger nocturnal predators.

Band of brothers

The cheetah's slight frame also makes it vulnerable to larger predators such as lions and hyenas; so solitary females with cubs are constantly on the lookout for danger. Males often band together for life, forming "coalitions" of 2 to 5 animals—sometimes related— which offers them greater protection. Once found throughout Asia and Africa, this species is now confined mainly to 25 African countries, with a critically endangered population of Asiatic cheetahs in Iran.

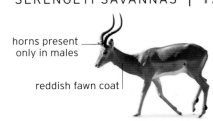
horns present
only in males

reddish fawn coat

short, rounded ears

Impala

Aepyceros melampus

A medium-sized antelope, the impala is distinguished by its black-tipped ears, rump and tail stripes, and black tufts above its rear hoofs. Male impala grow beautiful ridged, lyre-shaped horns that are up to 36 in (90 cm) long. These superbly agile mammals can change direction almost instantly and leap long and high over shrubs, bushes, and even other impala.

Impala rest and graze during the day and night. They eat grass in the wet season and feed on shrubs, bushes, fruit, and acacia pods during drier periods.

Spring and fall ruts

Mating takes place in a twice-yearly "rut," when males fight each other for access to females. They become noisier than usual, snorting and bellowing to advertise and defend territories. Successful males mate with several females in spring and fall, and the young are born about seven months later.

Outside the mating season, impala divide into smaller herds of bachelor males and larger herds of females and calves. The herd provides protection from predators, such as lions, hyenas, and leopards—an alert impala "barks" a warning that sets the entire herd fleeing.

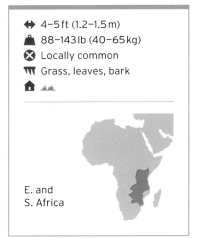

↔ 4–5 ft (1.2–1.5 m)
⚖ 88–143 lb (40–65 kg)
✗ Locally common
🌾 Grass, leaves, bark
🏠 🌾

E. and
S. Africa

↔ 4–5 ft (1.2–1.5 m)
⚖ 46–160 lb (21–72 kg)
✗ Vulnerable
🌾 Gazelles, antelopes
🏠 🌵 🌾

Africa and
SW. Asia

△ BORN TO RUN
The "greyhound of cats" is the fastest mammal on land. The cheetah can reach speeds of more than 70 mph (115 km/h) in three seconds. An average sprint lasts about 20 seconds.

◁ TEAR LINES
The distinctive black lines on a cheetah's face may protect its eyes from the sun's glare and also help it to focus on prey.

▽ LEAPING TO SAFETY
Impala flee from predators into dense vegetation. They can leap as far as 30 ft (9 m) and as high as 8 ft (2.5 m).

Impala **release scent signals** as they **kick and leap**, which are thought to **lay trails** for other **herd members**

sharp, curved horns

long white beard

Wildebeest
Connochaetes mearnsi

▷ **BLUE WILDEBEEST**
All wildebeest males bellow and snort to retain mating rights, but will fight each other if required. These blue wildebeest (*C. taurinus*) in South Africa have locked horns.

The Serengeti white-bearded wildebeest is on its feet within three to seven minutes of birth, can run at 40 mph (65 km/h), and migrates up to 1,000 miles (1,600 km) annually. This is enabled by several physical adaptations. High shoulders, a thick neck, and a large head place the bulk of its weight toward the front, while its back slopes to narrow, muscular hips. Mount this arrangement on long, thin legs and you get a bearded antelope that run effortlessly, sharing a similar build with that of a key predator, the spotted hyena.

Super herd formation
The broad mouth, wide row of incisors, and flexible lips are adapted to grazing on the Serengeti short grass, which is rich in phosphorus. This diet compels the wildebeest to follow short grass growth, which depends on seasonal rains, leading to spectacular migrations across the Serengeti plains of Kenya and Tanzania. The wildebeest merge with other grazers such as zebra to form a "super herd" of 1.25 million animals—the vast number keeps individuals relatively safe from predators.

At the end of the rainy season, all females become sexually receptive for two to three weeks—but each is fertile for just one day. Males set up small mating territories within the super herd. Most calves are born about eight months later, within a two- to three-week period, and can keep up with the herd within two days.

▽ **MASS CROSSING**
As many as 5,000 to 10,000 wildebeest may make the perilous crossing of the Mara river in Kenya at a time, but hundreds of Nile crocodiles lie in wait for them.

↔ 5–8 ft (1.5–2.4 m)
⬛ 265–606 lb (120–275 kg)
✖ Locally common
🌾 Grass
🏠 ⛰

E. Africa

△ RITUALIZED "NECKING"
Male giraffes reach sexual maturity at three to four years. To establish dominance, rivals engage in a ritual battle that involves slamming their necks against each other.

prehensile
upper lip

Giraffe
Giraffa camelopardalis

Giraffes are the world's tallest living animals, with adult males reaching 16–20 ft (5–6 m) and adult females growing to 15–16 ft (4.5–5 m). Even the calves are 5–6 ft (1.5–1.8 m) tall at birth. Much of this height comes from the giraffe's massively elongated neck and legs. It has thick blood vessels, high blood pressure, and a powerful heart to pump blood all the way to its brain.

Despite their size, giraffes are threatened by predators. A pride of lions can bring down an adult, and young calves are vulnerable to hyenas and leopards. If alarmed, giraffes can gallop at speeds of up to 35 mph (55 km/h).

Unique markings

The Masai giraffe (*G. c. tippelskirchi*) is one of nine subspecies, each of which has a different pattern of red-brown or almost black markings, with straight or fuzzy edges, on a white or yellow background. It lives in small herds in the Serengeti savanna and open woodland, and can browse leaves from trees that are out of reach of antelopes and other browsers. Giraffes have a prehensile upper lip and an extremely long, tough, and mobile tongue, which enables them to strip leaves from thorny acacia trees with ease.

Both sexes have a pair of blunt, skin-covered horns, called ossicones, which are larger in males. The females mate with the dominant bull in their home range, giving birth to a single calf after 16 months, usually in the dry season. She will have weaned the calf by the time it is 13 months old.

distinctive skin pattern
of Masai giraffe

long black
tail tuft for
whisking
away flies

↔ 12¹/₂–15¹/₂ ft (3.8–4.7 m)
🏋 Up to 2.1 tons (1.9 metric tons)
✖ Common
🌾 Tree leaves
🏠 ᎶᏏᏗ

markings fade
toward feet

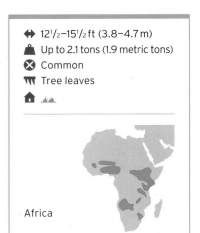

Africa

▷ STANDING TALL
As well as their great height, giraffes are distinguished by their large eyes and ears, short body, and a back that slopes steeply from shoulder to rump.

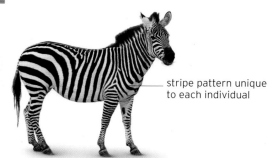

stripe pattern unique
to each individual

Grant's zebra

Equus quagga boehmi

Grant's zebras migrate to find food, traveling up to 1,800 miles (3,000 km) in search of the coarse long grass that they are best-adapted to eat. The smallest of the plains zebras, they are highly adaptable, and are able to survive in harsh conditions on the plains and in woodland at sea-level and on the slopes of Mount Kenya at heights of up to 13,000 ft (4,000 m).

Easily recognized by their black-and-white striped bodies (the function of which is not known for certain), zebras are social animals. They form close-knit family units that graze in large herds across East and Southern Africa. They are often joined by wildebeest, giraffes, and Thomson's gazelles, which benefit from the zebras' warning "bray-bark" when a predator is spotted. Zebras can also maintain a top speed of 35–40 mph (55–65 km/h), outlasting short-burst predators such as lions.

A family unit consists of a dominant stallion and several mares—the harem—and their foals. Males leave to join bachelor herds at between one and three years of age. Adult males try to lure females away, or take over a harem, resulting in violent fights. Most foals are born during the rainy season, after a year-long gestation.

△ **CHAPMAN'S ZEBRA**
A less-common subspecies of the plains zebra, *E. q. chapmani* has dark stripes alternating with fainter shadow stripes.

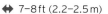

↔ 7–8 ft (2.2–2.5 m)
🏋 385–850 lb (175–385 kg)
✖ Common
🌾 Grass
🏠

E. Africa

◁ **DEADLY DUEL**
Fighting between stallions over mating rights is fierce, involving bites, powerful kicks, and strikes that frequently cause damage–and sometimes kill.

◁ **SAFETY IN NUMBERS**
Zebras have superb eyesight, hearing, and a sharp sense of smell, which help detect predators. Living in a herd means more senses at work, making it safer for members.

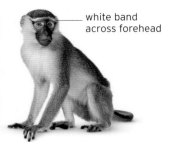
white band across forehead

Vervet monkey

Chlorocebus pygerythrus

Africa's most widespread monkey, vervets thrive in a variety of environments. They prefer scrub forests bordering rivers, but are found in habitats as diverse as semidesert and swamp, from sea level to altitudes up to 14,750 ft (4,500 m). Vervets eat all plant parts, from root to fruit, but also feed on insects, lizards, eggs, and small mammals. However, their appetite for sweet potatoes and bananas often brings them into conflict with farmers.

United we stand

A highly social species, vervets travel, feed, drink, groom, and rest in troops of as few as seven or as many as 75 individuals. Adult females rule the troop, which includes a smaller number of males (with their own hierarchy), juveniles, and offspring. While females stay with their troops for life, males leave at around age five, often in twos or threes to avoid an attack by a high-status female. They transfer mainly during the mating season (April to June), when dominant females are less prone to attack them.

Vervet monkeys have **specific vocal warnings** for **specific predators**

↔ 14–26 in (35–66 cm)
⚖ 7–17 lb (3.2–7.7 kg)
✖ Common
🌾 Plants, insects, lizards
🏠 🌳 🌵 🌾 ≈ 🏠

E. and
S. Africa

△ **SHARP AS A KNIFE**
Adult male vervets have longer canines than females. They reveal them in dominance displays and will use them as a weapon.

◁ **INHERITED RANK**
High-status females receive the best of everything, from food to sleeping trees, and their offspring inherit this status.

forward-curving tusks

trunk ends in two fingerlike tips

African savanna elephant

Loxodonta africana

The world's largest land animal, African savanna elephants are capable of carving paths through dense undergrowth, clearing shrubs, and excavating waterholes. They also help to replant forests because they excrete the seeds of fruit that they eat—many species of tree depend on African elephants for survival.

The elephant's range is shrinking rapidly due to expanding human population. As many as 3–5 million elephants roamed Africa less than a century ago, but today an estimated 470,000–690,000 are confined to fragmented areas south of the Sahara. More elephants die annually from hunting and ivory poaching than are born.

Complex anatomy

The African elephant's head weighs up to half a ton and its brain is larger than any other land animal's—about four times the size of the human brain. Its trunk —a fusion between upper lip and nose—contains a staggering 40,000 muscle bundles. The trunk is so adaptable that the elephant can pluck a grape-sized fruit without damaging it or throw a 12-in- (30-cm-) thick tree limb. Besides breathing, the elephant uses its trunk to smell, touch, and caress its family members, as well as to feed and drink. Its enormous ears are full of blood

Elephants **care for and aid** wounded relatives

vessels that radiate excess heat, while its tusks are used for tearing the bark and limbs of trees as well as for defense. Both male and female African elephants have tusks, although the female's tusks are shorter.

Females rule elephant society, which is highly social and family-based, with a matriarch leading related females and calves. The young are dependent on their mother for 8–10 years, learning how to behave, where to find water, and what to eat. Females remain with their birth herd, while most males leave at around 14 years old, joining other bulls in loose-knit bachelor herds and only coming into contact with females to mate.

Elephants are highly vocal communicators, with calls ranging from high-pitched squeaks to low-frequency "infrasound" rumbles. The deep rumbles can travel more than 2 miles (3 km) in the air and three times that distance through the ground, and elephants detect these vibrations through their feet and trunk.

▷ **REFRESHING SHOWER**
Bathing after drinking is a common activity. Elephants frequently use their trunks to spray themselves and each other with water.

◁ **MIGHTY TUSKER**
A fully grown bull African elephant with enormous tusks is a formidable opponent, capable of charges up to 25 mph (40 km/h).

↔ 13–16$\frac{1}{2}$ ft (4–5 m)
⚖ 4–7 tons
✕ Vulnerable
🌾 Grass, fruit, flowers

Sub-Saharan Africa

Black-capped social weaver

Pseudonigrita cabanisi

distinctive white beak

black tail

Its name says a lot about this small, neat, handsome bird. The black cap, red eye, and pale beak give the black-capped social weaver a unique look. It shares the nest-building habit of all weavers, although the nests that this social weaver builds have a rough, unfinished appearance as compared to some weavers' more precise constructions. Like other weavers, this is a gregarious bird, living in flocks, nomadic when not breeding, and nesting in colonies that are a few to 60 pairs strong. The need for social stimulation seems to be strong among them. Perching birds often squeeze together shoulder to shoulder and occasionally even preen each other.

Restricted range

The black-capped social weaver is a very localized bird found only in a small part of East Africa, very nearly restricted to Kenya and Tanzania, where it inhabits low-lying dry thorn bush plains. In this limited range, it is common in suitable habitats. Flocks of birds feed on the ground, foraging for seeds and a few grasshoppers; however, they frequently dash up to perch on treetops if disturbed. They should be a familiar bird to many safari-goers, but are often overlooked in parks and reserves where more glamorous big game claim most of the attention.

Expert builders

Breeding males create an insignificant, buzzy chattering from nesting trees, often flapping their wings; however, courtship is generally undistinguished. Nests often hang from tips of long, pendulous branches in a spreading acacia. A pair adds material all year round, using nests as roosts when not breeding. A new nest is built up above a slender twig in an arch and extended into a tubelike structure, with an entrance at the bottom. Eventually, the weight pulls the twig downward and the upper end of the tubeis closed off. Up to four eggs are laid, but little is known about the chicks.

Large nests may contain more than 9,000 grass stems

▷ **AT HOME**
Black-capped social weavers use prickly grass stems to make an unlined, conical nest. When used for roosting it has two entrances; one is sealed off for breeding.

◁ **NESTING TREE**
Often, the largest tree in a wide area forms the basis for a breeding colony, holding up to 60 nests.

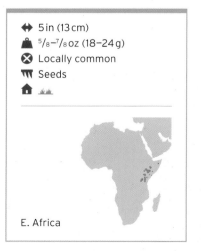

↔ 5 in (13 cm)
⚖ 5/8–7/8 oz (18–24 g)
✗ Locally common
🌾 Seeds
🏠

E. Africa

Red-billed hornbill

Tockus erythrorhynchus

bright beak used to impress mates

long tail

Groups of red-billed hornbills, sometimes numbering hundreds, wander through thorn bush and grasslands looking for food, which is mostly taken on the ground.

They build their nests in tree-holes or hollow logs. The female seals herself inside with mud up to 24 days before laying eggs, which take about the same time to hatch. All this time, the male brings her food. She breaks out 21 days later, when the oldest chick is ready to fly.

↔	16–19 in (41–48 cm)
⚖	4–8 oz (113–227 g)
✗	Common
⋔	Dung beetles, seeds
🏠 🌳 🌿	
◉	Sub-Saharan Africa

◁ **FLAP-AND-GLIDE FLIGHT**
Hornbills hunt prey on the ground during the day, but they fly back to trees to roost at night.

Helmeted guineafowl

Numida meleagris

tiny head

large, rounded body

Abundant in bushy savannas, helmeted guineafowl are named for the bony casque on their head. They need drinking water, thick cover to escape into if threatened, and trees to roost in at night. They eat seeds and shoots, but prefer grasshoppers and termites when abundant.

↔	21–25 in (53–64 cm)
⚖	2–3 lb (0.9–1.4 kg)
✗	Common
⋔	Seeds, shoots, insects
🏠 🌿	
◉	Sub-Saharan Africa

▷ **BOLTING AWAY**
Guineafowl live in busy, noisy groups on the ground. They run rather than fly from danger, unless sorely pressed.

Secretary bird

Sagittarius serpentarius

The secretary bird strides along elegantly on extraordinarily long legs in grassy plains, its head bobbing back and forth. It feeds mainly on grasshoppers, mice, and voles, but will eat anything it can kill. Long, bare legs help protect it from snakes, even deadly cobras, which it kills by stomping.

Each breeding pair needs about 20 sq miles (50 sq km) of "home range" for nesting. They drive out rival birds from their territories, jumping and kicking if they catch an intruder.

↔	4–5 ft (1.2–1.5 m)
⚖	9 lb (4 kg)
✗	Vulnerable
⋔	Grasshoppers, mice, voles
🏠 🌿 🌱	

Sub-Saharan Africa

quill-like crest

long, powerful legs

△ **SNAKE SNACK**
Secretary birds stalk determinedly across open grassland in search of prey, which even includes venomous snakes.

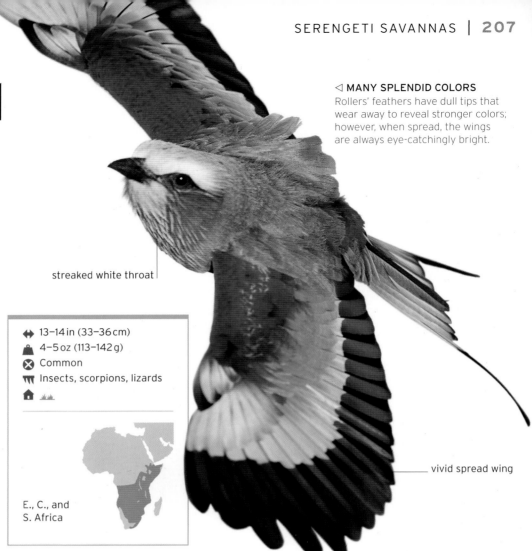

Lilac-breasted roller

Coracias caudatus

Several similar kinds of rollers occupy Africa at various times of the year, distinguished by their tail shapes and minor color differences. The lilac chest is the identifying feature of the lilac-breasted roller, but it shares elongated tail streamers with the Abyssinian roller. It prefers bushy savanna and dry, open woodland, and perches prominently on trees. It is a very territorial and pugnacious bird.

Disperse after breeding

Lilac-breasted rollers build their nest in a cavity in a decaying stump or termite mound, which is left unlined. Both parents incubate the eggs for 18 days, and the chicks fly when they are 35 days old. Although lilac-breasted rollers do not migrate as such, they disperse widely after breeding, finding feeding territories which they defend individually or in pairs. Rollers are generalist and opportunistic feeders. They swoop to the ground to catch big insects, scorpions, centipedes, small reptiles, and occasionally, a small bird.

streaked white throat

vivid spread wing

↔ 13–14 in (33–36 cm)
⚖ 4–5 oz (113–142 g)
✖ Common
🐛 Insects, scorpions, lizards
🏠 🌾

E., C., and
S. Africa

Black mamba

Dendroaspis polylepis

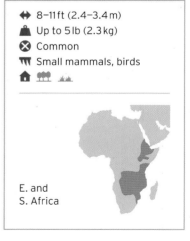

streamlined body with smooth scales

Strong, fast, agile, and deadly, the black mamba is Africa's longest venomous snake, and second only to the king cobra worldwide. Its "racing slither"—usually used to escape danger rather than to pursue prey—has been timed at 9 mph (14 km/h) and it may exceed 12 mph (20 km/h). Its somewhat drab olive, green, gray, or brown coloration has subdued, if any, markings.

Africa's deadliest snake

The black mamba is found in varied habitats, from rocky hills to coastal scrub. It rests at night in a home lair in a termite mound, small mammal burrow, tree root hollow, or rocky crevice. By day, the snake lurks in cover to strike out at passing victims. Its two fixed, hollow, upper fangs inject exceptionally toxic venom—it can kill a human in 30 minutes. The black mamba holds smaller prey for a few minutes until lifeless, but bites larger ones and withdraws, following them until the venom acts. The black mamba climbs well to hunt for nesting birds and squirrels. If threatened, it rears up, spreads its small "hood" cobra-fashion, opens its mouth, and hisses.

↔ 8–11 ft (2.4–3.4 m)
⚖ Up to 5 lb (2.3 kg)
✖ Common
🐛 Small mammals, birds
🏠 🌳 🌾

E. and
S. Africa

◁ BLACK BITE
Hissing, gaping, tongue erect, upper fang tips visible—it is the dark interior of the mouth that gives the "black" mamba its name.

CONGO BASIN
The dark green heart of Africa

The Congo Basin was carved by glaciers into a vast depression about the size of Europe. Much of the 78 in (2,000 mm) of rain that falls over the area each year ultimately drains into the Congo River, the second largest in the world. The river defines the character of the entire region, but it also represents an ecological barrier, with many groups of species found only on one side or the other —for example, chimpanzees live to the north of the river, while bonobos, or pygmy chimpanzees, occur only to the south.

Abundance under threat

Up to 10,000 plant species grow in the Congo Basin, about a third of which are found nowhere else. More than 1,000 bird species live here, as well as 700 known species of freshwater fish. New species of mammal are being discovered regularly in the basin, including fairly large animals that had remained unknown until relatively recently. The okapi was first described in 1901, followed by the bonobo in 1929, yet the forest elephant was not discovered until 2001.

In addition to its vast amounts of wildlife, the Congo Basin has been inhabited by humans for more than 20,000 years and is currently home to or supports more than 75 million people. Although new flora and fauna species undoubtedly exist in large areas of rainforest that remain unexplored, as the human population continues to grow, many are likely to become extinct before discovery. This is due to exploitation of land for agriculture, mining, fossil fuels, logging, and hunting for the bushmeat trade.

The forest in the Congo Basin is **so dense, only 1% of sunlight** reaches the ground

SITATUNGA

Contains the second-largest block of rainforest in the world

ADAPTABLE ANTELOPE
Sitatunga emerge from forests to graze in wet grasslands and swamps at night. Their long, splayed hooves and flexible foot joints allow them to walk on waterlogged ground without sinking. They are excellent swimmers and use the water to escape predators.

BONOBO

GUTS OF THE MATTER
Bonobos, or pygmy chimpanzees, are highly social, fruit-eating apes endangered by habitat loss and hunting. Threats to bonobos affect the entire ecosystem: the seeds of many tree species cannot germinate unless they pass through the apes' guts.

Home to around half of Africa's elephant population

AFRICAN CHERRY

THE MEDICINE TREE
The African cherry grows widely in the Congo Basin's mountain forests. Its bark is used in African medicine to treat everything from chest pains to mental illness, and it shows promising cancer-fighting properties.

LEAP OF FAITH
The black colobus lives high in the forest canopy, but has small thumbs for an animal that relies on good grip. This is thought to reduce the risk of injury when grabbing branches mid-leap.

BLACK COLOBUS MONKEY

More than 900 butterfly species live here

SALT OF THE EARTH
Occasional natural clearings in the forest are usually filled with wet grassland and swamp. They often contain important minerals, which attract a variety of wildlife. Forest elephants dig or even dive underwater to find the richest salt deposits.

FOREST ELEPHANT

Congo trees store an estimated 8% of the Earth's forest-trapped carbon

WATERS OF LIFE
The Congo is richer in fish than any other African river, with around 700 known species, many found nowhere else on earth. These include elephantfish, which use electric fields to sense surroundings, Goliath tigerfish, whose teeth grow up to 1 in (2.5 cm) long, and the planet's largest freshwater pufferfish.

FRESHWATER PUFFERFISH

LOCATION

Central Africa, between the Gulf of Guinea and the African Great Lakes; mostly within the Democratic Republic of Congo (DRC) and neighboring countries.

NIGERIA

CHAD

0 km 500
0 miles 500

SOUTH SUDAN

Yaoundé · Bangui

ATLANTIC OCEAN

· Kinshasa

TANZANIA

ANGOLA

CLIMATE

The Congo Basin is unrelentingly hot and humid, with average daytime temperatures reaching 70–80°F (21–27°C) year round. The humidity rarely drops below 80 percent, thanks to frequent rainfall, which peaks in spring and particularly fall.

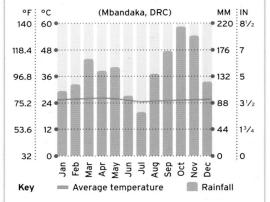

°F	°C	(Mbandaka, DRC)	MM	IN
140	60		220	8½
118.4	48		176	7
96.8	36		132	5
75.2	24		88	3½
53.6	12		44	1¾
32	0		0	0

Jan Feb Mar Apr May Jun Jul Aug Sep Oct Nov Dec

Key —— Average temperature ▬ Rainfall

HUMANS IN THE CONGO

The Congo is home to more than 250 ethnic groups. The lifestyle of modern hunter-gatherer peoples such as the seminomadic Bayaka and Bagyeli (formerly known as "pygmies") requires small groups of people to live sustainably on the land. They exchange forest goods for farmed produce grown in more settled communities.

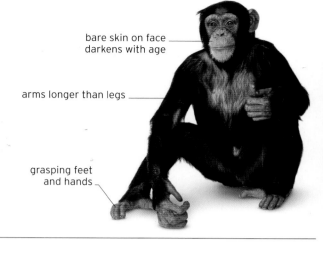

bare skin on face
darkens with age

arms longer than legs

grasping feet
and hands

Chimpanzee

Pan troglodytes

Our closest living relatives, chimpanzees are great apes that share numerous features with humans, such as large brains, expressive faces, a prominent "brow ridge" over the eyes, and dextrous hands with opposable thumbs. They also share some human biology—they go bald and get arthritis with old age, and suffer many human diseases. They display some aspects of human behavior, too, such as an ability to walk upright and play.

Making and using tools

Chimpanzees live in communities of about 35 members, although exceptionally large groups may have up to 150. Active by day, they spend half of it foraging in the forest for plants and animals. Some groups are known to eat as many as 200 types of food. Each evening, they construct sleeping nests in treetops.

British primatologist Jane Goodall's study at Gombe Stream, Tanzania, found that chimpanzees band together to hunt other primates, mainly colobus monkeys. Males do most of the hunting, and share the meat with the group. Goodall was also the first to record tool use in chimpanzees—they deploy stone anvils to crack nuts, hold up leaves as umbrellas, and use sticks to fish termites out of tree trunks or extract honey from bees' nests.

Chimpanzees share more than 98.5 percent of their DNA with humans

Females are sexually mature at between seven and eight years old, but only bear their first single infant at 13–14 years, after a gestation of about eight months. Babies are dependent on their mothers, sharing the maternal nest at night, and are weaned when four or five years old. Juveniles learn tool-use and other complex behavior by watching older relatives. If food is plentiful, chimpanzees can breed all year round.

Fragmented range

Up to the early 1900s, chimpanzees occurred throughout the tropical forests of West and Central Africa. Today their range is highly fragmented due to decades of deforestation, capture for zoos, circuses, and medical research, and hunting for the bushmeat trade. About 200,000–300,000 remain in the wild, and populations continue to fall.

▷ **HIGHLY INTELLIGENT**
After humans, chimpanzees are the most intelligent primate, with a sophisticated language of facial expressions, gestures, and vocalizations. They may live more than 50 years in the wild.

△ **BONOBO**
Bonobos, or pygmy chimpanzees (*P. paniscus*), are more agile than chimpanzees, and spend more time walking upright. They are rarer, confined to the Congo Basin, where about 30,000 may survive.

▷ **BABY CHIMPANZEE**
Young chimps are inquisitive and playful, engaging in frequent bouts of roughhousing with playmates of their age.

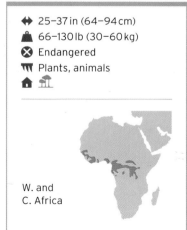

↔ 25–37 in (64–94 cm)
⬍ 66–130 lb (30–60 kg)
✖ Endangered
🌾 Plants, animals
🏠 🏛

W. and
C. Africa

grasping hand with
semi opposable thumb

Western gorilla

Gorilla gorilla

In the past, gorillas were often portrayed as brutish and dangerous, a reputation not helped by the early King Kong films, but they are, in fact, highly intelligent, peaceful, and almost entirely vegetarian. Western gorillas live in lowland forests and swamps in Central Africa and feed mainly on ripe fruit, along with some plant shoots and leaves. Their grinding teeth and massive jaw muscles are adapted for chewing vegetation. The only animals they eat are ants and termites.

Nonaggressive displays

Although the western gorilla is the heaviest and most powerfully built of all the great apes, the huge mature males rely on ritual displays rather than aggression to assert their dominance. They take 18 years to reach their full size and are known as silverbacks after the pale patches of fur on their backs. Adult females are only around half the size.

A typical gorilla family group consists of a single silverback and up to 12 adult females and their offspring of various ages. The bonds between the family members are very strong, and many group members stay together for life.

Western gorillas are threatened by deforestation, illegal poaching for the bushmeat trade, and some human diseases such as the ebola virus, which affects apes as well as humans.

△ **DEPENDENT YOUNG**
Young gorillas depend on their mothers for three to five years, suckling throughout. This is one of the longest nursing periods of any mammal.

△ **RITUAL DISPLAY**
Dominant male gorillas advertise their status by standing upright, baring their long canine teeth, thrashing vegetation, and beating their broad chests with their hands.

◁ **ON THE MOVE**
Gorillas travel mainly on foot, covering an average of 1 mile (2 km) a day in search of food. The young ride piggyback on their mothers, or cling to their undersides.

subordinate male has paler muzzle

Mandrill

Mandrillus sphinx

Mandrills live in large groups in tropical forest and forest-savanna mosaic habitats. They spend time on the ground and in trees where they feed mainly on fruit and insects, but will also eat small vertebrates. Groups number several hundred and even more than a thousand adult females and their young. Adult males may be solitary except during the mating season.

Size and color

Mandrills exhibit marked differences between the sexes: in addition to their colorful faces and yellow beards, the genital region and rump of the dominant males are a kaleidoscope of blue, red, pink, and purple. The dominant males are also roughly twice the size of the females, which are plain in comparison. When the females are ready to mate, the skin around their genitalia becomes swollen and red.

↔ 2–4 ft (55–110 cm)
🏋 24–73 lb (11–33 kg)
❌ Vulnerable
🍴 Fruit, eggs, small animals
🏠 🌳

W. Central Africa

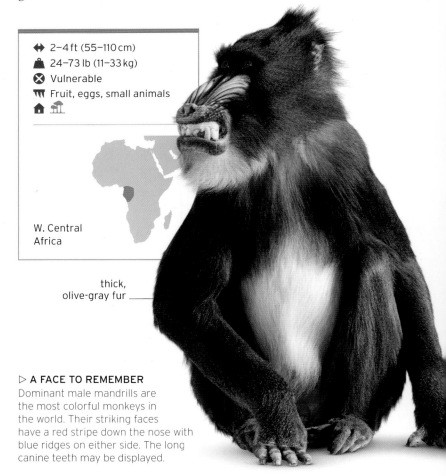

thick, olive-gray fur

▷ **A FACE TO REMEMBER**
Dominant male mandrills are the most colorful monkeys in the world. Their striking faces have a red stripe down the nose with blue ridges on either side. The long canine teeth may be displayed.

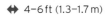

↔ 4–6 ft (1.3–1.7 m)
🏋 125–420 lb (57–190 kg)
❌ Critically endangered
🍴 Fruit, leaves, seeds, termites
🏠 🌳

Western gorillas feed on the fruit of more than **100 plant species**

C. Africa

paler background
color on underparts

Leopard

Panthera pardus

One of the smallest and strongest climbers of the big
cats, leopards are famed for their spots or "rosettes,"
but not all have the same type. Some are solid,
others have light patches in the center, but all spots
camouflage this hunter in habitats ranging from
rainforest to desert, from Africa to the Himalayas.

Night hunter

Solitary except during the mating season, leopards are
mainly nocturnal. Like all cats, they have a membrane
called the tapetum lucidum at the back of their eyes
that reflects twice as much light through their retinas,
giving them superb night vision. They eat fish, birds,
reptiles, hooved mammals such as antelope as well as
wild pigs and baboons, and carrion. Long-bodied and
powerfully built, leopards hunt by stealth, pouncing
on their prey and quickly suffocating it. They can pull
275 lb (125 kg) giraffe carcasses up into trees.

Each leopard has a home territory, and its boundaries
overlap with those of nearby leopards. Females give
birth to two or three smoky-gray cubs, keeping them in
a variety of den sites to protect them from predators. By
the age of six to eight weeks, cubs regularly leave their
den site and begin to eat solid food. They remain with
their mother for the first two years of their lives.

↔ 3–6 ft (0.9–1.9 m)
⚖ 82–200 lb (37–90 kg)
⊗ Near threatened
🐾 Deer, baboons, fish, birds

Africa, S. Asia

Leopards can catch prey up to **10 times their own weight**

△ **AT EASE**
Leopards are very comfortable
in trees, often hauling their kills
into branches to keep them
safe from lions and scavengers
such as hyenas.

▷ **OPEN WIDE**
The leopard's long canines are
used for stabbing and gripping.
The rough tongue is used to
lick scraps of meat from bones
and for grooming.

Red river hog
Potamochoerus porcus

Tufted ears, a fox-red coat, and a white spinal stripe make Africa's smallest wild pig a striking animal. What the red river hog lacks in size, it makes up for in strength. Its muscular, stocky body and wedge-shaped head are designed to dig up the hardest ground for roots, tubers, and other food.

Nocturnal foragers

Mostly active at night, red river hogs are strong swimmers, and can forage in water as well as on land. Small family groups are usually found resting in a burrow or undergrowth during the day. Unfortunately, their fondness for agricultural crops brings them into conflict with humans, their main persecutors.

↔ 3–5 ft (0.9–1.5 m)
⚖ 100–290 lb (46–132 kg)
✕ Common
🍴 Grass, roots, tubers, snails
🏠 🏛

W. to
C. Africa

long, pointed ears with prominent white tufts

facial hair fluffed out when threatened, making hog appear larger and more intimidating

▷ **DOMINANT BOAR**
Only male red river hogs have large warts in front of their eyes, whereas both sexes have tusks.

Common pangolin
Manis tricuspis

↔ 10–17 in (25–43 cm)
⚖ 4–7 lb (1.8–3.2 kg)
✕ Vulnerable
🍴 Termites, ants
🏠 🏛 🌿 ≈

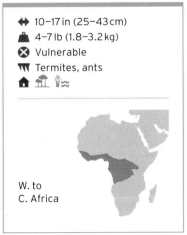

W. to
C. Africa

Pangolins are covered in overlapping scales made of keratin, a material found in hair and fingernails. When threatened, these burrowing mammals roll themselves up into a ball to protect their underparts—the only area of their body that is not covered in tough scales.

The common African pangolin feeds mainly on termites and, to a lesser extent, ants, gathering the insects with its long, sticky, muscular tongue. It is able to seal its nostrils and ears shut to protect them from stings and bites as it feeds. The pangolin has no teeth, and special muscles in its mouth keep insects in place once sucked inside. Its muscular stomach contains keratin spines, and the pangolin also swallows stones to help crush its food, ready for digestion.

◁ **FIFTH LIMB**
The common pangolin uses its long, strong, prehensile tail to maneuver around in trees.

Okapi

Okapia johnstoni

The closest relative of the giraffe, the okapi lives a solitary life, following well-trodden paths through dense forests. Like the giraffe, it uses its long, prehensile tongue to strip leaves from twigs. Okapis gather to mate at the end of the spring rainy season. Although silent at other times, adults make soft coughing calls to attract mates. Gestation lasts for 14 months, and a single calf is born between August and October.

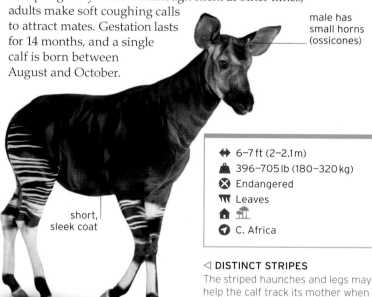

male has small horns (ossicones)

short, sleek coat

↔ 6–7 ft (2–2.1 m)
⚖ 396–705 lb (180–320 kg)
✖ Endangered
🍃 Leaves
🏠 🛖
◉ C. Africa

◁ **DISTINCT STRIPES**
The striped haunches and legs may help the calf track its mother when walking through the undergrowth.

Collared sunbird

Anthreptes collaris

This sunbird darts between flowers growing on tangled creepers and bushes at the forest edge. Acrobatically searching through cobwebs, dead leaves, and foliage, it gleans whatever it can eat. It suspends a tiny purse of plant fibers, leaf mold, and moss, knitted together with cobwebs, to hold two eggs, which hatch after 12 days.

▷ **VARIED DIET**
Its small, spiky bill makes the collared sunbird a generalist feeder. Although it feeds at flowers, it takes small insects, spiders, and snails more than nectar.

iridescent green plumage

↔ 4 in (10 cm)
⚖ ¼–³/₈ oz (6–10 g)
✖ Common
🍃 Insects, nectar
🏠 🛖 🌿 ≋
◉ Africa

Emperor scorpion

Pandinus imperator

Aptly named, this fearsome-looking creature is the world's biggest scorpion, although at least one more slender species is longer. Its front end is dominated by immense clawed pincers while, at the back, the tail-like telson is frequently curled menacingly forward over the body to display the curved stinger. However, the large size does not make this scorpion more deadly—its venom is not as potent as some other, smaller scorpions. A sting is painful to humans, but has few further ill effects. The emperor scorpion reserves its venom for self-defense or to incapacitate prey, and uses the crushing power of its pincers to kill it.

Feeling its way

Emperor scorpions are nocturnal and have poor eyesight. Touch-sensitive hairs are especially thick on the pincers and legs. These are used to detect prey in the dark, along with help from the comblike pectines under the body that are used to sense vibrations running through the ground.

Mating involves an elaborate dance, where the male leads the female by her pincers to a patch of flat ground where sperm can be transferred. After seven to nine months, she gives birth to between nine and 32 live young, which are white in color.

upper claw fixed; lower claw moves to grip

↔ 8 in (20 cm)
✖ Not known
🍃 Arthropods, mice, lizards
🏠 🛖

W. to C. Africa

◁ SAFE TRIP
Baby scorpions ride on their mother's back, and remain under her protection until their first molt gives them a darker, waterproof exoskeleton.

▽ LIQUID FEEDER
A scorpion's mouthparts cannot chew, so it uses its chelicerae to tear off small bits of prey. Digestive enzymes are regurgitated onto the food in a special cavity and the resultant liquid then enters the mouth.

rear walking leg

chelicerae (pair of pincerlike appendages in front of mouth)

massive pedipalps (pincers)

The emperor scorpion's **courtship dance** may last for **several hours**

OKAVANGO DELTA

The wetland jewel of southern Africa

River deltas are so called due to their triangular shape, which resembles the Greek letter Δ, or delta. Most form where rivers deposit vast amounts of silt and sand close to the point at which they meet the sea, but the Okavango River in Botswana never finds the coast. Instead, it drains into a depression in the Kalahari Desert, fanning out to create the greatest oasis in Africa—a vast complex of permanent and seasonal swamps, reed beds, forests, and grasslands. The precise pattern of its waterways changes constantly from year to year as channels become blocked by sand, silt, and vegetation, and the slow-moving water backs up and is forced to find an alternative route.

Breathing space

Much of the water in the Okavango Delta's permanent swamps is oxygen-poor, so the fish and aquatic invertebrates that live there are adapted to extract oxygen from the air. The waters support an estimated 35 million fish of 80 species, while the greatest abundance and diversity of terrestrial life is found in marginal areas, where swamps populated byhippopotamus and crocodiles are fringed with forest. This, in turn, gives way to open savannas, where huge herds of grazing animals attract top predators such as cheetahs, lions, hyenas, leopards, and wild dogs.

One of the **world's largest inland river deltas,** it swells to **three times its size** during winter

An estimated 482 bird species live here

More than 97% of water flowing into the delta evaporates or seeps away

GIANT TERMITE MOUND

MASTER BUILDERS
In low-lying deltas, slight variations create land high enough to support plants and animals. Many such mounds owe their existence to termites, whose nests rise several feet above ground, often sprouting trees, which contribute the organic material needed to form soil.

COMMON WARTHOG

GLORIOUS MUD
Warthogs roll in mud to cool off and gain a protective skin covering, creating hollows in the process that may be enlarged by elephants. Old wallows quickly fill with water when the rains return, often transforming into permanent water holes.

PAPYRUS

FLOOD CONTROL
Papyrus grows in flooded areas, filling channels so that water moves elsewhere, fixing carbon, and reducing evaporation. Its submerged stems provide nurseries for fish, while birds roost on its flower heads.

FISH SNATCHER
Forest-fringed swamps are perfect habitats for Pel's fishing owl, a huge bird capable of grabbing fish weighing 2–5 lb (1–2 kg) in its talons.

PEL'S FISHING OWL

Swamps make up 27% of the delta › Highly endangered black and white rhinoceros have adapted to wetland life here ‹

FRIEND OR FOE?
Often seen on the backs of hoofed grazers, oxpeckers are small perching birds that specialize in feeding on ticks and other skin parasites that afflict mammals. Their services may not be entirely benign: they also peck at wounds as a source of blood.

RED-BILLED OXPECKER

BORN SURVIVOR
A lungfish thrives in oxygen-poor waters due to a lunglike offshoot of the gut that extracts oxygen as the fish gulps air. During droughts, the fish squirms into mud and forms a slime cocoon to hold air and moisture that keep it alive until water returns.

WEST AFRICAN LUNGFISH

LOCATION
The Okavango River rises in the highlands of Angola, and flows southeast into Botswana, where it spreads out to form the vast delta landscape.

ANGOLA

Katima Mulilo

Shakawe

NAMIBIA

BOTSWANA

Maun

0 km 100
0 miles 100

CLIMATE

Most of the rain reaching the delta falls in the Angolan part of the Okavango river catchment area during the hot, humid summer months (December–February). Winters are dry and mainly mild, though nighttime temperatures may approach freezing.

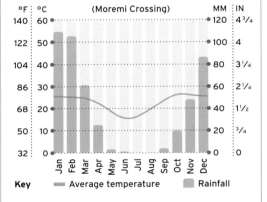

°F	°C	(Moremi Crossing)	MM	IN
140	60		120	4¾
122	50		100	4
104	40		80	3¼
86	30		60	2¼
68	20		40	1½
50	10		20	¾
32	0		0	0

Jan Feb Mar Apr May Jun Jul Aug Sep Oct Nov Dec

Key —— Average temperature ▮ Rainfall

NO WAY OUT

The Okavango Delta is an endorheic basin: a closed water system that does not involve the sea. Rain falling over such an area drains via rivers into a low point, forming a lake, inland sea (such as the Caspian), or a swamp. There is no route by which water can flow to the ocean, and all water flowing in is lost through evaporation or gradual seepage into the ground.

Cape buffalo

Syncerus caffer

large, curved horns

relatively short legs

The Cape buffalo is a massively built, oxlike hoofed mammal, and one of Africa's largest herbivores. Adult males mature at about five years of age, and weigh two-thirds more than females. Both sexes have a pair of formidable, curved horns, which in bulls almost meet across the top of the forehead, spanning up to 4 ft (1.3 m) in length. Bulls establish their dominance by displaying their horns in various threat positions and rarely fight.

Cape buffaloes have poor eyesight, and largely rely on their keen hearing to detect lions—their chief predators. Mixed herds comprise cows, their calves, and males of various ages. At certain times of the year, their numbers may reach hundreds or even thousands of animals. Bachelor herds contain five to 10 bulls.

↔ 8–11 ft (2.4–3.4 m)
⚖ 1,100–1,985 lb (500–900 kg)
✗ Common
🌾 Grass, leaves
🏠 🌳 ⛰ 🌾 〰

E. to S. Africa

▽ **QUENCHING THEIR THIRST**
Cape buffaloes eat huge quantities of grass. Their diet is thirst-inducing and they travel long distances to drink at rivers or waterholes They also rest for many hours, digesting their food.

△ **ON THE RUN**
Red lechwes have water-repellant hairs on their lower legs that prevent the legs becoming waterlogged as they run further into the swamp away from predators, giving them an advantage.

↔ 4–6 ft (1.3–1.8 m)
⚖ 115–298 lb (52–135 kg)
✗ Locally common
🌾 Aquatic plants, grasses
🏠 🌾 〰

C. Africa

▷ **BATTLE FOR SUPREMACY**
Two mature males fight to take possession of a prime breeding territory. A couple of male onlookers await the outcome with interest, while the females keep their heads down and carry on grazing.

male has long, swept-back, deeply ringed horns

Red lechwe
Kobus leche

This medium-sized antelope seldom moves far from water. In the rainy season, the red lechwe often feeds in the water, grazing on plants breaching the surface. If its shallow swampy habitat is heavily flooded, it will retreat to higher ground as it waits for the water to recede. When the water levels drop further in the dry season, the red lechwe is forced out again to forage on land. However, it has to drink regularly in hot weather and always stays within running distance of water.

Water crossing
The water is the red lechwe's primary defense. The lechwe has long, flattened hooves which provide a firm footing on the soft waterlogged ground, and it runs with a bounding gait that carries it over the shallow water. Although this way of running makes it ungainly on land, it is very effective for crossing shallow water quickly to escape attack from predators such as lions, African wild dogs, spotted hyenas, and leopards. The females and young tend to stay closer to the water than the usually solitary males.

Red lechwes breed during the rainy season between December and May. At this point, each mature male takes up a breeding territory, or lek. Male lechwes mature at five years or older, but females do so at 18 months, and so outnumber the mature males. Driven into the center of the lek—sometimes by harassing, immature males—where the dominant males hold court, the females are safe from attack as predators target the males left at the edge. Calves are born eight months later, toward the end of the dry season.

85 percent of the wild population lives in the Okavango Delta

growing horn
of young rhino

three-toed feet

White rhinoceros

Ceratotherium simum

↔ 12–13 ft (3.7–4 m)
⚖ Up to 5,000 lb (2,300 kg)
✖ Near threatened
🌾 Grasses
🏠 ⛰ 〰

E. and S. Africa

The white rhinoceros is one of the biggest mammals on earth, outweighed only by elephants and the semiaquatic hippopotamus. White rhinos are paler than their fellow African black rhinoceros, but still a dull lead gray. "White" is probably a misinterpretation of the Dutch/Boer term *wijd*, which means wide, referring to the animal's broad mouth unlike the black rhino's narrow, pointed lip. White rhinos graze with their heads held low, whereas black rhinos are browsers, grasping and twisting foliage from thorny scrub. Their large size as well as a process of hind-gut fermentation allows them to extract sufficient nutrition from a high-volume yet low-quality grass diet.

Both African rhinos have two horns. The one in front can be exceptionally long, especially in females. Rhino horn, which is made of a hairlike material, is used in traditional medicine in some Asian countries. In an attempt to save the rhino, conservationists in some reserves remove the horn under anesthetic, thereby giving poachers no reason to kill the animal.

◁ **BLACK RHINOCEROS**
Slightly smaller and rounder than
the white rhino, the black rhino
(*Diceros bicornis*) is identified by
its narrow, pointed lip.

More than **1,000 rhinos were killed** by poachers in South Africa in 2014

Group dynamics

White rhinos follow a complex system of social organization. Females and calves live in groups of five or six. Although the ranges of adult females overlap, there is little contact between the groups. The female gives birth to a single calf after a gestation of 16 months and the young stay with their mothers for two to three years. Adolescents form "friendships" or accompany cows that are without calves. Adult bulls, however, are solitary unless on the lookout for a breeding female.

They may tolerate one or two subordinate males close by—so long as they do not pose a challenge. Bulls mark their territories vigorously and stand horn-to-horn with intruding males, screaming defiance. It is safer for the weaker ones to back off than to turn tail, which invites a chase and heavy, damaging strikes from the fearsome horn. Adult white rhinos are effectively immune from attack by predators because of their huge size—humans are their only enemy—and healthy animals can live for around 45 years.

▽ **LITTLE AND LARGE**
Females are aggressively protective of their young, vulnerable calves, but chase them away after two to three years, before breeding again.

uniquely patterned coat gives alternative name of painted dog

African wild dog

Lycaon pictus

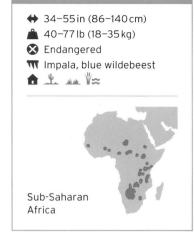

↔ 34–55 in (86–140 cm)
⚖ 40–77 lb (18–35 kg)
✖ Endangered
🍴 Impala, blue wildebeest
🏠 ⊥ ⋯ V≈

Sub-Saharan Africa

Highly adaptable, African wild dogs live in a variety of habitats across sub-Saharan Africa. Like many members of the dog family, African wild dogs live in packs and hunt cooperatively. A pack consists of four to nine adults with one dominant breeding pair and their pups. New packs usually form when siblings of the same sex leave their birth pack and join with a group of the opposite sex from another pack— a behavior that reduces inbreeding.

Wild dog packs require large home ranges—typically around 290 sq miles (750 sq km). Medium-sized antelope such as impala and Thomson's gazelles make up the majority of their prey. However, some packs have developed specialized skills for hunting different savanna animals such as zebras and ostriches. Wild dogs are threatened by habitat loss, human persecution, traffic, and diseases such as rabies and canine distemper; the latter is caught from domestic dogs.

△ **FACE OFF**
Notoriously tough-skinned and aggressive in defense, a pair of honey badgers fight off an attack by a pack of wild dogs despite their inferior size.

▷ **RARE AGGRESSION**
Fights, either for dominance or for food, are rare within a pack. African wild dogs rely on cooperation for their survival.

African jacana

Actophilornis africanus

Equipped with long toes and sharp claws, jacanas move elegantly over floating leaves, but are as likely to perch on top of a swimming hippopotamus. The jacana eats whatever it can reach in the water and on submerged stems and leaves. It snatches bees from lily flowers, dipping them into the water before swallowing. Typically, several jacanas feed on a marsh, but keep their distance, calling and chasing should another venture too near.

Female jacanas mate with several males and lay about four eggs in each of their nests. The male incubates them over 21–26 days. He also cares for the chicks, often carrying his brood beneath his wings, which are specially adapted for this purpose.

↔ 12 in (30 cm)
⚖ 5–9 oz (150–250 g)
✖ Common
🍴 Insects, mollusks
🏠 V≈
🧭 Sub-Saharan Africa

◁ **LILY TROTTER**
As one leaf gradually sinks beneath it, the lily-trotting jacana steps to the next, curling over leaf edges with its beak to find snails and beetles.

Red-billed quelea

Quelea quelea

Known as Africa's "feathered locust," the red-billed quelea is perhaps the world's most abundant bird. It is nomadic, descending on areas covered with tall seeding grasses or, if they cannot be found, cultivated cereal crops. Although individual birds only eat about ⅝oz (18g) of seed a day, a flock of 2 million birds can consume around 40 tons (36 metric tons). In South Africa alone, more than 180 million queleas are killed each year in pest control operations.

Flocks of red-billed queleas, millions strong, look like billowing clouds of smoke. The birds at the rear constantly leapfrog forward, to take a turn at the front, as the feeding flock forges ahead. Breeding birds weave a ball-shaped nest out of grass when the seasonal rains arrive.

↔ 5in (12cm)
⚖ ½–1oz (15–30g)
✖ Common
🍴 Seeds, insects
🏠 🌱 🌵 🌿 🏚
🧭 Sub-Saharan Africa

▷ **SEED CRACKER**
The quelea's thick beak is ideal for cracking and peeling seeds held by the tongue. Its red color is simply to impress a potential mate.

thick red beak of breeding male

African skimmer

Rynchops flavirostris

Although it looks "broken" at first glance, the African skimmer's bill is a specialized tool, used for fishing at the surface of calm water. Fine, parallel grooves on each side reduce friction, so that the bird can fly with the elongated tip of the lower mandible dipped in the water without tipping forward. Skimmers nest on remote, exposed sandbanks, often in temperatures above 95°F (35°C).

↔ 14–17 in (36–43 cm)
⚖ 4–7 oz (100–200 g)
✖ Near threatened
🍴 Fish
🏠 🌾 ≈ ≈
➤ Sub-Saharan Africa

▽ **SNATCHING FISH**
When the African skimmer's lower mandible touches a fish, it triggers a reflex mechanism to snatch the prey.

Leopard tortoise

Stigmochelys pardalis

This large tortoise prefers drier habitats, where it eats grassy plants, herbs, flowers, seeds, and berries. Males compete for females by butting one another until one is overturned. The female lays up to six clutches of between five and 25 eggs in a season, burying each clutch in a burrow. The eggs hatch after about nine to 14 months, depending on temperature, rainfall, and location, and the young mature in five to six years. The maximum lifespan of the leopard tortoise is more than 100 years.

↔ 12–28 in (30–71 cm)
⚖ 44 lb (20 kg)
✖ Not known
🍴 Grasses, fruit, seeds
🏠 🌵 🌾 ⛰
➤ E. to Southern Africa

high-domed shell with raised scutes

▷ **HIGHLY PATTERNED**
The scutes of the shell have rosettes similar to those of a leopard: straw yellow or tan-brown with black.

Nile monitor

Varanus niloticus

powerful front legs used for digging

whiplike tail used for swimming and defense

Fiercely defiant, the powerful Nile monitor readily defends its meal against crocodiles and big cats. Food can be almost any meat from insects, snails, and crabs to fish, amphibians, turtles, snakes, small mammals, and bird and reptile eggs as well as carrion. This huge lizard—the largest in Africa—stalks prey quietly and then strikes in a flash. It bites hard with its peglike teeth set in crushing jaws, writhes its muscular body, whips its long tail, and slashes violently with its sharp-clawed feet.

Generally found in or near slow-moving rivers and lakes, the semiaquatic Nile monitor can swim as fast and expertly as it runs and climbs. They bask in the sun on exposed sections of a bank or on nearby rocks or tree stumps. In cooler parts of their range, Nile monitors hibernate in communal dens.

Sealed in for safety

After the August–September rains, male Nile monitors wrestle and grapple for the right to mate. The female digs a hole in a damp termite mound and lays up to 60 eggs—the largest number of any lizard in a single clutch. The termites repair the mound, sealing in the eggs so they incubate in stable conditions. The eggs hatch in six to nine months, but the hatchlings, which are about 12 in (30 cm) long, remain in the nest until fresh rains soften the soil enough for them to dig their way out.

A **threatened** Nile monitor will **squirt fetid material** from its **cloaca**

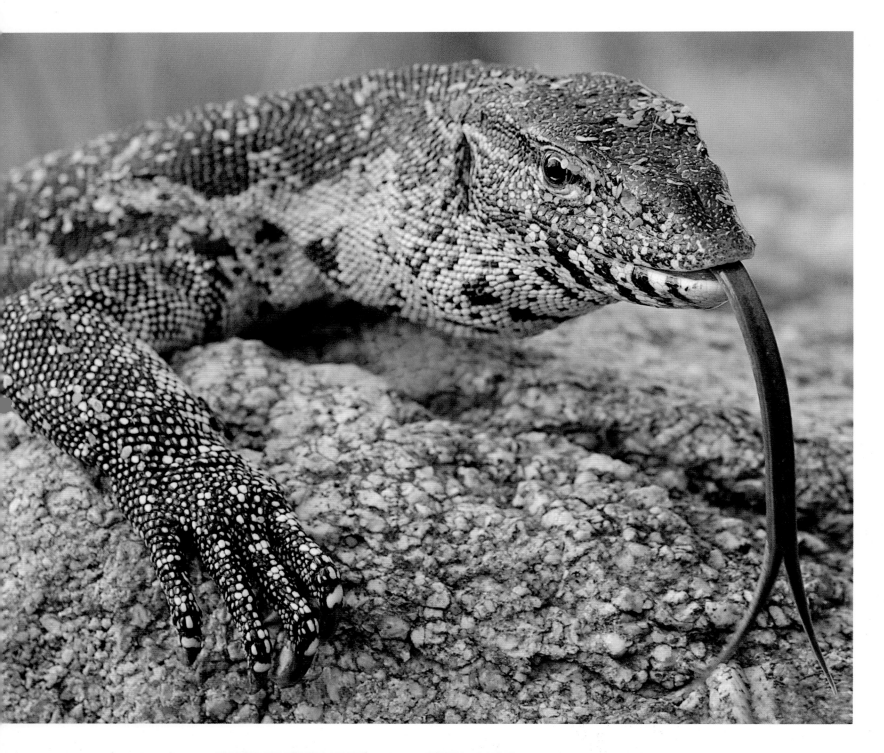

- ↔ 6–8 ft (1.8–2.4 m)
- 🏋 Up to 33 lb (15 kg)
- ✖ Common
- 🍴 Amphibians, birds, mammals
- 🏠 🌾 ≈ ≈

Sub-Saharan
Africa

△ **FORKED TONGUE**
Monitor lizards have a long, forked tongue, which they use to test their surroundings and to detect prey or carrion or the presence of predators such as crocodiles and pythons.

◁ **AT HOME IN WATER**
Nile monitors spend much of their time in water. They are reputed to be able to stay submerged underwater for up to one hour.

KALAHARI DESERT
A thirsty land where life finds a way

Covering an area of about 350,000 sq miles (900,000 sq km) in southern Africa, the Kalahari comprises a mixture of dry savanna and extensive areas of sand dunes. In summer, daytime temperatures can exceed 104°F (40°C), but the heat is moderated by altitude, with most of the region lying above 2,630 ft (800 m). The name Kalahari comes from the local Tswana language: *Kgalagadi* means waterless place. However, although it is commonly called a desert on account of its aridity, the Kalahari supports a far greater range of plant and animal life than a true desert.

Temporary greening

The Kalahari has a summer rainy season, when 4–20 in (100–500 mm) of rain may fall and parts of the region may become relatively green. However, the rains may fail completely in some years and as a result, the plants and animals have numerous adaptations to periodic drought.

For example, the plants of the dry savanna conserve water by producing tough, succulent or needlelike leaves and they take advantage of the rains to store water in roots, tubers, stems, and large, watery fruits such as melons and cucumbers.

The area has a diverse range of animals, including large herbivores such as antelopes and elephants, as well as predators such as lions, cheetahs, leopards, hyenas, wild dogs, and birds of prey. Other notable animals include aardvarks, ostriches, and meerkats. In recent years, the movement of larger herbivores has been restricted by cattle fencing, and wild predators have been persecuted by livestock farmers.

SURVIVAL FOOD
The deep roots of the camel thorn acacia help it to survive droughts, when its flowers and large seed pods become vital survival food for many of the Kalahari's herbivores. The leaves are protected by thorns, which deter browsers.

CAMEL THORN ACACIA

SAFE REFUGE
Colonies of 100 or more pairs of sociable weavers breed in a huge, multichambered nest, usually woven around the branches of a tree. Parent birds are aided by unrelated adults and older offspring, allowing them to raise up to four broods in succession.

SOCIABLE WEAVE

GEMSBOK

Contains the world's largest unbroken expanse of san

More than 400 species of plants

KEEPING A COOL HEAD
Among a variety of adaptations to the heat, the gemsbok pants through its nose to cool blood in the fine capillaries in the nostrils. Blood entering the brain is cooled by a close-knit network of vessels below it.

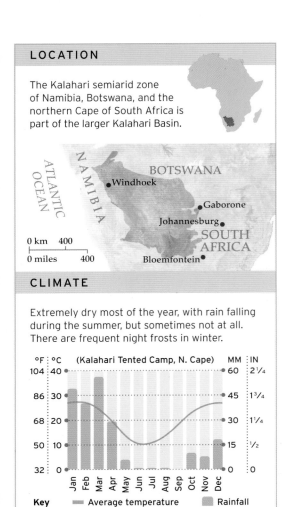

ATLANTIC OCEAN

NAMIBIA

BOTSWANA

● Windhoek

● Gaborone

Johannesburg ●

SOUTH AFRICA

Bloemfontein ●

0 km 400
0 miles 400

CLIMATE

Extremely dry most of the year, with rain falling during the summer, but sometimes not at all. There are frequent night frosts in winter.

(Kalahari Tented Camp, N. Cape)

°F	°C		MM	IN
104	40		60	2¼
86	30		45	1¾
68	20		30	1¼
50	10		15	½
32	0		0	0

Jan Feb Mar Apr May Jun Jul Aug Sep Oct Nov Dec

Key ▬ Average temperature ▬ Rainfall

Caracal
Caracal caracal

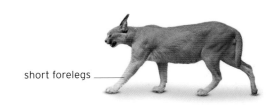

short forelegs

Africa's second-largest small cat, the caracal can bring down prey up to three times its own size. Speed and agility allow it to run down faster animals such as hares and small antelopes, while powerful muscles in its long hind legs enable it to leap up to 10 ft (3 m) in the air to grab flying birds with its large front paws. The caracal's hunting skills so impressed Persian and Indian royalty that many were trained to hunt gamebirds for royal families.

↔ 2–4 ft (0.6–1.2 m)
⚖ 13–44 lb (6–20 kg)
⊗ Common
♢ Birds, mammals

Africa, SW. Asia

◁ EAR TUFTS
The long, black ear tufts may be used as protection against flies, camouflage in long grass, or even as a tool for communication.

Aardvark
Orycteropus afer

Short, stocky legs and a flattened snout inspired South Africa's Dutch settlers to give this mammal a name that means "earth pig." Yet the solitary, night-foraging aardvark is not related to pigs or even anteaters, though it feeds mainly on ants, using its long, sharp claws to tear into their mounds. It extracts the ants with its 12-in (30-cm) long, sticky tongue, and an adult can eat up to 50,000 in one night. The food is ground up by a muscular area of the aardvark's stomach.

↔ 3–5 ft (0.9–1.5 m)
⚖ 88–143 lb (40–65 kg)
⊗ Common
♢ Ants, termites

Sub-Saharan Africa

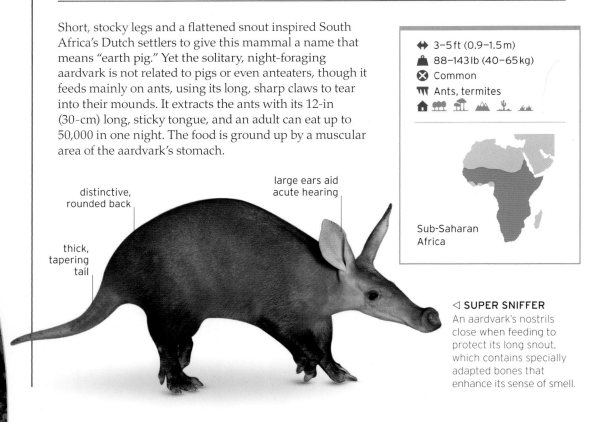

large ears aid acute hearing

distinctive, rounded back

thick, tapering tail

◁ SUPER SNIFFER
An aardvark's nostrils close when feeding to protect its long snout, which contains specially adapted bones that enhance its sense of smell.

DESERT SLEEPER
African bullfrogs survive droughts in a dormant state known as estivation. They seal themselves underground inside a watertight cocoon made of shed skin. Here, they can survive for up to 10 months until roused by fresh rainfall.

Too wet to be a true desert

AFRICAN BULLFROG

Common warthog
Phacochoerus africanus

protective warty
pad on cheek

Despite its rugged appearance, the common warthog is more likely to flee than fight if threatened, reaching speeds of up to 35 mph (55 km/h) on its long legs. If cornered, however, it uses its two sets of tusks to defend itself. Warthogs have reason to run—besides being hunted by humans for bushmeat, their natural predators include lions, leopards, hyenas, and crocodiles. The warthog is the only pig adapted for grazing. It "kneels" when eating grass or rooting with its tough snout, developing calluses on its wrists.

Facial armor
The warthog's facial "warts" are lumps of tissue that provide protection during fights. The warts are larger in adult males, which compete for mating rights. Females live in family groups called "sounders," with one or more litters of piglets, and individuals communicate using squeaks, grunts, and squeals.

↔ 3–5 ft (1–1.5 m)
⚖ 110–330 lb (50–150 kg)
✖ Common
🍴 Grass, roots, small animals
🏠 🌵 🌾

Sub-Saharan
Africa

◁ **SOLITARY BOAR**
Males leave their birth group after about two years and join a bachelor herd. Adult males, however, are solitary and mix with female-dominated sounders mainly to mate.

Kalahari springbok
Antidorcas hofmeyri

The name springbok refers to the way this antelope makes high, stiff-legged leaps when excited or threatened by predators, which include leopards, cheetahs, hyenas, and lions. It can leap 13 ft (4 m) through the air and reach speeds of 60 mph (100 km/h) when running away. The Kalahari springbok looks and lives much like the common springbok found to the east and south. However, this species is slightly larger and is a pale brown compared to its cousin's chestnut-red, and the band on its flank is closer to black. These are presumably adaptations to help it blend in among the arid sands and sparse vegetation of the Kalahari.

Kalahari springbok breed throughout the year. Females leave their herd when ready to give birth, usually to a single calf. They leave the calf hidden under a bush when feeding, and rejoin the herd when the calf is three or four weeks old. Calves are weaned when five or six months old, but usually stay with their mother until she next gives birth.

↔ 5 ft (1.5 m)
⚖ 67–105 lb (30.5–47.5 kg)
✖ Common
🍴 Grass, roots, tubers
🏠 🌵 🌾

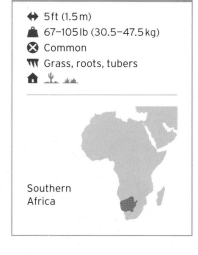

Southern
Africa

▷ **RACING AHEAD**
Springboks spend most of the year in single-sex herds. This male herd is on the move; any stragglers will be more at risk from predators.

Cape porcupine
Hystrix africaeaustralis

porcupine raises
quills to make
itself look bigger

This impressive rodent has taken defense to the extreme. All along its back are sharp spines called quills, which are modified hairs up to 12 in (30 cm) long. If threatened, the Cape porcupine flicks these out to form a black-and-white crest, while stomping its feet and shaking its hollow tail quills like a rattle. This dramatic display is enough to deter most predators. Porcupines are born with soft quills and stay in the family burrow for around two months until their quills have hardened. Adults live in pairs and form a close bond.

↔ 25–32 in (63–81 cm)
⚖ 22–53 lb (10–24 kg)
✖ Common
♱ Roots, bulbs, tubers, fruit

C. to Southern
Africa

◁ **WATCH OUT!**
If an inexperienced predator such as a leopard or lion cub attacks a porcupine, it risks a paw- or face-full of quills. If the wounds become infected, it may even die.

dark bands
on back

Meerkat

Suricata suricatta

Small enough to sit in the palm of a human hand, meerkats are feisty, highly territorial mongooses that live in complex groups, known as mobs, clans, or gangs, of up to 50 animals. Each clan consists of a dominant male and female, with subordinate "helpers" of both sexes. In smaller clans, the alpha female gives birth to most litters, while the male tries to prevent other males from mating. The female also releases pheromones that stop young females from coming into season. If this fails, she attacks ovulating or pregnant females, often killing their pups. During late pregnancy, she drives off other females to safeguard her young. They rejoin the clan later.

Mob mentality

Meerkat society relies on cooperation, and helpers play a crucial role in raising pups to adulthood. Some young females produce milk to help feed the dominant female's pups, while helpers of both sexes alert them to predators, teach them to forage, protect them, and bring them food during the weaning process.

Meerkats depend on their clan in many vital ways. A gang digs a series of multilevel tunnel-and-room burrows in its territory—usually with many entrances—where all its members sleep at night and rest during the hottest part of the day. In the morning, they emerge to warm up in the sun. They spend the day foraging and taking turns on lookout duty. While the clan searches for beetles, lizards, and scorpions, or digs for tubers and roots that supply much-needed water, sentry meerkats keep watch for predators such as jackals, snakes, and, especially, birds of prey. When alerted to danger by an alarm call, clan members retreat to a nearby bolthole or mob together to ward off the predator. If an adult is surprised, it may use its own body to shield nearby pups.

A meerkat clan may have as many as
1,000 boltholes in its territory

△ GROUP ATTACK
A meerkat mob acts as a single unit to ward off predators. All members arch their backs, raise their tails, and growl and hiss to intimidate the enemy.

▷ OLD AND YOUNG
Meerkats are highly social and the father may take an active role in guarding their pups. Nonbreeding members of the clan also look after the young.

↔ 8–12 in (19–29 cm)

⚖ 22–28 oz (620–800 g)

✖ Common

🦷 Insects, eggs, plants

🏠 ⚘ ⚶

Southern
Africa

◁ **ON GUARD**
While its clan forages,
a sentry meerkat finds
a good vantage point
and keeps watch for
predators, often staying
at its post for hours,
and squeaking to alert
the group to danger.

Ostrich
Struthio camelus

long legs and two-toed
feet adapted for sprinting

The largest living bird, the ostrich is immensely heavy and unable to fly. Standing more than 6½ ft (2 m) tall, ostriches are the tallest keen-sighted plains animals, except for giraffes. A bolting ostrich—reaching speeds of 45 mph (70 km/h)—alerts all prey species to danger.

Males attract females and repel rivals by making a deep boom. Akin to the roar of a lion, the "ohh-oooh-ooooooo" can be heard 2 miles (3 km) away.

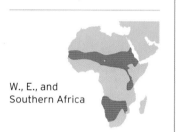

↔ 6–9 ft (1.7–2.7 m)
⚖ 220–353 lb (100–160 kg)
✖ Common
🍴 Plants, insects
🏠 🌵 🌱

W., E., and
Southern Africa

△ **CHOOSING HER MATE**
In the breeding season, a female ostrich bends her neck forward, flaps her wings backward, and makes a clapping noise when she selects a displaying male.

Cape cobra
Naja nivea

The Cape cobra prefers dry, scrubby habitats, where it hunts by day for small prey, such as colonial weaver bird eggs and nestlings. Like other cobras, it has fixed (not tilting) front fangs that inject nerve-disabling venom. After mating in early spring, the female lays 10–20 eggs in midsummer, usually in a rodent burrow or termite nest. Young Cape cobras have a characteristic dark throat patch that fades with age.

◁ **STANDING ITS GROUND**
A threatened Cape cobra rears up, spreads its hood, gapes, and hisses. Predators include meerkats, snake eagles, and secretary birds.

↔ 4–5 ft (1.2–1.5 m)
⚖ 5–7 lb (2–3 kg)
✖ Not known
🍴 Rodents, reptiles, birds
🏠 🌵
🧭 Southern Africa

▽ **DEFENSIVE MEASURES**
Body arched, mouth holding tail but ready to bite, scale edges sharp and forbidding, and foot claws ready to scratch—all these form the armadillo lizard's excellent defense mechanism.

tail gripped in
powerful jaws to form
protective hoop

broad, triangular head

thick, hard
head shield

Armadillo lizard

Ouroborus cataphractus

Large, thick, sharp-edged scales around the body and a
habit of curling up when threatened give this distinctive
reptile its common name. The armadillo lizard is
a type of girdled lizard. Its hard scales, reinforced
with bony plates, form bands or rings that encircle
its body. With such defenses the armadillo lizard
usually lives an unhurried life. It basks in the
sun or ambles around its dry scrub habitat in
search of small prey, especially termites,
then rests in a rocky crevice, empty burrow,
or among tree roots by night.

Social lizards

Armadillo lizards are unusual in both
their social and breeding habits. Extended
family groups numbering three or four
to occasionally 50 or more, of all ages and
both sexes, rest together in crevices. The
territorial males within a group generally
defend their small areas peaceably, but
are extremely aggressive to unrelated
intruding males. Also unusually for
a reptile, the female gives birth to just
one or two large young. Mating occurs in
early spring and the offspring are born
six to seven months later.

spines protect
soft underside

↔ 6–8 in (15–20 cm)
⚖ 3–4 oz (85–113 g)
✖ Vulnerable
🍴 Insects, millipedes, plants
🏠 🌵

Southern
Africa

MADAGASCAN DRY FOREST
Evolution in isolation

Madagascar is the world's fourth largest island. In the 135 million years since it separated from the continent of Africa, its plants and animals have diversified, producing a unique collection. The natural vegetation in the drier, western part of this tropical island is dominated by dry deciduous forests interspersed with wetlands. The geology of the area is mostly karst, a type of limestone, which means that surface water rapidly drains into underground rivers.

Baobabs, lemurs, and chameleons
Madagascar's trees include the gigantic baobabs—six species of which are endemic—and the spiny, succulent pachypodiums. The dry forests once extended from the coastal plain to about 2,600 ft (800 m) of altitude, but have been widely replaced by grazing pasture. Today, only three percent of the original forests remain, and they are of global ecological importance because of the hundreds of endemic plants and animals they support. These include lemurs—a group of primates found only in Madagascar. The forests are also home to a range of specialist insectivores and carnivores, and the world's most endangered tortoise, the plowshare tortoise—and two-thirds of the world's chameleon species.

Some of the more unusual wildlife is partly protected from persecution by traditional beliefs that place a *fady*, or taboo, on certain species. However, this has not protected the animals from the indirect threat of forest clearance for firewood and charcoal production, and some are still collected for the pet trade.

WORLD'S RAREST TORTOISE
This critically endangered tortoise has a wild population of just 200 adults, living in scraps of rocky scrub where they feed on grasses. Eggs and young are predated by introduced bush pigs, and individuals are still poached for the pet trade.

PLOWSHARE TORTOISE

MINIATURE MARVEL
With a total length of 2 in (5 cm), it is no surprise the dwarf chameleon escaped scientific attention until as recently as 1996. One of the world's smallest reptiles, it hunts in the leaf litter at night and climbs into low leafy branches to hide by day.

DWARF CHAMELE...

Baobabs can store up to 26,400 gallons (100,000 liters) of water in their trunk

95% o...

BAOBABS

THE MAGNIFICENT SEVEN
Madagascar's seven species of baobab are a symbol of the island. During wet periods, the fibrous wood swells with stored water, causing the trunk to bloat. Baobabs are deciduous, and shed their leaves in the dry season to reduce water loss.

LOCATION

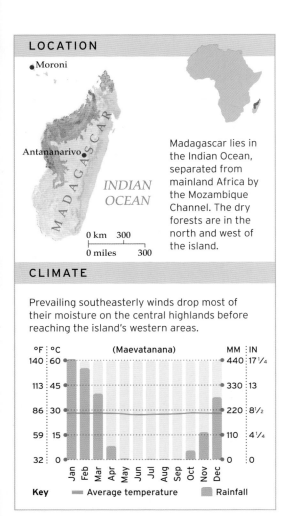

- Moroni

Antananarivo

MADAGASCAR

INDIAN OCEAN

0 km 300
0 miles 300

Madagascar lies in the Indian Ocean, separated from mainland Africa by the Mozambique Channel. The dry forests are in the north and west of the island.

CLIMATE

Prevailing southeasterly winds drop most of their moisture on the central highlands before reaching the island's western areas.

°F	°C	(Maevatanana)	MM	IN
140	60		440	17¼
113	45		330	13
86	30		220	8½
59	15		110	4¼
32	0		0	0

Jan Feb Mar Apr May Jun Jul Aug Sep Oct Nov Dec

Key — Average temperature ■ Rainfall

Fosa
Cryptoprocta ferox

Although they look like cats, fosas belong to a group of mammals thought to have evolved from a prehistoric mongooselike ancestor. Madagascar's largest predator, the fosa is active both day and night, and is able to hunt small mammals, birds, and reptiles in trees as well as on the ground. Because they occasionally take domestic poultry, fosas are targeted by local farmers as a pest.

↔ 28–32 in (71–81 cm)
⚖ 12–19 lb (5.5–8.5 kg)
✗ Vulnerable
♨ Lemurs, tenrecs, birds
🏠 🌳 🌴

Madagascar

▷ **UNIQUE FEATURES**
The fosa's catlike head ends in a doglike snout, and when walking slowly, it keeps its heels on the ground like a bear—or a human.

semiretractable claws provide good grip in trees

Berthe's mouse lemur
Microcebus berthae

The smallest living primate, this solitary nocturnal mammal spends its life in trees, searching for food around 33 ft (10 m) off the ground. Berthe's mouse lemurs enter a state of torpor during the day, lowering their metabolism and temperature to conserve energy.

▽ **TINY PRIMATE**
Berthe's mouse lemurs use all four limbs to run quickly along branches, leaping to flee from predators such as owls or fosas.

↔ 4 in (10 cm)
⚖ 1 oz (28 g)
✗ Endangered
♨ Fruit, gum, honeydew
🏠 🌳 🌴

Madagascar

BURROWING RAT
The Malagasy giant jumping rat occupies a similar burrowing niche to rabbits, which are absent from Madagascar. This endemic rodent's feeding and burrowing behaviors are important in seed dispersal and soil aeration.

...tile species are endemic

GIANT JUMPING RAT

↔ 16–18 in (39–46 cm)

⚖ 6–8 lb (2.5–3.5 kg)

✖ Endangered

🌿 Leaves, fruit, flowers

S. and SW.
Madagascar

▷ ON THE MOVE
Ring-tailed lemur troops cover
4 miles (6 km) a day in search
of food. When traveling, ringtails
raise their tails like flags to ensure
that the troop stays together.

Ring-tailed lemur

Lemur catta

dark, triangular eye patch

tail used for signaling

With their distinctive black-and-white faces and long, striped tails, ring-tailed lemurs are the most recognizable of all the lemur species. Covered in thick, gray-brown fur, they move so easily both on the ground and in trees that they seem like a cross between a cat and a raccoon. In fact, ring-tailed lemurs belong to the primates—the order that includes monkeys, apes, and humans. This means that, just like humans, lemurs have fingerprints and vision is their prime sense, although smell is also important to them.

Girl power

Native only to Madagascar, ring-tailed lemurs are found mainly in bush and dry forests, where these highly sociable animals live in groups of several males and females. Females rule the troop, winning fights with males, getting the best food, and ultimately deciding which males to mate with. During the mating season, males have "stink fights"—rubbing their tails over scent glands in their genitals and wrists, then flicking them at each other. Mating occurs between mid-April and June. In August or September, females give birth to one or two babies, weighing less than 4 oz (100 g) each. Females tend to raise their young jointly, often caring for groups of infants and carrying each other's offspring.

Sunshine and socializing

Unlike most other lemurs, ring-tails sunbathe in the morning, socializing at these times with a wide range of vocalizations and facial expressions. Ringtails are mainly plant eaters, including flowers and even bark and sap, but the fruit of the tamarind tree is a favorite. Sometimes they eat insects or small vertebrates such as lizards and, rarely, birds.

The main predators of ringtails are fossas—catlike carnivores also native to Madagascar—and large birds of prey, but devastation of habitat by humans is the chief threat to these and all other lemur species. On average, ring-tails live for 16–19 years in the wild, but they have been known to survive to the age of 27 in captivity.

△ **BLACK-AND-WHITE RUFFED LEMUR**
Unlike ring-tails, which spend much of their time on the ground, black-and-white ruffed lemurs (*Varecia variegata*) prefer to live high up in the tree canopy.

◁ **EARLY MORNING RITUAL**
Ring-tailed lemurs sit upright and expose their bellies to the warmth of the sun before beginning the search for their first meal of the day.

long tail used for balance when leaping

Verreaux's sifaka

Propithecus verreauxi

One of the largest members of the lemur family, the Verreaux's sifaka lives in the dry and spiny forests of south and southwest Madagascar. Sifakas are active during the daytime, feeding in trees—mainly on leaves, flowers, and fruit. They extract moisture from the leaves of succulent plants or by licking water droplets that have condensed on their woolly fur.

In leaps and bounds

Sifakas venture to the ground to cross open spaces in their distinctive bipedal leaping gait. In the trees, they move by clinging vertically and leaping with their long, strong hindlegs, covering gaps of up to 33 ft (10 m). Although their large hands and feet can be used for grasping, sifakas rarely use them in feeding. Instead they lean the whole body forward and pick up food directly with the mouth. Females are dominant in sifaka social groups. Groups of sifakas tend to spread out while traveling and searching for food, but come together in the same tree to rest.

Sifakas live in small groups of a few females and two or three males, one of which may be a "stain-chested" male, so-called because it produces scent from a gland in its throat which it uses in marking. All sifakas scent-mark their territories with urine and use it to signal to members of their own social group. They also communicate through calls, including a barklike "shi-fak" call which gave them their name.

Like many lemurs, the Verreaux's sifaka is at risk from destruction of its habitat due to slash-and-burn agriculture and timber felling.

About **30 percent** of Verraux's sifakas are **killed by fosas** in their **first year**

Aye-aye
Daubentonia madagascariensis

The world's largest nocturnal primate, the aye-aye is superbly adapted to locating insect larvae, in particular beetle grubs, beneath the bark of trees. It taps the tree trunk with its elongated middle finger and listens for the echo of a larva tunnel before chiseling away at the wood with its incisors and extracting the grub. The aye-aye's teeth and fingers are also useful when opening nuts and hard-shelled fruit. Aye-ayes are mainly solitary and spend the day in treetop nests made of twigs.

↔ 16–19 in (41–48 cm)
⚖ 7–11 lb (3.2–5 kg)
✖ Endangered
🍴 Leaves, fruit, flowers, bark
🏠

SW. and S. Madagascar

↔ 12–15 in (31–38 cm)
⚖ 5–6 lb (2.3–2.7 kg)
✖ Endangered
🍴 Grubs, fruit, nuts, fungi
🏠
◉ NW. and E. Madagascar

▷ **NOCTURNAL PROWLER**
Large eyes and ears help the aye-aye to see and hear in the gloom of the forest at night.

△ **COQUEREL'S SIFAKA**
Like all sifakas, Coquerel's sifakas (*P. coquereli*) have one young at a time. At first, it is carried across the mother's underside, then later rides on her back.

◁ **DANCING MALE**
When crossing open ground, a Verreaux's sifaka gracefully "dances" sideways on its strong hindlegs with its forearms held out for balance. Its tail is almost as long as its body.

Greater hedgehog tenrec
Setifer setosus

Greater hedgehog tenrecs rely on their long whiskers as well as smell and sound to find prey at night. These expert climbers nest in tree hollows or on the ground. They lower their body temperature during the day and for weeks at a time during cooler times to conserve energy.

↔ 6–9 in (15–23 cm)
⚖ 6–10 oz (170–284 g)
✖ Locally common
🍴 Earthworms, insects, fruit
🏠
◉ Madagascar

▽ **SHIELD OF SPINES**
Like true hedgehogs, greater hedgehog tenrecs can roll into a prickly ball for protection when threatened.

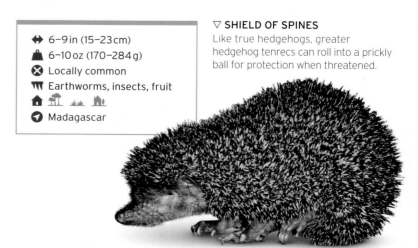

opposing fused
toes give feet
pincerlike grip

Panther chameleon
Furcifer pardalis

independently
moving eyes
give almost
360° view

△ **DAZZLING DISPLAY**
Male panther chameleons are more
colorful than females. They are at
their brightest when competing with
another male or courting a female,
and least colorful when hunting.

The panther chameleon's impressive color changes are affected by its mood, such as when it is being aggressively territorial, dealing with a threat, or courting a mate. Temperature, humidity, light levels, and—to a lesser extent than popularly believed—matching the colors of its surroundings as a means of camouflage are also influencing factors.

An aid to recognizing coloration changes in other individuals is excellent eyesight, which is also important for capturing prey. The two turretlike eyes move independently to look in different directions simultaneously, or are both aimed at prey to judge its distance and motion. Then, the muscular, catapultlike tongue—which is longer than the chameleon's body—flicks out and back with the prey in just 0.007 seconds. Panther chameleons feed mostly on insects, such as

crickets and beetles, and spiders, but they will also eat small vertebrates such as frogs, baby lizards (including other chameleons), and rodents. They are active during the day, spending most of their time in low trees or bushes hunting for prey. At night, they sleep with their tail coiled tight around a thin branch.

Ducking and bobbing

Panther chameleons live mostly alone and the males will display to, and even physically fight, others that intrude into their territory. However, during the breeding season (January–May), the aroused males—which are up to twice the size of the females—duck and bob to impress potential partners. The female lays up to six clutches of 10–50 eggs buried in moist soil, and the young hatch six to 12 months later.

△ **ON TARGET**
The chameleon shoots out its elastic tongue onto the prey, which adheres to the sticky cuplike end before the tongue springs back into the mouth.

thick, muscular tail base typical of males

16–21 in (41–53 cm)

5–8 oz (142–227 g)

Locally common

Insects, small vertebrates

N. and E. Madagascar, Reunion Island

prehensile tail acts as fifth limb when climbing

Henkel's leaf-tailed gecko

large, triangular head

Uroplatus henkeli

Henkel's leaf-tailed gecko's remarkable camouflage is heightened by the "frill" of skin along the sides of its head— giving it a "beard"—and part of its body. When resting during the day, lying flat on a mossy, lichen-covered rock or tree trunk, these features break up the otherwise recognizable lizard-shaped outline. It hunts at night, mainly for insects, usually several feet above ground.

11 in (28 cm)

1¹/₂–1³/₄ oz (40–50 g)

Vulnerable

Insects, snails

N. and W. Madagascar

△ **STICKY TOES**
Henkel's gecko's large, adhesive toe pads, typical of the gecko family, stick even to glossy leaves and crumbly bark and so help in climbing trees.

Tomato frog

Dyscophus antongilii

The tomato frog's bright orange-red skin is a warning to predators, such as snakes. When threatened, its first line of defense is to puff itself up to look larger, and this also makes it difficult to swallow. If taken into a predator's jaws, the frog exudes a sticky liquid from its skin that clogs up the attacker's mouth and inflames its skin. The liquid can cause swellings and rashes in humans.

2–4 in (5–10 cm)

Rainy season

Near threatened

Insects

N. and E. Madagascar

plump body

▷ **RED ALERT**
Female tomato frogs, such as the one shown here, are larger and more brightly colored than males.

Northern Thailand
Two Asian elephants wander into a jungle
clearing as the sun rises. Elephants are highly
social mammals–females stay with their
families, headed by a matriarch, for life.

Asia

LAND OF EXTREMES
Asia

Asia is the world's largest continent, covering around 30 percent of the Earth's land area. It extends nearly 4,000 miles (6,500 km) from the polar regions in the north of Siberian Russia, through the subtropics and tropics to the islands of Southeast Asia, which lie on and below the equator. Due to its vast size, parts of Central Asia experience a continental climate with extremes of heat in the summer and cold in the winter.

To the south of the Siberian plateau lies a sparsely populated landscape of mountain and plateau, desert, and steppe. The southern parts of Asia are geologically much younger. Tectonic activity to the east and southeast has created numerous volcanic island arcs that form the western side of the Pacific Ring of Fire. The Himalayas isolate the Indian subcontinent from the rest of Asia, and have a profound effect on the climate of Asia as a whole. More than 100 mountains have summits higher than 23,600 ft (7,200 m), and little moisture is left in the air flowing over them into Central Asia during the summer.

SIBERIAN TUNDRA

Running along the coast of northeastern Russia, this subarctic tundra is a breeding ground for migratory birds and a temporary home to herds of reindeer.

FEATURED ECOREGIONS

- Arabian Highlands ›› p248-53
  Montane woodland, desert scrub
- Terai-Duar Savanna ›› p254-65
  Subtropical grassland
- Eastern Himalayas ›› p266-71
  Temperate broadleaf, mixed forest
- Upper Yangtze Forests ›› p272-77
  Temperate broadleaf, mixed forest
- Gobi Desert ›› p278-83
  Desert, scrub
- Nihonkai Montane Forest ›› p284-91
  Temperate broadleaf, mixed forest
- Bornean Rainforest ›› p292-301
  Tropical, subtropical moist broadleaf forest
- Sulu-Sulawesi Seas ›› p302-09
  Marine, coral reefs

ARABIAN PENINSULA

Much of this peninsula is desert, but mountain ranges around the margins have woodlands with plants and birds found nowhere else.

MONSOON CLIMATE

India and Southeast Asia have a monsoon climate. In summer, the land is warmer than the sea. Rising warm air creates low pressure systems that draw in cool moist air from the oceans, resulting in torrential rainfall. In winter, the sea is warmer than the land and so the air flow reverses, causing the dry season.

Map labels

Central Siberian Plateau
berian Plateau
Siberia
h Siberian Lowland
Kolyma
Lena
Kamchatka
Sea of Okhotsk
Sakhalin
Kuril Islands
Amur
Lake Baikal
Manchurian Plain
Plateau of Mongolia
Gobi
Lake Khanka
Sea of Japan (East Sea)
Hokkaido
Altai untains
ASIA
Qinghai Hu
Yellow River
Great Plain of China
Yangtze
Yellow Sea
Japan
Mekong
Yangtze
East China Sea
Ryukyu Islands
5
Taiwan
Brahmaputra
Irrawaddy
Hainan
Philippine Sea
Philippines
of gal
Andaman Islands
Sulu Sea
Gulf of Thailand
Mouths of the Mekong
South China Sea
Malay Peninsula
Nicobar Islands
Celebes Sea
PACIFIC OCEAN
New Guinea
Borneo
Celebes
Moluccas
Sumatra
Java
Timor Sea

KEY DATA

ECOSYSTEMS

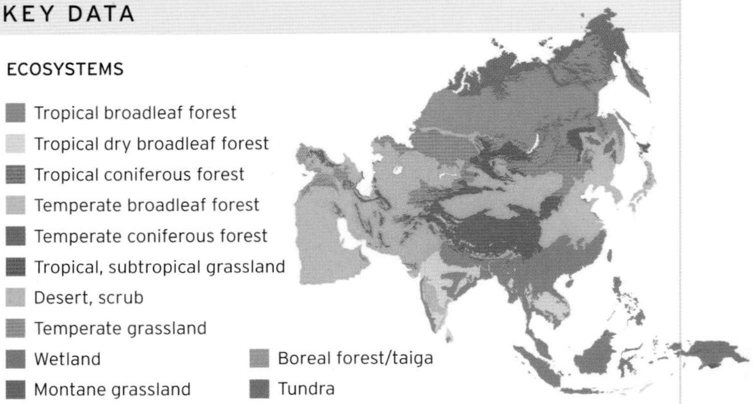

- Tropical broadleaf forest
- Tropical dry broadleaf forest
- Tropical coniferous forest
- Temperate broadleaf forest
- Temperate coniferous forest
- Tropical, subtropical grassland
- Desert, scrub
- Temperate grassland
- Wetland
- Montane grassland
- Boreal forest/taiga
- Tundra

AVERAGE RAINFALL

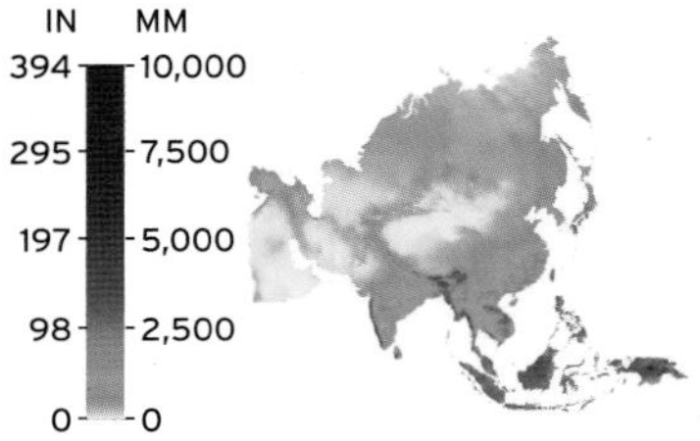

IN	MM
394	10,000
295	7,500
197	5,000
98	2,500
0	0

AVERAGE TEMPERATURE

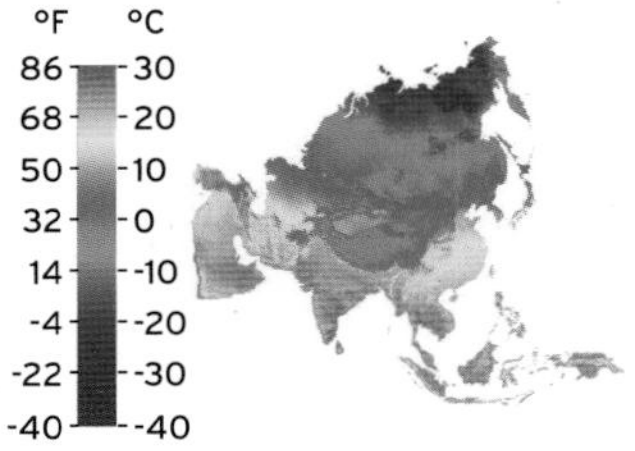

°F	°C
86	30
68	20
50	10
32	0
14	-10
-4	-20
-22	-30
-40	-40

VOLCANIC ISLAND ARCS

Volcanic island arcs form when one oceanic plate moves beneath another. Mantle rocks at the base of the overriding plate melt and the molten rock rises to create volcanic islands. The lake-filled volcanic caldera shown here is part of one of the volcanic arcs that make up Japan. This arc was formed by the Pacific plate moving under one of the plates on which Japan sits.

WALLACE'S LINE

Distinct groups of animals inhabit the islands to the west and east of Wallace's Line. Deep water channels between Borneo and Sulawesi and between Bali and Lombok meant animals were not able to cross.

ARABIAN HIGHLANDS
A moisture-laden haven for wildlife and plant species

The Arabian Highlands are a collection of mountain ranges, ridges, and plateaus rising around the fringes of the Arabian Peninsula. They stretch inland from the coastal "fog desert" and surround the Empty Quarter, the peninsula's vast sandy desert. Due to their altitude, the highlands are cooler and damper than the nearby deserts and are able to support a greater diversity of plant and animal life. Moisture-laden oceanic winds are forced up and over the mountains, producing seasonal rainfall, and low nighttime temperatures cause fog and dew formation.

Vital juniper woodland
Unusually, it is the highest areas of this ecoregion that are covered with woodland. Here juniper trees are particularly abundant and provide vital cover and food for several bird species. Drier, south-facing slopes are home to more succulent plants, such as aloe and euphorbia,

while the foothills are covered with shrubland and savanna. Many of the area's plant and bird species are found nowhere else in the world, but the peninsula also serves as an important land bridge between Africa and Eurasia for migrating birds, many of which follow the ridge of the Asir Mountains that run parallel to the Red Sea coast. In terms of mammal species, the Arabian Highlands are home to several large carnivores, including the caracal, the rare Arabian wolf, and the striped hyena. They also form one of the last strongholds of the critically endangered Arabian leopard.

ACACIA EATER
The slender mountain gazelle lives throughout the Arabian Highlands, especially where acacia is found. As well as its main food plant, the leaves and seed pods, it eats succulent plants and digs for bulbs and corms, especially when water is scarce.

MOUNTAIN GAZELLE

CLIMBING SERPENT
The Arabian cat snake is an agile, stealthy predator, able to climb trees and rock faces in search of prey such as rodents, lizards, fledgling birds, and bats. This nocturnal species kills with its venomous fangs and is widespread in the region.

ARABIAN CAT SNA[KE]

Arabian oryx

41 reptile species live here ›

Home to more than 2,000 plant species ›

EUPHORBIA AMMAK

SPIKY SUCCULENT
Reaching up to 33 ft (10 m) in height, Euphorbia ammak resembles a cactus, but is actually a succulent treelike plant from the spurge family. Its thick, spiny stems contain an unpleasant-tasting sap that discourages herbivores from browsing on it.

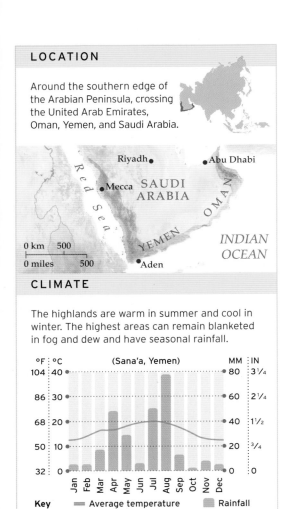

CLIMATE

The highlands are warm in summer and cool in winter. The highest areas can remain blanketed in fog and dew and have seasonal rainfall.

(Sana'a, Yemen)

Key — Average temperature   ▮ Rainfall

Hamadryas baboon
Papio hamadryas

doglike muzzle

Full-grown male Hamadryas baboons are among the world's most impressive monkeys, with a muscular build, sharp canine teeth, and a magnificent cape of silvery fur that contrasts with their bright pink faces. Both sexes have pads of bare reddish skin on their buttocks, which swell in females to advertise when they are sexually receptive.

↔ 20–38 in (51–97 cm)
⚖ 20–47 lb (9–21.5 kg)
✖ Common
🍴 Grass, fruit, insects

E. Africa, SW. Asia

Harems and bands

Hamadryas baboons were well known to the ancient Egyptians, who featured them in religious hieroglyphic carvings and paintings—they are also called sacred baboons. Like other baboon species, they spend most of their time on the ground and forage widely, eating grass, crops, and almost any small animals they find. At night many harems band together and climb cliffs for safety—in some places, a few hundred Hamadryas baboons may sleep on the same rock face.

The big dominant males jealously guard their females from rival males. They use visual threats such as yawning to reveal their large canine teeth and aggressive displays such as neck bites.

Dominant male baboons **lip-smack to reassure** their females

▽ GROOMING IN PROGRESS
Two female baboons groom a resplendent adult male as an act of loyalty and submission. Each adult male rules over a harem of several smaller, olive-brown females.

KEEPING COOL
Although relatively small compared to other gray wolf subspecies, the Arabian wolf has proportionately larger ears to disperse heat and help keep it cool during hot summers. In winter, its coat thickens to withstand freezing conditions.

were reintroduced in 1980

ARABIAN WOLF

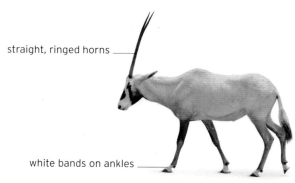

straight, ringed horns

white bands on ankles

Arabian oryx

Oryx leucoryx

Few large mammals are so well adapted to survive in the extreme heat and drought of the desert as the Arabian oryx. It has wide shovel-shaped hooves for plodding great distances over loose sand. The oryx is not a great runner—its only natural predators, wolves and striped hyenas, are few in number.

The bright, almost luminous white coat helps reflect away the sun's heat, but also makes the Arabian oryx stand out against the barren landscape, even in the dark. The benefit to the antelopes of seeing their herd mates easily outweighs any risk of attracting the attention of predators. If a predator does appear on the horizon, the oryx has nowhere to hide. It takes the threat side-on, showing its full size in an attempt to deter attack.

Following the leader

An oryx herd is led by an older female and contains a few other females and their young, the dominant male, and some subordinate males. When food is plentiful after rainfall, the herd can swell into hundreds, and males defend small territories, mating with any female that comes along. In favorable conditions, females can give birth to a single calf once a year, after about 34 weeks of gestation. However, births are rare in years with low rainfall. Outside of the breeding season, herd members are tolerant of each other, with both sexes adopting a simple hierarchy based on horn length. The lack of rivalries lets a small herd cluster in the shade of a tree during the warmest part of the day. When it is cooler, members spread out to graze, always staying within sight of each other. When it is time to move on, the lead female sets off, but stops regularly to ensure the others in her herd are following close behind.

The Arabian oryx can smell rain falling up to 50 miles (80 km) away. The herd follows the scent, covering 20 miles (30 km) in one go, mostly during the night. When they arrive, the oryxes graze on the newly sprouting desert plants. Oryxes also dig up roots and tubers using their shovel-like hooves. They can go for weeks without water, extracting the moisture they need from their food.

Operation oryx

The Arabian oryx was one of international conservation's earliest success stories. By 1972, trophy hunters had made the species extinct in the wild. By the following decade, a captive-born herd was reintroduced to a protected reserve in Oman, and they eventually spread into the wild.

Arabian oryx can **smell rain** more than **two days' walk away**

- ↔ 5–8 ft (1.5–2.4 m)
- ⚖ 120–165 lb (54–75 kg)
- ✖ Vulnerable
- 🌿 Grass, leaves, buds, roots
- 🏠 🌱

W. Asia

▷ **LOCKING HORNS**
Dominance is established with visual displays by individuals showing off their impressive horns. However, when the males are establishing territories, all-out fights do take place.

◁ **KEEPING COOL**
Young oryxes often rest near a shrub. They make a shallow pit to lie in, scraping away the hot surface sand to expose the cooler layer below.

dark brown or
black throat patch

Striped hyena
Hyaena hyaena

▷ **SPOTTED HYENAS**
Spotted hyenas
(*Crocuta crocuta*) are
the largest and most
powerful members
of the hyena family.
They are native to
sub-Saharan Africa.

Found from Africa to Central Asia and India, the
striped hyena has the largest range of the world's four
hyena species and frequents the widest variety of
habitats. However, it is now extinct in many areas and
populations are declining in
most places. Like other hyenas,
the striped hyena resembles a
lanky, big-eared dog. Its front legs
are longer than those at the back,
giving it a front-heavy profile with
a sloping back.

Bone cruncher

The striped hyena is primarily
a scavenger, using its massively
powerful jaw muscles to tear into
carcasses, rip apart tough sinews, and
crunch up bones. It also hunts small
prey and forages for dates, melons,
and other fresh fruit. Usually found
alone or in small groups, striped
hyenas are strictly nocturnal and
roam large distances in search of food.

The female gives birth to one to four
young in a rocky den or a burrow. The cubs
start eating meat when they are around 30 days old.
They may suckle for as long as a year while learning
important foraging skills from their mother. Most
striped hyenas are killed by lions or humans.

forelegs longer
than hindlegs

- ↔ 3–4 ft (1–1.2 m)
- ⚖ 57–90 lb (26–41 kg)
- ⊗ Near threatened
- 🍴 Carrion, hares, insects, fruit
- 🏠 ⛰ 🌵

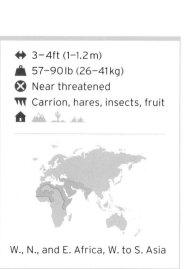

W., N., and E. Africa, W. to S. Asia

▷ **AGGRESSIVE STANCE**
Striped hyenas have extremely
shaggy fur, creating a mane along
the back. This is raised during
aggressive encounters with other
hyenas or predators such as lions.

dense coat

Rock hyrax
Procavia capensis

The tiny, tail-less rock hyrax makes its den in crevices and cavities in rocky outcrops or cliffs, which offer protection from predators such as leopards, snakes, and eagles. Rocks also help hyraxes to regulate their body temperature by providing basking places in cold weather and shade in hot conditions. The moist, rubberlike soles of their feet enable hyraxes to climb with ease. Despite their thick coats, hyraxes are sensitive to temperature extremes, avoiding cold winds and rain as well as midday heat.

A typical day begins with an hour or two of sunbathing, followed by an hour's foraging, then resting before feeding again in the afternoon.

pale brown coat with vertical flank bars

- ↔ 12–23 in (30–58 cm)
- ⚖ 7–11 lb (3–5 kg)
- ⊗ Common
- 🌾 All vegetation
- 🏠 ⛰ 🌵 🌱

W., S., and E. Africa, W. Asia

◁ **GROUP HUDDLE**
Young hyraxes stay close to their mother. After resting together in the sun, this family is getting ready to resume feeding.

Arabian partridge
Alectoris melanocephala

This is a bird of vegetated wadis, valleys, high slopes, and cultivated desert fringe, especially scrubby juniper forest. Currently common, the Arabian partridge is threatened by droughts and changes in its habitat caused by cultivation and overgrazing. It escapes predators by running rather than flying. Most feeding and drinking takes place in the cooler morning and evening. Females lay five to eight eggs in a nest hidden in low vegetation.

white band above eye

dark barring on flanks

- ↔ 16–17 in (40–43 cm)
- ⚖ 18–20 oz (500–570 g)
- ⊗ Common
- 🌾 Seeds, grass, small insects
- 🏠 🌱
- ◐ SW. Asia

▷ **UNIQUE APPEARANCE**
A neat, pale, red-legged bird of dry places, the Arabian partridge has a distinctively striped head and neck.

TERAI-DUAR SAVANNAS

Home to the world's tallest grasslands

This narrow region at the base of the Himalayas comprises a mosaic of river grassland, savannas, and forests. Much of the grassland is unusually high, which provides excellent cover for both predators and their prey. The Terai-Duar is home to numerous species of hooved mammals, including at least five different deer species, the endangered Asiatic wild buffalo, and the Indian rhinoceros. At the top of the Terai food chain is the tiger, populations of which are increasing here, especially in established national parks such as Chitwan and Bardia in Nepal. Leopards and the rare clouded leopard are also resident. Three bird species—the spiny babbler, the gray-crowned prinia, and the Manipur bush-quail—have ranges that are restricted to the Terai-Duar and neighboring regions.

Fertile floodplain

Alluvial or floodplain grasslands are submerged during monsoon rains and replenished with fertile silt, prompting rapid grass growth once the waters retreat. However, the moist, nutrient-rich soil is ideal for cultivation, and much of the land has been converted to agriculture. The survival of the Terai-Duar's wildlife depends on an extensive network of protected areas connected by wildlife corridors so that species such as tigers, elephants, and rhinoceros can move freely between reserves, with as little interaction with humans as possible.

The Terai-Duar is one of Earth's most **biologically outstanding habitats**

EGYPTIAN VULTURE

PLIGHT OF THE VULTURES
India's vulture populations crashed spectacularly in the 1990s after veterinary drugs used to treat cattle were ingested by birds that fed on livestock carcasses. Although one drug has since been banned, it will take time for the slow-breeding species to recover.

Has Asia's highest populations of tigers and rhinos

SWAMP DEER

ENDANGERED DEER
Terai grasslands are home to the barasingha, or swamp deer, which has large, splayed hooves that can cope with its swampy habitat. A vital prey species for tigers and leopards, barasingha numbers are threatened by habitat loss and hunting.

Manipur bush-quail was thought extinct until found here in 2006

MUGGER CROCODILE

ENDANGERED REPTILE
Mugger crocodile populations declined in the 1950s and 60s mainly due to hunting for their skin. Despite improved protection and captive breeding programs, the mugger still suffers because of habitat loss.

SMALL AND RARE
Standing just 10 in (25 cm) at the shoulder, the critically endangered pygmy hog is the smallest member of the pig family. Its range is restricted to a national park in northwest Assam, and as few as 150 animals survive.

PYGMY HOG

Home to mugger crocodiles and rare gharials

ICONIC GRASSES
The dominant grasses of the Terai-Duar are actually members of the sugarcane family. Kans grass grows up to 10 ft (3 m) high; baruwa grass is smaller, but both are important food for animals, including the Indian rhinoceros and pygmy hog. The grasses grow quickly after the monsoon rains.

KANS GRASS

Six of India's nine species of vulture live in the Terai-Duar grasslands

REJUVENATING NEWT
The Himalayan newt inhabits streams and paddy fields in the region. It possesses a remarkable ability to regrow lost limbs. Its wounds heal quickly thanks to a peptide called tylotoin that scientists have isolated from its skin, leading to speculation about its future use in speeding up human wound treatment.

HIMALAYAN NEWT

The Terai-Duar savannas are situated in a narrow belt of lowland in front of the Himalayas of southern Asia, where India borders Nepal, Bhutan, and Bangladesh.

CHINA

NEPAL

New Delhi

Kathmandu

Lucknow

Patna

INDIA

0 km 200
0 miles 200

CLIMATE

The Terai-Duar has a humid, subtropical climate with year-round warm temperatures averaging 72°F (22°C). Most of the rainfall takes place during the monsoon season, which occurs between June and September.

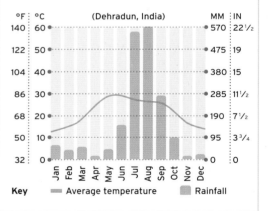

(Dehradun, India)

°F	°C		MM	IN
140	60		570	22½
122	50		475	19
104	40		380	15
86	30		285	11½
68	20		190	7½
50	10		95	3¾
32	0		0	0

Jan Feb Mar Apr May Jun Jul Aug Sep Oct Nov Dec

Key — Average temperature ▮ Rainfall

CULTIVATING CLIMATE CHANGE

Rice is cultivated in the Terai in flooded paddy fields. Microscopic soil organisms in the paddies are a major source of the greenhouse gas methane. Because methane levels increase with rising atmospheric carbon dioxide and warmer temperatures, rice cultivation is likely to fuel global warming. Seasonal drainage of the paddies helps to reduce their methane production.

single horn averages 10 in
(25 cm) in both sexes

Indian rhinoceros

Rhinoceros unicornis

Of all five rhinoceros species, the Indian rhino is second in size only to Africa's white rhino. It is also the one most at home in water—a trait seemingly at odds with its appearance. Its skin is 3 in (8 cm) thick and develops deep folds speckled with lumps, giving it an armor-plated look. Nevertheless, Indian rhinos are good swimmers and like to wallow. They are also surprisingly agile on land, able to turn quickly and charge at high speed. Since they have relatively poor eyesight, Indian rhinos rely on keen hearing and an excellent sense of smell to navigate their surroundings. A semiprehensile upper lip makes them adept at grasping grass stems.

Still at risk

Due to stricter protection laws, Indian rhino numbers have recovered from fewer than 200 in the early 20th century to more than 3,000 in the wild. Poaching, however, is still a problem, despite the fact that the Indian rhino's horn—which it uses mainly for foraging—is relatively small.

↔ 11 ft (3.4–3.5 m)
⚖ 4,400 lb (2,000 kg)
✖ Vulnerable
🌾 Grasses, shrubs, fruit
🏠 🌳 ⛰ 〰

S. Asia (Terai and Brahmaputra basins)

Blackbuck
Antilope cervicapra

pointed hoof

Once India's most numerous hoofed mammal, the blackbuck has become extinct in many areas due to habitat loss and hunting. However, it is recovering in protected areas, and introduced populations thrive in Argentina and Texas. Males are larger and darker than females, and have spiralled horns. Herds may contain both sexes, only females with young, or just bachelors.

↔ 4 ft (1.2 m)
⚖ 55–77 lb (25–35 kg)
✕ Near threatened
🌾 Grass, seed pods
🏠 ⛰
🧭 S. Asia

▽ WARNING LEAP
A high leap is a danger alert; smaller leaps follow before the herd gallops away at up to 50 mph (80 km/h).

△ AT PEACE
Although generally solitary, several Indian rhinos may wallow or graze near each other without fighting if food is plentiful in the area.

▽ STAY CLOSE
A rhino calf is vulnerable to predators such as tigers, and remains with its mother for up to two years.

hair only on rims of ears, tip of tail, and as eyelashes

heavy neck folds provide protection

Gaur
Bos gaurus

dewlap under chin extends to forelegs

One of the largest, most heavy-set of wild cattle, gaurs mostly live in herds of between five and 12 animals, led by a single bull. Usually active during the day, when humans encroach on their habitat, gaurs become nocturnal to avoid hunters.

↔ 8–11 ft (2.5–3.3 m)
⚖ 1,430–2,200 lb (650–1,000 kg)
✕ Vulnerable
🌾 Grasses, fruit, twigs, bark
🏠 🌳 🌲 ⛰
🧭 S. and SE. Asia

◁ HAZARDOUS HORNS
Both male and female gaurs have curved horns that grow up to 24 in (60 cm) long. Unfortunately, these are prized by hunters.

Red muntjac

Munitiacus muntjak

The red muntjac is one of few deer that are habitually omnivorous. A solitary animal, the deer supplements its diet of shoots, seeds, and fruit with the occasional bird egg, rodent, or a meal of carrion.

Breeding occurs at all times of the year, with males scent-marking to attract a harem of receptive females. Fights between rutting males involve both butting and biting, leading to frequent injury. Gestation lasts seven months, and the single offspring is weaned early for deer at just ten weeks after birth. Sexual maturity is reached at the age of two.

▷ **SIMPLE ANTLERS**
The short, simple antlers are seen only in males. The males also have long upper canine teeth and a scent gland under each eye.

↔ 3–4 ft (0.9–1.2 m)
🏋 44–62 lb (20–28 kg)
❌ Common
🍴 Leaves, fruit, eggs, carrion
🏠

S. to SE. Asia

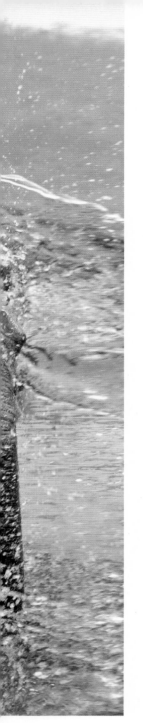

Asian elephant

Elephas maximus

long, flexible trunk
used like a fifth limb

Asia's largest land mammal, the Asian elephant spends most of the day eating up to 330 lb (150 kg) of plant material, including grass and fruit. It also eats cultivated crops such as bananas, causing conflict with humans. About 20 percent of the world's human population lives either in or near the Asian elephant's habitat, forcing these animals into increasingly fragmented areas. Poaching is also a threat, although, unlike African elephants, only male Asian elephants grow tusks, and some males lack them altogether. Females and some males grow "tushes"—small tusks that rarely extend beyond their mouths. Asian elephants also differ from African elephants in that they have arched backs, double-domed heads, and smaller ears.

Males leave their birth group when they are six or seven years old, living alone or in loose groups with other bulls. Females stay with their families, headed by a matriarch, who leads the herd to water and browsing areas. Females stay bonded to family members for life, using their trunks to greet and caress each other.

◁ **HEAVY DRINKERS**
Adult Asian elephants need to drink 18–24 gallons (70–90 liters) of water daily, spraying it into their mouth with their trunk.

▷ **MALES AT PLAY**
Young elephants, particularly bull calves, spend much of their time at play, often charging, sparring, or trunk-wrestling with one another.

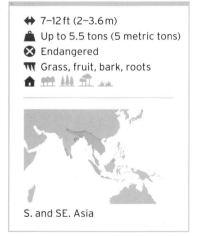

↔ 7–12 ft (2–3.6 m)
⬛ Up to 5.5 tons (5 metric tons)
✖ Endangered
🌾 Grass, fruit, bark, roots

S. and SE. Asia

Terai sacred langur

Semnopithecus hector

Like other species of langur and the related leaf monkeys, the Terai sacred langur (also called the Hanuman langur) feeds mainly on leaves. Its large stomach is separated into two chambers: an upper one, where the leaves are fermented by bacteria, and a lower acidic chamber. This system, like that found in cows and sheep, helps to break down the tough cellulose found in leaves. Because leaves are low in nutrients, langurs have to spend much of their day feeding in trees. However, they can eat many types of leaves and fruit that would be toxic to other species.

long,
slender
limbs

▷ **BLACK FACE**
According to Hindu mythology, the langur's face was scorched as punishment for stealing a mango.

↔ 23–30 in (58–76 cm)
⬛ 37–38 1/2 lb (17–17.5 kg)
✖ Near threatened
🌾 Leaves, fruit, flowers, shoots

S. Asia

↔ 5–9ft (1.4–2.8m)

⚖ 275–530lb (125–240kg)

✖ Endangered

🍖 Deer, wild pigs, ground birds

🏠 🌲 🌴 🌿 ≈ ⛰

S. and E. Asia

▷ **WATER FIGHT**
Tigers are usually solitary, so if
a stranger ignores the boundary
scent marks and wanders into
another tiger's territory, a fierce
fight often ensues.

no two tigers have the same markings

tail used for balance when chasing prey or climbing

powerful forelegs, big feet, and large claws enable tiger to grip prey securely

Bengal tiger

Panthera tigris tigris

The tiger is the largest of all the big cats. Five subspecies remain alive today, of which the Bengal tiger is the most common. It is found in a wide range of forest and mangrove habitats in India and Bangladesh. The Bengal tiger's distinctive coat is a deep orange with white undersides, chest, throat and parts of its face, and dark stripes. The Amur tiger (*P. t. altaica*), which lives to the north in the coniferous forests of Siberia, Russia, is the largest of the five. It is the lightest in color and has the longest, thickest coat to cope with the freezing winters. The southernmost subspecies, the Sumatran tiger (*P. t. sumatrae*), is also the smallest, being a good 30 percent smaller and weighing about 50 percent less than its massive cousins to the north.

Ambush attacker

Tigers are chiefly nocturnal but will hunt by day in places where they are undisturbed by daytime human activities. The tiger uses its sense of smell and hearing to detect and track prey. Its great strength and speed mean it can bring down prey that is at least as large as it is, sometimes more so. The Bengal tiger typically hunts hoofed animals, such as gaur, sambar, chital, and wild boar, and stalks them while hidden by the undergrowth. Once the tiger is close enough, it will launch a lightning strike, surging out of cover and using its weight to knock the prey to the ground. The tiger then delivers a deadly bite to the throat, which crushes the windpipe, leading to death by strangulation, or breaks the neck. Small prey are often killed with a bite to the neck. The tiger then hauls the carcass back into the undergrowth to eat. Despite the tiger's great killing potential, only one in 20 ambushes is a success.

Solitary cat

An adult tiger lives alone. It marks out a territory by scratching marks on tree trunks and rocks with its claws and leaving piles of feces in prominent places. The tiger also scent marks by spraying squirts of urine mixed with oils from a scent gland under the tail, and it gives out roars that can be heard 1 mile (2 km) away.

A tigress breeds every two or three years, and changes in her scent will attract a nearby male. The pair roar to each other as they get near and will live together for a few days, mating around 20 times before going their separate ways. Tigresses give birth to litters of up to six cubs, but half of them will not reach two years. Surviving cubs stay with their mother for up to two years, learning to hunt alongside her from the age of six months. They may breed when four or five years old.

△ **SUMATRAN TIGRESS AND CUB**
The smaller size of the Sumatran tiger (*P. t. sumatrae*) is an adaptation to life in the dense undergrowth of the swamp forests of Sumatra.

Tiger **cubs often have practice fights**, gaining the **speed and agility** they will need as **territorial adults**

short, rounded ears
closed in dusty places

Indian gray mongoose
Herpestes edwardsii

The Indian gray mongoose is a dietary opportunist—eating lizards, eggs, and fruit as well as larger mammals such as hares and venomous cobras. Mongooses are so adept at preying on rodents and snakes that they are used as a form of pest control in some areas.

Head clamp
While its molars are used to crush insects, its strong jaws and sharp, protruding canines give the mongoose an edge when fighting snakes, allowing it to clamp onto a snake's head and puncture its skull. Although not immune to snake venom, highly reactive reflexes help them avoid being bitten. Mongooses are solitary except during mating season. Females bear litters of two to four pups up to three times a year.

Mongooses **crack large eggs by throwing** them between their hindlegs **against a hard surface**

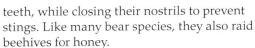
long, rough fur

Sloth bear
Melursus ursinus

The sloth bear is a solitary, elusive forest dweller, but the slurping sounds it makes when feeding can be heard up to 650 ft (200 m) away. These shaggy-looking members of the bear family use their long, curved claws to dig out ants, termites, and other insects, sucking them up through flexible lips and a special gap in their teeth, while closing their nostrils to prevent stings. Like many bear species, they also raid beehives for honey.

Sloth bears mate during the summer months. Females bear one or two cubs, which stay with their mother for up to four and a half years. They are the only bears known to carry cubs on their backs.

- ↔ 5–6 ft (1–1.9 m)
- ⚖ 110–320 lb (50–145 kg)
- ⊗ Vulnerable
- ☵ Ants, termites, fruit, honey

S. Asia

▷ **LONG, MOBILE SNOUT**
Sloth bears use their nostrils to blow dust and earth out of the way before sucking up insects to eat.

Side panel (sloth bear data)

- ↔ 14–18 in (35.5–45 cm)
- ⚖ 1–9 lb (0.5–4 kg)
- ⊗ Common
- ☵ Rodents, snakes, frogs, fruit

SW. and S. Asia

▽ **STRATEGIC COMBAT**
Mongooses defeat cobras by agility and endurance—dodging away each time a snake strikes, then biting into its skull once it tires.

Sarus crane
Grus antigone

mainly gray plumage in adults

long, trailing legs

At 6 ft (1.8 m), the sarus crane is the tallest flying bird on earth. It has dramatic displays: rhythmic bowing leading into two-footed leaps, with head extended and wings half open, while making loud trumpeting calls.

The sarus crane is a declining bird, being confined to wet paddy fields and reservoir edges as marshlands are drained and rice cultivation becomes more intensive. Breeding pairs occupy territories and forage for aquatic plants, insects, and frogs, mainly in natural vegetation, but occasionally in cultivated fields.

- ↔ 5 ft (1.5 m)
- ⚖ 14 lb (6.5 kg)
- ⊗ Vulnerable
- ☵ Roots, tubers, insects, frogs

S. and SE. Asia, N. Australia

△ **TAKING OFF**
Although long legs and broad wings power its take off, the sarus crane uses a steady, efficient action once airborne.

Great Indian hornbill
Buceros bicornis

This large hornbill relies on forest fruit for food and essential moisture. Fruiting trees attract scores of birds whose droppings, in turn, help disperse seeds throughout the forest. The function of the angular casque is uncertain, but the larger bones in the bill have networks of hollow cavities, combining lightness with strength.

sickle-shaped bill

casque

▷ **LIGHT AND SHADE**
Horizontal bands create effective camouflage in the light and shade of a forest canopy.

- ↔ 38–47 in (95–120 cm)
- ⚖ 7 lb (3 kg)
- ✖ Near threatened
- ♒ Figs, lizards, frogs, rodents
- 🏠 🌳 🌿
- 🧭 S. and SE. Asia

Indian cobra
Naja naja

Found in habitats from remote uplands to urban sprawl, the Indian cobra's diet ranges from tiny frogs to large rats. Females lay 12–20 eggs in a tree hollow, rodent burrow, or termite mound, and guard them. Hatchlings can immediately spread their hood and strike with venom.

- ↔ 6–7 ft (1.8–2.2 m)
- ⚖ 5–7 lb (2–3 kg)
- ✖ Not known
- ♒ Frogs, rats, lizards, birds
- 🏠 🍄 🌿 🏛
- 🧭 S. Asia

◁ **SPECTACLED HOOD**
This classic "snake charmer" species is also called the spectacled cobra from the markings on the rear of the hood and often on the front as well.

△ **SAFETY ISLAND**
Parents care for the young for the first few weeks, escorting them on their first swims. However, many other crocodilians nurture their offspring for longer periods.

▷ **FISH TRAP**
The gharial's 100–110 teeth are small and sharp—ideal for snagging fish, which are bitten several times to subdue them, then tossed around to be swallowed head first.

Gharial
Gavialis gangeticus

male has bulbous tip on long, narrow snout

↔ 12–23 ft (3.6–7 m)
⚖ 353–397 lb (160–180 kg)
✖ Critically endangered
🍴 Fish, waterbirds

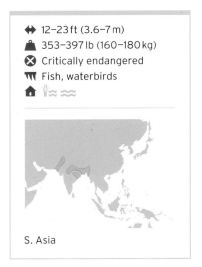

S. Asia

The gharial's unique long, narrow jaws—designed to make sudden sideways snaps at passing fish—make it instantly recognizable. It is more aquatic than its robust crocodile cousins and is highly adapted to move in water. Its rear feet are well webbed and the long tail has finlike keel scales along the top for powerful propulsion. On land, its limbs are not strong enough to lift its body in a high walk, so it pushes forward on its belly instead.

Females mature at eight to 10 years and are around 12 ft (3.6 m) long; males take another three to five years to mature and grow longer. At mating time, territorial male gharials intimidate rivals and display to females with much noise and thrashing. The male's bulbous snout—locally known as the "ghara," a type of pot—helps to make enticing bubbles to attract a mate.

Still on the brink
The gharial was on the verge of extinction in the 1970s due to habitat loss, poaching, and falling fish stocks. Captive breeding programs have led to more than 3,000 animals being released back into the wild since 1981, but the species is still critically endangered.

EASTERN HIMALAYAS
Earth's highest mountains support a variety of rare species

The peaks and steep-sided valleys of the world's highest mountain range are home to varied but vulnerable plants and animals. The lower and middle elevations of the Eastern Himalayas are covered with various types of forest. Depending on latitude and altitude, they might be subtropical or temperate, evergreen, or deciduous. Oaks and rhododendrons dominate the forests, which support a diverse array of wildlife. Even above the treeline, seemingly inhospitable rocky slopes are home to such elusive creatures as the snow leopard and blue sheep.

Vital water regulators

The mountains and their forests are also important for the region's water supply. They catch and gradually release rainwater to tributaries of some of Asia's most iconic rivers, including the Ganges and the Brahmaputra. The plants and animals of the high Himalayas are likely to experience great challenges due to climate change, as the melting of glaciers accelerates and they are forced to adapt to warmer temperatures, if they can.

There are 163 globally threatened species in the Eastern Himalayas, and a quarter of their original habitat remains intact. The challenge for conservationists is to protect sufficiently large areas and corridors between them to sustain animals that range over large areas. The main threat to the forests and their wildlife comes from poaching, collection of wood for fires and charcoal, and habitat loss or damage resulting from agricultural practices.

NATURAL CAMOUFLAGE
The Himalayan blue sheep's gray-blue coat provides superb camouflage against its rocky environment. This agile animal is able to climb up steep cliffs when trying to escape predators such as the snow leopard.

HIMALAYAN BLUE SHEEP

BLOOMING PARTNERSHIP
The higher elevations of the Himalayas feature a diversity of rhododendron species. More than 50 flourish in the Indian state of Sikkim and 60 in Bhutan. Rhododendron forests support insects and birds that pollinate the flowers when feeding on nectar.

RHODODENDRON

WILD YAK

ADAPTED TO THE COLD
The wild yak conserves body heat in the cold mountain climate—generating it uses valuable energy. It stores fat beneath its skin, and its thick, dark fleece has a layer of soft insulating down and another of coarse outer hair.

Boasts 9 of the world's 10 highest peaks

Home to 10,000 plant species and nearly 1,000

LOCATION

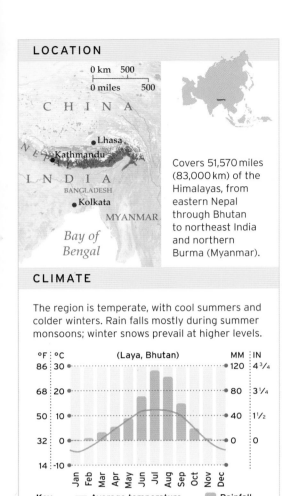

0 km 500
0 miles 500

CHINA

Lhasa

Kathmandu

NEPAL

INDIA

BANGLADESH

Kolkata

MYANMAR

Bay of Bengal

Covers 51,570 miles (83,000 km) of the Himalayas, from eastern Nepal through Bhutan to northeast India and northern Burma (Myanmar).

CLIMATE

The region is temperate, with cool summers and colder winters. Rain falls mostly during summer monsoons; winter snows prevail at higher levels.

(Laya, Bhutan)

°F	°C		MM	IN
86	30		120	4¾
68	20		80	3¼
50	10		40	1½
32	0		0	0
14	-10			

Jan Feb Mar Apr May Jun Jul Aug Sep Oct Nov Dec

Key ▬ Average temperature ▬ Rainfall

CHANGING ALTITUDES

Many species migrate up and down the Himalayas to avoid the worst of the winter weather and exploit summer food sources. One example is the satyr tragopan, a pheasant that moves to low-altitude forests in winter and high areas in summer.

...d and 300 mammal species

SATYR TRAGOPAN

Golden langur
Trachypithecus geei

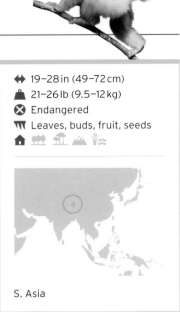

The golden langur's coat varies from cream-colored in summer to burnished gold in winter. This elusive, long-tailed monkey was not recognized as a species until the 1950s, and very little is known about it even today. Golden langurs live in groups of 3–40, and rarely come to the ground, a strategy that helps them avoid predators such as tigers. They are severely threatened by habitat loss.

↔ 19–28 in (49–72 cm)
⚖ 21–26 lb (9.5–12 kg)
⊗ Endangered
🌿 Leaves, buds, fruit, seeds

S. Asia

◁ **TREETOP DWELLER**
Golden langurs spend most of their time high in the forest canopy, only rarely descending to the ground to drink or lick up mineral salts.

Bhutan takin
Budorcas whitei

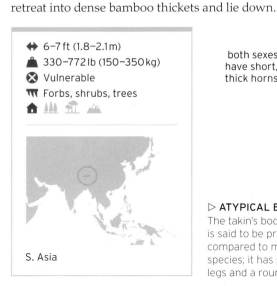

barrel-shaped body covered in shaggy hair

During spring, large mixed herds of takin—robust relatives of wild goats—congregate in sunny clearings high up in bamboo forests. As winter approaches, they fragment into fours and fives and head for lower areas. If threatened, they retreat into dense bamboo thickets and lie down.

↔ 6–7 ft (1.8–2.1 m)
⚖ 330–772 lb (150–350 kg)
⊗ Vulnerable
🌿 Forbs, shrubs, trees

both sexes have short, thick horns

S. Asia

▷ **ATYPICAL BODY**
The takin's body shape is said to be primitive compared to most hooved species; it has short, stocky legs and a rounded snout.

↔ 3–4 ft (0.9–1.2 m)
⚖ 55–165 lb (25–75 kg)
✖ Endangered
♆ Wild sheep, wild goats
⌂ ⛰

C. Asia

▷ **MOUNTAIN GHOST**
Snow leopards are nomadic
creatures, constantly on the move in
search of food. In territory where prey
is scarcest, one leopard may patrol as
much as 400 sq miles (1,000 sq km).

thick fur coat

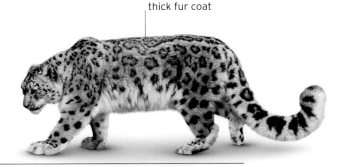

Snow leopard

Panthera uncia

To local people, snow leopards are "mountain ghosts" because they are so well camouflaged that they are as good as invisible even at close range. They are the most elusive, most secretive, and smallest of the big cats— and the only one that cannot roar. Snow leopards are among the planet's most endangered species. The estimated 4,000–7,000 remaining in the wild live mainly in the harsh mountain ranges of Central Asia, at elevations of 10,000–16,400 ft (3,000–5,000 m). They are still hunted illegally in "retribution" for killing livestock or for use in traditional medicine and for their pelts.

Fighting the cold

The snow leopard's thick, creamy gray coat dotted with brown and gray-black spots blends in seamlessly with a rocky or scrub-filled landscape, while its dense, white underside hair merges into the snow. Even the pads of its feet are covered with fur, as is the long, thick tail, which serves both as a balancing aid and a furry scarf, wrapping around its body and face when the animal is at rest. Short, rounded ears, also covered in dense fur, minimize heat loss, and a wider-than-average nasal cavity warms incoming air before it reaches the lungs. Short forelimbs and huge, snowshoelike forepaws give

The snow leopard is the **only big cat that cannot roar**

snow leopards extra traction in the snow. The longer, powerful hind legs let it leap as far as 50 ft (15 m) while chasing after prey such as wild sheep (argali and bharal) or wild goats such as ibex.

Lone hunters

Aside from the mating season and mothers raising cubs, snow leopards live and hunt alone, traveling far in search of food. Due to the harsh nature of their environment, which stretches across the Himalayas to the Hindu Kush mountains, a snow leopard will patrol an average home range of 100 sq miles (260 sq km), marking the landscape with urine and feces that act as scent signals to other snow leopards. Females have litters of two or three cubs, which stay with their mother until they are 18–22 months old.

△ **ATTRACTING A MATE**
When a female snow leopard is ready to mate, she may climb to a ridge or peak and make long, wailing cries to attract nearby males.

◁ **MISSED OPPORTUNITY**
Although wild sheep and goats are preferred prey, snow leopards eat small mammals such as lemmings and hares—and birds when they can catch them.

Red panda
Ailurus fulgens

soft, dense fur

alternating light and dark rings on tail

Once thought to be related to giant pandas, the red panda has closer genetic links to weasels and raccoons. Also called the firefox in China, this slow-moving mammal spends most of its life in trees in Asia's mountain forests, where its striking reddish brown fur allows it to blend in with the moss-covered branches of its arboreal home.

Red pandas move slowly to conserve energy as the bamboo shoots and leaves that make up most of their diet are so indigestible. They eat up to 30 percent of their body weight daily, but use only about a quarter of bamboo's available nutrients; yet, they rely on the plant to survive when other food is scarce. In winter, red pandas can lose up to 15 percent of their body weight due to lack of food, so they slow down their metabolism to compensate as temperatures fall.

Red pandas mate on the ground, but females return to their nest to give birth to between one and four cubs, which stay with their mother for a year or more.

↔ 20–29 in (51–73 cm)
⚖ 7–13 lb (3–6 kg)
✖ Vulnerable
🍴 Bamboo, fruit, insects, eggs
🏠 🌳 🌲 ⛰

S. to SE. Asia

◁ **WATCHFUL GAZE**
Although they regularly use scent marking, red pandas also communicate with each other using "stare downs" accompanied by head bobbing and vocalizations.

red-and-white markings provide camouflage

△ **MOVING A CUB**
Female red pandas move their cubs to different nests to avoid discovery by predators such as martens and snow leopards.

fanned crest

iridescent eyespots

Indian peafowl

Pavo cristatus

Peafowl have been collected for ornamental purposes for more than 3,000 years. This, combined with artificial introductions into other parts of the world, has made the peacock's display familiar to millions who have never visited its Asian homeland. Here, peafowl live in open or riverside woodland and close to human habitation, in orchards and cultivated land. Drawing attention with their loud, off-key calls, they may be seen flying into trees at dusk to find a safe roost for the night.

Ground nesters

By day, peafowl forage on the ground. Females visit several displaying males at a lek before choosing the one with most eyespots on its tail. Males play no part in nesting or caring for the young. The nests are made on the ground in dense vegetation. Up to six eggs hatch after four weeks, and the chicks quickly learn to find food for themselves.

Peacock blue is one of the most intense blues in the world

↔ 6–8 ft (1.8–2.4 m)

⚖ 9–13 lb (4–6 kg)

✖ Common

🍴 Seeds, fruit, plants, insects

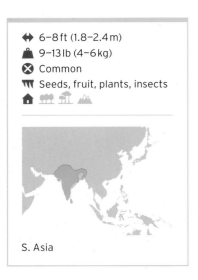

S. Asia

▷ **IRIDESCENT TRAIN**
The peacock's "tail" is actually a train of elongated feathers supported by a short, stiff tail beneath.

UPPER YANGTZE FORESTS
Home to China's national treasure, the giant panda

The Upper Yangtze Forests ecoregion comprises three areas: the Qinling Mountains, the Daba Mountains, and the Sichuan Basin. All three form a watershed between the drainage basins of the Yellow River to the north and the Yangtze River to the south. The climate is cooler and more temperate in the north of the region, where the forests are predominantly made up of deciduous trees. To the south are subtropical evergreen forests that flourish in this area's warmer temperatures and plentiful rain.

Rare lowland species
The lowlands of the Sichuan Basin are the most heavily populated. Here most of the land has been turned over to agriculture, but fragments of evergreen and broadleaf forest remain, particularly on the steeper hillsides and on any mountains considered sacred by local people. This area is home to the dawn redwood, an unusual

deciduous conifer that was known only from fossil records until the 1940s, when groups of the trees were discovered growing in Sichuan province.

The Upper Yangtze Forests' most famous inhabitant is the giant panda, and the Wolong Nature Reserve near Chengdu is dedicated to the preservation of this iconic yet rare black-and-white bear. The middle elevations of the Qinling forests in Shaanxi province have a dense bamboo understory, which provides a home and food to a distinctive type of giant panda that has dark- and light-brown fur. The smaller, tree-dwelling red panda also lives in the Upper Yangtze Forests.

HIDDEN FORAGER
The common but elusive Chinese bamboo partridge inhabits hillside forests, feeding on seeds, shoots, leaves, and insects. If it cannot remain hidden from predators, it flies uphill but is much more often heard than seen.

CHINESE BAMBOO PARTRIDGE

SEX-LINKED STRIPES
The Chinese green tree viper is a venomous snake endemic to Asia. Males and females can be distinguished from one another by a stripe that runs along the side of their bodies. In males, it is orange or brown and white; females' stripes are just white.

GREEN TREE VIPER

YELLOW-THROATED MARTIN

Home to the world's largest amphibian, the Chinese giant salamander › Contains one-fif

GROUP THREAT
The large, brightly colored yellow-throated marten eats eggs and fruit as well as small prey, such as rodents, reptiles, and ground-nesting birds. Sometimes hunting in small groups, it also kills deer fawns, wild boar piglets, and even giant panda cubs.

short, stumpy nose

Golden snub-nosed monkey

Rhinopithecus roxellana

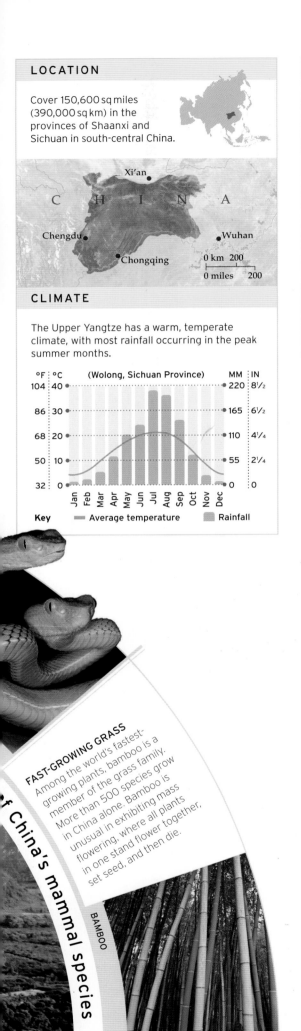
This Chinese monkey lives its entire life in a series of groups, the size of which waxes and wanes depending upon the season. During the warmer months, a single group's numbers can swell to 200 or even 600 individuals. In winter, this splits into several groups of 60–70 monkeys, which are further divided into small family troops of a single male, several females, and their offspring or all-male groups.

Startling appearance

With vertical nostrils and dark, almond-shaped eyes set in a striking blue face framed by blazing red-gold fur, golden snub-nosed monkeys look more like alien elves than primates. Yet for all their unique features, because they live in high mountainous forests and spend over 95 percent of their time in trees, snub-nosed monkeys are heard more than they are seen. Their calls are eerily humanlike, and frequently compared to the cries of young children or babies. Highly prized by hunters, their fur is so long across the back and shoulders that when they leap from one branch to another it gives the appearance of wings.

↔ 19–33 in (48–84 cm)
⬆ 13–42 lb (6–19 kg)
✖ Endangered
🌾 Lichen, leaves, fruit, bark
🏠 🌳 🌲 ⛰

SE. Asia

▽ **GROOMING SESSION**
Golden snub-nosed monkeys regularly check each other for parasites, a practice usually accompanied by whining and squealing.

Snub-nosed monkeys can **vocalize** **without moving their faces** or bodies

↔ 5–6 ft (1.6–1.9 m)
⚖ 155–275 lb (70–125 kg)
✖ Critically endangered
🎋 Bamboo
🏠 🌳 🌲 ⛰️

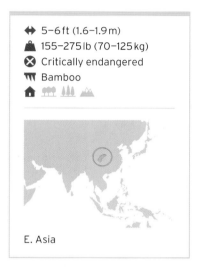

E. Asia

△ JUVENILE PANDAS
Panda cubs don't move much until they are three months old. By five to six months, they are able to climb trees, and may sit there for hours.

▷ FEEDING TIME
Large molars and strong jaw muscles help giant pandas cope with even the toughest bamboo stems. Giant pandas also occasionally eat rodents, eggs, and birds.

distinctive rounded face

front limbs more muscled than rear limbs, for climbing

Giant panda

Ailuropoda melanoleuca

The giant panda—one of the most endangered and rarest mammals—is found only in six small, densely forested regions of central China. Estimates place the number of giant pandas remaining in the wild at 1,000–2,500. Once common in lowland areas, human activity has fragmented their habitat and pushed them up into the mountains.

The giant panda has the most distinctive coat of all bear species, but for decades its unique black and white markings, rounded face, and largely vegetarian diet led many scientists to conclude it was not a bear at all, until genetic testing settled the debate.

Slower than the average bear

The giant panda's diet continues to be a puzzle. It has the canine teeth and short digestive tract of a carnivore (meat-eater), but 99 percent of its food is bamboo, which, for pandas, is nutritionally poor. Carnivores, including giant pandas, lack special gut bacteria that would allow them to process grasses such as bamboo. This means that giant pandas get only about 20 percent of a meal's energy; if they ate meat, this would shoot up to 60–90 percent. It is not surprising, then, that the giant panda is slow-moving, spends most of the day eating up to

Giant pandas spend up to **16 hours a day** eating bamboo

40 lb (18 kg) of bamboo, then rests for 8–12 hours. Its diet also prevents it from sleeping through the winter as it cannot put on enough fat to go without food for long. However, adults are truly bear-sized, and they are agile climbers and good swimmers as well.

Milk for two?

Giant pandas reach sexual maturity when they are between five and six years old. Although generally solitary, males and females spend two to four days together during the mating season from March to May. One or two tiny cubs are born around five months later, but the mother will abandon one cub if she cannot produce enough milk for both. A cub is fully dependent on its mother for the first few months, and may stay with her for up to three years.

◁ **MOTHER AND CUB**
Born hairless and blind, a newborn weighs just a few grams. New reserves and conservation work in China and zoos abroad are helping to boost the giant panda population.

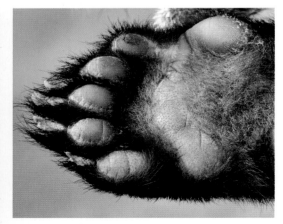

△ **PSEUDO-THUMB**
An enlarged wrist bone in the giant panda's forepaw acts like a human thumb and helps it to manipulate bamboo stems.

long tail
helps balance

long face compared
to other, smaller cats

Indochinese clouded leopard

Neofelis nebulosa

While they share a name and markings that allow them to blend in with their environment, clouded leopards and other leopards are not directly related. In fact, the Indochinese clouded leopard is unique in many ways. Relative to its size, this solitary cat has the longest upper canine teeth of any living felid—around 2 in (5 cm). It also has an impressive gape of almost 100 degrees, whereas a lion's mouth, for example, only opens to an average of 65 degrees.

Short, powerful legs, broad paws, and a thick, densely furred tail that is often as long as its body make the clouded leopard an excellent climber. It is able to move along the underside of branches, run headfirst down trees, and hang upside down by its hind feet, which rotate backward courtesy of flexible ankle joints. Clouded leopards are also superb swimmers.

Secretive cat

Since they are such experts at blending into their dense forest habitat, little is known about clouded leopard behavior, although males show a high degree of aggression toward females in captivity. Once believed to be nocturnal hunters, recent evidence suggests that they may hunt during the day as well, taking prey on the ground despite being such good climbers.

↔ 28–43 in (71–110 cm)
⬛ 24–51 lb (11–23 kg)
✖ Vulnerable
ⵣ Mammals
🏠 🌳 🌴 ⛰ ⛰ 🌾

S. and SE. Asia

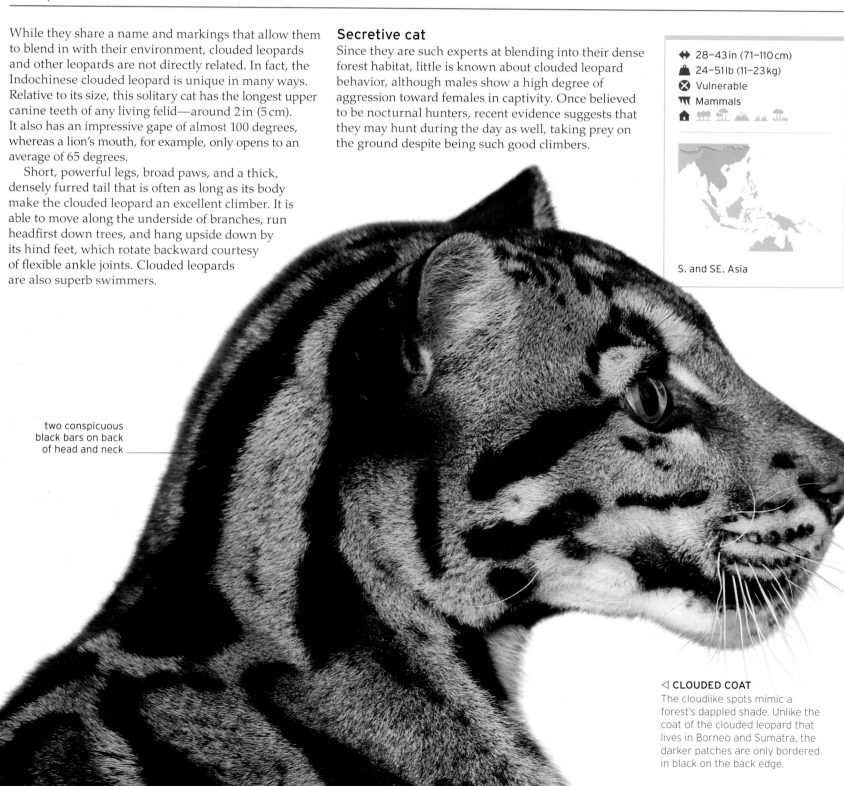

two conspicuous
black bars on back
of head and neck

◁ **CLOUDED COAT**
The cloudlike spots mimic a forest's dappled shade. Unlike the coat of the clouded leopard that lives in Borneo and Sumatra, the darker patches are only bordered in black on the back edge.

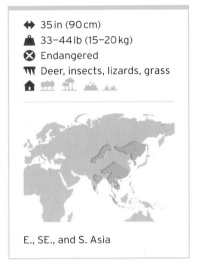

dholes living at higher
altitudes have thicker coats

Dhole
Cuon alpinus

With fewer than 2,500 individuals thought to exist in
the wild, the dhole is one of the world's rarest canids.
Also called the Asian red dog because of its tawny or
dark red coat, it differs from other canids in having
a much shorter jaw and two fewer molar teeth.
Like wolflike dogs and foxes, however, the dhole
has been persecuted as a pest, and is now found in
just 40 percent of its former range.

Strength in numbers

Dholes are extremely social mammals, forming
territorial, day-active packs of 5–10 individuals
(occasionally up to 30), usually with just one breeding
female. Group members readily cooperate to hunt, often
chasing deer, but also killing animals up to 10 times
their own body weight and aggressive species such as
wild boar. Good swimmers, dholes frequently drive deer
into water to gain an advantage. They also scavenge
from Asian elephant and wild cattle carcasses.

   As well as a high-pitched whistle used to call pack
mates, dholes use a remarkable range of vocalizations,
including mews and screams.

Dholes are nicknamed "whistling hunters"

↔ 35 in (90 cm)
⚖ 33–44 lb (15–20 kg)
✖ Endangered
♜ Deer, insects, lizards, grass

E., SE., and S. Asia

◁ **PLAY FIGHTING**
Social rank within a dhole pack is
not established by using aggression—
instead it is achieved by pushing
or restraining another pack member.

Golden pheasant
Chrysolophus pictus

Few birds are as showy as the male golden pheasant,
but ironically, when these gamebirds were brought to
Europe for their bright colors, they proved very hard
to see in dense conifer forest.

   Golden pheasants feed on the ground, picking up
food with a precise, chickenlike action. Although
tending to run rather than fly if approached, they seek
safety and shelter in treetops at night. Males have loud,
crowing calls and use ritualized, rhythmic posturing
to impress the mottled-brown females. They repeatedly
run to "corner" a hen, stretching up on tiptoe and
spreading the colorful ruff, or cape, over their head
to produce a shiny orange semicircle
with concentric blue-black rings.

↔ 24–43 in (60–110 cm)
⚖ 20–25 oz (566–709 g)
✖ Common
♜ Green shoots, insects

S. to SE. Asia

tail roughly
twice as long
as female's

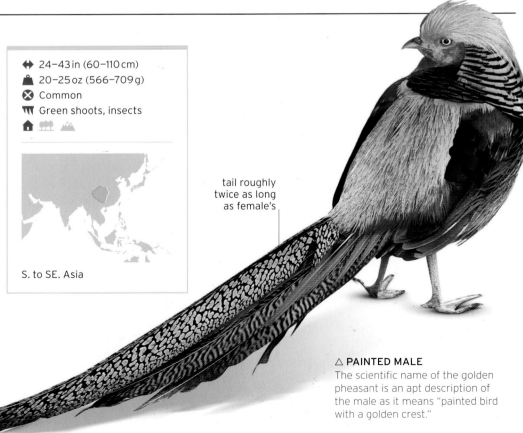

△ **PAINTED MALE**
The scientific name of the golden
pheasant is an apt description of
the male as it means "painted bird
with a golden crest."

GOBI DESERT

A high, mainly rocky desert that is the largest in Asia

Stretching across part of northern China and into southern Mongolia, the Gobi is the largest desert in Asia and the fifth largest in the world, with an area of around 500,000 sq miles (1.3 million sq km). It is located on a high-altitude plateau, which means that temperatures can fluctuate wildly: in summer they may reach 122°F (50°C) and in winter may fall as low as -40°F (-40°C). Most rain falls during the summer, but annual rainfall diminishes across the region, ranging from around 10 in (250 mm) in the east to just ⅜ in (10 mm) in the west.

Rocky and harsh

The land is primarily rocky rather than sandy. The stony ground supports sparse vegetation in the form of hardy, drought-adapted shrubs and grasses. Despite the scanty plant life and harsh climate, many animals make the desert their home. Smaller mammals, such as the dwarf hamster and midday gerbil, burrow into sandy ground to escape the searing daytime heat in summer and to hibernate during winter. They benefit the environment by aerating the soil and recycling plant nutrients. Larger animals, such as the Bactrian camel, Mongolian saiga, and Przewalski's wild horse, range far and wide over the desert plains to find sufficient food and water.

The Gobi Desert is expanding by around 1,400 sq miles (3,600 sq km) a year, with the result that devastating dust storms are becoming increasingly frequent. This desertification is also being accelerated by human activities, including deforestation and overgrazing.

STABILIZING TREE
One of the few trees able to grow in the Gobi Desert, the saxaul has thick bark that stores water. Its network of horizontal roots helps to stabilize sandy soil, so it is planted by people in an effort to fix sand dunes and slow down desertification.

SAXAUL

VITAL MARMOTS
The Mongolian marmot is a key species in the Gobi. Not only is it a food source for predators; it also provides shelter to corsac foxes, which use their old burrows. The two species are closely connected: when marmot numbers decline, so do foxes.

MONGOLIAN MARMOTS

HARASSED HERDS
Herds of khulan, or Mongolian wild ass, roam across the southern Mongolian part of the Gobi Desert. Populations are at risk from poaching and damage to their habitat from grazing livestock. Khulan dig holes in dry riverbeds to obtain water.

KHULAN

Temperatures vary by more than 63°F (35°C) in a day > Dinosaur eggs first found here >

Gobi bear
Ursus arctos gobiensis

limbs longer
than grizzly's

Smaller and lighter than other brown bears, Gobi bears have short, golden coats and proportionally longer limbs. They mainly eat plants, such as wild rhubarb, roots, and berries. The species is threatened by droughts, climate change, habitat destruction, and cubs being killed by wolves—fewer than 30 Gobi bears are thought to survive today.

▽ **GENETIC MYSTERY**
DNA hair analysis indicates that Gobi bears are related to but distinct from other brown bears. No other brown bear could survive the Gobi Desert's harsh environment.

↔ 5–7 ft (1.5–2.1 m)
⬛ 110–350 lb (50–160 kg)
✖ Critically endangered
🎋 Plants, rodents, insects
🏠 🌵

C. Asia

LOCATION

Lying in northern China and southern Mongolia, the Gobi is bordered by the Tibetan Plateau to the southwest.

Ulan Bator

Ürümqi

Beijing

C H I N A

0 km   500
0 miles   500

CLIMATE

The Gobi is a cold, dry desert, and temperatures fluctuate wildly on both a daily and a seasonal basis.

°F	°C	(Mandalgovi, Mongolia)	MM	IN
86	30		60	2¼
68	20		40	1½
50	10		20	¾
32	0		0	0
14	-10			
-4	-20			

Jan Feb Mar Apr May Jun Jul Aug Sep Oct Nov Dec

Key ▬ Average temperature ▬ Rainfall

Yarkand gazelle
Gazella yarkandensis

This antelope is one of three "goitered" species, named after the way males develop a swollen larynx for making loud bellows in the breeding season. Female Yarkand gazelles have tiny horns compared to males.

▽ **RACING AHEAD**
Unlike other gazelles, this species does not use a prancing running style to confuse chasing predators. It escapes threats with a flat-out sprint.

↔ 3–4 ft (0.9–1.2 m)
⬛ 44–66 lb (20–30 kg)
✖ Vulnerable
🎋 Grasses, leaves, herbs
🏠 🌵

C. Asia

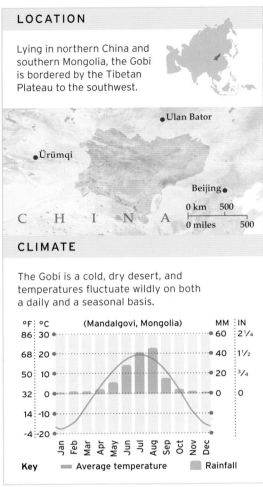

BIG EARS
The tiny long-eared jerboa has one of the largest ear-to-body ratios of any mammal. It spends the day in tunnels, emerging at night to hunt insects. Small hairs on its feet help it move on sand, hopping like a kangaroo.

95% of the desert is rocky

LONG-EARED JERBOA

Mongolian saiga

Saiga mongolica

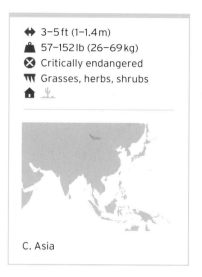
coat becomes thicker and paler in winter

The saiga is unmistakable. The males of this "goat-antelope" have pointed, ringed horns that are waxy and translucent. Both sexes sport long, drooping nostrils. The fleshy proboscis contains convoluted air passages lined with hairs. In summer, the hairs filter out dust that blows across the steppes. In winter, the long nasal passages warm the air before it reaches the lungs.

Saiga gather in huge herds and spend the winter—which is also the mating season—in the south of their range to avoid the worst of the weather.

↔ 3–5 ft (1–1.4 m)
⚖ 57–152 lb (26–69 kg)
✗ Critically endangered
🌾 Grasses, herbs, shrubs
🏠 🌵

C. Asia

Due to **human activity**, only **750 Mongolian saigas remain** in the wild

▷ **GRAZING MALE**
Saiga graze in the morning and afternoon —often traveling up to 50 miles (80 km) a day —and spend the middle of the day resting to aid digestion. As night falls, they scrape a shallow hollow to sleep in.

◁ **POINTED HUMPS**
Bactrian camels have erect humps that are much more pointed than those of feral and domesticated camels.

▽ **DESERT CROSSING**
Domesticated Bactrian camels are used for transportation in cold regions from China to Turkey. They are shorter and more well-built than the wild camels.

Bactrian camel
Camelus bactrianus

two toes on each foot cushioned by fatty pads

The Bactrian camel roams the dry, rocky plains and hills of Central Asia, especially the Gobi Desert of China and Mongolia, where vegetation is scarce. The two humps on its back store fat, which is converted to water and energy to sustain the camel during droughts. The humps shrink as the fat is used up.

Little is known about the Bactrian camel's behavior as it is difficult to study due to its nomadic lifestyle and remote habitat. It does not defend a territory, but lives in small herds that travel long distances in search of food. Mature breeding males spit at, bite, and kick rivals in battles. The strongest males gather a harem of females around them to mate with.

The Bactrian camel obtains most of the water it needs from its diet of leaves. It seldom sweats, to help conserve fluids during hot desert summers. However, after a drought, when it finally reaches water, it can drink up to 36 gallons (135 liters) of water in just 15 minutes. It can also tolerate drinking much saltier water than domesticated camels can. The desert winters are bitterly cold, so the Bactrian camel grows a long, thick, woolly coat. The two broad toes on each foot spread out to prevent it from sinking in snow or sand.

Tamed existence

Fewer than 1,400 Bactrian camels remain in the wild and the population continutes to decline, but the species is widely domesticated as a hardy transportation animal. Its relative, the one-humped dromedary, is now an entirely domesticated species found in North Africa, the Middle East, and Central Asia, and has been introduced to Australia.

↔ 11–12 ft (3.2–3.5 m)
⚖ 400–500 kg (880–1,100 lb)
✗ Critically endangered
🌾 Herbs, shrubs

C. Asia

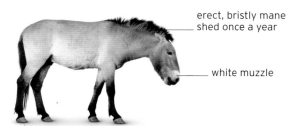

erect, bristly mane
shed once a year

white muzzle

Przewalski's wild horse

Equus przewalskii

For centuries, these stocky mammals grazed grassy plains ranging from Germany to China and Mongolia, but due to severe winters, habitat loss, and excessive hunting, their numbers fell during the 18th century. In 1969, the species was declared extinct in the wild. Thanks to cooperative captive breeding programs in Europe, the US, and Australia, since 1985 small herds have been reintroduced to China, Mongolia, Kazakhstan, and Ukraine. Today, more than 300 Przewalski's wild horses roam their historic range in Mongolia.

Dangerous union

Although closely related, Przewalski's differ from domestic horses at a genetic level: they have 66 chromosomes in each body cell, while domestic horses have 64. The two species can interbreed, producing fertile offspring, and interbreeding is considered a major threat to the remaining Przewalski's wild horses. Physical differences from domestic horses include a smaller, more compact body; a shorter, thicker neck; a short, erect mane; and all individuals being the same color.

In the wild, Przewalski's horses constantly roam in search of water and the short grasses that form the bulk of their diet. Herds consist of a dominant stallion, a harem of one to three females, and their offspring, which stay with the family group for two to three years.

△ **FIGHTING FOR DOMINANCE**
If ritualized signaling fails to deter a bachelor challenger, the dominant stallion will defend his right to lead a harem by fighting, often resulting in severe injuries.

All pure Przewalski's wild horses alive today are descended from just 12 individuals

▷ **MOTHER AND FOALS**
Foals stay close to their mothers for food, warmth, and protection against predators such as wolves. Sometimes, herds join forces in search of food.

Przewalski's wonder gecko

Teratoscincus przewalskii

Sheltering in a burrow by day, this gecko emerges at night to hunt. Its toes have fringes rather than the expanded pads seen in other geckos to help it dig and move easily over loose sand.

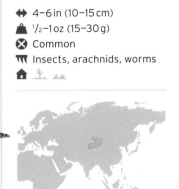

↔ 4–6 in (10–15 cm)

⚖ ½–1 oz (15–30 g)

✖ Common

🍴 Insects, arachnids, worms

🏠 🌵 🌿

C. Asia

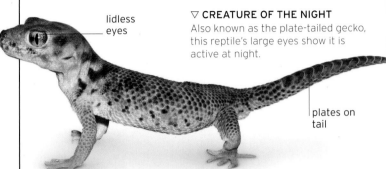

lidless eyes

plates on tail

▽ **CREATURE OF THE NIGHT**
Also known as the plate-tailed gecko, this reptile's large eyes show it is active at night.

Great bustard

Otis tarda

↔ 30–39 in (76–100 cm)

⚖ 7–40 lb (3.2–18 kg)

✖ Vulnerable

🍴 Seeds, insects, frogs, beetles

🏠 🌵 🌿

Europe, Asia

With the heaviest males reaching 46 lb (21 kg), the great bustard can be the world's heaviest flying bird, but many are leaner and lighter and females smaller still. All are big birds, but size can be deceptive in the wide open spaces they inhabit. Great bustards have a slow, stately walk and tend to run, not fly, when disturbed, but they are strong flyers with powerful wingbeats. Although extensive cereal fields are now their preferred habitat, they are disturbed by human activity and agricultural improvement. Asian populations migrate south and west to avoid bitter winters.

Males gather at leks to display and find a mate. Dominant males mate with several females, each of which lays two eggs in a scrape on the ground.

▽ **SPARRING MALES**
Before raising their tails and wings to become big balls of white in full display, males fight to establish dominance.

↔ 7–9 ft (2.2–2.8 m)

⚖ 440–660 lb (200–300 kg)

✖ Endangered

🍴 Grass, leaves, buds

🏠 🌵 🌿

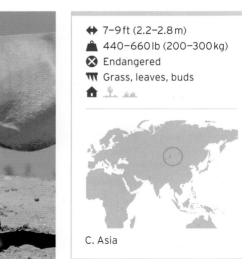

C. Asia

NIHONKAI MONTANE FOREST
A hilly ecoregion that experiences harsh winters

This deciduous forest ecoregion covers 31,800 sq miles (82,300 sq km) of the mountainous backbone of Japan's main island, Honshu, and a small portion of the more northerly island of Hokkaido. Two-thirds of Japan is covered with forest, although only a quarter is original, or primary, natural forest; the rest is secondary forest or plantations. Japan has a total of seven different natural forest ecoregions, including several evergreen and deciduous types and subtropical moist forest.

Wet summers, snowy winters
The Nihonkai montane forest is characterized by trees, shrubs, and grasses that flourish in warm, wet summers and then shed their leaves to survive throughout cold, snowy winters. The most numerous deciduous tree in the Nihonkai ecoregion is the Japanese cherry, which is now widely cultivated as an ornamental in parks and gardens

around the world. Other trees typically found in the forests include Japanese beech, katsura, and Japanese hornbeam. Many forest animals feed on the nuts and fruits produced by the trees, and so play an important role in dispersing their seeds.

In addition to the montane forest's canopy of mature full-sized trees, there is a lower layer of trees that are yet to reach full size, a shrub layer, and an understory of grasses and herbs. Biodiversity is greatest near the forest floor, unlike in tropical rainforests, where the number of species is highest in the canopy. The most iconic animal of the Nihonkai forest is the Japanese macaque.

POPULATION BOOM
More than 100,000 sika deer are estimated to live in Japan. Their numbers have boomed since the extinction of their main predator, the gray wolf, around a century ago. They are now considered a pest in their natural forest habitat and on farmland.

SIKA DEER

TRANSIENT BEAUTY
The Japanese cherry, or sakura, has profuse but short-lived displays of white or pink blossoms in spring. To the Japanese, their temporary beauty symbolizes the ephemeral nature of life and is celebrated in the hanami, or flower viewing, festival.

CHERRY BLOSSOM

SEASONAL DIET
One of the most widespread and abundant birds in Japan, the white-eye is seldom seen on the ground. It forages in trees and shrubs, searching for insects in summer and berries in fall, and feeding on blossoms, particularly cherry, in spring.

JAPANESE WHITE-EYE

One of seven forest ecoregions in Japan

Japanese cherry is the most common deciduo

LOCATION

Extends from Hiroshima in the west of the island of Honshu, eastward and northward to the most southerly tip of Hokkaido.

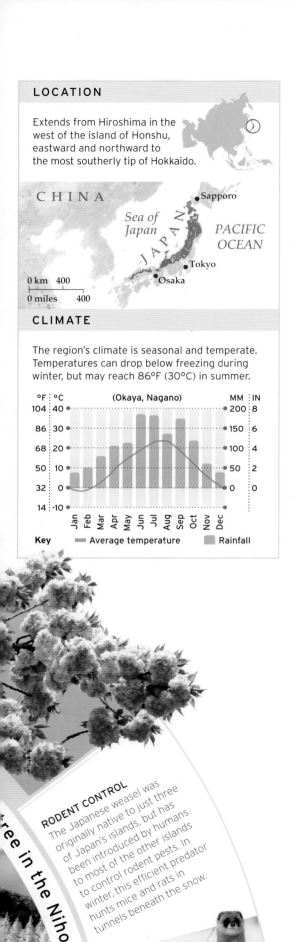

CHINA

Sea of Japan

JAPAN

Sapporo

PACIFIC OCEAN

Tokyo

Osaka

0 km 400
0 miles 400

CLIMATE

The region's climate is seasonal and temperate. Temperatures can drop below freezing during winter, but may reach 86°F (30°C) in summer.

°F	°C	(Okaya, Nagano)	MM	IN
104	40		200	8
86	30		150	6
68	20		100	4
50	10		50	2
32	0		0	0
14	-10			

Jan Feb Mar Apr May Jun Jul Aug Sep Oct Nov Dec

Key — Average temperature ▢ Rainfall

RODENT CONTROL

The Japanese weasel was originally native to just three of Japan's islands, but has been introduced by humans to most of the other islands to control rodent pests. In winter, this efficient predator hunts mice and rats in tunnels beneath the snow.

tree in the Nihonkai forest

JAPANESE WEASEL

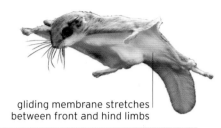

gliding membrane stretches between front and hind limbs

Siberian flying squirrel
Pteromys volans

Using its sail-like gliding membrane and flattened tail for lift, the flying squirrel is capable of gliding 245 ft (75 m) or more between trees. Old-growth forests are this nocturnal mammal's preferred habitat, as the trees provide food as well as woodpecker holes, which it uses as a nest site.

↔ 5–9 in (13–23 cm)
⚖ 3–6 oz (85–170 g)
✖ Common
〰 Nuts, buds, leaves
🏠 🌳 🌲

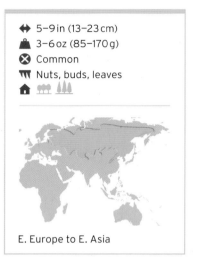

E. Europe to E. Asia

◁ **SEASONAL EATER**
In summer, the Siberian flying squirrel feeds mainly on fresh aspen, birch, and alder leaves.

white woolly ruff around neck

Japanese serow
Capricornis crispus

A small relative of goats, both male and female serows have short horns, and a long, woolly coat to withstand harsh winters. Diurnal browsers, they often retreat to a cave at night. They mark their territory with scent, chosen so they can exploit a wide range of plant food sources.

↔ 4 ft (1.2 m)
⚖ 68–106 lb (31–48 kg)
✖ Locally common
〰 Grass, leaves, acorns
🏠 🌳 🌲 ⛰

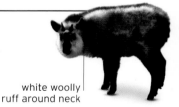

E. Asia (Japan)

◁ **GOING SOLO**
In winter, serows adopt a solitary lifestyle to make the most of the scarce food resources in their territory.

△ **IN THE SNOW**
Just like human children, young Japanese macaques
play with snowballs, and are often seen rolling them
or carrying them around.

face darker red during mating season

◁ **WARMING UP**
Japanese macaques regularly exploit hot springs to keep warm and rid themselves of parasites. High-ranking individuals within a troop are allowed greater privileges at the springs.

Japanese macaque

Macaca fuscata

Native to the Japanese islands, the Japanese macaque is also known as the snow monkey—with good reason. This short-tailed monkey lives in snowy regions farther north than any other nonhuman primate species on the planet. Northern Honshu in particular can be snow-covered for a third of the year, and the Japanese macaque's dense gray-brown coat, which covers its entire body except the face and rump, grows thicker as the temperature falls. This allows it to survive temperatures as low as -4°F (-20°C).

Its habitat ranges from subtropical forests in southern Japan to subarctic woods in the north. The females spend more time in trees, while males prefer to stay on the ground; however, all Japanese macaques sleep in trees whenever possible to avoid predators such as feral dogs. They are true omnivores, although they eat more plants than animals. Their preferred diet consists of seasonal fruit, nuts, seeds, and leaves, but they will eat fungi, insects, shellfish, fish, roots, and even soil, for minerals, when necessary.

Inherited rank
The males are slightly larger and heavier than females, and social groups, known as troops, are made up of both sexes. However, the rank, or standing, in a troop passes from mothers to daughters. One troop may have several of these "matrilines" arranged in a hierarchy, with members of one matriline outranking all lower-ranking matrilines. Males within a troop also follow a dominance system, led by an alpha male. Females stay in their troops for life, but males join different ones when they reach sexual maturity.

Female Japanese macaques decide which males to mate with, and will not necessarily choose an alpha male. Mating takes place on the ground or in trees, and a single infant (or twins in rare cases) is born five to six months later. Infants begin foraging for themselves at around seven weeks, but they depend on their mothers for about 18 months. Grandmothers sometimes raise their abandoned grandchildren—the first nonhuman primate known to do so.

Versatile communicator
An intelligent species, Japanese macaques use a number of sounds and calls to communicate, as well as to alert troop members to danger. They also learn behavioral techniques from each other, such as bathing in hot springs, rolling snowballs, and washing food in fresh water before dipping it in salt water to enhance the taste.

Japanese macaque troops in **different locations have different accents,** just like humans do

◁ **WINTER FORAGING**
The diet of Japanese macaques changes with the seasons—in winter they eat mainly tree bark and buds.

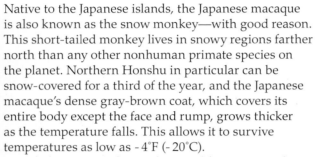

↔ 19–28 in (47–72 cm)
⚖ 18–24 lb (8–11 kg)
✖ Common
🍴 Plants, insects, shellfish
🏠

Japan

△ **ICE HOUSE**
Hollow trees or ground burrows provide shelter and sleeping dens for the primarily nocturnal Japanese marten, as well as protection from predators such as feral dogs.

▷ **STEPPING STONES**
Powerful leg muscles enable Japanese martens to leap several times their own body length, while sharp claws give them excellent traction. This means crossing thawing rivers poses no problem.

cream-colored neck patch

Japanese marten

Martes melampus

Although they belong to the weasel family, whose members are known for catching small mammals, Japanese martens are opportunists when it comes to food, adapting their diets to the seasons and whatever is available where they live. In spring, for example, birds may feature as prey of some populations, while insects make up a large part of their diet in summer.

Dispersal agents

Martens do eat small mammals such as field mice, as well as birds, eggs, fish, frogs, and crustaceans. However, their droppings, or scat, contain a wider variety of whole plant and fruit seeds than other native flesh-eating mammals, making the martens vital seed dispersers, particularly for plants producing flesh-rich fruits.

Japanese martens were once bred for their fur, which varies from yellowish to dark brown among the three subspecies, but very little is known about these agile and elusive mammals in the wild. They regularly mark their boundaries with scat, are thought to be highly territorial, and prefer broadleaf woodland to conifers due to the wider array of food choices the former offers.

Males are larger than females, which bear one to five kits per litter. Other than females with kits, Japanese martens live and hunt alone. They are threatened by the rise in the number of conifer plantations, increased use of agrochemicals, and overhunting for the fur trade.

In **Japanese folklore, martens** are said to have **shapeshifting abilities**

↔ 19–22 in (48–55 cm)
🏋 2–3 lb (1–1.5 kg)
✖ Locally common
〃 Mammals, birds, plants
🏠 🌳 🏘

E. Asia

face has black "mask" like a raccoon

Raccoon dog

Nyctereutes procyonoides

Native to East Asia, the raccoon dog is so adaptable that it is now widespread in eastern and northern Europe, where it was initially introduced by the fur trade. This member of the canid (dog) family is a distant cousin of wolves and dogs, but several characteristics set it apart. It is the only canid to semihibernate in winter, going into a state of lethargy unless its fat reserves are too low. It does not bark, but whines, mews, or growls. Raccoon dogs have smaller teeth and longer intestines than other canids—traits found in animals that consume plant matter. During fall in their native range, fruit and berries make up a large part of their diet.

long winter coat with thick fur undercoat

↔ 20–28 in (50–71 cm)
🏋 7–28 lb (3–12.7 kg)
✖ Common
〃 Birds, rodents, frogs, fruit
🏠 🌳 🌲 🏔 🌿 🏕

E. Asia

◁ **READY FOR WINTER**
Due to their relatively poor eyesight, raccoon dogs rely on their sense of smell to find enough food in fall to fatten up for winter.

female
much less
colorful

male has
spiky ruff

triangular orange
sails

Mandarin duck

Aix galericulata

Like many brightly patterned birds, mandarin ducks are surprisingly inconspicuous in the wild. They usually keep well out of sight beneath overhanging lakeside vegetation, or perch high up in trees. In spring, they nest in cavities in old trees. Males defend occupied nests at first, but do not incubate the eggs and leave the area before they hatch. Mandarins feed on small invertebrates, seeds, acorns, and other vegetable matter, taken from shallow water or while grazing on nearby short grass. They fly quickly through trees and across open water, making high-pitched, squeaky, quacking calls.

Numbers game

Habitat loss and exploitation have caused a dramatic decline in the mandarin's natural range, but, being an ornamental bird, it has been introduced into parts of Europe. Some mandarins escaped from collections to establish wild populations in North America. Normally, such out-of-range introductions turn out to be ecologically damaging, but in the mandarin's case, they may prove to be the species' salvation in the long term.

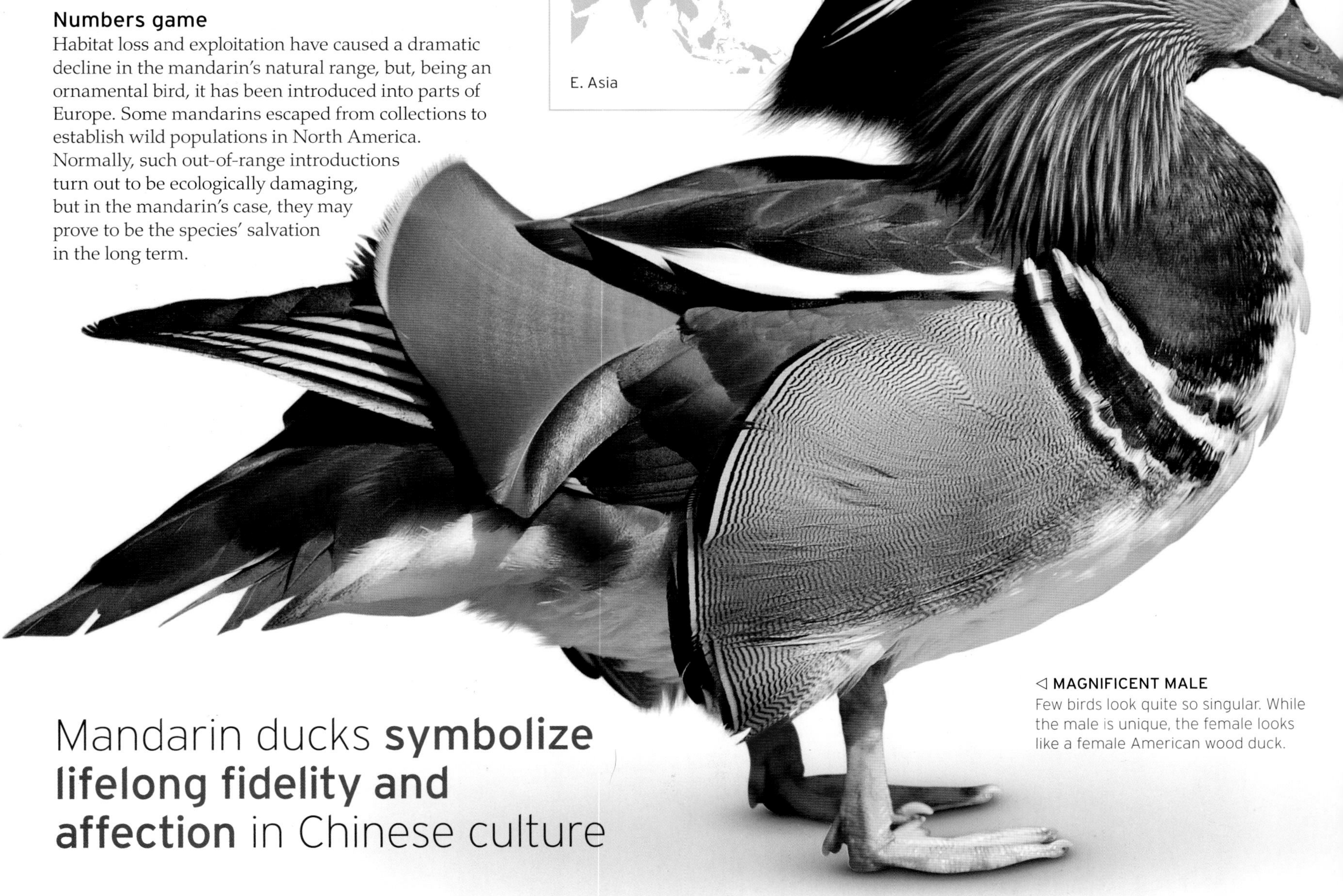

↔ 16–20 in (41–50 cm)
⚖ 22 oz (625 g)
✕ Common
🍴 Seeds, nuts, insects, snails

E. Asia

broad white
crescent of male

◁ **MAGNIFICENT MALE**
Few birds look quite so singular. While the male is unique, the female looks like a female American wood duck.

Mandarin ducks **symbolize lifelong fidelity and affection** in Chinese culture

Asian tiger keelback
Rhabdophis tigrinus

The Asian tiger keelback is a very unusual snake. It is both venomous (from its rear-fanged bite) and poisonous. Known as *yamakagashi* in Japan, the keelback absorbs toxins from its poisonous toad prey and stores it in its neck glands. When threatened, the snake arches its neck and oozes the poison as a deterrent. The female lays two to 40 eggs (average 10–14), which hatch after 30–45 days.

↔ 2–4 ft (0.7–1.2 m)
⚖ 2–28 oz (60–800 g)
✗ Not known
🐾 Amphibians
🏠 🌳 🌲 🌿 〰
◉ E. and SE. Asia

▽ **TRANSFERRING TOXINS**
The black-banded keelback can pass on the toxins derived from toads to its offspring via the egg yolk.

Alpine black swallowtail
Papilio maackii

iridescent scales

This large butterfly lives along forest edges and in grasslands where there are plentiful bushes. There are two broods per year, one hatching in late spring and the other in late summer. The adults survive for two weeks, feeding on nectar and gathering in crowds to mate. Eggs are laid on prickly ash and cork oak leaves— the preferred food of the caterpillars.

↔ 5–6 in (12–14 cm)
✗ Not known
🐾 Prickly ash leaves, nectar
🏠 🌳 🌲 🏔
◉ E. Asia

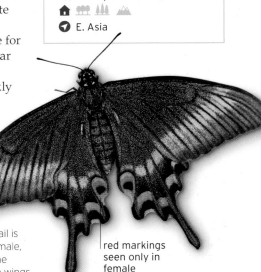

△ **FANCY FEMALE**
The female alpine black swallowtail is more vibrantly colored than the male, with red and blue spots behind the green band that runs across both wings.

red markings seen only in female

Japanese giant salamander
Andrias japonicus

↔ 3–5 ft (1–1.5 m)
🌙 Late summer
✗ Near threatened
🐾 Fish, insects, crustaceans
🏠 〰 〰 🏭

E. Asia (Japan)

This freshwater monster is the second largest amphibian on earth after the Chinese giant salamander. It breathes exclusively through its skin, which restricts it to living in cold, fast-flowing, oxygen-rich rivers. Between August and September, adults congregate at underwater nest sites to spawn. Females lay their eggs in burrows in riverbanks. These are fertilized and guarded by males until they hatch. The young remain as larvae for four to five years, and mature 10 years later.

bulbous head

wrinkled skin exudes milky fluid when salamander is threatened

forelimbs same length as hind limbs

△ **SENSITIVE SKIN**
The salamander's tiny eyes are no use in finding prey. Instead, it uses its sense of smell and sensors in its skin that pick up water currents produced by passing prey.

BORNEAN RAINFOREST
Southeast Asia's treasure trove of rare species

At around 140 million years of age, Borneo's lowland rainforest is one of the oldest and most biodiverse in the world. But the forest's diversity is also what makes it attractive to commercial exploitation. The lowland forests boast 267 species of large hardwood trees, 60 percent of which are endemic to Borneo. Estimates put forest loss in the region at 30 percent since 1970, due mainly to the logging of hardwoods for the global timber market and the conversion of land to agricultural use. Increasing fragmentation of the rainforest presents difficulties for endangered wide-ranging species such as orangutans, which require large, continuous tracts of forest for survival. Also, there is a staggering 99 percent drop in species diversity just a couple of yards into a plantation compared to the untouched rainforest.

High, green island heart
Currently just over half of the island retains its forest cover, with the majority consisting of lowland rainforest below 3,300 ft (1,000 m). The cooler, higher-altitude center of the island—now known internationally as the Heart of Borneo—is covered with unbroken mountainous rainforest, which has so far suffered less from logging and the encroachment of agriculture, mainly because the terrain is less suitable. Other important habitats for wildlife in Borneo include swamp forests and mangroves.

18 mammal species in Borneo's mountain rainforest exist nowhere else on Earth

SHRUB FROG

IMMUNE TO DANGER
Pitcher plants use bright colors and sweet smells to attract insects to their sticky, fluid-filled "pitchers." Prey that drowns in the liquid is digested by the plant. Shrub frogs are unaffected by the fluid, and lay their eggs in the pitchers, where they develop safely from predators.

The third-largest island on Earth

SUN BEAR

HONEY HUNTER
The Borneo sun bear is found only in the island's rainforests. It uses its large claws to rip open beehives and termite nests in search of honey and insects to eat. It also consumes fruit from various rainforest trees and plays an important role in seed dispersal.

44 of which are found nowhere else in the world

221 mammal species live here,

SLIPPER ORCHID

WONDERFUL ORCHIDS
Borneo has 2,500–3,000 orchid species; 51 new kinds were discovered between 2007 and 2010. The region is home to rare flowers, such as the Rothschild's slipper orchid—beautiful and endangered.

USELESS SCALES
Sunda pangolins have declined more than 50% in the last 15 years due to poaching. Their scales are illegally sold to buyers in China, and the medicines they are used in are useless.

SUNDA PANGOLIN

Called "Kalimantan" in Indonesian, or "burning-weather island"

FOREST GIANT
The titan arum's 10 ft (3 m)-tall inflorescence is actually a collection of small flowers on a fleshy stem, surrounded by a single petal-like structure called a spathe. The blooms give off an odor of rotting flesh that attracts flies to pollinate it.

TITAN ARUM

Home to about 15,000 species of flowering plants

SEED DISPERSER
Eight species of hornbill live in Borneo. Like the sun bear, bushy-crested, helmeted, and great rhinoceros hornbills are important dispersers of seeds. In addition to facing habitat loss, the birds are hunted for their feathers and meat.

RHINOCEROS HORNBILL

LOCATION

Borneo is located in Southeast Asia, southwest of the Philippines and north of Java. Politically the island is divided among three countries: Indonesia, Malaysia, and Brunei.

South China Sea

Bandar Seri Begawan

Kuching

Sulawesi Sea

Banjarmasin

0 km 250
0 miles 250

CLIMATE

Borneo's rainforest has a severely hot, tropical climate, with warm temperatures and significant rainfall occurring year round. The island's average annual rainfall is 118 in (2,992 mm), with an average temperature of 80°F (26.7°C).

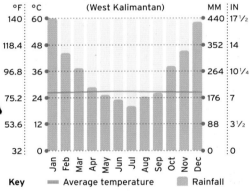

°F	°C	(West Kalimantan)	MM	IN
140	60		440	17½
118.4	48		352	14
96.8	36		264	10¼
75.2	24		176	7
53.6	12		88	3½
32	0	Jan Feb Mar Apr May Jun Jul Aug Sep Oct Nov Dec	0	0

Key — Average temperature ▮ Rainfall

THE PROBLEM WITH PALM OIL

Vast tracts of Borneo's forests have been destroyed to make way for oil-palm plantations. Palm oil, extracted from the fruit and seed kernels of the palms, is used globally in the food and cosmetics industries. Demand for cheap vegetable oils is expected to increase as human population grows.

Large flying fox
Pteropus vampyrus

Unlike the smaller microbats, flying foxes do not echolocate to find their way around in the dark. Instead, they use their big eyes and sensitive noses to find fruit and flowers to eat in the rainforest. This diet gives them their other common name: fruit bat. Flying foxes spend the day roosting upside down in large, noisy groups in trees. They can move around by using the thumbs on the edges of their wings to cling onto branches. At night they fly to feeding trees, which may be many miles away from their roost.

↔ 17 in (43 cm)
🏋 1–3 lb (0.5–1.4 kg)
✖ Near threatened
🍴 Fruit, flowers, nectar
🏠 🏝 🌲 🌾 🏜

SE. Asia

▷ **HANGING AROUND**
One of the largest bats in the world, the large flying fox has an average wingspan of 5 ft (1.5 m).

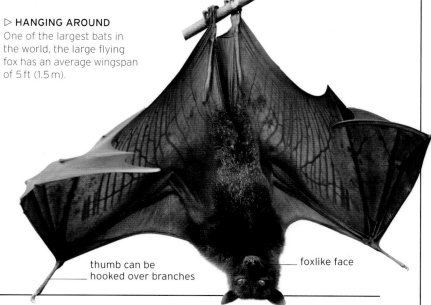

thumb can be hooked over branches

foxlike face

Western tarsier
Cephalopachus bancanus

Relative to its size, the western tarsier has the largest eyes of any mammal—each is slightly heavier than its brain. The eyes cannot move, but this nocturnal primate can turn its head to look backward for possible predators or prey. It also locates prey with its keen hearing, grabbing or leaping on its victim.

Leaping is the tarsier's main form of locomotion—it can jump across distances almost 40 times its body length. Mainly tree-dwelling, it has slender fingers and its toes have pads, nails, and sharp claws, for gripping branches.

Females have one offspring at a time. At first, the baby is carried by the mother, but it soon learns to cling to her fur.

↔ 5 in (13 cm)
🏋 4–5 oz (113–141 g)
✖ Vulnerable
🍴 Insects, bats, snakes, birds
🏠 🏛

SE. Asia

▷ **CLINGING ON**
The agile western tarsier easily holds on to vertical trunks, using its long tail as a support.

↔ 61–76 cm (24–30 in)
🏋 10–24 kg (22–53 lb)
✖ Endangered
🍴 Leaves, unripe fruit, seeds
🏠 🏝 🌾

SE. Asia

adult male has orange face and enormous nose

Proboscis monkey

Nasalis larvatus

Proboscis monkeys are as complex as their facial features are unusual. Both sexes have exceptional noses. The females' and juveniles' noses are long for primates but upturned, while adult males sport the clownlike, pendulous proboscis that gives the species its common name. Its purpose is still uncertain, but it may function as an "echo chamber," amplifying the males' calls and helping them attract mates.

Deceptive appearance

Males are much larger than females. Due to the high volume of leaves they consume coupled with a very slow digestive rate, both sexes have large, swollen stomachs that make them look perpetually pregnant.

A mature male heads a harem of several females and their young. Unusually for primates, females in a harem compete with each other for mating opportunities with the male, and may join several harems during their lifetimes. As they mature, males form bachelor groups before vying for harems of their own. Although rival males engage in noisy displays, they are not fiercely territorial. Several groups often come together at dusk, sleeping high up in the trees for safety.

Proboscis monkeys are never far from water and they are remarkable swimmers, aided by their partially webbed feet.

△ **ADOLESCENT SQUABBLE**
Bonds are forged and broken as juveniles grow in size, get stronger, and learn new skills.

△ **MIGHTY LEAP**
Leaping from trees and belly flopping into water is a common activity. Proboscis monkeys can swim up to 65 ft (20 m) underwater when threatened.

◁ **BABY FACE**
Both sexes are born with a "normal" monkey nose, and black fur and blue faces. The nose grows and the coloration changes with age.

An adult male's **nose is often so long** it has to be **pushed aside** to allow its owner **to eat**

Bornean orangutan

Pongo pygmaeus

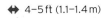

arms twice as long as legs

The orangutan is the only great ape to live in Asia. Its name means "man of the forest" in Malay. This shaggy, red-haired ape is found in the forests of Borneo and Sumatra. The Bornean species outnumbers the Sumatran orangutan (*P. abelii*) by almost 10 to one. However, with a population of around 55,000, Bornean orangutans are still highly endangered.

Life in the trees

Orangutans spend the day climbing up branches in search of food and sleep in trees at night. Their arm span is considerably longer than their height—an adult male's arms can span around 7 ft (2.2 m)—so they can reach for branches and swing across precipitous drops with relative ease. Weighing about the same as an adult human, although six times stronger, orangutans cannot reach the very top of trees safely and so spend most of their time in the lower 130 ft (40 m) of the forest. Older males are too heavy to climb that high, and in Borneo, where there are no large predators to speak of, the males spend long periods on the ground. Females and younger males, by contrast, may not touch the ground for weeks on end.

Orangutans feed primarily on fruit, using their dextrous hands and their teeth to remove the peel and expose the flesh. They also eat leaves, bark, and flowers, as well as honey, birds' eggs, insects, and fish.

Solitary ape

Adult male orangutans stay out of each other's way, using a series of calls to advertise their presence and warn off neighbors. Some male Bornean orangutans do not develop facial flaps when mature. They are less vocal and use stealth tactics to approach and mate with a female while the other males are vying with each other for mating rights. Female orangutans may spend short periods feeding in small groups, letting their young play together. A female orangutan cares for her young for about seven years, and will not have another until the previous offspring has become independent.

↔ 4–5 ft (1.1–1.4 m)
🏋 88–176 lb (40–80 kg)
✖ Endangered
🌿 Plants, eggs, insects
🏠 🏯

SE. Asia (Borneo)

◁ **MATURE MALE**
There is considerable physical difference between male and female orangs. Most males develop wide facial flaps at the age of 14, and grow a thin moustache and beard.

△ **NIGHT NEST**
Orangutans sleep in nests made of folded branches. They make a fresh one every night.

◁ **A SIP OF RAIN**
A young orangutan drinks rainwater dripping from forest leaves. Orangutans often use a leafy branch as an umbrella in heavy downpours.

Müller's gibbon
Hylobates muelleri

arms one-and-a-half ___
times as long as legs

The smallest members of the ape family, gibbons are among the most acrobatic primates, able to bridge gaps of more than 33 ft (10 m) between trees by flinging themselves across with their long arms. Müller's gibbon is one of four gibbon species native to Borneo, where it inhabits tall rainforest and tropical forest canopies. Since it rarely comes down to the ground, this species is mainly threatened by loss of habitat due to forest clearance.

While touch and grooming play vital roles in other ape species, gibbons bond and communicate largely by vocalizing, or "singing," and each species has its own unique song. Adults are serial monogamists, and mated pairs defend their territory with morning duets. The male begins singing shortly before dawn and is joined by the female after sunrise for an average of 15 minutes, before the daily search for food begins.

Gibbons use the same **vocalization techniques as operatic sopranos**

↔ 16–25 in (41–64 cm)
⚖ 10–16 lb (4.5–7.3 kg)
✖ Endangered
🍴 Ripe fruit, leaves, flowers

SE. Asia (Borneo)

◁ **KING OF THE SWINGERS**
Gibbons are highly agile and move by brachiation, or arm-swinging, traveling through trees at speeds of up to 34 mph (55 km/h).

Common flying dragon
Draco volans

▷ **CONTROLLED GLIDE**
As it glides, the dragon's chest muscles extend and tilt the ribs to curve the wings for lift, if air currents allow, and for directional control, aided by the tail and feet.

Rather than flying like its mythical namesake, this lizard glides between tree trunks to find food or mates, or to avoid territorial conflicts or predators. Its wings consist of stretchy skin supported by elongated ribs. Common flying dragon glides have been measured at more than 33 ft (10 m), with anecdotal records exceeding 165 ft (50 m). When not airborne, the wings are folded along the sides of the body for protection. They also aid camouflage, both with their coloration and by disrupting the typical body shape of a lizard. The dragon's favorite foods are tree ants and termites, usually caught morning and evening.

Mating displays
At breeding time the territorial male head-bobs, unfurls his wings, and fans out his bright yellow dewlap (chin flap) to repel rival males and attract females. After mating, the female climbs down to the ground and digs a shallow hole with her snout for her eggs.

↔ 6–8 in (15–20 cm)
⚖ $^3/_{16}$–$^3/_8$ oz (5–10 g)
✖ Common
🍴 Ants, termites, small insects

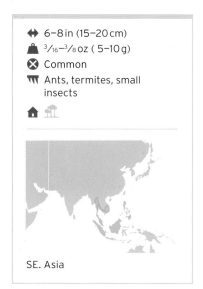

SE. Asia

Black-and-red broadbill

Cymbirhynchus macrorhynchos

Named for the wide, flattened bill designed to scoop up insects and other prey, this strikingly colored broadbill is surprisingly inconspicuous in thick foliage. It is often silent, but has a distinctive low song. Perched upright, taut and slim, with its tail pointing down, the male peers around, twisting his large head, then stretches and partially opens his bill to produce a brief phrase of buzzing notes.

↔ 10 in (25 cm)
⚖ 2–3 oz (57–85 g)
✖ Common
🍴 Insects, fruit, crabs, fish
🏠 🏞 〰 🍄〰
◉ SE. Asia

△ **MATCHED PAIR**
Black-and-red broadbills nest in tree stumps near water. The males help incubate the eggs and feed the chicks.

Stork-billed kingfisher

Pelargopsis capensis

Although it dives for fish, this kingfisher hunts in drier, wooded places, too, for a variety of prey. It is usually located by its loud, fast cackle of alarm and a regularly repeated low, three-note call. Aggressively territorial, it chases other birds, even birds of prey, from its patch.

large head compared to body

▷ **TOP HEAVY**
With the largest bill of any kingfisher, the stork-billed kingfisher can handle prey almost as big as itself.

↔ 14 in (35 cm)
⚖ 5–7 oz (142–200 g)
✖ Common
🍴 Fish, frogs, crabs, rodents
🏠 🏞 🏞 〰 〰 🍄〰
◉ S. to SE. Asia

Wallace's flying frog

Rhacophorus nigropalmatus

Juvenile froglets have
brown granular skin
more suited to life
among mud and soil
than the smooth
green skin of the
tree-living adult.

Named after its discoverer A.R. Wallace, the English naturalist who developed the theory of evolution with Charles Darwin, the flying frog is a perfect example of how species can adapt to their environments. The webbed feet used for swimming by the frog's ancestors are repurposed as parachutes, allowing it to leap long distances between trees. Adults need never come down to the ground—they can leap away from predators or toward new feeding areas. During the rainy season, eggs are laid inside a foam nest whipped up on a branch from the female's mucus secretions. When the tadpoles hatch, they fall into a pond or waterhole below.

↔ 3–4 in (8–10 cm)
☁ Rainy season
✕ Locally common
🐜 Insects, spiders

SE. Asia

◁ **PARACHUTING ADULT**
The splayed webbed feet allow
Wallace's flying frogs to make leaps
up to 50 ft (15 m). Large toe pads
provide a strong grip on landing.

Atlas moth

Attacus atlas

feathery antennae
of male

Named after the Greek demigod who carried the world on his shoulders, this species once held the title of the largest living moth; however, the Hercules moth of New Guinea and Australia has the biggest wing area of all. Nevertheless, the female Atlas moth can cover a dinner plate (the males are smaller).

Adult Atlas moths do not feed, and they live for a week at most, so they need to breed as soon as possible; males can track the scent of females several miles away with their feathery antennae. The females lay around 250 tiny eggs on the underside of leaves, particularly of citrus and other fruit trees.

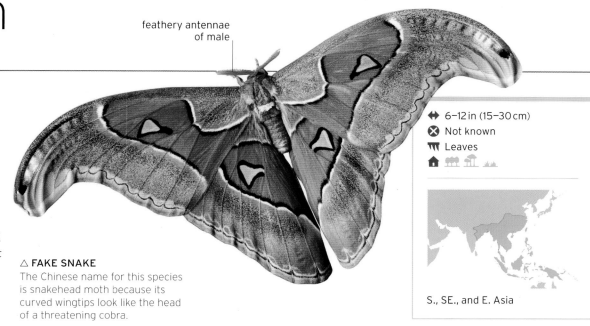

↔ 6–12 in (15–30 cm)
✕ Not known
🐜 Leaves

S., SE., and E. Asia

△ **FAKE SNAKE**
The Chinese name for this species
is snakehead moth because its
curved wingtips look like the head
of a threatening cobra.

Malaysian orchid mantis

Hymenopus coronatus

With its fine pink and cream shading, this mantis is a master of disguise. It resembles a forest orchid, with the back legs flattened to look like petals, and the plump abdomen resembling a ripening bud. The trick this insect plays not only keeps it hidden from predators that might snatch it from plants, but also fools its prey, which fly straight to it thinking it is a nectar-filled bloom.

Killer mimic

This strategy is known as aggressive mimicry. The Malaysian orchid mantis climbs around a plant until it finds a cluster of flowers. It can fine-tune its color from pink to brown to match its location, making it indistinguishable even when viewed in the ultraviolet spectrum by its insect prey. The mantis sways with the flimsy blooms, making it even harder to spot. Pollinating insects appear to approach the mantis as frequently as they do the real flowers —and are snatched up with lightning speed.

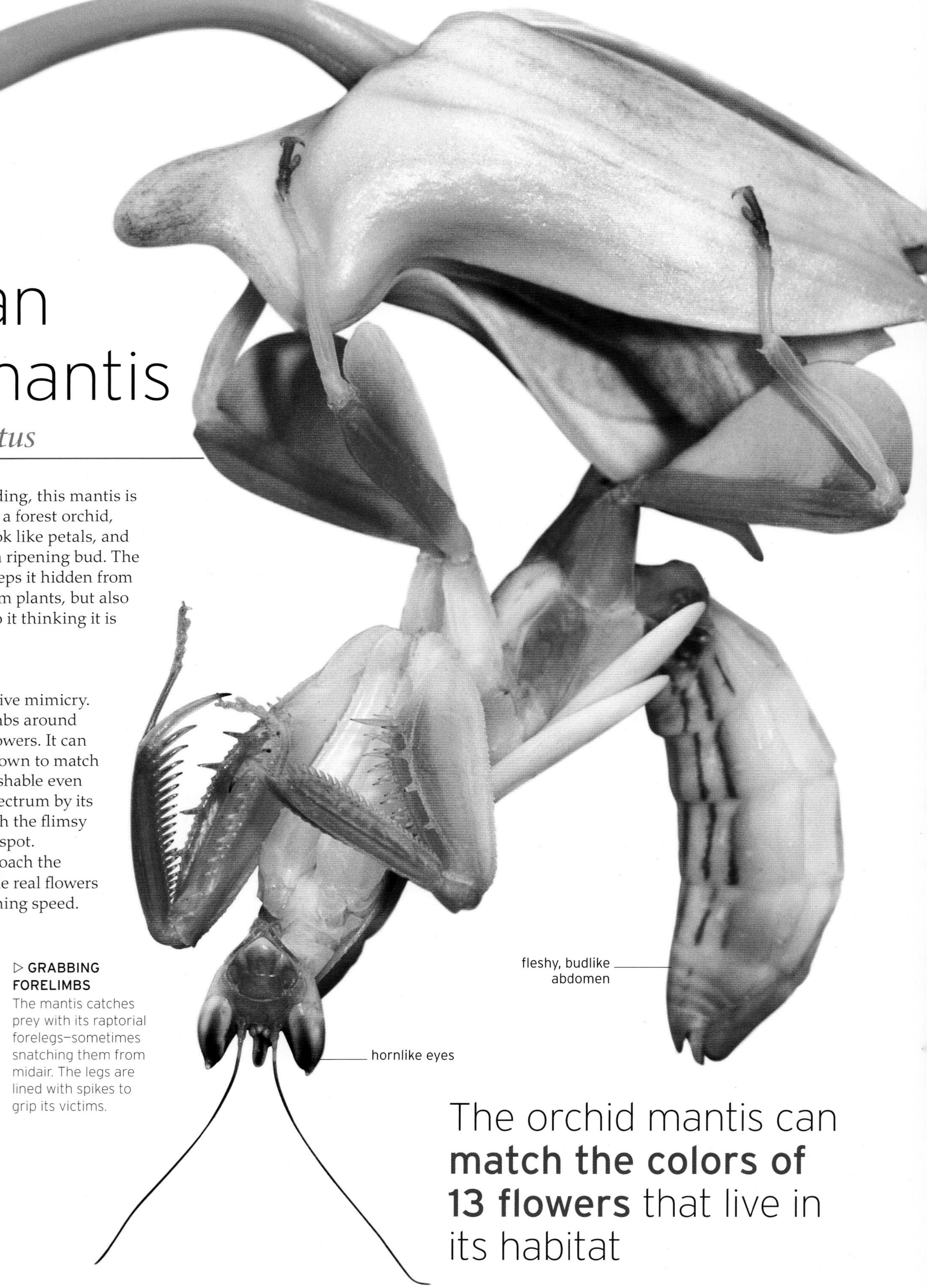

↔ 1–2 in (3–5 cm)
✖ Not known
🎚 Insects
🏠 🏛

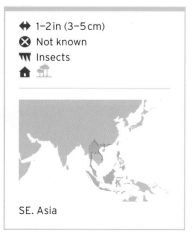

SE. Asia

▷ **GRABBING FORELIMBS**
The mantis catches prey with its raptorial forelegs–sometimes snatching them from midair. The legs are lined with spikes to grip its victims.

fleshy, budlike abdomen

hornlike eyes

The orchid mantis can **match the colors of 13 flowers** that live in its habitat

SULU-SULAWESI SEAS
The world's most biodiverse marine ecoregion

The Sulu-Sulawesi marine ecoregion covers around 660,000 sq miles (900,000 sq km) of the Sulu and Sulawesi seas and the inland seas of the Philippines. It sits at the top of the Coral Triangle of Southeast Asia. Its complex mix of marine habitats includes seagrass plains, coral reefs, deep sea trenches, seamounts, active volcanic islands, and mangrove forests. The diverse habitats support astonishing underwater biodiversity with more than 2,000 species of marine fish and 400 species of coral represented. The seas are also home to five of the world's seven sea turtle species, and the dugong and Irrawaddy dolphin—both vulnerable marine mammals.

reefs and islands. Many of the reefs are popular dive sites, and the Tubbata Reefs in the Sulu Sea were declared UNESCO World Heritate Site in 1993. Fishermen exploit the large populations of commercial fish, such as tuna.

Tourism and growing local populations put pressure on the marine environment through the development of coastlines and the use of coral for building. There is also increased pollution from untreated sewage and industrial and agricultural runoff into the sea. Efforts are being made by conservationists to curb harmful fishing techniques that use dynamite or cyanide, which damage the coral reefs and kill marine life indiscriminately.

Threatened paradise

The water is predominantly warm and clear thanks to the tropical climate. Such bountiful and beautiful waters draw crowds of tourists that come to experience the coral

OVERFISHING
Along with commercial fishing for the international food market, local people catch fish for their own consumption, and coral reef fish are sought for the aquarium trade. The sardine population is approaching collapse.

SARDINES

LIVING FOSSIL
Discovered in 1997, the Sulawesi coelacanth is one of two survivors of a group of fish that was thought to be extinct. It has become a flagship species for the better management and protection of the Bunaken National Park where it is found.

COELACANTH

LOCH'S CHROMODORIS

Home to around 2,000 species of fish

Five species of

More than 400 species of coral

TOXIC SEA SLUG
The colorful Loch's chromodoris is a sea slug that lives on coral reefs. It feeds on sponges and is able to ingest their toxins into its own body, making it inedible to potential predators. Its bright coloration serves as a warning that it is poisonous.

Spinner dolphin

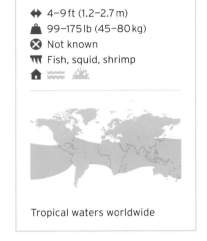

triangular dorsal fin

pointed flippers

Stenella longirostris

Spinner dolphins get their name from their ability to twirl several times in midair as they leap clear of the sea. Like most dolphin species, spinners are highly social, grouping together in schools that may range from under 200 to 1,000 or more individuals. They often swim with other dolphins and whales as well as fish such as yellowfin and skipjack tuna—a habit that results in many of these mammals dying in commercial tuna nets as bycatch.

Shallow sleepers, deep feeders

Although they are deep-water feeders, spinner dolphins retreat to areas safe from predators to rest during the day, usually frequenting the same area such as an inlet, bay, or shallow water. Hunting and feeding occur mainly at night, which is also when they do most of their leaping. Spinner dolphins use touch, such as nudges or flipper rubbing, whistles, and also echolocation to keep in contact with members of their group. They mate year round, and females give birth to a single calf, which stays with its mother for around seven years.

↔ 4–9 ft (1.2–2.7 m)

⚖ 99–175 lb (45–80 kg)

✗ Not known

🍴 Fish, squid, shrimp

🏠 〰 🌊

Tropical waters worldwide

Spinner dolphins make a **series of leaps**, often as many as **14 in a row**

▽ **AQUATIC ACROBAT**
Theories for the reason behind the spinner's trademark leaps include communication with other dolphins, parasite-removal, or sheer joy.

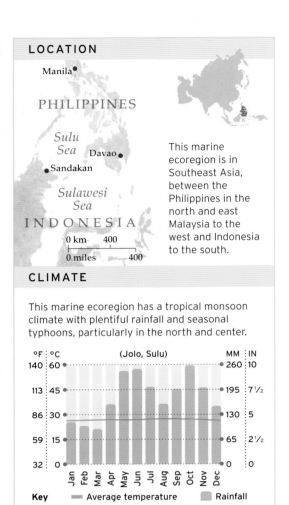

MULTIFACETED GRASS
Seagrass beds are vital to the marine ecosystem. They are a food source for dugongs and turtles and a nursery habitat for young fish. They also clean the water of chemicals, recycle nutrients, and help stabilize sandy sediments on the seafloor.

turtle live in these waters

SEAGRASS

Dugong

Dugong dugon

thick bristles on snout used to detect food

The dugong, a close relative of the elephant, is often called the sea cow, because it feeds almost exclusively on seagrass in shallow coastal tropical waters. Dugongs have torpedo-shaped bodies, broad heads, stubby flippers, and fleshy, bristled lips.

When dugongs dive, their valved nostrils seal themselves off. However, these large mammals can stay underwater only for about three minutes. Adult dugongs have few natural enemies because of their size and dense bones, though crocodiles, sharks, and killer whales attack calves and juveniles. Dugongs do not

mate until they are at least six years old, and only one calf is produced every three to seven years. Born in shallow water, after a 14-month gestation, the calf is immediately helped to the surface for its first breath by its mother.

Dugongs can live up to 70 years. However, their low reproductive rate, the loss of seagrass due to human activity, collisions with boats, drownings from fish net entanglements, and hunting mean that dugong populations are in decline. Today the largest numbers are concentrated around Australia's Great Barrier Reef.

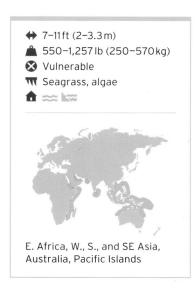

- ↔ 7–11 ft (2–3.3 m)
- 🏋 550–1,257 lb (250–570 kg)
- ✗ Vulnerable
- 🍴 Seagrass, algae
- 🏠 ≈ ≈

E. Africa, W., S., and SE Asia, Australia, Pacific Islands

◁ **KEEPING COMPANY**
Dugongs are often flanked by golden trevallies. These brightly colored fish feed on the creatures dugongs disturb when grazing.

▷ **MOTHER AND CALF**
Dugongs communicate with each other using trills, whistles, barks, and chirps, each at a different frequency and amplitude.

Ribbontail stingray

Taeniura lymma

- ↔ Up to 28 in (70 cm)
- 🏋 Not known
- ✗ Near threatened
- 🍴 Fish, crustaceans
- 🏠 ≈ ≈

Indo-Pacific Oceans

Viewed from below, a ribbontail stingray's white underside disappears into sunlit waters; from above, its speckled back blends into coral reefs. During low tide, stingrays seek shelter in reefs, moving into shallower water to feed as the tide rises.

A ribbontail stingray's mouth contains numerous tooth rows arranged in plates, ideal for crushing crustacean shells. Rays can sense food by detecting the prey's electrical field. They have few natural predators; only the hammerhead shark is known to eat them. They breed in late spring and summer. A female delivers up to seven live pups that hatch from eggs inside her body.

▽ **SPOTTED WARNING**
A ribbontail stingray's bright-blue spots serve as a warning to predators.

venomous tail spine

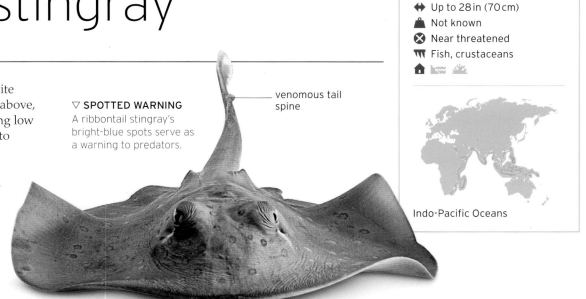

Mandarinfish
Synchiropus splendidus

↔ 3 in (6 cm)
⚖ Not known
✖ Not known
🍴 Crustaceans, worms, snails
🏠 🪸

Indonesian Ocean

The small, colorful mandarinfish lives on shallow lagoons and inshore reefs. It hides among dead coral during the day, but small groups gather to forage at night. A weak swimmer, it often "walks" along the bottom on its large pectoral fins. A small mouth limits its diet to small prey, such as tiny crustaceans.

The skin cells of the mandarinfish contain a blue pigment. This and one closely related species are the only fish known to produce this colored chemical. The color pattern is also a warning to predators. Its skin is coated in a protective layer of mucus. Filled with noxious chemicals, the mucus smells—and tastes—unpleasant. The slime also keeps off external parasites, which might exploit a sleeping fish.

▷ **PREPARING TO SPAWN**
The fish remain in bodily contact as they swim up from the reef, releasing eggs and sperm into the open water.

skin mottled with pale spots

Whale shark

Rhincodon typus

Possibly the most misnamed aquatic creature in the world, the whale shark is not a whale, but a fish, although it resembles whales in terms of size. It belongs to the same class as sharks, skates, and rays. The word "shark" brings to mind a toothy, prey-crunching predator that could be a threat to humans, but the whale shark is in fact a gentle giant. This docile, slow-swimming filter feeder allows divers to grasp its large dorsal fin without displaying any signs of aggression. Ironically, the largest living fish in the world survives on a diet made up entirely of the ocean's smallest organisms—tiny algae and animals known as phytoplankton and zooplankton.

Filter feeding

Relatively little is known about the whale shark's life and behavior. The average adult can be up to 39 ft (12 m) in length—although there are unverified reports of specimens as long as 75 ft (23 m)—and weighs around 10 tons (9 metric tons). The whale shark's huge, flat head ends in a mouth that is almost as wide as its body and contains hundreds of minuscule teeth, the function of which is unknown. It has specialized, sievelike filter pads lining the gill arches, which separate food from seawater. Unusually for a shark, its mouth is at the end of its snout rather than underneath. As well as non- or slow-moving microscopic organisms, whale sharks also eat small fish, tiny squid, fish eggs, and larvae—in short,

anything small enough to flow in with water but large enough to be trapped by their filter pads. Mostly solitary, whale sharks are occasionally seen in loosely organized schools of up to 100 individuals where food is plentiful.

Whale sharks migrate thousands of miles through the world's oceans. Individuals can be tracked using satellite tags and can be identified by the pattern of spots on their bodies—no two patterns are alike, just like human fingerprints. Adult males can be distinguished from females by the presence of "claspers"—external protrusions on their undersides that channel sperm into the female during mating. Little is known about when and how whale sharks breed, but a female retains up to 300 eggs inside her body until they hatch—a characteristic known as ovoviviparity. She then gives birth to live young or "pups," although it is believed that not all the pups are born at the same time.

Uncertain future

Once it has reached sexual maturity, which is at about 30 years of age, the whale shark's primary predator is man. They are hunted for food supplements, such as shark liver oil; their fins, which are made into soup; their meat; and their skin, which is made into leather. However, many adult whale sharks carry scars that suggest they were attacked, possibly by orcas or other sharks, at some point in their lives. It is believed that whale sharks can live up to 70–100 years in the wild.

△ **SPECIALIZED GILLS**
Cartilage rods support the spongy filter pads, which trap food such as plankton and tiny fish and squid.

△ **KEEPING COMPANY**
Schools of small fish often swim around the heads of whale sharks, possibly for protection.

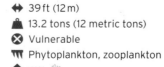
↔ 39 ft (12 m)
⚖ 13.2 tons (12 metric tons)
⊗ Vulnerable
🌾 Phytoplankton, zooplankton
🏠 〰 🌊

Tropical and temperate waters worldwide

◁ **SUCTION FEEDING**
A whale shark often holds its mouth close to the surface during suction feeding, opening and closing it to suck in water as well as food.

When feeding, a whale shark **filters enough water to fill an Olympic-sized swimming pool** every 100 minutes

Great barracuda
Sphyraena barracuda

adult has stiff
front dorsal fin

flat-topped,
elongated skull

This long, torpedo-shaped fish hunts alone or in packs. By day, great barracudas gather in large schools that patrol the periphery of warm-water coral reefs, opting for safety in numbers over the chance to make a kill. By night, the school fragments, and lone adults glide over the reef to ambush fish at close quarters, while juveniles maraud in smaller groups that harass schools of fish.

Toothy jaw
The great barracuda's long, streamlined body, along with short, stiff fins that provide stability, make it capable of many modes of swimming, from a steady cruise to a lightning fast surge—all powered by the large, triangular tail fins. The barracuda's jaw has a distinctive underbite with the lower jaw poking out in front of its head. This gives the fish a wide gape and exposes needlelike teeth, which are embedded in

the jaw bones and the roof of the mouth. The long, toothy jaw is ideal for gripping small, struggling fish, but is also capable of delivering a powerful bite that can cut through larger prey. Occasionally, a lone barracuda will give a diver a nasty bite if it mistakes a hand or shiny diving watch for a small, silvery fish.

Great barracudas spawn in open water, and the eggs are left to drift unattended. The fry shelter in estuaries until they are 3 in (8 cm) long, then they head out to sea.

The **flesh of large barracudas** contains **lethal toxins**

↔ Up to 7 ft (2 m)
⚖ Up to 110 lb (50 kg)
✕ Not known
♨ Fish
🏠

Tropical and subtropical waters worldwide

Boxer crab
Lybia tessellata

walking legs covered in short hairs

The boxer crab's slender pincer-bearing legs are of no use for attack or defense. Instead, it uses a pair of sea anemones as bodyguards. It grips them in its front pincers and thrusts their stinging tentacles at anything threatening. This relationship also benefits the anemones as they are carried through the water, allowing them to collect food particles suspended in it. The crab cannot catch its own food and so uses its long mouthparts to collect some of the food scraps snared by the anemones.

↔ ³/₈–1 in (1–2.5 cm)
✕ Not known
⊤ Plankton
🏠 🪸

W. Indian Ocean, W. and S. Pacific Ocean

△ **STINGING GLOVES**
Without the anemones, the crab is more or less defenseless, with little more than a picket of spines around the edge of its carapace.

Green humphead parrotfish
Bolbometopon muricatum

The largest of all parrotfish, the green humphead is one of the most social—feeding, sleeping, and spawning in large groups. This makes it an easy target for spearfishers, and overfishing has led to a decline in numbers. Like all parrotfish, green humpheads eat live coral; they use their forehead bulge to ram reefs, breaking the coral down into small pieces, which they crush with their beaklike front teeth.

↔ Up to 4 ft (1.2 m)
⚖ Up to 101 lb (50 kg)
✕ Vulnerable
⊤ Coral, algae
🏠 🪸

▷ **REEF CRUNCHER**
An adult parrotfish consumes around 6-7 tons (5-6 metric tons) of coral each year. Any hard, undigested material is passed out in the fish's feces, adding sediment back to the reef ecosystem.

Indian Ocean, S. Pacific Ocean

△ **SLY PREDATOR**
The barracuda's silver scales reflect the water, helping it blend into the background, and the narrow head gives prey little chance of seeing it coming.

△ **HERDING SCHOOL**
Groups of barracudas will work together to herd schools of smaller fish into shallow waters, where they are easier to catch.

Vatuira, Fiji Islands
The warm, clear waters of coral reefs support an
incredible variety of life. The bright coloration of
fish that live in reefs helps them recognize
members of their species.

Australasia

FEATURED ECOREGIONS

- New Guinea Montane Forest **»p314-19**
  Tropical moist broadleaf, mixed forest
- North Australia Savannas **»p320-27**
  Tropical grassland, scrub
- Great Sandy-Tanami Desert **»p328-33**
  Desert, scrub
- East Australian Forests **»p334-43**
  Temperate broadleaf, mixed forest
- Great Barrier Reef **»p344-53**
  Marine, coral reef
- New Zealand Mixed Forest **»p354-59**
  Temperate broadleaf, mixed forest

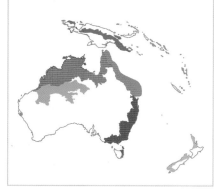

ARNHEM LAND

Within 930 miles (1,500 km) of the equator, this north-central region has a fiercely seasonal, monsoon tropical climate. Its intricate mix of coastal landscapes and hills harbors dozens of unique species, from rock rats to snakes. It also provides an important conservation habitat for dugongs, nesting turtles, and migratory birds.

Timor Sea

Arafura Sea

INDIAN OCEAN

Melville Island

Arnhem Land

Barkly Tableland

Kimberley Plateau

Tanami Desert

Great Sandy Desert

Macdonnell Ranges

A U S T R

WESTERN COASTAL DESERTS
Starved from rain due to cold ocean currents and prevailing offshore winds, there is little coastal vegetation and arid conditions extend throughout.

Hamersley Range

Gibson Desert

△ Uluru (Ayers Rock) 867m

Simpso Desert

Great Victoria Desert

Nullarbor Plain

Darling Range

NULLARBOR PLAIN
This vast plain, with much bare rock, has no permanent water. Life is sparse and restricted to a narrow coastal strip.

Kangar Islar

KEY DATA

ECOSYSTEMS

- Tropical broadleaf forest
- Temperate broadleaf forest
- Mediterranean woodland, scrub
- Tropical, subtropical grassland
- Temperate grassland
- Desert, scrub
- Montane grassland

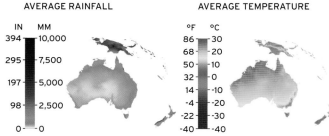

AVERAGE RAINFALL

IN	MM
394	10,000
295	7,500
197	5,000
98	2,500
0	0

AVERAGE TEMPERATURE

°F	°C
86	30
68	20
50	10
32	0
14	-10
-4	-20
-22	-30
-40	-40

SHARK BAY

The shallow, sheltered conditions in Shark Bay encourage the formation of curious concretions called stromatolites. These mounds of layered sediment with surface films of cyanobacteria are almost identical to ones that formed more than 3 billion years ago. The cyanobacteria were among the first organisms to inhabit Earth.

New Guinea

Solomon Islands

Torres Strait

Cape York Peninsula

Coral Sea

Great Barrier Reef

Great Dividing Range

ALIA

Fraser Island

e Eyre in

rs

anges

Darling

Murray

Great Dividing Range

△ Mount Kosciuszko 2,228m

Bass Strait

Flinders Island

GONDWANA RAINFOREST

Only remnants of these southern supercontinent forests survive, with prehistoric ferns and conifers and ancient flowering plants. Among birds, the lyrebird, bowerbird, and catbird lineages stretch back more than 60 million years.

GREAT MOUNTAIN RANGE

More than 2,200 miles (3,500 km) long, the continent's only major uplands moisten the climate to the east, while aridity increases westwards.

MURRAY-DARLING BASIN

Named for its two major rivers, the wetlands here are seasonal and ephemeral.

TASMANIA

Australia's southern island state has dense rainforest and cool deciduous woodlands. They provide refuges for species once also on the mainland, such as the Tasmanian devil.

Tasmania

THE RED CONTINENT
Australasia

Australasia consists of the mainland, or large island, of Australia, together with Tasmania, New Zealand, the huge tropical island of New Guinea, and a few other nearby islands. All of these, aside from New Zealand, make up the Australian continent. It is the smallest of the continents and also, on average, the driest inhabited continent: about one-third has a desertlike climate and another third is semi-arid. On the mainland of Australia, appreciable rain falls only around the eastern margins, while the great interior, or outback, is often parched.

The Australian continent has a unique evolutionary history. It split from the rest of the southern supercontinent of Gondwana more than 80 million years ago, taking with it plants and animals common at the time, especially marsupial mammals. What are now the Australian mainland and New Guinea remained linked by land bridges until 6,000 years ago, when sea levels rose after the last ice age. Consequently, they share much of their wildlife, a high proportion of which consists of endemic species—most of the continent's plants and mammals and a high proportion of its birds are found nowhere else.

Much more isolated, lying more than 1,300 miles (2,100 km) to the southeast of the Australian mainland, is New Zealand. It, too, boasts many unique plants and animals, including kiwis and other flightless birds.

NEW ZEALAND ALPS

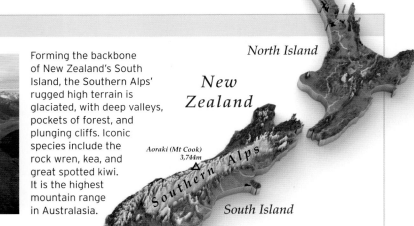

Forming the backbone of New Zealand's South Island, the Southern Alps' rugged high terrain is glaciated, with deep valleys, pockets of forest, and plunging cliffs. Iconic species include the rock wren, kea, and great spotted kiwi. It is the highest mountain range in Australasia.

North Island

New Zealand

Aoraki (Mt Cook) 3,744m △

Southern Alps

South Island

NEW GUINEA MONTANE FOREST
Remote tropical highlands form a biodiversity stronghold

Situated almost on the equator, New Guinea is the world's second-largest island. Politically it is divided into two halves: Indonesia in the west and Papua New Guinea in the east. The island's biodiversity, among the richest in the world, is a blend of Australian and Asian wildlife, which arrived here hundreds of thousands of years ago before the continents and New Guinea diverged.

Protected by terrain
Despite two centuries of encroachment by logging, agriculture, livestock, and mineral exploitation—which is persistently increasing—around two-thirds of New Guinea is still cloaked in forest, due mainly to the island's inaccessibly mountainous terrain. The upland forests are broadly organized into the Vogelkop (Bird's Head) montane rainforests in the northwest Doberai Peninsula, the Central Ranges rainforests along the backbone of the

island, and the Huon Peninsula rainforests in the northwest. The moist, tropical climate encourages riotous growth. Populations of plants and animals, isolated in steep, remote valleys and on scattered peaks, have evolved into thousands of species found nowhere else on the planet.

Active volcanoes and earthquakes continue to create new land forms, encouraging further diversity. So does altitude; lower hills are hot and steamy, while taller peaks are cooler and cloud-shrouded. These forests harbor more than 6,000 plant species and dozens of unique birds and mammals, including egg-laying echidnas and marsupials such as tree-kangaroos.

BOWER BUILDER
The Vogelkop bowerbird assembles a highly designed structure, or bower, of twigs, stems, and leaves decorated with flowers, shells, and other bright items. All his effort is aimed at one thing: to impress females enough to attract a mate.

VOGELKOP BOWERBIRD

POCKET PREDATOR
Dasyures are Australasian carnivorous marsupials, such as the quoll and Tasmanian devil. One of the smallest is New Guinea's speckled dasyure, a Central Ranges inhabitant that hunts various species of insects, worms, and grubs.

SPECKLED DASYU...

Home to all four echidna species

Dozens of new species found here each year

HOODED PITOHUI

POISONOUS BIRD
Tests in the late 1980s showed that the hooded pitohui's skin and feathers exude the nerve poison homobatrachotoxin, which causes numbness and tingling if touched by humans. Furthermore, the toxin has since been found in other pitohui species.

LOCATION

New Guinea's montane rainforests run west to east at altitudes of 3,280–9,840 ft (1,000–3,000 m), mainly along the Central Ranges.

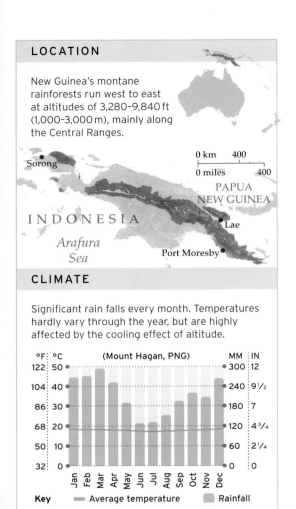

0 km 400
0 miles 400

PAPUA NEW GUINEA

Sorong

INDONESIA

Arafura Sea

Lae

Port Moresby

CLIMATE

Significant rain falls every month. Temperatures hardly vary through the year, but are highly affected by the cooling effect of altitude.

°F	°C	(Mount Hagan, PNG)	MM	IN
122	50		300	12
104	40		240	9½
86	30		180	7
68	20		120	4¾
50	10		60	2¼
32	0		0	0

Jan Feb Mar Apr May Jun Jul Aug Sep Oct Nov Dec

Key — Average temperature ▮ Rainfall

Common spotted cuscus

Spilocuscus maculatus

male's coat more spotted and patched than female's

A mainly nocturnal, tree-living marsupial, the common spotted cuscus has a woolly pelt that is prized by hunters, who also kill it for its meat. The cuscus sleeps on branches with its head tucked between its legs, often pulling large leaves around itself to hide from predators.

▷ **TELLING TAIL**
As well as its five-toed feet, the cuscus climbs with its prehensile tail—the lower half is naked on the inside to better grip branches.

↔ 14–18 in (36–45 cm)
⚖ 3–8 lb (1.4–3.6 kg)
✖ Common
🍽 Fruit, flowers, leaves

Papua New Guinea, N. Australia

Long-beaked echidna

Zaglossus bartoni

Protective white spines cover the eastern long-beaked echidna's head, back, and sides, but are almost hidden beneath its coarse, dark fur. This species is the largest of the monotremes, the group of egg-laying mammals that also includes the duck-billed platypus. Males have hind ankle spurs, and both female and male long-beaked echidnas use the electroreceptors in their snout to detect their prey's electric fields.

▽ **WORM HUNTER**
When foraging for earthworms, echidnas probe the soil with their long snout. They grasp the worms with their tongue, which has a spinelike structure at the back.

↔ 24–39 in (61–100 cm)
⚖ 11–22 lb (5–10 kg)
✖ Critically endangered
🍽 Earthworms

New Guinea

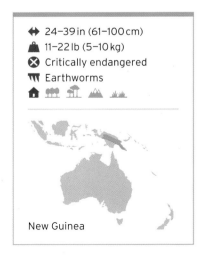

RARE BUTTERFLY
New Guinea has a diverse array of birdwings, or large swallowtail butterflies. The rare Rothschild's birdwing, which has a wingspan of 6–7 in (15–18 cm), is found only at 8,200 ft (2,500 m) in the Doberai Peninsula.

World's highest island

ROTHSCHILD'S BIRDWING

ears swivel to
detect prey

Sugar glider
Petaurus breviceps

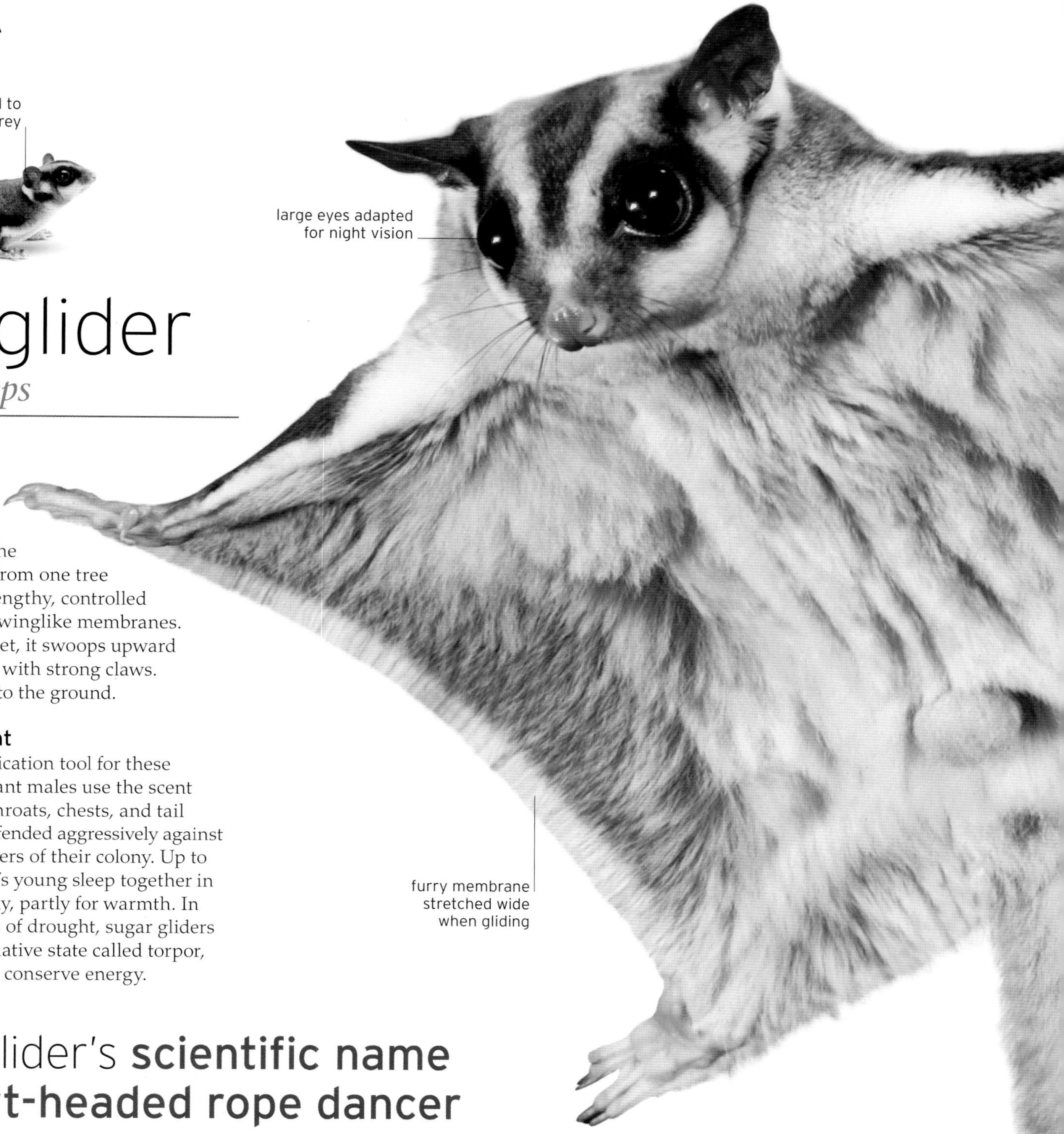

large eyes adapted
for night vision

The most widespread of all glider species, this highly social marsupial's most striking characteristic is its method of locomotion. The sugar glider launches itself from one tree and coasts to the next in a lengthy, controlled glide, courtesy of two furry winglike membranes. Just before it reaches its target, it swoops upward to land, clinging to the bark with strong claws. Sugar gliders rarely venture to the ground.

The importance of scent
Smell is a complex communication tool for these nocturnal possums. Dominant males use the scent glands on their foreheads, throats, chests, and tail region to mark territory—defended aggressively against intruders—as well as members of their colony. Up to seven adults and the season's young sleep together in leaf-lined tree hollows by day, partly for warmth. In cold or wet weather or times of drought, sugar gliders can enter a daily semihibernative state called torpor, lasting for up to 13 hours, to conserve energy.

furry membrane
stretched wide
when gliding

The sugar glider's **scientific name** means **short-headed rope dancer**

long rudderlike tail
helps control
direction of glide

◁ **HITCHING A RIDE**
Young sugar gliders, called joeys, frequently cling to their mother's back as she goes in search of food.

△ **LICKING SAP**
Sugar gliders use large incisors to chisel into tree bark, exposing the sap that makes up a large part of their diet.

Goodfellow's tree kangaroo
Dendrolagus goodfellowi

With its broad face, short muzzle, and rounded ears, Goodfellow's tree kangaroo's head resembles that of a bear more than that of a ground-dwelling kangaroo. Shorter, independently moving hindlegs, powerful shoulders, and longer, muscular front legs are other differences—as is the fact that it spends much of its time in trees, feeding mainly on leaves, as well as fruit and flowers. It is largely nocturnal and solitary except when breeding, which occurs year-round.

Flexible climber

Goodfellow's tree kangaroo climbs by grasping a trunk or branch with its strong front claws, then "walking" up or along it with its hindlegs. Flexible ankle joints and greater dexterity allow easy movement among branches, and it has a larger brain in proportion to body size than many marsupials. It also descends to the ground to find food, where it both walks and hops.

Like most tree kangaroos, Goodfellow's is most at risk from habitat loss due to logging and other forms of forest clearance. It is also hunted for meat.

▷ **BALANCING ACT**
Broad, padded hindfeet give tree kangaroos excellent grip, while a long tail aids stability on branches.

↔ 21–32 in (53–81 cm)
⚖ 14–32 lb (6.5–14.5 kg)
✖ Endangered
🌱 Leaves, fruit, flowers, grass
🏠 🏛 ⛰

New Guinea

◁ **GLIDING AROUND**
The gliding membrane stretches from wrist to ankle, allowing the sugar glider to parachute between trees up to 295 ft (90 m) apart.

↔ 6–9 in (15–23 cm)
⚖ 3–6 oz (85–170 g)
✖ Common
🌱 Sap, flowers, insects, spiders
🏠 🌳 🏛 🏡

SE. Asia, New Guinea, N. to W. Australia

Crested berrypecker
Paramythia montium

As is typical of animal species living at varying altitudes, crested berrypeckers in high forests are bigger than those lower down. Groups join mixed flocks to roam the forest canopy or gather in fruiting trees.

Crested berrypecker pairs are monogamous, building open, cup-shaped nests of moss and other plant materials. The female incubates the eggs alone, but both parents care for the chicks, which fledge after 15 days.

▷ **COURTING APPEAL**
Normally slim and sleek, the male stretches upright, puffs out his plumage, and raises his crest to maximize his appeal when courting.

↔ 9 in (23 cm)
⚖ 1–2 oz (28–61 g)
✖ Locally common
🌱 Fruit, berries, insects
🏠 🏛 ⛰

New Guinea

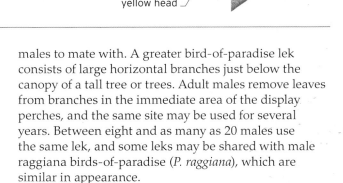

raised yellow plumes

black and
yellow head

Greater bird-of-paradise

Paradisaea apoda

More than 40 species of birds-of-paradise survive today, almost all in the dense forests of New Guinea, although a few extend into Indonesia and northern Australia. The greater bird-of-paradise is the largest in its family, and is roughly the size and shape of a crow, with strong, scaly legs and feet and a pointed beak. It is chiefly vegetarian, eating fruit and seeds as well as a few small insects.

Some species are relatively drab and form stable breeding pairs. Others are polygynous, with the more ornate males mating with several females. The males of these species boast beautiful feathers that have evolved into many kinds of plumes and springlike shafts, loops, spirals, and extensive iridescent shawls. Male greater birds-of-paradise have spectacular plumes that extend back from their flank, but which can be raised and spread, giving the impression that their whole body is adorned with long, wide sickles of maroon, white, and golden yellow. The females are dark maroon-brown and free of such eye-catching adornments.

Display perches

The males of polygynous species display at special sites called leks, where females assess their remarkable courtship dances and choose only the brightest, fittest males to mate with. A greater bird-of-paradise lek consists of large horizontal branches just below the canopy of a tall tree or trees. Adult males remove leaves from branches in the immediate area of the display perches, and the same site may be used for several years. Between eight and as many as 20 males use the same lek, and some leks may be shared with male raggiana birds-of-paradise (*P. raggiana*), which are similar in appearance.

Frenetic performance

Lekking male greater birds-of-paradise wave their wings and raise their long plumes, then briefly pose with spread plumes and arched, half-open wings. Competing males leap around each other, bouncing on a branch, flapping their wings and shaking their plumes. When they lean over and hang upside down, it is sometimes hard to tell which end is which. They keep up a chorus of loud, echoing *wa-wa-wa-wa-wah* sounds, while the females watch quietly then pick a favored male to mate with.

As with all the polygynous species, the male plays no part in nesting or the raising of young. The female builds a basin-shaped nest out of leaves and vine tendrils and lays one or two eggs.

Rumors of **"visitors from paradise"** reached Europe before these birds were first **described by naturalists**

◁ **DAWN DISPLAY**
During courtship, the male curves his yellow flank plumes over drooped wings and builds up to a trembling, shuddering performance designed to win a female's favors.

↔ 17–18in (42–45cm)

🗍 6oz (170g)

✖ Locally common

🍴 Fruit, seeds, insects

🏠 🏛

SE. Asia, New Guinea

NORTH AUSTRALIA SAVANNAS
Unique tropical grasslands where insects rule

In most regions, grasslands tend to be dominated by a few species of grasses and large grazing mammals. In Australia's tropical north, these savannas stretch roughly 0.6 million sq miles (1.5 million sq km) and harbor a more mixed range of plants and animals, and a greater variety of scenery, from typical rolling plains to rocky gorges hiding secret, almost rainforestlike thickets.

The Wet and the Dry
The scattered trees that dot the savanna and clumps of sparse woodland are mostly eucalypts, or gums. "The Wet," or rainy season, is reliable, with evergreen trees and shrubs thriving where there are occasional floods and temporary lakes, and acacias grow in the drier south. During six to eight months of "the Dry," grasses shrivel to gray-brown and some trees shed leaves to curtail water loss.

This seasonality, along with generally poor soils, and Australia's distinctive wildlife due to its prehistoric isolation, mean that large native mammals, chiefly kangaroos, wallaroos, and wallabies, are relatively few in variety. Instead, most plant consumption and recycling is carried out by insects, especially termites. Their mounds, the tallest sometimes reaching 16 ft (5 m), dot the landscape in thousands, and their underground lifestyles and foraging for dead wood and plant matter allow them to survive the Dry. In addition, a rich variety of reptiles, such as the inimitable frilled lizard, and small marsupials, also live here.

POINTING NORTH
So-called "magnetic termites" build 7 ft (2 m) tall mounds, facing north-south —not to do with Earth's magnetic field but to control temperature. The Sun's heat is side-on at midday so the mound stays cool.

TERMITE MOUNDS

COMPETING CATS
With so many smaller marsupial mammals in the tropical savannas, these are a rich hunting ground for introduced cats. In particular, feral cats compete with a native "marsupial cat," the northern quoll, whose numbers are declining.

NORTHERN QUOL

Temperatures often exceed 122°F (50°C)

More tr

JARRAH

Six times the size of the UK

LIFE AFTER FIRE
Like many local trees, the jarrah (a eucalypt tree) is adapted to occasional lightning-sparked fires—its underground part, or lignotuber, grows back. More frequent, extensive burns by livestock farmers threaten it and other vegetation species.

Dingo
Canis lupus dingo

irregular white patches on feet

Dingoes originated thousands of years ago in mainland Asia, where populations still remain. However, interbreeding with domestic dogs has made genetically pure numbers impossible to estimate. Persecuted as a pest, this species is vital to Australia's biodiversity, helping to keep introduced animals such as feral cats, European rabbits, and red foxes under control, which devastate indigenous wildlife.

↔ 3 ft (0.9 m)

⚖ 21–43 lb (9.5–19.5 kg)

✖ Vulnerable

♈ Rabbits, mice, wallabies, birds

🏠 🌳 🌿 🌾

SE. Asia, Australia

◁ **WATCHING OVER THE PUPS**
Only the dominant female in a dingo pack breeds and gives birth, and her pups are cared for by all pack members.

Spectacled hare wallaby
Lagorchestes conspicillatus

A spectacled hare wallaby is built to conserve water. It has the most efficient kidneys of all mammal species, allowing this nocturnal marsupial to extract moisture from food, and then produces concentrated urine. It also recycles its own breath moisture straight to its stomach. During the day, when temperatures soar, hare wallabies shelter under thick clumps of grass, which also hide them from predators such as nonnative cats and foxes.

↔ 16–19 in (40–48 cm)

⚖ 3–10 lb (1.4–4.5 kg)

✖ Common

♈ Grass, herbs, fruit

🏠 🌾

SW. Australia

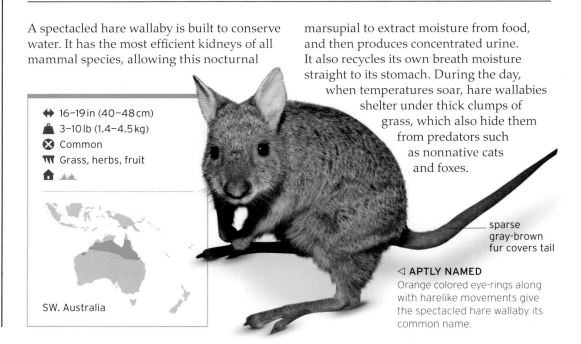

sparse gray-brown fur covers tail

◁ **APTLY NAMED**
Orange colored eye-rings along with harelike movements give the spectacled hare wallaby its common name.

LOCATION

The savannas cover one-fifth of the continent, blending into deserts to the west and forests to the east.

Timor Sea

Darwin

Gulf of Carpentaria

Cairns

Townsville

0 km   500
0 miles   500

AUSTRALIA

CLIMATE

With steady tropical temperatures and pronounced wet and dry seasons, over four-fifths of rain falls between December and March.

°F	°C	(Katherine, Northern Territory)	MM	IN
122	50		260	10
104	40		208	8
86	30		156	6
68	20		104	4
50	10		52	2
32	0		0	0

Jan Feb Mar Apr May Jun Jul Aug Sep Oct Nov Dec

Key   — Average temperature   ▢ Rainfall

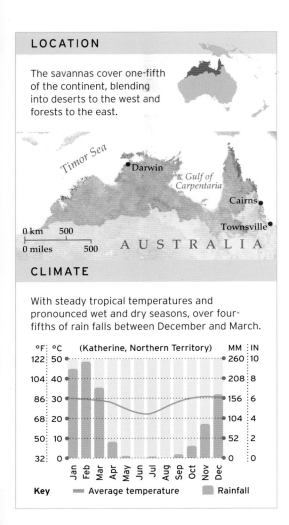

SEED EATERS
More than half of Australia's 90-plus species of seed-eating birds such as the Gouldian finch frequent the tropical savanna, flying extensively between productive areas. Like so much wildlife, they are at risk from new burning regimes.

bird species live here

GOULDIAN FINCH

male has pale neck; female's is black

Emu
Dromaius novaehollandiae

Australia's largest bird, the emu, has thin, double-shafted feathers, like its equally flightless relatives, cassowaries. Unlike the rounder feathers of Africa's ostrich and South America's rheas, the emu's plumage is more like coarse hair, with a part along the back.

Emus form large flocks only when forced to move in search of food or water. The female initiates pair formation, circling a male and making low drumming sounds. Later, booming calls, amplified by an inflatable sac, can be heard 1 miles (1.6 km) away. Females fight fiercely for access to males, or to repel potential competitors. Pairs stay together for several months before egg laying. Incubating males do not eat or drink for eight weeks, but females play no part in caring for the chicks, unlike the "major hen" in ostrich groups, and may move on to mate with another male.

Problems and solutions

In 1932, cereal farmers in Western Australia asked the army to exterminate the state's emus because they were damaging crops, but the initiative failed. Today, many of the birds are fenced into "emu refuges," but these enclosures can prove lethal during a drought as the emus are not free to find water. Their natural predators include dingoes and wedge-tailed eagles, as well as reptiles, which try to take the eggs.

powerful joints

▷ **DESIGNED TO RUN**
Emus have calf muscles and three-toed feet designed for running. They can cover long distances with a trotting speed of around 5 mph (8 km/h). They can also bolt at up to 30 mph (48 km/h) with 9 ft (2.7 m) strides.

◁ **WATCHFUL FATHER**
The male emu incubates the eggs and protects growing chicks, even chasing off the female.

↔ 6–7 ft (1.8–2.1 m)
🏋 66–132 lb (30–60 kg)
✖ Common
🌾 Seeds, berries
🏠 🌳 🌵 🌿

Australia

Blue-winged kookaburra

Dacelo leachii

Kookaburras, famous for their rising and falling "jackass" braying calls, are "tree kingfishers" of Australia and New Guinea. They perch conspicuously in trees, looking around from side to side, and drop to the ground to catch their prey. They concentrate especially on big insects, small reptiles, and frogs, although anything from worms to small birds and rodents are dealt with by the wide, heavy beak. The blue-winged kookaburra is slightly smaller than the more familiar laughing kookaburra, and has a particularly prolonged, manic laughing and cackling call.

Helpful big brother

Kookaburras pair for life and are assisted in defending their nest and raising their young by one or two male "helpers" from earlier broods, an uncommon system in birds. The female incubates her eggs in a hollow in a high tree branch, where they are vulnerable to snakes. Usually two or three chicks survive and fly after 36 days, but it takes 10 weeks before they are fully independent.

↔ 15–17 in (38–43 cm)
⚖ 11 oz (310 g)
✖ Common
🍴 Insects, reptiles, frogs, fish

S. Papua New Guinea, NW. to NE. Australia

◁ **BEGGING FOR FOOD**
Chicks compete with each other for food, and two or three older chicks may kill the weakest, youngest one while they are still in the nest.

Plumed whistling-duck

Dendrocygna eytoni

Although whistling-ducks often graze on dry land, they require easy access to water. They feed mainly at night and may fly up to 20 miles (30 km) to reach favored feeding places. Their nests are lined with soft grass, not with down plucked from the female's own body.

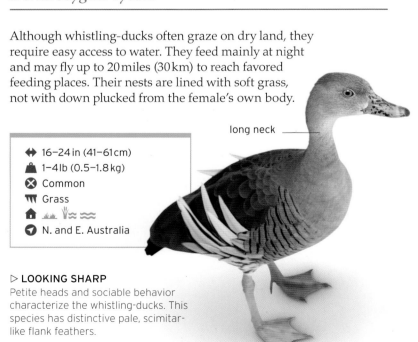

long neck

↔ 16–24 in (41–61 cm)
⚖ 1–4 lb (0.5–1.8 kg)
✖ Common
🍴 Grass
📍 N. and E. Australia

▷ **LOOKING SHARP**
Petite heads and sociable behavior characterize the whistling-ducks. This species has distinctive pale, scimitar-like flank feathers.

Purple-crowned fairy wren

Malurus coronatus

One of 14 species of fairy wrens that forage in dense low growth, the purple-crowned fairy wren is found in long grass close to a river. Males have brilliant blue patterns. A male and female form a pair to raise the young, but each mates with other birds and helps raise the chicks from those pairings too, creating a complex social structure.

↔ 6 in (15 cm)
⚖ $5/16$–$7/16$ oz (9–13 g)
✖ Common
🍴 Insects
📍 N. Australia

◁ **UPRIGHT TAIL**
The cocked tail seemed familiar when Europeans first reached Australia, but fairy wrens are not related to Northern Hemisphere wrens.

A **frilled lizard** can give a **painful bite** with two long, **fanglike teeth** in its lower jaw

△ **ESCAPE MODE**
When fleeing, this mainly tree-living lizard runs on two legs. As it picks up speed, its front end lifts off the ground so it is propelled only by its hindlegs.

mouth held open when frill erected to intimidate predators

long tail raised
when threatened

Frilled lizard

Chlamydosaurus kingii

This iconic member of the agamid or "dragon" family—which also includes Australia's moloch or thorny devil—is famous for its remarkable self-defense display. When threatened, the frilled lizard erects and flutters its highly colored throat-and-neck ruff of elastic skin, using muscles attached to its jaws, tongue, and the rods of cartilage that support the frill. It opens its large mouth wide to show the pale inner lining, raises and flicks its tail or swipes it against the ground, and hisses loudly. The lizard may also stand almost erect on its hindlegs, or hop from one leg to the other, while waving its front limbs to scare off predators, such as snakes, lizards, eagles, feral cats, and quolls (catlike marsupials).

Designed to startle

The sudden, intimidating threat display startles many of the lizard's enemies into pausing. This gives it time to run away, usually up a nearby trunk—trees are its main home and hunting place—or among rocks. At these times, the umbrellalike frill lies furled almost flat over the upper back and shoulders.

The frilled lizard uses its frill-erecting display for other reasons as well as defense: males repel intruders from their territory with it, and at breeding time it helps to deter rival males. Both sexes display to impress potential mates. The neck frill also plays an important role in controlling body temperature, acting at times as a sunshade, absorber of the sun's warmth, or radiator of excess body heat.

Temperature dependence

Breeding usually occurs from September to November, as the rains promise an abundance of food, especially insects such as ants, termites, cicadas, and caterpillars. After mating, the female digs a nest hole in loose soil and lays 5–20 soft-shelled eggs, then leaves—there is no maternal care. The eggs take around 10 weeks to hatch. The sex of the young is partially dependent on temperature. Both sexes develop from eggs incubated at temperatures of 84–95°F (29–35°C), but at temperatures above and below this range, the young produced are exclusively female. When the babies dig their way out of the nest, they are capable of putting on a full-frontal frill display straight away.

◁ **THREAT DISPLAY**
When in danger, the lizard may display its frilled neck and simply stand its ground, or it may lunge at the adversary in mock attack, snapping its jaws, and scratching with its claws.

▷ **ARBOREAL LIFESTYLE**
A frilled lizard spends up to 90 percent of its time on trees. When lying still, or resting, it is very well camouflaged as bark. The lizard can be speedy and agile when it is in search of ants and bugs.

↔ 28–36 in (71–91 cm)
⚖ 18–28 oz (510–794 g)
⊗ Common
Insects, spiders, amphibians

S. New Guinea,
N. Australia

Green tree frog

Litoria caerulea

The large, docile green tree frog is a common sight in the tropical regions of Australia. It spends the day hiding from the sun in damp crevices and emerges at night to hunt. Green tree frogs call all year, but only do so from the ground during the late summer breeding season. Eggs are glued to vegetation in still waters, and the tadpoles transform into adults in six weeks.

↔ 2–4 in (5–10 cm)
🍂 Spring and summer
✖ Common
🐛 Insects, mice
🏠 🌳 🌴 🌾 🌱 ≈ ≋ 🏚
⊘ S. New Guinea, N. and E. Australia

◁ **CLINGING ON**
This frog usually lives in woodland trees close to water sources, but is often found in outside bathrooms.

Redback spider

Latrodectus hasseltii

This small but potentially deadly species is one of the highly venomous widow spiders, so named because the female often eats the male after mating. The male is less than a third the size of the female and lurks cautiously on the periphery of her untidy web hoping to steal leftover scraps from the insects she snares.

↔ ⅛–⅜ in (0.3–1 cm)
✖ Common
🐛 Insects
🏠 🏭 🌾 🏚
⊘ Australia

▽ **KILLER BITE**
The female kills prey with a venom that is powerful enough to endanger humans unless an antivenin is taken.

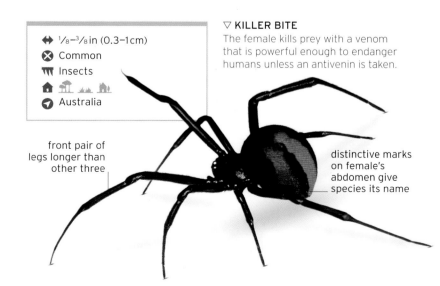

front pair of legs longer than other three

distinctive marks on female's abdomen give species its name

Green jumping spider

Mopsus mormon

female has dark red and white face mask

This is the largest jumping spider in Australia. Generally, a jumping spider's fangs are too tiny to pierce human skin, but this species can manage it and delivers a painful, although ultimately harmless, bite. The green jumping spider hunts on leaves and stalks for insect prey, ambushing them with a long jump that can be several times the spider's body length. Wherever it goes, the spider lets out a safety line of silk in case it loses its footing. However, jumps are seldom off target thanks to the acute vision afforded by two huge forward-facing eyes, supported by six others elsewhere on the head.

Long courtship

Jumping spiders are cautious of each other, and males must spend a lot of time earning their mate's trust. The male begins by plucking love messages on the female's nest and silk lines and by stroking her abdomen. This courtship generally occurs while the female is still a nonbreeding subadult. The male sets up home next to the female's nest and waits for her to molt into a fully mature form and is ready to mate.

The nest is a crudely woven sheet of silk made on the concave side of long, narrow leaves. It has three sections. The female lives at one end and guards the middle section that will house the eggs. The male builds the far end.

↔ ⅜–¾ in (1.2–1.8 cm)
✖ Common
🐛 Insects
🏠 🌳 🏚

N. Australia

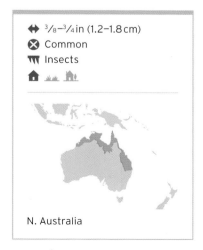

▷ **SNATCHING A BITE**
A large but delicate damselfly succumbs to the swift strike of a green jumping spider camouflaged on a green patch of leaf.

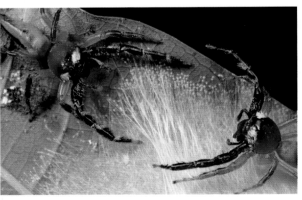

△ **BY A WHISKER**
Males sport side whiskers and a hairy top knot not seen in females. This sexual difference allows males to identify rivals easily.

◁ **BATTLE FORMATION**
Two male green jumping spiders size each other up before a fight. Interactions between members of this species are frequently aggressive.

GREAT SANDY-TANAMI DESERT
Australia's vast northwestern deserts are rich in wildlife

The Great Sandy and Tanami deserts sport a range of semiarid to arid habitats, from shifting dunes of loose sand to windswept bare rock to low rolling plains dominated by shrubby hummocks of Australia's endemic dryland grass known as spinifex. In various forms, spinifex covers almost one-fifth of the entire continent. In the far southeast of the ecoregion squats the glowing sandstone mound of Uluru, formerly known as Ayers Rock.

Grass-based food chain
Spinifex's sharp, silica-rich, abrasive leaves deter many large grazing animals, yet the soft new shoots and plentiful seeds produced after rain feed a myriad of small creatures. These range from ants, termites, beetles, and cicadas to small parrots such as the budgerigar, or parakeet, as well as the painted firetail and the omnivorous dusky grass wren. Tiny native mice, including

the spinifex hopping mouse and sandy inland mouse, also depend on it. Grass-dwelling insects feed reptiles such as thorny devils and knob-tailed geckoes, and also the smallest marsupial: the shrewlike long-tailed planigale. Farther up the food chains are larger hunters such as the desert death adder, gray falcon, and Australia's largest bird of prey, the wedge-tailed eagle.

This web of life is diverse but sporadic, thriving after downpours, then struggling to survive for months, even years, if the summer rains fail. In recent decades the desert ecology has been unbalanced by introduced grazing animals that can survive on spinifex, especially feral donkeys and camels.

ELUSIVE HUNTER
The gray falcon is a keen hunter of small birds and some small mammals. Because it has a large range and is difficult to identify in the wild, estimated numbers are problematic. Due to habitat loss, however, they are thought to be declining.

GRAY FALCON

NOMADIC FLOCKS
More familiar as a caged bird, the budgerigar is a native of Australian deserts. Large, colorful, chattering flocks fly between seed-rich areas and oases in the wild, and livestock water supplies have helped to extend their range.

BUDGERIGARS

BLACK-FOOTED ROCK WALLABY

Has dune ridges up to 30 miles (50 km) long

One of Australia's least populated areas

DESERTED WALLABIES
The black-footed rock wallaby feeds during darker, cooler, and damper hours and gains what water it needs from food. Increasing numbers of introduced grazing animals have fragmented its dwindling populations.

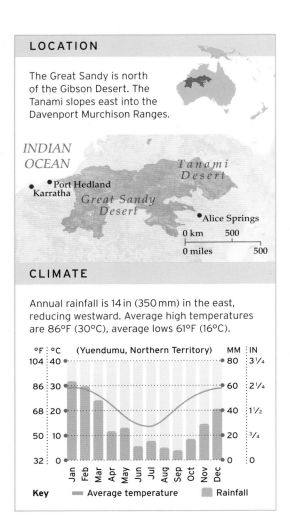

INDIAN
OCEAN

Port Hedland
Karratha
*Tanami
Desert*
*Great Sandy
Desert*
Alice Springs

0 km   500
0 miles   500

CLIMATE

Annual rainfall is 14 in (350 mm) in the east, reducing westward. Average high temperatures are 86°F (30°C), average lows 61°F (16°C).

(Yuendumu, Northern Territory)

°F	°C		MM	IN
104	40		80	3¼
86	30		60	2¼
68	20		40	1½
50	10		20	¾
32	0		0	0

Jan Feb Mar Apr May Jun Jul Aug Sep Oct Nov Dec

Key — Average temperature   ▉ Rainfall

Fat-tailed dunnart
Sminthopsis crassicaudata

Despite its mouselike appearance, the fat-tailed dunnart is a marsupial that mainly feeds on insects, but also eats small lizards. Found in habitats ranging from open woodland and grassland to desert, these nocturnal mammals conserve energy by huddling in communal nests built under logs or rocks during colder weather; they can also enter a state of torpor for up to a few days when food is short.

↔ 2–4 in (5–10 cm)
⚖ ³⁄₈–¾ oz (10–20 g)
✖ Common
🐾 Moths, beetles, lizards

Australia

pointed snout

◁ **FAT STORE**
A dunnart's tail holds excess fat, which supplies it with energy when food is scarce.

Southern marsupial mole
Notoryctes typhlops

creamy yellow to golden fur

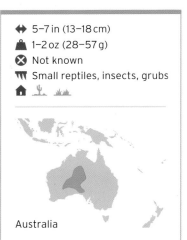

Southern marsupial moles resemble true moles, but belong to a separate order, Notoryctemorphia. These underground dwellers are effectively blind, with vestigial eyes, and also lack external ears. They do not use tunnels; instead, the soil collapses behind them as they move forward.

↔ 5–7 in (13–18 cm)
⚖ 1–2 oz (28–57 g)
✖ Not known
🐾 Small reptiles, insects, grubs

Australia

◁ **DIGGING FOR DINNER**
A horny nose-shield, rigid neck, and huge, spadelike foreclaws allow southern marsupial moles to power through sandy soil in search of food.

SPIKY SHELTERS
Hugely important for so many arid Australian habitats, spinifex sends roots down 7 ft (2.1 m) or more for moisture. In doing so, it stabilizes wind-whipped sand and provides food and shelter for a myriad of small creatures.

A rich haven for lizards

SPINIFEX GRASS

large, sensitive ears

long, strong tail

Red kangaroo

Macropus rufus

Standing up to 7ft (2m) tall, the red kangaroo is the world's largest marsupial and the largest land animal in Australia. Its huge, muscular hindlegs enable it to hop along at speeds of up to 35mph (60km/h) for several minutes, covering several feet in a single bound, with its three-foot-long tail held out behind as a counterbalance.

Australia's sandy plains, semideserts, savanna, and scrubland are extremely harsh environments, but the red kangaroo is well adapted to these hot, dry, and largely barren landscapes. Mostly active at dawn and dusk, it retreats to the shade of trees or rocks during the hottest part of the day. It repeatedly licks its forelegs to regulate its body temperature—as the saliva evaporates, the blood flowing just under the skin is cooled.

Boomers and mobs

A highly nomadic species, the red kangaroo has no fixed home range. It roams large distances in search of fresh grass and leaves. The kangaroo lives in small groups of up to 10 animals that usually consist of one large adult male, known as a boomer, and several smaller females, which are only about half as heavy, plus a few young. If food is plentiful, several groups may join together to form a larger unit known as a mob.

Arrested development

Breeding is determined by the availability of food—red kangaroos may not breed at all during droughts. However, a reproductive system in which a female can have three offspring at the same time all at different stages of development allows maximum production of young when times are favorable. A female gives birth to a single baby following a short gestation of 32–34 days. This tiny joey climbs into its mother's pouch, attaches to a teat, and continues to develop. The female then mates again within days of giving birth, but development of this new embryo is suspended until the female's existing joey leaves the pouch at about eight months old. It will still be suckling from its mother when the next baby is born— the female's teats are able to produce milk independently of one another, allowing her to provide milk specific to the needs of each offspring.

More than **11.5 million red kangaroos live** in Australia's **hot, arid landscapes**

◁ **SWIFT HOPPER**
Hopping is very energy-efficient, especially at higher speeds. The hindlegs act like springs and so the thrust delivered when leaping uses little energy.

▷ **POUCHED JOEY**
The joey first pokes its head out of the pouch when it is about five months old. It leaves the pouch at eight months, but suckles milk for another four months.

- ↔ 3–5ft (1–1.6m)
- 🏋 55–200lb (25–90kg)
- ⊗ Common
- 🌾 Grasses, leaves
- 🏠 🌵 🌱

Australia

Thorny devil
Moloch horridus

Secure in its all-over prickly protection, the thorny devil moves with a characteristic slow, swaying, stiff-legged gait. If it senses danger, it stands still, relying on its superb camouflage. Faced with a predator such as a bird of prey or a goanna (a type of monitor lizard), this spiky lizard puffs up its body with air to make itself look bigger—and even harder to swallow. If attacked, it dips its head between its front legs to present the "fake head" on its neck; this fat-filled hump recovers quickly from any minor injury.

Trail meal

The thorny devil eats ants almost exclusively, feeding during the day, when ants are on the move. A favorite tactic is to locate a trail of foraging worker ants, stand next to it, then lick up each ant in turn, which it chews with its strong, shearing rear teeth. Solitary except when mating, the thorny devil shelters in a burrow or secluded place at night and also for several weeks during midsummer and midwinter. This desert-dweller obtains most of the water that it needs from fog that condenses on its scales when it emerges in the cool hours of early morning.

Thorny devils mate in late winter to early summer, with the smaller males approaching females to see if they are receptive. Females dig a burrow up to 8 in (20 cm) deep, lay 5–10 eggs, and fill it with sand. The hatchlings emerge three to four months later and take up to five years to grow to full size.

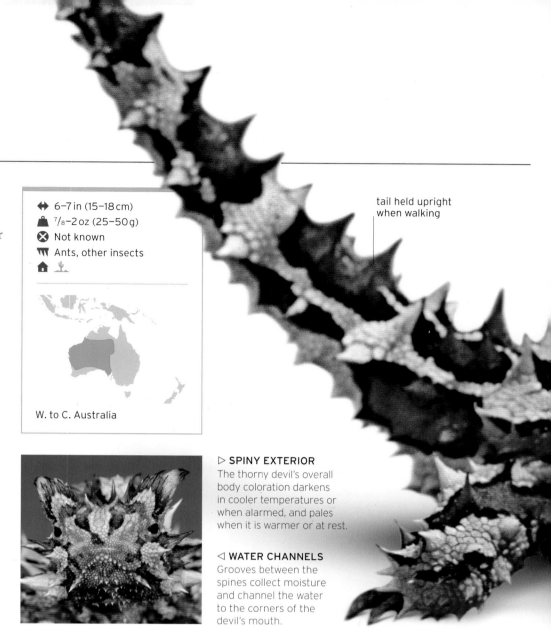

tail held upright when walking

↔ 6–7 in (15–18 cm)
⚖ ⁷⁄₈–2 oz (25–50 g)
✕ Not known
🐾 Ants, other insects
🏠 🌵

W. to C. Australia

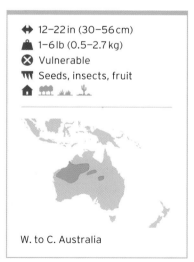

▷ **SPINY EXTERIOR**
The thorny devil's overall body coloration darkens in cooler temperatures or when alarmed, and pales when it is warmer or at rest.

◁ **WATER CHANNELS**
Grooves between the spines collect moisture and channel the water to the corners of the devil's mouth.

Greater bilby
Macrotis lagotis

The only survivor of Australia's six native bandicoot species, the greater bilby inhabited 70 percent of the country before European settlement. Today, mainly due to habitat loss and predation by introduced species such as the domestic cat, it occurs in less than 20 percent of its original range.

A nocturnal marsupial, the bilby uses its strong, three-clawed forelimbs to dig long, spiraling burrows where it sleeps during the day and shelters from dust storms. Huge ears, which give it the alternative name of rabbit-eared bandicoot, help it detect predators and prey, such as termites and ants, which it digs out with its claws. One of its favorite foods is the yalka, or bush onion, a bulb that only germinates in desert soil after fires.

↔ 12–22 in (30–56 cm)
⚖ 1–6 lb (0.5–2.7 kg)
✕ Vulnerable
🐾 Seeds, insects, fruit
🏠 🌳 ⛰ 🌵

W. to C. Australia

◁ **SNIFFING THE AIR**
A long, tapering snout and keen sense of smell make up for the bilby's poor eyesight, while long whiskers help bilbies navigate their environment.

A hungry devil can **lick up more than 1,000 ants** in one feeding session

fake head

spiky horns above eyes

brown, tan, and yellow coloration mimics sandy habitat

Woma python
Aspidites ramsayi

The nocturnal Woma python consumes mainly other reptiles, but its specialty is killing rodents in their burrows by crushing them against the wall. After winter mating, like most pythons, the female coils around her eggs to protect them and keep them warm by "shivering" until they hatch in spring.

↔ 5 ft (1.5 m)
⚖ 7–11 lb (3–5 kg)
✖ Endangered
🍖 Reptiles, birds, mammals
🏠 🌵 🌾
➤ Australia

muscular coils

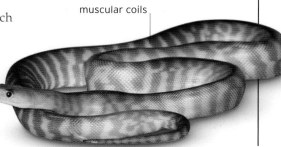

▷ **MARKED BANDING**
The Woma python has a slim head, distinctive banding along the powerful body, and a short, thin tail.

Blistered grasshopper
Monistria pustulifera

Also known as the arid painted pyrgomorph, this flightless, locustlike insect specializes in defoliating strong-scented emu, poverty, and turkey bushes. Blistered grasshoppers are cone-headed and have short antennae, known as horns. Females, which are almost twice as large as the males, lay eggs in soil and only hatch after a cold snap.

↔ Up to 3 in (7.6 cm)
✖ Not known
🍖 Leaves, shoots
🏠 🌵
➤ Australia

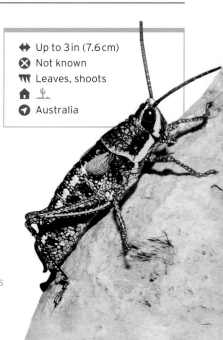

▷ **SPOTTED WARNING**
The "blisters" are yellow patches that warn potential predators of this grasshopper's foul-tasting flesh.

EAST AUSTRALIAN FORESTS

A damp corner of the drought continent

As moisture-laden winds from the Pacific Ocean rise over Australia's southeastern and eastern coast toward the Great Dividing Range, water vapor condenses into rain. This is especially true in the Australian Alps, where rainfall may exceed 90 in (2,300 mm) yearly, and in the Blue Mountains, near Sydney. Tasmania's hills commonly have winter snows, while 1,240 miles (2,000 km) north in southern Queensland, the climate is subtropical.

Eucalypt patchwork

Within this moist, warm mosaic are patches of temperate forest, dominated by more than 120 kinds of eucalypts, or gum trees. Upland eucalypts, especially the tall mountain ash gum, cloak rocky crags and steep gorges. More gum forests and acacia woods, including the golden wattle, grow on lower slopes, as well as ferns, banksias, and grevilleas. This ecoregion is home to some of Australia's most famous animals, including the Tasmanian devil, koala, duck-billed platypus, short-beaked echidna, laughing kookaburra, and Albert's lyrebird. However, human expansion has meant felling and conversion of forest to farmland, while introduced pests such as rabbits, foxes, and cats ravage the native wildlife.

More than **a fifth of Australia's eucalypts grow here,** but are threatened by **climate change**

LITTLE RED FLYING FOX

POLLINATING BAT
The little red flying fox visits eucalypt blossoms to lap up nectar and pollen and transfers the latter between trees in the process. This sometimes balances out the damage caused by its dense roosting habit, where dozens of the bats crowd on a few boughs of a tree.

Volatile eucalyptus oils give the Blue Mountains a colorful haze

WOLLEMI PINE

LIVING FOSSIL
The Wollemi pine caused a sensation when it was discovered by a Blue Mountains field officer in 1994. The sole survivor of a group dating from the dinosaur era, it grows only in a few locations.

Total area exceeds 193,000 sq miles (500,000 sq km)

EUCALYPTUS

THREATENED TREES
Eucalypt species range from the ice-hardy snow gum to frost-tender tallow-wood. Food for many animals, including koalas and possums, these forests are now heavily harvested and rarely regrow once felled.

NECTAR FACTORIES

Many banksias have large, colorful flower spikes with hundreds of nectar-producing blooms. This energy-packed liquid is vital food for marsupials such as honey and pygmy possums, and sugar and squirrel gliders, as well as bats.

The world's second-tallest tree, the mountain ash gum, grows here

HONEY POSSUM

COOPERATIVE FEEDERS

More than 20 honeyeater species coexist in the Blue Mountains, lapping up honey (nectar) with their brush-tipped tongues. They avoid competition by living at different altitudes, breeding at different times of year, and migration; regent honeyeaters, for example, prefer wetter, lowland sites.

REGENT HONEYEATER

Home to the endangered Leadbeater's possum

FOREST MAINTENANCE

One of the first marsupials to be described by European settlers, the long-nosed potoroo eats mycorrhizal fungi. These trufflelike underground fungi provide minerals to tree roots, receiving carbohydrates in return. The potoroo excretes fungal spores in its feces, thus spreading them to new trees.

LONG-NOSED POTOROO

LOCATION

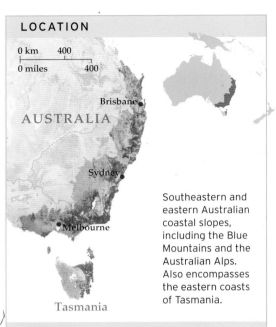

0 km 400
0 miles 400

AUSTRALIA

Brisbane

Sydney

Melbourne

Tasmania

Southeastern and eastern Australian coastal slopes, including the Blue Mountains and the Australian Alps. Also encompasses the eastern coasts of Tasmania.

CLIMATE

Southeastern Australia is generally warm and temperate, with plenty of rainfall throughout the year. Temperatures range from the subtropical in southern Queensland to low enough for snowfall accumulation in Tasmania's hills. Higher altitudes have the most rainfall.

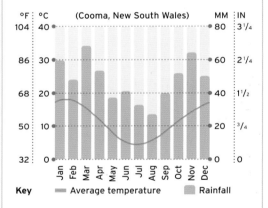

(Cooma, New South Wales)

°F	°C		MM	IN
104	40		80	3 1/4
86	30		60	2 1/4
68	20		40	1 1/2
50	10		20	3/4
32	0		0	0

Jan Feb Mar Apr May Jun Jul Aug Sep Oct Nov Dec

Key — Average temperature ▢ Rainfall

RABBIT PLAGUE

Perhaps Australia's worst invasive species, the European rabbit has devastated huge areas of vegetation, killed trees by bark-ringing, and outcompeted many herbivores. Even if 90 percent are destroyed in an area, the remainder restore the original population in 12-18 months because of the rabbits' rapid rate of reproduction.

Duck-billed platypus

Ornithorhynchus anatinus

With its ducklike bill, thick fur, and webbed feet, the platypus is one of Earth's most unusual animals, yet it possesses even more distinctive traits. One of just two living monotremes, or egg-laying mammals (the other is the echidna), the average body temperature of the platypus is 89.6°F (32°C), which is lower than most mammals, and its legs extend out, not down. These features are more common in reptiles. Males have a horny spur on the inside of each hind ankle that delivers a venomous sting to rivals vying for their breeding territory. Extremely painful to humans, the venom is strong enough to kill a domestic dog.

Sensory perception

A duckbilled platypus spends most of the day in its burrow, which it digs into an earth bank using its strong front claws. On land, the paddlelike webbing of the front feet folds beneath them, allowing the platypus to walk. It emerges to feed at night, rootling through the muddy bottom of shallow pools, where it detects prey with its bill's highly sensitive electroreceptors. These are capable of spotting the tail-flick of a crayfish from 6–8 in (15–20 cm) away. The platypus stores all the food it catches in its cheek pouches, at the back of the jaw. When it surfaces to breathe, the platypus uses the horny pads and ridges in its mouth to grind up the food before swallowing.

Platypuses mate during spring, and the female lays up to three eggs in a nesting burrow about three weeks later. She incubates them until they hatch, then feeds the young with milk, although not from nipples like other mammals. Female platypuses ooze milk directly through the skin on either side of their belly; the milk is sucked up by their young.

↔ 16–22 in (41–56 cm)
⚖ 2–5 lb (1–2.3 kg)
✖ Common
🍴 Insect larvae, crayfish
🏠 🌿 〰 〰

E. Australia, Tasmania

waterproof coat
with dense underfur

▽ **SOME HOAX**
Aboriginal legend says the platypus was born after a female duck mated with a water rat. When the first platypus skin arrived in Britain in 1799, it was thought to be a hoax.

smooth,
suedelike
skin covering

The **bill** of a platypus is **soft and rubbery**, not hard like a duck's

Common wombat
Vombatus ursinus

Common wombats spend up to two-thirds of their lives underground, in burrows excavated with sturdy front claws. An efficient digestive system allows them to extract the maximum energy from the nutrient-poor grasses that make up the bulk of their diet. Thick fur and a high tolerance for low-oxygen environments help them to survive underground, avoiding predators such as dingoes, red foxes, and Tasmanian devils. Despite their cuddly appearance, common wombats are solitary and fairly cantankerous, readily defending food sources or burrows; actual fighting, however, is rare.

They emerge mainly at dusk to feed, grazing on short grasses and other plants thanks to a split in their upper lip. Their rootless teeth keep growing throughout their lifetime.

△ **GRACEFUL SWIMMER**
A platypus moves easily through water using its heavily webbed front feet, while the hindfeet and tail help it change direction.

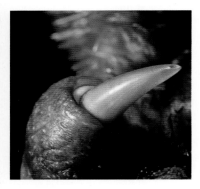

△ **UNIQUE STINGER**
Of all mammals, only male platypuses can deliver a venomous sting. Male echidnas also have horny ankle spurs, but lack functional venom glands.

- ↔ 28–47 in (71–119 cm)
- ⬛ 55–88 lb (25–40 kg)
- ✕ Common
- ᗰ Grass, sedges, roots, tubers
- 🏠 🌳 🌿

E. Australia, Tasmania

◁ **MOTHER AND JOEY**
Born the size of a jellybean, common wombat joeys remain with their mothers until they are around 17-20 months old.

broad tail acts as rudder when swimming

Parma wallaby
Macropus parma

small, thin forelimbs

The "parma" in this marsupial's name comes from an Aboriginal word for the species, rather than the city of Parma, Italy. Once thought to have been hunted to extinction, parma wallabies were rediscovered in New South Wales in 1967.

Mainly nocturnal, wallabies prefer forests with a dense, grassy understory that shields them from predators such as dingoes, red foxes, and some birds of prey. In addition to the grasses and herbs that make up the bulk of its diet, the parma wallaby also eats trufflelike fungi, the spores of which it helps to spread—and fertilize— via its feces.

- ↔ 18–21 in (45–53 cm)
- ⬛ 7–13 lb (3.2–6 kg)
- ✕ Near threatened
- ᗰ Grass, herbs, leaves, bark
- 🏠 🌳 🌳

E. Australia

◁ **WEIGHED DOWN**
A parma wallaby joey leaves the maternal pouch permanently only around the age of seven months.

▷ **EMBRYONIC BOND**
A baby koala spends six to seven months in its mother's pouch, which has a strong muscle at the entrance to keep the small joey from falling out.

rounded, white-tufted ears

short, powerful limbs

Koala

Phascolarctos cinereus

Koalas are marsupials that have evolved the unique ability to eat a plant that would poison other animals. They feed almost exclusively on eucalyptus leaves, but not just any eucalyptus will do. Koalas are choosy eaters, feeding only on a few of the 600-plus eucalyptus species found in Australia. They also avoid eating leaves from trees growing in poor soil because these are the most toxic.

Special adaptations

A fiber-digesting organ known as the cecum helps koalas to feed on eucalyptus without ill effects. In humans, this small pouch at the beginning of the large intestine is about 3 in (6.25 cm) long, but in koalas, it reaches 80 in (200 cm). The cecum contains millions of bacteria that break down the leaf fiber and toxic oils and enable absorption of nitrogen. A slow metabolic rate keeps food within the digestive system for extended periods. Even so, a koala absorbs only about 25 percent of what it consumes—so one animal must eat up to 1 lb (up to 500 g) of eucalyptus leaves a day in order to survive.

Fortunately, the koala's teeth are made for the job. Sharp front incisors cut leaves from stems, while molars shear and crush, breaking the food down before it reaches the cecum. While it chews, a koala stays safely anchored in a tree to avoid ground predators such as dogs. As well as sharp, curved claws, its paws have rough pads that grasp bark and branches. The front

paws have two digits that oppose the other three to give the animal a firm, fistlike grip. The koala's dense, thick coat varies from light gray in northern animals to dark-brown in southern ones. The soft, long, fur protects the koala from extreme temperatures as well as rain.

Mainly nocturnal, koalas are highly territorial animals; each adult maintains a home range within a breeding group, marking the trees it visits regularly with scratches. The males also scent-mark from a brown gland in the middle of their chests, which they rub on the base of trees.

Joey in a pouch

The breeding season lasts from August to February, punctuated by frequent bellowing from males. Females give birth to a single hairless, embryonic joey, roughly 1 in (2 cm) long and weighing less than a gram. The tiny joey climbs from the birth canal to its mother's pouch and once inside, latches on to one of her two teats. It stays there and develops, for about 22–30 weeks, when it begins to feed on "pap" as well as milk. Pap, a special type of dropping the mother produces, contains the microbes needed to digest eucalyptus leaves. Once large enough to leave the pouch, the joey rides on its mother's back, and stays with her until her next joey is born.

The main threats koalas face today are habitat loss and fragmentation due to logging and increasing urbanization—an estimated 4,000 koalas a year are killed by dogs and car accidents.

△ **TIME TO REST**
Eucalyptus leaves provide little energy, so when koalas are not sleeping up to 18 hours a day, they rest between bouts of feeding, cushioned on a dense pad of rump fur, to conserve energy.

◁ **FAVORITE FOOD**
A koala's diet is made up almost entirely of eucalyptus leaves, but it occasionally eats tea tree and wattle leaves as well.

↔ 26–32 in (65–82 cm)
⬛ 9–33 lb (4–15 kg)
✖ Common
🍴 Eucalyptus leaves
🏠 🌳

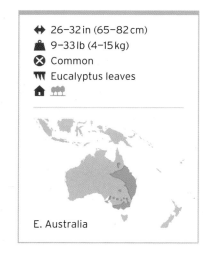

E. Australia

Koalas eat such large quantities of **eucalyptus leaves** that their body oil **smells like cough drops**

white patches on chest, sides, and rump

Tasmanian devil

Sarcophilus harrisii

The world's largest living carnivorous marsupial gets its name from the screeches and growls it produces during hunts for food. Tasmanian devils are predominantly scavengers, using their strong, wide jaws to devour the flesh, fur, and bone of often rotting animal carcasses. However, they will eat whatever is available, from insects to mammals, including "imps": young Tasmanian devils. Devils are equally unfussy about their habitat, provided they can find shelter during the day and food by night.

Uncertain future

Once common throughout Australia, today the species exists only in Tasmania, where it is critically endangered in the wild due to a contagious cancer called devil facial tumor disease (DFTD), spread from animal to animal through biting—a common occurrence when devils meet. To preserve the species, a national conservation program has established a DFTD-free captive "insurance population."

most powerful bite relative to body size of any animal

△ **HIDING OUT**
Young Tasmanian devils shelter in caves, hollow logs, or burrows to avoid predators such as eagles or other devils.

Tasmanian devils can **eat 40 percent of their body weight** in half an hour

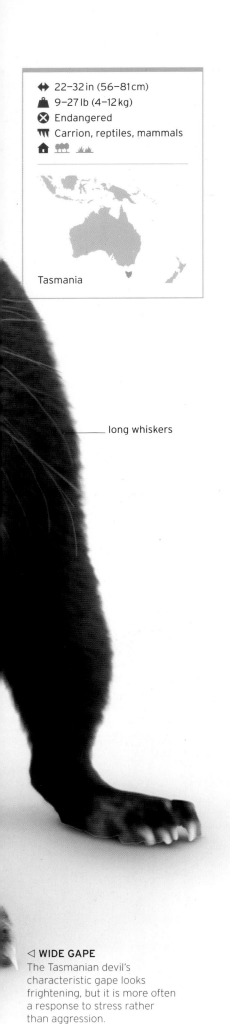

- 22–32 in (56–81 cm)
- 9–27 lb (4–12 kg)
- Endangered
- Carrion, reptiles, mammals

Tasmania

long whiskers

◁ **WIDE GAPE**
The Tasmanian devil's characteristic gape looks frightening, but it is more often a response to stress rather than aggression.

Tiger quoll

Dasyurus maculatus

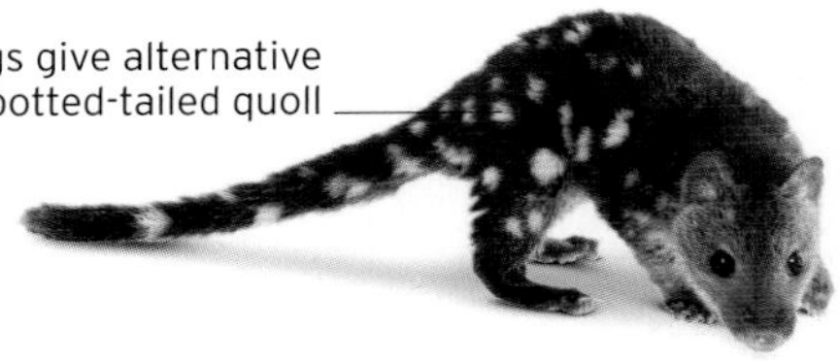

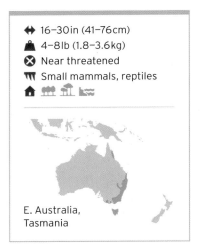

markings give alternative name of spotted-tailed quoll

The largest of six quoll species, the tiger quoll is a fierce nocturnal hunter that is as at home in trees as it is on the ground. This carnivorous marsupial prefers woodland habitats, and will venture into cleared farmland in search of food, despatching small mammals such as bandicoots and gliders with a powerful bite to the head or neck. Forest clearance is a major threat.

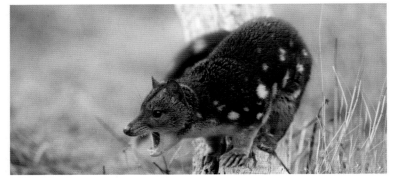

△ **HOLDING HER OWN**
Although much smaller than males, female tiger quolls are no less aggressive and have been seen chasing Tasmanian devils away from carcasses.

- 16–30 in (41–76 cm)
- 4–8 lb (1.8–3.6 kg)
- Near threatened
- Small mammals, reptiles

E. Australia, Tasmania

Sulfur-crested cockatoo

Cacatua galerita

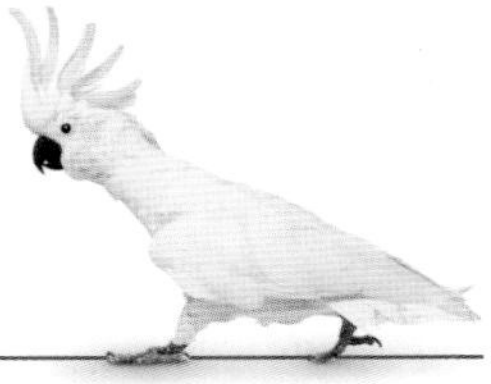

Sulfur-crested cockatoos have excellent foot-eye-bill coordination as they feed on seeds and fruits. They form large flocks in parts of Australia, and are sometimes dealt with as pests on cereal crops. The distinctive crest is usually held flat, but is raised in a fan up to 6 in (14 cm) high when the birds are excited, such as when mating.

- 20 in (50 cm)
- 34 oz (960 g)
- Common
- Seeds, nuts, fruit, crops

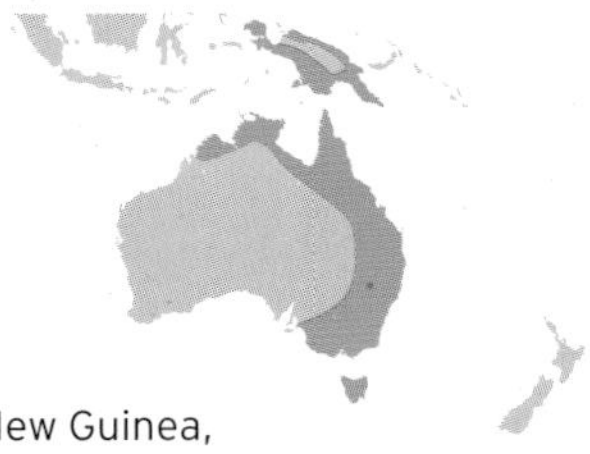

New Guinea, Australia, Tasmania

primrose yellow underwing

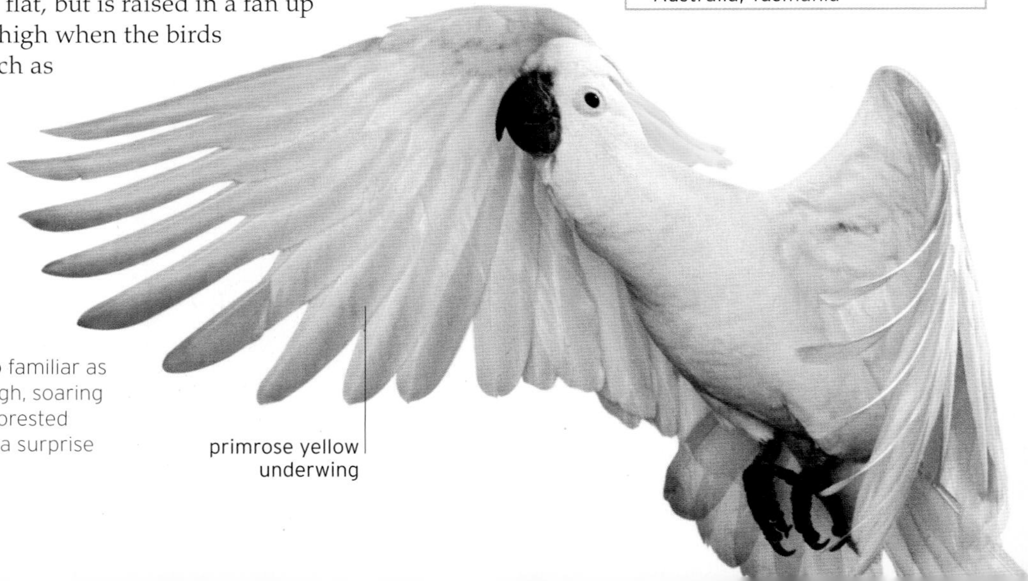

▷ **AIMING HIGH**
Cockatoos are so familiar as pets that their high, soaring flight far above forested slopes comes as a surprise in the wild.

long legs and claws for climbing

long, narrow tail aids swimming

Australian water dragon
Intellagama lesueurii

True to its name, this large lizard frequents many flowing freshwater habitats, from cool upland streams to city rivers, and even occasional estuaries. It is a proficient swimmer and also a capable climber.

Basking then hunting

The water dragon basks on rocks (or a road or patio) until it is warm enough to hunt—in trees, on the ground, and along the water's edge. It searches for snails and crabs as well as small vertebrates such as frogs and chicks. In some locations, however, fruit and vegetation comprise up to half of its diet. To avoid danger, the water dragon races up a tree or dives underwater, where it can stay submerged for more than an hour. In winter, water dragons living to the south of their range hide in a burrow, or among roots or rocks, and brumate (similar to hibernation); in the north, they remain active all year. In spring, territorial males display to rivals and to attract females with much head-bobbing, tail-flicking, and leg-flourishing. Hatchlings mainly eat insects until they are about half grown.

↔ 3 ft (1 m)
⚖ 2–3 lb (1–1.4 kg)
⊗ Not known
🍴 Small animals, fruit, plants
🏠 🌱 ≈ ≈ 🏘 🏔

E. Australia

large tympanum (external eardrum)

◁ SNUB-NOSED PROFILE
The short, deep snout and angular head is accentuated by a central crest of scales that runs from head to tail, enlarging considerably from the neck rearward.

Sydney funnelweb spider
Atrax robustus

This funnelweb is a member of the mygalomorph spider group, whose prominent fangs point straight down rather than diagonally as in other spiders. It spins its tube-shaped web in a cool, moist, shady site, under a rock or log—or an outhouse. Repeated bites quickly subdue its small prey; untreated, the venom may be fatal to humans.

In late summer, the smaller, longer-legged, wider-roaming male mates with the more sedentary female. She keeps the 100–150 eggs in a silken egg sac safe in her burrow. They hatch in three to four weeks and the spiderlings remain for a few more months.

▷ **GOOD VIBRATIONS**
Silk thread trip lines fan out from the web entrance and alert the funnelweb spider to passing prey.

↔ 1–2 in (2.5–5 cm)
✖ Not known
🍴 Insects, snails, frogs, mice

🏠 🌳 🏚️

SE. Australia

Macleay's specter
Extatosoma tiaratum

spiny legs kick in defense —

Also known as the giant prickly stick insect, Macleay's specter is well camouflaged by the twigs of its favorite food trees: eucalyptus. Females are longer, twice as heavy, and spinier than males, and their small wing buds mean they cannot fly. The slimmer, winged males fly readily, especially to find a mate. The female flicks her abdomen when releasing her eggs so they reach the forest floor. The eggs are gathered by spider ants, which carry them to their colony, then eat the outer layer but leave the rest of the egg intact. Hatching nymphs mimic the colors of their hosts, protecting them until they leave the colony in search of food trees.

◁ **GREEN LICHEN FORM**
Among the colored forms of this species, *E. t. tiaratum* is hard to spot amid green leaves, lichens, and mosses.

forelegs raised for defensive strike

female has small wing buds

↔ 3–7 in (7.6–18 cm)
✖ Not known
🍴 Leaves, especially eucalyptus

🏠 🌳 🏛️

leg flaps mimic leaves

E. Australia

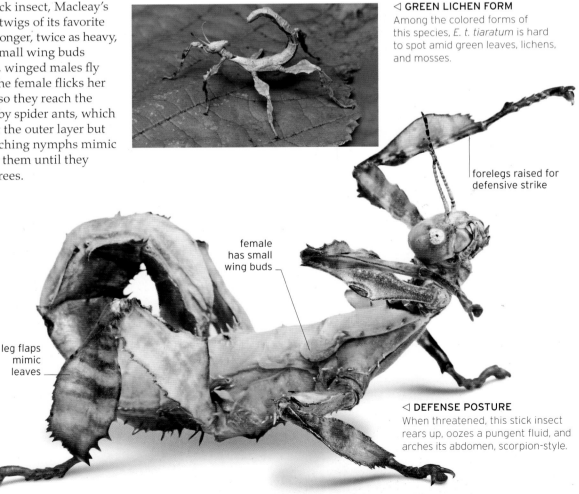

◁ **DEFENSE POSTURE**
When threatened, this stick insect rears up, oozes a pungent fluid, and arches its abdomen, scorpion-style.

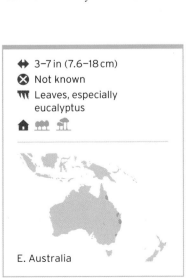

GREAT BARRIER REEF

The world's most famous reef system

Possibly Earth's most massive single ecoregion, the Great Barrier Reef—actually 3,000 interlinked reefs—is 1,430 miles (2,300 km) long, more than 62 miles (100 km) wide in parts, and covers 133,200 sq miles (345,000 sq km). More than 400 species of coral polyps (small anemone-like creatures) constructed the reef system among 900 islands. Its waters are warm, sunlit, clear, and bathed by mild currents. Dazzling reef fish, shrimp, starfish, sea slugs, and other sea creatures hide, feed, and claim territories here, while more than 100 species of shark and ray hunt among them. Around 200 species of bird also live here all year round.

Complex ecosystems

Along the reef, temperatures climb several degrees from south to north, and the seabed profile continually changes. Mingling with the reefs themselves are inshore waters averaging 115 ft (35 m) deep, sandy cays, seagrass meadows, sponge gardens, and mangrove stands, all giving way to continental slopes plunging down 6,560 ft (2,000 m). As one of the planet's most complex and biodiverse ecoregions, the Great Barrier Reef is carefully managed and conserved in some respects, but industrial and agricultural pollution, while declining, are still large-scale problems. In addition, rising water temperature and acidity linked to climate change, which causes environmental upheaval, are intensifying threats.

The Great Barrier Reef receives more than **2 million tourists** every year

CROWN-OF-THORNS STARFISH

The Great Barrier Reef is the largest living structure on the planet

SPINY ENEMY
Crown-of-thorns starfish periodically plague the reef. By eating polyps, they have destroyed up to one-quarter of its coral cover. Land nutrient run-off aids their increase in numbers, because it increases plankton, which in turn feeds larval starfish.

BLACK NODDY

BIRD BREEDING HUB
The Great Barrier Reef supports over one-quarter of Australia's tropical breeding birds, and more than half the population of one species, the black noddy. Noddy nests are made of leaves, twigs, and debris cemented with their own droppings.

Declared a UNESCO World Heritage Site in 1981

BRAIN CORAL

CORAL DIVERSITY
The reef's builders are 450-plus species of stony or hard corals. Their polyps construct limestone cups and calcareous skeletons around their soft bodies. Coral colonies grow into patterns that resemble antlers and even brains.

HELPFUL PARTNERS

Guard crabs scavenge debris, defend their cauliflower coral hosts against intruders, and occasionally help catch prey. The corals provide shelter and the crabs share meals.

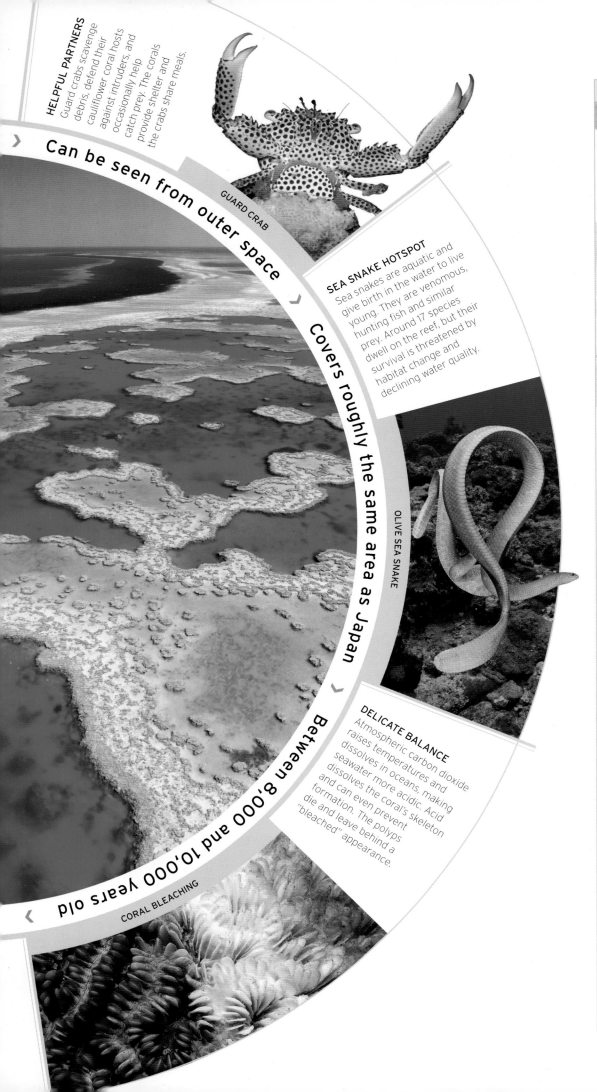

GUARD CRAB

Can be seen from outer space

Covers roughly the same area as Japan

Between 8,000 and 10,000 years old

CORAL BLEACHING

SEA SNAKE HOTSPOT

Sea snakes are aquatic and give birth in the water to live young. They are venomous, hunting fish and similar prey. Around 17 species dwell on the reef, but their survival is threatened by habitat change and declining water quality.

OLIVE SEA SNAKE

DELICATE BALANCE

Atmospheric carbon dioxide raises temperatures and dissolves in oceans, making seawater more acidic. Acid dissolves the coral's skeleton and can even prevent formation. The polyps die and leave behind a "bleached" appearance.

LOCATION

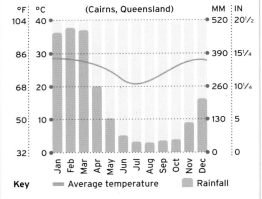

PAPUA NEW GUINEA

Coral Sea

Great Barrier Reef

Cairns

Townsville

AUSTRALIA

Brisbane

0 km 400
0 miles 400

Roughly parallel to Australia's northeast coast, south from Cape York to Fraser Island. The reef's edge extends from 18-155 miles (30-250 km) from the mainland.

CLIMATE

Almost entirely within the tropic zone, the climate is moist and warm to hot most of the year, averaging 73-79°F (23-26°C), and rarely below 63°F (17°C) or above 90°F (32°C). In the wettest months of December to April, rain reduces the salinity of the more isolated lagoons.

(Cairns, Queensland)

°F	°C		MM	IN
104	40		520	20½
86	30		390	15¼
68	20		260	10¼
50	10		130	5
32	0		0	0

Jan Feb Mar Apr May Jun Jul Aug Sep Oct Nov Dec

Key ── Average temperature ▮ Rainfall

LIFE ON THE REEF

Thousands of species live on the reef year-round, their numbers boosted by annual visitors such as humpback and dwarf minke whales. The smallest fish include permanent residents such as pygmy seahorses and gobies; the largest would be a passing whale shark.

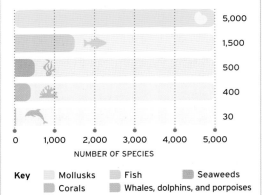

5,000
1,500
500
400
30

0 1,000 2,000 3,000 4,000 5,000
NUMBER OF SPECIES

Key ▮ Mollusks ▮ Fish ▮ Seaweeds
▮ Corals ▮ Whales, dolphins, and porpoises

Green sea turtle

Chelonia mydas

elongated
front limbs
modified
into flippers

The world's second largest turtle (after the leatherback), the green sea turtle is mostly solitary, swimming from one feeding area to another. Adult sea turtles graze inshore on marine plants using their toothless, horny, sharp-edged beaks, which have serrations on the lower jaw. When young, they are partly carnivorous, eating jellyfish, crustaceans, worms, and sponges.

Green sea turtles have a streamlined, teardrop-shaped carapace (upper shell). The common name comes from the layer of green fat between their shell and organs. The turtles swim using a flap-twist motion of the front flippers, with the shorter rear flippers acting as rudders. Their cruising speed is 1–2 mph (2–3 km/h)—in mid-migration they can cover 50 miles (80 km) daily—but can reach 20 mph (30 km/h) if threatened. Sea turtles can hold their breath for more than five hours when resting

underwater, although they surface every three to five minutes when feeding and traveling, and often sleep under a ledge or on the sea floor.

Distinct populations

Two green sea turtle populations occur in the Pacific and Atlantic oceans. Individuals roam widely, some covering more than 5,000 miles (8,000 km) yearly between their traditional feeding and mating-nesting areas. When mature, they return to their natal (hatching) beach. Many males arrive every year, females every two to three years. Hundreds gather up to 1 mile (2 km) offshore to mate. The female crawls onto the sandy beach at night, digs a hole with her flippers, deposits 100–200 eggs, fills the pit, and returns to sea. Depending on the temperature, hatching occurs 45–70 days later.

↔ 3–4 ft (1–1.2 m)
⚖ 143–286 lb (65–130 kg)
✖ Endangered
♨ Seagrass, seaweed
⌂ 🗺 〰

Temperate and tropical
waters worldwide

Turtle-headed seasnake

Emydocephalus annulatus

This fully aquatic snake's high-snouted, blunt-nosed head and sharp-edged jaw scales are adapted to scrape up its specialized food: fish eggs, laid in seabed nests. Unlike almost all other seasnakes, it has no need to disable prey, so its venom glands are reduced and its fangs are less than 1/25 in (1 mm) long. Each individual lives in a small area, where it seems to memorize which eggs are laid where and in which season.

↔	24–47 in (61–119 cm)
⚖	Up to 3 lb (1.4 kg)
✕	Common
⋔	Fish eggs
⌂ 🪸	
◉	Philippines, Timor Sea, Coral Sea

▽ **LONG LUNG**
A single lung that runs almost the length of their body lets seasnakes stay submerged for up to two hours.

△ **REEF COURTSHIP**
Male and female green sea turtles are similar-sized, although males have longer tails. Rival males bite and flipper-slap, then the winner shadows the female before grasping her shell with his flipper claws to mate.

◁ **RACE FOR LIFE**
Hatchlings flailing to the sea are feasted on by crabs, lizards, snakes, gulls, and other predators. In the sea lie more perils including sharks, kingfish, and dolphins.

Ocean sunfish

Mola mola

After a deep feeding dive, the world's heaviest bony fish basks at the surface to warm up with its disklike body lying side-on. The sunfish's fused jaw teeth form a "beak," which it uses to seize its main prey, jellyfish, and to break up its food. The female releases more eggs than almost any other animal—up to 300 million.

↔	Up to 13 ft (4 m)
⚖	Up to 2.2 tons (2 metric tons)
✕	Not known
⋔	Jellyfish
⌂ 〰	
◉	Philippines, Timor Sea, Coral Sea

△ **SCULLING ACTION**
The sunfish's tail is reduced to just a fleshy frill. It swims by moving its elongated dorsal and anal fins from side to side.

▷ **DAY SCHOOL**
Female scalloped hammerheads spend the day in large schools that gather along the edges of coral reefs. At night the sharks disperse to hunt alone.

▽ **SHELL HEAD**
The scalloped hammerhead is named for the notches in the leading edge of its hammer. This, combined with grooves running down to the mouth, give the hammerhead's underside the look of a scallop shell.

pointed upper tail lobe

eye on side of hammer-shaped head

Scalloped hammerhead shark

Sphyrna lewini

There are few fish as iconic as a hammerhead shark, and the scalloped hammerhead is one of the most widespread. Contrary to their reputations as lone killers, these sharks are highly social—at least the females are. Groups develop around older, dominant females, with the lowest ranked individuals out on the edge. Hammerhead sharks display dominance by swimming in a corkscrew or ramming each other. Weaker individuals submit with a shake of the head.

Love bite

Male scalloped hammerheads reach maturity at the age of six—a full 10 years before the females, which are normally 7 ft (2 m) long before they are ready to breed. A mature male swims into the school of females, sweeping toward the center in an S-shaped path. When he meets a likely mate, he secures himself to her by biting on one of her pectoral fins. Scalloped hammerheads give birth to live young and about 25 pups are born after an 8–12 month gestation.

At birth, the pups are only 16 in (40 cm) long, but fully formed with the distinctive hammerhead. They receive no parental care and have to fend for themselves. Most hunting takes place at night, with younger scalloped hammerheads feeding in shallow water, while the older ones move further out to sea.

The hammer feature has benefits in both habitats. The wide head acts like a hydrofoil—an underwater wing that creates lift, keeping the shark afloat. The head also acts as a communication dish, allowing the shark's senses to work better.

Prey detector

Hammerheads, like other sharks, have an excellent sense of smell. They can detect tiny quantities of chemicals in the water with two nostril-like slots called nares, which are located toward the ends of the hammer just in front of the eyes. The large distance between the nares means that a scent coming from a particular direction arrives at each nare at different times. This allows the hammerhead to zero in on the exact source of the scent.

Tiny pits arrayed along the underside of the hammerhead are filled with electrical sensors called the ampullae of Lorenzini. The large scanning surface provided by the head greatly enhances the sensitivity of these sensors, which can detect very tiny electrical currents produced by the nerves and muscles of all animals. By sweeping its head over the seabed like a metal detector, the hammerhead locates prey buried in the sand and takes hold of it, sometimes pinning it down with its head.

Scalloped hammerheads' teeth are more suited to seize prey than to rip it apart

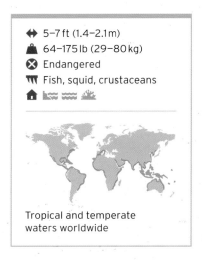

↔ 5–7 ft (1.4–2.1 m)
⚖ 64–175 lb (29–80 kg)
⊗ Endangered
🍴 Fish, squid, crustaceans
🏠 🌾 〜〜 🏭

Tropical and temperate waters worldwide

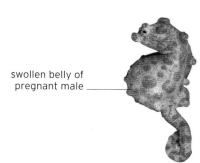

swollen belly of
pregnant male

Bargibant's pygmy seahorse
Hippocampus bargibanti

Found on coral reefs at depths of 53–130 ft (16–40 m), Bargibant's pygmy seahorse is so adept at mimicry that it was only discovered by chance in the late 1960s, when a laboratory researcher examining a gorgonian—a piece of soft, fanlike coral—realized that this tiny fish was attached to it. In addition to their much shorter, flattened snouts, pygmy seahorses differ from larger seahorse species in that the male's downward-facing brood pouch, in which he nurtures the fertilized eggs after mating, is located on his body cavity and not at the base of the tail. Their fleshier bodies lack easily distinguished segments, and they cling only to gorgonians, or sea fans, of the *Muricella* genus.

Little is known about the Bargibant's behavior, but like many other seahorse species, it anchors itself to corals with its prehensile tail, feeding on tiny crustaceans that float past.

↔ 1in (2.5 cm)
🏋 Not known
✖ Not known
🍴 Microscopic crustaceans
🏠

Indo-Pacific oceans

△ **DENISE'S PYGMY SEAHORSE**
At first believed to be a juvenile Bargibant's, Denise's pygmy seahorse (*H. denise*) is, at just ½ in (1.6 cm) in length, the smallest known seahorse species–and an equally effective camouflage artist.

▷ **MASTER OF DISGUISE**
Bargibant's pygmy seahorses are covered in wartlike tubercles that resemble the color and polyp texture of their host gorgonians so closely as to make them almost invisible.

Barrier Reef anemonefish

Amphiprion akindynos

two black-edged white bands encircle body

Also known as clownfish, Barrier Reef anemonefish live in groups among anemones in reef waters up to 80 ft (25 m) deep. All anemonefish are born male, but some change to females as required. The largest fish in a group becomes the dominant female and the second-largest, her mate. When the female dies, the dominant male changes sex to take her place.

↔ 2–5 in (5–13 cm)
⚖ 1 oz (28 g)
✕ Not known
🍴 Algae, zooplankton
🏠

SW. Pacific Ocean (Coral Sea)

◁ **SAFE SHELTER**
By blending anemone mucus into their skin's own mucus coating, anemonefish avoid stings–and predators.

Peacock mantis shrimp

Odontodactylus scyllarus

↔ 1–7 in (2.5–18 cm)
✕ Not known
🍴 Crabs, gastropods, fish
🏠

Indo-Pacific oceans

Peacock mantis shrimp are as complex as their colors. Their compound eyes have 12 different color photoreceptors (humans have three), which process infrared, ultraviolet, and polarized light, and they communicate using muscle-generated vibrations. Their "smasher" claws generate underwater explosions that can crack aquarium glass.

hinged smasher folded against body

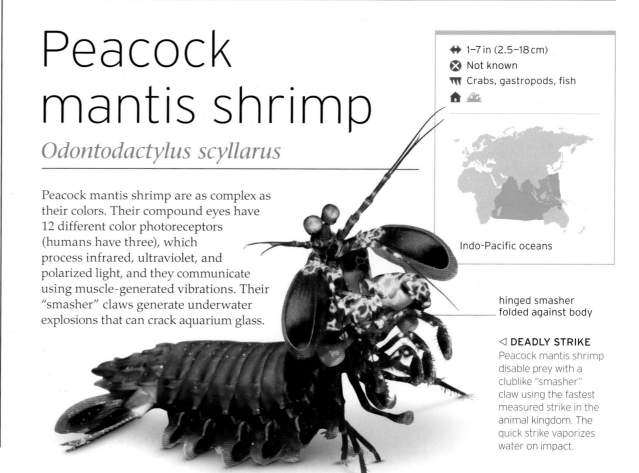

◁ **DEADLY STRIKE**
Peacock mantis shrimp disable prey with a clublike "smasher" claw using the fastest measured strike in the animal kingdom. The quick strike vaporizes water on impact.

Greater blue-ringed octopus

swims by jet propulsion

Hapalochlaena lunulata

Although small enough to fit in a teacup, this species poses the greatest danger to humans of any octopus. It rests by day in rocky crevices close to the shore, piling up a wall of stones for extra privacy. If disturbed, the octopus can give a deadly bite. Fatalities are rare, but its saliva contains tetrodotoxin, a poison 10,000 times more toxic than cyanide. It hunts on the seabed, catching prey with its beak or paralyzing it by releasing poison into the water.

↔ 6–8 in (15–20 cm)
✖ Not known
🍴 Fish, crabs, shrimp
🏠 ▨ ▨
🧭 Indo-Pacific, S. Australia coasts

▷ **BLUE ALERT**
If the octopus is alarmed, its rings turn electric blue, warning that a deadly bite will follow.

Giant clam

ridged shell covered in seaweed

Tridacna gigas

The giant clam is the largest living mollusk. Its immense shell is opened and closed by a powerful muscle, and animals sometimes get trapped, although the giant clam is not carnivorous. It feeds by filtering suspended food items from seawater. Adult giant clams also get nutrients from algae that live inside their fleshy tissues. These single-celled plants need light to photosynthesize, which restricts the clams to shallow, sunlit areas.

△ **SPAWNING**
Giant clams start life as males and later become hermaphrodites. However, they only release either eggs or sperm during a spawning session to avoid self-fertilization.

↔ 3–5 ft (1–1.5 m)
✖ Vulnerable
🍴 Algae, plankton
🏠 ▨
🧭 Indo-Pacific, Pacific Ocean

Portuguese man o' war

Physalia physalis

This relative of jellyfish floats on the surface of the ocean, snaring fish in its stinging tentacles that trail for 33 ft (10 m) or more below the surface. It is named after a passing resemblance between its gas-filled float and the distinctive curved sails of an 18th-century fighting ship. The Portuguese man o' war is unable to power its own movements, and the float, or pneumatophore, is also a sail of sorts, intended to catch the wind, which takes the organism wherever it may.

Colonial creature

A man o' war looks like a single animal but is actually a colony of several individual polyps, all of which connect beneath the float. There are three polyp types, each adapted for a particular job. The dactylozooids develop the long blue-green tentacles. These are lined with stinging cells, which are primed to fire barbed venomous darts into anything that touches them. The tentacles are used in defense and can inflict thousands of painful stings on anyone who tangles with them. The stingers also gather food, which is slowly hoisted up the tentacle to the gastrozooids, the feeding polyps. These engulf prey of all sizes and secrete enzymes to digest them.

The third polyp type—the reproductive gonozooid—has male and female parts, which produce new larval individuals that bud off from the main body to start life on their own.

↔ 33–165 ft (10–50 m)
✖ Not known
🍴 Small fish, plankton
🏠 ▨

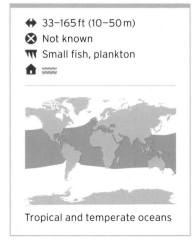

Tropical and temperate oceans

▷ **DRIFTING DANGER**
The float is mostly air, topped up with carbon monoxide. If attacked at the surface, the gas is released so the man o' war can sink safely underwater.

NEW ZEALAND MIXED FOREST
Remnants of vast tree cover provide evergreen oases

Aligned almost south-north, and 1,000 miles (1,600 km) long, New Zealand straddles considerable latitude and experiences a wide temperature range as a consequence. The annual average is below 50°F (10°C) in the far south, yet nearly double this at the northern tip. Since the country's greatest width is 250 miles (400 km), nowhere is far from the Pacific Ocean. The result is a cool-to-warm, generally moist climate where temperate forests thrive.

Main forested regions
On South Island, the Richmond temperate forests cloak the northeast. The damper west becomes more rugged southward, through the Westland temperate forest ecoregion to the Fjordland National Park alpine zone in the far southwest. In the far north of North Island is the flatter, milder Northland temperate kauri forests. These mixed forests are home to many kinds of indigenous conifers, such as the totara, rimu, and giant kauri—all in the pine group—as well as silver, red, black, and hard beeches. The majority of these trees are evergreen, so the forest floor remains in shade all year, with a dense understory of mosses, ferns, and small shrubs.

Much unique New Zealand wildlife thrives in these forests, from grasshopperlike wetas, to the bold kea and flightless kakapo parrots and ground-based kiwis. Before humans arrived, mixed temperate forests covered more than three-quarters of New Zealand. Burning, logging, and conversion to agriculture mean that today only a quarter remains.

PLAGUE POSSUMS
To launch a fur trade in the 1830s, brushtail possums were introduced from Australia. These omnivorous marsupials have been a disaster for New Zealand's native ecology, damaging trees and eating eggs, insects, snails, and even bats.

BRUSHTAIL POSSUM

Kauris may live for 1,500 years

SEED STIMULATION
Certain trees, such as the rimu, depend on a few native animal species, including New Zealand pigeons, to distribute their seeds. The seeds must pass through the birds' gut and be expelled in droppings before they can germinate.

NEW ZEALAND PIGEON

New Zealand is home to more species of flightless birds

SNAILS IN PERIL
Unique to New Zealand forests, fist-sized amber snails–a type of land snail– are carnivores, feeding on earthworms. However, introduced possums, rats, hedgehogs, and other animals have devastated their numbers.

AMBER SNAIL

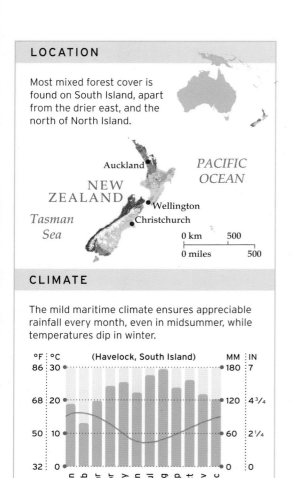

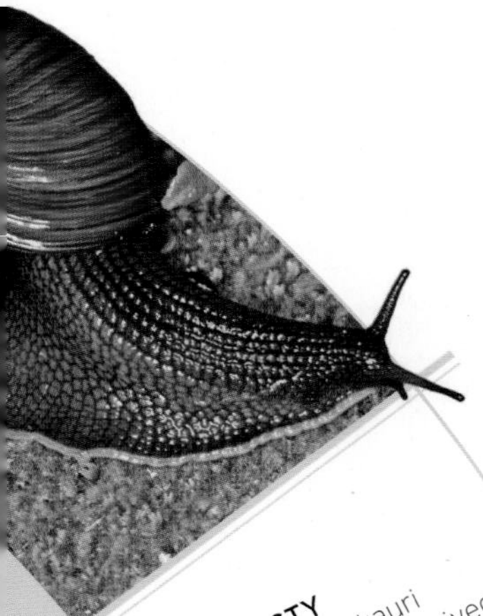

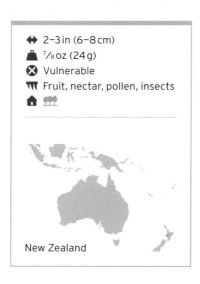

KAURI MAJESTY
In Northland, giant kauri conifers, which have survived from Jurassic times, reach heights of 165 ft (50 m) with diameters up to 66 ft (20 m). Their numbers have been so ravaged by logging that only five percent remain.

than any other country

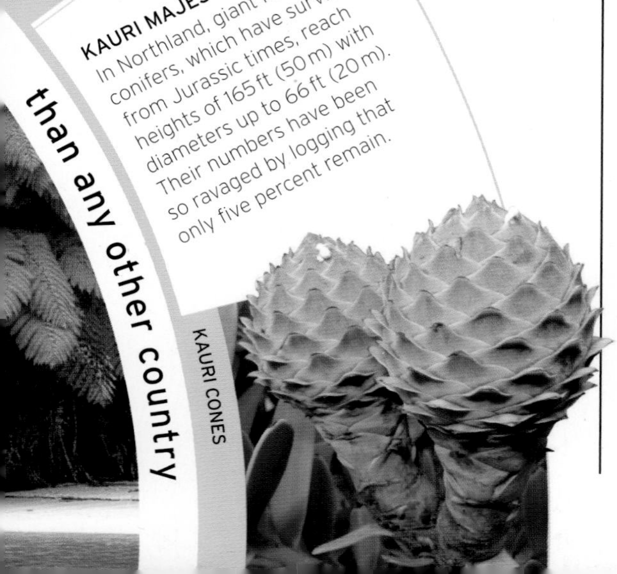

KAURI CONES

Lesser short-tailed bat
Mystacina tuberculata

The lesser short-tailed bat spends about 30 percent of its feeding time foraging among deep leaf litter on the forest floor. The talons on the claws of its thumbs and feet aid its agility on the ground.

▽ **GROUND FEEDER**
The short-tailed bat's folded wings are protected from damage by a leathery sheath when it moves on the ground.

↔ 2–3 in (6–8 cm)
⚖ ⅞ oz (24 g)
⊗ Vulnerable
🍴 Fruit, nectar, pollen, insects
🏠 🌳

New Zealand

talon on side of claw gives extra grip

tubular nostrils

Welcome swallow
Hirundo neoxena

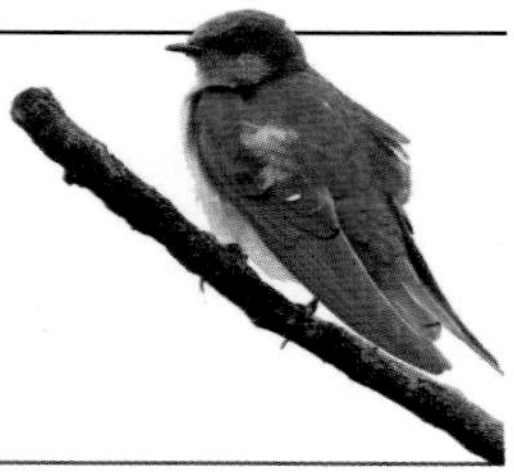

Australia's familiar rural and suburban swallow remains all year in most of its range. Unlike swifts, it perches on wires and bare branches, but it is a harvester of airborne insects, swerving elegantly at low level in pursuit of flies, and rising higher in humid conditions.

↔ 6 in (15 cm)
⚖ ⁷⁄₁₆–⅝ oz (12–17 g)
⊗ Vulnerable
🍴 Insects
🏠 🌳 🏔 🌾 🌊 🌲 🏚

Australia, New Zealand

◁ **FEEDING TIME**
Chicks from nests in sheds and car ports line up on wires, and call out to be fed whenever a parent appears.

"scaly" body feathers

Kea
Nestor notabilis

The only alpine parrot, the kea is a great tourist attraction—investigating cars, bags, and clothing with its hooked bill—but many locals deem it a pest. Keas eat roots, berries, and insects, but came under scrutiny in the 1860s because of suspicions that they attacked sheep. Bounties were offered and more than 150,000 were killed between 1870 and 1970. By then there were only 5,000 keas left and protective measures were taken, but their numbers still declined and have yet to recover.

- ↔ 19 in (48 cm)
- 🏋 29 oz (825 g)
- ✖ Vulnerable
- 🍴 Fruit, insects, grubs, carrion
- 🏠 🌳🌳 ⛰ ᨆ 🏘
- 📍 New Zealand

◁ **ALPINE SURVIVOR**
The kea is exceptionally intelligent —a quality that is vital to its survival in its harsh mountain habitat.

Kakapo
Strigops habroptila

blunt, round, owl-like head

The biggest, heaviest, and only flightless parrot, the kakapo is one of the world's longest-lived birds—averaging 95 years and reaching 120. Males compete for females in a lek, digging shallow bowls in the ground, perhaps to help amplify their calls, which continue for up to eight hours a night for several months.

- ↔ 25 in (64 cm)
- 🏋 5 lb (2 kg)
- ✖ Critically endangered
- 🍴 Plants
- 🏠 🌳🌳 ⛰
- 📍 New Zealand

◁ **RARE BIRD**
Just 126 kakapos were known in 2014, with only six chicks having hatched since 2011. The best chance of the species' survival rests on the birds having been moved to offshore islands free from predators.

Kiwis are the **only birds** in the world with **external nostrils** at the **tip of the bill**

soft, furlike
plumage

△ **LITTLE SPOTTED KIWI**
The little spotted kiwi (*A. owenii*) often lays two eggs,
three weeks apart, on a bed of moss. Each egg is a
quarter of the female's weight.

North Island brown kiwi

Apteryx mantelli

Nothing else looks remotely like a kiwi, but they share
their origins with other flightless birds and are most
closely related to emus and cassowaries. Kiwis prefer
rainforest, but habitat loss has forced them into scrub
and pine plantations, from coasts to alpine regions.
They need high humidity, well-drained soil for digging
nesting burrows and daytime dens, and moist leaf litter
in which to find food such as worms and grubs at night.
They detect prey by sound, smell, and touch, leaving
a trail of holes where they have probed with their bill.

Extraordinary eggs

Kiwis form life-long pairs in fixed territories, digging
burrows months or years before using them for
nesting, so new growth disguises the entrance.
Females are bigger than males, and produce eggs
four times as large as might be expected for the
bird's size. The North Island brown kiwi's egg
may be 20 percent of the body weight, its yolk
an exceptional 60 percent of the egg's volume.
The egg takes a month to develop, and in
this time the grossly distended female stops
feeding. Incubation is by the male, using a
temporary brood patch on his belly to keep the
egg warm, and may last 90 days.

↔ 20–26 in (51–66 cm)
🏋 6–8 lb (2.7–3.6 kg)
✖ Endangered
🐛 Insects, worms, millipedes
🏠 🌳 🌾

N. New Zealand

large feet with
fleshy pads and
long, sharp claws

long, slender bill

△ **NATIONAL ICON**
New Zealand's national bird, the kiwi's
big round body, small head, and long,
slim bill make it instantly recognizable
around the world.

Tuatara
Sphenodon punctatus

Although it looks like a fairly standard if rather chunky lizard, the tuatara belongs to an ancient order of reptiles of which it is the sole survivor. Differences in its teeth, skull bones, and other anatomy—little changed from its group's origins some 200 million years ago—set it apart from lizards and snakes.

Island strongholds

Tuataras inhabit around 30 New Zealand offshore islands, chiefly those without invasive pests such as rats that eat their eggs and young. Breeding tuataras have recently been discovered at a release site on the mainland, where they are protected by a mammalproof fence.

The tuatara is better adapted than any other reptile to a cool, damp climate, remaining active at just 41°C (5°C) and showing heat stress above 77°C (25°C). In winter, it lies torpid in its home burrow—self-dug or usurped from a seabird—sometimes for several weeks. Tuataras have a lengthy breeding cycle, reaching sexual maturity at 10–20 years. Females lay eggs only once every three to four years, which take at least a year to hatch. Juveniles are at risk of being cannibalized by adults, otherwise tuataras may live for more than 100 years.

light-sensitive organ, or "third eye", covered by scales

△ **POWERFUL BUILD**
Clawed toes, strong legs, a muscular build, and a crushing, tenacious bite make tuataras formidable adversaries.

Auckland tree weta
Hemideina thoracica

This cricket is a common sight in backyards and scrublands. Mostly nocturnal, it spends the day inside burrows—known as galleries—in branches and trunks. Each gallery contains up to 10 wetas, with a single male living with a harem of females and juveniles. The insects enlarge a natural hollow or burrows vacated by a beetle grub, using their powerful biting mouthparts to snip away the bark. Tree wetas are mostly wingless, although a few grow small wings unsuited to flight. The female has what looks like a large stinger on her abdomen. This is actually the ovipositor, which is used to lay eggs into rotting wood or soil. Both sexes hiss and may bite when threatened, often flicking forward their spiky back legs to scratch attackers.

↔ 2 in (5 cm)
⊗ Not known
♨ Leaves, fruit, seeds, insects
🏠 🌳

N. New Zealand

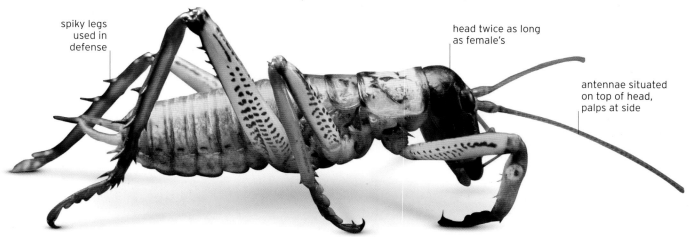

spiky legs used in defense

head twice as long as female's

antennae situated on top of head, palps at side

◁ **MALE TREE WETA**
The male Auckland tree weta has a much larger head and mouthparts than the female, which it uses to defend its harem and gallery from interloping males.

soft, jagged crest along back and tail, larger in male

stout limbs and sharp-clawed toes for burrowing

20–24 in (51–61 cm)

⅞–2 lb (0.4–1 kg)

Locally common

Spiders, insects, worms

New Zealand (coastal islands)

The tuatara's closest **relatives died out** more than **60 million years ago**

△ **BONY TEETH**
The sharp teeth are fused to the jaw bone and are not shed and regrown as in most other reptiles.

---

wings point backward at rest

Blue damselfly
Austrolestes colensonis

The largest damselfly in New Zealand, the blue damselfly can be seen fluttering around reeds and rushes in areas of still water. Frequently confused with dragonflies, damselflies are less powerful fliers and hold their wings along the body, rather than out sideways, when at rest. The blue damselfly can change color to control its temperature—the blue males and greener females turn darker when the weather is cold in order to absorb more heat from their surroundings.

Aerial hunters
Adult damselflies live only for a couple of weeks. They are aerial hunters, snatching smaller insects, using their enormous round eyes to track moving targets. Mating couples can be seen flying together over still water—the male guards the female as she lays her eggs, ensuring no other mate is able to copulate with her. The nymphs spend the winter underwater, breathing with gills that are located on the tip of their abdomen. They hunt on the bottom using a specialized mouthpart to skewer prey. In spring, the wingless nymphs climb out of the water to molt into the adult form.

2 in (5 cm)

Common

Water fleas

New Zealand

◁ **LOVER'S EMBRACE**
During mating the male clasps the female just behind her head and she then reaches around with her flexible abdomen to accept a packet of sperm from him.

Southern Ocean
Chinstrap penguins spend winter out at sea hunting for krill, fish, and squid. Their main predator is the leopard seal, from which they take refuge on large icebergs.

Antarctica

SNOW ALGAE

Some species of single-celled algae can survive in snow and ice. Some produce red pigments that mask green chlorophyll and resist frost and deadly ultraviolet rays that penetrate snow. Barely visible in winter, algae rise to the surface in summer, creating algal blooms that color whole snowbanks red, pink, orange, green, or gray.

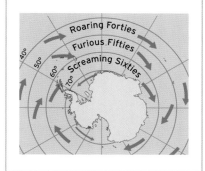

ANTARCTIC PLANTS

The coastal fringe of the peninsula is the only area free of permanent ice. Mosses and lichens dominate the tundra vegetation. Swards of Antarctic hair grass and cushions of Antarctic pearlwort are the only flowering plants.

ROARING WINDS

Westerly winds sweep unimpeded around the Southern Ocean. The Roaring Forties is the area between 40° and 50° latitude south. Now, due to a shift in weather patterns caused by climate change, these winds appear to be moving south, becoming stronger, and merging with the Furious Fifties.

CIRCULAR OCEAN MOVEMENT

The winds around Antarctica drive the Antarctic Circumpolar Current, sealing off the Southern Ocean and creating the world's roughest seas.

FEATURED ECOREGIONS

■ Southern Ocean Islands **p364-69**
Tundra, ice

■ Antarctic Peninsula **p370-75**
Tundra, ice

ROSS SEA AND ICE SHELF

The vast Ross Ice Shelf shelters an abundance of invertebrate life below. Winds driving away sea-ice next to the ice shelf can create ice-free areas of water called polynyas. The summer sun brings forth blooms of phytoplankton and the Ross Sea bursts into life, supporting whales, seals, penguins, petrels, fish, and more than 1,000 species of invertebrate.

Scotia Sea

South Orkney Islands

Eimbulisen

Bransfield Strait

Graham Land

Antarctic Peninsula

Palmer Land

Alexander Island

Maudheimvidda

Dronning Maud Land

Weddell Sea

Filchner Ice Shelf

Berkner Island

Ronne Ice Shelf

Bellingshausen Sea

Pensacola Mountains

Vinson Massif 4,897m

South Pole

Peter I Øy

Ellsworth Land

Whitmore Mountains

Transantarctic

SOUTHERN OCEAN

Thurston Island

West Antarctica

Queen Maud Mountains

Amundsen Sea

Marie Byrd Land

Rockefeller Plateau

Ross Ice Shelf

Roosevelt Island

Mount Erebus 3,794m

Ross Sea

Roaring Forties
Furious Fifties
Screaming Sixties
40° 50° 60° 70°

LAND OF ICE AND SNOW
Antarctica

The Antarctic ice-sheet, which covers most of the continent, is the largest mass of ice on Earth. It is 3 miles (4.8 km) thick in places, its volume is more than 7.2 million cubic miles (30 million cubic km), and it holds more than 70 percent of Earth's fresh water. The ice-sheet is separated into two parts by the Transantarctic Mountains, most of which are hidden, but several peaks more than 13,000 ft (4,000 m) high emerge from the ice. How the mountains formed is debated, but an active rift on the West Antarctica side of the range is thought to have played a part. The rift may be causing a plate to be pushed under East Antarctica, causing uplift. West Antarctica is low-lying; East Antarctica is a larger, higher region of ancient rocks overlain in places by sandstones, shales, limestones, and coal laid down during warmer times.

Plant, dinosaur, and marsupial fossils provide further evidence of Antarctica's warm past, before it broke from the Gondwana supercontinent and moved south. Now it is typically below freezing all year round and recorded temperatures have plunged to -129 °F (-89 °C). Small wonder that, with the exception of a few researchers, Antarctica is uninhabited.

LAKES UNDER THE ICE
Vast lakes deep within the ice, sealed from the atmosphere for thousands of years, retain complex communities of thousands of microbes.

TRANSANTARCTIC MOUNTAINS
The curved belt of mountains separates East and West Antarctica.

KEY DATA

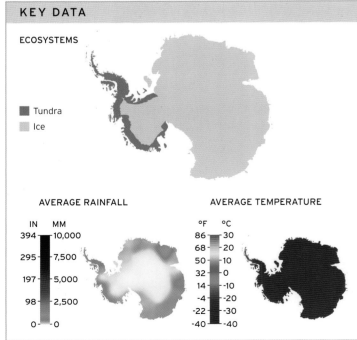

ECOSYSTEMS

- Tundra
- Ice

AVERAGE RAINFALL

IN	MM
394	10,000
295	7,500
197	5,000
98	2,500
0	0

AVERAGE TEMPERATURE

°F	°C
86	30
68	20
50	10
32	0
14	-10
-4	-20
-22	-30
-40	-40

SOUTHERN OCEAN ISLANDS
Inhospitable to man, last refuges for threatened species

Remote, mostly uninhabited volcanic islands, many with glaciers, ice caps, and snow fields year round, are dotted north of the 60 degrees south latitude line that marks the boundary of the Southern Ocean. They include South Georgia, South Sandwich, Bouvet, Prince Edward, and Kerguelen islands, and Heard Island. Situated close to the Antarctic Convergence, where cold Antarctic waters sink under warmer seas, these islands are home to a great variety and number of fish, birds, and mammals.

Lynchpin of the food chain

The food chain for the survival of all these creatures is based on tiny plankton and vast numbers of krill—small, shrimplike crustaceans. Krill form the staple diet of petrels and albatrosses, crabeater seals, and humpback, right, blue, fin, sei, and minke whales arriving from tropical seas for the Antarctic summer. Ironically,

whales were hunted from these islands until they were declared commercially extinct by 1965. This created a surplus of Antarctic krill, so other marine species subsequently increased. For example, fur seals, once thought extinct, now breed here in their millions. Yet even a krill surplus may not help slow-breeding whales. Human exploitation has now shifted to the krill itself, threatening the basis of all Antarctic sea life.

VULNERABLE TO RATS
The South Georgia pintail is found only on the South Georgia and South Sandwich islands, preferring freshwater areas with tussock grass, and coastal bogs, but often feeding offshore. Introduced rats threaten this duck as they eat eggs and chicks.

SOUTH GEORGIA PINTAIL

SIEVING THE SEA
The most abundant seal species in the world, crabeater seals eat krill by taking in seawater and squeezing it out between interlocking teeth, which act like sieves to retain the prey. When not feeding, they rest on floating sea ice.

CRABEATER SEAL

The total weight of Antarctic krill is more than tha

Home to millions of crabeater seals

SPERM WHALE

DIVING FOR DINNER
Earth's deepest-diving mammal, the sperm whale can hold its breath for up to an hour or more as it dives in search of squid, a main food source. Its lungs collapse to cope with crushing water pressure at depths of up to almost 2 miles (3,000 m).

Southern elephant seal

Mirounga leonina

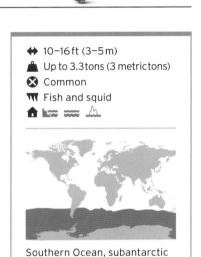

proboscis amplifies mating roars

The largest of the pinnipeds, or flipper-footed marine mammals, the southern elephant seal shows the greatest sex-related size difference of all mammals. Males weigh up to 10 times as much as females, and only mature bulls bear the trunklike inflatable proboscis that gives the species its common name.

Fighting to breed

Southern elephant seals may reach depths of up to 6,550 ft (2,000 m) in search of food, aided partly by their special, oxygen-rich red blood cells. They spend up to 90 percent of their lives at sea, often sleeping underwater, but like all seals, they haul out on land to molt, breed, and give birth. Adult males fight for mating rights to groups of females, but only 2–3 percent are successful. The largest harems are controlled by a single dominant bull known as a "beachmaster." While females and pups can be injured or even killed during these fights, the breeding season is tough on both sexes: males lose an average of 26 lb (12 kg) a day—more than 40 percent of their body weight.

↔ 10–16 ft (3–5 m)
⚖ Up to 3.3 tons (3 metric tons)
✖ Common
⋔ Fish and squid

Southern Ocean, subantarctic oceans

Southern elephant seals are able to **stay underwater for up to two hours** at a time

LOCATION

Island groups situated between Antarctica to the south and New Zealand, South Africa, and South America to the north.

SOUTH AMERICA

Bouvet Island
Prince Edward Islands
South Georgia and South Sandwich Islands
Crozet Islands
South Orkney Islands
Kerguelen

PACIFIC OCEAN
Peter I Island
ANTARCTICA
INDIAN OCEAN

0 km 2000
0 miles 2000

Scott Island
Balleny Islands
Macquarie Island
AUSTRALIA

CLIMATE

With strong winds and temperatures only slightly above freezing at times, this polar tundra climate has no true summer.

°F	°C	(Grytviken, South Georgia)	MM	IN
59	15		144	5¾
50	10		108	4¼
41	5		72	2¾
32	0		36	1½
23	-5		0	0

Jan Feb Mar Apr May Jun Jul Aug Sep Oct Nov Dec

Key — Average temperature — Rainfall

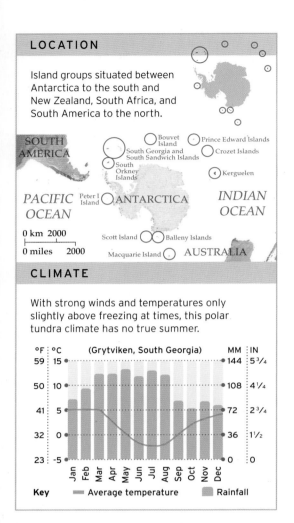

COLORFUL SWARM
The sea often turns orange-red as vast swarms of Antarctic krill gather in summer. Just 2 in (5 cm) long, krill are shrimplike creatures that feed on phytoplankton (microscopic plants), but they can go up to 200 days without food.

of all the humans on Earth

KRILL

▽ **DUELING FOR DOMINANCE**
Male elephant seals fight for breeding rights early in the mating season. They raise more than half of their body off the ground and inflict wounds to an opponent's neck and face with their teeth.

Wandering albatross

Diomedea exulans

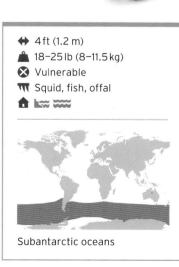

stands upright on
large webbed feet

With a wingspan of up to 12 ft (3.5 m), the wandering albatross is the largest flying bird in the world. Old males become so white they have been called "snowy albatrosses," but the bird's scientific name comes from the Latin term for "living as an exile." This refers to the fact that wandering albatrosses spend months at a time on the wing in the world's southern oceans.

Male wandering albatrosses are 20 percent heavier than females, but with only slightly larger wings. They forage farther south than females and their 12 percent greater wing loading (body weight related to wing area) seems to help them deal with stronger winds. Immature birds circle the southern hemisphere before becoming old enough to breed at 10 years. Wandering albatrosses form large breeding colonies on remote islands, creating nest mounds out of mud and vegetation. Pairs mate for life, then breed every two years, incubating one egg for around 80 days and sharing parental duties.

Longline fishing threat

Albatrosses have a very good sense of smell thanks to their large, tubular external nostrils, and most of their diet is fish and squid taken at the ocean's surface or in shallow dives. Scavenging around fishing boats for fish and other unwanted sea creatures that are thrown aside gives these seabirds an easy feeding option, but has increased risk. With just 8,000 pairs nesting in any year and a slow reproductive rate, wandering albatrosses, in particular, are extremely vulnerable to threats such as drowning when caught on baited hooks from long-line trawlers.

↔ 4 ft (1.2 m)
⚖ 18–25 lb (8–11.5 kg)
⊗ Vulnerable
🍴 Squid, fish, offal
🏠 〰〰

Subantarctic oceans

△ **DYNAMIC SOARING**
Instead of beating their wings, albatrosses hold them out stiffly and fly by dynamic soaring, exploiting air currents rising over ocean waves. Getting airborne, however, relies on a headwind.

△ **INFREQUENT MEAL**
Chicks are fed every two to four days at first, less often as they grow. They remain at the nest for as long as 9-11 months.

◁ **COURTSHIP RITUAL**
An elaborate ritual involving spread wings, clapping bill, and moaning calls is much the same for all large albatross species.

Rockhopper penguin

Eudyptes chrysocome

strong webbed feet
with sharp claws
give good grip

After six months at sea, chasing shrimplike krill and fish, rockhopper penguins must begin nesting promptly once melting sea ice allows them access to firm land. Of around 3.5 million pairs, some 2.5 million breed in the Falkland Islands. Males return first, to begin building nests of stones, grass, and fish bones. Courtship is short, but caressing, billing, and other rituals reaffirm past pair-bonds and establish new ones—vital if pairs are to act in concert to rear their chick.

Each parent incubates two eggs while the other is away feeding at sea for 7–17 days. They may forage up to 155 miles (250 km) from the colony. With such long periods between meals, only the stronger chick survives. Unusually among birds, the second egg, laid several days after the first, can be 70 percent heavier and hatches first. Scientists speculate whether the species is still evolving a single-egg clutch. The chick is brooded constantly for three weeks before being moved into a nursery, where "aunties" strive to protect vast numbers of chicks from giant petrels, skuas, and gulls. Only the parents feed their chick, and the first few days between parental guarding and establishment in the nursery expose it to the greatest risk of predation.

distinctive black
and yellow crest and
yellow eyebrow

↔ 20 in (51 cm)
⬛ 6 lb (2.7 kg)
✖ Vulnerable
♨ Fish, crabs, squid
⌂ ≋

S. South America;
S. Pacific, S. Atlantic,
S. Indian, Southern oceans

▷ **HURRYING HOME**
Having escaped predatory leopard seals lurking inshore, these rockhoppers are heading back to the colony with a belly full of fish.

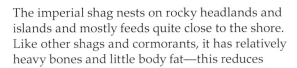

Imperial shag
Phalacrocorax atriceps

old brown feathers replaced by new black ones during molt

The imperial shag nests on rocky headlands and islands and mostly feeds quite close to the shore. Like other shags and cormorants, it has relatively heavy bones and little body fat—this reduces buoyancy and makes it a more efficient underwater forager. Unlike terns and gannets, which locate fish from the air by sight, the shag dives deep and searches systematically for prey.

△ **GOING FISHING**

These stocky little penguins use their short, strong legs to make double-footed kangaroo hops across rocks when going to and from the ocean.

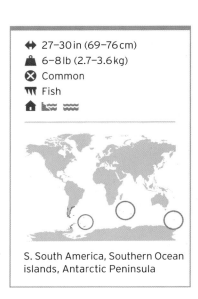

↔ 27–30 in (69–76 cm)
⚖ 6–8 lb (2.7–3.6 kg)
⊗ Common
🍴 Fish
🏠

S. South America, Southern Ocean islands, Antarctic Peninsula

△ **EGG CUPS**

Each nest is a mound of seaweed, grass, and mud liberally mixed with white excrement, with a shallow bowl for two or three eggs.

Antarctic tern
Sterna vittata

The southern equivalent of the Arctic tern, the Antarctic tern does not undertake vast migrations from north to south. It breeds in November and December when the northern species is "wintering" at sea. Some birds remain close to nesting colonies, while others move far out to sea, feeding along the edges of the pack ice and often resting on ice floes.

↔ 14–16 in (36–41 cm)
⚖ 5–6 oz (150–175 g)
⊗ Common
🍴 Fish
🏠

SE. South America, Southern Africa, Southern Ocean islands, Antarctic Peninsula

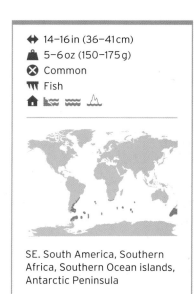

◁ **BREEDING ADULT**

In its summer plumage, the Antarctic tern looks very similar to its Arctic cousin. It breeds on rocky islands in the Southern Ocean.

ANTARCTIC PENINSULA
The coldest, most remote continent is ruled by ice

More than 99 percent of Antarctica—Earth's driest, coldest, windiest continent—is covered by ice. Only the 1,240-mile (2,000-km) long Antarctic Peninsula reaches beyond the Antarctic Circle, pointing north toward Cape Horn. Life here is shaped by extremes. Antarctica's interior is elevated, with air so cold it cannot hold moisture, yet the coastal belt is damp. Cold air falls from the interior in blistering gales. Rain, fog, and blizzards alternate with sunny days when temperatures reach 41°F (5°C). Months of darkness give way to summers of 24-hour daylight, but even the best summer conditions are still challenging.

Life among the ice
The waxing and waning of sea ice is the driving force for most Antarctic life. Pack ice expands by up to 3 miles (4.8 km) per day, thickening to 7 ft (2.1 m), with fallen snow on top. For much of the year, ice locks away feeding areas and breeding sites for many creatures. Most seals and penguins, skuas, and other birds only breed when the ice melts to reveal solid rock, so they move away from land as the ice expands. Emperor penguins, however, head south, where the males endure the worst winter conditions as they incubate eggs and fast for 65 days while the females go back to the ocean to feed. Weddell seals remain, using breathing holes so they can live under the ice all winter.

While approximately 300 species of algae, 200 lichens, 85 mosses, and 25 liverworts are known to exist in this icy landscape, only two flowering plant species are considered to be native to the Antarctic.

LOYAL MATE
Snow petrels nest farther south than any other bird, with many colonies along the peninsula. Mated pairs remain faithful for life, and lay one egg per year in a rock crevice. Their pure white plumage camouflages them against snow and ice.

SNOW PETREL

WHITE-BLOODED FISH
Blackfin icefish survive in temperatures that would freeze most other fish solid. Glycoproteins prevent their body fluids from freezing, and although their blood lacks hemoglobin (red blood cells), it is more fluid and so uses less energy to circulate.

BLACKFIN ICEFISH

ANTARCTIC PEARLWORT

Antarctica holds 90% of the planet's ice and mo...

So dry it is classified as a cold desert

EXPANDING BLOOMS
One of only two flowering plants on the entire continent, Antarctic pearlwort forms green cushions, seen more and more frequently on the Antarctic fringe. This white-blossomed plant is widening its range due to a warming climate.

Weddell Sea

SOUTH AMERICA

PACIFIC OCEAN

ANTARCTICA

0 km   2000
0 miles   2000

CLIMATE

Summer temperatures average 34°F (1°C); winter temperatures can drop to 5° to -4°F (-15° to -20°C) in the northern tip, lower in the south.

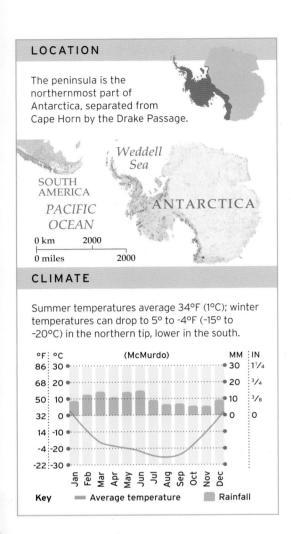

°F	°C	(McMurdo)	MM	IN
86	30		30	1¼
68	20		20	¾
50	10		10	⅜
32	0		0	0
14	-10			
-4	-20			
-22	-30			

Jan Feb Mar Apr May Jun Jul Aug Sep Oct Nov Dec

Key — Average temperature ▮ Rainfall

Leopard seal
Hydrurga leptonyx

head has no forehead

Named for its spotted coat, this aquatic mammal is an expert hunter, thanks to its almost snakelike head and wide, powerful jaws with long canine teeth. Although it is the only true seal that feeds on other seals, up to half of a leopard seal's diet consists of tiny, shrimplike krill, and it has a set of specially adapted cheek teeth that serve as a sieve for feeding on them.

Different strokes

Unlike other true seals, the leopard seal swims not by propelling itself solely with its hindquarters, but by strong, simultaneous strokes of its large, elongated front flippers. This technique gives the seal increased speed and agility in the water, but makes it difficult for the animal to move around on land. Females are slightly larger than males —the opposite of size differences in most true seals. Females give birth on pack ice to single pups, which are suckled for three to four weeks.

Although they are the most formidable carnivores in their ecoregion, leopard seals are occasionally hunted by killer whales. Seals are protected from commercial hunting, but juveniles, which depend largely on krill to survive, may also be threatened by a decrease in krill numbers due to commercial overfishing.

↔ 8–12 ft (2.4–3.7 m)
⚖ 440–1,000 lb (200–455 kg)
✖ Common
🦷 Krill, squid, seals, penguins

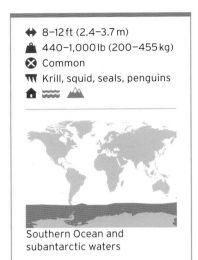

Southern Ocean and subantarctic waters

▽ **OPPORTUNISTIC PREDATOR**
Leopard seals patrol penguin rookeries in search of young, newly fledged penguins, which are more vulnerable to attacks.

Leopard seals **vocalize underwater**, making **long-lasting calls**, some of which can be **felt through ice**

FLIGHTLESS INSECT
Antarctica's only insect is flightless and so avoids the constant buffeting winds. It tolerates high salinity and loss of body water, and its black color absorbs heat. By living in shallow burrows, the midge survives temperatures just below freezing.

...han 70% of its fresh water

ANTARCTIC MIDGE

55-68 throat grooves

Blue whale
Balaenoptera musculus

Aside from the tiny, shrimplike krill it eats, everything about the blue whale is supersized. The largest animal on Earth, the blue whale is roughly the size of a jumbo jet. It weighs twice as much as the biggest dinosaurs; even its tongue weighs 4 tons (3.6 metric tons). A human could swim through its blood vessels, which carry 11 tons (10 metric tons) of blood, circulated by a heart that weighs up to 2,000 lb (900 kg)—about the size of a small car.

Despite their huge size, blue whales are almost perfectly hydrodynamic—the long, streamlined body moves through seawater with minimal resistance, propelled by the strong tail. They travel either alone or in small groups, but occasionally up to 60 animals may come together to feed. Blue whales produce the loudest vocalizations on the planet—up to 188 decibels —via a series of low-frequency calls that can be heard underwater for hundreds of miles.

Back from the brink
Their massive proportions kept blue whales safe from human threats until the mid-19th century, when the invention of the exploding harpoon focused the whaling industry's attention on the species. Thousands of blue whales were slaughtered, and despite a 1966 global ban on hunting them, today's population has decreased by an estimated minimum of 70 percent, possibly as much as 90 percent. There have, however, been signs of very slow recovery in recent years, and current blue whale numbers are thought to be around 10,000–25,000.

◁ **HIGHEST SPOUT**
At 30-40 ft (9-12 m), blue whales have the highest "blow" or spout of any whale. It happens when the whale expels air through the two blowholes.

↔ 105–108 ft (32–33 m)
⚖ 124–165 tons (113–150 metric tons)
✖ Endangered
🦐 Krill, copepods
🏠 〰 ⛰

Oceans worldwide, except Arctic

Hourglass dolphin
Lagenorhyncus cruciger

white pattern give species its name

Usually seen far out at sea, hourglass dolphins live in colder, deeper Antarctic and subantarctic waters. They are often found in groups of seven or eight, although schools of 60 to 100 dolphins have also been sighted. They excel at bow-wave riding and frequently approach boats, as well as larger cetaceans such as fin whales, to "catch a ride." Although little is known about its behavior, research has revealed that this species' echolocation clicks allow it to find prey at over twice the distance of other dolphins.

↔ 5–6 ft (1.5–1.8 m)
⚖ Up to 207 lb (94 kg)
✖ Common
🦐 Fish, squid, crustaceans
🏠 ▬ 〰 ⛰
◉ S. Pacific, S. Atlantic, S. Indian, Southern oceans

▷ **PORPOISING**
Hourglass dolphins swim at speeds of up to 14 mph (22 km/h), leaping out of the water when riding a bow wave.

Adelie penguin
Pygoscelis adeliae

white ring around eyes

Adelie penguins nest on large ice-free areas of rock, often far from shore, in colonies up to 280,000 pairs strong. Although new scientific bases and tourism cause disturbance, more than 2 million pairs breed around Antarctica. Their insulation is so good that falling snow does not melt but simply covers them.

↔ 18–24 in (46–61 cm)
⚖ 9–12 lb (4–5.5 kg)
✖ Near threatened
🦐 Krill, small fish
🏠 ▬ ⛰
◉ Circumpolar around Antarctica

△ **FEEDING IN SHIFTS**
Both parents take turns to feed their chick for 16–19 days until it is ready to join a nursery of juveniles.

golden cheek patch

white front and dark back help camouflage penguins when swimming

Emperor penguin
Aptenodytes forsteri

Adapted to some of the most challenging conditions on Earth, the emperor penguin is the only bird that breeds during the severe Antarctic winter. It is the largest of the penguins, but has the same upright pose, short legs, waddling walk, and stiff wings held like arms at its sides, as well as an incurably inquisitive nature.

Built for survival

When moving from ice-cold water into the warmth of the sun, penguins may wave their wings to dissipate heat and they also pant to keep cool. In cold conditions, emperor penguins tilt back onto their heels and tails, avoiding contact between the ice and their feet. The dark plumage absorbs heat from the sun and beneath the dense feathers is a trapped layer of insulating warm air. Beneath this they have a thick layer of fat—creating the familiar rotund, streamlined shape—that is indispensable for survival in temperatures as low as -76°F (-60°C).

Emperor penguins live in a narrow band of ice floes and frozen bays surrounding the Antarctic continent. The rookeries get further from the open sea as it freezes, forcing these flightless birds to undertake annual treks to establish their colonies in March or April, and then make repeated and longer marches—up to 37 miles (60 km) each way—to bring food back to their chick.

Teamwork

The female lays a single egg, which she transfers to the male before heading to the open ocean on a feeding trip that lasts about two months. The male incubates the egg in his brood pouch, a fold of featherless skin just above his feet. Emperor penguin colonies may be several thousand strong, with the incubating males huddling together over large open areas. They stand almost motionless for days in low temperatures and raging blizzards. When the female returns, care of the newly hatched chick transfers to her and the near-starving male goes off to feed.

After 45 days, when it is well grown and covered in down, the chick joins a nursery, but it is still fed by its parents. The nursery breaks up after five months, when the parents abandon their chick and leave for the open sea. The chicks eventually follow and, having acquired adult plumage, take to the water.

Emperor penguins **dive deeper than any other bird** to find food

◁ **BUBBLE POWER**

Penguin feathers release a stream of air bubbles when the birds head back to the surface from a deep dive. This increases their speed of ascent sufficiently for them to clear the water and land safely on the ice.

▷ **KEEPING WARM**

The solitary emperor penguin chick is hatched almost naked. It is kept warm by a parent until it is covered with down and big enough to join a nursery.

↔ 4 ft (1.1 m)
🏋 66–88 lb (30–40 kg)
✖ Near threatened
🍴 Krill, fish, squid
🏠 ▰▰ ⛰

Circumpolar around Antarctica

Yellowstone National Park

A lone American bison crosses the Grand Prismatic Spring in Yellowstone, Wyoming. The national park—the first in the US and the world—is one of the bison's last strongholds.

The Animal Kingdom

MAMMALS

No class of vertebrates has conquered the world's wild places like mammals. Warm blood, a big brain, and well-nurtured offspring help them succeed practically wherever life is possible. They thrive in places too cold for reptiles, and a fifth of their kind—the bats—can fly as expertly as birds. Others are runners, climbers, burrowers, and swimmers. Oceangoing mammals, such as the whales, are the biggest animals on the planet, and a few marine mammals can even dive up to a mile below the water's surface, holding their breath for an hour or more.

Anatomy

Mammals evolved from lizardlike ancestors—a transition that required considerable changes to the skeleton. Parts of the reptilian jaw became miniaturized in mammals and reassigned to the middle ear to help transmit sound signals. This left mammals with just a single pair of bones in their lower jaw—but resulted in a stronger, more flexible, chewing action. The reptiles' uniform teeth changed too. Mammals now have ridged, grinding molars at the back and stabbing canines at the front—helping some to eat tough, fibrous plants and others to be bone-crushing predators.

Proficient feeding provides fuel for the body, and a mammal's metabolism generates a lot of heat. This makes mammals warm blooded, while a complex system of self-regulation keeps their temperature constantly high. Most mammals have a coat of hairs to trap this warmth close to the body, and because of this, unlike cold-blooded vertebrates, they can stay active even when their surroundings change. Their high oxygen demand is satisfied by a powerful four-chambered heart and lungs that are inflated by a muscular diaphragm located below the chest cavity.

zygomatic arch

teeth to crush bone

canine teeth for gripping or tearing

△ LION'S SKULL
Mammals have especially effective jaws—and specialized teeth for crunching or stabbing. The strong zygomatic arch of a lion's skull supports muscles for a powerful bite.

Reproduction

Mammals are typically devoted parents. Most give birth to live young after a pregnancy period, during which the unborn are carried in the womb and nourished by an advanced blood-filled organ called the placenta. Marsupials are born at a more premature stage of their development, and in monotremes, the young hatch from eggs. However, all mammalian mothers suckle their offspring after birth with nutrient-rich milk secreted from the mammary glands. Many mammals give birth to one or a few offspring and can therefore give a relatively large amount of care to each individual. The single young of a large ape, such as an orangutan, could remain with its mother for many years. In contrast, small rodents—with a speedy reproductive cycle—can produce litters of a dozen babies, which are ready to breed themselves in just a few weeks.

Behavior

Like their early ancestors, most living mammals use well-developed senses of hearing and smell to interact with others as well as to hunt at night. Although some, such as monkeys, evolved to be active during the day, the sense of smell is still important in the life of most mammals, and many communicate socially by using scent. In a warm-blooded body, the temperature-sensitive brain has evolved to carry out sophisticated tasks, making mammalian behavior highly complex. This means that mammals can learn as well as solve problems. Infants pick up life skills by watching their parents or other individuals, but mammals vary in their social behavior. Most cats, for example, are solitary, fiercely territorial, and only form temporary bonds for the purpose of mating. Conversely, many hooved mammals socialize in herds and, in places, gather to form some of the biggest aggregations of wildlife seen on the planet.

△ PIGGYBACKING LITTER
Litter size varies in mammals. Opossums have up to a dozen infants—carried first, like most marsupials, in their mother's pouch, but then on her back.

◁ FIERCE BATTLE
Mammalian social behavior varies with species and sex. Male gemsboks—a type of desert antelope—clash in disputes over mates, while females socialize in small herds.

MAMMAL CLASSIFICATION

There are more than 5,000 species of mammals, divided into 29 orders. In the table below, the seven orders of marsupials have been collected together.

Egg-laying mammals » p380
Order Monotremata **Species** 5

Marsupials » pp380–81
Orders Didelphimorphia/Peramelemorphia/
Dasyuromorphia/Diprotodontia/Notoryctemorphia/
Microbiotheria/Paucituberculata **Species** 320

Sengis » p381
Order Macroscelidea **Species** 15

Tenrecs and golden moles » p381
Order Afrosoricida **Species** 53

Aardvark » p381
Order Tubulidentata **Species** 1

Dugong and manatees » p382
Order Sirenia **Species** 4

Elephants » p382
Order Proboscidea **Species** 3

Hyraxes » p382
Order Hyracoidea **Species** 4

Armadillos » p382
Order Cingulata **Species** 21

Sloths and anteaters » p382
Order Pilosa **Species** 11

Rabbits, hares, and pikas » p383
Order Lagomorpha **Species** 92

Rodents » pp382–87
Order Rodentia **Species** 2,272

Colugos » p388
Order Dermoptera **Species** 2

Tree shrews » p388
Order Scandentia **Species** 20

Primates » p388–92
Order Primates **Species** 382

Bats » p392–93
Order Chiroptera **Species** 1,117

Hedgehogs and relatives » pp394
Order Erinaceomorpha **Species** 24

Shrews and moles » p394
Order Soricomorpha **Species** 418

Pangolins » p395
Order Pholidota **Species** 8

Carnivores » p395–402
Order Carnivora **Species** 285

Hooved mammals » p402–06
Order Perissodactyla/Artiodactyla **Species** 393

Cetaceans » p407
Order Cetacea **Species** 85

◁ **TENDER MOMENT**
A placenta nourishes most mammalian pregnancies. Even so, a giant panda is born tiny—and so relies on the mother's rich milk for most of its growth.

Egg-laying mammals

Order Monotremata

Marsupials

Orders Didelphimorphia/Peramelemorphia/Dasyuromorphia/Diprotodontia/Notoryctemorphia/Microbiotheria/Paucituberculata

Short-beaked echidna
Tachyglossus aculeatus

- ↔ 12–18 in (30–45 cm)
- ◑ Australia (including Tasmania), New Guinea
- ✕ Common

Bristling with long, thick defensive spines, the short-nosed echidna is a low-slung, solitary insect-eater that feeds mainly on ants and termites. It hunts by day and night, locating its prey among the leaf litter with its snout and scooping it up with its long, sticky tongue. It is the most widespread of the monotremes: a group of five mammal species found in Australasia.

Other species
- ● Duck-billed platypus
  Ornithorhynchus anatinus » p336
- ● Eastern long-beaked echidna
  Zaglossus bartoni » p315

Virginia opossum
Didelphis virginiana

- ↔ 13–20 in (33–50 cm)
- ◑ W., C., and E. US, Mexico, Central America
- ✕ Common

This cat-sized marsupial is the biggest of the American opossums, and the one species found in North America north of Mexico. It is still expanding its range in the US, thanks to its ability to thrive in urban habitats. It often nests in outbuildings and can eat virtually anything, ranging from insects and fruit to kitchen scraps. It is famous for "playing possum," or feigning death when threatened.

hairless, partly prehensile tail

Eastern quoll
Dasyurus viverrinus

- ↔ 11–18 in (28–45 cm)
- ◑ Tasmania
- ✕ Near threatened

The six species of quolls are carnivorous marsupials closely related to the Tasmanian devil. The catlike eastern quoll is one of the smallest. Once widespread in southeastern Australia, it now survives only in Tasmania, where it hunts by night for small mammals and also eats some plant material and scavenges from carcasses.

Eastern barred bandicoot
Perameles gunnii

- ↔ 11–14 in (27–35 cm)
- ◑ SE. Australia, Tasmania
- ✕ Near threatened

Named for the bars on its rump, the eastern barred bandicoot is an omnivorous marsupial that uses its sensitive nose to probe the soil for insects, worms, and seeds at night. By day, it retreats to its nest. It has been almost wiped out on the Australian mainland by foxes but still thrives in fox-free Tasmania.

Water opossum
Chironectes minimus

- ↔ 10–16 in (26–40 cm)
- ◑ S. Mexico to C. South America
- ✕ Common

The slender, long-legged water opossum, or yapok, is the only marsupial adapted for hunting in water. Active by night, it uses its long, webbed hindfeet to swim in pursuit of fish, frogs, and freshwater crustaceans, seizing them with its handlike forefeet.

Common cuscus
Phalanger orientalis

- ↔ 15–19 in (38–48 cm)
- ◑ New Guinea, Solomon Islands
- ✕ Locally common

Native to the densely forested island of New Guinea, this monkeylike marsupial has strong, grasping fingers and toes and a prehensile tail for clinging to branches. It feeds at night, climbing carefully in search of leaves and fruit. Its color is very variable; some island races are black, while others are almost white.

Numbat
Myrmecobius fasciatus

- ↔ 8–11 in (20–28 cm)
- ◑ SW. Australia
- ✕ Endangered

Sleek and bushy-tailed, with a pattern of white stripes around its red-brown body, this solitary, day-active marsupial is specialized for eating termites. Using its large-clawed forefeet, it rips their nests open and licks them up with its tongue. It is remarkable for having 52 teeth—more than any other land mammal—but they are very small. Predation by introduced red foxes has made it extremely rare.

pattern of bands unique on each individual

elongated, pointed snout

Honey possum
Tarsipes rostratus

- ↔ 3–4 in (6.5–9 cm)
- ◑ SW. Australia
- ✕ Locally common

This mouselike marsupial feeds on pollen and nectar, which it gathers from flowers with its bristle-tipped tongue. This diet is unusual for a mammal, because it relies on flowers being available all year, but—unlike birds and insects—the possum cannot fly to cover a wide foraging area. An excellent climber, it uses its sharp-clawed grasping feet and long prehensile tail to grip twigs and stems.

Western gray kangaroo
Macropus fuliginosus

- ↔ 3–5 ft (0.9–1.4 m)
- ◑ S. Australia
- ✖ Locally common

One of the four largest kangaroos, this is also one of the most numerous. Widespread across southern Australia, it lives in groups of up to 15 in mixed habitats that offer shade in the day and good grazing at night. Like all kangaroos, the female nurtures her young in a pouch on her belly. Males are bigger than the females and fight over them by grappling, pushing, and kicking their rivals.

short forelegs

long, powerful tail

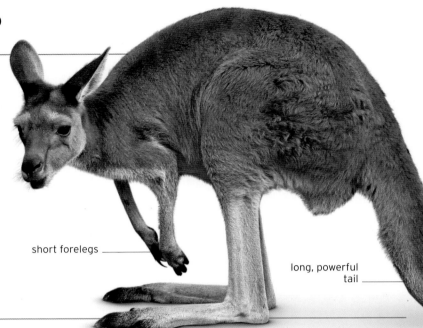

Other species
- **Common spotted cuscus** *Spilocuscus maculatus* » p315
- **Common wombat** *Vombatus ursinus* » p337
- **Fat-tailed dunnart** *Sminthopsis crassicaudata* » p329
- **Goodfellow's tree kangaroo** *Dendrolagus goodfellowi* » p317
- **Greater bilby** *Macrotis lagotis* » p332
- **Koala** *Phascolarctos cinereus* » pp338–39
- **Parma wallaby** *Macropus parma* » p337
- **Red kangaroo** *Macropus rufus* » pp330–31
- **Southern marsupial mole** *Notoryctes typhlops* » p329
- **Spectacled hare wallaby** *Lagorchestes conspicillatus* » p321
- **Sugar glider** *Petaurus breviceps* » p316
- **Tasmanian devil** *Sarcophilus harrisii* » p340
- **Tiger quoll** *Dasyurus maculatus* » p341

Quokka
Setonix brachyurus

- ↔ 16–22 in (40–54 cm)
- ◑ SW. Australia
- ✖ Vulnerable

The quokka is a miniature kangaroo with a compact body the size of a domestic cat. Like other kangaroos, it hops on its hindlegs when moving fast, but it can also climb into shrubs to reach juicy leaves and fruit. It feeds by night in swamps and woodland in southwestern Australia, but is now numerous only on a few islands such as Rottnest Island near Perth.

Sengis
Order Macroscelidea

Karoo rock sengi
Elephantulus pilicaudus

- ↔ 4–6 in (10.5–14.5 cm)
- ◑ South Africa
- ✖ Not known

The Karoo rock sengi is one of the elephant shrews—small mammals with very long snouts, which they use to probe the ground for prey such as earthworms and insects. This species is restricted to the semidesert Karoo region of South Africa, living on the boulder-strewn slopes of rocky mountains. Until 2008, it was thought to be a local race of the very similar but more widespread Cape sengi.

Other species
- **Rufous sengi** *Elephantulus rufescens* » p182

Tenrecs and golden moles
Order Afrosoricida

Common tenrec
Tenrec ecaudatus

- ↔ 10–16 in (26–39 cm)
- ◑ Madagascar
- ✖ Locally common

Resembling a large shrew but with sharp spines among its coarse gray fur, this is the biggest of about 30 species of tenrecs that are mainly native to Madagascar. It lives in a variety of habitats ranging from virgin forest to urban yards, using its long, mobile snout to root for insects, worms, and similar animals. It may also hunt small vertebrates such as frogs and mice. If threatened, the tenrec squeals, bristles up the spines on its neck into a crest, jumps and bucks, and readily bites. It shelters by day in a nest of grass and leaves under a log, rock, or bush.

Cape golden mole
Chrysochloris asiatica

- ↔ 4–6 in (9–14 cm)
- ◑ Southern Africa
- ✖ Locally common

Although it is not closely related to the true moles, the Cape golden mole is similarly adapted for tunneling below ground. Its short front limbs have stout claws for digging—two on each foot—and it has short, soft fur that allows movement in either direction below ground. It is quite blind and relies on its nose and sensitivity to vibrations to locate soil animals, which are its main prey.

Other species
- **Greater hedgehog tenrec** *Setifer setosus* » p241

Aardvark
Order Tubulidentata

Aardvark
Orycteropus afer

- ↔ 5 ft (1.6 m)
- ◑ Sub-Saharan africa
- ✖ Common

With its piglike snout and digging skills, the solitary, nocturnal aardvark deserves its name, which means "earth-pig." It feeds on ants and termites, scooping them up with its sticky tongue.

Dugong and manatees
Order Sirenia

Amazonian manatee
Trichechus inunguis

- ↔ Up to 10 ft (3 m)
- ◑ Amazon basin
- ✕ Vulnerable

Sirenians, or sea cows, are seal-like aquatic mammals related to elephants. They feed on water plants in swamps and shallow coastal seas. The only fully freshwater sirenian, this manatee feeds in the extensive floodwaters of the Amazon river system during the rainy season.

Other species
- ● **Dugong** *Dugong dugon* » p304
- ● **West Indian manatee** *Trichechus manatus* » p67

Elephants
Order Proboscidea

African forest elephant
Loxodonta cyclotis

- ↔ 10–13 ft (3–4 m)
- ◑ W. and C. Africa
- ✕ Not known

Although similar to the African savanna elephant (*Loxodonta africana*), this species is smaller in size and has smaller, oval ears and darker skin as well. Compared with the savanna elephant, the African forest elephant's tusks are harder and straighter, adaptations that allow it to push through the dense vegetation of its tropical forest habitat. Mature males are known to have tusks that almost reach the ground. The forest elephant eats more fruit than the bush elephant and is an important agent of seed dispersal.

Other species
- ● **African savanna elephant** *Loxodonta africana* » pp202–03
- ● **Asian elephant** *Elephas maximus* » p259

Hyraxes
Order Hydracoidea

Southern tree hyrax
Dendrohyrax arboreus

- ↔ 16–28 in (40–70 cm)
- ◑ E. and Southern Africa
- ✕ Common

Hyraxes are small, stocky mammals that resemble guinea pigs, but they are actually most closely allied to elephants. This East African species lives mainly in forests, where it forages in the trees at night for fruit, leaves, and other plant matter. It rarely comes down to the ground, retreating to tree-holes by day to avoid predators such as lions, jackals, hyenas, and eagles.

Other species
- ● **Rock hyrax** *Procavia capensis* » p253

Armadillos
Order Cingulata

Giant armadillo
Priodontes maximus

- ↔ 30–39 in (75–100 cm)
- ◑ N. and C. South America
- ✕ Vulnerable

By far the biggest armadillo, this widespread species has 11–13 bands of hinged plates on its body, with others covering its head, neck, and tail. It uses its long, curved front claws to dig for small prey such as ants and worms, but will also eat small snakes and lizards.

Sloths and anteaters
Order Pilosa

Maned sloth
Bradypus torquatus

- ↔ 18–20 in (45–50 cm)
- ◑ E. South America
- ✕ Vulnerable

Restricted to the coastal rainforests of eastern Brazil, this is one of four species of three-toed sloth. Like all sloths, it is a leaf-eater that spends nearly all its time hanging from the branches of trees by its strong, hooklike claws. Green algae growing on its coat camouflages it well from predators, but if attacked, it lashes out with its claws.

Other species
- ● **Giant anteater** *Myrmecophaga tridactyla* » p116
- ● **Hoffman's two-toed sloth** *Choloepus hoffmanni* » p79
- ● **Silky anteater** *Cyclopes didactylus* » p86

Big hairy armadillo
Chaetophractus villosus

- ↔ 9–16 in (22–40 cm)
- ◑ S. South America
- ✕ Common

Named for the long, coarse hair that protrudes from between the plates of its body armor, this is one of the most common armadillos in southern South America. When threatened, it protects its soft underside by pressing its body into the ground.

Other species
- ● **Six-banded armadillo** *Euphractus sexcinctus* » p117

Collared anteater
Tamandua tetradactyla

- ↔ 21–35 in (53–88 cm)
- ◑ N. and E. South America
- ✕ Least concern

Although similar to the giant anteater in both appearance and feeding habits, this smaller, more agile species often feeds in the trees of the tropical rainforest. It uses its strong prehensile tail to grip the branches as it breaks into the nests of tree-living ants, termites, and bees with its long claws, extracting them with a wormlike tongue that may be up to 16 in (40 cm) long.

Rabbits, hares, and pikas
Order Lagomorpha

Black-lipped pika
Ochotona curzoniae

↔ 6–8 in (15–20 cm)
◑ E. Asia
✖ Common

The black-lipped pika is sandy brown above and dull yellow-white on the underside, with a rust-hued patch behind the ear and a dark nose and lips. Native to the bleak, cold grasslands of the Tibetan plateau, this small, hamsterlike relative of rabbits and hares has special physiological adaptations that help it to survive in habitats where temperatures frequently plunge well below freezing. A plant-eater, it lives in family groups that occupy a single burrow system. Some of these groups can be very large, because the females are each capable of bearing up to five litters of eight young in a season. Unlike other pika species, both parents care for the young. In some areas, this pika is so numerous as to be considered a pest.

Brown hare
Lepus europaeus

↔ 19–28 in (48–70 cm)
◑ Europe, Australia, New Zealand, North and South America
✖ Common

At first glance similar to a rabbit, the brown hare is bigger, with longer legs and longer, black-tipped ears. It is essentially a solitary animal of open habitats that rests by day in a hollow rather than an underground burrow. It feeds mainly by night on plants, relying on its speed to escape enemies. In spring, courting males are often fought off by females in stand-up fights.

gray ears with black tip

long, tawny or rusty fur

Arctic hare
Lepus arcticus

↔ 17–26 in (43–66 cm)
◑ N. Canada, Greenland
✖ Common

Specialized for life in its hostile, snowbound habitat, the Arctic hare has a thick coat of dense fur and shorter ears, reducing heat loss. In the north of its range, its coat stays white all year, but further south it turns gray-brown in summer. It eats a variety of plant material, and even carrion when food is scarce. Unlike other hares, it sometimes gathers in groups of 300 or more that move together as coordinated flocks.

Eastern cottontail
Sylvilagus floridanus

↔ 15–20 in (38–51 cm)
◑ SE. Canada to Mexico, Central America, N. South America
✖ Common

The most widespread and adaptable of the 13 cottontail species, the eastern cottontail usually lives in grassy areas with shrubs for cover. It eats green plants in summer, and bark and twigs in winter. Unlike the European rabbit, which it resembles, it prefers not to dig its own burrows, relying on those excavated by other animals. When breeding, it nests in a shallow depression dug among the grass, which it lines with fur.

European rabbit
Oryctolagus cuniculus

↔ 14–20 in (34–50 cm)
◑ Europe, NW. Africa, Australia, New Zealand, S. South America
✖ Near threatened

Previously restricted to southwest Europe and nearby northwest Africa, the European rabbit has now been introduced throughout much of the world.

Other species
● **American pika** *Ochotona princeps* » p40
● **Black-tailed jackrabbit** *Lepus californicus* » p63

Rodents
Order Rodentia

Yellow-bellied marmot
Marmota flaviventris

↔ 14–20 in (34–50 cm)
◑ SW. Canada to W. US
✖ Common

This rodent spends much of its time in a burrow and hibernates all winter. It usually feeds in the morning and late afternoon, on grasses and other low-growing plants. Each male may live with up to four females in a small colony.

Woodchuck
Marmota monax

↔ 13–21 in (33–53 cm)
◑ Alaska and W. Canada to E. Canada to E. US
✖ Common

Also known as the marmot or groundhog, the woodchuck is a type of ground squirrel that favors open habitats, where it feeds on seeds, grass, fruit, and insects. In winter it retreats to a deep burrow to hibernate. When they emerge, rival males often fight for dominance, and a woodchuck will defend its burrow by threatening trespassers with chattering, bared teeth.

Eastern chipmunk
Tamias striatus

↔ 6 in (15.2 cm)
◑ SE. Canada to C. and E. US
✖ Common

This small ground squirrel is widespread in deciduous woodland, especially in rocky areas with plenty of crevices where it can hide from predators. It lives alone in a burrow, hibernating over winter and emerging in spring. Its loud, staccato alarm calls are valuable to other small animals, alerting them to predators.

bushy tail

bold, black-bordered body stripes

Eastern gray squirrel
Sciurus carolinensis

↔ 9–11 in (23–28 cm)
➐ S. and SE. Canada to S. US, Europe
✖ Common

Introduced to parts of Europe over a century ago, this North American tree squirrel has become an invasive species in many regions, displacing native squirrels. It is an agile, resourceful, and opportunistic feeder, taking a wide variety of natural foods such as nuts, seeds, fruit, and fungi, as well as raiding bird feeders. The squirrel often hoards surplus food, carrying it in its mouth and burying it in scattered underground caches.

thick, bushy tail helps in balance

pale-gray to white ears

pale fur on underside

Cape ground squirrel
Xerus inauris

↔ 8–12 in (20–30 cm)
➐ Southern Africa
✖ Common

Found in the semideserts of southern Africa, this bushy-tailed ground squirrel shelters from the midday heat in a burrow system dug with its strong claws. It lives in small colonies of up to 30 animals, feeding by day on a variety of plant matter such as seeds, bulbs, and roots, though it also takes insects and bird eggs. The squirrel extracts the water it needs from the food, so it rarely has to drink—a valuable asset in such a dry habitat.

Indian giant squirrel
Ratufa indica

↔ 14–16 in (35–40 cm)
➐ S. Asia
✖ Common

Remarkable for its striking two-tone coloration—dark above and pale below—and its very long, bushy tail, the Indian giant squirrel is an agile climber that forages for fruit, nuts, insects, and eggs in the trees. It can leap up to 20 ft (6 m) between branches, enabling it to move from tree to tree without descending to ground level. It also sleeps and breeds in the trees, building a large nest (drey) of twigs and leaves.

Hazel dormouse
Muscardinus avellanarius

↔ 2–3 in (5–7.6 cm)
➐ Europe
✖ Common

Widespread across Europe, the hazel dormouse is a small, bushy-tailed rodent that spends most of its time foraging in the trees. It searches for flowers, insect grubs, and bird eggs in spring and summer, then switches to fruit, nuts, and seeds before hibernating in a nest on the ground throughout the winter. The dormouse may also sink into a deep sleep to survive periods of bad weather or food scarcity in summer.

Large pocket gopher
Orthogeomys grandis

↔ 4–14 in (10–35 cm)
➐ Mexico to Central America
✖ Locally common

Named for its external cheek pouches used for carrying food, this stocky rodent is specialized at burrowing, with large-clawed forefeet and permanently exposed incisor teeth for digging. It emerges above ground at night to feed on vegetation. Usually solitary, the large pocket gopher forms breeding groups of up to four females and one male. Each female bears two or more young.

Eurasian beaver
Castor fiber

↔ 33–39 in (83–100 cm)
➐ Europe to C. Asia
✖ Common

Like its very similar American relative, the big, bulky European beaver is an aquatic rodent that uses its large, orange, chisel-like incisor teeth to gnaw through wood and fell small trees. The beaver uses these to dam streams, creating small lakes that surround and protect its stick-and-mud lodges. In areas with many natural waterways, however, it often makes a riverbank burrow with an underwater entrance.

Chinese bamboo rat
Rhizomys sinensis

↔ 9–16 in (22–40 cm)
◔ E. Asia
✕ Common

The stocky, soft-furred bamboo rat is well-named, for it lives in bamboo thickets and feeds almost entirely on bamboo shoots and roots. It digs extensive burrow systems up to 150 ft (45 m) long, breeding in a nest chamber lined with bamboo leaves. Widespread across southern China and Southeast Asia, this rat can be common enough to be regarded as a plantation pest in some areas.

Golden hamster
Mesocricetus auratus

↔ 5 in (13 cm)
◔ W. Asia
✕ Vulnerable

Native to the borderlands between Syria and Turkey, this golden-furred rodent is far more familiar as a pet. It has a broad diet including seeds, nuts, and insects, and lives in a burrow that can be as deep as 7 ft (2 m). In the wild, it feeds mainly at night, but carries food back to the nest in its large cheek pouches to eat during the day.

stout body

White-footed mouse
Peromyscus leucopus

↔ 3–4 in (7.6–10.1 cm)
◔ SE. Canada to Mexico
✕ Common

Common and widespread throughout central and eastern North America, aside from the far north, this small mouse usually lives in pairs in a sheltered den beneath tree roots or stones, or in a burrow. The mice stay hidden by day and forage at night for seeds, berries, and insects. They often take food back to the den, covering it with soil to hide it.

Giant South American water rat
Kunsia tomentosus

↔ 12 in (30 cm)
◔ C. South America
✕ Locally common

This large rat is found in wet grasslands in Brazil and Bolivia. Despite its name, the giant water rat is a burrower rather than a swimmer, spending most of its time below ground, where it tunnels beneath plants and eats their roots. During the tropical rainy season, the rat's tunnels are often inundated by floodwater, forcing it to feed on grasses and green shoots of other plants on the surface.

Muskrat
Ondatra zibethicus

↔ 10–14 in (25–35 cm)
◔ North America, W. Europe to N. and E. Asia
✕ Common

The largest of the voles, the beaver-like muskrat is specialized for swimming with webbed hindfeet and a flattened tail that it can use as a rudder. It lives in family groups, in riverbank burrows or in mounds of twigs, reeds, and mud. Mainly active by night, it eats water plants such as reeds and water lilies, plus a few small aquatic animals. Native to North America, it has been introduced to Eurasia, where it is now widespread.

Eurasian water vole
Arvicola amphibius

↔ 5–9 in (12–23 cm)
◔ W. Europe to W. and N. Asia
✕ Common

As its name indicates, the water vole is adapted for life in slow-moving rivers, streams, and wetlands and is an adept swimmer and diver. It feeds on a variety of waterside plants, consuming up to 80 percent of its body weight every day. Water voles that mainly burrow in meadows and woods are almost half the size of those that live in river banks. Both types have thick fur, which is gray, brown, or black on the upperparts and dark gray to white below.

Common vole
Microtus arvalis

↔ 4–5 in (10–13 cm)
◔ W. Europe to W. and C. Asia
✕ Common

The small, stocky, blunt-snouted common vole is very common on Eurasian grasslands, farmland, and other open habitats. Its main food is grass, but it also eats a variety of leafy farm crops, as well as soft bark in winter. The common vole makes tunnel-like runways through the grass for easy access to feeding areas and maintains them even under snow cover in winter. It also digs shallow burrows for sleeping, breeding, and storing food.

soft, dense gray-brown fur

blunt snout

Brown lemming
Lemmus sibiricus

↔ 5–6 in (12–15 cm)
◔ N. Asia
✕ Common

The short, rounded body of this volelike rodent is the ideal shape for conserving body heat in the Arctic tundra. In winter, it forages beneath the snow, which insulates it from the bitterly cold wind and hides it from predators such as snowy owls. It feeds on plants, breeding prolifically when food is plentiful. The brown lemming migrates to higher ground in summer, but does not make mass migrations, unlike some other lemming species.

Fat-tailed jird
Pachyuromys duprasi

↔ 4–5 in (10–13 cm)
◔ N. Africa
✕ Common

Adapted for life in the North African desert, this small, soft-furred rodent has a pointed snout and long rear feet. It is named for its stout, hairless tail, which stores energy-rich body fat like the hump of a camel. The jird spends most of the day in a burrow, insulated from the burning sun, and emerges at dusk to hunt through the night for insects and spiders. It also eats some plant matter such as leaves and seeds.

Harvest mouse
Micromys minutus

↔ 2–3 in (5–8 cm)
➤ W. Europe to E. Asia
✖ Common

The tiny, reddish brown harvest mouse is specialized for climbing through tall grasses and other ground vegetation to feed on seeds, berries, and small insects. It is the smallest and lightest European rodent and the only one with a prehensile tail that it can wrap around a grass stem to support it as it feeds. It weaves a spherical nest of shredded grass, suspended above ground level by plant stems.

Black rat
Rattus rattus

↔ 7–10 in (16–24 cm)
➤ Worldwide (except Polar regions)
✖ Common

Sometimes known as the ship rat, this dark, long-tailed, pink-footed rodent has been carried around the globe in ships' cargoes and now lives almost worldwide. Able to climb and swim well, it exploits urban habitats, where it often nests in roof cavities. It prefers plant matter, such as seeds and fruit, but will eat almost anything,

black to tawny brown colour, with lighter underparts

including carrion and human refuse. Black rats gather in "packs" of 20–60 and may intimidate larger animals such as dogs. This rodent's fleas are carriers of diseases such as bubonic plague, responsible for the deaths of millions of people in the past.

Brown rat
Rattus norvegicus

↔ 8–11 in (20–28 cm)
➤ Worldwide (except Polar regions)
✖ Common

Bigger than the black rat, the brown rat favors damp habitats near or below ground level. It is extremely common in urban areas, where it often infests sewer systems. Mostly active by night, it is an opportunistic feeder on a variety of plant and animal matter and will even hunt in packs for live animals such as rabbits. Unlike the black rat, it does not transmit bubonic plague, but it does carry other human diseases and is a serious pest worldwide.

Spinifex hopping mouse
Notomys alexis

↔ 9–17 cm (3½–7 in)
➤ W. and C. Australia
✖ Common

Named after the tough, spiky spinifex grass typical of its Australian desert habitat, this large mouse is well adapted for survival in the arid landscape. It conserves body fluids by producing very concentrated urine; this allows it to get all the moisture it requires from the leaves, berries, and seeds that it eats, so it never needs to drink water.

House mouse
Mus musculus

↔ 3–4 in (7–10.5 cm)
➤ Worldwide (except Polar regions)
✖ Common

Like the black and brown rats, the house mouse has been unwittingly spread around the world by humans and thrives in artificial habitats. House mice live in family groups that multiply very fast, with females capable of producing 10 litters of up to eight young per year. The mice mark their territory with scent and urine, damaging any foodstuffs that they do not eat.

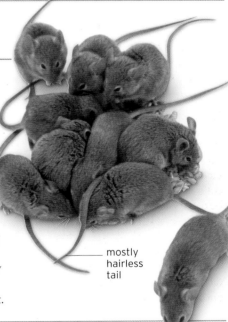

mostly hairless tail

Lesser Egyptian jerboa
Jaculus jaculus

↔ 4–5 in (10–12 cm)
➤ N. Africa to W. Asia
✖ Common

Also known as the desert jerboa, this rodent resembles a miniature kangaroo, with long hindlimbs that it uses to hop across the desert, balanced by its long, bushy-tipped tail. Its feet have broad pads of hair to stop them from sinking into the desert sand. It feeds at night on seeds and roots, and retreats to a burrow during the day, plugging the entrance to keep out the heat and predators.

North American porcupine
Erethizon dorsata

↔ 26–32 in (65–80 cm)
➤ Canada, US
✖ Common

Covered with sharp, hollow spines, which can be up to 3 in (8 cm) long on its head, this rodent is adapted for climbing trees, with strong, broad feet and sharp claws to improve its grip. In winter, it feeds on conifer needles and bark, but in summer it also eats roots, leaves, flowers, seeds, and water plants. It is unusually vocal, especially during the courtship season, when it screeches, snorts, grunts, and hoots.

Brazilian guinea pig
Cavia aperea

↔ 8–12 in (20–30 cm)
➤ NW. to E. South America
✖ Common

The probable ancestor of the domestic guinea pig (*Cavia porcellus*), but with a slightly more elongated body, this blunt-snouted, brown-furred rodent lives in shrubby grasslands across a wide swathe of South America. It feeds on a variety of leaves, grasses, flowers, and seeds, and also gnaws at bark. Guinea pigs share a feeding range, using communal runways through the grass, but each individual has its own nest.

Long-tailed chinchilla
Chinchilla lanigera

- ↔ 8–9 in (22–23 cm)
- ⬗ SW. South America
- ✕ Critically endangered

Restricted to the mountains of central Chile, the chinchilla has been hunted for centuries for its thick, soft, silver-gray fur, essential for survival in its cold mountain habitat. Although widely bred in captivity, it is now very rare in the wild, where it lives in colonies of 100 or more in rocky terrain, sheltering in crevices. Active at night, it nibbles grass, leaves, and other plant material, often holding them in its forepaws like a squirrel.

bushy tail

Argentine plains viscacha
Lagostomus maximus

- ↔ 2 in (5 cm)
- ⬗ C. and S. South America
- ✕ Common

Plains viscachas have mainly gray fur with badgerlike black-and-white facial stripes. They live in noisy colonies of 20–50, in extensive burrow systems that are used for many generations. They stay below ground during the day, coming out to feed at night. They often return with sticks, stones, and even bones, which they pile up around the entrances to their burrows.

Desmarest's hutia
Capromys pilorides

- ↔ 22–24 in (55–60 cm)
- ⬗ Locally common
- ✕ Caribbean

Found only in Cuba, this big, stocky, short-legged rodent resembles an oversized vole. It has sharp, curved claws with which it grips the bark as it climbs trees in search of nutritious leaves, fruit, soft bark, and the occasional small animal such as a lizard. In northern Cuba, this animal lives mainly among coastal mangrove forests, but it favors more open habitats in other locations.

Naked mole rat
Heterocephalus glaber

- ↔ 3 in (7.6 cm)
- ⬗ E. Africa
- ✕ Common

This rodent is specialized for living underground, with very sparse hair on its wrinkled, pale skin, tiny eyes, and big incisor teeth used for tunneling through the dry East African soil. It lives in large colonies, organized in a similar way to ant colonies, with one breeding queen, two or three breeding males, and up to 80 nonbreeding workers of both sexes. The female workers are reproductively suppressed, but if the queen dies, one of them takes over and develops the ability to breed.

large incisor tooth

Coypu
Myocastor coypus

- ↔ 19–23 in (47–58 cm)
- ⬗ S. South America
- ✕ Common

The beaverlike coypu is adapted for swimming, with webbed hindfeet and eyes and ears set high on its head, clear of the water. In its native South American wetlands, it lives in family groups in riverbank burrows and feeds on water plants. It has been farmed for its dense brown fur in many other parts of the world, where escaped animals have established breeding colonies in the wild.

Springhare
Pedetes capensis

- ↔ 11–16 in (27–40 cm)
- ⬗ C. and E. Africa to Southern Africa
- ✕ Common

Looking like a cross between a rabbit and a kangaroo, the springhare lives in the deserts of southeastern Africa, where it has a mixed diet of seeds, bulbs, plant stems, and insects. It can hop fast on its long hindlegs, covering up to 10 ft (3 m) in a single bound, but despite this, it rarely travels far from the burrows where it hides during the day. Its speed is mainly for defense, allowing it to bolt for cover at the first hint of danger.

Other species

- Alpine chipmunk
  Tamias alpinus » p56
- Alpine marmot
  Marmota marmota » p160
- American beaver
  Castor canadensis » p41
- Black-tailed prairie dog
  Cynomys ludovicianus » p48
- Cape porcupine
  Hystrix africaeaustralis » p231
- Capybara
  Hydrochoerus hydrochaeris » p101
- Eurasian red squirrel
  Sciurus vulgaris » p142
- Northern viscacha
  Lagidium peruanum » p109
- Patagonian mara
  Dolichotis patagonum » p117
- Siberian flying squirrel
  Pteromys volans » p285

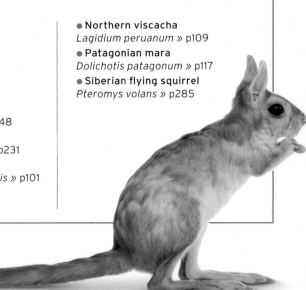

Colugos
Order Dermoptera

Malayan colugo
Galeopterus variegatus

↔ 13–17 in (33–43 cm)
◐ SE. Asia
✖ Common

Once known as the flying lemur, this tropical tree-dweller has a broad membrane of skin between its digits that, when outstretched, allows it to glide from tree to tree without losing much height. The single young clings to its mother as she moves between the trees.

Tree shrews
Order Scandentia

Indian tree shrew
Anathana ellioti

↔ 7–8 in (17–20 cm)
◐ S. Asia
✖ Locally common

More closely related to primates than to true shrews, this small, furry-tailed mammal resembles a squirrel with a pointed muzzle, large eyes, and furred ears. It is speckled with yellow and brown on the upper parts and has a distinctive cream-colored

slender build
bushy tail

shoulder stripe. It is not particularly arboreal, foraging for insects and seeds on the ground and among bushes,

as well as in trees. Typically solitary, it is mainly active by day, sleeping in a tree hole or rocky den at night.

Primates
Order Primates

Calabar angwantibo
Arctocebus calabarensis

↔ 9–10 in (22–25 cm)
◐ W. Africa
✖ Locally common

One of only two *Arctocebus* species, the Calabar angwantibo is orange to yellow on its upper parts and buff beneath. A distinctive white line of fur extends from its forehead to the tip of the nose. A relative of

the lorises and potto, it is a slow-moving, nocturnal primate that climbs deliberately through the trees of the African rainforest in search of fruit and insects as well as snails and lizards. It targets caterpillars, carefully rubbing off any irritating hairs before swallowing them. It prefers to forage at a low level among new growth, which lets it colonize areas of secondary forest that are regenerating after being cleared.

Sunda slow loris
Nycticebus coucang

↔ 10–15 in (26–38 cm)
◐ SE. Asia
✖ Vulnerable

Unusual among primates for its slowed-down lifestyle, this big-eyed climber spends its entire life up in the trees, sleeping by day and creeping through the branches at night. It has an unusually cautious climbing technique, clinging to branches with at least three limbs at a time. It lives alone or in pairs, although several males may pursue a single female.

West African potto
Perodicticus potto

↔ 12–16 in (30–40 cm)
◐ W. and C. Africa
✖ Common

Like the lorises, the potto is a careful, nocturnal tree climber, which feeds on sugary sap, fruit, and insects. It has strong hands and feet and unusually mobile limb joints that allow it to reach out in any direction to grasp a branch. Secretive and solitary, it relies on immobility to avoid detection by predators, but it can defend itself by lowering its head and jabbing at an enemy with hard, sharp-pointed structures covering its neck bones.

Thick-tailed greater galago
Otolemur crassicaudatus

↔ 10–16 in (25–40 cm)
◐ C., E., and Southern Africa
✖ Locally common

This is the largest of the galagos, a group of nocturnal climbers that are also known as bushbabies. It has huge eyes and sensitive ears, which it uses to locate insects in the trees at night, seizing them with a swift movement of its hand. It also uses its comblike, protruding lower incisors to scrape gum and sap from tree bark, and eats fruit such as figs.

fur on back varies from silver to gray or brown

Indri
Indri indri

↔ 24 in (60 cm)
◐ E. Madagascar
✖ Critically Endangered

One of the biggest lemurs, the indri or babakoto ("little father") has dense, silky fur with a striking black-and-white pattern. It has a short tail but very long hindlegs, which it uses to make dramatic leaps between trees. The indri feeds mainly on leaves during the day, but has long periods of inactivity. Males and females mate for life, and live in pairs with their immature young in a territory defended by the male.

Fat-tailed dwarf lemur
Cheirogaleus medius

↔ 7–10 in (17–26 cm)
➊ W. and S. Madagascar
✖ Locally common

No bigger than a squirrel, the fat-tailed dwarf lemur, or the lesser dwarf lemur, is one of the smallest primates, with big, dark-ringed eyes for locating food in the forest at night. During the tropical rainy season, it searches trees and shrubs for fruit, flowers, and insects, building up a reserve of fat in its tail. This sustains it through the eight-month dry season, when it enters a state of dormancy similar to hibernation.

fat stored in tail

Betsileo sportive lemur
Lepilemur betsileo

↔ 10 in (26 cm)
➊ E. Madagascar
✖ Endangered

The sportive lemurs owe their name to the athletic habit of using their hindlimbs to leap from one tree trunk to another. Named after the Malagasy Betsileo people, this species lives in the humid rainforests of eastern Madagascar, feeding mainly on leaves and flowers. Gray-brown with a black tail, the sportive lemur is solitary while awake but gathers in groups to sleep.

Black lemur
Eulemur macaco

↔ 12–18 in (30–45 cm)
➊ N. Madagascar
✖ Vulnerable

Like many lemurs, this species is found only in Madagascar. The males are black, while the females are red, brown, or gray; however, both sexes have a distinctive pale ruff around the neck and shoulders. Groups of up to 15 individuals forage together in trees for fruit, as well as leaves and flowers, gathering them with their hands. They often feed at night, which is unusual for lemurs and possibly a response to human disturbance. Lemurs are also hunted for food.

Monk saki
Pithecia monachus

↔ 15–19 in (38–48 cm)
➊ N. and W. South America
✖ Locally common

The Monk saki is covered in long, coarse, black fur that falls around its face like a monk's hood. It has a thick, bushy tail which, unlike that of many New World monkeys, is not prehensile. Despite this, it spends most of its time on treetops, staying high in the canopy and keeping very quiet, although it can make a loud alarm call if threatened by a high-flying predator.

Bald uakari
Cacajao calvus

↔ 15–23 in (38–57 cm)
➊ NW. South America
✖ Vulnerable

Instantly identifiable by its bright red face and bald crown, which contrast with its shaggy red-brown or white fur, the bald uakari lives in seasonally flooded forests bordering rivers and swamps in the west of the Amazon basin. It forages by day in mixed-sex troops of 10 to 20, but sometimes up to 100, searching the trees for seeds, fruit, flowers, and insects.

Southern muriqui
Brachyteles arachnoides

↔ 22–24 in (55–61 cm)
➊ C. South America (SE. Brazil)
✖ Endangered

Also known as woolly spider monkeys, the two species of muriquis live only in the Atlantic coastal forests of Brazil near São Paulo, where both are now endangered by habitat destruction. Locally known as the charcoal monkey because of its black face, the brown-furred southern muriqui has a heavy body, long limbs, and hooklike fingers with no external thumb. Its prehensile tail helps it to climb through the trees as it feeds on fruit, seeds, and tender leaves.

Guatemalan black howler
Alouatta pigra

↔ 21–25 in (53–64 cm)
➊ Mexico, Central America
✖ Endangered

This is the biggest of the howler monkeys—a group of New World monkeys famous for the phenomenal volume of the males' territorial whoops and howls. Twice the weight of the female, each male controls a troop of about seven females and juveniles, and calls at dawn and dusk to warn off neighboring troops. Howler monkeys feed mainly on leaves, but also take ripe fruit.

Gray woolly monkey
Lagothrix cana

↔ 20–26 in (50–65 cm)
➊ C. South America
✖ Endangered

large forehead and braincase

Named for their thick, close-curled fur, woolly monkeys live in the tropical forests of South America, where they feed mainly on fruit in the treetops. The gray woolly monkey's fur is gray with black flecks, with a darker head, hands, feet, and tail tip. It is an agile climber, with powerful shoulders and hips, and a prehensile tail capable of supporting its weight from a branch while it gathers food. It lives in mixed troops, with a hierarchy based on age.

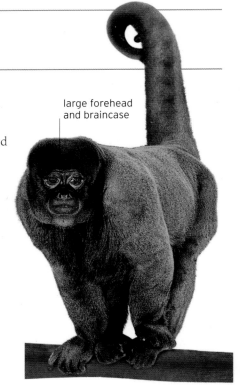

Guianan weeper capuchin

Cebus olivaceus

↔ 15–18 in (38–46 cm)
◑ NE. South America
✕ Locally common

This sociable, intelligent monkey lives in troops of 20 or more in the rainforests of northern South America. It owes its name to the plaintive, weeping calls that the troop uses to stay in contact while moving through the tree canopy in search of food. Males are bigger than females and compete for dominance; typically, only one dominant male in each troop gets the chance to breed.

Black-capped squirrel monkey

Saimiri boliviensis

↔ 11–13 in (27–33 cm)
◑ W. to C. South America
✕ Locally common

The small, agile squirrel monkey feeds mainly on fruit and small animals such as insects, flushing them out from the foliage with twittering, clicking calls as it moves through the trees in large troops. These can number 50 or more, sometimes up to 200—much bigger than that of any other South American monkey. They also follow other monkey troops to snatch any insects they disturb.

small white face patch with dark crown above

tail longer than head and body

Goeldi's marmoset

Callimico goeldii

↔ 8–9 in (22–23 cm)
◑ NW. South America
✕ Vulnerable

Goeldi's marmoset is larger than most marmosets and tamarins. Unknown to the scientific community before 1904, this black-furred species lives in scattered groups in dense undergrowth such as creeper-tangled bamboo. It has a mixed diet of small animals, fruit, and tree sap, which it gathers by using its incisor teeth to make gashes in the bark and licking up the sap that flows from the wounds.

Cotton-top tamarin

Saguinus oedipus

↔ 8–10 in (20–25 cm)
◑ NW. South America
✕ Critically endangered

Found only in a small part of northwest Colombia, the cotton-top tamarin is unmistakable, thanks to the crest of long white hair that flows down its shoulders. It lives in troops of 2 to 15. When there are more than two adults, males or females may have more than one mate. It feeds on small animals and fruit, searching for food by day. It is constantly on the alert, with one member of the group always keeping watch for danger.

Red-bellied titi

Callicebus moloch

↔ 8–10 in (20–25 cm)
◑ N. South America
✕ Critically endangered

Speckled brown, with mainly orange underparts, this monkey has such a thick, soft coat that its ears are almost hidden by fur. It lives in dense forests near rivers, swamps, and pools, where it feeds on fruit, leaves, seeds, and insect grubs. Males and females form strong pair-bonds, staying close to each other and singing a "duet" before dawn to defend their territory. The newborns are carried by the male.

Lemurine night monkey

Aotus lemurinus

↔ 12–17 in (30–43 cm)
◑ Central America to NW. South America
✕ Vulnerable

Sometimes called the owl monkey because of its huge, forward-facing brown eyes and hooting calls, this species and its close relatives are the world's only nocturnal monkeys. Most active at twilight and on moonlit nights when food is easier to see, it climbs cautiously through the forest trees looking for fruit and insects.

De Brazza's monkey

Cercopithecus neglectus

↔ 50–59 cm (20–23 in)
◑ C. to E. Africa
✕ Common

This tropical forest monkey has a black crown, an orange stripe across its forehead, and a luxuriant white beard and moustache. Most of the rest of its body is covered with speckled gray fur. The male is much bigger than the female, and the species usually lives in small groups headed by a dominant male. De Brazza's monkeys communicate using deep, booming calls.

Patas monkey

Erythrocebus patas

↔ 23–35 in (60–88 cm)
◑ W. to E. Africa
✕ Common

This slender, long-legged monkey can run at speeds of up to 34 mph (55 km/h), making it the fastest primate. It lives on the ground in open areas, where cover is scarce and speed is often the only effective defense. Troops often consist of females, their young, a single breeding male, and extra group males. If threatened, the male often distracts the predator while the rest of the troop escapes.

Myanmar snub-nosed monkey
Rhinopithecus strykeri

- ↔ 22 in (56 cm)
- ◔ S. Asia
- ✗ Critically endangered

Discovered in 2010 in northern Myanmar, this rare and endangered monkey is mostly black, with a contrasting white mustache, beard, and ear tufts. It has an upturned nose, which, according to local people, makes it prone to sneezing in rainy weather. It lives in mountain forests in summer, and spends the winter at lower, warmer altitudes. Its known population is less than 500, making it vulnerable to extinction.

Bengal gray langur
Semnopithecus entellus

- ↔ 20–31 in (50–78 cm)
- ◔ India
- ✗ Common

Also known as the hanuman langur, this slender, long-tailed monkey has a striking black face that contrasts with its gray or brown fur. It occurs in a wide variety of habitats ranging from semideserts to tropical forests, often living near villages, where it makes the most of any discarded food. Elsewhere, it feeds mainly on leaves and fruit. It lives in groups of varying sizes, spending most of the daylight hours on the ground, but sleeping in trees at night.

Chacma baboon
Papio ursinus

- ↔ 24–32 in (60–82 cm)
- ◔ Southern Africa
- ✗ Common

Found in open habitats in southern Africa, this is the biggest of the baboons—ground-dwelling monkeys with long, doglike snouts and protruding nostrils that typically live in large troops. The chacma baboon mostly forages on the ground by day and has a broad diet ranging from fruit and seeds to small gazelles, although hunting is rare. Intelligent and adaptable, it may throw stones to deter intruders.

Celebes crested macaque
Macaca nigra

- ↔ 21–23 in (53–58 cm)
- ◔ SE. Asia
- ✗ Critically endangered

Covered with black fur but having big, expressive, red-brown eyes, this short-tailed monkey lives in tropical forests. A crest runs from the forehead back over the crown. Usually flat, the crest rises when the animal is aroused. A sociable animal, it lives in groups of 60–80, but sometimes forms mixed-sex troops of 100 or more. It mainly feeds on fruit and invertebrates, but it may also eat other small animals.

dense, woolly coat

Guereza
Colobus guereza

- ↔ 21–23 in (53–58 cm)
- ◔ C. and E. Africa
- ✗ Locally common

Mainly black with a white ruff around its naked black face, this monkey is also known as the eastern black and white colobus. It has a fringe of long, white, silky hair along its flanks and a matching white tuft at the tip of its long tail. It mainly eats tough, fibrous leaves, which it can digest thanks to a complex, three-part stomach containing gut microbes that break down the fiber.

Lar gibbon
Hylobates lar

- ↔ 17–23 in (42–59 cm)
- ◔ SE. Asia
- ✗ Endangered

Like all gibbons, this is a superb arboreal acrobat, able to swing through trees using its long arms and, thanks to its opposable big toes, walk upright along branches. It usually lives in monogamous pairs, which reinforce their pair-bond each morning with loud hooting duets that are repeated many times. Deforestation and hunting by humans are major threats to this primate.

Sumatran orangutan
Pongo abelii

- ↔ 4–5 ft (1.2–1.5 m)
- ◔ N. Sumatra
- ✗ Critically endangered

Slimmer than the Bornean orangutan, and with longer chestnut hair, the Sumatran orangutan is also more sociable than its largely solitary relative. Big groups may come together to feed in fruiting fig trees, moving slowly through the canopy and often using their weight to bend a branch within reach of the next one. These orangutans are almost exclusively arboreal—females virtually never travel on the ground and adult males rarely do so. Now restricted to the north of their native island, Sumatran orangutans are critically endangered by the destruction of their rainforest habitat to create oil palm plantations.

grasping hands

coarse, shaggy coat

Eastern gorilla
Gorilla beringei

↔ 4–6 ft (1.2–1.8 m)
◐ C. and E. Africa
✕ Endangered

The eastern gorilla lives in the Rift Valley region near Lake Victoria, and is divided into two races: the mountain gorilla and the eastern lowland gorilla. Both types live in family groups, led and defended by a dominant male gorilla with pale gray fur on his back. Known as a silverback, the dominant male fathers most or all the young in the group. Adult males are much bigger than females, weighing up to 460 lb (210 kg). Gorillas mainly eat plant material including leaves, fruit, nuts, berries, and juicy roots, and occasionally insects such as termites and ants.

Bonobo
Pan paniscus

↔ 28–33 in (70–83 cm)
◐ C. Africa
✕ Endangered

A close relative of the chimpanzee, and thought to be the same species until 1929, the bonobo is slimmer, with longer limbs. It has mostly black skin, and the hair on its crown has a distinctive central part. The bonobo feeds chiefly on the ground and has a varied diet of fruit, seeds, leaves, flowers, fungi, bird eggs, and small animals. Groups of up to 100 bonobos gather to sleep at night, but they generally split up into smaller groups to forage for food, mainly on the ground. Females are dominant and leave their family groups when mature; males tend to stay on.

Other species

● **Aye-aye**
Daubentonia madagascariensis » p241
● **Berthe's mouse lemur**
Microcebus berthae » p237
● **Bornean orangutan**
Pongo pygmaeus » pp296–97
● **Chimpanzee**
Pan troglodytes » pp210–11
● **Emperor tamarin**
Saguinus imperator » p92
● **Gelada**
Theropithecus gelada » pp180–81
● **Golden langur**
Trachypithecus geei » p267
● **Golden snub-nosed monkey**
Rhinopithecus roxellana » p273
● **Hamadryas baboon**
Papio hamadryas » p249
● **Hooded capuchin**
Sapajus cay » p102
● **Japanese macaque**
Macaca fuscata » pp286–87
● **Mandrill**
Mandrillus sphinx » p213

● **Müller's gibbon**
Hylobates muelleri » p298
● **Olive baboon**
Papio anubis » p185
● **Proboscis monkey**
Nasalis larvatus » p295
● **Pygmy marmoset**
Cebuella pygmaea » p92
● **Red howler monkey**
Alouatta seniculus » p93
● **Ring-tailed lemur**
Lemur catta » pp238–39
● **Terai sacred langur**
Semnopithecus hector » p259
● **Verreaux's sifaka**
Propithecus verreauxi » p240
● **Vervet monkey**
Chlorocebus pygerythrus » p201
● **Western gorilla**
Gorilla gorilla » p212
● **Western tarsier**
Cephalopachus bancanus » p294

Bats
Order Chiroptera

Rodrigues flying fox
Pteropus rodricensis

↔ 14 in (35 cm)
◐ Indian Ocean (Rodrigues Island)
✕ Critically endangered

The flying foxes are named for their foxy, pointed faces, which differ from those of most other bats. This species is a fruit bat, found only on Rodrigues Island, where it feeds at

hooklike foot claws permit roosting without muscle tension

brown fur

night on ripe fruit and returns at dawn to roost in trees. Human disturbance and destruction due to tropical cyclones has made it rare.

Egyptian rousette
Rousettus aegyptiacus

↔ 6–7 in (15–18 cm)
◐ W. Asia, N. Africa (Egypt), W., E., and Southern Africa
✕ Common

The Egyptian rousette and a few of its close relatives are the only fruit bats to use a form of echolocation, which is similar to that used by insectivorous bats. This helps it to find its way around and roost in dark caves. More widespread across Africa than its name suggests, it is seen as a pest by fruit farmers.

Proboscis bat
Rhynchonycteris naso

↔ 1½–2 in (3.5–5 cm)
◐ Mexico to C. South America
✕ Common

Found across most of Amazonia and parts of Central America, the proboscis bat owes its name to its long, pointed nose. This insect-eater lives in small groups that use echolocation to hunt for airborne insects at night, usually over water. By day, the groups of up to 40 roost together on a branch or a wooden beam, typically lying nose-to-tail.

Lesser mouse-tailed bat
Rhinopoma hardwickii

↔ 2–3 in (5–8 cm)
◐ W. to S. Asia, N. and E. Africa
✕ Common

The mouse-tailed bats are a small group of insectivorous bats that are unique for their thin, trailing tails, like those of mice. Favoring dry habitats, this species preys mainly on beetles and moths; when these are scarce in the dry season, it lies dormant, sustained by body fat built up when food is abundant.

Lesser horseshoe bat
Rhinolophus hipposideros

↔ 2 in (5 cm)
◐ Europe, N. Africa to W. Asia
✕ Common

Named for its horseshoe-shaped nose leaf, this is one of the smallest insectivorous bats. It hunts at night for small insects and spiders. Widespread across the warmer parts of Europe, it roosts by day in tree holes, caves, and manmade structures. It hibernates in deep caverns throughout the winter.

Ghost bat
Macroderma gigas

↔ 4–5 in (10–13 cm)
◐ W. and N. Australia
✕ Vulnerable

This long-winged bat can seize frogs, mice, small snakes, and even roosting birds in its long, curved claws. It locates them at night by sight and by using echolocation, and kills them with a neck bite. It is called the ghost bat as the skin of its wings is unusually thin, giving it a ghostly appearance as it flies overhead in the moonlight.

Greater bulldog bat
Noctilio leporinus

↔ 2½–3 in (6–8 cm)
◑ Central America, N., E., and C. South America
✕ Common

Remarkably, this tropical American bat is a specialist at catching fish. It targets them at night using echolocation to detect leaping fish and the ripples they make, then scoops them from the water with its sharp-clawed back feet. It can catch fiddler crabs and shrimp in the same way, but also takes insects and even scorpions. It has velvety fur with a distinct pale stripe along the middle of its back.

Common pipistrelle
Pipistrellus pipistrellus

↔ 1–2 in (2.5–5 cm)
◑ Europe to N. Africa, W., and C. Asia
✕ Common

One of the most widespread Eurasian bats, this small insect-eater lives in a range of habitats from dense forests to city parks and suburban yards. It can squeeze its tiny body into the narrowest crevices, slipping between overlapping tiles to roost by day in roof spaces, and is one of the first bats to emerge at dusk to prey on midges, small moths, and other flying insects. It hibernates throughout the winter and forms

large breeding colonies of up to 1,000 females, each nursing a single baby.

Pallid bat
Antrozous pallidus

↔ 2–3 in (5–8 cm)
◑ W. North America to Mexico, Cuba
✕ Common

The pallid bat lives in arid habitats, where it hunts on the ground at night, flying low and using its eyes and ears. It targets large insects, spiders, centipedes, scorpions, and even lizards and mice, swooping down to seize them and carry them off to a favorite perch where it can eat them. By day, the bats gather in groups and retreat to roost in rock crevices, old buildings, and tree cavities, giving clearly audible cries as they go.

Daubenton's bat
Myotis daubentonii

↔ 2–3 in (5–8 cm)
◑ Europe to N. and E. Asia
✕ Common

This widespread Eurasian bat specializes in hunting over water, flying low over ponds, lakes, and waterways to catch flying insects in its mouth or scoop them up with its tail or wing membrane. It even targets small fish, skimming over the surface and grabbing them with its large feet. By day, it often roosts beneath bridges but also uses abandoned buildings and trees. It flies up to 180 miles (300 km) to its winter hibernation site, usually a deep cave or an old mine.

gray flight membrane

pale underside

Brown long-eared bat
Plecotus auritus

↔ 1½–2 in (4–5 cm)
◑ Europe, C. Asia
✕ Common

The enormous ears of this small woodland bat—almost as long as its body—give it incredibly sensitive hearing. They allow it to detect the faint sounds made by insects such as moths and beetles as they feed on vegetation at night, so it can pick them off the leaves. It then usually takes its prey to a perch to eat. It roosts in caves, trees, and outbuildings and spends the winter hibernating in a deep cave, abandoned mine, or disused basement or cellar.

Angolan free-tailed bat
Mops condylurus

↔ 3 in (8 cm)
◑ W., C., E., and Southern Africa
✕ Common

Named for its long, mouselike tail, which is not attached to any flight membranes, the Angolan free-tailed bat is widespread across Africa south of the Sahara. It gathers in large numbers to roost by day, emerging each evening in noisy, flapping groups

Common noctule
Nyctalus noctula

↔ 3 in (8 cm)
◑ Europe to W., E., and S. Asia
✕ Common

This high-flying bat lives in woodland, roosting alone in tree cavities by day. At night it hunts by swooping down on insects such as large moths. It hibernates in groups in better-insulated places, such as caves, and may travel 1,200 miles (2,000 km) or more to find a suitable site, returning in spring.

designed to confuse potential predators such as hawks and owls. It preys on flying insects, discarding the hardest, most inedible parts as it eats them on the wing.

Other species
● **Large flying fox**
Pteropus vampyrus » p294
● **Lesser short-tailed bat**
Mystacina tuberculata » p355
● **Vampire bat**
Desmodus rotundus » p115
● **White bat**
Ectophylla alba » p79

Hedgehogs and relatives
Order *Eulipotyphla*

Moonrat
Echinosorex gymnura

↔ 10–18 in (26–46 cm)
◐ SE. Asia
✕ Common

The moonrat is one of a small group of mainly insectivorous mammals closely related to hedgehogs but without the spines. It has harsh, rough, coarse outer fur and a long, scaly, almost hairless tail. The moonrat hunts at night in the tropical forests of Southeast Asia, catching insects on the ground but also pursuing aquatic animals, including fish, in the water. It marks its territory with a pungent scent of ammonia, similar to that of rotting onions.

Long-eared hedgehog
Hemiechinus auritus

↔ 6–11 in (15–28 cm)
◐ S. Asia
✕ Locally common

This prickly mammal is adapted for life in the desert. Its large ears act as radiators, helping it to lose excess heat, and it gets most of the water it needs from its insect food. Spending the day in its burrow, it emerges at dusk to hunt. When prey is scarce, it can become dormant, but this state rarely lasts long.

> **Other species**
> ● European hedgehog
> *Erinaceus europaeus* » p156

Shrews and moles
Order *Eulipotyphla*

Eurasian shrew
Sorex araneus

↔ 2–3 in (5–8 cm)
◐ Europe to N. Asia
✕ Common

Also known as the common shrew, this tiny, frenetically active animal has such a fast rate of metabolism that it must eat 80–90 percent of its body weight in food every 24 hours, or it will starve. It hunts day and night, taking short rests between regular bursts of activity when it uses its long, bristly, sensitive snout to search for insects, worms, slugs, and snails. Adults are normally solitary except during a brief courtship period in spring or early fall. The common shrew is territorial—it defends itself vigorously, biting if cornered.

Eurasian water shrew
Neomys fodiens

↔ 3–4 in (8–10 cm)
◐ Europe to N. Asia
✕ Common

Adapted for hunting in pools and streams, the water shrew has water-repellent outer fur and thick underfur that keeps it warm when submerged. Its back and sides are dark, but it has a white underside. It propels itself underwater with its hair-fringed hindfeet, pursuing aquatic insects, small fish, and frogs. It has venomous saliva that immobilizes the prey it seizes in its teeth. It also hunts on land for beetles and worms.

short, dense fur

Armored shrew
Scutisorex somereni

↔ 4–6 in (10–15 cm)
◐ C. to E. Africa
✕ Common

This large shrew has a highly unusual spine adaptation—each backbone has interlocking flanges above, below, and on each side, making it immensely strong. The adaptation's function is unknown, but studies suggest it may help the shrew lever dead logs off the ground to get at worms hiding below.

Russian desman
Desmana moschata

↔ 7–9 in (18–23 cm)
◐ E. Europe to C. Asia
✕ Vulnerable

Native to river systems to the north of the Black Sea, the desman is part of the mole family, but hunts in the water. It swims well, propelled by its webbed hindfeet and laterally flattened tail. It uses its sensitive nose to probe for aquatic insects and crayfish among the stones of the riverbed. It lives in groups, which may share a riverbank burrow.

Bicolored white-toothed shrew
Crocidura leucodon

↔ 2–7 in (5–18 cm)
◐ Europe to W. Asia
✕ Common

The name of this shrew refers to the sharp divide between the brown fur of its upperparts and the creamy white underfur. It is one of a large subfamily of shrews that have white teeth; those of the other subfamily have red-tipped teeth. It hunts by night for worms and insect grubs.

Star-nosed mole
Condylura cristata

↔ 7–8 in (18–20 cm)
◐ E. Canada, NE. US
✕ Common

The nose of this functionally blind mole ends in 22 fleshy tentacles equipped with thousands of microscopic sensory organs that are highly responsive to touch and help the mole detect prey. This mole digs a network of tunnels through the soil. It is also an excellent swimmer, and hunts mainly in the water for insects, worms, and small fish.

Hispaniolan solenodon
Solenodon paradoxus

↔ 11–13 in (28–33 cm)
◐ Caribbean (Hispaniola)
✕ Endangered

This shrewlike insectivore was first described in 1833. It hunts at night for insects and small vertebrates, half-paralyzing them with a venomous bite that it also uses for defense. It is one of just two species of solenodon, the other being found on the nearby island of Cuba.

European mole
Talpa europaea

- 4–7 in (12–18 cm)
- Europe to N. Asia
- Common

long, cylindrical body

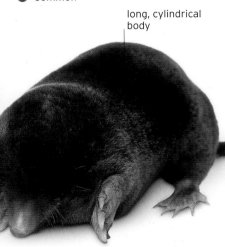

Specialized for living underground, this virtually blind mole uses its powerful, spadelike feet to dig a network of tunnels radiating from a central chamber. It pushes the excavated soil up to the surface, forming a series of distinctive molehills. Its short, dense black fur can lie in either direction, allowing the mole to move forward or backward through the soil. It feeds on worms, insect grubs, and other animals that fall into the tunnels, detecting them by touch, smell, and sound. The female gives birth to three or four young.

Pangolins
Order Pholidota

Ground pangolin
Manis temminckii

- 20–24 in (50–61 cm)
- E. to Southern Africa
- Vulnerable

Pangolins are insect-eating mammals with a unique body armor of large, overlapping scales made of keratin. If threatened, they can roll up into an armored ball. This species eats ants and termites, using its large claws to rip open their nests. It laps them up with a sticky tongue about 16 in (40 cm) long—half the length of its body.

Other species
- **Common pangolin**
  Manis tricuspis » p215

Carnivores
Order Carnivora

Fennec fox
Vulpes zerda

- 10–16 in (25–41 cm)
- N. Africa
- Common

Native to the arid lands of the Sahara, the fennec is the smallest of all foxes. It is remarkable for its big, sensitive ears, which it uses to detect prey such as insects and mice in the desert night; they may also help it to dissipate heat. It has a broad diet, eating fruit and seeds as well as small animals. It is adapted to minimize water loss, which means that it rarely needs to drink.

huge, batlike ears to radiate body heat

long, thick hairs protect from cold

Rüppels fox
Vulpes rueppellii

- 25 in (64 cm)
- N. and E. South America
- Common

Also called the sand fox, Rüppels fox is similar to the red fox but slighter in build. It has soft, dense, sandy or silver-gray fur to match its arid habitat, black patches on the sides of the muzzle, and a white tail tip. In some regions, this species forms monogamous pairs, but in others, it gathers in groups of up to 15. It eats a variety of food from grass to insects, reptiles, and mammals.

Crab-eating fox
Cerdocyon thous

- 25 in (64 cm)
- N. and E. South America
- Common

Widespread on the grasslands and open woodlands of tropical South America, this medium-sized fox is an opportunist hunter that often preys on crabs, both in freshwater habitats and on the coast. It also takes various other prey, ranging from insect grubs to small mammals and fish as well as eggs and fruit. It is usually grayish brown above and white below.

Bush dog
Speothos venaticus

- 23–30 in (58–76 cm)
- N. and C. South America
- Near threatened

This long-bodied, short-snouted, short-legged wild dog lives in packs of up to 12 in the tropical forests of the Amazon. This powerful and persistent hunter hunts by day, using group tactics that enable it to bring down large animals such as deer and capybaras. Each pack has a mated pair and offspring of various ages; only the dominant pair breeds, but other members of the pack help to defend and feed the youngest pups.

Black-backed jackal
Canis mesomelas

↔ 18–35 in (45–90 cm)
◔ E. and Southern Africa
✖ Common

An adaptable and resourceful species, the black-backed jackal is a common sight in eastern and southern Africa, from city suburbs to remote deserts. Males and females mate for life and live as a pair, hunting their own prey and scavenging from the kills of others. They eat a huge variety of animals, as well as fruit and berries. Each pair has its own territory, centered on a den, such as an old aardvark hole, where they rear their family.

Red wolf
Canis rufus

↔ 3–4 ft (1–1.2 m)
◔ Reintroduced to E. US
✖ Critically endangered

Smaller than the gray wolf, and with a red tinge to its gray-brown fur, the red wolf once lived throughout the eastern states of the US but was reduced to near-extinction by hunting and interbreeding with coyotes. Reintroduced to the wild in North Carolina from 1987, the species built up a small wild population, but its future is still in serious doubt. It lives in family-based packs and hunts mammals such as rabbits and raccoons.

Bat-eared fox
Otocyon megalotis

↔ 18–26 in (46–66 cm)
◔ E. and Southern Africa
✖ Common

This long-legged, small-headed African fox is a specialized insect-eater. It uses its huge ears to pinpoint the location of its prey on the savanna, targeting the harvester termites that swarm over the grasslands. It also eats other insects such as dung beetles and grasshoppers. Compared with other foxes, it has smaller teeth and more of them (with up to eight extra molars), an adaptation to its small prey.

Sun bear
Helarctos malayanus

↔ 4–5 ft (1–1.5 m)
◔ SE. Asia
✖ Vulnerable

Mainly black or rusty-brown with a U-shaped pale patch on its chest, the sun bear is the smallest of the bears and the only one adapted for life in tropical rainforests. A good climber, it sleeps in trees and feeds mainly on fruit and insects. It breaks into termite mounds for prey and rips hollow trees apart to get at the nests of bees so it can devour their honey and larvae.

Asiatic black bear
Ursus thibetanus

↔ 4–6 ft (1.2–1.8 m)
◔ E., S., and SE. Asia
✖ Vulnerable

Also known as the moon bear because of the white crescent on its black chest, this species is similar to the American black bear. It spends much of its time in trees, foraging for nuts and fruit, but also eats bamboo shoots, grasses, and insects. Deforestation has destroyed much of its forest habitat, and as a result, it sometimes raids farm crops, coming into direct and sometimes fatal conflict with humans.

Common seal
Phoca vitulina

↔ 5–6 ft (1.5–1.8 m)
◔ North Atlantic, North Pacific
✖ Common

Also known as the harbor seal, this is the most widespread of the seals, ranging along the coasts of both the northern Pacific and Atlantic oceans, as well as some Arctic seas. The common seal has a small, rounded, catlike head with large eyes and distinctive V-shaped nostrils and is very variable in color. It preys mainly on fish, which it catches on short dives lasting just three to four minutes each.

pale gray-brown fur with small rings and blotches

Crabeater seal
Lobodon carcinophaga

↔ 7–9 ft (2.1–2.7 m)
◔ Antarctic and subantarctic waters
✖ Common

Despite its name, this Antarctic true seal is specialized for catching the shrimplike krill that form vast swarms in the Southern Ocean. Its elaborately lobed teeth interlock to form a sieve when its jaws are closed, allowing it to strain the krill from the water rather than seizing them individually. It rests and breeds on drifting pack ice and is a regular target for killer whales and leopard seals.

Weddell seal
Leptonychotes weddellii

↔ 8–10 ft (2.5–3 m)
◔ Antarctic and subantarctic waters
✖ Common

The deep-diving Weddell seal hunts fish and other marine animals beneath the sea ice that fringes the Antarctic coast. It can stay underwater for over an hour, but must maintain a breathing hole in the ice above. To do this, the seal enlarges cracks in the ice with its teeth—as a result, many Wendell seals suffer from worn teeth and dental abscesses, which can prove fatal.

Baikal seal
Pusa sibirica

↔ 4–5 ft (1.2–1.5 m)
◔ E. Asia (Lake Baikal)
✖ Locally common

Although closely related to the ringed seal of the Arctic Ocean, this small, sleek seal lives only in Lake Baikal in Siberia, the deepest freshwater lake in the world. Like all true seals, it swims effortlessly, propelling itself with its rear-facing hindlimbs. The males stay in the water all winter, hunting fish beneath the ice, but in late winter, the females haul out onto the ice to bear their white-coated pups.

Brown fur seal
Arctocephalus pusillus

↔ 6–8 ft (1.8–2.4 m)
◑ Southern Africa, SE. Australia
✕ Locally common

Like all fur seals and sea lions, brown fur seals have powerful forelimbs and long hindlimbs that can be rotated forward. This allows them to walk on all fours on land, unlike the more fishlike true seals. They gather on rocky shores in colonies of a thousand or more during the breeding season. The males are bigger than the females, and compete to secure territories that give them control over harems of females.

South American sea lion
Otaria byronia

↔ 8–9 ft (2.4–2.8 m)
◑ W., S., and E. South America, Falkland Islands
✕ Common

This species is probably the original "sea lion"—the male has a huge head with a luxuriant mane and weighs twice as much as the female. As with other sea lions and fur seals, the biggest males fight to control as many females as possible. South American sea lions favor sandy beaches for resting and breeding, and go out to sea to prey on fish, squid, and the occasional seabird. The mothers coax their pups into the water after 1–2 months, which is a relatively early age for a sea lion.

California sea lion
Zalophus californianus

↔ Up to 2.4 m (7³/₄ ft)
◑ W. US
✕ Locally common

Ranging from Alaska to Mexico, the California sea lion is far more widespread than its name suggests. It preys mainly on squid and shoaling fish such as herring, catching them on short dives to depths of about 75 m (245 ft). This species rarely strays more than 16 km (10 miles) out to sea and often enters harbours and estuaries for food and shelter. Compared to the sleek females, the males are bigger and generally darker, with more robust forequarters, which prove useful during territorial disputes. The juveniles are a uniform tan colour.

small external ear

streamlined body tapers from shoulder to tail

Humboldt's hog-nosed skunk
Conepatus humboldtii

↔ 10–15 in (25–38 cm)
◑ S. South America
✕ Locally common

Named for its piglike naked nose pad, adapted for rooting in the ground for insects, this skunk is black or reddish brown with a prominent white stripe extending along each flank, from its crown to its bushy tail. Solitary and nocturnal, it spends the day hidden in a burrow or a den beneath rocks. Like other skunks, it can defend itself with a foul-smelling spray.

Eastern spotted skunk
Spilogale putorius

↔ 12–14 in (30–36 cm)
◑ E. to C. US, NE. Mexico
✕ Common

Smaller and sleeker than the more familiar striped skunk, the eastern spotted skunk has a similar pattern of black-and-white fur, broken up into large patches that vary from one individual to another. The striking pattern warns predators to leave it alone, or risk being sprayed with a noxious fluid from its anal glands. It has a mixed diet of small animals, bird eggs, and fruit.

Palawan stink badger
Mydaus marchei

↔ 14–18 in (36–46 cm)
◑ Philippines (Palawan and Busuanga Islands)
✕ Locally common

Genetic studies show that this stocky, badgerlike animal belongs to the same family as the skunks, which accounts for its ability to drive off its enemies with a pungent secretion squirted from its anal scent glands. It uses its long, flexible, almost hairless snout to probe for small animals in the soil and lives alone in a rocky den or abandoned burrow.

Ringtail
Bassariscus astutus

↔ 12–17 in (30–43 cm)
➔ C. and W. US to S. Mexico
✖ Common

This slim, agile North American hunter is a relative of the raccoons and has a similar black-and-white ringed tail. Otherwise mainly brown, it has big eyes surrounded by black rings and striking white eyebrows. It hunts at night for small mammals, birds, and reptiles, but it has a broad diet and also forages for insect grubs, fruit, and nuts.

Crab-eating raccoon
Procyon cancrivorus

↔ 18–35 in (45–90 cm)
➔ Central America to C. South America
✖ Common

Similar to the common raccoon, with a ringed tail and black-masked eyes, this crab-eater lives up to its name by hunting crabs along seashores and the edges of rivers and marshes. It feels for prey in the shallows with its sensitive, nimble front paws. Solitary and nocturnal, it retreats to a tree hole by day.

Stoat
Mustela erminea

relatively long neck

↔ 7–10 in (18–25 cm)
➔ North America, Greenland, Europe to N. and E. Asia
✖ Common

The long, slender, flexible body of this widespread predator is well adapted for pursuing other small mammals, such as voles, through their burrows. It also kills rabbits, even though they often far outweigh it. It is red-brown above and creamy white below, but in the snowy north of its range, it molts to pure white in winter, aside from the tip of the tail, which is always black; this white form is known as an ermine.

Least weasel
Mustela nivalis

↔ 7–10 in (18–25 cm)
➔ North America, Europe to N., C., and E. Asia
✖ Common

Similar to a stoat, but with an even smaller, slimmer, brown and white body and tiny head, the least weasel can enter the smallest mouse or vole burrow in search of prey. It specializes in hunting these small rodents, which are so abundant and widespread that the least weasel consequently has a huge range across both North America and northern Eurasia. In the far north, it turns white in winter for camouflage in the snow —this is for its own protection as well as to conceal it from potential prey. It lives alone, using several nests in crevices or old burrows.

European polecat
Mustela putorius

sinuous body

↔ 14–20 in (35–51 cm)
➔ Europe
✖ Common

This relatively large member of the weasel family has long dark outer fur with creamy-yellow underfur visible as it moves and a black mask across its eyes. Its sinuous body and short legs allow it to enter rabbit holes in search of prey. A domesticated form of the polecat—the ferret— is used by hunters to flush rabbits out of their burrows. It also runs and swims well. If threatened, it defends itself with a foul-smelling product of its anal glands. Male and female polecats defend separate territories, but the males' territories usually overlap those of the females.

American mink
Neovison vison

↔ 12–22 in (30–56 cm)
➔ North America; introduced to Europe
✖ Common

Native to North America, this adaptable relative of the weasels has become widespread across Eurasia as a result of escapes from fur farms. Normally dark brown to almost black, it resembles a smaller, darker otter, and often uses its partly webbed feet to hunt in the water for frogs, fish, and water voles. An excellent swimmer, it can stay submerged for distances of up to 98 ft (30 m). It also takes a wide variety of prey on land and is widely seen as a threat to native wildlife in its introduced range.

dark, glossy fur

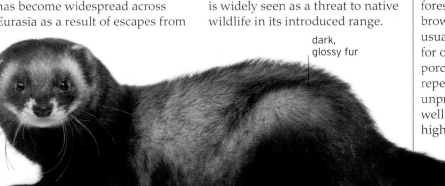

Fisher
Martes pennanti

↔ 19–30 in (48–76 cm)
➔ Canada to N. US
✖ Common

The cat-sized fisher is the biggest of the martens—a long, low-slung forest predator with dense, dark brown fur and a bushy tail. It usually hunts on the ground for other mammals, including porcupines, which it kills by repeatedly biting at their unprotected faces. It can climb well and often makes its den high in a hollow tree, where it also raises its young.

Sable
Martes zibellina

↔ 13–18 in (33–46 cm)
➔ N. and E. Asia
✖ Common

This is the northeast Asian equivalent of the fisher, famous for its dense, brown-black fur, which made it a prime target for fur-trappers over several centuries. Fast and agile, it hunts in the forests for small mammals such as hares and rodents, scavenges from the kills of wolves, and also eats fruit. It often adopts an abandoned burrow as a breeding nest, but makes temporary dens for shelter from the cold when foraging for food in winter.

front claws adapted
for digging

African zorilla
Ictonyx striatus

↔ 11–15 in (28–38 cm)
◑ W. to E. and Southern Africa
✗ Common

The zorilla resembles a small skunk, both in appearance and in its defense tactics. Like a skunk, it drives away attackers by spraying them with a foul secretion from its anal glands, while hissing and screaming. Mainly nocturnal, it digs out prey such as insect grubs from among dead leaves with its long front claws.

Honey badger
Mellivora capensis

↔ 24–30 in (61–76 cm)
◑ W., C., E., and Southern Africa, W. and S. Asia
✗ Common

The martenlike honey badger has a striking two-tone pattern of silver-gray upperparts, sharply contrasting with black below. It eats a variety of prey ranging from insect grubs to snakes and porcupines, but it owes its name to its taste for wild honey. It digs large burrows, but may also live in rock crevices and holes in tree roots. It defends itself fearlessly, sometimes producing an offensive smell to deter predators.

Greater grison
Galictis vittata

↔ 19–22 in (48–56 cm)
◑ S. Mexico, Central and northern South America
✗ Common

Grizzled gray above and black below, with a white U-shaped stripe dividing the two on its forehead and neck, this is a sleek, sinuous hunter with a slim, pointed head and relatively short legs. An agile runner, swimmer, and climber, it forages on the ground, usually by day, for small mammals such as agoutis and opossums, as well as insects, worms, frogs, birds, and some fruit. It usually lives alone, or in pairs. Its sounds include snorts, growls, screams, and barks.

American badger
Taxidea taxus

↔ 17–28 in (43–71 cm)
◑ SW. Canada to US, N. Mexico
✗ Common

Like other badgers, this species is stocky and powerful, with short, strong legs, shaggy gray fur, and a black-and-white striped face. It usually lives on open grasslands, where it uses its powerful claws to dig for burrowing prey such as ground squirrels, pocket gophers, voles, and even ground-nesting birds, such as burrowing owls. It also eats a lot of insects and some seeds. It typically forages at night, spending the day in a burrow.

Hog badger
Arctonyx collaris

↔ 22–28 in (55–70 cm)
◑ SE. and E. Asia
✗ Near threatened

This forest dweller has a long, black-striped white face with a pink, piglike snout and protruding lower teeth—the ideal tool for digging in soft soil for insect grubs, worms, seeds, and juicy roots. It also seizes other small animals, such as mice. It is an expert digger, using its very long front claws to create elaborate burrow systems. A nocturnal species, it spends the day sheltering in these burrows. The hog badger regularly falls prey to tigers and leopards but fights back vigorously if cornered.

Sea otter
Enhydra lutris

↔ 22–51 in (56–130 cm)
◑ North Pacific
✗ Endangered

The heaviest of all otters but the smallest marine mammal, the sea otter hunts in coastal seas. Its extremely dense fur keeps it warm, enabling it to stay at sea for many hours. It hunts for shellfish such as clams and especially the sea urchins that swarm beneath the submerged forests of giant kelp (seaweed) that grow in north Pacific coastal waters. Bringing the shellfish to the surface, it often breaks them open with a stone, while floating on its back.

African clawless otter
Aonyx capensis

↔ 29–37 in (73–95 cm)
◑ W., E., C., and Southern Africa
✗ Common

This otter has short claws on its hindfeet, but its clawless front toes are more like fingers, with a sensitivity that enables the animal to feel for prey in muddy water. The otter's long, sinuous body and muscular tail make it an excellent swimmer and diver, allowing it to chase after fish and frogs underwater. It also preys on crabs and lobsters on coasts, cracking their shells open with its strong jaws.

Asian small-clawed otter
Aonyx cinereus

- ↔ 29–37 in (73–95 cm)
- ➤ W., E., C., and southern Asia
- ✖ Vulnerable

The claws of this small otter are so short that they do not protrude beyond the fleshy pads of its webbed feet. It feeds mainly on mussels, clams, and crabs, catching them in its forefeet and crushing them with its broad cheek teeth; it also eats large insects, frogs, rodents, and small fish. Small-clawed otters live in extended family groups of about 12, which can often be seen

playing on riverbanks. Male-female pair bonds in these groups are especially strong.

outer guard hairs provide water-proofing

long, muscular tail

Falanouc
Eupleres goudotii

- ↔ 19–22 in (48–56 cm)
- ➤ E. and N. Madagascar
- ✖ Near threatened

Restricted to tropical rainforests and marshes on the island of Madagascar, this elusive hunter has a bushy tail and a long, slim snout. Its tiny, cane-shaped teeth are flattened to cope with gripping slimy invertebrate prey such as earthworms and slugs. Its single young is born with its eyes open and is able to follow its mother after only two days.

Yellow mongoose
Cynictis penicillata

- ↔ 9–13 in (23–33 cm)
- ➤ Southern Africa
- ✖ Common

Similar to the meerkat, the yellow mongoose also has a habit of standing on its hindlegs for a better view of its surroundings and possible danger. It often occupies a burrow system—originally dug by meerkats—and sometimes shares it with them. The mongoose lives in extended family groups, each comprising a main breeding pair, their young, and nonbreeding adults. It preys on small animals—mainly insects such as termites, beetles, and locusts, but also frogs, lizards, birds, and mice.

Banded mongoose
Mungos mungo

- ↔ 12–18 in (30–45 cm)
- ➤ Africa
- ✖ Common

This sociable mongoose is named for the pattern of dark bands across its brownish gray back. Widespread across Africa in open forests and grasslands, it lives in groups of 20 or so that forage together, twittering and chirping as they seek out food such as insects and other small animals. It also eats bird eggs, cracking open the shells by throwing them against rocks.

Common palm civet
Paradoxurus hermaphroditus

- ↔ 17–28 in (43–71 cm)
- ➤ S., E., and SE. Asia
- ✖ Common

Grayish brown, but mottled with darker spots and black stripes, and with a dark mask across its face, this bushy-tailed civet is widespread across a varied range of habitats. It mainly eats small animals and fruit—especially figs and the fermented juice of palm tree flowers. An accomplished climber, it often takes refuge in a tree or roof by day, searching for food at night.

Common genet
Genetta genetta

- ↔ 16–22 in (40–55 cm)
- ➤ W., E., and Southern Africa, W. Europe
- ✖ Common

The slender, sharp-faced common genet has a body with bold black spots and a long, black-banded tail, like that of a raccoon. It climbs like a cat and forages mainly at night for a variety of small mammals, birds, eggs, insect grubs, and fruit. By day, it hides away in a hollow tree or a den made in a tangle of roots among dense bushes. Adaptable and opportunistic, it has a wide distribution ranging from South Africa to central France.

Eurasian lynx
Lynx lynx

- ↔ 3–4 ft (0.9–1.2 m)
- ➤ N. Europe to E. Asia
- ✖ Common

This is the biggest of the four lynx species, with a striped, spotted, or plain yellow-brown coat, and prominent black ear tufts. The lynx is adapted for life in the northern Eurasian forests, where it copes with the cold winters by growing an extra-long coat; its big, broad feet enable it to walk on deep snow. Unusually, it can bring down deer

and similar prey up to four times its own size, but it also hunts smaller animals such as hares.

dense fur

Serval
Leptailurus serval

↔ 24–39 in (61–100 cm)
➤ Africa
✖ Common

Lean and long-legged like a small cheetah, the serval often hunts among the tall reeds and rushes of wetlands, where its dark-spotted, yellowish coat provides excellent camouflage. It catches a variety of prey ranging from locusts and frogs to small birds, but usually targets rats and other rodents. The serval, one of the tallest cats, detects much of its prey with its long, mobile ears, but also uses its height to see over tall vegetation. The females bear an average litter of two young after a 73-day gestation period.

black markings run from top of head

slender, agile body

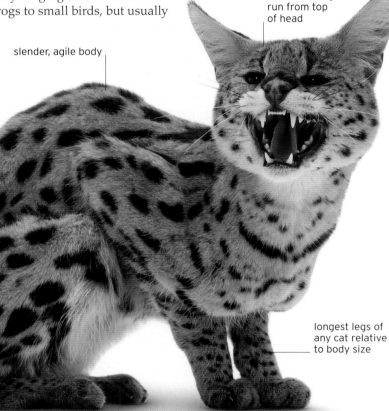

longest legs of any cat relative to body size

Sand cat
Felis margarita

↔ 18–23 in (46–58 cm)
➤ N. Africa, W., C., and SW. Asia
✖ Near threatened

This small, short-legged, blunt-clawed, sandy gray cat is adapted for life in the desert. It digs or takes over a burrow in the sand for shelter from the scorching sun by day and hunts at night—mainly for rodents such as gerbils and jerboas, although it also takes lizards, snakes, and a few insects. It gets most of the moisture it needs from its prey, so it does not need to live near a water source.

Fishing cat
Prionailurus viverrinus

↔ 30–34 in (75–86 cm)
➤ S. to SE. Asia
✖ Endangered

The stocky, powerful fishing cat lives in freshwater wetlands and tidal mangrove swamps, where it hunts fish and other aquatic animals such as frogs, crabs, crayfish, and even snakes. It swims well, but has few physical adaptations for its way of life—its teeth, for example, are not well suited to seizing slippery fish, and it usually catches prey with its sharp-clawed forepaws.

Margay
Leopardus wiedii

↔ 18–31 in (46–79 cm)
➤ S. US to Central and South America
✖ Near threatened

Big-eyed and marked with leopardlike clusters of spots, this small cat lives in tropical forests, where it hunts mainly in the trees. It is an unusually agile climber, able to descend head-first down a trunk like a squirrel or hang by its hindfeet from a high branch. It ambushes opossums, young sloths, squirrels, and small birds, and also preys on invertebrates such as large insects and spiders.

Jaguarundi
Puma yagouaroundi

↔ 22–30 in (55–77 cm)
➤ S. US to South America
✖ Common

The jaguarundi has an unusually long body and short legs for a cat. Widespread across South America in forests, wetlands, and arid scrub, it occurs in several color forms ranging from black to pale gray-brown, to match its habitat. Active by day, it usually hunts on the ground for any small animals it can catch, including large insects, rodents, rabbits, lizards, and ground-feeding birds.

Brown hyena
Hyaena brunnea

↔ 5 ft (1.5 m)
➤ Southern Africa
✖ Near threatened

Resembling a large dog, but with a long, shaggy, dark brown coat and short back legs, this southern African hyena ranges far into the Kalahari and Namib deserts in search of carrion and occasional small prey. It can scent a carcass from more than 8 miles (13 km) away and is aggressive enough to steal the prey of a leopard. It lives in small clans with various structures, but always including 1–5 females and their offspring.

Spotted hyena
Crocuta crocuta

↔ 5 ft (1.5 m)
➤ W. to E. and Southern Africa
✖ Common

The biggest and most powerful of the hyenas—with massive jaws and teeth capable of cracking large bones—the spotted hyena is both a scavenger and an accomplished pack-hunting predator. It lives in female-dominated clans with up to 80 members in prey-rich savanna. The clan shares a communal den, and members work together to bring down prey, such as wildebeest, or drive larger predators, such as lions, off their kills. The animal makes

many sounds, including the famous hyena's "laugh," which signifies submission to a senior clan member.

Aardwolf

Proteles cristata

⬌ 26 in (67 cm)
◉ E. and S. Africa
✗ Locally common

This small, striped relative of the hyenas has the typical hyena body form, with short hindlegs and a sloping back, exaggerated by a crestlike mane on its back. But it is much more lightly built, with small teeth, and instead of scavenging for carrion, it preys almost exclusively on termites. Hiding in a burrow by day, it emerges at dusk to search the dry grasslands for harvester termites, which it licks up from the ground with its long, sticky tongue.

Other species

● **African wild dog**
Lycaon pictus » p224
● **American black bear**
Ursus americanus » p55
● **Arctic fox**
Alopex lagopus » p27
● **Bengal tiger**
Panthera tigris tigris » pp260–61
● **Black-footed ferret**
Mustela nigripes » p48
● **Bobcat**
Lynx rufus » p37
● **Caracal**
Caracal caracal » p229
● **Cheetah**
Acinonyx jubatus » p196
● **Coati**
Nasua nasua » p86
● **Coyote**
Canis latrans » p49
● **Culpeo**
Pseudalopex culpaeus » p109
● **Dhole**
Cuon alpinus » p277
● **Dingo**
Canis lupus dingo » p321
● **Ethiopian wolf**
Canis simensis » p182
● **Eurasian otter**
Lutra lutra » p167
● **European badger**
Meles meles » p165
● **European pine marten**
Martes martes » p165
● **Fosa**
Cryptoprocta ferox » p237

● **Galapagos sea lion**
Zalophus wollebaeki » p123
● **Giant otter**
Pteronura brasiliensis » p102
● **Giant panda**
Ailuropoda melanoleuca » pp274–75
● **Gobi bear**
Ursus arctos gobiensis » p279
● **Gray seal**
Halichoerus grypus » p135
● **Gray wolf**
Canis lupus » p37
● **Grizzly bear**
Ursus arctos horribilis » p36
● **Harp seal**
Pagophilus groenlandicus » p31
● **Iberian lynx**
Lynx pardinus » pp154–55
● **Indian gray mongoose**
Herpestes edwardsii » p262
● **Indochinese clouded leopard**
Neofelis nebulosa » p276
● **Jaguar**
Panthera onca » pp94–95
● **Japanese marten**
Martes melampus » p288
● **Kit fox**
Vulpes macrotis » p61
● **Leopard**
Panthera pardus » p214
● **Leopard seal**
Hydrurga leptonyx » p371
● **Lion**
Panthera leo » pp194–95
● **Maned wolf**
Chrysocyon brachyurus » pp118–19

● **Meerkat**
Suricata suricatta » pp232–33
● **Northern grey fox**
Urocyon cinereoargenteus, » p67
● **Northern raccoon**
Procyon lotor » pp68–69
● **Ocelot**
Leopardus pardalis » p80
● **Polar bear**
Ursus maritimus » pp28–29
● **Puma**
Puma concolor » p62
● **Raccoon dog**
Nyctereutes procyonoides » p289
● **Red fox**
Vulpes vulpes » p168
● **Red panda**
Ailurus fulgens » p270
● **Sloth bear**
Melursus ursinus » p263
● **Snow leopard**
Panthera uncia » pp268–69
● **Southern elephant seal**
Mirounga leonina » pp365
● **Spectacled bear**
Tremarctos ornatus » p87
● **Striped hyena**
Hyaena hyaena » p252
● **Striped skunk**
Mephites mephites » p54
● **Walrus**
Odobenus rosmarus » p32
● **Wildcat**
Felis silvestris » p143
● **Wolverine**
Gulo gulo » p38

Hoofed mammals

Orders Perissodactyla/Artiodactyla

Tibetan wild ass

Equus kiang

⬌ 7–8 ft (2–2.4 m)
◉ W., C., and S. Asia
✗ Common

Native to the deserts of central Asia, this relative of the domestic horse is specialized for life in dry habitats. It is a nomad that wanders the arid lands in herds looking for food such as grass and succulent desert plants. The herds are made up of females and their young, or bachelor males; the mature males are more solitary.

buff, tawny, or gray coloration

African wild ass

Equus africanus

⬌ 7–8 ft (2–2.4 m)
◉ NE. Africa
✗ Critically endangered

The probable ancestor of the domestic donkey, with a similar gray coat and a dark, bristly mane, the African wild ass lives in rocky east African deserts where the temperature on the ground can exceed a scorching 122°F (50°C). It survives by eating virtually any plant food it can find, from grasses to thorny acacia foliage and it is capable of going without drinking water for several days.

Plains zebra

Equus quagga

⬌ 7–8 ft (2–2.4 m)
◉ E. to Southern Africa
✗ Locally common

This is the most common and widespread of the zebras. It roams the African savannas in herds alongside wildebeest and gazelles, feeding mainly on grass. A typical zebra herd is made up of a male, his harem of females, and several young. The herds may stay together for several years, but the male must regularly fight off challenges from the younger males that live in their own bachelor herds.

Sumatran rhinoceros
Dicerorhinus sumatrensis

↔ 8–10 ft (2.4–3 m)
➤ S. and SE. Asia
✖ Critically endangered

The smallest rhinoceros, and the hairiest, this two-horned species was once widespread across Southeast Asia, but is now extremely rare and localized. It is a solitary animal of forests and swamps, spending the day in a mud wallow to keep cool. It feeds mainly in the evening and early morning, gathering leaves, tender shoots, and fruit, and often uses its weight to push over young trees so it can get at their foliage.

Lowland tapir
Tapirus terrestris

↔ 6–7 ft (1.8–2.1 m)
➤ N. and C. South America
✖ Vulnerable

pale brown on cheeks, throat, and chest

This bristly, brown-coated animal has white-tipped ears and a short, narrow mane. Like other tapirs, it has a long, mobile snout, which it uses to browse selectively for nutritious leaves, shoots, and fruit. It prefers waterside habitats and is a good swimmer—it dives into the water to escape predators such as jaguars, but is often taken by the black caiman. Females give birth to single young, which are born with white spots and stripes. These provide camouflage in the dappled shade.

Malayan tapir
Tapirus indicus

↔ 6–8 ft (1.8–2.4 m)
➤ SE. Asia
✖ Endangered

The largest and only Old World tapir, this species is black with a sharply contrasting white back and rump. The effect is striking, but in the Malayan tapir's shady forest habitat, it acts as camouflage, breaking up the animal's outline so it is not recognizable by predators such as tigers. The Malayan tapir is a solitary browser that feeds on a variety of soft twigs and young leaves of bushes and saplings, as well as fallen fruit.

Giant forest hog
Hylochoerus meinertzhageni

↔ 4–7 ft (1.2–2.1 m)
➤ W., C., and E. Africa
✖ Locally common

Perfectly described by its name, the giant forest hog is the biggest of the wild pigs and lives almost entirely in the African tropical forests. Its dark skin is covered with coarse black hair, and it has enlarged canine teeth forming tusks that grow up and out from each jaw. Unlike most pigs, it does not root in the ground for food, but eats grasses, leaves, and occasionally cultivated crops.

Bushpig
Potamochoerus larvatus

↔ 4–5 ft (1.2–1.5 m)
➤ E., C., and Southern Africa
✖ Common

The long-snouted bushpig is similar to the Eurasian wild boar, with a coat of coarse dark hair, a paler, bristly mane, and a pale head with white face markings. It lives in forests and swamps, in groups of up to 12 that usually consist of several females, juveniles, and a single adult male. Bushpigs use their snouts to poke around in the soil for roots, bulbs, tubers, and insect grubs, but may also scavenge for carrion.

Moluccan babirusa
Babyrousa babyrussa

↔ 3–4 ft (0.9–1.2 m)
➤ SE. Asia
✖ Vulnerable

This wild pig is notable for the male's tusks, which curve upward from its upper jaw to its forehead; they may be up to 12 in (30 cm) long. It has shorter, sharper tusks in its lower jaw for fighting rivals, and uses the upper tusks for defense. Males usually live alone, but females and their young travel in small groups. They eat a range of leaf, root, fruit, and animal foods, but do not root in the ground for them.

Collared peccary
Pecari tajacu

↔ 30–39 in (75–100 cm)
➤ SW. US to S. South America
✖ Common

Built like a small wild boar, with a barrel-shaped body, slim legs, and a pale band around its neck, this omnivore thrives in a range of habitats. Extremely sociable, it lives in tightly knit mixed-sex groups for mutual defense against enemies such as pumas. It feeds mostly on plant material, but also eats worms, lizards, and snakes.

Pygmy hippopotamus
Choeropsis liberiensis

↔ up to 5 ft (up to 1.5 m)
➤ W. Africa
✖ Endangered

The pygmy hippopotamus is much smaller and rarer than its big relative, with a more compact head and narrower feet with fewer webbed toes. A solitary animal, it follows well-worn forest trails to forage at night for leafy foliage and fruit, retreating to a muddy swamp during the day. Like its larger cousin, it has delicate skin that dries out easily in the sun, so it must keep the skin moist by staying close to water.

Guanaco
Lama guanicoe

↔ 3–7 ft (0.9–2.1 m)
➤ W. to S. South America
✖ Common

This slender, brown-coated relative of the domestic llama is specialized for life in the cold, arid foothills of the Andes, where it is found at altitudes of up to 15,000 ft (4,500 m) or more. It lives in family groups of one breeding male and up to seven adult females and young; unmated males live in separate herds. Guanacos feed mainly on grasses and shrubs, but some also survive in the hostile Atacama Desert, where they eat cacti and lichens.

Dromedary
Camelus dromedarius

↔ 7–11 ft (2.1–3.4 m)
➤ N. and E. Africa, W. and S. Asia
✖ Not known

Although widespread across north Africa and the Middle East, this one-humped camel is extinct in the wild. The only place where it lives in the wild is Australia, where captive dromedaries, imported to work in the desert, have formed feral breeding populations. The dromedary is superbly adapted for desert life. The hump stores fat that can be broken down into water and energy, allowing the camel to survive for weeks without drinking.

Alpine musk deer
Moschus chrysogaster

- ↔ 28–39 in (70–100 cm)
- ◔ S. Asia
- ✕ Endangered

This species is remarkable for the long canine teeth in the upper jaw of both males and females. Those of males can be up to 4 in (10 cm) long; they are used in displays and fights between rivals. The deer live on forested mountains with rocky slopes, and have unusually big toes that can be spread for a secure footing on rocks and soft snow. The name refers to a musky secretion of the males, used to attract females.

Common fallow deer
Dama dama

- ↔ 5–6 ft (1.5–1.8 m)
- ◔ North and South America, Europe, Southern Africa, Australia, and New Zealand
- ✕ Common

Native to the Near East but introduced widely elsewhere, the common fallow deer is brown with white spots in summer, becoming darker in winter. Mature males have antlers, which fall off in spring and regrow by the end of summer. During the fall breeding season, rival males use them to fight over small territories,

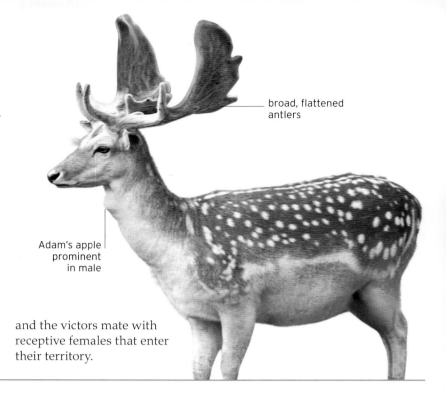

broad, flattened antlers

Adam's apple prominent in male

and the victors mate with receptive females that enter their territory.

Mule deer
Odocoileus hemionus

- ↔ 3–7 ft (1–2.1 m)
- ◔ W. North America
- ✕ Common

The mule deer is named for its large ears, which reminded American settlers of the ears of a mule. Rusty brown in summer, and gray-brown in winter, it has a large, white rump patch and black tail tip. Widespread and adaptable, it lives in a broad variety of habitats, ranging from cactus deserts to the boreal forests of Canada, and eats an equally broad range of plants.

Marsh deer
Blastocerus dichotomus

- ↔ Up to 7 ft (2.1 m)
- ◔ C. and E. South America
- ✕ Vulnerable

Adapted for life in wetlands, the marsh deer has long legs and broad hooves that allow it to wade easily through swamps and walk over soft mud. It is also a capable swimmer. Reddish brown with dark lower legs and a black muzzle, it is the largest South American deer. It eats a variety of grasses, water plants, and leaves gathered from bushes, feeding alone or in groups of two or three.

Southern pudu
Pudu puda

- ↔ 34 in (86 cm)
- ◔ SW. South America
- ✕ Vulnerable

Pudus are the world's smallest deer. There are two species—northern and southern—both native to the Andes of South America. The southern pudu of Chile and Argentina is buff to reddish or dark brown, with rounded ears. The male has short antlers that are just spikes, used to defend territory against other males. It lives alone or in pairs, browsing on leaves, buds, flowers, and fruit.

Bongo
Tragelaphus eurycerus

- ↔ 6–8 ft (1.8–2.4 m)
- ◔ W. and C. Africa
- ✕ Near threatened

This is the largest forest antelope and also the most striking because of the pattern of narrow, vertical white stripes on its chestnut-brown body. In addition, it has a white chest crescent, cheek spots, nose chevron, and leg bands. Both sexes have spiral, lyre-shaped horns, although those of the male are longer. It lives in tropical forests with dense undergrowth and is mainly a selective browser on the tender young leaves of bushes and low-growing trees.

Common eland
Tragelaphus oryx

- ↔ 7–11 ft (2.1–3.5 m)
- ◔ C., E., and S. Africa
- ✕ Common

Resembling a cow but with a smaller, dark-crowned head and tightly spiraling horns, the common eland is an antelope of open grassland, where it eats grass during the rainy season, but switches to browsing on leaves in the dry season. During droughts, it can allow its body temperature to rise by up to 44°F (7°C) to avoid losing body moisture as sweat, reducing its need for water. It typically lives in large herds of up to 500 for mutual protection

against hunters such as lions. Herds mainly consist of females with calves and juveniles; males may be solitary.

Greater kudu
Tragelaphus strepsiceros

- ↔ 2–2.5 m (6½–8¼ ft)
- ◔ E. to Southern Africa
- ✕ Common

A woodland browser, the greater kudu is one of the tallest antelopes. The height of the male is increased by a spectacular pair of spiral horns that can be well over 120 cm (47 in) long. The male uses these horns to impress rivals, forcing any antelopes with shorter horns to give way. If two equally matched males confront each other, they may fight; sometimes they lock horns so tightly that they cannot free themselves and die as a result.

Asian wild buffalo
Bubalus arnee

↔ 8–10 ft (2.4–3 m)
◑ S. Asia
✕ Endangered

The big, powerful Asian wild buffalo is the ancestor of the domestic water buffalo, but while the latter is widespread and common, its wild counterpart is now very rare. It is adapted for eating lush marsh vegetation, with broad, splayed feet that help stop it from sinking into the mud. Females live in herds with their young, while young males form bachelor groups. Older males are

solitary; they compete for females by sparring with their horns, which can span more than 79 in (200 cm).

Wisent
Bison bonasus

↔ 7–11 ft (2.1–3.4 m)
◑ E. Europe
✕ Vulnerable

The wisent is the European bison, a very close relative of the similar American bison. Driven to extinction in the wild by the 1920s, it was reintroduced to the Bialoweiza forest in eastern Europe using animals bred from bison held captive in zoos. Small wild populations have also been established elsewhere. It feeds on grasses and the leaves of forest trees and shrubs, and lives in small herds.

Yak
Bos mutus

↔ Up to 11 ft (3.4 m)
◑ C. Asia
✕ Vulnerable

The larger, wild form of the domestic yak is now extremely rare and restricted to the desolate, bitterly cold steppe grasslands of the Tibetan plateau and part of neighboring Kashmir. It is one of the wild cattle, but specialized for its hostile habitat with a coat of long, shaggy, black or dark brown hair concealing a dense, soft undercoat. It grazes on plants and eats snow when it cannot find water.

Nilgai
Boselaphus tragocamelus

↔ 6–7 ft (1.8–2.1 m)
◑ S. Asia
✕ Common

Also known as the bluebuck or blue bull, this large antelope has an oxlike appearance, but with longer legs and a much smaller head. Females are tawny with a white throat and a dark mane; males are larger and bluish gray, with a pair of short horns. Nilgai live in open woods, where they feed on leaves, fruit, and grasses while staying sharply alert for powerful predators, such as tigers.

Bush duiker
Sylvicapra grimmia

↔ 2–4 ft (0.7–1.2 m)
◑ W., C., E., and Southern Africa
✕ Common

The common duiker is a small antelope with a dark stripe down its nose and short, sharp horns. It has a wide range across Africa. Its diet ranges from various plant foods to occasional small animals. The duiker can survive without water for long periods, obtaining all the moisture it needs from its food. The males use their horns to defend territories against rivals; females use them to defend their young.

Common waterbuck
Kobus ellipsiprymnus

↔ 4–8 ft (1.3–2.4 m)
◑ W., C., and E. Africa
✕ Common

The waterbuck is adapted for wet habitats. It has skin glands that secrete a musky-smelling oil, which waterproofs its long, coarse fur. When threatened, it leaps into the nearest water body, where it either swims to safety or submerges except for its nose. It feeds on grass and lives in herds of 6–20 animals. Males use their long, ridged and ringed horns to fight for dominance, sometimes inflicting deadly wounds.

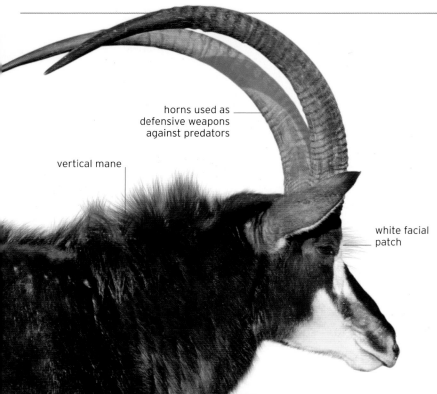

horns used as defensive weapons against predators

vertical mane

white facial patch

Southern sable antelope
Hippotragus niger

↔ 6–9 ft (1.8–2.7 m)
◑ E. to SE. Africa
✕ Common

A mature male southern sable antelope is black all over, except for its cheeks, chin, and underparts; females are smaller and browner, but both sexes have heavily ringed horns that curve up and back from the forehead. In the rainy season, males compete for territories, and the victors dominate small herds of females. During the dry season, they switch from grazing to browsing, sometimes gathering in larger, mixed-sex herds of 100 or more.

Gemsbok
Oryx gazella

↔ 5–8 ft (1.5–2.4 m)
◑ SW. Africa
✕ Locally common

The big, long-horned gemsbok roams in nomadic herds across the deserts of southwest Africa, searching for the grass, leaves, and fruit that appear after sporadic rainstorms. It relies on fruit such as wild melons and cucumbers to supply much of its water, although it is well adapted to avoid moisture loss, not sweating until its body temperature reaches 113°F (45°C). Like many desert species, gemsbok breed opportunistically, and year-round when food is available.

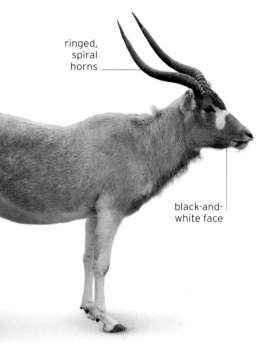

ringed, spiral horns

black-and-white face

Addax
Addax nasomaculatus

↔ 5–6 ft (1.5–1.8 m)
🧭 NW. Africa
✖ Critically endangered

Like the gemsbok, the spiral-horned addax is specialized for life in deserts, with a nomadic lifestyle and physiological adaptations to help it conserve body moisture. It rarely drinks, getting nearly all the water it needs from succulent desert plants. Grayish brown in winter, it turns almost white in summer, with a white facial patch and a dark crown. Always elusive, it is now on the brink of extinction.

Southern gerenuk
Litocranius walleri

↔ up to 5 ft (1.5 m)
🧭 E. Africa
✖ Near threatened

Also called the giraffe-gazelle, the slender, elegant gerenuk is highly adapted for browsing on foliage that is out of reach of most antelopes. It has a very long, slim neck and a modified spine that allows it to stand vertically on its long hindlegs for long periods to pluck young, tender leaves with its sharp teeth. It lives in dry shrubland and semidesert, where it feeds mainly on thorny bushes and trees such as acacia.

Alpine ibex
Capra ibex

↔ 4–6 ft (1.2–1.8 m)
🧭 S. Europe
✖ Locally common

Famous for its fearless agility on steep mountain terrain, this wild goat lives in the Alps at altitudes of up to 22,000 ft (6,700 m). Both sexes have long, curved, ridged horns, but those of the male grow to over 39 in (100 cm) long. Males use them to spar with rivals—in general, the male with the longest horns dominates the others.

scimitar-shaped horns

woolly beard

Markhor
Capra falconeri

↔ 5–6 ft (1.5–1.8 m)
🧭 C. and S. Asia
✖ Endangered

The spiral horns of the male markhor can be up to 63 in (160 cm) long. The female's horns are much shorter; she is also only half the male's weight and lacks the shaggy mane that falls from the male's neck and chest almost to his feet. Now rare, markhors live in the mountains to the west of the Himalayas, mainly in oak and pine forest.

Barbary sheep
Ammotragus lervia

↔ 4–6 ft (1.2–1.8 m)
🧭 N. Africa
✖ Vulnerable

This reddish brown wild goat lives in the mountains of north Africa, where it feeds on grass, herbaceous plants, and the foliage of desert bushes. Both sexes have crescent-shaped horns, but those of the males are bigger. They are used for ritual combat as the males charge each other to determine status and gain access to females.

Other species

- **Alpine chamois**
  Rupicapra rupicapra » p159
- **American bison**
  Bison bison » pp46–47
- **Arabian oryx**
  Oryx leucoryx » pp250–51
- **Bactrian camel**
  Camelus bactrianus » p281
- **Bhutan takin**
  Budorcas whitei » p267
- **Bighorn sheep**
  Ovis canadensis » p53
- **Blackbuck**
  Antilope cervicapra » p257
- **Camargue horse**
  Equus caballus » p147
- **Cape buffalo**
  Syncerus caffer » p220
- **Impala**
  Aepyceros melampus » p197
- **Common warthog**
  Phacochoerus africanus » p230

- **Gaur**
  Bos gaurus » p257
- **Grant's zebra**
  Equus quagga boehmi » p200
- **Hippopotamus**
  Hippopotamus amphibius » pp186–87
- **Indian rhinoceros**
  Rhinoceros unicornis » p256
- **Japanese serow**
  Capricornis crispus » p285
- **Kalahari springbok**
  Antidorcas hofmeyri » p230
- **Ethiopian klipspringer**
  Oreotragus saltatrixoides » p179
- **Giraffe**
  Giraffa camelopardalis » p201
- **Moose**
  Alces alces » p39
- **Mountain nyala**
  Tragelaphus buxtoni » p179
- **Mountain tapir**
  Tapirus pinchaque » p85

- **Muskox**
  Ovibos moschatus » p26
- **Okapi**
  Okapia johnstoni » p216
- **Reindeer**
  Rangifer tarandus » p26
- **Pronghorn**
  Antilocapra americanus » p45
- **Przewalski's wild horse**
  Equus przewalskii » p282
- **Iberian ibex**
  Capra pyrenaica » p153
- **Red lechwe**
  Kobus leche » p221
- **Red muntjac**
  Muntiacus muntjak » p258
- **Red river hog**
  Potamochoerus porcus » p215
- **Mongolian saiga**
  Saiga mongolica » p280

- **Vicuña**
  Vicugna vicugna » p110
- **Western red deer**
  Cervus elaphus » p141
- **Western roe deer**
  Capreolus capreolus » p153
- **White-lipped peccary**
  Tayassu pecari » p101
- **White rhinoceros**
  Ceratotherium simum » p222–23
- **White-tailed deer**
  Odocoileus virginianus » p40
- **Wild boar**
  Sus scrofa » p169
- **Wildebeest**
  Connochaetes mearnsi » p198
- **Yarkand gazelle**
  Gazella yarkandensis » p279

Cetaceans
Order Cetacea

Gray whale
Eschrichtius robustus

- 43–49 ft (13–15 m)
- North Pacific
- Locally common

This coastal Pacific species is one of the larger filter-feeding whales, albeit one with an unusual foraging technique. As well as sifting small planktonic animals from open water, it dives to the shallow seabed and scoops up mouthfuls of mud; it then strains the mud for animals such as worms, starfish, and shrimp. In summer, it migrates north along the coast to feed in the Arctic seas north of Alaska, returning south in winter to breed in the warm waters off Mexico.

mottled gray skin

Southern right whale
Eubalaena australis

- Up to 59 ft (18 m)
- Southern Ocean
- Common

One of two species of right whale, this mammal lives in the Southern Ocean around Antarctica, but avoids the very coldest waters; the other species lives in the Arctic. It feeds on small planktonic animals by straining food-rich water through the bristlelike baleen that lines its mouth in place of teeth. Unusually, up to eight males may mate with each female—there is no rivalry between the males.

Amazon river dolphin
Inia geoffrensis

- 7–9 ft (2–2.7 m)
- South America (Amazon and Orinoco basins)
- Locally common

One of five river dolphin species, this pink or gray mammal has a long, slim snout and a flexible neck. It uses echolocation to find its way in muddy rivers and seasonal floodwaters, probing submerged vegetation for freshwater crabs, fish, and turtles. It seizes prey with peg-like teeth at the front of its jaws and crushes it with bigger cheek teeth.

Bowhead whale
Balaena mysticetus

- 46–59 ft (14–18 m)
- Arctic and subarctic waters
- Common

This large filter-feeding whale gets its name from its high-arched upper jaw—part of a massive head that accounts for 40 percent of the animal's length. It lives near the edge of the Arctic pack ice, where it feeds by swimming with its mouth open to force water in at the front and out through the mesh of baleen at each side. This traps swarming animals, such as shrimplike copepods, which it then swallows.

Pantropical spotted dolphin
Stenella attenuata

- 5–9 ft (1.5–2.7 m)
- Temperate and tropical waters worldwide
- Common

Widespread in all warm oceans, this slender dolphin swims in large schools, often associating with schools of tuna to hunt smaller fish. Once threatened by industrial tuna fishing—thousands were trapped and drowned in tuna nets—"dolphin friendly" techniques have allowed it to recover.

Humpback whale
Megaptera novaeangliae

- 43–46 ft (13–14 m)
- Worldwide (except Mediterranean, Baltic, Red Sea, Arabian Gulf)
- Common

The humpback whale has a knobbly head and unusually long pectoral flippers. It feeds by using its expandable, pleated throat to engulf large quantities of water, which it then strains for small prey. Groups also herd fish to the surface by blowing bubbles around them, and lunge upward through the water to swallow them. Vocal and sociable, it communicates using various sounds, including "whale songs" performed by the males.

Short-beaked common dolphin
Delphinus delphis

- 8–9 ft (2.4–2.7 m)
- Temperate and tropical waters worldwide
- Common

A typical fast-swimming, sociable dolphin, this species has a dark back and a distinctive wavelike pattern of yellow on each flank, overlapping with a similar pattern in gray nearer the tail. It hunts offshore in deep waters, pursuing schooling fish and squid in large schools. The dolphins stay in contact with a variety of clicking, squeaking, and croaking calls that are loud enough to be heard from nearby boats.

Short-finned pilot whale
Globicephala macrorhynchus

- 16–23 ft (5–7 m)
- Temperate and tropical waters worldwide
- Not known

This stocky relative of the dolphins has a very short snout topped with a bulbous forehead. It is black or dark gray all over, aside from an anchor-shaped pale patch on its throat. It feeds mainly on deep-water squid, diving to depths of 1,600 ft (500 m) to pursue them through the oceanic twilight zone. Males weigh almost twice as much as females, and scars on their bodies may be evidence of fights between rivals.

Sperm whale
Physeter macrocephalus

- 36–65 ft (11–20 m)
- Deep waters worldwide
- Vulnerable

The largest of the toothed whales, this oceanic giant has an enormous, boxy head and a long, narrow lower jaw armed with 20–26 pairs of large, conical teeth. It uses them to catch squid, octopus, and fish, diving to depths of well below 3,300 ft (1,000 m), sometimes staying submerged for almost an hour. It regularly targets deep-water giant squid—many sperm whales bear big circular scars inflicted by the giant squid's toothed suckers.

Other species
- **Beluga**
  Delphinapterus leucas » p31
- **Blue whale**
  Balaenoptera musculus » p373
- **Harbor porpoise**
  Phocoena phocoena » p135
- **Hourglass dolphin**
  Lagenorhynchus cruciger » p372
- **Narwhal**
  Monodon monoceros » p30
- **Orca**
  Orcinus orca » p136
- **Spinner dolphin**
  Stenella longirostris » p303

BIRDS

Birds are perhaps the most strikingly conspicuous of all land vertebrates. The first feathered birds evolved from a small group of hollow-boned dinosaurs. These warm-blooded flying animals went on to become one of the most species-rich of vertebrate classes—many with dazzling colors or melodious calls. Today, most birds have a high-speed metabolism suited for a frenetic lifestyle. Some rank among the fastest vertebrates on the planet and they combine speed with impressive brain power to find food and raise a family.

Anatomy

Birds are unique among vertebrates in many respects. Their skin is feathered, their bones contain air spaces to make them lightweight, and their tail vertebrae are fused into a stump —the so-called "Parson's nose." All birds

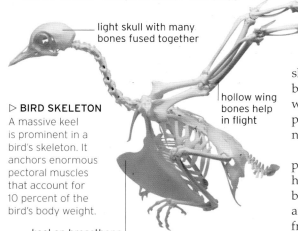

light skull with many bones fused together

▷ **BIRD SKELETON**
A massive keel is prominent in a bird's skeleton. It anchors enormous pectoral muscles that account for 10 percent of the bird's body weight.

hollow wing bones help in flight

keel on breastbone

walk, run, or perch on their hindfeet, while their forelimbs are adapted as wings—with the wrist and "hand" modified for greater rigidity. A few birds are flightless, but the vast majority are aerobatic and have a prominent keel on their breastbone for supporting the massive muscles needed to flap. Tiny hummingbirds, beating their wings up to 50 times per second, can even fly backward. A bird's head contains a large brain and big eyes—and is supported by a long, flexible neck with more neck vertebrae than in mammals. Its jaws are toothless and have a horny covering that makes up the bill. The shape of the bill varies a great deal, depending on dietary habits—for example, sharply hooked in predators, strong and stubby in seedeaters.

Like mammals, birds have a warm-blooded body and a strong, four-chambered heart. In order to maximize oxygen intake, their respiratory system also has a complex arrangement of sacs in the chest and abdomen, which helps flush stale air out of the lungs and replace it with fresh air.

Reproduction

Birds are the only class of vertebrates that are exclusively egg-laying. Their eggs have hard, chalky shells and extra yolk to support the developing embryo. Virtually all birds take advantage of their warm-bloodedness to incubate their eggs, and many build elaborate nests to house them. Some, such as weaver birds, are particularly skilful in their nest-building. However, a few birds—such as cuckoos and the finchlike whydahs—have evolved to be brood parasites, which lay their eggs in the nests of other species.

Like mammals, most birds are dedicated parents. They care for both their eggs and hatchlings. More primitive ground-dwelling birds hatch precocious chicks that are feathered and capable of running soon after breaking from the shell. But most birds, including almost all tree-dwellers, hatch "altricial" chicks, which are born naked, blind, and entirely dependent on the parents to provide them with food.

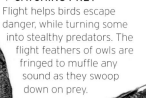

▽ **CATCHING PREY**
Flight helps birds escape danger, while turning some into stealthy predators. The flight feathers of owls are fringed to muffle any sound as they swoop down on prey.

▷ **DANCE DISPLAY**
Bird courtship involves displays of song or even– as in great crested grebes–displays of dance. Such rituals help seal the cooperative bonds needed to raise a family.

Behavior

Birds exhibit complex behavior that is made possible by good senses of sight and hearing. The higher parts of their brain—including the cerebellum, the part involved in the coordination of complex movements and important for flying—are especially well developed. Many combine flight with impressive navigational skills to accomplish long-distance migrations. The Arctic tern's migration—longer than that of any other bird —takes it between the Arctic and Antarctic summers every year. It sees more daylight than any other animal. Some birds demonstrate skills that can only be developed by learning and a few—like some mammals—even use tools to manipulate their environment and find food.

Birds vary widely in the type and extent of their social behavior. Many use elaborate courtship displays to find a mate—showing off with colorful plumage, rich calls and songs, or even ritual dances. Breeding for most birds is a private, monogamous affair—even for species that flock together for the rest of the year. But others—such as many seabirds —nest communally, raising their families in noisy, crowded rookeries.

BIRD CLASSIFICATION

In most systems, bird species are classified into 29 orders. One of these orders, the passerines, contains more species than all the others put together.

Tinamous » p410
Order Tinamiformes **Species** 45

Kiwis » p410
Order Apterygiformes **Species** 5

Cassowaries and emus » p410
Order Casuariiformes **Species** 4

Ostrich » p381
Order Struthioniformes **Species** 1

Rheas » p382
Order Rheiformes **Species** 2

Gamebirds » p410
Order Galliformes **Species** 290

Waterfowl » p411
Order Anseriformes **Species** 174

Penguins » p411
Order Sphenisciformes **Species** 17

Albatrosses and petrels » p412
Order Procellariiformes **Species** 133

Divers » 412
Order Gaviiformes **Species** 5

Grebes » p413
Order Podicipediformes **Species** 22

Flamingos » p413
Order Phoenicopteriformes **Species** 6

Herons and relatives » p413
Order Ciconiiformes **Species** 121

Pelicans and relatives » p413–14
Order Pelecaniformes **Species** 67

Birds of prey » p414–16
Order Falconiformes **Species** 319

Cranes and relatives » pp416
Order Gruiformes **Species** 228

Waders, gulls, and auks » p417–18
Order Charadriiformes **Species** 379

Pigeons » p418
Order Columbiformes **Species** 321

Sandgrouse » p419
Order Pteroclidiformes **Species** 16

Parrots » p419
Order Psittaciformes **Species** 375

Cuckoos and turacos » p419
Order Cuculiformes **Species** 170

Owls » p420
Order Strigiformes **Species** 202

Nightjars and frogmouths » p420
Order Caprimulgiformes **Species** 125

Hummingbirds and swifts » pp420
Order Apodiformes **Species** 447

Mousebirds » p421
Order Coliiformes **Species** 6

Trogons » p421
Order Trogoniformes **Species** 40

Kingfishers and relatives » p421
Order Coraciiformes **Species** 218

Woodpeckers and toucans » p421–22
Order Piciformes **Species** 411

Passerines » p422–25
Order Passeriformes **Species** c.6,000

◁ **NOISE AND COLOR**
With a good sense of vision and hearing, birds use color and voice to communicate—turning a flock of green-winged macaws into a noisy rainforest spectacle.

Tinamous
Order Tinamiformes

Elegant crested tinamou
Eudromia elegans

↔ 15–16 in (38–41 cm)
◑ S. South America
✕ Locally common

Resembling a large partridge with dark-speckled plumage, this plump ground bird is identified by the slender, forward-curving crest on top of its head. A relatively shy bird, it usually lives in small to moderately large groups that search dry grassland and woodland for seeds and insects. Both sexes may have several mates. The male incubates the eggs and guards the young, which can feed themselves within minutes of hatching.

Kiwis
Order Apterygiformes

Great spotted kiwi
Apteryx haastii

↔ 26–28 in (65–70 cm)
◑ South Island, New Zealand
✕ Vulnerable

This is the largest of five kiwi species. Like all kiwis, it has a big, round body, small head, and slim bill. Pairs defend large territories, sleeping by day in burrows. At night, they probe for invertebrates using their sense of smell and by detecting vibrations with their bills.

Other species
● **North Island brown kiwi**
Apteryx mantelli » p357

Cassowaries and emus
Order Casuariiformes

Southern cassowary
Casuarius casuarius

↔ 4–6 ft (1.2–1.8 m)
◑ New Guinea, NE. Australia
✕ Vulnerable

The cassowaries are ostrichlike flightless birds that live in dense, tropical forests. This is the biggest and most powerful, with coarse, bristly black feathers and a large, hornlike crest. It has naked, bright blue skin on its head and neck, with two dangling red wattles. It feeds mainly on fallen fruit that it finds on the forest floor, and defends itself with a lethally sharp claw on the inner toe of each foot.

Other species
● **Emu**
Dromaius novaehollandiae » p322

Rheas
Order Rheiformes

Darwin's rhea
Rhea pennata

↔ 35–39 in (90–100 cm)
◑ W. and S. South America
✕ Locally common

Rheas are the South American equivalents of the African ostrich. The smaller of two extant species, Darwin's rhea lives in flocks of up to 30 on the grasslands and mountains of Patagonia feeding on fruit and insects. This flightless bird runs to escape predators, but may also squat under a bush and flatten its body against the ground. It eats shrubs and seeds as well as small vertebrates such as frogs.

Other species
● **Greater rhea**
Rhea americana » p121

Gamebirds
Order Galliformes

Malleefowl
Leipoa ocellata

↔ 24 in (61 cm)
◑ W. and S. Australia
✕ Vulnerable

The chicken-sized malleefowl is one of a small group of birds that incubate their eggs in mounds of decaying vegetation. The decay process generates the warmth that the eggs need to develop. The male heaps up a mound of sticks and leaves— 15 ft (4.5 m) across and 5 ft (1.5 m) high—and the female lays her eggs in it. The male then tends the mound for up to 11 weeks, adding more vegetation if it needs more heat, and removing some if it gets too hot. When the young hatch, however, they have to dig their own way out of the mound.

black, white, and chestnut barred feathers

Wild turkey
Meleagris gallopavo

↔ 4 ft (1.2 m)
◑ North America
✕ Common

Ancestor to the domestic turkey, this big gamebird has bronze plumage and, in males, a bald blue head and a naked red wattle. Male turkeys are much larger than females and try to mate with as many as possible, courting them with strutting, fan-tailed displays while giving the characteristic gobbling and booming calls.

Common quail
Coturnix coturnix

↔ 7 in (18 cm)
◑ Europe, Asia, Africa, Madagascar
✕ Common

This small, streaky brown bird is so secretive that it is rarely seen and is usually detected by the male's characteristic "whit wit-wit" call. The common quail lives on the ground, preferring to slip into cover rather than fly from danger. Yet it is one of the few gamebirds that makes long migratory flights, with the birds that breed in Europe flying all the way from Africa or India.

Red junglefowl
Gallus gallus

- ↔ 32 in (80 cm)
- ◑ S. and SE. Asia
- ✕ Common

Native to the tropical forests of southern Asia, the red junglefowl was first raised in captivity at least 5,000 years ago, to become the ancestor of the domestic chicken. In spring—the breeding season—the male looks much like many farmyard cockerels, with a golden cape, and a fleshy comb and red wattles on his head. He also performs the same "cock-a-doodle-doo" when displaying to rival males and the less colorful females. Hens and chicks use calls to keep in contact and signal danger. The species lives in mixed flocks during the nonbreeding seasons.

long tail feathers

Other species
- ● Arabian partridge
  Alectoris melanocephala » p253
- ● Golden pheasant
  Chrysolophus pictus » p277
- ● Greater sage-grouse
  Centrocercus urophasianus » p50
- ● Helmeted guineafowl
  Numida meleagris » p207
- ● Indian peafowl
  Pavo cristatus » p271
- ● Ptarmigan
  Lagopus muta » p161
- ● Western capercaillie
  Tetrao urogallus » p145

Waterfowl
Order Anseriformes

Black swan
Cygnus atratus

- ↔ 4–5 ft (1.2–1.5 m)
- ◑ Australia (including Tasmania), New Zealand
- ✕ Common

With its sinuous neck and elegant appearance, this is a typical swan. Its plumage is black, aside from white flight feathers that are hidden when its wings are folded; it has a uniquely bright red bill with a white bar near the tip. It feeds on aquatic plants, often in large groups.

Canada goose
Branta canadensis

- ↔ 22–39 in (55–100 cm)
- ◑ North America, N. Europe, NE. Asia, New Zealand
- ✕ Common

This dark, black-necked goose is native to North America, but has been introduced to other regions where its adaptability has enabled it to thrive in a wide range of habitats, from remote wetlands to urban parks. It lives in flocks, eating mainly grasses and aquatic plants. In its native range, it migrates north to breed and returns south for the winter, flying

Common teal
Anas crecca

- ↔ 14–15 in (36–38 cm)
- ◑ North America, Europe (including Iceland), Asia, N. to C. Africa
- ✕ Common

Much smaller than most wild ducks, the teal is widespread on lakes and wetlands throughout Eurasia, gathering in large flocks in winter. In the breeding season, the male develops a chestnut head, with metallic green around the eyes, and a speckled gray body with a bright green wing patch. The female is mainly brown but has the same green wing patch. The common teal eats seeds in winter and small animals in summer.

in V-formations with loud honking calls. Males and females of this species tend to mate for life, and pairs remain together year round.

Other species
- ● King eider
  Somateria spectabilis » p137
- ● Mandarin duck
  Aix galericulata » p290
- ● Mute swan
  Cygnus olor p148
- ● Plumed whistling-duck
  Dendrocygna eytoni » p322
- ● Snow goose
  Chen caerulescens » p33

Penguins
Order Sphenisciformes

Macaroni penguin
Eudyptes chrysolophus

- ↔ 28 in (71 cm)
- ◑ S. Chile, South Atlantic, S. Indian Ocean
- ✕ Vulnerable

The macaroni penguin is distinguished by its conspicuous crest of golden plumes and its large, orange-brown bill. Like all penguins, it hunts at sea, but forms large breeding colonies on the Antarctic Peninsula and the sub-Antarctic islands to the south of Africa and South America. Noisy and aggressive, it competes for breeding territory with loud, braying calls. Females lay two eggs, and both sexes share incubation duties—although, unlike in other penguin species, females take the first shift.

Chinstrap penguin
Pygoscelis antarctica

- ↔ 28–30 in (71–76 cm)
- ◑ Circumpolar around Antarctica
- ✕ Common

Named for the black line around its chin, this penguin feeds mainly on swarming, shrimplike krill in the waters around the Antarctic peninsula. It lives at sea most of the year, resting on the floating pack ice that covers the Southern Ocean in winter. In spring, the chinstrap penguin makes its way to dense colonies on ice-free shores, laying two eggs in nests made of small stones and feathers.

Other species
- ● Adelie penguin
  Pygoscelis adeliae » p372
- ● Emperor penguin
  Aptenodytes forsteri » p374-75
- ● Galapagos penguin
  Spheniscus mendiculus » p124
- ● Rockhopper penguin
  Eudyptes chrysocome » p368

Albatrosses and petrels

Order Procellariformes

Atlantic yellow-nosed albatross

Thalassarche chlororhynchos

- ↔ 32 in (81 cm)
- ◑ South Atlantic Ocean
- ✕ Endangered

One of the smallest of the southern albatrosses, this black-and-white species has a distinctive orange-tipped yellow ridge along the top of its black bill. It lives in the South Atlantic, ranging widely over the ocean in search of fish, squid, and krill, as well as scraps scavenged from fishing fleets. In the breeding season, it nests in colonies on remote islands, each pair building a column-shaped nest of mud and vegetation for their single egg. Both parents rear the chick, which is able to fly within about four months.

dark brown plumage

white U-shaped patch

Wilson's storm petrel

Oceanites oceanicus

- ↔ 7 in (18 cm)
- ◑ Pacific, Atlantic, Indian, and Southern oceans
- ✕ Common

Only slightly bigger than a sparrow, this seabird has a vast distribution across the southern oceans, ranging north of the equator in the northern summer. Dark brown with a white patch on its rump, it flies over the ocean surface in search of small prey, often pattering on the water with its dangling feet. It nests in coastal colonies in Antarctica and nearby islands, in rock crevices and shallow burrows.

Northern fulmar

Fulmarus glacialis

- ↔ 18–20 in (45–50 cm)
- ◑ Arctic, North Pacific, North Atlantic oceans
- ✕ Common

Although it looks like a gull, the northern fulmar is a petrel, more closely related to the albatrosses. It is a superb flier, soaring on updrafts near cliffs on stiff, straight wings. It hunts at sea for small fish, jellyfish, and squid, seizing most of its prey at the surface, but sometimes plunging into the water. It also follows fishing fleets to feast on discarded fish scraps. This habit has led to a rapid increase in its population.

Other species
- Wandering albatross
  Diomedia exulans » p366–67
- Waved albatross
  Phoebastria irrorata » p125

Divers

Order Gaviiformes

Red-throated diver

Gavia stellata

- ↔ 22–28 in (55–70 cm)
- ◑ North America, Greenland, Europe, Asia
- ✕ Common

In breeding plumage this sleek, elegant diving bird has a gray head set off by red eyes, vertical black and white stripes on the hindneck, and a brick-red patch at the base of its thick, long neck. It is the smallest of the divers—birds so specialized for hunting fish underwater that they are almost helpless on land. It feeds at sea in winter, but nests by freshwater lakes and marshes in the far north, claiming its territory with loud wailing cries. The nests are usually a simple platform of reeds, rushes, and grass.

Grebes

Order Podicipediformes

Little grebe

Tachybaptus ruficollis

- ↔ 10–12 in (25–30 cm)
- ◑ Europe, Asia, Africa, Madagascar, New Guinea
- ✕ Common

The plump, almost tailless grebe appears buoyant on the water, but is in fact a skilful diver, staying underwater for up to half a minute as it hunts for aquatic insects and similar freshwater prey. It stands and walks on land more easily than other grebes, and is also more likely to fly outside of migration. Although wary and secretive, it often reveals its presence with a high-pitched trill during the summer breeding season.

Western grebe

Aechmophorus occidentalis

- ↔ 22–30 in (55–75 cm)
- ◑ C. and S. North America
- ✕ Common

This is the largest North American grebe. It is black and white with a long, slim neck and a long, sharp yellow bill. It has a spectacular courtship display, during which the courting pair rear up out of the water and, holding themselves erect, run across the surface together for 66 ft (20 m) or more. They build their nest on the water, anchored to reeds. The parents take turns carrying the newly hatched young on their backs for the first two to four weeks.

Hoary-headed grebe

Poliocephalus poliocephalus

- ↔ 12 in (30 cm)
- ◑ Australia (including Tasmania), S. New Zealand
- ✕ Common

This species is a specialized water bird; an expert diver, but clumsy on land. It breeds in large colonies, building floating nests of vegetation on the floodwaters that rise after heavy rain.

Other species
- Great crested grebe
  Podiceps cristatus » p157
- Titicaca grebe
  Rollandia microptera » p111

Flamingos
Order Phoenicopteriformes

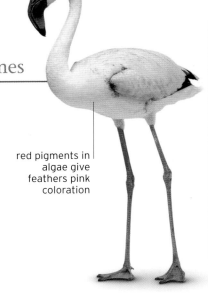

red pigments in algae give feathers pink coloration

Puna flamingo
Phoenicoparrus jamesi

↔ 4 ft (1.1 m)
◐ W. South America
✕ Near threatened

Also known as James' flamingo, this was once believed to be extinct, but in 1956, it was discovered in a remote part of the Andes. It lives in the salt lakes of the high Andean plateau —locally known as the puna—where it feeds on microscopic algae by sifting the water through filters in its bill. The female lays a single egg on a mound of mud, and both parents feed the chick.

> **Other species**
> ● **Greater flamingo**
> *Phoenicopterus roseus* » p149
> ● **Lesser flamingo**
> *Phoenicopterus minor* » p188

Herons and relatives
Order Ciconiiformes

Gray heron
Ardea cinerea

↔ 35–39 in (90–98 cm)
◐ Europe, Asia, Africa
✕ Common

Found in wetlands throughout most of its range, this tall, long-legged bird typically hunts in shallow water, either wading slowly or watching for prey such as fish. On spotting a victim, it darts its head forward on its long neck to seize it in its sharp bill and swallows it whole. Gray herons usually nest high in trees in small colonies; they pair for life, returning to the same nest each spring.

American bittern
Botaurus lentiginosus

↔ 24–34 in (61–86 cm)
◐ North and Central America, Caribbean
✕ Common

The American bittern is a type of heron but with a shorter neck and legs. This marshland bird is camouflaged among dense reedbeds, with streaked and mottled brown plumage. If disturbed, it enhances the effect by standing with its neck extended and bill pointing up, and even swaying in the wind with the surrounding reeds.

Wood stork
Mycteria americana

↔ 34–43 in (85–100 cm)
◐ North, Central, and South America, Caribbean
✕ Common

One of the largest North American wading birds, the wood stork is white with a black tail and flight feathers. It has a naked, dark gray head and a long, heavy gray bill, which it uses to probe in the mud for food. It feels for prey such as fish with its sensitive bill tip and snaps up any animal it touches. It favors wooded marshland habitats, resting and nesting in the trees.

Sacred ibis
Threskiornis aethiopicus

↔ 26–35 in (66–89 cm)
◐ Sub-Saharan Africa, Madagascar, Aldabra Island, W. Asia
✕ Common

Similar to the wood stork, with white plumage, black legs and tail, and a naked black head and neck, this bird has a long, downcurved bill adapted for searching wet mud for prey. However, it has learned to exploit other food resources, including carrion and edible refuse. It also stalks across grasslands in the wake of fires, looking for animals killed by the flames.

African spoonbill
Platalea alba

↔ 30–36 in (76–91 cm)
◐ Sub-Saharan Africa, Madagascar
✕ Common

Like all spoonbills, this graceful, red-legged white bird is specially adapted for feeding in shallow water by sweeping the spoon-shaped tip of its long bill from side to side to snap up shrimp and other small animals. It may also create currents that bring small fish within striking range. The broad bill develops as the bird grows; when it hatches, it has a short bill resembling that of an ibis.

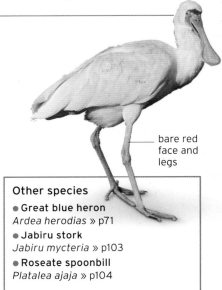

bare red face and legs

> **Other species**
> ● **Great blue heron**
> *Ardea herodias* » p71
> ● **Jabiru stork**
> *Jabiru mycteria* » p103
> ● **Roseate spoonbill**
> *Platalea ajaja* » p104

Pelicans and relatives
Order Pelecaniformes

Hamerkop
Scopus umbretta

↔ 16–22 in (40–56 cm)
◐ Sub-Saharan Africa, Madagascar, SW. Asia
✕ Common

The short, heavy bill and long crest of this brown bird give its head an unusual shape; this is reflected in the name hamerkop, which means "hammerhead." It feeds in shallow water, raking the mud at the bottom with its bill for frogs and fish. Breeding pairs use twigs, mud, and grass to build an enormous domed nest in a tree, up to 6 ft (2 m) high and wide—the largest roofed nest made by any bird.

dark brown primary feathers

Great cormorant
Phalacrocorax carbo

↔ 32–39 in (80–100 cm)
◐ E. North America, S. Greenland, Europe, Asia, Southern Africa, Australia
✕ Common

A specialized fisheater, this goose-sized bird can swallow a large eel whole. It pursues its prey underwater, propelling itself on large webbed feet. Its loose plumage is easily wetted, allowing water to penetrate and reduce its buoyancy for easy diving.

Red-billed tropicbird
Phaethon aethereus

- ↔ 31–32 in (78–81 cm)
- ◓ E. Pacific, C. Atlantic, and N. Indian oceans
- ✕ Common

This seabird spends most of its time in the air, flying over the tropical oceans in search of fish and squid that it catches by plunge-diving into the sea. Both sexes have white plumage, black wingtips, and two long, white tail streamers that create a spectacular effect as they flick from side to side during the birds' aerial courtship displays. Like many ocean birds, it breeds in large colonies on remote islands.

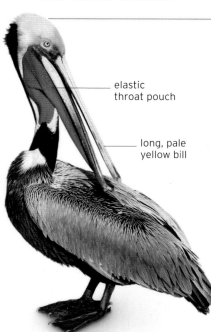

elastic throat pouch

long, pale yellow bill

Dalmatian pelican
Pelecanus crispus

- ↔ 5–6 ft (1.5–1.8 m)
- ◓ SE. Europe, S. and SW. Asia, NE. Africa
- ✕ Vulnerable

Silvery white, with black wingtips, this is one of the largest flying birds. Its expandable throat pouch turns a rich reddish orange in the breeding season. Sociable and intelligent, the pelican feeds in small flocks that often cooperate to drive fish into shallow water, where they are more easily caught. Each bird scoops up a mass of water and fish, filling its throat pouch, which it then drains of water by tipping its head back.

Brown pelican
Pelecanus occidentalis

- ↔ 3–5 ft (1–1.5 m)
- ◓ North, Central, and South America, Caribbean
- ✕ Common

Although similar to other pelicans in build, this is the only pelican that feeds by plunge-diving instead of fishing from the surface. Typically, it searches for prey by gliding low over the water. When it sights a fish, it flies up to gain height, then folds its wings back and plunges into the sea. As it enters the water, it opens its bill to trap its victim in its expanded throat pouch.

Northern gannet
Morus bassanus

- ↔ 32–35 in (80–90 cm)
- ◓ N. Atlantic, Mediterranean
- ✕ Common

This big, long-billed seabird is specialized for plunge-diving, with a highly streamlined head and body, and shock-absorbing air sacs under its skin. These adaptations allow it to plunge into the sea from heights of 100 ft (30 m) or more, scything into the water with swept-back wings at speeds of up to 60 mph (100 km/h). It plunges deep beneath the surface to catch fish, swallowing them underwater. The northern gannet breeds in large, densely packed colonies on small islands and remote clifftops. Once paired, a male and female will remain together for years.

Other species
- ● Great white pelican
  Pelecanus onocrotalus » p189
- ● Shoebill
  Balaeniceps rex » p190

buff-colored head and neck

black, tapering wingtips

webbed feet

Birds of prey
Order Falconiformes

California condor
Gymnogyps californianus

- ↔ 4 ft (1.2 m)
- ◓ W. US (California, Arizona)
- ✕ Critically endangered

Rescued from certain extinction by captive breeding and released back into the wild, this relative of the majestic Andean condor is the largest flying bird in North America and also one of the most endangered. It searches for carrion by soaring high over open country on its broad black wings and once ranged as far east as Florida. Now reduced to just a few hundred individuals, its future is still in the balance; many have died from lead poisoning as a result of eating animals killed by hunters using lead ammunition. California condors generally mate for life, producing one chick every two years.

distinctive black eyestripe

brown plumage

Osprey
Pandion haliaetus

- ↔ 22–25 in (56–64 cm)
- ◓ Worldwide (except Antarctica)
- ✕ Common

This large bird of prey has an almost worldwide range. It is found on coasts, lakes, and large rivers. The osprey is a fish hunter, famous for the way it plunges into the water feet-first to seize large fish with its powerful curved talons. Its feet have spiny soles that give it a firm grip on its prey as it flies off to a perch to tear it apart with its hooked bill. During the breeding season, pairs mate following dramatic courtship displays by the males.

Snail kite
Rostrhamus sociabilis

↔ 16–18 in (40–45 cm)
➤ SE. US (Florida), Cuba, Central America, South America
✖ Common

Widespread across South and Central America, with a small population in Florida, this broad-winged kite is adapted for flying slowly over marshland in search of its only prey —large aquatic snails. Snatching them up with one foot, it carries them to a perch. Its hooked bill has a long, narrow tip, which it slips into the snail's shell to sever the attachment muscle, allowing it to extract the soft body.

fine, heavily curved bill

squarely tipped tail

long legs

African fish eagle
Haliaeetus vocifer

↔ 25–29 in (63–73 cm)
➤ Sub-Saharan Africa
✖ Locally common

Well known in Africa for its loud, penetrating, yelping calls, the African fish eagle has a unique and distinctive plumage, with a white head and breast contrasting with broad black wings and a chestnut belly and back. It habitually perches in trees overlooking rivers, watching for fish, which it catches by swooping down and seizing them in its talons. This bird also eats small mammals, birds, and carrion, and steals fish from other eagles.

Egyptian vulture
Neophron percnopterus

↔ 23–28 in (58–70 cm)
➤ Europe, Africa, Asia
✖ Endangered

The relatively small, mostly white Egyptian vulture shares the scavenging habits of its bigger relatives, but as it cannot compete with them for food, it has to wait its turn at sharing the carcass. It makes up for this with its versatility, taking all kinds of scraps and even eating live prey such as mice and lizards. It also steals the nestlings and eggs of other birds and is well known for its habit of dropping stones on ostrich eggs to break them open.

Northern goshawk
Accipiter gentilis

↔ 19–28 in (48–70 cm)
➤ Canada to Mexico, Europe, Asia
✖ Common

This gray-backed forest hawk is adapted for hunting on the wing in woodland, with relatively short, rounded wings for swerving between trees and a long tail for steering and braking hard. It is adept at plucking forest animals off the ground and even snatching squirrels from branches. The female is larger than the male; in this species, she is up to 50 percent heavier. Goshawks are mainly secretive and often go unseen.

white brow

white front with gray barring

Harpy eagle
Harpia harpyja

↔ 35–39 in (89–100 cm)
➤ S. Mexico to C. South America
✖ Near threatened

The massively built harpy eagle has hugely powerful feet and talons, ideal for its preferred hunting technique of swooping into a tropical forest tree to rip a sloth or monkey from its perch. It is strong enough to carry off an adult howler monkey weighing 20 lb (9 kg) and even seizes small deer. Largely black above and white below, it has a gray head crowned with an impressive crest of darker feathers.

Wedge-tailed eagle
Aquila audax

↔ 32–39 in (81–100 cm)
➤ S. New Guinea, Australia (including Tasmania)
✖ Common

Australia's largest bird of prey, the wedge-tailed eagle is a huge, dark brown bird with a distinctive diamond-shaped tail. It hunts a variety of small animals such as rabbits and wallabies, searching for them by soaring overhead or watching from a high perch. Young eagles also eat a lot of roadkill and other carrion, acting as the Australian equivalent of vultures.

Southern caracara
Caracara plancus

↔ 20–23 in (51–58 cm)
◑ South America
✕ Common

Although a member of the highly aerial falcon family, this large, crested, mainly dark bird of prey spends most of its time on the ground, scavenging for carrion like a crow. It has long legs with strong feet, well suited to walking and investigating carcasses. An opportunistic scavenger, it will often dig for food or chase other birds, including raptors and vultures, to steal it. It also preys on live frogs and reptiles, as well as feeding on road kill, rotting vegetables, dead and dying fish, worms, and insects. Its name is based on its harsh, cackling call.

> **Other species**
> ● **Andean condor**
>   *Vultur gryphus* » p112
> ● **Bald eagle**
>   *Haliaeetus leucocephalus* » p42–43
> ● **Golden eagle**
>   *Aquila chrysaetos* » p162
> ● **Lammergeier**
>   *Gypaetus barbatus* » p183
> ● **Peregrine falcon**
>   *Falco peregrinus* » p144
> ● **Secretary bird**
>   *Sagittarius serpentarius* » p206
> ● **Turkey vulture**
>   *Cathartes aura* » p56

dark brownish black wings

finely barred breast

bare legs

Cranes and relatives
Order Gruiformes

Common crane
Grus grus

↔ 4 ft (1.2 m)
◑ Europe, Asia, N. Africa
✕ Common

A tall, long-legged, elegant gray bird with a red spot on top of its black-and-white head, the common crane can gather in huge flocks in winter to feed on crops such as grain. In spring, it moves to wetlands to pair up and breed, each pair performing a courtship display in which they walk in circles with wings raised, bobbing and pirouetting, while picking up small objects and tossing them over their heads. The performance is accompanied by loud, trumpeting calls, given with their bills pointing skyward. The sound is amplified by an enlarged windpipe that is fused with the breastbone.

Sandhill crane
Grus canadensis

↔ 4 ft (1.2 m)
◑ North America, NE. Asia
✕ Common

Similar to the common crane, but with no black on its head, this is a widespread species with several distinctive subspecies. Like most cranes, it is an opportunistic feeder, gleaning a range of plant foods and prey from the ground. In winter, the birds that breed in Alaska and Canada migrate southward, gathering at stopover sites and wintering grounds in large flocks.

Limpkin
Aramus guarauna

↔ 22–28 in (56–71cm)
◑ SE. US (Florida), Central and South America
✕ Common

Named for its curious limping walk, this wetland bird has brown, white-speckled plumage and a long, curved, slender bill, which it uses to pry aquatic snails from their shells. However, it also eats other prey such as freshwater mussels, insects, and frogs. The male is highly territorial, defending his patch with loud calls and fighting off intruders and rivals.

Corncrake
Crex crex

↔ 11–12 in (28–30cm)
◑ Europe, W. to C. Asia, SE. Africa
✕ Common

Superbly camouflaged by its streaky brown plumage, the corncrake is hard to see in its grassland habitat. But where it is still common, the male is easily heard in spring as he raises his head to advertise his territory with the loud, rasping, "krek-krek" call reflected in the species' scientific name. Although widespread in summer across Europe and western Asia, it has been badly hit by modern farming practices involving the destruction of old, species-rich grasslands.

tawny back with bold black streaks

legs trail behind body in flight

Kori bustard
Ardeotis kori

↔ 4 ft (1.2 m)
◑ E. and Southern Africa
✕ Near threatened

The kori bustard is a very large, long-legged, mainly gray and brown bird of dry grasslands and deserts, where it typically lives alongside large grazing animals and preys on the insects disturbed by their hoofs. It also inhabits areas that have recently been burned, eating the new shoots of grass and insects exposed by the lack of vegetation. Adult males may weigh up to 44 lb (20kg), making them among the heaviest of all flying birds. Like its relatives, however, it lives on the ground and is reluctant to fly unless in serious danger. The males perform dramatic courtship displays to attract the much smaller females, inflating their throats like feathery white balloons.

> **Other species**
> ● **Great bustard**
>   *Otis tarda* » p283
> ● **Gray crowned crane**
>   *Balearica regulorum* » p189
> ● **Purple gallinule**
>   *Porphyrio martinica* » p71
> ● **Red-legged seriema**
>   *Cariama cristata* » p120
> ● **Sarus crane**
>   *Grus antigone* » p263

Waders, gulls, and auks
Order Charadriiformes

Wattled jacana
Jacana jacana

↔ 7–10 in (18–25 cm)
➲ S. Central America, South America
✕ Common

In many ways similar to the moorhen, this tropical waterbird has enormously elongated toes. These spread its weight so effectively that it can walk on floating vegetation as it searches for aquatic insects and snails. Unusually, the females are larger than the males, defend territories, and compete with rivals for mates; each may mate with up to three males, which incubate the eggs and care for the young.

red wattle

dark plumage

extremely long toes

Black-winged stilt
Himantopus himantopus

↔ 14–16 in (36–41 cm)
➲ Europe, Asia, Africa, North, Central, and South America
✕ Common

The long, pink legs of this black and white wader allow it to feed in much deeper water than most of its competitors. It gathers small aquatic animals by sweeping its slender, straight black bill through the water, detecting them by touch—although it also seizes insects from the surface. The black-winged stilt may also forage on land, but has to bend its legs awkwardly to pick prey off the ground.

Eurasian oystercatcher
Haematopus ostralegus

↔ 16–19 in (40–48 cm)
➲ Europe, NW., N., and E. Africa, SW., C., E., and S. Asia
✕ Common

Recognizable by its piping calls, this bird has a long bill adapted for feeding on shelled mollusks, such as limpets, with a sharp tip, which it uses to detach them from rocks or pry them apart to sever the shell-closing muscle within. But some oystercatchers probe for prey in sand and mud, and their bills are more pointed.

pied black-and-white plumage

Common ringed plover
Charadrius hiaticula

↔ 7–8 in (18–20 cm)
➲ N. North America, Greenland, Europe, Asia, Africa, Madagascar
✕ Common

When this compact, short-necked plover is feeding on a mudflat, the contrasting white collar and black bands on its head and breast can be conspicuous. But on a shingle beach, where it nests, the pattern disrupts its outline so effectively that the bird is almost invisible. Nesting pairs rely on this for protection, but when their young hatch, the adults may lure predators away from them with a "broken wing" display that makes them look like temptingly easy prey.

clean white underparts

Eurasian curlew
Numenius arquata

↔ 20–24 in (51–61 cm)
➲ Europe, Asia, Africa
✕ Near threatened

This large, brown-streaked wader has a long, downcurved bill—the perfect tool for probing coastal sand or mud for burrowing prey such as worms, clams, and tiny crabs. The curlew also feeds on the surface, especially in summer, when breeding adults move to inland nesting sites and feed on insects, earthworms, and berries. This bird has a loud ringing "courli" call.

Australian pratincole
Stiltia isabella

↔ 9 in (23 cm)
➲ Australia, Indonesia, Malaysia, Papua New Guinea
✕ Common

This sandy-brown bird has very long, pointed black wings, a white underside, and a vent with a chestnut-and-black patch at the side. When breeding, the bill is bright red at the base. Non-breeding birds are duller, with a mostly black bill, black spotting on the throat, and smaller flank markings. Pratincoles feed on invertebrates.

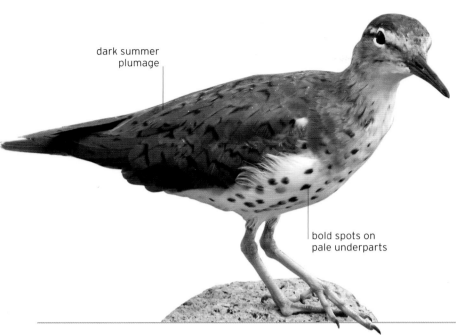

dark summer plumage

bold spots on pale underparts

Spotted sandpiper
Actitis macularius

- 7–8 in (18–20 cm)
- North, Central, and South America
- Common

Breeding across most of North America and migrating to the tropics in winter, this small, active, white and brown wader is common in a wide variety of habitats ranging from city parks to the Arctic tundra—although it is nearly always near water. As with some other waders, the female courts the male with quivering wings and fanned tail, and may mate with several different males; each male then incubates a clutch of eggs.

Herring gull
Larus argentatus

- 22–26 in (55–67 cm)
- North and Central America, Europe, NE. and E. Asia
- Common

Few seabirds are as familiar as the herring gull—a large, gray and white bird with a loud bugling call that is one of the emblematic sounds of northern shores. Highly adaptable, it will eat almost anything and has become an expert at surviving on refuse scavenged from city streets and garbage dumps. This allows it to forage well inland, and it often nests on rooftops in coastal towns.

Sooty tern
Onychoprion fuscatus

- 14–18 in (35–45 cm)
- Worldwide, in tropical seas
- Common

Mainly black above and white below, with a long, forked tail, this tropical tern is one of the world's most abundant seabirds. It lives out on the open ocean in large flocks, snatching small prey from the surface rather than plunge-diving like a typical tern. It remains at sea for most of the year, returning to remote islands to breed in noisy colonies that may have more than a million pairs.

Guillemot
Uria aalge

- 16–17 in (41–43 cm)
- North Atlantic, North Pacific
- Common

One of the auks—northern counterparts of the penguins—this neat, black-and-white seabird uses its short wings for swimming underwater in pursuit of fish and other prey. It breeds in large colonies on coastal cliffs, each pair incubating their single egg on a narrow ledge of bare rock. The egg has a conical form, so it rolls in a circle if dislodged rather than falling off the ledge. The young leave the cliff nest site when they are just three weeks old, leaping into the sea on half-fledged wings.

dark brown to black head

dark rump with narrow white sides

Other species

- **African jacana** *Actophilornis africanus* » p224
- **African skimmer** *Rynchops flavirostris* » p226
- **Antarctic tern** *Sterna vittata* » p369
- **Atlantic puffin** *Fratercula arctica* » p138–39
- **Pied avocet** *Recurvirostra avosetta* » p149

Pigeons
Order Columbiformes

Rock dove
Columba livia

- 12–14 in (30–36 cm)
- North, Central and South America, Africa, Europe, Asia, Australia
- Common

Also known as the rock pigeon, this species is the wild ancestor of the common feral pigeon, found in cities worldwide. In its wild form, it is largely gray, with iridescent feathers on its neck and upper breast. The wild birds feed on seeds and nest on sea cliffs and in river gorges—a habit that was readily adaptable to urban landscapes, where their feral counterparts nest on buildings.

black bars on wings

Common wood pigeon
Columba palumbus

- 16–18 in (41–45 cm)
- Europe, NW. Africa, W. and C. Asia
- Common

The throaty, cooing calls of the wood pigeon are a familiar feature of the countryside throughout most of its wide range. Originally a woodland bird, it has adapted so well to feeding on farmland that it has become a pest, with big flocks raiding fields for the seeds of cereals and other crops. Males perform distinctive gliding, wing-clapping displays, which are sometimes echoed by females.

Southern crowned pigeon
Goura scheepmakeri

- 26–29 in (66–74 cm)
- S. New Guinea
- Vulnerable

This big, blue and maroon tropical pigeon owes its name to its flamboyant crest of lacy blue-gray feathers. It feeds on the ground in small groups, searching the forest floor for seeds, fallen fruit, and small animals. It retires to a roost in the branches during the hottest part of the day and nests high in a tree. Like other pigeons—and flamingos—it feeds its young on "milk" secreted from its crop.

Sandgrouse
Order Pteroclidiformes

Crowned sandgrouse
Pterocles coronatus

↔ 11–12 in (27–30 cm)
🧭 N. Africa, W. to. S. Asia
✖ Common

This partridgelike desert bird can survive air temperatures of up to 122°F (50°C), thanks to its ability to conserve moisture and drink the salty water formed by evaporation under the desert sun. It feeds on seeds and the tips of plants that sprout after rare rainstorms.

Rainbow lorikeet
Trichoglossus haematodus

↔ 12 in (30 cm)
🧭 New Guinea, SE. Asia, SW. Pacific, Australia (including Tasmania)
✖ Common

This long-tailed parrot is named for its multicolored plumage, with patches of blue, green, yellow, orange, and bright red. But it is very variable, with 22 distinct races across its large range. Like most lorikeets, it has a brush-tipped tongue for gathering nectar and pollen from flowers, and typically feeds in noisy flocks on treetops.

Parrots
Order Psittaciformes

Galah
Eolophus roseicapilla

↔ 14 in (35 cm)
🧭 Australia (including Tasmania)
✖ Common

Elegant in pale gray with deep rose-pink underparts and a paler pink crown, this cockatoo is one of the most abundant and widespread Australian parrots. The sexes are similar, differing only in eye color: brown in the male and red in the female. The galah lives in large,

screeching flocks in open or thinly wooded terrain, feeding on seeds, buds, and insects, as well as juicy roots, which it digs up with its bill. The expansion of arable farming in Australia has dramatically increased its food supply, and the galah is commonly seen as an agricultural pest.

gray wings

short, square tail

Gray parrot
Psittacus erithacus

↔ 13 in (33 cm)
🧭 W. to C. Africa
✖ Vulnerable

Renowned for its ability to imitate human speech and perform tricks, this stocky, short-tailed African parrot is gray overall aside from its bright red tail and black wingtips. It lives in flocks in tropical lowland forests and mangroves, as well as farmland, feeding on seeds, nuts, and oil palm fruit. In some parts of its range, it spends the night in roosts of up to 10,000 birds.

Red-and-green macaw
Ara chloropterus

↔ 35 in (90 cm)
🧭 N. and C. South America
✖ Common

This big, long-tailed parrot is similar to the scarlet macaw but has green wing patches contrasting with its mainly red and blue plumage. It lives in tropical forests, where it forages in the tree canopy for fruit and seeds, usually in pairs that stay together for life. The mated pairs generally nest in tree holes, but in some regions, they use crevices in rock faces.

Other species

● **Kakapo**
Strigops habroptila » p356
● **Kea**
Nestor notabilis » p356
● **Scarlet macaw**
Ara macao » p97
● **Sulfur-crested cockatoo**
Cacatua galerita » p341

Cuckoos and turacos
Order Cuculiformes

Common cuckoo
Cuculus canorus

↔ 32–33 cm (12½–13 in)
🧭 Europe, Asia, NW. and Southern Africa
✖ Common

A medium-sized, dark gray bird, the common cuckoo is more often heard than seen. The hollow, breathy, two-note "cuck-coo" call of the male is a welcome sign of spring in its Eurasian breeding range. But it is less welcome to many small birds, for the common

cuckoo is a notorious brood parasite. The female removes an egg from the nest of another species and lays one of her own; when the cuckoo chick hatches, it throws out the other eggs so it can eat all the food brought to the nest by its foster parents. Adult cuckoos resemble small-headed hawks in flight; the male has gray plumage and a dark-barred breast, while the female is browner.

pointed wings

Hoatzin
Opisthocomus hoazin

↔ 24–28 in (62–70 cm)
🧭 N. South America
✖ Common

This heavy-bodied tropical forest bird feeds almost entirely on leaves, digesting them with the help of bacteria in its gut. It nests on branches overhanging water; if threatened, the young dive into the water, then climb up through the vegetation using tiny wing claws.

Other species

● **Greater roadrunner**
Geococcyx californianus » p63

Owls
Order Strigiformes

Barn owl
Tyto alba

- ↔ 12–18in (30–46cm)
- ◑ North, Central, and South America, Europe, Asia, Africa, Australia
- ✖ Common

The most widespread of all owls, the barn owl has a white, heart-shaped face with black eyes and typically buff upperparts mottled with gray. It usually hunts by night, flying low over the ground in search of small prey such as voles, locating them mainly by sound. Barn owls often nest in barns and other buildings, but may also use holes in trees.

Spectacled owl
Pulsatrix perspicillata

- ↔ 17–21in (43–53cm)
- ◑ S. Mexico to C. South America
- ✖ Common

Deep chocolate brown above and creamy white below, with a dark head and pale "spectacles" around its big yellow eyes, this forest bird has unusually striking plumage for an owl. The pattern helps to conceal it from enemies as it roosts by day on treetops. At night, it hunts from a perch, ambushing birds sleeping on trees and swooping down to the forest floor.

Great horned owl
Bubo virginianus

- ↔ 20–24in (50–60cm)
- ◑ North, Central, and South America
- ✖ Common

The largest of all American owls, the great horned owl occurs in a variety of habitats ranging from rocky deserts to the cold northern conifer forests. It has a similarly wide range of prey, taking anything from beetles to jackrabbits. It hunts at night, usually from a perch, seizing and killing its victims with its strong talons. Large prey are ripped apart, while smaller ones are swallowed whole.

> **Other species**
> - **Burrowing owl**
>   *Athene cunicularia* » p121
> - **Great gray owl**
>   *Strix nebulosa* » p58
> - **Snowy owl**
>   *Nyctea scandiaca* » p33

long, feathery, hornlike ear tufts

Nightjars and frogmouths
Order Caprimulgiformes

European nightjar
Caprimulgus europaeus

- ↔ 10–11in (25–28cm)
- ◑ Europe, W. to E. Asia, NW., W., and SE. Africa
- ✖ Common

Rarely seen because of its excellent camouflage, this nocturnal summer visitor to Europe reveals its presence after nightfall with a churring song. It hunts for airborne insects such as moths, scooping them up in its gaping mouth as it flies on long, pointed wings. Males display in the air, clapping their wings together and gliding to show off the white spots on their wingtips and tail feathers.

Tawny frogmouth
Podargus strigoides

- ↔ 14–21in (36–53cm)
- ◑ S. New Guinea, Australia (including Tasmania)
- ✖ Common

Related to nightjars, the tawny frogmouth has a similar nocturnal hunting habit. Instead of patrolling the air, however, it hunts from a perch, gliding down to catch prey on the ground. Its large mouth lets it swallow animals as big as mice and even snakes. By day, it sits still on a tree, where its cryptic, mottled plumage matches the bark and makes it all but invisible.

Hummingbirds and swifts
Order Apodiformes

Ruby-throated hummingbird
Archilochus colubris

- ↔ 4in (10cm)
- ◑ S. Canada, C. and E. US, Mexico to S. Central America
- ✖ Common

In many ways a typical small hummingbird, with a diet of nectar, sweet tree sap, and a few small insects, this species is remarkable for the long migrations between Central America and its breeding grounds, which may lie as far north as Canada. For some birds, this involves crossing the Gulf of Mexico, in a nonstop flight of some 530 miles (850km) on tiny, whirring wings. Both sexes are green above and mainly grayish white below, but only the male has a ruby-red throat.

Crimson topaz

Topaza pella

↔ 9 in (23 cm)
➤ N. South America
✖ Common

The male crimson topaz is one of the most striking hummingbirds, with an iridescent crimson-purple breast and upperparts, a yellow-green throat, and a pair of long, dark tail feathers that curve in to cross over near their tips. The female is far less conspicuous, with mainly green plumage and a shorter tail. A denizen of tropical forests, the crimson topaz feeds in the middle and upper canopy, taking nectar from a wide variety of flowers. It is rarely seen on the ground.

Common swift

Apus apus

↔ 7 in (18 cm)
➤ N. and Southern Africa, Europe, W. to C. Asia
✖ Common

A familar summer sight in many northern towns, the common swift hunts in the air for small insects and carries them back to its young. But this is the only time the swift returns to a perch, for it is the most aerial of all birds—able to eat, drink, sleep, and even mate in flight.

> **Other species**
> ● **Booted racket-tail**
> *Ocreatus underwoodii* » p88

Mousebirds

Order Coliiformes

Speckled mousebird

Colius striatus

↔ 12–16 in (30–40 cm)
➤ C., E., and Southern Africa
✖ Common

This bird owes its name to the way it scrambles through vegetation like a mouse, searching for insects, flowers, and fruit. The effect is enhanced by its mainly brown plumage, although it has a very long, stiff tail. It often roosts in groups of up to 20, hanging together in a cluster from a branch.

Trogons

Order Trogoniformes

Violaceous trogon

Trogon violaceus

↔ 9–10 in (23–25 cm)
➤ SE. Mexico to C. South America
✖ Common

The male violaceous trogon is dark blue and green above and yellow below, with black wings and a yellow eye-ring; the female, by contrast, is mostly gray. Usually solitary, it lives in the rainforests of Amazonia and adjacent regions. The trogon usually nests in a tree hole, but may also use an old wasp or termite nest. It feeds on fruit, insects, and other invertebrates.

> **Other species**
> ● **Resplendent quetzal**
> *Pharomachrus mocinno* » p81

Kingfishers and relatives

Order Coraciiformes

Common kingfisher

Alcedo atthis

↔ 7 in (18 cm)
➤ Europe, Asia, N. Africa
✖ Common

Mainly blue above, but with bright orange underparts, this short-tailed, heavy-billed bird can be surprisingly inconspicuous as it sits quietly on a perch overlooking the water, watching for prey. But when it spreads its wings, it reveals a vivid, electric-blue streak down its back, catching the eye as it skims across the water in fast, direct flight. It dives to seize small fish, returning to beat the victim against its perch before swallowing it head first. It supplements its diet with insects, crustaceans, and amphibians.

Southern yellow-billed hornbill

Tockus leucomelas

↔ 20–24 in (51–61 cm)
➤ Southern Africa
✖ Common

This long-tailed hornbill has a much smaller horny crest—or casque—than most hornbills. It has a bright red patch of naked skin around its eyes and on each side of its throat. Widespread on the savannas of southern Africa, it forages on the ground for seeds, fruit, and insects, occasionally catching larger animals such as mice and even scorpions. It sometimes forms foraging parties with dwarf mongooses, which flush out locusts on which the birds feed. The hornbill, in turn, warns them of approaching danger.

Blue-crowned motmot

Momotus momota

↔ 19 in (48 cm)
➤ Central America to C. South America, Trinidad and Tobago
✖ Common

Like many of its close relatives, this tropical forest bird has elongated central tail feathers that are bare except for the tips. It spends much of its time perched among the trees, barely moving aside from slowly swinging its extended tail from side to side. It eats insects and spiders, gleaning them from tree trunks or the ground; it often immobilizes them by hitting them against a branch before swallowing them.

> **Other species**
> ● **Blue-winged kookaburra**
> *Dacelo leachii* » p323
> ● **European bee-eater**
> *Merops apiaster* » pp150–51
> ● **Great Indian hornbill**
> *Buceros bicornis* » p264
> ● **Hoopoe**
> *Upupa epops* » p157
>
> ● **Lilac-breasted roller**
> *Coracias caudatus* » p207
> ● **Red-billed hornbill**
> *Tockus erythrorhynchus* » p206
> ● **Stork-billed kingfisher**
> *Pelargopsis capensis* » p299

Woodpeckers and toucans

Order Piciformes

Yellow-bellied sapsucker

Sphyrapicus varius

↔ 9 in (23 cm)
➤ North and Central America, Caribbean Islands
✖ Common

This species mainly eats sugary sap, which it obtains by drilling holes in the bark of trees such as maples and waiting for the sap to ooze out. It also snaps up any insects attracted by the sap. The holes may be tended to keep them open and renewed on

pale yellow underparts

barred black-and-white body

return from migration. The yellow-bellied sapsucker claims its territory in spring by drumming on a dead branch with its bill.

Chestnut-eared aracari

Pteroglossus castanotis

↔ 13–16 in (33–40 cm)
➤ N. to C. South America
✖ Common

This relatively small toucan has a long, slim, gently curved bill with serrated edges and yellow markings resembling teeth. Its name refers to the brown patch behind each eye; otherwise it is mainly dark with yellow underparts and a red band across its chest. Small parties forage together in the forest canopy for insects and fruit, often hanging upside down from branches to reach it.

light build

Other species

● **Andean flicker**
Colaptes rupicola » p111
● **Black woodpecker**
Dryocopus martius » p169
● **Toco toucan**
Ramphastos toco » p96

Passerines

Order Passeriformes

Eurasian magpie

Pica pica

↔ 18 in (46 cm)
➤ Europe, NW. Africa, Middle East, C. and E. Asia
✖ Common

Boldly pied in black and white, with a blue-purple sheen on its wings and a harsh, chattering call, the long-tailed Eurasian magpie is common and conspicuous across its wide range. It is an intelligent, resourceful bird with a broad diet of small animals, carrion, bird eggs, fruit, and seeds. Notorious for being attracted to shiny objects, the magpie also has a reputation for stealing the eggs and nestlings of other birds, but this has been exaggerated. It is a territorial bird; it forms flocks after the breeding season and roosts in groups.

iridescent sheen to wings and tail

Carrion crow

Corvus corone

↔ 19–21 in (48–53 cm)
➤ Europe, W. and C. Asia
✖ Common

The carrion crow and the similar hooded crow were once considered subspecies of the same bird, but have been reclassified as separate species. The carrion crow has a heavy black bill. Like many crows, it is highly intelligent, exploiting a huge range of food resources—on coasts, for example, it drops shellfish onto rocks to crack them open. The crow lives in many habitats including woodland, moorland, farmland, and towns. Although usually seen alone or in pairs, it may feed in loose flocks in winter. A solitary nester, it usually makes its home in a tree, although cliff ledges are often used in mountainous areas.

Wilson's bird-of-paradise

Cicinnurus respublica

↔ 7 in (16 cm)
➤ Indonesia
✖ Near threatened

Like all its relatives, this bird is renowned for the male's dazzling plumage. Its black and crimson back, emerald green breast, and yellow neck patch contrast strikingly with the bare crown on its head, which is turquoise with a pattern of black lines. It also has a pair of spiral, wirelike tail feathers that it flicks when displaying to females.

Blue tit
Cyanistes caeruleus

↔ 5 in (13 cm)
⬏ Europe, N. Africa, Middle East, parts of Central Asia
✖ Common

Mainly yellow below, the blue tit has a bright blue cap and greenish blue wings and tail; the blue of a breeding male's plumage is brighter than that of the female. It is naturally a woodland bird, but is widespread on farmland and in backyards. Pairs may raise large broods of up to 16 in tree holes, but the survival of the young depends on a continuous supply of caterpillars —each nestling can eat up to 100 caterpillars a day. Both parents help to feed the young, making several excursions a day to collect food.

greenish blue upperparts

House martin
Delichon urbicum

↔ 5 in (13 cm)
⬏ Africa, Europe, SE. and northern Asia
✖ Common

Closely related to the swallows, this small, highly aerial, black-and-white bird is a common sight in European towns in summer, where small groups gather to swoop and dive in pursuit of airborne insects. It usually nests on buildings, high up beneath overhangs that provide shelter from the rain; the nest is a cup built from pellets of mud attached to the wall. At the end of summer, it migrates to Africa.

Eurasian skylark
Alauda arvensis

↔ 7–8 in (18–20 cm)
⬏ N. Africa, Europe, parts of Asia; introduced to Australia and New Zealand
✖ Common

Celebrated for its liquid, silvery song, performed while rising high in the air on fluttering wings, the skylark is a common grassland bird across most of Eurasia, although its numbers have declined due to changes in farming regimes. Its streaky brown plumage makes it inconspicuous on the ground, where it nests in the shelter of a grass tussock or similar cover.

Eurasian wren
Troglodytes troglodytes

↔ 3 in (8 cm)
⬏ Europe, Asia, N. Africa
✖ Common

This tiny, brown, short-tailed wren is frequently seen darting between shrubs on whirring wings or searching for insect prey among dense thickets near the ground. The male draws attention with his pugnacious posturing, bobbing his head with his tail cocked and delivering an astonishingly loud song for his size. In winter, wrens often gather in communal night roosts to keep warm.

Eurasian nuthatch
Sitta europaea

↔ 6 in (15 cm)
⬏ Europe, C. and E. Asia
✖ Common

This small woodland bird uses its powerful bill to probe for insects in tree bark and hammer into nuts. It is very agile, climbing up and down tree trunks and branches with distinctive jerky movements, clinging on with its sharp claws and often descending head first. Blue-gray above with rich buff underparts and a black streak through its eye, it often gives itself away with loud, fluting calls.

Northern mockingbird
Mimus polyglottos

↔ 10 in (26 cm)
⬏ North America, Mexico
✖ Common

Mainly gray with paler underparts and a white bar across each wing, the northern mockingbird possesses remarkable vocal skills. It has a wide repertoire, made up of original phrases combined with mimicry of almost anything it hears, from other birds to sounds such as car alarms; it typically repeats each phrase several times. It thrives in a variety of habitats from semideserts to city centers.

Common myna
Acridotheres tristis

↔ 10 in (25 cm)
⬏ Southern Asia
✖ Common

This dark, yellow-billed grassland starling is a native of southern Asia, but has been widely introduced to other regions such as Australia, where it is now so common that it is considered a pest. In the wild, it eats fruit, seeds, and insects, but it is an adaptable opportunist, scavenging for scraps of all kinds in towns. At dusk it gathers in large tree roosts, calling noisily with a cacophony of gurgling, squawking, and clicking sounds.

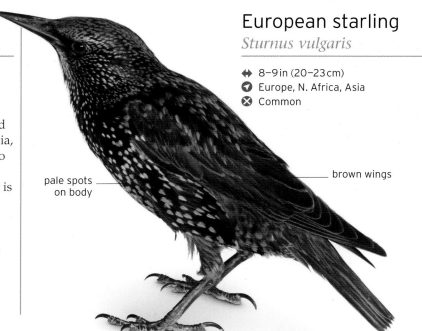
pale spots on body

brown wings

European starling
Sturnus vulgaris

↔ 8–9 in (20–23 cm)
⬏ Europe, N. Africa, Asia
✖ Common

Common, widespread, and invasive, the European starling has spread to every continent (except Antarctica), in some cases through deliberate introduction. In North America, for example, 60 birds released in 1890 have multiplied to an estimated 150 million. Glossy iridescent black in summer, with pale spots in winter, the starling is a swaggering, quarrelsome, yet sociable bird that feeds in flocks, often probing the ground for insect grubs. It forms huge communal roosts, preceded at dusk by spectacular mass aerial displays resembling clouds of smoke. In the wild, these birds are hole-nesters, although they also nest in buildings and nest boxes.

Blackbird
Turdus merula

- ⬌ 10–12in (25–30cm)
- 🧭 Europe, N. Africa, Asia; introduced in Australia, New Zealand, and South America
- ✖ Common

The blackbird is a type of thrush instantly recognizable in the case of the male by its all-black plumage and contrasting yellow bill and eye-ring. The female is a well-camouflaged brown. Common in backyards, it feeds on earthworms and other small animals and also eats berries in fall. The male has a rich, musical song, usually performed from a high perch.

brown upperparts in both sexes

short tail, brown above and pale below

boldly spotted creamy underside

Song thrush
Turdus philomelos

- ⬌ 8–10in (20–25cm)
- 🧭 Europe, N. Africa, northwest Asia; introduced in Australia and New Zealand
- ✖ Common

This small thrush is well-known for its habit of smashing the shells of garden snails on large stones and bricks, returning to the same stone time after time to build up a litter of shell fragments. The sexes look alike, but the male has a loud, inventive song made up of a variety of phrases, each repeated two to four times before moving on to the next.

Nightingale
Luscinia megarhynchos

- ⬌ 7in (18cm)
- 🧭 S. Europe, C. Africa, W. Asia
- ✖ Common

Secretive and inconspicuous, with a habit of hiding in dense cover, this small, brown, russet-tailed bird reveals its presence with one of the most beautiful and varied of all bird songs. Often performed at night as well as by day, it is an arresting combination of slow, rich, fluting notes, throaty croaks and gurgles, and rapid trills and whistles. It nests in tangled thickets, often returning to the same site each year after spending the winter in Africa.

Northern wheatear
Oenanthe oenanthe

- ⬌ 6in (15cm)
- 🧭 N. North America, Asia, Central Africa
- ✖ Common

One of the world's great migrants, the northern wheatear breeds in the far north—often on Arctic tundra—yet flies south to spend the winter in sub-Saharan Africa. While on migration, it stops off to feed in many regions in between. Elegant in black, white, and pinkish-buff plumage, and with a blue-gray back in the male, it feeds mainly on the ground, searching for insects and often perching on rocks or anthills with a bold, upright stance.

House sparrow
Passer domesticus

- ⬌ 6in (15cm)
- 🧭 Europe, C. and S. Asia
- ✖ Common

The sociable, noisy house sparrow has been spread far beyond its original Eurasian range through its association with humans and now flourishes on every continent except Antarctica. Very adaptable, it feeds mainly on seeds, but often gathers to eat household scraps or crumbs from picnic sites. It naturally nests in tree holes and rock crevices, but takes readily to nest boxes and cavities in buildings. Both sexes have a brown back streaked with black.

Zebra finch
Taeniopygia guttata

- ⬌ 4in (10cm)
- 🧭 Australia
- ✖ Common

black patch on breast of male

Named for its barred black-and-white tail, this small, largely gray bird is the most common of Australia's grass finches—birds that typically live on open grasslands with scattered bushes and trees. It primarily feeds on plants and has a stout red bill that it uses to crack and remove the husks of small seeds, but it also eats insects and even catches termites on the wing. It forages in lively, noisy flocks and breeds at any time of the year after periods of heavy rain that stimulate plant growth. Unlike most other birds, it drinks by sucking rather than scooping up water in its bill.

Chaffinch
Fringilla coelebs

- ⬌ 6in (15cm)
- 🧭 W. Europe and N. Africa
- ✖ Common

Like that of many small songbirds, the breeding plumage of the male chaffinch is much brighter than the female's, with pink underparts, a blue-gray cap, chestnut back, green rump, and white bars on its mainly black wings. Breeding males sing loudly from perches to claim their territories. Chaffinches prey mainly on insects in summer, but feed in flocks on seeds in winter.

Common yellowthroat
Geothlypis trichas

↔ 4 in (10 cm)
◐ N. and C. America
✖ Common

This New World warbler is common among damp thickets and reedbeds across most of North America. Mainly greenish brown, the common yellowthroat has a bright yellow chin, throat, and breast which, in the male, are set off by a striking black face mask, edged with white. It feeds close to the ground on small insects, usually in dense cover, but is often betrayed by its "wichity-wichity-wichity" song.

Crested oropendola
Psarocolius decumanus

↔ 14–20 in (36–51 cm)
◐ N. and E. South America
✖ Common

Looking mainly black from a distance, but with a striking yellow tail and a long, heavy white bill, this Amazonian bird's breeding colonies consist of up to 100 intricately woven hanging nests suspended from a tree. The tree is usually isolated from the forest edge to deter arboreal predators such as snakes; it may also be chosen because it contains the extra defense measure of a nest of hornets.

Yellowhammer
Emberiza citrinella

↔ 7 in (18 cm)
◐ Europe and Central Asia
✖ Common

The yellowhammer can be a conspicuous feature of farmland and bushy heaths—especially the bright yellow male singing with a rapid, repeated "tzi-tzi-tzi-tzi-tzi-tzeeee." On sunny summer days, it may sing nonstop for hours. Yellowhammers join other buntings and finches in flocks that forage on the ground for seeds, especially in arable fields with plenty of weeds and spilled grain.

Spotted towhee
Pipilo maculatus

↔ 9 in (23 cm)
◐ W. US, SW. Canada, Mexico, Guatemala
✖ Common

The spotted towhee was considered to be the same species as the Eastern towhee, but differences in their voice and plumage resulted in their separation into distinct species. However, the two species hybridize where their range overlaps. Spotted towhees forage on the ground to feed on insects, caterpillars, and seeds. They move in pairs or alone, but small family groups stay together after the nesting season.

Painted bunting
Passerina ciris

↔ 5 in (13 cm)
◐ S. North America and Mexico
✖ Near threatened

Aptly named, the male painted bunting is the most colorful North American bird, with a vivid blue head, bright green mantle, and scarlet rump and underparts. Yet, despite its striking appearance, it can be difficult to see among the dense foliage that it favors; the confusion of colors helps to disguise its outline. The female is even less visible, being green overall. It feeds mainly on seeds, supplemented by small animals, but nurtures its young exclusively on insects.

Scarlet tanager
Piranga olivacea

↔ 7 in (18 cm)
◐ North and South America
✖ Common

A male scarlet tanager in breeding plumage is a striking sight, with a bright crimson head and body, and contrasting black wings and tail. Outside the breeding season, it exchanges the red for green, to resemble the far less flamboyant female. These birds feed on insects, which they find in treetops, along with some fruits. After breeding in the deciduous woodlands of eastern North America, they migrate south to winter in the tropical forests of western Amazonia.

pointed red crest in male

Northern cardinal
Cardinalis cardinalis

↔ 9 in (23 cm)
◐ North America
✖ Common

One of North America's most eye-catching birds, the northern cardinal is instantly recognizable by its crest and crimson color. Its exotic appearance makes it look like a summer migrant, but it is actually a year-round resident throughout most of its range. Females are olive-brown with darker wings and tails. Like males, they have conspicuous, pointed crests.

Other species

● **Andean cock-of-the-rock**
Rupicola peruvianus » p89
● **Black-and-red broadbill**
Cymbirhynchus macrorhynchos » p299
● **Black-capped social weaver**
Pseudonigrita cabanisi » p204–05
● **Collared sunbird**
Anthreptes collaris » p216
● **Greater bird-of-paradise**
Paradisaea apoda » p318–19
● **Mountain chickadee**
Poecile gambeli » p56
● **Red-billed quelea**
Quelea quelea » p225
● **Scottish crossbill**
Loxia scotica » p143
● **Welcome swallow**
Hirundo neoxena » p355
● **Woodpecker finch**
Camarhynchus pallidus » p125
● **Yellow-billed chough**
Pyrrhocorax graculus » p161

REPTILES

Reptiles occupy a pivotal position in the history of vertebrate life—they were the first vertebrates to truly conquer the world's driest places. In their heyday, they evolved into dinosaurs—the biggest animals that have ever lived—but they diversified into birds and mammals as well. Although dinosaurs may have been warm-blooded, all modern reptiles rely more on the warmth derived from the sun than from their metabolism to stay active. Their scaly skin—largely impervious to moisture—helps many to thrive in deserts, but thousands of species also live in wet, humid rainforests.

Anatomy

The archetypal reptile is a lizard—an elongated, scaly-skinned, long-tailed vertebrate that crawls on land on all four limbs, its body hanging close to the ground. The scales erupt from the outer layer of its skin and are reinforced with a tough protein called keratin—the same substance found in hair, feathers, and finger-nails. Reptiles replace their old scales either by shedding their outer skin in flakes or by sloughing it in one piece. In some kinds of lizards, the hindlimbs—or both sets of limbs—have been lost. All snakes lack limbs, but some primitive constrictors retain clawlike rudiments of the hindlegs. Turtles and tortoises have toothless beaks, but most reptiles have teeth—conical, needlelike, or jagged, but never differentiated into molars and canines as in mammals. The teeth of many snakes are modified as fangs for injecting venom.

Some lizards have particularly big scales, so they look armor-plated, but reptilian armor is especially solid in the bony shells of turtles and tortoises. The shells are usually covered with horny plates, but some are soft and leathery. Their upper shell is fused to the ribs in such a way that these reptiles have to breathe by pumping the muscles at the top of their legs. Crocodilians, the largest living reptiles, are armored differently: they have plates—called osteoderms—that are reinforced with bone.

Reproduction

All reptiles reproduce by internal fertilization that involves copulation. Unlike the soft-coated eggs of amphibians, reptiles produce eggs that are surrounded by a protective membrane, called an amnion, derived from the developing embryo.

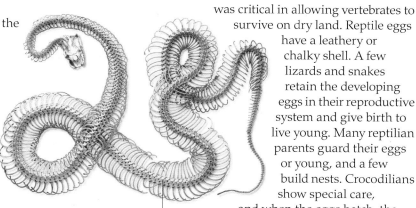

unusually long
vertebral column

△ **SKELETON WITHOUT LIMBS**
Reptiles have a bony skeleton, which is highly modified in limbless snakes. Pythons and related constrictors, however, retain claw-like remnants of the pelvic girdle.

Reptiles share this feature with birds and mammals, so these vertebrates are collectively called amniotes. The evolution of the amnion was critical in allowing vertebrates to survive on dry land. Reptile eggs have a leathery or chalky shell. A few lizards and snakes retain the developing eggs in their reproductive system and give birth to live young. Many reptilian parents guard their eggs or young, and a few build nests. Crocodilians show special care, and when the eggs hatch, the mother carries the hatchlings to a nearby pool for release.

Behavior

Although tortoises and some lizards are herbivorous, most reptiles are predatory. Reptiles have well-developed senses for tracking their prey on dry land. The sense of smell is especially well developed—most lizards and all snakes have a forked tongue that collects

▽ **SENSING DIRECTION**
Typical of other snakes—and most lizards—the mangrove snake's forked tongue enables it to sense scent molecules coming from different directions, helping it to track its prey.

△ **BREAKING OUT**
Although some reptiles—such as sea turtles—have conquered the oceans, their eggs must hatch—and hence, are laid—on land. Only live-bearing sea snakes are permanently aquatic.

▷ **PROTECTIVE COVERING**
Waterproof skin lets reptiles cope with some of the driest habitats. Some reptiles, such as this agama lizard, use colorful skin to make territorial claims.

scent molecules and transfers them to a sensory organ, called Jacobson's organ, in the roof the mouth. Some snakes also have sensory pits on their head that detect the infrared radiation given out by warm-blooded prey.

Most reptiles have a sluggish metabolism compared to mammals and birds, so they generate limited body warmth. They rely on the environment to raise their body temperature to a level at which they can become active. Most achieve this by basking in the sun.

REPTILE CLASSIFICATION

There are four orders of reptiles. Most species belong to one of these orders, the squamates, which includes lizards, snakes, and amphisbaenians.

Tortoises and turtles » p428
Order Testudines **Species** 341

Tuataras » p381
Order Rhynchocephalia **Species** 1

Snakes and lizards » p429-35
Order Squamata **Species** c.9,810

Crocodiles and alligators » p435
Order Crocodilia **Species** 25

Tortoises and turtles

Order Chelonia

Common snake-necked turtle

Chelodina longicollis

↔ 8–10 in (20–25 cm)
🧭 S. New Guinea, N. Australia
✖ Not known

With a neck nearly two-thirds the length of its shell when fully extended, this Australian river turtle has a long reach for catching invertebrates, frogs, and fish. Like other snake-necked turtles, it withdraws its neck sideways into its shell—but cannot retract its head entirely. This turtle has earned the local name of "stinker" because it releases a foul-smelling defensive fluid when disturbed.

neck covered with short nodules

black to light brown oval carapace

Matamata

Chelus fimbriata

↔ 12–18 in (30–45 cm)
🧭 N. South America
✖ Not known

Unlike other side-necked turtles, the matamata rarely swims in open water. Instead it stays still on the bottom of stagnant wetlands until prey gets close enough to grab with its wide mouth. Its bizarre fleshy adornments camouflage it against the background of weedy debris. In the shallows, its long neck can reach the surface to breathe with its tubular, snorkel-like snout. Female matamatas lay up to 28 eggs in a single nesting.

Loggerhead turtle

Caretta caretta

↔ 28–39 in (71–100 cm)
🧭 Tropical, subtropical, and temperate waters worldwide
✖ Endangered

The world's biggest, hard-shelled sea turtle is named for its large head, armed with powerful jaws for crunching crustaceans and mollusks. Like all other sea turtles, its limbs are modified into flippers for swimming, but females must "beach" themselves to lay eggs. Loggerheads breed only every two years—sometimes longer.

Alligator snapping turtle

Macrochelys temminckii

↔ 16–32 in (40–80 cm)
🧭 SE. US
✖ Vulnerable

The weightiest freshwater turtle is an aggressive predator. It crawls along the bottom of swamps for prey, waiting among water weed with its mouth open. A wriggling appendage on its tongue then lures fish in. To make a catch, the turtle's head shoots forward and the jaws snap with a powerful bite.

European pond turtle

Emys orbicularis

↔ 6–8 in (15–20 cm)
🧭 N. Africa, Europe, W. Asia
✖ Near threatened

This species ranges further north than most other freshwater turtles, and populations in the coldest parts survive the winter by hibernating in shallow water. Typical of many reptiles, this turtle routinely basks in the sun. It spends more time on land than other, more strictly aquatic, species—often wandering miles away from wetlands.

Leatherback sea turtle

Dermochelys coriacea

↔ 4–6 ft (1.2–1.8 m)
🧭 Tropical, subtropical, and temperate waters worldwide
✖ Vulnerable

This jellyfish-eating predator is the biggest of all turtles—and the fastest swimming reptile. Its muscles generate enough body heat to stay active even in the cold ocean. Its blood circulation also traps this heat close to vital organs, giving it the stamina to dive deep and travel far.

African helmeted turtle

Pelomedusa subrufa

↔ 8–13 in (20–33 cm)
🧭 Sub-Saharan Africa
✖ Not known

This turtle can retract its neck completely by folding it sideways under the leading edge of the shell. It is an opportunistic marshland predator and will even grab birds that come down to drink, pulling them underwater to drown them. It lives in rain pools and watering holes in Africa's open country. During the rainy season, it wanders from pool to pool foraging for prey. It may estivate in dry conditions by burying itself in mud.

Red-footed tortoise

Chelonoidis carbonaria

↔ 16–20 in (41–51 cm)
🧭 N. to C. South America
✖ Not known

This tortoise ranges widely in South American grasslands and open woodland, but is absent from the wettest parts of the Amazon basin. The orange or yellow color pattern is highly variable, and a closely allied species—the yellow-footed tortoise (*C. denticulata*)—may occur in the same habitat. This group of tropical American tortoises also includes the ancestors of the giant tortoises of the Galapagos Islands.

Indian star tortoise

Geochelone elegans

↔ Up to 11 in (28 cm)
🧭 S. Asia
✖ Common

Named for the striking pattern on its shell, this tortoise lives in dry scrubby forests, where its yellow, starlike markings camouflage it against the leaf litter on the forest floor as it feeds on grasses and low-growing succulent plants. The plates of its shell are raised into distinct peaks—which help the animal to right itself if it falls on its back. This tortoise needs plenty of water and is most active during the monsoon season. In drier weather, it stirs only in the morning and late afternoon.

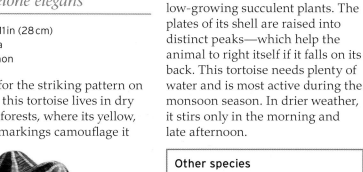

Other species

● **Common snapping turtle**
Chelydra serpentina » p73
● **Galapagos tortoise**
Chelonoidis elephantopus » p127
● **Green sea turtle**
Chelonia mydas » p346
● **Leopard tortoise**
Stigmochelys pardalis » p227

Snakes

Suborder *Serpentes*

South American pipe snake

Anilius scytale

- 28–35 in (70–90 cm)
- SE. US
- Vulnerable

The sole member of the family Aniliidae, this snake of the Amazon basin, is also called the "false coral snake" due to its superficial resemblance to the vividly colored—and highly venomous—coral snakes. However, it lacks venom and is more closely related to constricting boas and pythons. It is a secretive, ground-dwelling species—preying on cold-blooded animals. It hunts in burrows, and its diet is thought to consist of small vertebrates, including snakes. It may be preyed upon by other snakes.

flattened head

Sunbeam snake

Xenopeltis unicolor

- 3–4 ft (1–1.2 m)
- SE. Asia
- Common

This snake spends much of its time in underground burrows, but when it emerges into sunlight, its iridescent scales shine with many colors—inspiring its name. The young have a distinctive white color that disappears once the skin has molted two or three times. This snake's flat head may help with burrowing. An egg-laying constrictor, it comes above ground only at night and preys on frogs, lizards, snakes, and small mammals.

Rainbow boa

Epicrates cenchria

- 3–7 ft (1–2.1 m)
- Central and South America
- Not known

Named for the colored sheen of its skin, the rainbow boa is a typical muscular constrictor. Its color varies across its range from plain brown to a pattern of orange, red, and black, depending upon subspecies. The back has black circles, while the flanks have light-centered spots. It climbs into low vegetation, but also inhabits open savanna. Like other boas, this snake bears live young, sometimes producing litters of over 20.

Burmese python

Python bivittatus

- 16–23 ft (5–7 m)
- S. and SE. Asia
- Vulnerable

One of the biggest of the Old World pythons, the Burmese python climbs well and swims—despite its bulk. Full-grown pythons can overpower pigs and goats—and backward-pointing teeth help grip the victim for swallowing whole. Like other pythons, this species lays eggs. The female vibrates her body to generate heat to warm the brood.

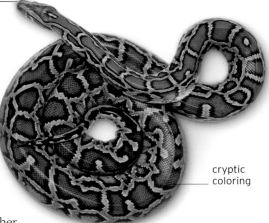

cryptic coloring

Common egg-eating snake

Dasypeltis scabra

- 28–39 in (70–100 cm)
- Africa and W. Asia
- Common

This toothless snake has a special feeding technique. Flexible jaws and throat allow it to swallow hard-shelled eggs whole—even ones wider than its head. Once in the throat, bony projections of the snake's spine puncture the shell, so the yolk and white can flow into the digestive system. The crushed remains of the shell are regurgitated.

Boomslang

Dispholidus typus

- 3–6 ft (1–1.8 m)
- Sub-Saharan Africa
- Not known

One of the most potently venomous of all climbing snakes, the boomslang—meaning "tree snake" in Afrikaans—spends much of its life among branches. Here, its agility and good binocular vision help it prey on climbing lizards, mammals, and birds during the day. It has large rear fangs and a wide gape. Its venom causes internal bleeding that can quickly lead to death. Females lay clutches of up to 14 eggs in tree hollows and dead vegetation.

Corn snake

Pantherophis guttatus

- 3–6 ft (1–1.8 m)
- C. and SE. US
- Common

The corn snake is so-called because it is often drawn to caches of corn and grain, where it kills rats and mice by constriction and can be effective at pest control. It is common in the eastern US, and in colder, northern parts of its range it hibernates during winter. This non-venomous snake is harmless to humans and its docile nature makes it a popular pet.

slender, muscular body

Golden flying snake
Chrysopelea ornata

↔ 3–4 ft (1–1.2 m)
◓ S. and SE. Asia
✗ Not known

Superbly adapted for climbing, this mildly venomous snake uses its underside scales to grip bark and branches—and is capable of scaling near-vertical surfaces. Once it reaches a high perch, it can even launch itself into the air and glide across forest clearings. By spreading its ribs, it pulls its underside to form a U-shape along its length so its body acts like a lengthened parachute.

Milksnake
Lampropeltis triangulum

↔ 1–7 ft (0.3–2.1 m)
◓ North America, Central America, N. South America
✗ Not known

One of the most widely distributed terrestrial snakes, the milksnake's colors mimic those of the venomous coral snakes—a feature that probably evolved to warn predators to stay away. Milksnakes feed on invertebrates, amphibians, and small rodents.

smooth scales

Common kingsnake
Lampropeltis getula

↔ 3–7 ft (1–2.1 m)
◓ W. and S. US, N. Mexico
✗ Common

Closely allied to milksnakes, this nonvenomous snake is harmless to humans—but is a formidable predator of small animals. It hunts warm-blooded mammals and birds, entering rodent burrows and killing the occupants by constriction. It also preys on amphibians and other reptiles—even venomous snakes. It is largely immune to their venom and may subdue them by biting down onto their jaws.

slender body

yellow collar

European grass snake
Natrix natrix

↔ 4–7 ft (1.2–2.1 m)
◓ Europe to C. Asia, NW. Africa
✗ Common

Widespread in open woodland and grasslands of Europe, this snake neither uses venom to kill prey nor constricts them—it swallows them alive. The snake targets amphibians, such as frogs, and stays close to their wetland habitat. It can also swim well. It rarely bites except when hunting; if molested by predators, it plays dead and releases a foul-smelling fluid from its anal glands.

Brown house snake
Boaedon capensis

↔ 3–4 ft (1–1.2 m)
◓ S. Africa
✗ Not known

House snakes—so called because of their fondness for entering buildings—are nonvenomous African snakes. They may bite if provoked, but are harmless to humans. It may be tan, brown, orange, or black with cream stripes on the sides of its head. It constricts and kills small mammals and may be significant in the control of mice and rats in towns and villages.

Australian copperhead
Austrelaps superbus

↔ 4–6 ft (1.2–1.8 m)
◓ SE. Australia, N. Tasmania
✗ Not known

This elapid snake—a relative of cobras and mambas—thrives in cool parts of eastern Australia. It is often seen flattening its body, perhaps as a way of increasing absorption of the sun's heat—but can stay active in lower temperatures where other snakes are dormant. Like other elapids, it has dangerously potent venom, but mainly hunts cold-blooded prey, such as amphibians, which it targets in wetland habitats.

Yellow-lipped sea krait
Laticauda colubrina

↔ 3–7 ft (1–2.1 m)
◓ S. and SE. Asia
✗ Common

Although oceangoing in habit, the yellow-lipped sea krait is less well adapted to an aquatic life than other sea snakes. It returns to shore to lay eggs, whereas most other sea snakes give birth to live young in the ocean. Its large belly scales help it to grip land. This sea krait is common on coral reefs, where it hunts at night using powerful venom to kill fish—particularly eels. However, it is very reluctant to bite humans.

South American coral snake
Micrurus lemniscatus

↔ 24–35 in (61–89 cm)
◓ N. and C. South America
✗ Common

Around 80 species of American coral snakes have their greatest diversity in the South American tropics. Each has a body pattern of vibrant red, yellow, and black bands—a warning that the venom of these front-fanged snakes is very potent. The South American coral snake is one of the most widespread coral snakes, but—like others—it is a shy ground-dweller that spends part of the day in a burrow and hunts other reptiles.

King cobra
Ophiophagus hannah

- 10–16 ft (3–5 m)
- S. and SE. Asia
- Vulnerable

The world's longest venomous snake is also a specialist hunter of other snakes. Like other cobras, it rears up when threatened, but its hood is narrower than that of other cobras. Females have an especially aggressive threat display when guarding their nests from intruders. They lay their eggs in warm mounds of woodland debris and remain in attendance until the eggs start to hatch.

tan, olive-brown, or black colored body

Puff adder
Bitis arietans

- 3–6 ft (1–1.8 m)
- Sub-Saharan Africa
- Not known

This ground-dwelling, highly venomous snake, often found near human habitations, is responsible for more fatal bites in Africa than any other species. It is a well-camouflaged, thick-bodied snake and, when threatened, it hisses and puffs before striking with considerable force. Like most other members of the viper family, this species bears live young, sometimes producing litters of more than 100 —more than any other snake.

Gaboon viper
Bitis gabonica

- 4–7 ft (1.2–2.1 m)
- W. and C. Africa
- Not known

A massive head and bulky body make the gaboon viper the world's heaviest venomous snake. It also has the biggest fangs of any snake —and delivers the greatest volume of venom. Its coloration and patterning camouflage it perfectly against the leaf litter of its woodland habitat. It strikes with lightning speed and keeps a hold of its victim, killing prey up to the size of small antelopes.

geometric patterning

triangular head

Southern copperhead
Agkistrodon contortrix

- 24–51 in (61–130 cm)
- C. and SE. US
- Common

This woodland snake hunts in the dark, targeting warm-blooded prey, such as rodents, using heat-seeking sensory "pits" on the sides of its head. Like other pit vipers, it waits for prey to approach within striking range before attacking. Its venom, although fatal to small animals, is less dangerous to humans than that of related species.

Sidewinder
Crotalus cerastes

- 18–32 in (45–80 cm)
- SW. US, NW. Mexico
- Locally common

The "side-winding" form of locomotion—where the snake moves in a diagonal direction with two parts of its body touching the ground at any one time—is a specialized technique used for moving quickly on unstable, shifting sand. The sidewinder, a species of rattlesnake, hunts desert rodents. Like other vipers, it is an ambusher—and attacks prey from the cover of clumps of shrubby vegetation.

South American bushmaster
Lachesis muta

- 8–12 ft (2.4–3.7 m)
- S. Central America, N. South America
- Not known

Widespread in forests and open country, the bushmaster is the longest venomous snake in the Americas. It exhibits the tail-shaking behavior of rattlesnakes when threatened, but lacks their noisy rattle. Like other pit vipers, it hunts warm-blooded animals, but differs from most by laying eggs instead of giving birth to live young.

Texas thread snake
Rena dulcis

- 6–11 in (15–30 cm)
- S. US, NE. Mexico
- Locally common

This earthwormlike snake has smooth skin and scale-covered eyes as adaptations for burrowing through the soil. It is one of nearly 300 species of superficially similar thread and blind snakes—a group that includes the world's smallest snake. It uses its tiny mouth to hunt underground ants and termites, and even releases a pheromone that pacifies the insects so it can invade their nests unmolested.

Other species

- **Asian tiger keelback**
  Rhabdophis tigrinus » p291
- **Black mamba**
  Dendroaspis polylepis » p207
- **Cape cobra**
  Naja nivea » p234
- **Common adder**
  Vipera berus » p145
- **Common garter snake**
  Thamnophis sirtalis » p50
- **Emerald tree boa**
  Corallus caninus » p97
- **Giant parrot snake**
  Leptophis ahaetulla » p105
- **Green anaconda**
  Eunectes murinus » p105
- **Indian cobra**
  Naja naja » p264

- **Mojave rattlesnake**
  Crotalus scutulatus » p65
- **Mountain kingsnake**
  Lampropeltis zonata » p59
- **Turtle-headed seasnake**
  Emydocephalus annulatus » p347
- **Woma python**
  Aspidites ramsayi » p333

Lizards
Order Lacertilia

Rainbow lizard
Agama agama

↔ 12–16 in (30–40 cm)
◐ W., C., and E. Africa
✕ Not known

Widespread in open countryside, this day-active lizard has strong limbs for climbing rocks and trees, where it hunts insects. During the breeding season, and especially in bright sunlight, males develop their most vivid colors—an orange head and a blue body—to attract females. This makes them one of the most distinctive of all African lizards. Rival males nod vigorously and sometimes clash with whipping tails.

Asian water dragon
Physignathus cocincinus

↔ 32–39 in (80–100 cm)
◐ SE. Asia (Thailand, Cambodia, and Vietnam)
✕ Not known

This long-tailed lizard climbs trees in dense forests, usually in pool-side thickets. Its emerald green skin camouflages it in the foliage, but if disturbed, it jumps into the water. Here, it swims well and can remain submerged for nearly half an hour. Larger males develop head crests to impress the females. The dragon is an opportunistic feeder—it hunts smaller lizards but also grazes on vegetation.

North African mastigure
Uromastyx acanthinura

↔ 12–16 in (30–41 cm)
◐ N. Africa
✕ Not known

Mastigures are mainly plant-eaters. This species grazes on succulent desert vegetation, supplemented with occasional insects. It rarely drinks, getting the water it needs from the plants it eats. Like other mastigures, it lashes out with its thick, spiny tail when threatened by predators. It also uses its tail to block the entrance of its underground burrows and may even inflate its body to wedge itself inside.

Jackson's chameleon
Trioceros jacksonii

↔ 8–12 in (20–30 cm)
◐ E. Africa, introduced in Hawaii
✕ Locally common

Like all chameleons, this lizard has eyes on turrets that can move independently of one another and an extendible, sticky-tipped tongue for catching insect prey. It is a large tree-dwelling species—opposable digits on its feet and a prehensile tail help it to grip branches. Males develop three head horns and flush with bright colors when courting females or showing off to rivals.

Smooth helmeted iguana
Corytophanes cristatus

↔ 12–16 in (30–41 cm)
◐ S. Mexico to N. South America
✕ Not known

A group of mainly tree-climbing lizards, largely confined to the American tropics, iguanas have well-developed gripping feet, but their tails are not prehensile. One of many species with a head crest, or casque, this iguana can change its color. It runs quickly and may even scurry away on two hindlegs when fleeing from predators.

Green anole
Anolis carolinensis

↔ 5–8 in (13–20 cm)
◐ SE. US
✕ Locally common

Nearly 400 species of anoles—small and medium-sized relatives of the iguanas—occur in tropical and subtropical parts of the Americas. The green anole is found further north than others and often frequents backyards in warmer US states. Like other anoles, it has a prominent fleshy colored fan on its throat—called a dewlap—that can be

slender body

toes have pads and claws for climbing

erected for displaying to other members of the same species. The dewlap is larger in the males than in the females.

Green basilisk
Basiliscus plumifrons

↔ 24–30 in (61–76 cm)
◐ Central America
✕ Locally common

A member of the so-called helmeted iguana family, this rainforest lizard climbs and swims well, hunting for insects and other small animals near river banks. It escapes from predators by running away on its hindlegs. Its feet have flaps of skin, which trap bubbles of air as it scampers across pools of water—this ability to run on water has earned it the name "Jesus Christ lizard." Green basilisks can live up to 10 years in captivity.

high crest on back

orange eyes

long hindlimbs for running

tail raised when running on two legs

Desert horned lizard
Phrynosoma platyrhinos

- ↔ 3–5 in (8–13 cm)
- ◔ SW. US
- ✖ Locally common

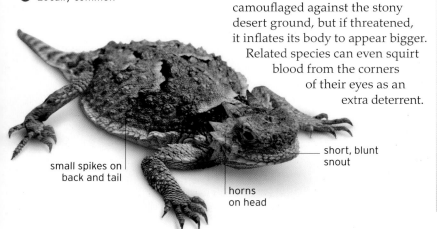

small spikes on
back and tail

horns
on head

A thorny-skinned reptile, the desert horned lizard gets all its nourishment by eating ants. It laps up columns of these insects in quick succession using an extendible tongue. The lizard is camouflaged against the stony desert ground, but if threatened, it inflates its body to appear bigger. Related species can even squirt blood from the corners of their eyes as an extra deterrent.

short, blunt
snout

Northern chuckwalla
Sauromalus ater

- ↔ 11–17 in (28–43 cm)
- ◔ SW. US, N.W. Mexico
- ✖ Locally common

A large, desert-living member of the iguana family, the chuckwalla feeds mainly on vegetation—including leaves, flowers, and fruit. Males are highly territorial and defend their areas from rivals using various threat displays, including head-bobbing, push-ups, and flushing with color. Like some other related species, the chuckwalla retreats to rocky crevices when a predator comes too close, where it secures itself by inflating its body.

Rhinoceros iguana
Cyclura cornuta

- ↔ 3–4 ft (1–1.2 m)
- ◔ Caribbean
- ✖ Vulnerable

One of the bulkiest of all iguanas, this species is confined to the dry, scrubby Caribbean habitat of Hispaniola. It is named for the raised scales on the head, which resemble horns. These "horns" are more prominent in the highly territorial males. The rhinoceros iguana is a ground-living vegetarian that is adapted to feed on the leaves of some plants that contain bitter alkaloids—toxic to many other animals.

African fat-tailed gecko
Hemitheconyx caudicinctus

- ↔ 6 in (15 cm), max 10 in (25 cm)
- ◔ W. Africa
- ✖ Common

Like the closely related leopard gecko, this desert lizard can store fat reserves in its tail to help it survive periods when food is scarce. Its tail is fattest when it is well fed, but shrinks as the stored nutrients are metabolized. It can also shed its tail when danger threatens, temporarily distracting a predator while it escapes.

Common leopard gecko
Eublepharis macularius

- ↔ 8–10 in (20–25 cm)
- ◔ S. Asia
- ✖ Locally common

This desert lizard belongs to a group of geckos that, unlike others, have fully working eyelids. Only adult geckos have the leopardlike spots; juveniles have saddlelike blotches instead. This gecko preys on insects and other invertebrates, hunting mainly at dusk and dawn. Under extreme temperatures, it stays underground, surviving by metabolizing the fat reserves built up in its tail. The common gecko's tail may be discarded in defense, but not as readily as in some other lizards.

tail contains
food reserves

eye protected by
movable eyelid

Common house gecko
Hemidactylus frenatus

- ↔ 5–6 in (13–15 cm)
- ◔ Tropical regions worldwide
- ✖ Common

This small, widespread gray or brown gecko is so-called because of its habit of entering human dwellings. The undersides of its feet are covered with rows of microscopic hairs, which allow the gecko to cling to flat, vertical surfaces. It climbs walls easily and can even cling to glass. House geckos often gather near electric lamps, drawn by the insects that are attracted there.

Tokay gecko
Gekko gecko

- ↔ 7–14 in (18–36 cm)
- ◔ SE. Asia
- ✖ Not known

One of Asia's largest geckos, this is a nocturnal lizard with a loud "tokay" call. Males are among the most vocal of geckos and call to attract females—or to defend their territories from other males. The species has a powerful bite and will attack other lizards that stray too close. When threatened by snakes and small, nocturnal mammals, it delivers a hard bite and, if grasped, it discards its tail. The male mates with several females. The females then attach a pair of spherical, hard-shelled eggs to a vertical surface, usually protected inside a crevice.

distinctive pattern
of orange spots

Northern leaf-tailed gecko
Saltuarius cornutus

- ↔ 6–9 in (15–23 cm)
- ◔ E. Australia
- ✖ Locally common

Named for its flattened tail, the leaf-tailed gecko is a tree-dweller and has a body pattern that camouflages it against lichen- and moss-covered tree bark. Its flattened body reduces shadow as it hugs the surface of a branch or trunk. Southern-ranging forms of leaf-tailed geckos hibernate during cooler months, but this species is active throughout the year in the tropical zone.

Kuhl's flying gecko

Ptychozoon kuhli

✦ 7–8 in (18–20 cm)
◐ SE. Asia
✖ Not known

Several species of so-called flying geckos have elaborate webbing of skin between their digits and along their body, which serve to help these tree-dwelling lizards glide from perch to perch. This species is widespread in rainforests of Southeast Asia and is colored for effective camouflage against the background of foliage and tree bark. It usually rests head-down on a tree trunk, in readiness to jump.

Rough-scaled plated lizard

Broadleysaurus major

✦ 16–19 in (40–48 cm)
◐ C., E., and Southern Africa
✖ Not known

Named for their prominent, shiny scales, about eight species of plated lizards live in dry, rocky habitats of Africa. This species eats leaves, fruit, and insects. Its armorlike skin protects it from predators—and keeps it wedged in rocky crevices when danger threatens. Males are highly territorial and flaunt a pink throat during the breeding season.

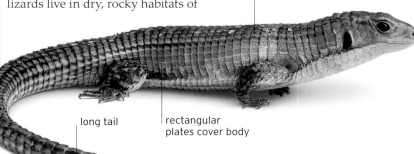

light brown to
medium brown body

long tail

rectangular
plates cover body

Sand lizard

Lacerta agilis

✦ 7–9 in (18–22 cm)
◐ Europe to C. Asia
✖ Common

In the northern part of its range, this lizard is confined to coastal sand dunes and sandy heaths, but further south it is more widespread in open country and yards; here, it is called the "agile lizard." There is considerable geographic variation in color, but males are always more vivid in the breeding season. The sand lizard is active by day, feeding on small insects and spiders, and—like related species—may shed its tail if attacked by predators.

Viviparous lizard

Zootoca vivipara

✦ 4–5 in (10–13 cm)
◐ Europe to C. and E. Asia (including Japan)
✖ Common

This species belongs to an Old World family of fast-running, so-called lacertid lizards. It is the only member of this family to have populations that give birth to live young; it ranges farther north than any other species of lizard—where it is too cold for eggs to develop properly. Close to the Arctic Circle, it survives the coldest periods in underground hibernation.

African fire skink

Lepidothryis fernandi

✦ 9–15 in (23–38 cm)
◐ W. and C. Africa
✖ Not known

The bright stripe of orange-red on its flank gives this African lizard its name. It belongs to a group of skinks characterized by a similar pattern. Like most other skinks, this is a slender-bodied, shiny-scaled lizard with small limbs. It lives among leaf litter on the ground and is active at twilight. It hunts for insect prey among tree roots in woodland, but may also venture into open grassland.

Eyed skink

Chalcides ocellatus

✦ 12 in (30 cm)
◐ S. Europe, N. and NE. Africa, W. Asia
✖ Not known

A native of dry Mediterranean scrub, this short-limbed skink is one of many species called "sand-swimming" skinks. In loose sand, it moves swiftly forward by undulating its body, like a snake. Above ground, it can use its feet for walking, but some related sand-swimmers lack limbs altogether. It is named for the pattern of eyelike spots that occur on its body.

Blue-tongued skink

Tiliqua scincoides

✦ 18–20 in (45–50 cm)
◐ N., E., and SE. Australia
✖ Not known

Unlike its smaller, nimble insect-eating cousins, this heavy-bodied, slow-moving skink mainly eats flowers, fruit, and berries, but may supplement this diet with small animals. In its native land, it is often seen basking on roads, where a flash of its bright blue tongue may help to deter predators. Like other giant skinks of the Australasian region, it gives birth to live young —after a 5-month gestation period.

Emerald tree skink

Lamprolepis smaragdina

✦ 7–10 in (18–25 cm)
◐ SE. Asia, New Guinea, Pacific islands
✖ Not known

This agile, tree-living skink climbs well and hunts for insects, flowers, and fruit. The species occurs on many islands throughout archipelagos of Southeast Asia and Australasia. Like other tree-living lizards, its dispersal through the region is perhaps facilitated by rafting over water on "islands" of floating vegetation.

green color
camouflages
against foliage

Slow worm

Anguis fragilis

✦ 12–20 in (30–50 cm)
◐ Europe to W. Asia, NW. Africa
✖ Not known

One of several legless lizards, the slow worm is often mistaken for a snake—but its eyelids serve to distinguish it as a true lizard. Its scientific name, *fragilis*, refers to its habit of shedding its tail when attacked. A new tail grows slowly, and so many of these lizards have a truncated appearance. Slow worms have a long lifespan, but they hibernate for nearly half the year in the coldest parts of their range.

Komodo dragon

Varanus komodoensis

✦ 7–10 ft (2–3 m)
◐ Indonesia (Komodo, Rinca, Padar, W. Flores)
✖ Vulnerable

The world's largest lizard is a powerful, clawed flesh eater, perfectly suited as the top predator on its native island habitat—where it preys on animals as big as deer. This giant monitor lizard delivers a savage bite with sharp teeth. Venom in its saliva, along with possible bacterial infections, means that the wound festers, eventually disabling the prey so the dragon can make an easier kill.

Savanna monitor

Varanus exanthematicus

↔ 3–5 ft (1–1.5 m)
➤ Sub-Saharan Africa
✕ Locally common

Monitors include some of the largest of lizards. They have powerful bodies and sharp claws —and most are opportunistic in their feeding habits. This species is widespread across Africa in open woodland and grassland, spending most of its time on the ground, but occasionally climbing into low trees. It also swims well and preys on anything that it can overpower

—including invertebrates and small vertebrates. Its chief predators are martial eagles and ratels, and it is sometimes eaten by humans, despite legal protection. Savanna monitors breed in the wet season. Females dig nests and lay about 20–50 eggs.

rows of circular, dark-edged yellow spots across back

Other species

- **Armadillo lizard**
  Ouroborus cataphractus » p235
- **Australian water dragon**
  Intellagama lesueurii » p342
- **Common flying dragon**
  Draco volans » p298
- **Fabian's lizard**
  Liolaemus fabiani » p113
- **Frilled lizard**
  Chlamydosaurus kingii » pp324–25
- **Gila monster**
  Heloderma suspectum » p64
- **Golden tegu**
  Tupinambis teguixin » p105

- **Henkel's leaf-tailed gecko**
  Uroplatus henkeli » p243
- **Jeweled lizard**
  Timon lepidus » p157
- **Marine iguana**
  Amblyrhynchus cristatus » pp128–29
- **Nile monitor**
  Varanus niloticus » p227
- **Panther chameleon**
  Furcifer pardalis » p242
- **Przewalski's wonder gecko**
  Teratoscincus przewalskii » p283
- **Thorny devil**
  Moloch horridus » p332

Amphisbaenians

Order Amphisbaenia

Speckled worm lizard

Amphisbaena fuliginosa

↔ 12–18 in (30–45 cm)
➤ N. South America, Trinidad
✕ Not known

Worm lizards are burrowing reptiles, with a superficial resemblance to earthworms or snakes—but they are most

closely related to the family that includes sand and viviparous lizards. Like other worm lizards, this species has poor vision, but can detect invertebrate prey by vibrations.

mosaiclike pattern

Saltwater crocodile

Crocodylus porosus

↔ 16–23 ft (5–7 m)
➤ SE. Asia to N. Australia
✕ Common

The world's largest living reptile is a formidable predator, capable of preying on large mammals. Once the victim is grabbed, the crocodile rolls in the water to drown the prey. Unlike most other crocodilians, it can swim considerable distances out to sea. This salt tolerance means the species can disperse between islands— and this has helped to make it widespread throughout Southeast Asia and Australasia.

Dwarf crocodile

Osteolaemus tetraspis

↔ 6 ft (1.8 m)
➤ W. and C. Africa
✕ Vulnerable

This shy, nocturnal reptile is one of the smallest of crocodilians and quickly dives under water when disturbed. It inhabits rainforest wetlands in tropical Africa, where

bony plates cover body

Crocodiles and alligators

Order Crocodylia

Black caiman

Melanosuchus niger

↔ 13–20 ft (4–6 m)
➤ N. South America
✕ Locally common

Caimans are members of the alligator family characterized by a bony ridge running from eyes to snout. Most are smaller than true

alligators—even though this species is one of the largest predators in wetlands of Amazonia, and a fully grown black caiman is capable of bringing down a small deer. Its dark color provides camouflage, and a wide, heavy head means it has a strong bite. The female lays and guards 30–65 eggs and stays with the young after they hatch.

it hides during the day in burrows or beneath tree roots. At night, it feeds near the water's edge. The dwarf crocodile hunts for fish during the wettest months, but turns to bankside crustaceans and amphibians during the dry season.

Other species

- **American alligator**
  Alligator mississippiensis » p72
- **Gharial**
  Gavialis gangeticus » p265
- **Nile crocodile**
  Crocodylus niloticus » p191
- **Yacare caiman**
  Caiman yacare » pp106–07

yellowish underside with black patches

blunt snout

AMPHIBIANS

The Age of Amphibians—when amphibian giants ruled the planet—belongs to the prehistoric past. However, amphibians still include more than 7,000 species today—a thousand more than all the known mammals. Moist, glandular skin helps many amphibians to absorb oxygen and protects some with deadly poison. It also makes them vulnerable to dehydration and prevents them from entering salty ocean waters. However, in moist habitats such as rainforests, amphibians have evolved into a multitude of frogs, toads, and salamanders, which includes some of the most exquisitely colorful species on the planet.

Anatomy

Six out of seven kinds of amphibians are frogs or toads, and they embody the essential aspects of amphibian biology: adults have lungs but can also breathe through their moist skin. Their soft eggs usually hatch into aquatic larvae. The frog's build—with its long hindlegs—is adapted for jumping, but many species use their legs for digging or even swimming.

Other groups of living amphibians are the wormlike caecilians and lizardlike newts and salamanders. Burrowing caecilians lack limbs, and their tiny eyes are sometimes hidden by a heavily roofed skull, which is used for bulldozing through soil. Salamanders—and their more aquatic relatives, the newts—are generally crawling amphibians with long tails. A few lack hindlegs and are eel-like swimmers.

As amphibians lack the sharp teeth and claws of reptiles, many rely on chemical defense to deter predators. Their skin is peppered with numerous glands, many of which secrete slime, but others produce toxins. The so-called "poison frogs" are notorious for their deadly toxicity—and advertise the fact by flashing bright warning colors.

△ ATTRACTING A MATE
Courtship in amphibians can be elaborate. Male frogs call for attention, but the smooth newt—like related species—uses color to impress a mate.

Reproduction

Amphibian eggs are coated with soft jelly that is not drought-resistant. This means that the eggs must be laid in water or moist places. Almost all frogs and toads—and most primitive salamanders—reproduce by external fertilization: sperm and eggs are released into water. Males of more advanced salamanders and newts deposit a packet of sperm, which the female manipulates into her genital opening. Caecilians, by contrast, are some of the only amphibians that practice internal fertilization by direct copulation.

Many rainforest frogs breed in puddles or pools that collect in leaves. Others lay eggs on moist ground—or in elaborate bubble nests made in vegetation, relying on their tadpoles being able to drop into a pool of water underneath. Some kinds hatch into tiny froglets instead of tadpoles and a few parents even carry their eggs or offspring around with them, piggyback fashion. A range of developmental changes occurs in salamanders: the eggs directly hatch into miniature versions of the parents, while a few give birth to live young.

Behavior

The aquatic larvae of amphibians retain some of the sensory features of fish—including their vibration-detecting lateral line system, which senses water currents. But the sensory emphasis in land-living adults is different. Burrowing caecilians rely on a sense of smell to hunt underground invertebrates or find mates—and have a tiny tentacle below each eye to collect this information. Frogs and toads usually have good vision and a very sharp sense of hearing—evident from their big eyes and conspicuous eardrums. Many are highly vocal and amplify their calls with bulbous, air-filled vocal sacs. Calls—ranging from insectlike chirps to barks and metallic peals—are species specific and the principal means of communication between individuals, especially when breeding.

Salamanders and newts rely more on underwater pheromones or sometimes visual cues. Their elaborate courtship rituals often involve flaunting bright, dramatic colors.

◁ FIRE BELLY
Some amphibians use shock tactics when under threat. The fire-bellied toad flashes its orange underside using various gymnastics—including flipping onto its back.

▽ COLORFUL WARNING
Otherwise largely defenseless, amphibians rely on poisonous skin to deter predators. Brightly colored poison frogs accumulate their potent toxins from the invertebrates they eat.

large, black eyes

▷ SPAWNING SITE
Many amphibians release sperm and eggs in open water. Communally breeding frogs spawn in thick masses, warming the eggs to speed up hatching.

AMPHIBIAN CLASSIFICATION

There are three orders of amphibians: frogs and toads, the largest group; the lizardlike newts and salamanders; and the wormlike caecilians.

Newts and salamanders » p438
Order Caudata **Species** 691

Caecilians » p439
Order Gymnophiona **Species** c.203

Frogs and toads » p439–41
Order Anura **Species** 6,481

Newts and salamanders
Order Caudata

Greater siren
Siren lacertina

↔ 20–35 in (50–90 cm)
◑ E. and SE. US
✖ Locally common

This large salamander of the lower Mississippi valley lacks hindlimbs and the entire pelvic girdle. It has tiny front feet and can move through the water with eel-like undulations of the body. Larval gills are retained into adulthood, growing large and feathery as the animal matures. The siren rarely

feathery, external gills

leaves the water, except during heavy rains—but can survive drought by cocooning in mud.

Hellbender
Cryptobranchus alleganiensis

↔ 12–29 in (30–74 cm)
◑ E. US
✖ Near threatened

America's largest salamander is a member of the same family as the Oriental giant salamanders, the biggest in the world. It rarely leaves the water. Adults have lungs, but in their oxygen-rich, fast-flowing river habitat, gaseous exchange is supplemented by absorption of oxygen across the flabby skin. The male uses his flat head to excavate a protective cavern beneath rocks, in which he fertilizes the female's eggs and guards them until they hatch.

Mudpuppy
Necturus maculosus

↔ 12–19 in (30–48 cm)
◑ S. Canada, C. and E. US
✖ Common

The mudpuppy is a water-breathing salamander—its feathery gills become bigger in stagnant habitats with lower oxygen concentration. An aggressive, nocturnal predator of small animals, it may become active by day when the water is muddy. Unlike many other exclusively aquatic salamanders, which disperse sperm into the water, the mudpuppy reproduces like newts—males produce a spermatophore (sperm package) for transferring sperm to the female's body.

short, stout limbs

yellow markings may consist of stripes, spots, or blotches

Fire salamander
Salamandra salamandra

↔ 7–11 in (18–28 cm)
◑ Europe
✖ Common

The bright warning spots of this woodland salamander mark the locations of glandular patches of skin that secrete toxic secretions, which are used in defense against predators. Fire salamanders typically develop from aquatic larvae. Adults are almost entirely terrestrial, except when breeding; however, some populations give birth to live young on land that are miniature versions of adults.

Alpine newt
Ichthyosaura alpestris

↔ 2–5 in (5–12.7 cm)
◑ Europe
✖ Not known

A typical newt, this amphibian leads a dual aquatic–terrestrial life. Outside the breeding season, the adults live on land, moving into ponds to breed. Here, the males grow a dorsal crest and develop brighter colors to court females. Eggs hatch into larvae, which metamorphose into terrestrial adult forms called efts. Only southern populations are truly alpine in habitat.

Eastern newt
Notophthalmus viridescens

↔ 3–5 in (7.6–12.7 cm)
◑ E. Canada, E. US
✖ Common

After metamorphosing from the aquatic larval stage, this newt develops into a tiny, terrestrial, lizardlike eft with red spots. The pattern may act as a warning to predators that the skin of this amphibian is extremely toxic. The efts spend up to four years of their life on land in woodland, but return to pools to grow into larger breeding adults; they retain the red-spotted colors.

Mexican axolotl
Ambystoma mexicanum

↔ 4–8 in (10–20 cm)
◑ Mexico (Lake Xochimilco)
✖ Critically endangered

Although the Mexican axolotl belongs to a family of mole salamanders that are typically terrestrial as adults, it remains aquatic and retains some larval characteristics into adulthood, including feathery gills and a finlike tail. Axolotls are popular pets, but the wild population—almost entirely confined to a lake near Mexico City—is critically endangered.

Eastern tiger salamander
Ambystoma tigrinum

↔ 7–14 in (18–35 cm)
◑ North America
✖ Common

Named for its vivid skin pattern, this typical burrowing mole salamander usually spends its adult life on land. Adults breed in ponds—often returning to their place of birth to do so. Most larvae metamorphose into terrestrial adults, but under some conditions—such as in the cool Rocky Mountains—they may stay aquatic and retain gills right into sexual maturity.

short, powerful limbs used for burrowing

Other species
- **Ensatina**
  Ensatina eschscholtzii » p59
- **Great crested newt**
  Triturus cristatus » p170
- **Japanese giant salamander**
  Andrias japonicus » p291

Caecilians

Order Gymnophiona

Ringed caecilian

Siphonops annulatus

↔ 8–16 in (20–40 cm)
◑ N. South America
✖ Common

Like all caecilians, this legless, burrowing amphibian preys on small invertebrates. Unusually for amphibians, caecilians reproduce by internal fertilization, with the male and female physically mating together. The female lays her eggs in the soil. The newly hatched infants are nourished by grazing on the outer layers of the mother's skin.

Frogs and toads

Order Anura

Oriental fire-bellied toad

Bombina orientalis

↔ 1–2 in (2.5–5 cm)
◑ E and SE. Asia
✖ Locally common

This small, vivid green toad of wet Asian forests uses color to startle predators and warn them of its skin's toxicity—just like several other species of fire-bellied toads. Its belly is bright red with black spots. When attacked, the toad flashes the pattern by flattening its body, lifting its legs, and sometimes even rolling onto its back. The male calls to attract a mate. The female lays eggs under rocks in streams.

rounded warts on back

Surinam toad

Pipa pipa

↔ 2–8 in (5–20 cm)
◑ N. South America
✖ Common

This entirely aquatic toad has remarkable breeding habits. A mating pair does somersaults in the water, and fertilized eggs attach to the back of the female— where they develop in honeycomb-like pockets. The eggs hatch into miniature toads; in related species, they release filter-feeding tadpoles.

Mexican burrowing toad

Rhinophrynus dorsalis

↔ 2–3 in (5–7.6 cm)
◑ S. US to Central America
✖ Common

This small-headed toad— the sole species in its family—has large feet for digging burrows. It feeds on underground insects, uniquely catching them by projecting its tongue through a gap at the front of its mouth—more like an anteater than a toad. In the rainy season, it emerges to breed in temporary pools. The eggs float singly on the surface and quickly hatch into filter-feeding tadpoles.

Common spadefoot toad

Pelobates fuscus

↔ 2–3 in (5–7.6 cm)
◑ C. and E. Europe, W. Asia
✖ Common

Spadefoot toads are so-called because their feet have a horny lump for pushing soil as they burrow backward into the ground. This common European species is also known as the "garlic toad" because of its distinctive odorous secretion, which may serve to repel predators. Like other spadefoot toads, this amphibian is most active above ground during rains, when it lays its eggs in ponds.

Parsley frog

Pelodytes punctatus

↔ 1–2 in (2.5–5 cm)
◑ W. and SW. Europe
✖ Common

Named for the parsleylike green flecks on its skin, this is a primitive burrowing frog—although it lacks the hardened feet of the related spadefoot toads. It also climbs well, its perching ability assisted by a suckerlike underside. During the breeding season, males call out from underwater to attract females, who answer back. Spawning is triggered by rainfall, when each female can produce over 1,000 eggs. These are laid in broad strips in ponds. The tadpoles grow for several months, often attaining lengths considerably bigger than those of metamorphosed adults. Like most frogs, this species is active at night, spends winter and dry spells hibernating underground, and feeds on insects and other invertebrates.

Holy cross frog

Notaden bennettii

↔ 2–3 in (5–7.6 cm)
◑ E. Australia
✖ Locally common

This small, round-bodied native of Australia has been named after the distinct, crosslike pattern of warts on its back. Like many of its relatives, this ground-dwelling species spends dry periods underground and emerges during very heavy rains to breed in temporary ponds. The holy cross frog feeds on ants and termites and produces a sticky, defensive secretion when handled.

South American bullfrog

Leptodactylus pentadactylus

↔ 3–9in (8–23cm)
◑ N. South America
✖ Common

Males of this large rainforest frog have spines on their chest and thumbs for fighting rivals. In its humid habitat, the species is adapted for laying eggs on land. While mating, a male and female whip watery mucus into a froth using their hindlegs. Fertilized eggs are deposited in this "bubble-nest." Eggs hatch during rainfall, and larvae get washed into pools to complete their development.

dry, warty skin

large parotid gland

toes not webbed

European common toad

Bufo bufo

↔ 3–8in (8–20cm)
◑ NW. Africa, Europe to C. Asia
✖ Common

This species belongs to a family of true toads, characterised by warty skin and two large glands behind the eyes; these release a toxic secretion that deters predators. Southern populations—regarded by some scientists as a separate species—have spiny warts for extra protection. This toad breeds in ponds, laying its eggs in "strings" of jelly that become entwined around water weeds.

Cane toad

Rhinella marina

↔ 2–9in (5–23cm)
◑ Central America, South America; introduced to Australia and elsewhere
✖ Common

Originally from South America (where it is known as the marine toad), one of the world's biggest toads has spread far and wide. It was introduced to control insect pests of sugarcane, but its voracious predatory habits and toxic skin have proved harmful to vulnerable wildlife. It lays clutches of up to 20,000 eggs in ponds.

Darwin's frog

Rhinoderma darwinii

↔ 1in (2.5cm)
◑ S. South America
✖ Vulnerable

Restricted to the cool, wet rainforests of southern Chile and Argentina, this pointed-nose frog resembles a dead leaf, which camouflages it against forest leaf litter. The female lays eggs on the moist forest floor. The attending father takes them into his vocal pouch—where they continue their development. Hatching froglets jump out of their father's mouth.

Paradoxical frog

Pseudis paradoxa

↔ 2–3in (5–8cm)
◑ N. and C. South America
✖ Common

This highly aquatic frog spawns in floating foam nests. The eggs have abundant yolk, which can sustain the tadpoles for weeks. If other food is available, they grow more quickly, reaching up to 10in (25cm) in length—the largest of any frog. During metamorphosis, their long tail is reabsorbed, so the fully developed frog is just a quarter of the tadpole's maximum length.

Spring peeper

Pseudacris crucifer

↔ ³⁄₄–2in (2–5cm)
◑ SE. Canada, E. US
✖ Common

The scientific name *"crucifer"* refers to the crosslike pattern on the back of the peeper. It belongs to a group of highly vocal frogs called "chorus frogs." The peeper retires under logs to hibernate during winter, even tolerating partial freezing in the northernmost reach of its range. When it stirs from dormancy, its high-pitched "peeping" call is a sign that spring has arrived.

plain green back and limbs can change to brown

Common tree frog

Hyla arborea

↔ 1–2in (2.5–5cm)
◑ W. Europe, Asia
✖ Common

True tree frogs make up a large family that have their greatest diversity in the tropical Americas —but this is a member of a small species group from Eurasia. Like its cousins, its eyes have horizontal pupils and its toes are tipped with small disks to help with climbing trees. The skin color varies from green to yellow or brown over its wide geographic range. During the breeding season, males make loud quacking sounds building up into a noisy chorus.

European common frog

Rana temporaria

↔ 2–4in (5–10cm)
◑ Europe, NW. Asia
✖ Common

Familiar in northern Europe as the archetypal frog, the distribution of this species reaches inside the Arctic Circle. The European common frog is common in wetlands and backyards across its range—and sometimes overwinters by hibernating in mud under water. Arctic frogs survive the bitter winter by staying inactive under the cover of tundra ice. In springtime, large numbers of this species gather in ponds to breed.

American bullfrog
Rana catesbeiana

↔ 4–8 in (10–20 cm)
◐ SE. Canada, W., C., and E. US; introduced to Europe, South America, and E. Asia
✖ Common

Males of North America's biggest species of frog are so vocal in defending their territories that their call has been likened to a roaring bull, inspiring the common name. Groups of males even call together in chorus. The American bullfrog is native to the eastern US, but has spread to other parts of the world—including Europe—where its predatory habits make it a destructive invasive species.

Wood frog
Lithobates sylvatica

↔ 2–3 in (5–8 cm)
◐ Canada, E. US
✖ Common

This frog's blood contains anti-freeze chemicals, enabling it to reach further north into the Arctic than any other American frog. It is one of the first frogs to emerge from hibernation in spring, when it favors temporary seasonal rain pools for breeding. These have the benefit of lacking predatory fish—but the strategy carries the risk of entire broods being lost if pools dry up too soon.

Marsh frog
Pelophylax ridibundus

↔ 4–6 in (10–15.2 cm)
◐ Europe, W. and SW. Asia
✖ Common

This frog is the largest in Europe—and big enough to take prey up to the size of mice, lizards, and snakes. It is related to the European common frog, but the marsh frog is larger and spends more time in water. It thrives in many aquatic habitats—including lakes, ditches, and streams—and can even tolerate the salty water around the shores of the Caspian Sea. Females lay up to 12,000 eggs in the water.

Goliath frog
Conraua goliath

↔ 4–16 in (10–40 cm)
◐ Cameroon, Equatorial Guinea
✖ Endangered

This rainforest amphibian grows bigger than any other species of frog or toad. In its native Cameroon, it inhabits clean, well-oxygenated, fast-flowing streams. Unusually for frogs, the goliath frog lacks a vocal sac—adults are silent, even when breeding. Males are larger than females and assemble stony nests to accommodate the female's eggs—perhaps as a way of stopping them from being washed downriver.

Green mantella
Mantella viridis

↔ 1 in (2.5 cm)
◐ N. and E. Madagascar
✖ Endangered

Mantellas are small, strikingly colored frogs that are confined to the island of Madagascar. Like the poison frogs of South America, their bodies harness toxins from the tiny invertebrates they eat—then store them in their skin. The colors warn of toxicity. This green or yellow species has a prominent black face mask and—like others—is endangered by habitat loss and the exotic animal trade.

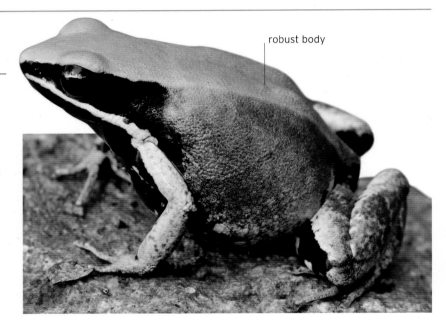

robust body

Gray foam-nest frog
Chiromantis xerampelina

↔ 2–4 in (5–10 cm)
◐ S. Africa
✖ Common

By laying eggs in a "foam nest" attached to a tree branch, this frog avoids losing its vulnerable clutch to aquatic predators, such as fish. The nest is built by the male as he mates with a female on her perch.

More than 10 males may gather in a mating frenzy to fertilize the eggs. Hatched tadpoles drop into a pool beneath the nest. Usually gray or pale brown, this frog can change color for camouflage.

prominent eyes

long, slender limbs

Tailed frog
Ascaphus truei

↔ 1–2 in (2.5–5 cm)
◐ SW. Canada, NW. US
✖ Locally common

This green, brown, gray, or reddish amphibian is the only aquatic frog that breeds by internal fertilization. During mating, the male uses his unique "tail"—an extension of his cloaca—to deposit sperm inside the female's cloaca. Eggs are laid in cold mountain streams, and the hatching tadpoles take two years to mature. The tadpoles have large, suckerlike mouths so they can attach themselves to the underside of rocks and avoid being swept away by fast-flowing currents.

Other species

- **Argentine horned frog**
  Ceratophrys ornata » p121
- **Couch's spadefoot**
  Scaphiopus couchii » p64
- **Dyeing poison frog**
  Dendrobates tinctorius » p98
- **Green tree frog**
  Litoria caerulea » p326
- **Midwife toad**
  Alytes obstetricans » p162
- **Red-eyed tree frog**
  Agalychnis callidryas » pp82–83
- **Tomato frog**
  Dyscophus antongilii » p243
- **Trueb's cochran frog**
  Nymphargus truebae » p89
- **Wallace's flying frog**
  Rhacophorus nigropalmatus » p300
- **Yellow-legged frog**
  Rana sierrae » p59

FISH

Fish are the vertebrates most perfectly adapted to living in water. They are also among the most advanced of all aquatic animals. Typically, they have a streamlined, muscular body for swimming and a set of fins to help control their movement in water. Fish were the first of the world's vertebrates to evolve and include the genetic stock from which all other land-living vertebrates emerged. Some deep-sea fish plumb depths traversed by no other vertebrate, and in some places, such as coral reefs and tropical rivers and lakes, they have evolved into an astonishing —sometimes richly colorful—variety.

Anatomy

A small minority of fish lacks jaws, but all others are jawed, making many formidable predators. Along with rays, sharks have a skeleton made largely from mineralized cartilage, while their

and their blood-rich, feathery gills extract it from water. A few fish can even supplement this by breathing air with lunglike structures.

◁ LIFE ON LAND
Fish have gills for breathing in water, but some can survive for short periods on land. The mudskipper breathes the air trapped in its modified throat.

vertebral column supports ribs and spine

dorsal fin

tail fin

rear anal fin

front anal fin

operculum

△ **BONY SKELETON**
Most fish have a bony skeleton. The rest, including sharks and rays, are cartilaginous. In all fish, skeletal rods, or spines, help support the fins.

skin is covered in hard, pricklelike scales that give it the texture of sandpaper. Bony fish—comprising 95 percent of living fish species—differ from cartilaginous fish in having a skeleton made of bone as well as a swim bladder, which is usually filled with gas, for controlling buoyancy. Their gills are covered by a shieldlike flap called the operculum. Their scales can be thick like armor or thin and flexible.

A few primitive fish rely on the support of a rubbery rod, called the notochord, instead of a spine. In all other vertebrates, the notochord is replaced by the spine during development. When muscles contract, the spine bends sideways, helping the body flex for swimming. Fish need plenty of oxygen to do this,

Reproduction

Most fish release eggs and sperm into the water, often in copious quantities to optimize fertilization. Ocean sunfish produce hundreds of millions of eggs per spawn—more than any other vertebrate. Other fish take better care of their brood and deposit their eggs in discrete clusters. Eggs, and sometimes fry, may be fiercely guarded. Some fish even make nests.

All sharks and rays reproduce through internal fertilization: the male grasps his mate and transfers sperm with the help of modified fins called claspers. Most sharks give birth to live young, but others produce egg capsules. Bony fish are mostly egg-layers with external fertilization, but there are exceptions. Males of a group of freshwater live-bearers, including the guppy, have a tubelike anal fin for channeling sperm into the female.

Behavior

Water transmits sound and vibrations, so fish sense underwater disturbances. A system of tiny, jelly-filled channels, called the lateral line, runs

down both sides of a fish's body. It contains microscopic "hair cells" that detect movement in the water. This helps fish to respond to water currents, as well as detect predators and prey.

Many fish are sensitive to chemical cues as well: sharks are drawn to blood in the water. Cartilaginous fish even have sensory pores for picking up the electrical activity of prey. Several fish species routinely use their underwater senses to gather and swim in coordinated schools, making it harder for predators to single out a target. The biggest schools of herrings and sardines may number hundreds of millions of individuals and stretch across miles of ocean.

▷ **TROPICAL DIVERSITY**
Warm, sunlit waters of tropical reefs host the planet's biggest diversity of marine fish, where many—such as blue-striped snappers—gather in large schools.

▷ **MOUTHFUL OF EGGS**
Fish from many different groups have independently evolved strategies to care for their young. The male jawfish is a mouthbrooder, tending eggs in his cavernous mouth.

FISH CLASSIFICATION

Unlike other vertebrates, fish are not a formally recognized group. Instead, they are a collection of three distinct classes that evolved separately.

Jawless fish » p444
Class Cyclostomata **Species** 123

Cartilaginous fish » pp444–45
Class Chondrichthyes **Species** c.1,235
   Sharks and rays
   Subclass Elasmobranchii **Species** c.1,182
   Chimaeras
   Subclass Holocephali **Species** 53

Bony fish » pp445–47
Class Osteichthyes **Species** c.32,075
   Fleshy-finned fish
   Subclass Sarcopterygii **Species** 8
   Ray-finned fish
   Subclass Actinopterygii **Species** c.32,067

Jawless fish

Class Cyclostomata

Sea lamprey
Petromyzon marinus

- Up to 4 ft (1.2 m)
- North Atlantic, Mediterranean
- Locally common

This is the largest species of lamprey. An adult sea lamprey uses its suckerlike mouth—armed with horny teeth—to clamp onto the sides of another fish, scrape a hole in the host's skin, and suck out flesh and fluids. Sexually mature individuals migrate upriver to spawn in fresh water. Here, larvae may live for more than five years before maturing into adults and moving out to sea. Lampreys breed only once and die after spawning.

Blacktip reef shark
Carcharhinus melanopterus

- Up to 3–4 ft (0.9–1.2 m)
- Tropical Indo-Pacific, E. Mediterranean
- Near threatened

Named for its black-tipped fins—its dorsal fin is often seen projecting above the surface—this is one of the most common predatory sharks of tropical Asian and Australasian waters. Individuals spend much of their time in a territorial patch of reef. Pregnant females move into shallow, sand-bottomed lagoons to give birth.

Smooth hammerhead
Sphyrna zygaena

- 7–8 ft (2.1–2.4 m)
- Tropical, subtropical, and temperate waters worldwide
- Vulnerable

The anatomy of a large hammerhead shark's skull is likely to provide extra lift as the shark swims. The "blade" of the head helps with maneuverability, while a battery of chemical and electrical receptors along its front edge detects prey, especially bottom-living stingrays.

Cartilaginous fish

Class Chondrichthyes

Spotted wobbegong
Orectolobus maculatus

- 4–6 ft (1.2–1.7 m)
- S. Australia
- Near threatened

Flattened like a ray, wobbegongs—sluggish inhabitants of tropical inshore waters of the Indo-Pacific—are among the most distinctive of sharks. This species' mottled skin pattern and tasseled body help it to blend in with seaweed and coral—ideally suited for ambushing smaller fish. It hunts on the bottom, sometimes using its paired pectoral fins to climb between rock pools, with parts of its body showing above the water.

Zebra shark
Stegostoma fasciatum

- 5–8 ft (1.5–2.4 m)
- Indo-Pacific
- Vulnerable

Only juvenile zebra sharks have a black-and-white striped body pattern—possibly to help keep predators away by mimicking the highly venomous banded sea snake. In adults, the stripes are replaced by leopardlike spots. A suction feeder, the shark draws bottom-living fish and invertebrate prey into its mouth cavity—located just behind the snout—with the help of powerful muscles.

Great white shark
Carcharodon carcharias

- 12–17 ft (3.7–5.2 m)
- Temperate and tropical waters worldwide; at times in cold waters
- Vulnerable

A formidable hunter, the great white shark has one of the most powerful bites of any living animal. It is a particularly efficient predator of marine mammals, such as seals, sea lions, and dolphins, although it will feed on any large creature that it can catch. A core of heat-generating body muscles keep it alert and active even in cold waters, while circulatory modifications help retain the heat. Although usually solitary, it may sometimes be seen in pairs or small groups feeding at a carcass, with larger individuals eating first.

Leopard shark
Triakis semifasciata

- Up to 7 ft (2.1 m)
- E. North Pacific
- Locally common

The spots on the leopard shark's body may help camouflage it among the weeds and corals of coastal waters. It hunts in schools for small fish and invertebrates, sometimes venturing into estuaries and bays as well. The shark shuns colder waters, and northern populations migrate to greater depths in winter, where temperatures are less extreme.

Giant manta ray
Manta birostris

- 13–23 ft (4–7 m)
- Tropical and sometimes warm temperate waters worldwide
- Vulnerable

The world's biggest ray virtually "flies" underwater by flapping its giant pectoral fins. The manta has vestigial teeth that are useless for processing food. Instead, it is a filter feeder—with the help of two lobe-like horns, small planktonic animals are channeled into the mouth and then trapped by the gill rakers.

Common eagle ray
Myliobatis aquila

↔ 2–6 ft (0.6–1.8 m)
➤ E. Atlantic, Mediterranean, SW. Indian Ocean
✖ Not known

Eagle rays have massively expanded triangular pectoral fins for swimming through open waters—most species of rays, in comparison, are bottom-dwellers. Eagle rays' jaws are armed with teeth that form plates for crushing the shells of mollusks and crustaceans. This species, like others, occasionally performs spectacular leaps from the water—perhaps as a way of escaping predators or clearing parasites from the surface of its body.

Smalltooth sawfish
Pristis pectinata

↔ 18–25 ft (5.5–7.6 m)
➤ W. Atlantic, Indo-Pacific
✖ Critically endangered

Sawfishes have a sharklike body, but are more closely related to rays. Like its relatives, the smalltooth sawfish—also called the wide sawfish—has an elongated snout that is about one-quarter of its body length. The snout is edged with 23–32 pairs of teethlike projections as well as sensory receptors for detecting prey. The smalltooth sawfish swims close to the bottom of inshore waters, where the "saw" is swept from side to side to disturb and immobilize prey living in the sediment.

Spotted ratfish
Hydrolagus colliei

↔ 7–24 in (18–61 cm)
➤ E. North Pacific
✖ Locally common

Ratfishes—also called chimaeras—are big-headed cousins of sharks. They share their cartilaginous skeleton, but differ from sharks in having their gill slits covered by a flap of skin and in having rubbery, instead of sandpaperlike, skin. Like other ratfish species, the spotted ratfish has a ratlike tail, wingslike pectoral fins, a dorsal fin spine, a downward-facing mouth equipped with platelike teeth for crushing hard-shelled invertebrates, and a sensory snout for detecting prey buried in sediment.

Other species
● **Ribbontail stingray**
Taeniura lymma » p304
● **Scalloped hammerhead shark**
Sphyrna lewini » p348–49
● **Whale shark**
Rhincodon typus » pp306–07

Bony fish
Class Osteichthyes

Coelacanth
Latimeria chalumnae

↔ Up to 6 ft (2 m)
➤ W. Indian Ocean
✖ Critically endangered

This "living fossil" belongs to a lineage of fish once thought to have died out 400 million years ago—until a living specimen was caught in 1938. The coelacanth is found at depths of 500–2,300 ft (150–700 m) along rocky slopes with submarine caverns swept by strong oceanic currents. It has fleshy fins and is closely related to lungfish, but the way it evolved in relation to other vertebrates is not completely understood. Today, it uses its fins as stabilizers in deep waters.

steel-blue body

iridescent white flecks

European sturgeon
Acipenser sturio

↔ Up to 11 ft (3.5 m)
➤ North Atlantic, Mediterranean, Europe
✖ Critically endangered

Sturgeons make up a family of northern circumpolar fish. Although classified with bony fishes, its skeleton is composed of both bone and cartilage. The skin lacks scales, but is covered with an armor of bony plates instead. The European sturgeon breeds in cold, gravel-bottomed river waters, where it produces an astonishing output of up to 6 million eggs at a single spawning.

Arapaima
Arapaima gigas

↔ Up to 10 ft (3 m)
➤ N. South America
✖ Not known

One of the biggest freshwater fish, the arapaima is a long-bodied predator of Amazon swamplands with particularly hard scales. A lunglike swim bladder and a specialized organ located above the gills that lets it take in air from the water surface help the arapaima to survive in warm, stagnant pools with little oxygen.

European eel
Anguilla anguilla

↔ Up to 3 ft (1 m)
➤ E. North Atlantic, Mediterranean, Europe
✖ Critically endangered

Eels are snakelike fish that lack pelvic fins and girdles. Most species live permanently in ocean waters, but the European eel spends its adult life in freshwater rivers. It migrates to saltwaters to breed, spawning in the North Atlantic's Sargasso Sea. Typical of eels, the eggs hatch into transparent larvae. These migrate back to European rivers, developing first into silvery, pigmented juveniles called elvers before maturing into adults.

narrow, pointed snout of adults

continuous dorsal, anal, and tailfin

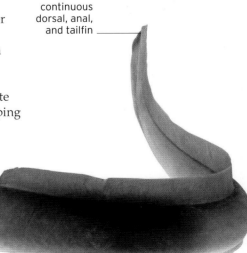

Atlantic herring
Clupea harengus

↔ Up to 18 in (46 cm)
◐ North Atlantic, North Sea, Baltic Sea
✖ Locally common

A typical open-ocean schooling fish, the Atlantic herring's behavior of gathering into large groups to confuse predators also makes it an important species in commercial fisheries. Other schooling members of the herring family, such as sardines, form some of the biggest aggregations of fish on the planet. Herrings spawn in schools too, laying adhesive eggs that form a thick mat on the seabed.

Common carp
Cyprinus carpio

↔ Up to 4 ft (1.2 m)
◐ W. Europe to SE. Asia
✖ Vulnerable

The deep-bodied common carp belongs to the cyprinid family—the largest family of freshwater fish, with over 2,000 species found in temperate America and across the Old World. This fish feeds on a wide range of invertebrates and pond plants using its protrusible mouth. The common carp has been introduced to many parts of the world as a source of food—in places, it has become destructively invasive.

Northern pike
Esox lucius

↔ Up to 4 ft (1.2 m)
◐ North America, Europe, Asia
✖ Common

No more than half a dozen species of pike live in cool weed-choked fresh waters around the northern hemisphere. All are elongated, big-mouthed predators of other fish that rely on ambushing prey from the cover of water plants. They have a distinct shovel-like snout and sharp teeth. The northern pike is the most widespread species—and the only one found in both North America and Eurasia.

Sockeye salmon
Oncorhynchus nerka

↔ Up to 33 in (84 cm)
◐ NE. Asia, North Pacific, NW. and W. North America
✖ Common

Salmonids, including salmon, trout, and chars, are cold-water fish of the northern hemisphere. Many live in fresh waters, while others spend their adult lives at sea, but return upriver to breed at sites where they hatched. Sockeye salmon migrate from the Pacific Ocean into North American rivers and lakes, flushing red when breeding.

Prickly lanternfish
Myctophum asperum

↔ Up to 4 in (10 cm)
◐ North and South Pacific, W. and E. Atlantic, Indian Ocean
✖ Not known

The skin of lanternfish carries light-producing organs, called photophores, which help them to communicate in the dark deep-water environment. This species migrates closer to the surface at night to feed on tiny planktonic crustaceans. During the day, they descend to depths of more than 2,450 ft (750 m).

Atlantic cod
Gadus morhua

↔ Up to 5 ft (1.5 m)
◐ North Atlantic, Arctic Ocean
✖ Vulnerable

This large, schooling, predatory fish with a huge head and overhanging upper jaw can live for more than 60 years. However, overfishing has reduced the average age and size of populations. Atlantic cod live in the water over the continental shelf and usually feed at 100–250 ft (30–80 m) above areas of flat mud or sand.

They spawn in schools in established breeding grounds, with each female releasing millions of eggs. The larvae spend time in the ocean's plankton, taking up to seven years to reach their adult forms.

Angler
Lophius piscatorius

↔ Up to 7 ft (2 m)
◐ E. North Atlantic, Mediterranean, Black Sea
✖ Not known

Anglerfish are so-called because their first dorsal fin spine is modified to form a line-and-bait structure for attracting prey. Many are found in deep water, but members of the monkfish family—including this European species—occupy the continental slope. They hunt on the seabed, using massive jaws equipped with hard backward-pointing teeth for grabbing large prey. They have even been known to lunge at diving birds.

Tropical two-wing flying fish
Exocoetus volitans

↔ Up to 12 in (30 cm)
◐ Tropical and subtropical waters worldwide
✖ Not known

Despite its name, this species does not actually fly; instead, this open-ocean fish uses its winglike pectoral fins to glide short distances across the water's surface—at full speed, it can glide for up to 12 seconds. This is used as an escape mechanism—the fish darts to the surface, where aerial launching is helped by a quivering tail that beats more than 50 times per second.

Stonefish
Synanceia verrucosa

↔ Up to 16 in (40 cm)
◑ Indo-Pacific, E. Africa
✖ Not known

A stout, slow-moving predator, this species is among the most dangerously venomous of fish. The aptly named fish lacks scales—instead, its body is covered in glandular warts, which afford perfect camouflage against the rocky background of its coral reef habitat. It usually stays motionless at the bottom, waiting to ambush passing prey, sometimes half burying itself in the seabed.

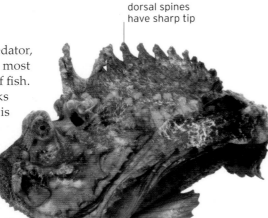

dorsal spines have sharp tip

Giant grouper
Epinephelus lanceolatus

↔ Up to 9 ft (2.7 m)
◑ Indian Ocean, W. and C. Pacific
✖ Vulnerable

One of the largest bony fish on coral reefs, the giant grouper is a widespread predator, ranging throughout the warm coastal waters of the Indo-Pacific region. Young fish have a black, white, and yellow beelike pattern, but adults are uniformly gray with some mottling. Like most other grouper species, this fish may be a sequential hermaphrodite, in which the gonads can change to produce either eggs or sperm.

Emperor angelfish
Pomacanthus imperator

↔ Up to 16 in (40 cm)
◑ Indian Ocean, Pacific
✖ Common

Large members of the butterflyfish family, marine angelfish are characterized by a side-flattened body, bright colors, small mouth, and comblike teeth. Juveniles have striking blue-and-white ringlike markings. However, after two years, they change to their adult form, with a yellow tail, longitudinal blue and yellow stripes, and a black face mask. Emperor angelfish graze on sponges and algae in their coral-reef habitat.

Atlantic bluefin tuna
Thunnus thynnus

↔ Up to 15 ft (4.6 m)
◑ Atlantic
✖ Endangered

The torpedo-shaped Atlantic bluefin tuna is one of the fastest fish, reaching speeds of at least 40 mph (70 km/h) in pursuit of mackerel and squid. Its tail helps propulsion, while its circulatory system helps it to retain body heat. Oxygen is extracted from water across thin-walled blood vessels, and high hemoglobin levels allow it to deliver oxygen to its muscles highly effectively.

Atlantic mudskipper
Periophthalmus barbarus

↔ Up to 10 in (25 cm)
◑ E. Atlantic
✖ Locally common

Mudskippers are amphibious members of the goby family. They can use their pectoral fins to "walk" out of water and can extract oxygen from air through their throat lining and skin. An enlarged gill cavity also works much like a lung. Like other mudskipper species, the Atlantic mudskipper uses these adaptations to stay active and to feed on mudflats at low tide.

Clown triggerfish
Balistoides conspicillum

↔ Up to 20 in (50 cm)
◑ Pacific, Indian Ocean
✖ Not known

This coral-reef fish gets its name from its colorful body, with yellow lips, and the triggerlike mechanism of its dorsal fin spines, which, when erected, can lock it into the safety of a rocky crevice as protection from predators. Its large head is covered with tough, protective scales and measures a third of its total length. Although its mouth is small, it has strong jaws and incisorlike teeth for crushing hard-shelled invertebrate prey, including crustaceans, mollusks, and echinoderms. Like other triggerfish, this species can be very territorial, especially during the mating season.

Atlantic halibut
Hippoglossus hippoglossus

↔ Up to 8 ft (2.4 m)
◑ North Atlantic, Arctic
✖ Endangered

This commercially valuable—but overfished—species is one of the largest of the flatfish. Juvenile flatfish are upright-swimming and have unmodified symmetrical anatomy. But as they develop, one eye migrates to the other side of the head. The adult fish settles on its "blind" side and becomes bottom-living. The Atlantic halibut has both eyes on its right side—other flatfish species may have eyes on their left or right side.

Other species

- **Arctic char**
  Salvelinus alpinus » p33
- **Atlantic salmon**
  Salmo salar » p137
- **Barrier Reef anemonefish**
  Amphiprion akindynos » p351
- **Electric eel**
  Electrophorus electricus » p98
- **Great barracuda**
  Sphyraena barracuda » p308
- **Green humphead parrotfish**
  Bolbometopon muricatum » p309
- **Mandarinfish**
  Synchiropus splendidus » p305
- **Ocean sunfish**
  Mola mola » p347
- **Zebra mbuna**
  Maylandia zebra » p191

INVERTEBRATES

Invertebrates are animals without backbones. They account for 97 percent of all animal species, almost covering the full range of animal diversity—from brainless jellyfish to flying insects. Beetle species alone may outnumber vertebrates ten to one. Invertebrates dominate by individuals too: at any one time, the ocean's shrimplike krill outnumber all the humans who have ever lived; and a single super-colony of ants can contain billions. Some invertebrates even occupy habitats too hostile for other life forms—including around boiling hot vents on the ocean floor or in lakes of hypersaline brine.

Anatomy

Invertebrates are defined by exclusion. They include all the species that are not classified as vertebrate (back-boned) animals, thus covering more than 30 phyla.

The lowliest of invertebrates— shapeless sponges— lack all bodily organs. The rest are muscular, animate creatures that can swim, burrow, walk, or fly. Jellyfish and anemones have a radial anatomy. Their tentacles encircle a single gut opening, so —anatomically—they have "up" and "down" but no "front" and "back." Most other animals have a "head end" that leads forward—with a brain that can coordinate the sensory information received from the surroundings.

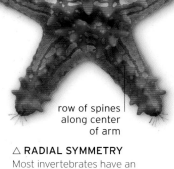

row of spines along center of arm

△ RADIAL SYMMETRY
Most invertebrates have an elongated body, running from head to "tail." However, some— such as starfish—have a radial body encircling a central gut cavity.

The biggest range of anatomical types among invertebrates occurs in the world's oceans, including animals that burrow in sediments or swim in open water, but groups from different phyla have invaded land too. On land, invertebrates need an especially effective skeleton for support—as well as protection from dehydration. Arthropods— jointed-legged invertebrates, such as insects and spiders—have their cuticle reinforced into a rigid exoskeleton. It makes them true conquerors of the planet—they now make up more than 80 percent of the world's animal life, the articulated parts of their jointed legs giving them superior mobility in running, digging, and swimming.

Reproduction

Some invertebrates can reproduce without sex: sponges and some flatworms can fragment, while aphids give birth to young without being fertilized. However, sexual reproduction, where sperm cells fuse with eggs, is more widespread because it has the benefit of mixing up genetic variety. It can be astonishingly productive.

Minute, anemonelike polyps of a coral reef eject billions of eggs and sperm at once, with external fertilization happening in open water. Other invertebrates transfer sperm directly into the female's body. This kind of internal fertilization is crucial on land but demands complex sexual parts. Slugs, for instance, jab their partners with "love darts" to facilitate sperm transfer.

Some invertebrates may live only for a few hours, but some ocean clams survive for centuries. The life of many invertebrates is punctuated by episodes of metamorphosis too, whereby larval forms undergo considerable reshaping as they develop into adults. For example, many kinds of marine worms, snails, and crustaceans start their lives as minute planktonic larvae.

Behavior

Invertebrates have varied and impressive sensory adaptations. Male moths can sense just a few molecules of sexual pheromone wafting from a

◁ GROWING UP
Larval invertebrate stages may be different from their adult forms. The mullein moth caterpillar is a colorful leaf-eater before metamorphosing into a drab, nectar-drinking adult.

female miles away, while predatory mantis shrimps see sun-dappled coral reefs using highly sophisticated color vision.

However, invertebrates generally have simple brains for habitual tasks—for example, a fairy wasp, which is the size of a period, has a brain with 10 billion times fewer neurons than that of a human. The wasp's behavior is genetically "hard-wired" and inflexible although still complex enough to parasitize the eggs of other insects. Many invertebrates—such as ants, termites, and bees and wasps—are highly social and exhibit a bigger behavioral repertoire by living in complex societies with division of labor. These colonies are made up of different "caste" members devoted to foraging, defense, and breeding—effectively meaning that the entire colony works more like a super-organism with a "super-brain."

◁ PREDATORY ACT
Although hard-wired, invertebrate behavior is complex. A spider-hunting hawk wasp drags its victim— paralyzed by stinging— to a nest to provide food for its larva.

▷ SUPERSIZED
The widest variety of invertebrate phyla is oceanic. Many are tiny, wormlike animals, but others—such as this octopus—grow large and exhibit complex behavior.

INVERTEBRATE CLASSIFICATION

Vertebrates form a single phylum, but the invertebrates are an informal group of about 30 phyla.

Sponges » p450
Phylum Porifera **Species** 10,000

Cnidarians » p450
Phylum Cnidaria **Species** 11,000

Flatworms » p450
Phylum Platyhelminthes **Species** 20,000

Segmented worms » p450
Phylum Annelida **Species** 21,000

Roundworms » p450
Phylum Nematoda **Species** 20,000

Velvet worms » p450
Phylum Onychophora **Species** 180

Rotifers » p450
Phylum Rotifera **Species** 2,000

Water bears » p451
Phylum Tardigrada **Species** 1,000

Bryozoans » p451
Phylum Bryozoa **Species** 6,000

Ribbon worms » p451
Phylum Nemertea **Species** 1,400

Brachiopods » p451
Phylum Brachiopoda **Species** 4,000

Spoonworms » p451
Phylum Echiura **Species** 200

Arrow worms » p451
Phylum Chaetognatha **Species** 150

Arthropods Phylum Arthropoda **»** pp452–55
  Mandibulates Subphylum Mandibulata
  - **Hexapods** Superclass Hexapoda
    > **Springtails** Class Collembola **Species** 8,100
    > **Proturans** Class Protura **Species** 760
    > **Diplurans** Class Diplura **Species** 975
    > **Insects** Class Insecta **Species** 1.1 million
  - **Myriapods** Superclass Myriapoda
    > **Centipedes** Class Chilopoda **Species** 3,149
    > **Millipedes** Class Diplopoda **Species** 9,973
  Crustaceans Subphylum Crustacea
  - **Malacostracans »** p454
    Class Malacostraca **Species** 38,032
  - **Other classes** Branchiopoda/Ostracoda/
    Maxillopoda
  Chelicerates Subphylum Chelicerata
  - **Sea spiders »** p454
    Class Pycnogonida **Species** 1,330
  - **Horseshoe crabs »** p454
    Class Merostomata **Species** 4
  - **Arachnids »** p454
    Class Arachnida **Species** 103,000

Mollusks Phylum Mollusca **»** p455
  - **Bivalves »** p455
    Class Bivalvia **Species** 15,000
  - **Gastropods »** p455
    Class Gastropoda **Species** 75,000
  - **Cephalopods »** p455
    Class Cephalopoda **Species** 750
  - **Other classes** Aplacophora/Polyplacophora/
    Monoplacophora/Scaphopoda

Echinoderms Phylum Echinodermata **»** p455
  - **Starfish** Class Asteroidea **Species** 1,853
  - **Sea urchins** Class Echinoidea **Species** 1,090
  - **Other classes** Crinoidea/Ophiuroidea/
    Holothuroidea

Acorn worms » p451
Phylum Hemichordata **Species** 130

Invertebrate chordates» p455
Phylum Chordata **Species** 2,900
Subphyla Urochordata/Cephalochordata

MORE THAN 10 OTHER MINOR INVERTEBRATE PHYLA

Sponges
Phylum Porifera

Species About 10,000
Occurrence Marine, freshwater

The simplest of all animals, these aquatic organisms consist of a variety of cells attached to a skeleton of collagen—the springy, absorbent material used as the original bath sponge. Specialized collar cells create water currents that flow into the body of the sponge through small pores, then pass out of a larger aperture; the collar cells filter the flow of food particles. Most sponges live in the sea, attached to rocks and other hard surfaces.

tube open at top

Stovepipe sponge *Aplysina archeri*

Velvet worms
Phylum Onycophora

Species About 180
Occurrence Moist forests, under stones

Although they have soft, wormlike bodies, velvet worms are equipped with up to 43 pairs of short, fleshy, clawed legs that they use for walking, like centipedes. They locate prey with their sensitive antennae and attack by spraying them with sticky slime. They live in warm, moist forests and are the survivors of a group of marine animals that were widespread during the Cambrian Period, more than 500 million years ago.

Cnidarians
Phylum Cnidaria

Species About 11,000
Occurrence Marine, freshwater

The cnidarians consist of the hydroids, sea anemones, corals, and jellyfish. Their bodies are composed of an inner and outer skin of cells, separated by a layer of jelly. Most are of a tubular form called a polyp, with a crown of stinging tentacles at the top that gather food. They live attached to rocks, either alone or—in the case of reef-building corals—in interconnected colonies. Free-swimming jellyfish have a bell-shaped form called a medusa;

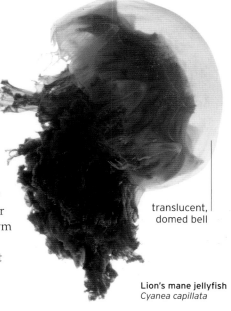

translucent, domed bell

Lion's mane jellyfish
Cyanea capillata

they trail long stinging tentacles to catch prey, and some are highly venomous.

Segmented worms
Phylum Annelida

Species About 21,000
Occurrence Soil, freshwater, marine

Typified by earthworms, these worms have long, fluid-filled bodies divided into many ringlike segments. In an earthworm, longitudinal muscles contract to shorten the body, while muscles encircling each segment squeeze and extend it, so it can push through the soil. The segments carry bristlelike structures, and many marine types, such as the ragworms, have long bristles that resemble legs.

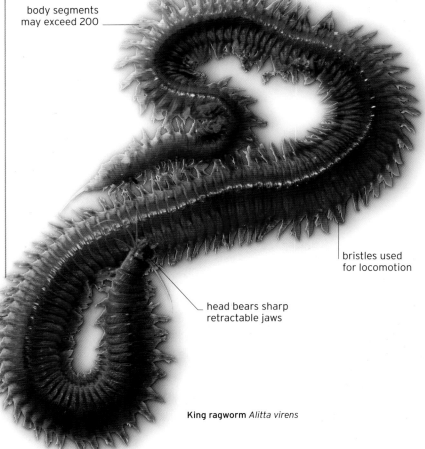

body segments may exceed 200

bristles used for locomotion

head bears sharp retractable jaws

King ragworm *Alitta virens*

Flatworms
Phylum Platyhelminthes

Species About 20,000
Occurrence Parasitic, freshwater

These are the simplest animals to have a distinct head and tail. The head contains sensory organs linked to a cluster of nerve cells that form a primitive brain, and the body may have a simple gut. Their entire body surface absorbs oxygen from their environment. Some flatworms absorb food in the same way; most of these are internal parasites, such as flukes and tapeworms. Free-living flatworms, such as *Dugesia*, have mouths for gathering food.

Roundworms
Phylum Nematoda

Species About 20,000
Occurrence Parasitic, aquatic

Roundworms have no body segments, and their smooth, tapering bodies cannot extend and contract; they move by wriggling like snakes, but less effectively. They have very basic senses, and many live as parasites inside other animals and humans, causing diseases. Others live in damp or aquatic habitats worldwide, where they eat organic detritus, plant fluids, or other animals.

Rotifers
Phylum Rotifera

Species About 2,000
Occurrence In vegetation in lakes, rivers, seas; freshwater habitats on land

Rotifers occur in large numbers in all kinds of watery habitats. These tiny animals are equipped with crowns of hairlike cilia that beat rhythmically to pump water into the mouth, where it is filtered for food. The crowns of beating cilia look like rotating wheels, so they are sometimes called wheel animals. Like water bears, they can survive years of desiccation and extremely low temperatures; some have revived after being frozen in Antarctic ice for a century or more.

Water bears
Phylum Tardigrada

Species About 1,000
Occurrence Freshwater, saltwater, wetlands

Similar to velvet worms, but microscopic, water bears have plump bodies and four pairs of short, fleshy legs, on which they crawl around. In damp terrestrial habitats, they feed on plant juices and other animals. Water bears have a remarkable tolerance to drought, being able to shrivel and survive in a state of dehydration for several years, then swelling up and resuming normal life when conditions improve. By being dormant for extended periods, they may live over 50 years.

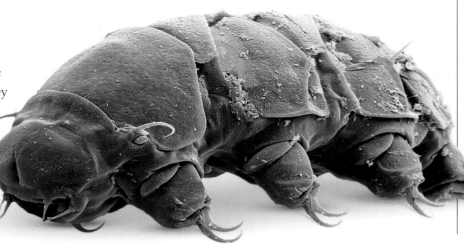

Moss water bear *Echiniscus* **species**

Bryozoans
Phylum Bryozoa

Species About 6,000
Occurrence Attached to hard surfaces in aquatic environments

Also known as moss animals, bryozoans are very small aquatic animals that live in colonies. Each animal occupies a boxlike case that forms part of a mat or ribbon of identical cases; typically, these encrust rocks, seaweed, or flooded tree roots, but some form branched, plantlike structures. The animals feed by extending crowns of feathery tentacles to filter food from the water.

Ribbon worms
Phylum Nemertea

Species About 1,400
Occurrence On bed, in surface or middle waters of seas, rivers and lakes; forests

Related to flatworms, these mainly marine worms are armed with a muscular proboscis that normally lies inside the animal's snout, but can be pushed out by hydraulic pressure to catch prey; in some forms, it is armed with venomous barbs to inject toxins. Most ribbon worms are less than 8 in (20 cm) long, but one species is known to grow to 177 ft (54 m), making it the longest of all known animals. Many ribbon worms are brightly colored.

Brachiopods
Phylum Brachiopoda

Species About 400
Occurrence Attached to hard surfaces or buried in sediments on the seabed

Enclosed in bivalved shells, these marine animals look like bivalve mollusks, but they are not related and their anatomy is quite different. A brachiopod lives attached to a rock or burrow by a muscular stalk, and its shells protect a loop of hollow, fringed tentacles, called the lophophore, which filters food from the water. Also known as lamp shells, brachiopods were once far more abundant than they are now.

Spoonworms
Phylum Echiura

Species About 200
Occurrence In burrows or other cavities on the seabed

The echiurans, or spoonworms, are soft-bodied marine animals that occur in seabeds throughout the world. Although some species inhabit rock crevices, most live in burrows in the mud. A few species even occur in brackish water. Spoonworms have bulbous, sausagelike bodies and a spoon-shaped, nonretractable, muscular proboscis, which they use to gather food from surrounding rocks and sediments. Although usually only about 6 in (15 cm) long, some can extend the proboscis for 39 in (100 cm) or more.

Green spoonworm *Bonellia viridis*

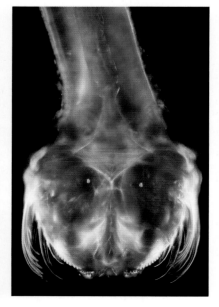

Arrow worm *Sagitta* **species**

Arrow worms
Phylum Chaetognatha

Species About 150
Occurrence In plankton, one genus on the seabed

Most of these small, torpedo-shaped animals drift in the oceans among the plankton, where they attack and eat other animals. Arrow worms are armed with a fearsome array of grasping spines around the mouth that help them to crush their prey. The spines are backed up by piercing teeth that inject a potent, paralyzing venom. Produced by symbiotic bacteria, this venom is called tetrodotoxin and is used by very few animals. Much of the prey of arrow worms consists of larval fish, which they devour in large numbers. Highly active predators, arrow worms can eat a third of their own body weight each day. Their size ranges from about 1/8 in (3 mm) to more than 4 in (100 mm); species inhabiting colder waters are generally larger than those from tropical seas. Widespread in open waters of oceans worldwide, their large numbers can have a significant ecological impact—for example, on fish larvae.

Acorn worms
Phylum Hemichordata

Species About 130
Occurrence In marine mud and sand, and other intertidal and subtidal habitats

Acorn worms are named after the pointed front ends of their bodies, which are separated from the rest of the body by a tubelike collar. Typical acorn worms live in mucus-lined burrows in soft seabeds and tidal flats. They consume sand and mud, ejecting anything inedible as a coiled cast. However, others feed by extending a proboscis from the burrow and trapping small drifting organisms in sticky mucus.

Arthropods
Phylum Arthropoda

Springtails
Class Collembola

Species About 8,100
Occurrence Grassland, leaf litter, soil

Springtails are named after their springy, fork-shaped tail, which is folded under the body and held there by a cliplike structure. When released, it flicks downward and catapults the insect into the air away from danger. Springtails swarm in damp places and water surfaces, feeding on organic plant material.

Silverfish
Order Thysanura

Species About 570
Occurrence Tree canopies, leaf litter, under stones, human dwellings

Silverfish differ from other insects in that they do not ever develop wings. Common in houses worldwide, they feed on starchy matter, such as flour, and various types of glue, such as wallpaper paste. Their scales detach easily, helping them to slip from the grasp of predators such as spiders.

Mayflies
Order Ephemeroptera

Species About 3,000
Occurrence Fresh water, on vegetation

Renowned for their short lifespans as flying adults, mayflies live for months as aquatic larvae. They turn into nonfeeding adults for the brief final stage of their lives, when they mate, lay eggs, and die within a few hours. Mayflies were among the first insects to evolve this type of metamorphosis from a wingless larva to a winged, sexually mature adult, which is now typical of insects. They also have a winged subadult stage.

three tails of equal length

Mayfly *Ephemera danica*

Damselflies and dragonflies
Order Odonata

Species About 5,600
Occurrence Still water, swamps, streams

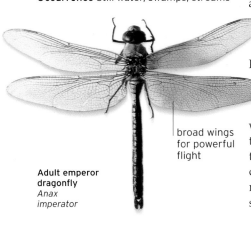

broad wings for powerful flight

Adult emperor dragonfly
Anax imperator

The earliest of these insects evolved at about the same time as the mayflies, and they have many similar features, such as aquatic larvae that turn into flying adults. However, their larvae are voracious predators, and unlike mayflies, the adults are accomplished hunters that live for several weeks. Dragonflies are fast fliers that seize other insects on the wing, targeting them with their huge compound eyes. Damselflies are more delicate, fly weakly, and pick small insects off vegetation.

Crickets and grasshoppers
Order Orthoptera

Species Over 25,000
Occurrence On ground, on vegetation, damp soil, under logs and stones

These insects are recognizable by their long hindlegs, which grasshoppers in particular use to leap away from danger. They are also well known for their chirping songs. Most can fly, and the specialized grasshoppers known as locusts are notorious for flying in vast swarms that destroy farm crops. Crickets and grasshoppers do not undergo metamorphosis; the young are wingless miniatures of adults.

grasshoppers have shorter antennae than crickets

Stripe-winged grasshopper *Stenobothrus lineatus*

Stick and leaf insects
Order Phasmatodea

Species 2,450
Occurrence On vegetation, particularly foliage of trees and shrubs

Many insects are camouflaged to elude predators such as birds, but few can match the cryptic perfection of the stick and leaf insects. Shaped and colored to look almost exactly like twigs or leaves, the insects also mimic the way they grow and sway in the breeze. They use their chewing mouthparts to feed on plant foliage, moving slowly to avoid detection, but if this fails, some may defend themselves by squirting noxious chemicals at

their enemies. If attacked, they can shed their legs, which soon grow back. In many species, males occur either rarely or not at all. The females typically scatter their eggs on the ground.

small forewings

transparent hindwings

leaflike expansions of legs

Javanese leaf insect *Phyllium bioculatum*

Earwigs
Order Dermaptera

Species About 1,900
Occurrence Leaf litter, soil, under bark or in crevices

Most of the slender-bodied earwigs have a distinctive pair of sharp-pointed pincers at the end of their abdomen, which are used for defense, in courtship, and for grooming. They have thin, fan-shaped hindwings that they normally keep folded beneath their much shorter, hardened forewings. Earwigs eat a wide variety of plant and animal matter. The females are unusually maternal, guarding their eggs and licking them clean.

Termites
Order Isoptera

Species About 2,900
Occurrence Trees, soil, underground

These social insects feed on dead or decaying wood and live in large colonies centered on a single breeding queen. Most of the other termites in the colony either defend the nest or maintain it and care for the young. Some tropical species build spectacular mounds of earth, containing fungus gardens cultivated by the termites for their own consumption and cooled by complex ventilation systems.

Parasitic lice
Order Phthiraptera

Species 5,200
Occurrence On a variety of hosts

The wingless parasitic lice feed on the skin or blood of their hosts, which include birds, wild mammals, and humans. Their legs and strong claws are adapted for gripping feathers or hair—most species are specialized to cling to a specific type of host. They usually spend their entire lives on one animal, but may move from host to host—some spread infections in this way.

Beetles
Order Coleoptera

Species 370,000
Occurrence Terrestrial, fresh water

Almost a quarter of all known animal species are beetles, making them the most successful animals on the planet. In their adult form, most species have a single pair of wings protected by two modified forewings forming tough, often shiny, wing cases. Beetles eat a range of plant and animal matter, and some have wood-boring larvae that can be destructive timber pests. Many have very effective chemical defenses for deterring predators.

Golden beetle
Chrysina resplendens

Bugs
Order Hemiptera

Species 88,000
Occurrence Terrestrial, fresh water

The true bugs are insects with piercing mouthparts for obtaining liquid food. Some, such as the aphids, cicadas, and shield bugs, are specialized for extracting plant sap. Others, such as the assassin bugs and pond skaters, attack animals—usually other insects—and inject them with digestive juices that liquefy their tissues. A few, such as the sap-sucking thorn bug, are cryptically shaped to avoid detection by birds.

Wart-headed bug
Phrictus quinquepartitus

bright patterns
on hindwings

Fleas
Order Siphonaptera

Species About 2,400
Occurrence On mammal and bird hosts, in lairs, burrows

All fleas are bloodsuckers of birds and mammals, highly specialized for life among their feathers or fur. A flea's body is flattened from side to side, enabling it to slip between hair or feather shafts, and strongly armored to resist scratching and grooming. Its long hindlegs have a unique adaptation that allow it to leap high in the air onto a new victim. In their pupal stage, fleas can lie dormant for a year or more waiting for a suitable host.

Flies
Order Diptera

Species 150,000
Occurrence Almost all habitats, namely vegetation, decaying matter, and water

Many insects are known as flies, but the true flies are distinguished by having a single pair of wings. The hindwings are reduced to a pair of club-shaped organs called halteres; these act as stabilizers and give many species phenomenal powers of flight. The group includes the well-known houseflies, blowflies, hoverflies, and mosquitoes, as well as midges, with a variety of diets and lifestyles. Some are vital pollinators of crops, while others carry deadly diseases.

Butterflies and moths
Order Lepidoptera

Species Over 165,000
Occurrence Open habitats, on vegetation

Butterflies and moths have large wings covered with small overlapping scales. The wing scales of many butterflies and day-flying moths are vividly colored in eye-catching patterns, while those of night-flying moths are cryptically colored for daytime camouflage. All species begin life as soft-bodied caterpillars that feed on leaves, growing rapidly until they turn into pupae. These develop into winged adults that sip nectar to fuel their courtship and breeding activities.

Bees, wasps, ants, and sawflies
Order Hymenoptera

Species About 198,000
Occurrence On plants, insect hosts

Notorious for their stings, but also of vital importance as pollinators, these insects are almost as numerous and diverse as the beetles. Social Hymenoptera, including ants and bees, live in highly ordered societies. All ants live in colonies controlled by a single breeding queen. Many wasps and bees—basically vegetarian wasps—do the same, including species such as hornets and honeybees. Others are solitary, and include hunting wasps that paralyze insects and spiders with their stings and bury them as food for their young. This group also includes some parasitic species that develop inside the bodies of other insects.

German wasp
Vespula germanica

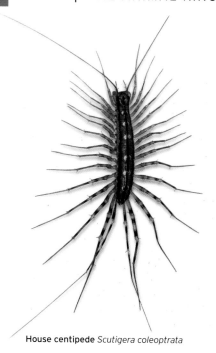

House centipede *Scutigera coleoptrata*

Centipedes
Class Chilopoda

Species 3,149
Occurrence Humid habitats on land

Unlike an insect, which has a three-part body and three pairs of legs, a centipede's body is made up of a long chain of similar segments, each equipped with a pair of legs. Some centipedes have more than 150 pairs. The front legs are modified into venomous claws that curve around the head for seizing prey such as worms and snails; large tropical centipedes can even catch and devour frogs, lizards, and nestling birds.

Millipedes
Class Diplopoda

Species 9,973
Occurrence Humid habitats on land

Similar to centipedes, but almost exclusively vegetarian, millipedes have two pairs of legs on each body segment. As a result, some have as many as 375 pairs of legs, or 750 in total. Despite this, they move much more slowly than centipedes, creeping along on rippling waves of leg movement. They avoid predation by coiling into tight armored balls, depending on length, or rely on glands that secrete toxic chemicals, including cyanide.

Maxillopods
Class Maxillopoda

Species 17,987
Occurrence Oceans, fresh water, hot springs, land

This group of crustaceans is largely made up of copepods and barnacles. Copepods swarm in the plankton of oceans and fresh waters worldwide; they are mostly very small, and feed on drifting algae. Barnacles are also planktonic when young, but then settle on rocks, where they grow a protective armor of hard shell plates. Common on tidal shores, they close up at low tide, but extend feathery limbs to gather drifting food particles when submerged.

Malacostracans
Class Malacostraca

Species 38,032
Occurrence Marine intertidal to abyssal zones, freshwater habitats

The largest class of crustaceans, this includes shrimp, crabs, lobsters, and crayfish, as well as less familiar forms such as krill, sandhoppers, and terrestrial woodlice. Many swim in open water, while others live on the seabed or on tidal shores. Some, such as most shrimp and prawns, are delicate, almost transparent, but the crabs and lobsters are heavily armored, with stout pincers for feeding and defense.

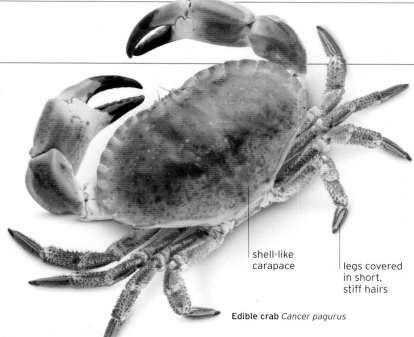

shell-like carapace

legs covered in short, stiff hairs

Edible crab *Cancer pagurus*

Sea spiders
Class Pycnogonida

Species About 1,330
Occurrence Coastal areas to deep oceans

Despite their name, sea spiders are not spiders (or even arachnids). A sea spider appears to be entirely composed of four or more pairs of legs, joined at the center. However, it does have a small cylindrical body and an even smaller head with four eyes and a sharp proboscis, flanked by a pair of palps and a pair of feeding claws. It uses these to prey on marine animals such as corals and sponges, tearing off pieces with its claws or simply stabbing into them and sucking their juices.

Horseshoe crabs
Class Merostomata

Species 4
Occurrence Shallow waters

Despite their name, these marine animals are not true crabs. They are distantly related to arachnids, such as spiders, but look quite different because of their body, which is covered by a broad, hinged shield, or carapace, with a long spinelike tail. Beneath the carapace are five pairs of legs and a pair of pincerlike chelicerae, which the crab uses to seize and cut up prey, such as clams, as it plows through the soft sediments of the seabed.

Scorpions
Order Scorpiones

Species 1,500
Occurrence Mainly deserts, forests

Scorpions are relatives of spiders, with eight legs, but instead of subduing their prey with venomous fangs as spiders do, scorpions have a stinger on the end of a long tail. The tail can arch forward over the body to sting and paralyze prey, but typically a scorpion prefers to seize its victims with its powerful pincers and tear them apart. The sting is more useful for defense, and the venom of some species is powerful enough to kill an adult human.

Harvestmen
Order Opilones

Species 6,125
Occurrence Mainly grasslands, semi-deserts, forests

The spiderlike harvestmen have very long, slender legs, attached to a small, almost spherical body. On top of the body is a turret with a single pair of eyes, but the main sense organs are the extra-long second pair of legs, which are used to feel for prey and edible scraps. If attacked, a harvestman may shed one or more legs to escape, or it may spray its attacker with noxious fluid.

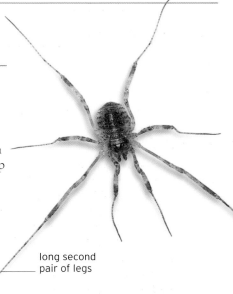

long second pair of legs

Horned harvestman *Phalangium opilio*

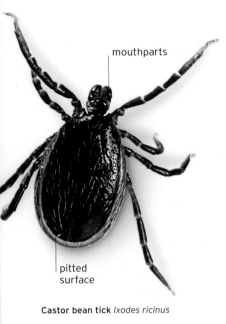

mouthparts

pitted surface

Castor bean tick *Ixodes ricinus*

Ticks and mites
Order Acari

Species 48,200
Occurrence Most terrestrial habitats

Many of the tiny, eight-legged mites and ticks are harmless, but some are parasites that latch onto warm-blooded animals—including humans—and suck their blood. A feeding tick can consume so much blood that it swells to up to 10 times its normal size before dropping off to breed. In the process, it may transmit infections such as Siberian tick typhus—a disease that can kill if not treated. Other, much smaller mites may cause itching diseases such as scabies.

Golden Orb *Nephila* **species**

Spiders
Order Araneae

Species About 42,000
Occurrence Most terrestrial habitats

The most familiar arachnids, spiders are eight-legged predators that either hunt down their prey or snare it in complex traps made of silk. They kill their victims with venom injected by a pair of sharp fangs, then flood the tissues with digestive juices to liquefy them—as, unlike insects, spiders cannot eat solid food. Normally only used for hunting, the venom of some species, such as the black widows, includes nerve toxins that can kill a human.

Mollusks
Phylum Mollusca

Bivalves
Class Bivalvia

Species 15,000
Occurrence Fresh- and seawater habitats

Mollusks have soft bodies that are protected by hard shells. A bivalve, such as a clam, has two shells hinged together so that they can be sealed shut to enclose the animal within. Most bivalves live attached to rocks or buried in soft sediments.

Gastropods
Class Gastropoda

Species 75,000
Occurrence Aquatic habitats; wet, damp, and dry regions on land

Gastropods such as snails have a single coiled shell into which they retreat to escape danger or stop themselves from drying out. They glide on a layer of mucus secreted by the flat "foot" beneath the body. Land snails and slugs eat plant material, but many marine snails are predators. Tropical cone shells have a powerful venom that they use to kill prey.

Cephalopods
Class Cephalopoda

Species About 750
Occurrence Open water or near seabed

Cephalopods have many flexible arms and often a pair of tentacles. A few, such as the tropical blue-ringed octopus, have a highly venomous bite. Squid can swim at high speed by jetting water from their bodies, and many species can change color instantly.

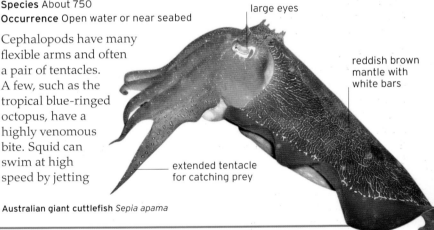

large eyes

reddish brown mantle with white bars

extended tentacle for catching prey

Australian giant cuttlefish *Sepia apama*

Echinoderms
Phylum Echinodermata

Starfish
Class Asteroidea

Species 1,853
Occurrence On the seabed

These spiny-skinned invertebrates have body segments that radiate like the spokes of a wheel from a central hub containing the mouth and main internal organs. This is most obvious in starfish, which typically have five long arms, although some have more than 40. They creep over the seabed on hundreds of small, hydraulic tube feet and prey on other invertebrates.

Sea urchins
Class Echinoidea

Species 1,090
Occurrence On or beneath seabed

A sea urchin has the same radial symmetry as starfish, but its body is roughly spherical and the radial elements are arranged like the segments of an orange. It has a shell-like skeleton under its skin, which supports sharp, protective spines. Most urchins eat seaweed and encrusting animals, rasping them from rocks.

Invertebrate chordates
Phylum Chordata
Subphyla Urochordata, Cephalochordata

Sea squirts
Class Ascidacea

Species 2,813
Occurrence Attached to coastal rocks and the seabed

Adult sea squirts have a spherical or cylindrical protective tunic, or test, that surrounds their bodies. They live attached to rocks and filter seawater for food—drawing water into their bodies, passing it through a sievelike structure, and then pumping it out again. However, when young they are completely different—free-swimming animals that resemble tadpoles. Remarkably, the tails of these larvae are strengthened by a rod called a notochord, which is a feature found in vertebrates such as fish. For this reason, the simple sea squirts are classified among the chordates—a phylum that includes all vertebrates, including humans.

GLOSSARY

A

ACID RAIN Most rain (and snow) is slightly acidic due to dissolved carbon dioxide. More strongly acidic rain results from atmospheric pollution or sometimes from gases released by volcanoes.

ACIDIFICATION Becoming more acid. The term is used especially in the context of the Earth's oceans and fresh waters.

ADAPTATION Any feature that helps an organism survive in its habitat or the process that allows it to do so.

ALGAE Any of a variety of plantlike life forms. They include single-celled species as well as larger forms such as seaweeds, and are especially important in the oceans.

ALTIPLANO The huge high-plateau region in the central Andes mountains of South America.

AMBUSH PREDATOR Any predator whose main feeding strategy is to stay in one place and wait for suitable prey to approach; also called a "sit-and-wait" predator.

AMPULLA (plural Ampullae) The enlarged end of a tube or duct.

ANTENNA (plural Antennae) The paired sensory "feeler" of insects, crustaceans, and some other invertebrates.

ANTLERS Paired bony structures, often branched, on the heads of most members of the deer family. Except for reindeer, only male deer have antlers. They are shed and regrown every year. See also *Horns*.

APEX PREDATOR A predator at the top of its food chain, hunted by no other animal (except humans).

ARACHNIDS The group of arthropods that includes spiders, scorpions, mites, and relatives. See also *Arthropods*.

ARCHIPELAGO A group of islands.

ARTHROPODS A major group of invertebrate animals having jointed legs and a hard outer skeleton. Arthropods include insects, crustaceans, and arachnids. See also *Exoskeleton*.

AXIL In plants, the upper angle between a leaf stalk and a stem, or between a side shoot and a main stem.

B

BACHELOR GROUP A group formed by immature males or males of the same species that have no sexual partners.

BILL The jaws of a bird, consisting of bone with a horny outer covering, also known as a beak. Also a similar structure in other animals, such as turtles.

BINOCULAR VISION The ability to see in 3D, which allows animals to judge distances.

BIODIVERSITY A general term for the variety of living things, either on the Earth as a whole, or in a particular region. Frequently it refers to the number of different species, but it can also be applied to genetic variety, ecological variety, and so on.

BIOMASS The total mass or weight of living organisms in a given area.

BIOME A large-scale ecosystem or set of ecosystems with characteristics determined by environmental factors, such as climate and geography. Deserts and tropical rainforests are examples of biomes.

BLOWHOLE The nostril(s) of cetaceans, situated on top of their heads.

BOG A mossy wetland, common in cooler regions, composed mainly of rotting plant material. It receives most of its water from rain and snow. Soils are nutrient-poor and acidic. See also *Fen*.

BOREAL Relating to or coming from the colder parts of the northern hemisphere, between the Arctic and temperate zones.

BOREAL FOREST The huge region of forest dominated by coniferous trees that circles the cooler regions of the northern hemisphere, between the tundra to the north and temperate broadleaved forests to the south. See also *Taiga*.

BRACKET FUNGUS Any of a variety of fungi that are relatives of toadstools and have spore-producing fruiting bodies that resemble shelves or brackets.

BROMELIAD A plant with numerous species, some of which grow in rainforests, using trees and shrubs for support. Typically they have rosettes of tough, waxy leaves in which rainwater collects. See also *Epiphyte*.

BROOD PARASITE An animal, such as the cuckoo, that makes use of other species to raise its young rather than raising its own young.

BRUMATION A state similar to hibernation that occurs in reptiles and other cold-blooded animals.

C

CAMOUFLAGE A means of being undetected used by predators, prey, and plants. It may involve color and/or pattern, shape, or even using a disguise. See also *Mimicry*.

CANID A member of the dog family, which includes foxes, wolves, and relatives.

CANINE (TOOTH) In mammals there is one canine tooth in each side of the upper and lower jaws. In carnivores it is enlarged and used for holding and/or stabbing prey.

CANOPY The part of the forest formed by the crowns of trees. It is also the name given to that part of a forest ecosystem.

CARAPACE A hard shield on the back of an animal's body—for example, in crabs and turtles.

CARNIVORE (1) A member of the Carnivora, the group of mammals that includes cats, dogs, bears, seals, and relatives. (2) Any flesh-eating animal.

CARRION Dead, decaying flesh.

CECUM A blind-ended part of the digestive tract, at the junction of the small and large intestines. See also *Hind-gut digestion*.

CETACEANS The group of mammals comprising whales, dolphins, and porpoises.

CHORDATE An animal that has a notochord, a rod support that runs the length of the body, for at least part of its life. See also *Notochord*.

CLASPERS In sharks and relatives, modified parts of the males' pelvic fins used to channel sperm to the female. In insects, claspers are structures used to hold the female during mating.

CLOVEN-HOOVED Having a hoof split into two halves, each containing one toe of the foot. This is a characteristic of two-toed herbivores, such as cattle and deer.

COALITION A cooperative alliance between individuals of the same species for defending or winning a territory or gaining access to females. Coalitions may be long or short term.

COLONY In zoology, any group of animals living together or in close association with one another, including birds such as emperor penguins in their breeding season; swarms of bees; and reef-forming coral polyps.

CONFLUENCE A place where two rivers, streams, or glaciers meet.

CONIFERS Predominantly evergreen trees and shrubs that produce seedbearing cones and have needle- or scalelike leaves. The most numerous of the nonflowering plants, including pines, firs, and spruces.

CORAL (1) Simple animals related to sea anemones and jellyfish. (2) The hard skeleton left behind by some coral polyps that can form large reefs.

CROP MILK A milklike substance rich in nutrients secreted by some birds in their lower throat (crop) and used to feed their nestlings.

CRUSTACEANS The dominant group of arthropods in the oceans, though they also live in fresh water and on land. Crustaceans include crabs, lobsters, shrimp, and krill. See also *Arthropods*, *Zooplankton*.

CURRENT A flow of water or air. In the oceans, large-scale currents exist on the surface and also at depth, driven either by the wind or by differences in temperature and salinity.

D

DECIDUOUS Trees and shrubs: having leaves that fall at a certain time of the year, such as winter or a dry season.

DELTA An often fan-shaped area at the mouth of a river that is built up by deposited sediment.

DIURNAL Active by day.

DIVERSITY See *Biodiversity*.

DREY A squirrel's nest.

DRY FOREST A forest growing in a region that has a long dry season.

E

ECHOLOCATION A method of detecting surrounding objects and prey, used by dolphins, bats, and some other animals, that involves emitting high-pitched sounds and interpreting their echoes.

ECOREGION Any geographical region defined on the basis of the particular ecosystems and distinctive flora and fauna that it contains.

ECOSYSTEM Any community of organisms considered together with the interactions between them and their associated physical environment.

EL NIÑO Phenomenon involving the waters of the eastern Pacific off South America that become warmer than usual every few years. It is part of a larger climatic cycle that seriously affects marine life and global weather patterns.

EMERGENT (1) In tropical forests, an emergent is a tall tree that grows higher than the surrounding tree canopy. (2) In freshwater ecosystems, emergent plants, such as the bulrush, grow out of the water into the air above. See also *Canopy*.

ENDEMIC A living species native to a particular region and only found in that region.

ENDOSKELETON An internal skeleton, such as the bony skeleton of vertebrates.

EPIPHYTE A plant that grows on another plant as a means of support.

EROSION The processes by which rocks or soil are loosened and transported to another location.

ESTIVATION A state similar to hibernation, but occurring in hot, dry seasons.

EVERGREEN Having some green leaves all the year round.

EVOLUTION Cumulative change over time brought about mainly by natural selection. Organisms with characteristics that not only enhance survival, but can also be inherited pass them on to their offspring. The genetic makeup of the population changes as these advantageous features spread through the population. See also *Adaptation*.

EXOSKELETON A skeleton situated on the outside of an animal, such as is found in insects and other arthropods. See also *Arthropod*.

EXOTIC In ecology, a term for any nonnative species.

F

FEN A type of wetland, formed when glaciers retreat, that receives its water supply mainly through groundwater seepage. Typically, it does not have standing water in the growing season, and is less nutrient-poor than a bog. See also *Bog*.

FERAL Term applied to an animal, or population of animals, living successfully in the wild but descended from a domestic species or breed.

FJORD A narrow, steep-sided, deep inlet of the sea, once occupied by a glacier.

FOOD CHAIN A food pathway that can be followed from its creation by plants to the apex predators.

FORAGING Activities concerned with seeking and obtaining food.

FORB Any herbaceous (nonwoody) plant other than grass, and especially such a plant growing naturally in grassland.

FRUGIVORE A fruit-eating animal.

FUMAROLE In volcanic regions, a small opening in the ground from which hot gases can escape.

G

GASTROPODS The group of invertebrate animals that includes snails and slugs.

GENUS The first level of traditional biological classification above species. A genus may contain one or more species. For example, lions belong to the genus *Panthera*.

GESTATION Pregnancy. In animals that produce live young, the gestation period is the time between fertilization and birth of the young.

GEYSER A jet of boiling water and steam that rises at intervals from the ground. It is powered by hot rocks heating groundwater.

GROOMING Behaviors that keep body coverings (fur, feathers, etc.) in good condition. In some species individuals may groom each other for social reasons.

H

HABITAT Any area that can support a group or community of living things.

HELICONIA A genus of plants mainly found in the American tropics, often having flower clusters with distinctive red bracts that are pollinated by hummingbirds.

HERBIVORE An animal that eats plants.

HERMAPHRODITE An animal that is both male and female at some point in its life. Species that are both sexes at once are called "simultaneous hermaphrodites;" those that change from one sex to the other are "sequential hermaphrodites."

HIBERNATION A state in which the bodily processes of an animal are drastically slowed down in winter, with the animal becoming completely inactive. The term is mainly applied to "warm-blooded" animals that drastically reduce their heart rate and let their body temperatures fall close to those of their surroundings. See also *Brumation, Estivation*.

HIND-GUT DIGESTION A type of digestion found in animals such as horses and elephants, in which tough plant food is fermented in the hind part of the gut, often in an enlarged cecum. See also *Cecum*.

HORNS Paired, permanent structures with a core of bone sheathed by a hard outer layer of keratin, found on the heads of cloven-hoofed animals such as antelope and cattle. Rhinoceros horns are not paired or attached to the skull, and they are sited on the nasal bones rather than the top of the head. Consisting only of keratin, there may be one or two depending on species. See also *Antlers, Keratin*.

HOTSPOT (1) In ecology, a region or location with a very high biodiversity, especially one that contains many endemic species and is under threat. (2) In geology, hotspots are fixed points that are unusually hot due to molten rock rising from deep within the Earth and are sites of volcanic activity.

HYBRIDIZATION Cross-breeding between different species or strains of organisms.

I

INDICATOR SPECIES A species whose presence or absence may define an ecoregion or indicate some significant feature, such as the presence of pollution.

INSECTIVORE An animal, especially a land vertebrate, that eats mainly insects.

INTRODUCED SPECIES A species introduced by humans to a particular region and now living successfully in the wild there. See also *Exotic*.

INVERTEBRATE Any animal without a backbone. Of the 30 or so major groups into which animals are classified, vertebrates (backboned animals) form only part of one single group (see *Chordate*): all other animals are invertebrates.

ISLET A small island.

J

JET STREAM High-altitude strong winds that are confined to a relatively narrow band within the atmosphere. Such winds blow in a winding course from west to east in both hemispheres, and their position influences the pattern of weather systems nearer the ground.

K

KARST A type of landscape that develops in regions where the underlying rock, most commonly limestone, is water soluble. Karst landscapes are characterized by deep gorges, underground rivers, and caves.

KERATIN A tough structural protein found in hair, claws, feathers, and horns.

KEYSTONE SPECIES Any species native to a particular ecosystem whose presence or absence has a major impact on the functioning of that ecosystem.

KINGDOM The second highest level in traditional biological classification. Originally there were the animal and plant kingdoms, but later, other kingdoms were introduced to cover fungi and other microorganisms.

KIT Name for the young of various mammals, such as mink and muskrat.

L

LARVA (plural Larvae) A young stage of an animal when it is completely different in form from the adult. Caterpillars and tadpoles are examples.

LEKKING Mating system found in some species that involves males gathering at traditional locations (leks) and competing for the attention of females by performing ritualized displays, building mounds, or undertaking other "show-off" activities.

LIGNOTUBER A swollen, woody base of a stem or trunk that occurs in some plants.

LITHOPHYTE A plant adapted to grow on rock surfaces.

LIVE-BEARER An animal species where the females give birth to live young, rather than laying or releasing eggs.

M

MANDIBLE A jaw or jawbone. In mammals it usually refers to the lower jaw, while in birds both the upper and lower parts of the bill are referred to as mandibles. Mandibles are also the chewing mouthparts of insects and other arthropods.

MANTLE (1) In geology, the layer lying between the Earth's crust and its core. The mantle is subject to high temperatures and pressures, and can slowly move. (2) In zoology, a protective skin layer in snails and relatives that secretes the shell.

MARSUPIALS The group of mammals that includes kangaroos, opossums, wombats, and relatives. Unlike most other mammals including humans, marsupials give birth to offspring in a relatively undeveloped state, and the young then typically continue their growth within an external pouch on the mother's body.

MEDITERRANEAN WOODLAND AND SCRUB A type of habitat found in warm temperate regions with hot dry summers and cool wet winters. As well as the Mediterranean area itself, this habitat is found in California, parts of Australia, and elsewhere.

METABOLISM The sum total of the biochemical processes taking place in the body.

METAMORPHOSIS Phenomenon in which an animal's body undergoes a major change in structure between the young and the adult form as in butterflies, or transforms more gradually, as in frogs. Metamorphosis occurs in many types of animals including crabs, starfish, frogs, and butterflies.

MID-OCEAN RIDGE A submerged range of mountains running along the deep-ocean floor. It is caused when tectonic plates move away from one another and new crust is created by upwelling of molten rocks from the Earth's mantle. See also *Mantle*.

MIGRATION Movements undertaken by an animal species on a regular seasonal or diurnal basis. Some migrations cover huge distances.

MIMICRY Phenomenon in which one species of animal has evolved to look very similar to another unrelated animal.

MIXED FORESTS Temperate forests in which a mixture of broadleaf and coniferous tree species grow.

MONOGAMY Situation where a male and female of a given species mate only with one other and not with other partners. The pairs thus formed may last for life or for a single season, depending on the species.

MONOTREMES The egg-laying mammals, comprising the platypus and the echidnas (spiny anteaters).

MONTANE Relating to or found in mountainous regions.

MONTANE GRASSLANDS Grassland habitats occurring high on mountains, in both tropical and temperate regions.

MORPH A physical variant of a species. Some species have several clearly defined morphs, which may differ in color or patterning, but can interbreed.

MOLTING Shedding or renewing the body covering, such as periodically replacing the feathers in birds, or shedding the exoskeleton to allow for growth in insects. A molt is any period when this happens.

MUTUALISM A close relationship between two different species in which both benefit.

N

NICHE The ecological "role" that a living thing plays. Ecological theory states that no two species can occupy the same niche, because one should outcompete the other.

NOCTURNAL Active by night.

NOTOCHORD A reinforcing rod that runs the length of the body, it is the defining feature of chordates. It is present in embryonic vertebrates, but later becomes incorporated into the backbone.

NYMPH An immature insect that looks similar to its parents except that it does not have functioning wings or reproductive organs. See also *Larva*.

O

OLD-GROWTH Term applied, especially in North America, to natural forests that have not been significantly altered by human activity. In Britain the equivalent term is ancient woodland.

OMNIVORE An animal whose natural diet includes a wide variety of animal and vegetable food.

OPERCULUM A cover or lid. In many snails, an operculum on the back of the foot is used to seal the shell when the animal has withdrawn inside. In bony fish and larval amphibians, there is an operculum on each side of the body to protect the gill chamber.

P

PARASITE Any organism that lives on or in the body of another organism and feeds off it for an extended period. The relationship is beneficial to the parasite, but not to its host.

PECTORAL FIN One of two sets of paired fins positioned on either side toward the front of a fish's body, often just behind its head. Pectoral fins are usually highly mobile and are normally used for maneuvering and braking.

PECTORAL MUSCLES Large, paired muscles that pull the forelimbs toward the chest. In birds they are the main flight muscles.

PEDIPALPS A pair of jointed structures found near the front of the body in spiders and relatives. They have various functions including sensing the environment and as aids in reproduction, depending on the species. The large "pincers" of scorpions are pedipalps.

PENINSULA An area of land jutting out into the sea or a lake.

PERMAFROST Permanently frozen ground (technically, ground that has remained frozen for at least two years). It is characteristic of polar regions. See also *Tundra*.

PHOTOSYNTHESIS The process by which green plants and algae utilize the sun's energy, carbon dioxide, and water to produce energy-containing sugars. Oxygen is a byproduct.

PHYTOPLANKTON Plantlike lifeforms of the plankton that produce their own food by photosynthesis. They are mainly microscopic algae. See also *Algae, Plankton, Zooplankton*.

PLANKTON Mainly microscopic floating lifeforms living in open water that cannot swim strongly (or at all) and so drift with the currents.

PLATE TECTONICS A concept that explains how the plates that make up the Earth's crust move. They are created at midocean ridges and destroyed where plates collide or slide by each other.

PNEUMATOPHORE (1) An aerial root produced by some trees living in waterlogged conditions to take in the air their roots need. (2) The large gas-filled float of the Portuguese man o' war (a relative of jellyfish).

POLYGAMY The situation where members of a species (male, female, or both sexes) have multiple sexual partners.

PREDATOR An animal that hunts and eats other animals.

PREHENSILE Capable of grasping, such as the tails of some monkeys.

PREY Any animal hunted for food by another animal or trapped by a carnivorous plant.

PROBOSCIS In mammals, an elongated nose or snout, such as that of an elephant, or an elongated mouthpart for sipping liquids as seen in many butterflies.

PUFFBALLS Fungi that produce globular fruiting bodies, which release spores in a dustlike cloud when they rupture.

PUNA GRASSLAND An ecoregion of the montane grasslands in the Andes mountains of South America.

PUP A name for the young of many animals, including sharks and seals as well as (more obviously) dogs.

PUPA In many insects such as flies and moths, a stage in which the larval body is broken down and rebuilt as an adult. See also *Larva*.

R

RANGE (1) The geographical distribution of a particular species. (2) The "home range" of an individual animal is the area within which it normally forages, which may or may not also be a territory. See also *Territory*. (3) In geology, a term applied to a mountain belt.

RAPTOR A bird of prey.

RUMINANT Cloven-hooved mammals, such as antelope and sheep, that have a specialized digestive system with a compartmented stomach. The first compartment, the rumen, contains microorganisms that help break down tough plant food. It is also regurgitated and rechewed, a process called ruminating or "chewing the cud."

RUT The breeding season of deer. Also called the rutting season, it is marked by intense rivalry between males for mates. It often involves roaring ("rut" is an old word for roar) and displaying. Equally matched males fight.

S

SALINE Of water, springs, or lakes: having a high concentration of dissolved salts.

SAVANNA A general term for all tropical grasslands. Most savannas also have scattered trees.

SCUTES Shieldlike plates or scales that form a hard covering on some animals.

SEAMOUNT An undersea mountain, usually formed from an extinct volcano.

SEXUAL DIMORPHISM Condition in which the males and females of a species differ obviously in appearance (for example, in color pattern, shape, or size).

SHIELD In geology, any large, stable region of ancient rocks that has not been altered by mountain-building in recent geological history. Shield regions are usually relatively flat and form the central parts of most continents.

SPAWN The eggs of fish, amphibians, and marine invertebrates, especially when laid as a large mass. "To spawn" is to lay such eggs.

SPECIATION The formation of new species.

SPECIES A species is the basic unit of biological classification. It is a group of organisms that are similar in appearance and behavior, usually breed only with each other, and differ in some way from other similar species.

SPERMATOPHORE A packet of sperm that is transferred either directly from the male to the female, or indirectly—for example, by being left on the ground. Spermatophores are produced by a range of animals, including squid, salamanders, and some insects.

STOOP Of a bird of prey: to swoop down swiftly on its target prey.

STRATIFIED GRAZING The different feeding levels (grasses, bushes, trees) and different parts and ages of plants (new shoots, older plants) eaten by various grazers and browsers in the same area.

STRIDULATE Of insects such as grasshoppers: to make a shrill or grating noise by rubbing modified parts of the body against one another. Some tarantula spiders and venomous snakes also stridulate.

STROBILURIN Any of several related chemical compounds used in agriculture to kill fungi.

SUBDUCTION The sinking of one tectonic plate beneath another when the two plates collide. See *Plate tectonics* and *Midocean ridge*.

SUBTROPICAL DRY BROADLEAF FORESTS Forests in warm subtropical regions where frost is still occasionally possible and where there is a long dry season, during which trees may shed their leaves.

SYMBIOTIC RELATIONSHIP A close living, relatively long-term relationship between two species. See also *Mutualism, Parasite*.

T

TAIGA Another term for boreal forest, though sometimes used just for the northern part of this, nearest the tundra.

TECTONIC PLATE Any of the large, rigid sections into which the Earth's surface is divided, such as the Pacific Plate.

TEMPERATE Relating to the regions of the Earth between the tropics and the polar regions.

TEMPERATE BROADLEAF FORESTS Forests in temperate regions that are dominated by broadleaf tree species.

TEMPERATE CONIFEROUS FORESTS Evergreen forests, often dominated by conifers, that occur in temperate regions with warm summers, cold winters, and typically plentiful rainfall.

TERRITORY A particular area or section of habitat defended by an animal or group of animals against rivals, usually of the same species. See also *Range*.

TROPICAL Relating to the warm regions of the Earth that lie between the Equator and the tropics of Cancer (to the north) and Capricorn (to the south).

TROPICAL DRY BROADLEAF FORESTS Tropical broadleaf forests growing in regions with a long dry season.

TROPICAL MOIST BROADLEAF FORESTS Tropical forests dominated by broadleaved trees and characterized by high rainfall and no long dry season.

TUNDRA A treeless habitat of low-growing, cold-tolerant plants widespread in the far north of North America, Russia, and the Antarctic peninsula. A similar habitat (alpine tundra) is found high on some mountain ranges as well.

TUSK In mammals, an enlarged modified tooth that often projects outside the mouth.

TYPHOON A tropical cyclone, especially in Pacific regions (equivalent to a hurricane in the Atlantic).

U

ULTRAVIOLET RADIATION Radiation of shorter wavelength than the light visible to humans, which other animals may be able to see.

UMBRELLA SPECIES A species whose protection and conservation has the side effect of protecting threatened habitats where it lives, and the other animals and plants that live there.

UNGULATE A hooved mammal.

V

VASCULAR PLANT Any plant with specialized tissues for transporting water and nutrients between its different parts. Most land plants except for mosses and their relatives are vascular plants.

VENOM Any toxic fluid produced by an animal that is actively transferred into the body of another. Venomous animals commonly deliver their venom via fangs, stings, or similar structures.

VENTRAL Relating to the lower surface or underside of an animal.

VERTEBRATE Any animal with a backbone (fish, amphibians, reptiles, birds, and mammals). See also *Chordate, Invertebrate*.

VIVIPAROUS Giving birth to live young, rather than laying eggs.

W

WARNING COLORATION Striking colors on an animal designed to warn potential predators that it is poisonous or otherwise dangerous.

WEANING The period of adjustment in young mammals' lives when they start taking solid food rather than relying on their mother's milk.

WORLD HERITAGE SITE A site designated by the United Nations Educational, Scientific, and Cultural Organization (UNESCO) as being of world importance either for cultural reasons (such as historic city centers) or for aspects of its natural heritage, such as its natural beauty, conservation value, or geological interest.

Y

YUNGAS The varied and biodiverse warm, moist broadleaf forests on the eastern side of the Andes mountains.

Z

ZOOPLANKTON Animals such as krill that are part of the plankton. See *Plankton*.

ZYGOMATIC ARCH Bony arch under the eye socket on each side of the face.

The IUCN (International Union for the Conservation of Nature) is the leading source of information on the conservation and status of animal and plant species. Scientists and organizations collect data on a species' population size, rate of habitat fragmentation and decline, and the IUCN assess the risk for each species using this information.

INDEX

Page numbers in **bold** refer to main entries.

U

ACKNOWLEDGMENTS

DK would like to thank:

Robert Dinwiddie for consultancy on main continent feature pages; Christopher Bryan for additional research; Sanjay Chauhan, Parul Gambhir, Alison Gardner, Meenal Goel, Konica Juneja, Roshni Kapur, Alexander Lloyd, Upasana Sharma, Riti Sodhi, and Priyansha Tuli for additional design assistance; Suefa Lee, Vibha Malhotra, and Ira Pundeer for editorial assistance; Katie John for proofreading; and the following people and organizations for allowing us to photograph:

British Wildlife Centre, Lingfield, Surrey, UK

The British Wildlife Centre is home to more than 40 species of native British wildlife, all housed in large natural enclosures that mimic their wild habitats. The centre actively manages or participates in several conservation programs for British wildlife, and focuses on education in all aspects of their work. The British Wildlife Centreis an excellent place to see Britain's wonderful wildlife up close and personal.
(Liza Lipscombe, Marketing and Information Officer; Matt Binstead, Head Keeper); Izzy Coomber (Senior Keeper)

Liberty's Owl Raptor and Reptile Centre, Hampshire, UK

Liberty's Owl, Raptor and Reptile Centre is located near Hampshire's New Forest National Park. It is named after Liberty, the Alaskan bald eagle who lives there. Liberty's houses a large collection of birds of prey including owls, hawks, falcons, and vultures, as well as a collection of reptiles and other small animals. The centre also offers falconry experience days, photographic experience days, and hawking days.
(Lynda Bridges and all the staff)

Wildlife Heritage Foundation, Kent, UK

Wildlife Heritage Foundation (WHF) is a centre of excellence dedicated to the captive breeding of endangered big cats within European Endangered Species Programs with the eventual aim of providing animals for scientifically based re-introduction projects. WHF is also a sanctuary for older big cats.
(The trustees, management, staff, and volunteers)

Blackpool Zoo, UK

Blackpool Zoo is a medium-sized collection of more than 1,000 animals that has been open for over 40 years on its current site. Species vary from those critically endangered such as Amur tigers, Bactrian camels, and Bornean orangutans to western lowland gorillas, Asian elephants, giraffes, and many other favorites. A growing and varied collection of birds includes the only Magellanic penguins in the UK, and Californian sea lions offer an educational display daily throughout the year.
(Judith Rothwell, Marketing & PR Coordinator; Laura Stevenson, Digital Marketing Executive; all the keepers)

Cotswolds Wildlife Park, Oxfordshire, UK

The Cotswold Wildlife Park was opened in 1970. It covers 160 acres (65 hectares) and is home to 254 species. Highlights include a breeding group of white rhinos and a collection of lemurs. The gardens are also highly regarded among the horticultural community. The park has its own charity that funds conservation work all over the world and also directly manages the Sifaka Conservation Project in Madagascar.
(Jamie Craig, Curator; Hayley Rothwell, Activities Coordinator)

Picture credits

The publisher would like to thank the following for their kind permission to reproduce their photographs:

(Key: a-above; b-below/bottom; c-center; f-far; l-left; r-right; t-top)

1 FLPA: Frans Lanting. **2-3 FLPA:** Minden Pictures / Tui De Roy. **4 Alamy Images:** Matthijs Kuijpers (cl); Life On White (fcr). **Corbis:** Joe McDonald (fcl). **Dorling Kindersley:** Thomas Marent (c). **Getty Images:** Tim Flach (ffcr). **SuperStock:** Animals Animals (cr). **5 FLPA:** ImageBroker (fcl); Minden Pictures / Chris van Rijswijk (fcr). **6 Corbis:** AlaskaPhotoGraphics / Patrick J. Endres (fcl); AlaskaStock (cr). **FLPA:** Minden Pictures / Ingo Arndt (cl). **Getty Images:** Gail Shumway (c). **7 Corbis:** Anup Shah (cl); Staffan Widstrand (c). **Getty Images:** Digital Vision / David Tipling (fcr). **National Geographic Creative:** Tim Laman (cr). **8 Carl Chapman:** (cl). **FLPA:** Frans Lanting (cb); Albert Visage (tl); Ben Sadd (tr); Minden Pictures / Thomas Marent (cla). **Getty Images:** Grambo Grambo (bl); Gail Shumway (tc). **naturepl.com:** Aflo (clb). **stevebloom.com:** (br). **9 Corbis:** Design Pics / Natural Selection William Banaszewski (cl); All Canada Photos / Wayne Lynch (cla). **FLPA:** Frans Lanting (bc); Minden Pictures / Steve Gettle (tl); Minden Pictures / Konrad Wothe (clb). **Tom & Pat Leeson Photography:** Thomas Kitchin & Victoria Hurst (c). **SuperStock:** Mark Newman (cb). **10 Alamy Images:** Bernd Schmidt (cr). **Getty Images:** Stocktrek Images (c). **11 Corbis:** Tim Graham (bl). **Dreamstime.com:** Viophotography (br). **FLPA:** Minden Pictures / Ingo Arndt (cra). **Getty Images:** Ascent Xmedia (ca). **iStockphoto.com:** Anita Stizzoli (cr). **12 FLPA:** Minden Pictures / Tim Fitzharris (cr); Minden Pictures / Konrad Wothe (clb). **12-13 Corbis:** Minden Pictures / Buiten-beeld / Wil Meinderts (b). **13 Alamy Images:** MShieldsPhotos (crb). **Dreamstime.com:** Isselee (cra). **FLPA:** ImageBroker (c). **naturepl.com:** Nick Upton (cl). **14 Dreamstime.com:** Iakov Filimonov (cla). **FLPA:** Imagebroker / Herbert Kratky (crb); Minden Pictures / Michael Durham (ca). **naturepl.com:** Onne van der Wal (clb). **14-15 Alamy Images:** Blaine Harrington III (b). **15 123RF.com:** Tatiana Belova (cr). **FLPA:** Bob Gibbons (cl); Minden Pictures / Richard Du Toit (c). **16 Dorling Kindersley:** Liberty's Owl, Raptor and Reptile Centre, Hampshire, UK (cra). **FLPA:** Dickie Duckett (c); Imagebroker / Peter Giovannini (crb). **Getty Images:** DC Productions (clb). **16-17 FLPA:** ImageBroker (b). **17 Dreamstime.com:** Subhrajyoti Parida (cla). **FLPA:** ImageBroker (cra); Minden Pictures / Michael & Patricia Fogden (c). **Getty Images:** Imagemore Co., Ltd. (crb). **18 Dreamstime.com:** Fabio Lotti (clb); Welcomia (c). **FLPA:** Minden Pictures / Kevin Schafer (cr). **18-19 Getty Images:** Design Pics / Vince Cavataio (bc). **19 FLPA:** Imagebroker / Alfred & Annaliese T (cl); Minden Pictures / Konrad Wothe (cr). **OceanwideImages.com:** Gary Bell (c). **20-21 SuperStock:** age fotostock / Don Johnston. **22 Alamy Images:** Charline Xia Ontario Canada Collection (cb). **23 123RF.com:** David Schliepp (bc). **Ardea:** (cra). **Getty Images:** Jad Davenport (tr). **24 Alamy Images:** Gary Tack (tr). **FLPA:** Biosphoto / Sylvain Cordier (c). **naturepl.com:** MYN / Carl Battreall (bc). **24-25 FLPA:** Minden Pictures / Jim Brandenburg (c). **25 Alamy Images:** Wildscotphotos (ca). **Corbis:** Tim Davis (br). **FLPA:** Minden Pictures / Jim Brandenburg (c). **Peter Leopold, University of Norway:** (bl). **naturepl.com:** MYN / Les Meade (tl). **26 Corbis:** All Canada Photos / Wayne Lynch (tr). **FLPA:** Minden Pictures / Jim Brandenburg (b). **27 Corbis:** AlaskaStock (tr); Tom Brakefield (tl). **Getty Images:** Photodisc / Paul Souders (b). **28 Corbis:** Cultura (tr); Jenny E. Ross (tc). **stevebloom.com:** (b). **30-31 National Geographic Creative:** Paul Nicklen (t). **30 FLPA:** Minden Pictures / Flip Nicklin (tl). **Getty Images:** National Geographic / Paul Nicklen (b). **31 Alamy Images:** Andrey Nekrasov (tr). **Corbis:** All Canada Photos / Wayne Lynch (bc). **Getty Images:** AFP / Kazuhiro Nogi (ca). **32 Corbis:** All Canada Photos / Wayne Lynch (b). **Dreamstime.com:** Vladimir Melnik (l). **FLPA:** Minden Pictures / Flip Nicklin (tr). **33 123RF.com:** Vasiliy Vishnevskiy (cra). **Alamy Images:** Blickwinkel (br). **Dorling Kindersley:** Liberty's Owl, Raptor and Reptile Centre, Hampshire, UK (tc). **Getty Images:** Universal Images Group (bl). **34 Margarethe Brummermann Ph.D.:** (c). **Corbis:** Joe McDonald (cb). **naturepl.com:** Ben Cranke (tr). **34-35 Alamy Images:** Nature Picture Library (c). **35 Corbis:** Jeff Vanuga (br). **FLPA:** Minden Pictures / Donald M. Jones (ca); Minden Pictures / Michael Quinton (bl); Fritz Polking (c). **36 FLPA:** Frans Lanting (b). **naturepl.com:** Andy Rouse (tr). **37 Corbis:** Charles Krebs (bc). **Dorling Kindersley:** Jerry Young (tl, tr). **38-39 Alaskaphotographics.com:** Patrick J. Endres (Moose). **38 Alamy Images:** Danita Delimont (tc). **Getty Images:** Robert Postma (bl). **39 Corbis:** Minden Pictures / Mark Raycroft (tr). **40 FLPA:** Minden Pictures / Donald M. Jones (tr). **naturepl.com:** Shattil & Rozinski (bl). **Robert Harding Picture Library:** James Hager (cr). **41 Ardea:** Tom & Pat Leeson (tr, b). **Dreamstime.com:** Musat Christian (tl). **42 Alamy Images:** franzfoto.com (tc). **Corbis:** Arthur Morris (b). **43 FLPA:** Frans Lanting (tr). **Getty Images:** Tom Murphy / National Geographic (tl). **44 FLPA:** ImageBroker (c); Photo Researchers (cl). **Getty Images:** Jake Rajs (b). **45 Alamy Images:** (bl, br). **Dreamstime.com:** Izanbar (tr). **naturepl.com:** Gerrit Vyn (clb). **46 FLPA:** Minden Pictures / Ingo Arndt (bl). **Ben Forbes:** (t). **National Geographic Creative:** Tom Murphy (br). **48 FLPA:** Minden Pictures / Donald M. Jones (b). **48-49 FLPA:** Paul Sawer. **49 123RF.com:** Steve Byland (tr). **50 123RF.com:** Melinda Fawver (cr); Benjamin King (br). **FLPA:** Minden Pictures / Donald M. Jones (bl). **SuperStock:** Animals Animals (tc). **51 Dreamstime.com:** Janice Mccafferty | (cr). **FLPA:** Minden Pictures / Ingo Arndt (b). **52 Corbis:** All Canada Photos / Glenn Bartley (clb). **naturepl.com:** Tom Vezo (cb). **Photoshot:** NHPA (bc). **53 123RF.com:** (tr). **Corbis:** Imagebroker / Michael Rucker (bl). **FLPA:** Minden Pictures / Donald M. Jones (br). **naturepl.com:** (clb). **54 Corbis:** First Light / Thomas Kitchin & Victoria Hurst (b). **FLPA:** S & D & K Maslowski (tc). **Getty Images:** Fuse (tl). **54-55 Alamy Images:** Melody Watson (t). **55 Ardea:** M. Watson (bc). **FLPA:** Minden Pictures / Donald M. Jones (tr); Minden Pictures / Konrad Wothe (bl). **56 Corbis:** 167 / Ralph Lee Hopkins / Ocean (bl). **FLPA:** Frans Lanting (br). **Paul Whalen:** (cl). **57 Getty Images:** mallardg500. **58 FLPA:** Jules Cox (b); Minden Pictures / Michael Quinton (tc). **Robert Royse:** (tr). **59 123RF.com:** Tom Grundy (crb). **Alamy Images:** Design Pics Inc (tr). **FLPA:** Minden Pictures / Sebastian Kennerknecht (bl). **60 Christopher Talbot Frank:** (bc). **Robert A. Klips, Ph.D.:** (clb). **Wikipedia:** Ryan Kaldari (cb). **61 FLPA:** Minden Pictures / Tim Fitzharris (clb); Minden Pictures / Kevin Schafer (br). **Getty Images:** Joel Sartore (tr). **Warren E. Savary:** (bc). **62 123RF.com:** Eric Isselee (l). **Corbis:** George H H Huey (br). **63 Alamy Images:** Jaymi Heimbuch (tc). **Corbis:** Minden Pictures / Alan Murphy / BIA (cr). **Getty Images:** Danita Delimont (tr). **Rick Poley Photography:** (b). **64 Dorling Kindersley:** Jerry Young (tc). **FLPA:** Photo Researchers (crb). **naturepl.com:** Daniel Heuclin (clb). **64-65 Dorling Kindersley:** Jerry Young (c). **65 Corbis:** Visuals Unlimited / Jim Merli (tr). **National Geographic Creative:** Joel Sartore (b). **66 4Corners:** Susanne Kremer (bc). **Alamy Images:** WaterFrame (cb). **FLPA:** Frans Lanting (clb). **67 Alamy Images:** F1online digitale Bildagentur GmbH (bl). **Corbis:** Design Pics / Natural Selection William Banaszewski (bc). **FLPA:** Mark Newman (clb). **Photoshot:** Franco Banfi (c). **68-69 Getty Images:** Life on White. **69 Alamy Images:** Arco Images GmbH (br). **Getty Images:** Craftvision (tr); Joe McDonald (bl). **70 123RF.com:** Tania and Jim Thomson (tr). **FLPA:** Imagebroker / Christian Hutter (tl). **70-71 FLPA:** Minden Pictures / Donald M. Jones (b). **71 123RF.com:** John Bailey (tr). **Alamy Images:** Blickwinkel (cr). **Getty Images:** Russell Burden (ca). **naturepl.com:** George Sanker (bc). **72-73 Alamy Images:** Jeff Mondragon (t). **72 Corbis:** Biosphoto / Michel Gunther (bc). **Dorling Kindersley:** Jerry Young (tl, crb). **73 Science Photo Library:** MH Sharp (br). **74-75 Corbis:** Jim Zuckerman. **76 Corbis:** Galen Rowell (cra). **77 Corbis:** Novarc / Nico Stengert (bc). **Oscar Fernandes Junior:** (tr). **Getty Images:** Pasieka (tc). **78-79 Photo Bee1, LLC / Myer Bornstein. . Photo Bee1, LLC / Myer Bornstein:** (cb). **78 FLPA:** Minden Pictures / Michael & Patricia Fogden (bc). **Paul Latham :** (cb). **naturepl.com:** Nick Garbutt (clb). **79 Lucas M. Bustamante / Tropical Herping:** (bl). **FLPA:** Minden Pictures / Konrad Wothe (ca); Minden Pictures / Suzi Eszterhas (br). **80 Corbis:** E & P Bauer (bl). **81 Corbis:** Minden Pictures / Stephen Dalton (br). **FLPA:** Minden Pictures / Juan Carlos Vindas (tr). **82-83 Dorling Kindersley:** Thomas Marent. **83 FLPA:** Minden Pictures / Michael & Patricia Fogden (tl); Minden Pictures / Ingo Arndt (tr). **84 Alamy Images:** All Canada Photos (clb). **Corbis:** Image Source / Gary Latham (bc). **National Geographic Creative:** Christian Ziegler (cb). **85 Ardea:** Kenneth W. Fink (cb, tr). **Flickr.com:** diabola62 / www.flickr.com / photos / bilder_heinzg / 11874681244 (clb). **Getty Images:** Joel Sartore (br). **Science Photo Library:** James H. Robinson (bl). **86 Corbis:** Kevin Schafer (ca). **FLPA:** Chris Brignell (b). **Photoshot:** Jany Sauvanet (tr). **87 Robert Harding Picture Library:** C. Huetter (br). **88 Dreamstime.com:** Suebmtl (tl). **Getty Images:** Mark J Thomas (r). **89 Alamy Images:** Wildlife GmbH (ca). **FLPA:** Minden Pictures / James Christensen (cb). **Getty Images:** Kim Schandorff (br). **90 Corbis:** JAI / Gavin Hellier (cb). **FLPA:** Robin Chittenden (c). **Keith Newton:** (tr). **90-91 Getty Images:** Elena Kalistratova (c). **91 FLPA:** Minden Pictures / Flip de Nooyer (c); Minden Pictures / Kevin Schafer (bl); Silvestre Silva (br). **92 Alamy Images:** Wildlife GmbH (cb). **Dorling Kindersley:** Gary Ombler, Courtesy of Cotswold Wildlife Park (tc, ca). **92-93 Ardea:** Thomas Marent (c). **93 FLPA:** Minden Pictures / Piotr Naskrecki (bc). **94 FLPA:** Frans Lanting. **95 123RF.com:** Anan

Kaewkhammul (tr). **Corbis:** Minden / Foto Natura / SA Team (clb). **FLPA:** Frans Lanting (br). **96-97 Alamy Images:** Steve Bloom Images (b). **97 Corbis:** Joe McDonald (crb). **FLPA:** Minden Pictures / Chris van Rijswijk (tc). **98 Dorling Kindersley:** Thomas Marent (cl). **Getty Images:** Gail Shumway (b). **SuperStock:** Mark Newman (cra). **99 123RF.com:** Mirosław Kijewski (tl). **Getty Images:** Tim Flach (c). **100 FLPA:** Mike Lane (clb); Malcolm Schuyl (c); Minden Pictures / Luciano Candisani (bc). **101 123RF.com:** Noppharat Manakul (bl). **Ardea:** François Grohier (tr). **Dorling Kindersley:** Courtesy of Blackpool Zoo, Lancashire, UK (bc). **FLPA:** Biosphoto / Sylvain Cordier (clb); Minden Pictures / Pete Oxford (c). **102-103 FLPA:** Minden Pictures / Pete Oxford (t). **102 Alamy Images:** DPA Picture Alliance (bc). **naturepl.com:** Angelo Gandolfi (crb). **103 Corbis:** Jami Tarris (cr). **FLPA:** ImageBroker (b); Frans Lanting (tr). **104 FLPA:** Minden Pictures / Steve Gettle (bc). **Getty Images:** Dickson Images / Photolibrary (r). **105 FLPA:** Minden Pictures / Pete Oxford (cra). **Getty Images:** Suebg1 Photography (br). **Andrew M. Snyder:** (cr). **John White:** (cl). **106-107 Corbis:** SuperStock / Nick Garbutt (b). **106 Corbis:** Minden Pictures / Tui De Roy (tr). **107 Corbis:** SuperStock / Nick Garbutt (tl). **FLPA:** Minden Pictures / Luciano Candisani (tr). **108 Ignacio De la Riva:** (cb). **FLPA:** Biosphoto / Denis Bringard (cr); Biosphoto / Alain Pons (clb); Imagebroker / GTW (cl); ImageBroker (bc). **109 Flickr.com:** Fernando Rosselot (br). **FLPA:** Biosphoto / Antoni Agelet (ca). **Pablo Omar Palmeiro:** (tr). **110-111 Getty Images:** Padmanaba01 (b). **111 Corbis:** All Canada Photos / Glenn Bartley (bc). **FLPA:** Minden Pictures / Tui De Roy (tl). **Paul B Jones:** (ca). **112 Getty Images:** Joel Sartore (tr). **naturepl.com:** Daniel Gomez (ca). **112-113 Alamy Images:** Blickwinkel. **113 Manuel Francisco Gana Eguiguren:** (c). **María de la Luz Vial Bascuñán www.fotonaturaleza.cl:** (br/ FabianLizard). **114 FLPA:** Carr Clifton (bc); Minden Pictures / Luciano Candisani (c). **naturepl.com:** Luiz Claudio Marigo (cl, clb). **115 Dreamstime.com:** Lunamarina (clb). **Flickr.com:** Yeagov C / www.flickr.com / photos / yeagovc / 15252486009 (bl). **FLPA:** Minden Pictures / Michael & Patricia Fogden (br). **naturepl.com:** Barry Mansell (tr). **116-117 Alamy Images:** Life On White. **117 Ardea:** (ca). **Corbis:** Tom Brakefield (tl). **Dreamstime.com:** Poeticpenguin (tr). **119 Dorling Kindersley:** Jerry Young (tr). **FLPA:** Minden Pictures / Tui De Roy (bc); Minden Pictures / Pete Oxford (br). **120 123RF.com:** Eric Isselee (tl). **FLPA:** Minden Pictures / Pete Oxford (tr). **Photoshot:** Picture Alliance (br). **121 FLPA:** Minden Pictures / Jim Brandenburg (bl). **Photoshot:** Juniors Tierbildarchiv (cra). **122-123 FLPA:** Frans Lanting (cb). **122 FLPA:** Frans Lanting (bc); Minden Pictures / Pete Oxford (clb); Minden Pictures / Tui De Roy (c). **123 FLPA:** Minden Pictures / Tui De Roy (tr, br); Minden Pictures / Pete Oxford (bl). **124 Corbis:** Kevin Schafer (tl). **FLPA:** Frans Lanting (br). **Dan Heller Photography:** (tr). **125 123RF.com:** Keith Levit (tr). **FLPA:** Minden Pictures / Tui De Roy (cra, bc). **126-127 SuperStock:** Mark Jones. **127 123RF.com:** Smileus (cra). **FLPA:** Minden Pictures / Tui De Roy (bc). **128-129 FLPA:** Frans Lanting (t). **128 FLPA:** Minden Pictures / Tui De Roy (bl, br). **129 FLPA:** Imagebroker / Ingo Schultz (tr). **130-131 naturepl.com:** Bruno D'Amicis. **132 FLPA:** Imagebroker / Hans Blossey (cl). **Getty Images:** Traumlichtfabrik (tl). **133 Corbis:** Imagebroker / Günter Lenz (bl). **FLPA:** Minden Pictures / Karl Van Ginderdeuren (bc). **134 Corbis:** imagebroker / Olaf Krüger (bc). **naturepl.com:** Espen Bergersen (cb). **Markus Varesvuo:** (bl). **135 Corbis:** Andrew Parkinson (ca). **FLPA:** Minden Pictures / Peter Verhoog (br). **naturepl.com:** Geomar / Solvin Zankl (bl). **136-137 Corbis:** AlaskaStock. **137 FLPA:** Harri Taavetti (cr). **National Geographic Creative:** Paul Nicklen (bc). **138 FLPA:** Minden Pictures / Luc Hoogenstein. **139 Fotolia:** Lux / Stefan Zeitz (tr). **Tomi Muukkonen:** (bc). **naturepl.com:** Asgeir Helgestad (br). **140 Corbis:** Fortunato Gatto / PhotoFVG (bc). **naturepl.com:** Arco / Meul (clb); Paul Hobson (cb). **141 Alamy Images:** (cb). **Corbis:** Niall Benvie (clb). **Dorling Kindersley:** British Wildlife Centre, Surrey, UK (tr, br). **FLPA:** Terry Whittaker (bl). **142 123RF.com:** Eric Isselee (tr). **FLPA:** Albert Visage (br). **Fotolia:** Eric Isselée (l). **143 Dorling Kindersley:** British Wildlife Centre, Surrey, UK (tc, cra). **FLPA:** Paul Hobson (bc). **144 Photoshot:** Picture Alliance (cr); Dave Watts (bc). **145 Alamy Images:** Christoph Bosch (tc). **Matt Binstead, British Wildlife Centre:** (br). **FLPA:** Desmond Dugan (tr). **146 123RF.com:** Wouter Tolenaars (bc). **Alamy Images:** Tim Moore (clb). **FLPA:** Fabio Pupin (cb). **147 Corbis:** JAI / Nadia Isakova (br). **FLPA:** Minden Pictures / Wim Weenink (clb); Minden Pictures / Wil Meinderts (bl). **148-149 naturepl.com:** 2020VISION / Fergus Gill (t). **148 FLPA:** Minden Pictures / Flip de Nooyer (br). **149 FLPA:** Imagebroker / Winfried Schäfer (tr); Minden Pictures / Ramon Navarro (br). **150 Dreamstime.com:** Geanina Bechea (tl). **150-151 FLPA:** Imagebroker / Franz Christoph Robi. **151 FLPA:** Rebecca Nason (tl). **Getty Images:** Joe Petersburger (tc). **152 Corbis:** JAI / Mauricio Abreu (bc). **Dorling Kindersley:** Thomas Marent (ch). **FLPA:** Minden Pictures / Lars Soerink (clb). **153 123RF.com:** Eric Isselee (tr). **Ardea:** Stefan Meyers (crb). **FLPA:** Bob Gibbons (bl); Minden Pictures / Willi Rolfes (cr). **naturepl.com:** Juan Carlos Munoz (clb). **Wild-Wonders of Europe, Staffan Widstrand:** (br). **154 FLPA:** Biosphoto / Jorge Sierra (tr). **Iberian Lynx Ex-situ Conservation Programme. www.lynxexsitu.es:** (bc). **naturepl.com:** Wild Wonders of Europe \ Pete Oxford (bl). **155 Marina Cano www.marinacano.com:** (r/lynx). **156 FLPA:** Paul Hobson (tr); Minden Pictures / Ingo Arndt (bc). **157 Corbis:** Biosphoto / Michel Gunther (b). **FLPA:** Gianpiero Ferrari (cl); Imagebroker / Bernd Zoller (tr). **158 FLPA:** Imagebroker / Bernd Zoller (clb); ImageBroker (cb). **Getty Images:** Look-foto / Andreas Strauss (bc). **159 FLPA:** Biosphoto / Remi Masson (bl); Imagebroker / Stefan Huwiler (tr). **naturepl.com:** Angelo Gandolfi (clb). **Wild-Wonders of Europe, Staffan Widstrand:** (bc). **160 123RF.com:** Eric Isselee (tl). **FLPA:** Minden Pictures / Misja Smits, Buiten-beeld (tr). **naturepl.com:** Alex Hyde (b). **161 Corbis:** Minden Pictures / BIA / Patrick Donini (cb). **FLPA:** Jurgen & Christine Sohns (cl). **naturepl.com:** Radomir Jakubowski (br). **162 Dreamstime.com:** Outdoorsman (tr). **FLPA:** Minden Pictures / Jelger Herder (bc). **162-163 age fotostock:** Blickwinkel / P Cairns (c). **163 Ettore Balocchi:** (br). **naturepl.com:** Stefan Huwiler (cr); Alex Hyde (b). **164 Corbis:** Novarc / NA / Martin Apelt (bc). **FLPA:** Imagebroker / Christian Hütter (clb); Gerard Lacz (cb). **165 Alamy Images:** Blickwinkel (ca); imagebroker (bl). **Dorling Kindersley:** British Wildlife Centre, Surrey, UK (tr). **FLPA:** ImageBroker (clb). **166 FLPA:** Minden Pictures / Ernst Dirksen. **167 123RF.com:** Eric Isselee (tr). **Alamy Images:** AGE Fotostock (bc, br). **168 James Kruger:** (b). **169 Ardea:** Duncan Usher (ca). **Dreamstime.com:** Isselee (tr). **FLPA:** Duncan Usher (br). **Photoshot:** Niko Pekonen (crb). **170-171 Heidi & Hans-Jürgen Koch:** (t). **170 Dorling Kindersley:** Frank Greenaway / Courtesy of the Natural History Museum, London (cb). **FLPA:** Minden Pictures / Jelger Herder (cla); Minden Pictures / Thomas Marent (bc). **171 Getty Images:** Bill Beatty (bl); Oxford Scientific (OSF) (bc). **172 Dom Greves:** (bc). **172-173 FLPA:** Minden Pictures / Thomas Marent. **174-175 Corbis:** Minden Pictures / Tim Fitzharris. **176 FLPA:** Imagebroker / Egmont Strigl (tr). **177 Alamy Images:** Steve Bloom Images (tr). **naturepl.com:** Rhonda Klevansky (bl, cr); Poinsignon & Hackel (clb). **178 Corbis:** Robert Harding World Imagery / Gavin Hellier (bc). **FLPA:** Imagebroker / Stefan Auth (clb). **Fran Trabalon:** (c). **179 Africa Image Library:** (crb). **Alamy Images:** Papillo (bc). **© Dr Viola Clausnitzer. :** (clb). **FLPA:** Ignacio Yufera (bl). **Rene Mantei www.zootierliste.de:** (cra). **180 Dorling Kindersley:** Andy and Gill Swash (tc). **FLPA:** Imagebroker / GTW (bc). **Getty Images:** Anup Shah (bl). **180-181 FLPA:** Ignacio Yufera. **181 FLPA:** Imagebroker / Christian Hütter (crb). **182 Corbis:** Biosphoto / Michel Gunther (ca). **Dorling Kindersley:** Andy and Gill Swash (tc). **FLPA:** Martin B Withers (cb). **Getty Images:** John Downer (bc). **182-183 Mitchell Krog www.mitchellkrog.com:** (b). **183 Photoshot:** Jordi Bas Casas (tl, tr). **184 Ardea:** Ian Beames (c). **FLPA:** Frans Lanting (bc); Jack Perks (clb). **185 FLPA:** Dickie Duckett (clb); ImageBroker (tr); Frans Lanting (crb). **Magdalena Kwolek-Mirek. :** (bl). **186 FLPA:** Frans Lanting (t). **186-187 FLPA:** Frans Lanting (b). **187 Corbis:** Minden Pictures / ZSSD (bc). **Fotolia:** Eric Isselée (tr). **188-189 Corbis:** Anup Shah (b). **FLPA:** Elliott Neep (t). **189 Getty Images:** Grambo Grambo (ca). **190 Alamy Images:** Sue O'Connor (bc). **FLPA:** Frans Lanting (tl). **191 Ardea:** Leesonphoto / Thomas Kitchin & Victoria Hurst (br). **192 123RF.com:** Mike Price (c). **Getty Images:** Claudia Uribe (tr). **naturepl.com:** Visuals Unlimited (bc, crb, cb). **192-193 FLPA:** Frans Lanting (c). **193 Corbis:** (cb); Anup Shah (bl). **Getty Images:** Joel Sartore (c). **Kimball Stock:** HPH Image Library (tc). **194 Ardea:** Chris Harvey (br). **FLPA:** Frans Lanting (bl). **195 Alamy Images:** Chris Weston. **196 Dorling Kindersley:** Wildlife Heritage Foundation, Kent, UK (tl). **FLPA:** Frans Lanting (c). **197 Dorling Kindersley:** Greg & Yvonne Dean (tr). **FLPA:** Minden Pictures / Stephen Belcher (cl); Minden Pictures / Richard Du Toit (crb). **198 123RF.com:** mhgallery (tl). **FLPA:** Minden Pictures / Tui De Roy (tr). **Photoshot:** Andy Rouse (b). **199 123RF.com:** Fabio Lotti (c). **Corbis:** Hemis / Denis-Huot (tr). **200 FLPA:** Biosphoto / Mathieu Pujol (cl). **Cain Maddern / wildfocusimages.com:** (tr). **201 Getty Images:** Angelika Stern (bc); Pal Teravagimov Photography (tr). **202-203 stevebloom.com. 203 FLPA:** Frans Lanting (tr). **Getty Images:** Danita Delimont (bc). **204-205 FLPA:** Bernd Rohrschneider. **205 FLPA:** Minden Pictures / Tui De Roy (cra, bc). **206 123RF.com:** Gerrit De Vries (cb). **Dorling Kindersley:** Frank Greenaway, Courtesy of the National Birds of Prey Centre, Gloucestershire (br). **FLPA:** Frans Lanting (bc). **naturepl.com:** Charlie Summers (cla). **207 Corbis:** Richard du Toit (tr). **naturepl.com:** Michael D. Kern (bc). **SuperStock:** Animals Animals (cr). **208 Ardea:** Chris Harvey (tr). **FLPA:** Frans Lanting (c). **Witbos Indigenous Nursery:** (br). **208-209 Getty Images:** Cultura Travel / Philip Lee Harvey (c). **209 Alamy Images:** Blickwinkel (bl). **FLPA:** Phil Ward (br). **naturepl.com:** Tim Laman (tc); Mark MacEwen (c). **210 FLPA:** Frans Lanting (bl); Minden Pictures / Konrad Wothe (bc). **211 FLPA:** Frans Lanting. **212-213 FLPA:** Minden Pictures / Cyril Ruoso (t). **212 Alamy Images:** Terry Whittaker (bc). **OceanwideImages.com:** Mark Carwardine (bl). **Thinkstock:** Matt Gibson (tl). **214 Corbis:** Jami Tarris (br). **Dorling Kindersley:** Jerry Young (tl). **naturepl.com:** TJ Rich (bl). **215 123RF.com:** Jatesada Natayo (tr). **FLPA:** Frans Lanting (bc). **216 FLPA:** Neil Bowman (bc). **Getty Images:** Joel Sartore (cla). **217 San Diego Zoo Global:** (tl/ EmperorScorpion). **218 FLPA:** Biosphoto / Sergio Pitamitz (tr); Biosphoto / David Santiago Garcia (c); David Hosking (br). **218-219 FLPA:** Frans Lanting (c). **219 FLPA:** Wendy Dennis (tc). **naturepl.com:** (c). **Science Photo Library:** Tom McHugh (bl); NASA (br). **220 123RF.com:** Nico Smit (tc). **Ardea:** Ferrero-Labat (bl). **220-221 FLPA:** Frans Lanting (t). **221 Alamy Images:** David Hosking (bl). **FLPA:** Imagebroker / Andreas Pollok (tr). **222-223 FLPA:** Minden Pictures / Tui De Roy (b). **223 Kevin Linforth:** (tc). **224 Corbis:** Minden Pictures / Suzi Eszterhas (c). **Dorling Kindersley:** Jerry Young (tl). **FLPA:** Minden Pictures / Martin Willis (bc). **225 123RF.com:** Alta Oosthuizen (br). **naturepl.com:** Tony Heald (t). **226 Dorling Kindersley:** Jerry Young (cra). **FLPA:** Chris Mattison (bc); Minden Pictures / Winfried Wisniewski (tc). **Chris Van Rooyen:** (cla). **227 naturepl.com:** Francois Savigny (b). **Shannon Wild:** (t). **228 FLPA:** Imagebroker / Winfried Schäfer (clb); Minden Pictures / Vincent Grafhorst (bc). **naturepl.com:** Philippe Clement (cb). **228-229 naturepl.com:** Ingo Arndt (c). **229 123RF.com:** Anan Kaewkhammul (tr). **Dorling Kindersley:** Courtesy of Blackpool Zoo, Lancashire, UK (bc). **Getty Images:** Heinrich van den Berg (ca). **Sharifa Jinnah:** (clb). **Photoshot:** Karl Switak (bl). **230 Corbis:** Imagebroker / Erich Schmidt (tc). **FLPA:** Frans Lanting (ca). **231 FLPA:** Minden Pictures / Richard Du Toit (b). **Getty Images:** Tim Jackson (ca). **232 FLPA:** Minden Pictures / Pete Oxford (tc). **naturepl.com:** Will Burrard-Lucas (bc); Charlie Summers (clb). **233 FLPA:** Ben Sadd. **234 Corbis:** Nature Picture Library / Tony Heald (ca); Ocean / 2 / Martin Harvey (bl). **234-235 Alamy Images:** Matthijs Kuijpers. **235 Corbis:** Biosphoto / Michel Gunther (tr). **236 FLPA:** Minden Pictures / Thomas Marent (clb). **naturepl.com:** Brent Stephenson (cb). **Photoshot:** Nick Garbutt (bc). **237 Dr. Melanie Dammhahn:** (br). **Dr. Jörn Köhler:** (clb). **naturepl.com:** Alex Hyde (tr). **238 FLPA:** Minden Pictures / Cyril Ruoso. **239 Corbis:** Nature Picture Library / Inaki Relanzon (bc). **Dorling Kindersley:** Courtesy of Blackpool Zoo, Lancashire, UK (tr). **FLPA:** Minden Pictures / Konrad Wothe (crb). **240 FLPA:** Frans Lanting (tl). **240-241 naturepl.com:** Nick Garbutt. **241 FLPA:** Frans Lanting (cb). **naturepl.com:** Nick Garbutt (cra, br). **242-243 FLPA:** Jurgen & Christine Sohns (c). **243 Corbis:** Biosphoto / Michel Gunther (tr); Visuals Unlimited / Simone Sbaraglia (tl). **Dorling Kindersley:** Thomas Marent (br). **Tom & Pat Leeson Photography:** Thomas Kitchin & Victoria Hurst (cra). **244-245 4Corners:** Andy Callan. **246 Dreamstime.com:** Horia Vlad Bogdan (tr). **FLPA:** Minden Pictures / Hiroya Minakuchi (bc); Winfried Wisniewski (tc). **247 Getty Images:** Datacraft Co Ltd (cr). **248 FLPA:** Imagebroker / Winfried Schäfer (bc). **Svein Erik Larsen www.selarsen.no:** (clb). **naturepl.com:** Hanne & Jens Eriksen (cb). **249 Dreamstime.com:** Lawrence Weslowski Jr (tr). **FLPA:** Biosphoto / Xavier Eichaker (bl); ImageBroker (br). **naturepl.com:** Michael D. Kern (clb). **250 123RF.com:** Sirylok (tc). **FLPA:** Biosphoto / Michel Gunther (bc). **250-251 Corbis:** Staffan Widstrand. **252-253 Ardea:** Jean Michel Labat (t). **Dreamstime.com:** Isselee (b). **253 Alamy Images:** Blickwinkel (bl). **FLPA:** Minden Pictures / Ingo Arndt (tr); Jurgen & Christine Sohns (c). **254 FLPA:** Bernd Rohrschneider (c). **naturepl.com:** Hanne & Jens Eriksen (tr); Axel Gomille (cb). **254-255 iStockphoto.com:** Danielrao (c). **255 Christopher Casilli:** (c). **Getty Images:** EyeEm / Damara Dhanakrishna (br). **naturepl.com:** Sandesh Kadur (tc). **256 123RF.com:** Carlos Caetano (tl). **256-257 FLPA:** John Zimmermann (b). **257 Dreamstime.com:** Shailesh Nanal (crb). **FLPA:** Biosphoto / Patrice Correia (tl); Minden Pictures / ZSSD (bc). **naturepl.com:** Bernard Castelein (cra). **258-259 FLPA:** Biosphoto / Stéphanie Meng (t). **258 Alamy Images:** Blickwinkel (bc). **259 Dreamstime.com:** (tr, bc). **FLPA:** Minden Pictures / Cyril Ruoso (c). **260-261 Dreamstime.com:** Happystock. **261 FLPA:** ImageBroker (bc). **262 Alamy Images:** Papillo (tr). **262-263 FLPA:** Biosphoto / Daniel Heuclin (b). **263 FLPA:** Harri Taavetti (br). **Gunnar Pettersson:** (tr). **Dyrk Daniels - Woodinville, WA:** (cra). **264 Alamy Images:** Arco Images

GmbH (ca). **Corbis:** Yannick Tylle (br). **Photoshot:** Bruce Coleman (bl). **264-265 Udayan Rao Pawar:** (t). **265 Dreamstime.com:** Lukas Blazek (cb). **266 Corbis:** Radius Images (bc). **naturepl.com:** Wim van den Heever (cb); Xi Zhinong (clb). **267 Alamy Images:** Luis Dafos (clb); Petra Wegner (bl); Kevin Schafer (tr). **James Cargin:** (crb). **Scott Klender:** (br). **naturepl.com:** Bernard Castelein (ca). **268-269 FLPA:** Paul Sawer. **269 Alamy Images:** Nature Picture Library (crb). **Dorling Kindersley:** Wildlife Heritage Foundation, Kent, UK (tr). **naturepl.com:** Jeff Wilson (bc). **270 Alamy Images:** Wildlife GmbH (br). **Dorling Kindersley:** Gary Ombler, Courtesy of Cotswold Wildlife Park (tr, b). **271 FLPA:** Frans Lanting (r). **272 Alamy Images:** Fuyu Liu (bc). **FLPA:** F1online (clb). **Natalia Paklina:** (cb). **273 FLPA:** Biosphoto / Emmanuel Lattes (bl); Minden Pictures / Cyril Ruoso (tr); Minden Pictures / Thomas Marent (br). **naturepl.com:** Michael D. Kern (clb). **274 FLPA:** Biosphoto / Juan-Carlos Munoz (clb). **274-275 FLPA:** Minden Pictures / Konrad Wothe. **275 FLPA:** Minden Pictures / Katherine Feng (bc); Minden Pictures / Thomas Marent (br). **Fotolia:** Eric Isselée (tr). **276 Dorling Kindersley:** Gary Ombler / Wildlife Heritage Foundation, Kent, UK (t, b). **277 123RF.com:** Iakov Filimonov (tr). **naturepl.com:** Mary McDonald (ca). **278 Alamy Images:** Cultura RM (cb). **FLPA:** Imagebroker / Stefan Auth (clb). **Getty Images:** Wan Ru Chen (bc). **279 FLPA:** Biosphoto / Eric Dragesco (clb, br). **naturepl.com:** Eric Dragesco (tr); Roland Seitre (bl). **Jenny E. Ross:** (cra). **280 FLPA:** Biosphoto / Eric Dragesco (tr). **naturepl.com:** Igor Shpilenok (bc). **Science Photo Library:** Anthony Mercieca (tc). **280-281 Corbis:** Yi Lu (b). **282 FLPA:** Imagebroker / Dieter Hopf (tr); Minden Pictures / ZSSD (br). **283 Alamy Images:** AGE Fotostock (br). **Vladimír Motyčka. Vladimir Motycka:** (ca). **284 Ardea:** Chris Knights (cb). **Corbis:** Amanaimages / Satoru Imai (bc). **FLPA:** Imagebroker / Klaus-Werner Friedri (clb). **285 Alamy Images:** Yuriy Brykaylo (clb); Interfoto (crb). **FLPA:** Imagebroker / Stefan Huwiler (bc). **naturepl.com:** Jussi Murtosaari (ca); Nature Production (bl, tr). **286 Corbis:** Nature Picture Library / Yukihiro Fukuda (b); T.Tak (tr). **FLPA:** Minden Pictures / Hiroya Minakuchi (tl). **287 Dreamstime.com:** Mikelane45 (tr). **288-289 naturepl.com:** Aflo (t). **288 naturepl.com:** Nature Production (b). **289 Alamy Images:** Prisma Bildagentur AG (br). **Ardea:** Stefan Meyers (tr). **Asian Nature Vision:** Masahiro Iijima (tc). **290 Alamy Images:** Bildagentur-online / McPhoto-Rolfes (tr). **FLPA:** ImageBroker (b). **291 Alamy Images:** Survivalphotos (cra). **Dreamstime.com:** Valeriy Kirsanov | (tr). **Getty Images:** Joel Sartore (b). **Kevin Messenger:** (cla). **292 FLPA:** Biosphoto / Berndt Fischer (crb); Minden Pictures / Chien Lee (tr). **naturepl.com:** Nick Garbutt (c). **292-293 FLPA:** Frans Lanting (c). **293 FLPA:** Biosphoto / Alain Compost (tc); Minden Pictures / Sebastian Kennerknecht (br). **naturepl.com:** Tim Laman (bl); Neil Lucas (c). **294 FLPA:** Frans Lanting (bc). **Getty Images:** Lucia Terui (ca). **294-295 FLPA:** Minden Pictures / Suzi Eszterhas (t). **295 FLPA:** Minden Pictures / Sebastian Kennerknecht (tr); Minden Pictures / Suzi Eszterhas (bl). **naturepl.com:** Anup Shah (bc). **296 FLPA:** Frans Lanting. **297 FLPA:** Biosphoto / Theo Allofs (tr); Frans Lanting (bc); Minden Pictures / Konrad Wothe (br). **298-299 FLPA:** Photo Researchers (b). **298 Johannes Pfleiderer www.zootierliste.de/en:** (tr). **SuperStock:** age fotostock (ca). **299 123RF.com:** Kajornyot (cr). **Alamy Images:** Panu Ruangjan (ca). **300 Corbis:** Minden Pictures / Stephen Dalton (cl). **FLPA:** Minden Pictures / Thomas Marent (bc). **Kurt (Hock Ping Guek) :** (tr). **301 FLPA:** Minden Pictures / Thomas Marent. **302 Alamy Images:** Steve Bloom Images (clb). **Didi Lotze, roundshot360.de:** Location: Wakatobi Dive Resort, Indonesia (bc). **Kar Seng Sim:** (c). **303 Corbis:** Robert Harding World Imagery / Michael Nolan (br). **Dreamstime.com:** Caan2gobelow (tr). **naturepl.com:** Constantinos Petrinos (bl). **SeaPics.com:** Mark V. Erdmann (clb). **304 FLPA:** Imagebroker / Fotoatelier, Berlin (tc); Imagebroker / Norbert Probst (c). **304-305 naturepl.com:** Doug Perrine (t). **305 FLPA:** Colin Marshall (br). **306 Dreamstime.com:** Torsten Velden (tl). **FLPA:** Reinhard Dirscherl (br). **Science Photo Library:** Alexis Rosenfeld (bl). **306-307 National Geographic Creative:** Brian J. Skerry. **308 FLPA:** Biosphoto / Tobias Bernhard Raff (t). **naturepl.com:** Pascal Kobeh (crb). **309 Alamy Images:** WaterFrame (tr). **Ardea:** Valerie Taylor (bl). **Dreamstime.com:** Teguh Tirtaputra (cra). **Photoshot:** Linda Pitkin (bc). **310-311 National Geographic Creative:** Tim Laman. **312 Corbis:** Nature Connect (tc). **FLPA:** Minden Pictures / Mitsuaki Iwago (br). **313 Alamy Images:** Clint Farlinger (c). **FLPA:** Imagebroker / FB-Fischer (bc). **314 FLPA:** Biosphoto / Daniel Heuclin (clb); Minden Pictures / Piotr Naskrecki (bc). **naturepl.com:** Richard Kirby (cb). **315 Alamy Images:** AGE Fotostock (bl). **FLPA:** Minden Pictures / Gerry Ellis (tr); Minden Pictures / Konrad Wothe (ca). **Markus Lilje:** (clb). **National Geographic Creative:** Tim Laman (br). **316 Corbis:** Nature Connect (bl). **Getty Images:** David Garry (bc); Imagemore Co., Ltd. (tl). **316-317 Getty Images:** Joe McDonald. **317 FLPA:** Minden Pictures / Otto Plantema (bc). **naturepl.com:** Roland Seitre (tr). **318-319 National Geographic Creative:** Tim Laman. **319 FLPA:** Biosphoto / Alain Compost (tr). **320 Dreamstime.com:** Metriognome | (clb). **FLPA:** Minden Pictures / Ingo Arndt (cb). **Getty Images:** UIG / Auscape (bc). **321 123RF.com:** Christian Musat (tr). **Ardea:** Hans & Judy Beste (clb). **Michael J Barritt:** (bc). **Photoshot:** Picture Alliance / I. Bartussek (ca). **322 FLPA:** Biosphoto / Jami Tarris (bl). **323 FLPA:** Minden Pictures / Martin Willis (tr). **Steve Murray:** (br). **324 Ardea:** Auscape (tl). **FLPA:** Biosphoto / Sylvain Cordier (c). **325 FLPA:** Malcolm Schuyl (bc). **326 123RF.com:** Christopher Ison (cl). **OceanwideImages.com:** Gary Bell (bl). **Steve and Alison Pearson Airlie Beach Queensland Australia:** (tr). **327 Michael Doe:** (t). **FLPA:** Minden Pictures / Mark Moffett (bl, br). **328 David Cook:** (ca). **Getty Images:** UIG / Auscape (bc). **Nathan Litjens:** (clb). **329 Alamy Images:** Auscape International Pty Ltd (bc). **Ardea:** Jean Michel Labat (cl). **FLPA:** ImageBroker (bl); Jurgen & Christine Sohns (clb). **OceanwideImages.com:** Gary Bell (ca). **Photoshot:** NHPA (crb). **330-331 Getty Images:** Tier Und Naturfotographie J & C Sohns. **331 Corbis:** Jami Tarris (bc). **332 Getty Images:** Theo Allofs (ca). **naturepl.com:** Roland Seitre (bc). **332-333 naturepl.com:** Steven David Miller (t). **333 Bill & Mark Bell. :** (br). **Stephen Mahony:** (bc). **334 Corbis:** Minden Pictures / Roland Seitre (tr). **Dreamstime.com:** Jeremy Wee (c). **FLPA:** Keith Rushforth (bc). **334-335 123RF.com:** Tim Hester. **335 Corbis:** Minden Pictures / BIA / Jan Wegener (c). **Dorling Kindersley:** Courtesy of Blackpool Zoo, Lancashire, UK (bl). **FLPA:** Martin B Withers (tc). **Getty Images:** Mike Powles (br). **338-339 FLPA:** Jurgen & Christine Sohns (t). **338 Alamy Images:** AGE Fotostock (br). **FLPA:** Minden Pictures / Suzi Eszterhas (bc). **339 Fotolia:** Eric Isselée (tr). **340 Corbis:** Laurie Chamberlain (clb). **National Geographic Creative:** Joel Sartore (tl). **Science Photo Library:** Gerry Pearce (r). **341 123RF.com:** Eric Isselee (cb). **Alamy Images:** Gerry Pearce (tr); David Sewell (ca). **Photoshot:** NHPA (br). **342 123RF.com:** Peter Zaharov (b). **343 Alamy Images:** Redbrickstock.com (tr). **Getty Images:** Oktay Ortakcioglu (cr). **Minibeast Wildlife:** Alan Henderson (ca). **naturepl.com:** Chris Mattison (b). **Koen van Dijken:** (cb). **344 Corbis:** Ocean / 167 / Jason Edwards (br). **FLPA:** Imagebroker / Norbert Probst (tr). **naturepl.com:** Dave Watts (c). **344-345 naturepl.com:** Inaki Relanzon (c). **345 naturepl.com:** Brandon Cole (c). **OceanwideImages.com:** Gary Bell (tc). **346-347 naturepl.com:** David Fleetham (t). **346 FLPA:** Minden Pictures / Pete Oxford (crb). **347 FLPA:** Minden Pictures / Tui De Roy (bl); Minden Pictures / Richard Herrmann (br). **SeaPics.com:** Gary Bell (cra). **348 Alamy Images:** Martin Strmiska (t). **348-349 OceanwideImages.com:** David Fleetham (b). **349 Robert Harding Picture Library:** David Fleetham (tr). **350 OceanwideImages.com:** Gary Bell (tc, cl). **350-351 Vickie Coker**. **351 Carl Chapman:** (ca). **Ecoscene:** Phillip Colla (tr). **FLPA:** (br). **352 Alamy Images:** Natural History Museum, London (tc). **Ardea:** D. Parer & E. Parer-Cook (bc). **353 Corbis:** Stephen Frink. **354 FLPA:** Minden Pictures / Sebastian Kennerknecht (cb). **Wim Kok, Vlaardingen:** (bc). **Photoshot:** Dave Watts (clb). **355 Tom Ballinger:** (bl). **FLPA:** Minden Pictures / Martin Willis (crb); Geoff Moon (ca). **naturepl.com:** Brent Stephenson (bc). **www.rodmorris.co.nz:** (clb). **356 123RF.com:** Eric Isselee (tc). **Alamy Images:** Frans Lanting Studio (cb). **FLPA:** Minden Pictures / Tui De Roy (cla). **Photoshot:** (bl). **356-357 123RF.com:** Eric Isselee. **357 Alamy Images:** Prisma Bildagentur AG (tc). **358 Jérôme Albre:** (b). **359 Alamy Images:** Bruce Coleman (cra). **Grahame Bell (www.grahamenz.com):** (bc). **Alastair Stewart www.flickr.com/photos/alstewartnz:** (crb). **360-361 Corbis:** Maria Stenzel. **362 Corbis:** Wolfgang Kaehler (bc). **Getty Images:** Ralph Lee Hopkins (cla); Henryk Sadura (tc). **364 Xavier Desmier :** (bc). **Linda Martin Photography:** (c). **naturepl.com:** Doug Perrine (bl). **365 FLPA:** Minden Pictures / Konrad Wothe (clb). **naturepl.com:** Charlie Summers (br); David Tipling (bl). **Rex Features:** Gerard Lacz (tr). **366-367 Corbis:** Ocean / 145 / Mike Hill (t). **366 FLPA:** Frans Lanting (cr). **367 Corbis:** National Geographic Creative / Paul Nicklen (crb). **FLPA:** Frans Lanting (bl). **368 FLPA:** Minden Pictures / Tui De Roy (tr). **368-369 Corbis:** Minden Pictures / Otto Plantema / Buiten-beeld (b). **369 Alamy Images:** Cultura RM (tl). **FLPA:** Bill Coster (bc); James Lowen (tr); Malcolm Schuyl (cra). **370 Corbis:** Ocean / 167 / Keenpress (bc). **Getty Images:** Daisy Gilardini (c). **Dr Roger S. Key:** (clb). **371 Corbis:** Momatiuk - Eastcott (tr); Nature Picture Library / Doug Allan (clb); Paul Souders (br). **Richard E. Lee:** (bl). **372 Phillip Colla www.oceanlight.com**. **373 Dreamstime.com:** Freezingpictures / Jan Martin Will (crb). **Graham Ekins:** (cra). **FLPA:** Minden Pictures / Hiroya Minakuchi (br). **Robert Harding Picture Library:** Anthony Pierce (tr). **374-375 National Geographic Creative:** Paul Nicklen. **375 FLPA:** Biosphoto / Samuel Blanc (bc). **PunchStock:** Photodisc / Paul Souders (tr). **376-377 Corbis:** Imagebroker / Christian Handl. **381 Dreamstime.com:** Farinoza (tr). **378 FLPA:** Philip Perry (b). **Getty Images:** Frank Lukasseck (cra). **379 FLPA:** Minden Pictures / Katherine Feng. **380 Dreamstime.com:** Julian W (bc); Marion Wear (ca). **381 Dorling Kindersley:** Blackpool Zoo, Lancashire, UK (br). **382 Corbis:** Kevin Schafer (cr). **Getty Images:** Luiz Fernando Souza Fernandes (tc); Per-Gunnar Ostby (bl). **383 FLPA:** Jim Brandenburg / Minden Pictures (c). **384 Dorling Kindersley:** Rollin Verlinde (br). **385 Dorling Kindersley:** The National Birds of Prey Centre, Gloucestershire (bl). **Dreamstime.com:** Farinoza (t); Susan Robinson (cr). **386 123RF.com:** Eric Isselee (bc). **Dorling Kindersley:** British Wildlife Centre, Surrey, UK (cl). **387 123RF.com:** Eric Isselee (br). **388 Dreamstime.com:** Chris Moncrieff (tr). **naturepl.com:** Rod Williams (cl). **389 Dreamstime.com:** Isselee (tc). **390 Dorling Kindersley:** Blackpool Zoo, Lancashire, UK (cl, br). **392 Dorling Kindersley:** Drusillas Zoo, Alfriston, West Sussex (c); Jerry Young (cr). **393 Dreamstime.com:** Plazaccameraman (tc). **394 Corbis:** Ken Catania / Visuals Unlimited (br). **Dorling Kindersley:** Rollin Verlinde (cra). **Dreamstime.com:** Dmitry Zhukov / Mite (bl). **395 Corbis:** Joe McDonald (br). **Dorling Kindersley:** Jerry Young (bl). **Getty Images:** David Paynter (tr). **396 Dorling Kindersley:** Whipsnade Zoo, Bedfordshire (bl). **397 Robert Harding Picture Library:** Pablo Cersosimo (bl). **398 Dorling Kindersley:** Rollin Verlinde (cl). **399 Dreamstime.com:** Kevin Gillot (tr). **FLPA:** Donald M. Jones / Minden Pictures (cb). **Getty Images:** Roger de la Harpe (br). **401 123RF.com:** petestock (tr). **402 Corbis:** Paul Souders (tl). **Dreamstime.com:** Lukas Blazek / Lukyslukys (bc). **404 Dreamstime.com:** Tony Campbell (cl). **406 Dorling Kindersley:** Greg and Yvonne Dean (tr). **Dreamstime.com:** Tossi66 (c). **407 Corbis:** Mike Paterson / National Geographic Creative (cl); Paul Souders (cr). **408 Dreamstime.com:** Josefpittner (bc); Mikelane45 (cra). **409 Dreamstime.com:** Pixattitude. **410 Dorling Kindersley:** E.J. Peiker (crb). **FLPA:** Eric Woods (bl). **411 123RF.com:** Dmytro Pylypenko (bc). **412 Dreamstime.com:** Mikelane45 (cr). **413 Dorling Kindersley:** Blackpool Zoo, Lancashire, UK (cr). **415 Alamy Images:** RGB Ventures / SuperStock (tc). **FLPA:** Tui De Roy (bl). **416 Dreamstime.com:** Musat Christian (tr); Farinoza (bl). **417 Dorling Kindersley:** The Natural History Museum, London (cr). **418 Dorling Kindersley:** Neil Fletcher (bc). **Dreamstime.com:** Menno67 (cr); Suebmtl (tl). **419 Alamy Images:** imageBROKER (bc). **Dorling Kindersley:** Blackpool Zoo, Lancashire, UK (tr). **420 Dorling Kindersley:** Liberty's Owl, Raptor and Reptile Centre, Hampshire, UK (bl). **421 Dorling Kindersley:** E.J. Peiker (c). **Dreamstime.com:** Mikelane45 (cra). **422 Alamy Images:** National Geographic Image Collection (br). **423 Dorling Kindersley:** Neil Fletcher (c). **424 Dreamstime.com:** Vosken75 (c). **425 Dreamstime.com:** Steve Byland (c, bl). **426 Alamy Images:** Matthijs Kuijpers (bc). **Dorling Kindersley:** The Natural History Museum, London (c). **428 Dorling Kindersley:** Jerry Young (bc). **429 Corbis:** Mattias Klum / National Geographic Creative (bl). **FLPA:** Piotr Naskrecki / Minden Pictures (tl). **430 Dreamstime.com:** Diverstef (bc). **432 Dorling Kindersley:** Paolo Mazzei (tl). **433 Dorling Kindersley:** Liberty's Owl, Raptor and Reptile Centre, Hampshire, UK (tr). **435 Dreamstime.com:** Amwu (ca). **436 Dreamstime.com:** Isselee (bl). **FLPA:** Wil Meinderts / Minden Pictures (ca). **437 FLPA:** Emanuele Biggi. **438 Dorling Kindersley:** Twan Leenders (tc). **439 Corbis:** Pete Oxford / Minden Pictures (cl). **Dorling Kindersley:** Jan Van Der Voort (bc); Jerry Young (tr). **440 Dorling Kindersley:** Paolo Mazzei (tc). **441 FLPA:** Thomas Marent / Minden Pictures (cr). **442 Dreamstime.com:** Chatchawin Pola (cra). **Robert Harding Picture Library:** Dave Fleetham (bc). **443 Dreamstime.com:** Ben Piek. **444 Getty Images:** Michael Aw (br). **445 123RF.com:** Svetlana Foote (tr). **Dreamstime.com:** Alessandrozocc (c). **446 Alamy Images:** Reinhard Dirscherl (bc). **Getty Images:** MyLoupe / Universal Images Group (cla). **447 Corbis:** Richard Herrmann / Minden Pictures (c). **Dorling Kindersley:** The Weymouth Sea Life Centre (cla). **Dreamstime.com:** Iliuta Goean (bc). **448 123RF.com:** vilainecrevette (bc). **449 Corbis:** Design Pics / Ed Robinson. **450 Dorling Kindersley:** Linda Pitkin (cl). **451 Corbis:** Wim van Egmond / Visuals Unlimited (bl); Solvin Zankl / Visuals Unlimited (cr). **Science Photo Library:** Steve Gschmeissner (tc). **452 Dorling Kindersley:** The Natural History Museum, London (tr); Oxford University Museum of Natural History (cl). **454 Dorling Kindersley:** Paolo Mazzei (tl). **455 Dorling Kindersley:** Richard Ling (cr). **Dreamstime.com:** Sarah2 (tl)

Jacket images: *Front:* **FLPA:** Frans Lanting; *Back:* **Getty Images:** Paul Souders cb; *Spine:* **FLPA:** Frans Lanting t

All other images © Dorling Kindersley

For further information see: www.dkimages.com